CRIMINAL LAW

CRIMINAL LAW

TJ McIntyre
Sinéad McMullan
Seán Ó Toghda

ROUND HALL

Published in 2012 by
Thomson Reuters (Professional) Ireland Limited
(Registered in Ireland, Company No. 80867.
Registered Office and address for service:
43 Fitzwilliam Place, Dublin 2, Ireland)
trading as Round Hall

Typeset by
Carrigboy Typesetting Services

Printed by
CPI Antony Rowe, Chippenham, Wiltshire

ISBN 978-1-85800-585-0

A catalogue record for this book
is available from the British Library

All rights reserved. No part of this publication may be reproduced or transmitted in any form or by any means, or stored in any retrieval system of any nature without prior written permission. Such written permission must also be obtained before any part of this publication is stored in a retrieval system of any nature.

Thomson Reuters and the Thomson Reuters Logo are trademarks of Thomson Reuters. Round Hall is a registered trademark of Thomson Reuters (Professional) Ireland Limited.

© Thomson Reuters (Professional) Ireland Limited, 2012

To Clodagh and Marcus
TJM

To my parents and Seamus
SMcM

To my parents Patrick and Joan
SÓT

FOREWORD

Forty years ago this October, when I attended my first lecture in Criminal Law, students were offered a choice of two British textbooks. There were no Irish options and we were entirely dependent on our lecturer, Senator Professor Mary Robinson, to introduce us to and guide us through Irish legislation and case law. Four years on when I entered the Law Library the situation was no better—a key objective for a newly qualified barrister was to get one's hand on an old copy of Archbold, one that pre-dated the English Theft Act of 1968.

Now, all is changed. Recent years have seen an explosion of activity in Irish legal publishing. Criminal Law has been a particular beneficiary and a number of first class texts became available covering aspects of both substantive and procedural Criminal Law. This publication is a very worthy edition to the Irish Criminal Law library and it is one for which its authors are to be highly commended.

There must have been times in recent years when authors and publishers allowed themselves to become a little frustrated as their labours were quickly overtaken by events. Successive Ministers for Justice anxious to respond to public concern at high crime rates and to leave their mark introduced major legislative changes. Now though, comes a textbook that is bang up to date.

T.J., Sinéad and Seán have produced a textbook that is at once authoritative, lively and accessible. Students and practitioners alike will find this a valuable tool.

All those who practice in the area of Criminal Law will be conscious of the frequency with which cases take unexpected directions. A surprising answer from a witness or even an unexpected or unusual formulation of a response to a question asked or a proposition put may bring a quite unexpected area of law into play, perhaps involving a defence which, up to then, had not been thought to arise. For that reason it is an unwise practitioner who enters court unarmed. A barrister or solicitor who slips a copy of this work into his or her briefcase before setting off for court will have taken a very shrewd decision. So equipped, the advocate will be in a position to respond effectively to whatever develops. For my part, I certainly intend to have a copy on the bench beside me at all times when sitting in the Central Criminal Court next term, and I expect to be taking it up frequently and referring to it.

The Hon. Mr. Justice George Birmingham

PREFACE

This book grew from two editions of a criminal law book written by TJ McIntyre and Sinéad McMullan in 2000 and 2005. That book was aimed at the student market and was part of the Round Hall Essential Law Text series. As such, both the word count and scope were limited. When we were asked to write a criminal law book to form part of the Round Hall University Core Text series we seized the opportunity to describe and comment on the law in a much more expansive manner. We hope that this book will not only be a definitive criminal law text for students but also form part of the library of the busy criminal practitioner. The many recent changes in criminal law, especially in areas such as sexual offences, self-defence in the home and insanity, mean that a comprehensive and up-to-date text is an essential tool for all those involved in every aspect of the criminal justice system. The focus of this book is on the substantive law—we have not addressed evidential or procedural issues in this text because of the array of excellent and recent Irish textbooks dealing with criminal evidence and procedure.

We are very grateful to Round Hall for their patience in awaiting this title. Frieda Donohue must be especially thanked for her forbearance. Both Frieda and Katie Bermingham-Thomas were a pleasure to work with.

A number of people very kindly read drafts of various chapters and their comments were much appreciated. A very big debt is owed to Fiona Murphy BL who took the time to read the book from cover to cover and made numerous invaluable suggestions. Many thanks to David Prendergast for his observations on the chapter on inchoate offences. Seán Ó Toghda wishes to express his gratitude and thanks to his colleagues for their advice and support, and in particular special thanks goes to Luigi Rea BL and Richard Downey BL. Sinéad McMullan would also like to thank Feichín McDonagh SC, Úna Ní Raifeartaigh SC and Cormac Quinn BL for their help and encouragement to her during her devilling years and throughout the past decade. Thanks is also due to the librarians of the Law Library for their help in finding obscure cases and articles.

We are very grateful indeed to Mr Justice George Birmingham for his kind and thoughtful Foreword.

We would be obliged if any inaccuracies or omissions could be brought to our attention so they can be taken into consideration for the next edition.

TJ McIntyre
Sinéad McMullan
Seán Ó Toghda
August 2012

TABLE OF CONTENTS

Foreword vii
Preface ix
Table of Cases xix
Table of Legislation xxxi

CHAPTER 1   **GENERAL PRINCIPLES** 1
Defining the Criminal Law 1
   Background 1
   Nature of the criminal law 3
   Effect of the civil–criminal distinction 5
   The indicia *of a criminal offence* 6
   Administrative penalties 8
   Tribunals of inquiry 11
   Proceeds of crime legislation 13
   *Criminal offences under the European Convention on
      Human Rights* 16
Classification of Crimes 20
   Felonies, misdemeanours and treason 20
   Summary and indictable offences 22
   Minor and non-minor offences 25
   Serious and non-serious offences 30
   Arrestable and non-arrestable offences 32
Fundamental Principles of Criminal Law 35
   The presumption of innocence 35
   The principle of legality 45

CHAPTER 2   **MENTAL ELEMENT OF CRIMES** 52
Introduction 52
Intention 53
   Defining "intention" 53
   The problem of indirect/oblique intention 54
   The English approach to oblique intention 54
   The Irish approach to oblique intention 57
   The presumption of intention 60
   Reform of intention 61
Recklessness 61
   Irish approach 62
   The approach in England and Wales 64
Criminal Negligence 68
Negligence 68
Strict or Absolute Liablity 68
   Introduction 68
   Strict liability versus absolute liability 69

	Determining whether an offence is one of strict liability........ 69
	*The Irish approach pre-*CC v Ireland..................... 71
	The constitutional status of strict liability offences and
	CC v Ireland.................................... 73
	The Irish approach since CC v Ireland 76
	The Doctrine of Transferred Malice........................ 77

CHAPTER 3   ACTION ELEMENT OF CRIMES................. 81
Introduction 81
Actus Reus as a State of Affairs............................ 81
Actus Reus and Mens Rea must coincide 83
The Actus Reus may be an Omission 84
    Duty of parents towards their children.................... 85
    Duty voluntarily assumed............................. 86
    Creation of a danger 87
    Duty under contract................................. 88
    Statutory duties to act............................... 89
    Is the act–omission distinction artificial? 89
Actus Reus and Causation 90
    Break in the chain of causation?—Novus actus interveniens 92
    Can a victim of crime break the chain of causation by his
        own actions? 94

CHAPTER 4   HOMICIDE................................ 96
General Principles...................................... 96
    Year-and-a day-rule................................. 96
    Absence of a body.................................. 97
Murder 97
    Of sound memory and of the age of discretion................ 97
    Unlawfully killeth.................................. 98
    Within any county of the realm......................... 98
    Any reasonable creature in rerum natura................... 98
    Under the King's peace 100
    With malice aforethought............................ 100
    Either expressed by the party or implied by law 101
    So as the party, wounded or hurt, etc. die of the wound or hurt,
        etc. within a year and a day after the same 102
    Attempted murder................................. 102
    Aggravated murder 102
    Murder and the defences 104
    Mandatory sentence for murder........................ 104
    The murder–manslaughter distinction................... 109
    Should the mens rea for murder include an intention to cause
        serious injury? 112
    Should the mens rea for murder be expanded to include
        other fault elements? 113
Manslaughter 114
    Manslaughter by criminal negligence 115
    Manslaughter by criminal and dangerous act 121
    Death on the roads................................ 125
Suicide 126

Table of Contents xiii

        Legality of suicide 126
        Suicide pacts... 126
        Assisted suicide 127
        Euthanasia 130
        Discontinuation of medical treatment 133
    Infanticide 136

CHAPTER 5   **SEXUAL OFFENCES** 141
    Rape 141
        Actus reus of common law rape 141
        Section 4 rape... 143
    Consent... 144
        Consent vitiated by fraud................................. 145
        Fraud as to existence of HIV or other diseases 146
        Consent vitiated by fear 149
        Incapacity to give consent 149
    Mens Rea of Sexual Offences 149
        Honest but unreasonable belief in consent 150
        Recklessness as to consent............................... 152
    Sexual Assault and Aggravated Sexual Assault................... 152
        Indecent assault at common law 153
    Incest 155
        Incest by a male 156
        Incest by a female....................................... 156
        Punishment of incest 156
        Reform 156
    Sexual Offences Against the Mentally Handicapped............... 157
    Sexual Abuse of Children 160
        Statutory rape—unlawful carnal knowledge 160
        Defilement of a child under the age of 15 years and defilement
            of a child under the age of 17 years..................... 162
        Reckless endangerment of children 164
        Child trafficking and pornography......................... 164
        Child sex tourism 165
        Register of sex offenders 165
    Human Trafficking... 166

CHAPTER 6   **OFFENCES AGAINST THE PERSON** 167
    Background 167
    Assault 167
        Consent.. 168
        Corporal punishment 168
        Force 169
        Immediacy 169
        Causes another to believe 170
        Can words alone amount to an assault? 170
        Indirect use of force 171
        Punishment.. 171
    Assault Causing Harm 171
        Punishment.. 172
    Causing Serious Harm 172

    Is consent a defence to causing serious harm? 173
    Punishment. 176
  Threats to Kill or Cause Serious Harm 176
    Punishment. 177
  Syringe Attacks And Related Offences 177
    Punishment. 178
    Possession of syringes 178
  Coercion. 179
    Punishment. 179
  Harassment. 179
    Mens rea. 180
    Persistently. 181
    Lawful authority or reasonable excuse 182
    Non-contact orders. 182
    Punishment. 183
  Demands for Payment of Debts. 183
  Poisoning 183
  Endangerment 184
  Endangering Traffic 186
  False Imprisonment 187
  Child Abduction. 188
  Assault with Intent to Cause Bodily Harm or Commit an Indictable
    Offence. 189
  Assault of Certain Classes of Workers. 189
  Blackmail. 190

CHAPTER 7   **OFFENCES AGAINST PROPERTY** 192
  Criminal Justice (Theft and Fraud Offences) Act 2001 192
    Introduction 192
  Theft. 192
    Background 192
    Dishonestly: without a claim of right made in good faith 193
    Intention to temporarily or permanently deprive. 195
    Actus reus of theft. 195
  Fraud Offences. 197
    Background 197
    Making a gain or causing a loss by deception. 198
    Obtaining services by deception 199
    Making off without payment. 199
    Unlawful use of a computer. 200
    False accounting 201
    Suppression, etc. of documents 201
    Handling stolen property. 201
    Possession of stolen property. 202
    Withholding information regarding stolen property 203
  Burglary. 203
    Trespass. 204
    Entering a building or part of a building. 206
    Burglary: the mental element. 208
    Aggravated burglary 209
  Robbery 211

Possession of Certain Articles 212
Forgery and Counterfeiting Offences....................... 212
Arson and Criminal Damage 213
   Defence of lawful excuse 214
   Damaging property 216
   Damaging property with intent to endanger life or recklessness
      as to whether life would be endangered................ 216
   Damaging property with intent to defraud.................. 217
   Arson 218
   Threats to damage property............................ 218
   Possessing any thing with intent to damage property 218
   Unauthorised accessing of data......................... 218

CHAPTER 8   OFFENCES AGAINST THE ADMINISTRATION OF JUSTICE 220
Perjury 220
   On oath or affirmation 220
   Before a competent court or authority in the course of a judicial
      proceeding 221
   Material to the matter in question 221
   Which to the knowledge of such person is false, or which,
      whether true or false, he does not believe to be true, or
      as to which he knows himself to be ignorant 221
   Case law 221
   Reform 222
Attempting to Pervert the Course of Justice 222
Contempt of Court 223
   Civil versus criminal contempt......................... 224
   Types of criminal contempt 226
   Scandalising the court 226
   Mens rea and criminal contempt 231
   Procedure... 232
   Reform of the law of contempt of court 234

CHAPTER 9   PUBLIC ORDER OFFENCES..................... 236
Core Offences Relating to Public Order 236
   Definition of "public place"........................... 236
   Intoxication in a public place.......................... 237
   Offensive conduct in a public place 238
   Offence of threatening, abusive or insulting behaviour in a
      public place 239
   Offence of breach of the peace contrary to common law........ 242
   Display of material which is threatening, abusive, insulting or
      obscene... 243
   Offence of failure to comply with direction of member of
      An Garda Síochána 244
   Obstruction offences................................ 246
Begging Offences....................................... 247
   Background 247
   Offence of begging................................. 248

```
        Offence of failure to comply with a Garda direction to desist
            from begging ........................................249
        Offences related to organised begging......................249
    Trespass Offences ............................................250
        Criminal trespass..........................................250
        Offence of entering a building or curtilage with intent to
            commit an offence ...................................252
        Offence of trespass on a building or curtilage causing fear in
            another person.......................................253
        Offences relating to entering and occupying land without
            consent .............................................254
    Riot, Violent Disorder and Affray ............................255
        Riot.......................................................255
        Violent disorder ..........................................256
        Affray ....................................................257

CHAPTER 10  DEFENCES SPECIFIC TO MURDER ...................260
    Introduction .................................................260
    Diminished Responsibility.....................................260
    Provocation ..................................................261
        Introduction ..............................................261
        Historical background .....................................262
        The Irish position on provocation: subjective test ............263
        Immediacy requirement ...................................267
    Excessive Self Defence .......................................268

CHAPTER 11  GENERAL DEFENCES.............................271
    Duress........................................................271
        Imminence of threats ....................................272
        The nature of the threats ................................273
        Objective or subjective test? .............................274
        Application to murder ...................................274
        Membership of a violent organisation .....................275
        Duress and marital coercion ..............................277
        Law Reform Commission recommendations .................277
    Necessity ....................................................279
        When can necessity be used as a defence?..................279
        Necessity and murder....................................281
    Lawful Use of Force .........................................283
        Defence of the person ...................................283
        Protection from trespass to the person; defence of property;
            prevention of crime..................................284
        Preparation in anticipation of an attack ...................285
        Self-induced self defence ................................285
        Force ...................................................286
        Criminal Law (Defence and the Dwelling) Act 2011 .........287
        Other defences preserved................................287
        Proportionality of response .............................288
        Mistake and self defence ...............................288
        Defence and the dwelling...............................288
```

Table of Contents

xvii

     Intoxication 293
         Dutch courage 294
         Basic/specific intent 294
         Intoxication under Irish law 297
         Intoxication by other drugs 299
         Involuntary intoxication 299
         Law Reform Commission 300
     Mistake 300
     Consent 302
     Infancy 302
     Entrapment 304
         Traditional approach to entrapment 304
         Modern English approach 305
         United States approach 305
         Influence of the European Convention on Human Rights 306
         Irish approach 307
     Automatism 309
         Definition 309
         Defence unavailable in cases of voluntary intoxication 310
         External factors versus internal factors 311
         Self-induced automatism 313
         Loss of control must be total 314
     Insanity 315
         Insanity under Irish law pre-2006 315
         Reform of defence of insanity 321
         Section 4 of the Criminal Law (Insanity) Act 2006: fitness to
            be tried 321
         Section 5: verdict of not guilty by reason of insanity 323
         Section 6: diminished responsibility 323
         Procedural aspects 324
     Unconstitutionality 326

CHAPTER 12 INCHOATE OFFENCES 328
     Introduction 328
     Attempt 329
         Introduction 329
         Actus reus of attempt 331
         Mens rea of attempt 335
         Identifying the types of offences that may be attempted 337
         Legal impossibility and factual impossibility 338
         Abandonment 338
     Conspiracy 339
         Introduction 339
         Actus reus of conspiracy: an agreement 339
         The object of conspiracy 342
         Mens rea of conspiracy 344
         Specific offences of conspiracy 345
         Impossibility 347
         Abandonment 348
     Incitement 348
         Introduction 348

Actus reus of incitement	350
Mens rea of incitement	351
Impossibility	353
Abandonment	354
Specific offences of incitement	354

CHAPTER 13   DEGREES OF COMPLICITY IN CRIME 355
                  Introduction 355
                      Criminal Law Act 1997 356
                      Innocent Agency 358
                      Elements of secondary liability 359
                      Secondary liability—the conduct element 360
                      Aiding 361
                      Abetting and counselling 363
                      Procuring 364
                      Failure to act or mere presence as an actus reus 365
                      Secondary liability—the mental element 369
                      The doctrine of common design/joint enterprise 373
                      Victims as participants in crime 378
                      Withdrawal 379
                      Assistance after a crime has been committed 380
                      Withholding information 382

CHAPTER 14   CRIMINAL LIABILITY OF CORPORATIONS 383
                  Introduction 383
                  The Identification Doctrine—Controlling Mind—Directing
                      Mind Theory 384
                  The Organisational—Aggregation Theory 386
                  Statutory Construction Approach 387
                  Restrictions on Corporate Liabilty 389
                      Where the corporation is incapable of committing the
                          particular crime 389
                      Where the corporation is the victim 390
                      Where employees act contrary to instructions 390
                  Punishment of Companies 390
                  Corporate Manslaughter and Homicide Act 2007 (UK) 391
                  The Irish Position 392
                      Common law 392
                      Law Reform Commission proposals 393
                      Corporate Manslaughter Bill 2011 394

INDEX 397

TABLE OF CASES

A v Arbour Hill Prison [2006] 4 I.R. 88 .... 326n
A v Governor of Arbour Hill Prison [2006] 4 I.R. 88 .... 161n
A (Children) (Conjoined Twins: Surgical Separation), Re [2001] 2 W.L.R. 480 282
Airedale NHS Trust v Bland [1993] 1 All E.R. 821 .... 89–90, 134
Ambard v Attorney General for Trinidad and Tobago [1936] A.C. 322 227
Attorney General v Able [1984] 1 Q.B. 795 .... 128, 360, 370n
Attorney General v Ball (1936) 70 I. L.T.R. 202 97
Attorney General v Byrne [1974] 1 I.R. 1 37
Attorney General v Capaldi (1949) 1 Frewen 95 351
Attorney General v Commane [1965] WJSC-CCA 388 270
Attorney General v Connolly [1947] I.R. 213 228
Attorney General v Crosbie and Meehan [1966] I.R. 490 122
Attorney General v Crosby (1961) 1 Frewen 231 .... 116, 125
Attorney General v Cunningham [1932] I.R. 28 242
Attorney General v Dermody [1956] I.R. 307 .... 142n
Attorney General v Dunleavy [1948] I.R. 95 .... 116, 117, 121, 125, 396
Attorney General v Dwyer [1972] I.R. 416 .... 268, 270, 292
Attorney General v England (1947) 1 Frewen 81 332
Attorney General v Fennell [1940] 1 I.R. 445 39
Attorney General v Hayes, unreported, Central Criminal Court,
    November 30, 1997 .... 318, 319
Attorney General v Keane (1975) 1 Frewen 392 .... 340n
Attorney General v Keatley [1954] I.R. 12 284
Attorney General v Maher (1937) 71 I.L.T. 60 121
Attorney General v Manning (1953) 89 I.L.T.R. 155 297
Attorney General v Newspaper Publishing Plc [1988] Ch. 333 .... 226n
Attorney General v O'Brien [1936] I.R. 263 .... 317, 318
Attorney General v O'Callaghan [1966] I.R. 501 .... 30, 37n
Attorney General v Oldridge [2000] 4 I.R. 593 .... 340, 345n, 347
Attorney General v Ryan (1966) 1 Frewen 304 367
Attorney General v Sullivan [1964] I.R. 169 .... 209n, 330n, 332–335, 338, 347,
                                                                           348, 353, 354
Attorney General v Thornton [1952] I.R. 91 .... 209n, 330n, 331n, 332, 335
Attorney General v Whelan [1934] I.R 518 .... 271, 272, 274, 275
Attorney General v X [1992] 1 I.R. 1 282
Attorney General (Shaughnessy) v Ryan [1960] I.R. 181 160
Attorney General (Society for the Protection of Unborn Children) v Open Door
    Counselling Limited [1988] I.R. 593 .... 49, 345n
Attorney General for Northern Ireland v Gallagher [1963] A.C. 349 294
Attorney General's Reference (No.1 of 1975) [1975] Q.B. 773 360,364
Attorney General's Reference (No.6 of 1980) [1981] Q.B. 715 .... 173n, 174n
Attorney General's Reference (No.3 of 1992) [1994] 1 W.L.R. 409 ...... 209n, 331n, 336
Attorney General's Reference (No.3 of 1994) [1998] 1 A.C. 245 .... 78–79, 100
Attorney General's Reference (No.2 of 1999) [2006] 3 All E.R. 182 388

Attorney General's Reference (No.3 of 2003) [2004] EWCA Crim 868 . . . . 67, 246n
Attorney General's Reference (No.60 of 2009) (Appleby) (2010)
   2 Cr. App. R. (S) 46 . . . . 123n

B v An NHS Hospital Trust [2002] EWHC 429 (Fam). 133
B v DPP [2000] 2 A.C. 428 301
Bates v Brady [2003] 4 I.R. 111. . . . . 245, 249n
Blakely and Sutton v DPP [1991] R.T.R. 405 369
Bowes v DPP and McGrath v DPP [2003] 2 I.R. 25 . . . . 125n
Brady v DPP [2010] IEHC 231 . . . . 242n
Bratty v Attorney General for Northern Ireland [1963] A.C. 386 . . . . 309n, 311, 313
Broome v Perkins [1987] Crim. L.R. 271 314
Brown v Putnam 6 A.L.R. 307 (Sup. Ct N.S.W. Ct App. 1975) 231
Brown v United States 256 U.S. 335 (1921) 288

C (A Minor) v DPP [1994] 3 W.L.R. 888 302
Cafferata v Wilson [1936] 3 All E.R. 149 . . . . 370n
Cagney v DPP [2008] 2 I.L.R.M. 293 . . . . 49n
Calder Publications Limited v Powell [1965] 1 Q.B. 509 . . . . 243n
Callan v Ireland and the Attorney General [2011] IEHC 190 104
Canadian Dredge & Dock Co. v R [1985] 1 S.C.R. 662 390
Cartmill v Ireland [1987] I.R. 192 29
CC v Ireland [2006] 4 I.R. 1 . . . . 4n, 73–76, 161, 162n, 232, 250n, 251n, 326
Chan Wing-Siu v R [1985] A.C. 168 . . . . 377n
Charlton v Ireland [1984] I.L.R.M. 39 29
Chief Constable of Avon an Somerset Constabulary v Shimmen (1987)
   84 Cr. App. R. 7 62
Churchill v Watson [1967] 2 A.C. 224. 344
Clifford v DPP [2008] IEHC 322. . . . . 58–59, 64, 239, 240, 241, 242n, 243
Clune v DPP and Clifford [1981] I.L.R.M. 17. 22
Collins v Wilcock [1984] 3 All E.R. 374 . . . . 168, 169
Conroy v Attorney General [1965] I.R. 411 . . . . 25, 26, 28
Cook v Stockwell (1915) 84 L.J.K.B. 2187. . . . . 370n
Corway v Independent Newspapers [1999] IESC 5 50
Cotterill v Penn [1936] 1 K.B. 53 . . . . 246n
Cruzan v Director, Missouri Department of Health (1990) 110 S. Ct. 2841 133

D (A Minor) v Ireland [2010] IEHC 101 137
Davey v Lee [1967] 2 All E.R. 423 . . . . 335n
Dental Board v O'Callaghan [1969] I.R. 181 307
Devlin v Armstrong [1971] N.I. 13 283
Dillon v DPP [2008] 1 I.R. 383 . . . . 247, 248
Director General of Fair Trading v Pioneer Concrete (UK) Limited [1995]
   1 A.C. 456. . . . . 387, 390
Director of Corporate Enforcement v Gannon [2002] 4 I.R. 439 72
D(M) (A Minor) v Ireland [2012] IESC 10 327
Dokie v DPP [2011] 1 I.R. 805 48
Donnelly v DPP [2006] IEHC 158 . . . . 222n
Doolan v DPP [1992] 2 I.R. 399 153
Doyle v Wicklow County Council [1973] IESC 1; [1974] I.R. 55 . . . .315, 317, 318, 320, 323
DPP v Armstrong [2000] Crim. L.R. 379 351

Table of Cases xxi

DPP v B [2011] IECCA 1 325
DPP v Bambrick [1999] 2 I.L.R.M. 71 ....261n, 265
DPP v Barnes [2006] IECCA 165 288
DPP v Barnes [2007] 3 I.R. 130.......................................289, 291
DPP v Bartley, unreported, Central Criminal Court, Carney J., June 13, 1997..........89
DPP v Beard [1920] A.C. 479 ....299n
DPP v Behan, unreported, High Court, Ó Caoimh J., March 3, 2003................73
DPP v Bignell (1998) 1 Cr. App. R. 1 ....218, 219
DPP v Boyle [2000] 2 I.R. 13 266
DPP v Byrne [1988] 2 I.R. 417 ....210n
DPP v Byrne, unreported, ex tempore, Court of Criminal Appeal, February 24, 2003...261
DPP v Byrne, Healy and Kelleher [1998] 2 I.R. 417............................43
DPP v C [2001] I.R. 345 145
DPP v Cagney and McGrath [2008] 2 I.R. 111 ....63, 185
DPP v Carew [1981] 1 I.L.R.M. 91....................................345, 346
DPP v Connaughton, unreported, Court of Criminal Appeal, April 5, 2001 125
DPP v Courtney, unreported, Court of Criminal Appeal, July 21, 1994 319
DPP v Creighton [1994] 2 I.R. 570 151
DPP v Crowe (Leigh) [2010] 1 I.R. 129 324
DPP v Cullagh, unreported, ex tempore, Court of Criminal Appeal, Murphy J.,
    March 18, 1999...116
DPP v Cumberton [1995] WJSC-CCA 495.............................373, 376
DPP v Curran [2011] IECCA 95 ....261, 266, 267
DPP v Daley and McGhie [1980] A.C. 237................................124
DPP v Davis [1993] 2 I.R. 1 291
DPP v Davis [2001] 1 I.R. 146 ....91, 230, 261n, 266, 267, 268
DPP v Delaney [2010] IECCA 123 ....261n
DPP v Dickey, unreported, Court of Criminal Appeal, March 7, 2003 274
DPP v Doohan [2002] 4 I.R. 463...101
DPP v Doohan [2002] WJSC-CCA 2022..............................373, 375
DPP v DO'T [2003] 4 I.R. 286 ....37n, 38
DPP v Douglas and Hayes [1985] I.L.R.M. 25 ....58, 102n, 337n
DPP v Doyle, unreported, Court of Criminal Appeal, March 22, 2002..............261n
DPP v Doyle (Gary) [1994] 2 I.R. 286 ....23n
DPP v Ebbs [2011] 1 I.R. 778 210–211
DPP v Eccles, McPhillips and McShane (1986) 3 Frewen 36.....................377
DPP v EF, unreported, Supreme Court, February 24, 1994......................153
DPP v Egan [1989] I.R. 681 ....361, 372, 373
DPP v Egan (Seán) [2010] IECCA 28....................................162n
DPP v F, unreported, Court of Criminal Appeal, May 27, 1993 151
DPP v Gaffney, unreported, Court of Criminal Appeal, May 10, 1991..............151
DPP v Gallagher [1991] I.L.R.M. 339.....................................324
DPP v Galligan, unreported, High Court, Laffoy J., November 2, 1995........245, 249n
DPP v Heaney [1999] WJSC-CCA 1795...................................266
DPP v Horgan [2007] 3 I.R. 568 122
DPP v Hull, unreported, Court of Criminal Appeal, July 8, 1996...................60
DPP v Independent Newspapers [2003] 2 I.R. 367............................230
DPP v Independent Newspapers (Ireland) Limited and Ors [2005] IEHC 128.........230
DPP v Independent Newspapers (Ireland) Limited, Gerard O'Regan
    and Anne-Marie Walsh [2009] 3 I.R. 598 ....229n, 231n, 233n, 235n
DPP v Jordan and Deegan [2006] 3 I.R. 425................................368

DPP v K [1990] 1 All E.R. 331 171
DPP v Kehoe [1992] I.L.R.M. 481 .... 261n
DPP v Kelly [2000] 2 I.R. 1 .... 261n, 266, 268
DPP v Kelly (Mary) [2011] IECCA 25 216
DPP v Kent and Sussex Contractors Limited [1944] 1 K.B. 146 384
DPP v Kieran Smyth Snr and Kieran Smyth Jnr [2010] 3 I.R. 688 42–45
DPP v Kieran Smyth Snr and Kieran Smyth Jnr [2011] 1 I.L.R.M. 81 .... 39n, 40
DPP v Kirwan [2005] IECCA 136 172
DPP v Lynch (Martin) [2008] IEHC 183 .... 51n
DPP v MacEoin [1978] I.R. 27 .... 261, 263, 264, 265, 266, 267
DPP v Madden [1977] I.R. 336 372
DPP v Majewski [1976] 2 All E.R. 142 .... 295, 296, 297, 298, 299n
DPP v McBride [1996] 1 I.R. 312 60
DPP v McDonagh [1996] 1 I.R. 565 151
DPP v McDonagh [2001] 3 I.R. 201 .... 61, 261n
DPP v McMahon [1986] I.R. 393 206
DPP v Morgan [1976] A.C. 182 .... 150, 151n
DPP v Mulder [2009] IECCA 45 .... 39n
DPP v Mullane, unreported, Court of Criminal Appeal, March 11, 1997 .... 261n
DPP v Mullane [1998] WJSC-CCA 5885 .... 264, 265, 266
DPP v Mulligan [2009] 1 I.R. 794 .... 249n
DPP v Murphy, unreported, Court of Criminal Appeal, July 8, 2003 ...... 293n, 297n
DPP v Murray [1977] I.R. 360 .... 53, 57, 62–63, 103, 104, 152, 173, 301, 376, 377
DPP v Murtagh [1990] 1 I.R. 339 350
DPP v Nally [2007] 4 I.R. 145 .... 289, 291
DPP v Nock [1975] A.C. 476 347
DPP v Noonan [1998] 1 I.L.R.M. 154 .... 261n, 265
DPP v O'Donoghue [2007] 2 I.R. 336 123
DPP v O'Mahony [1985] I.R. 517 .... 315n, 320
DPP v O'Toole, unreported, Court of Criminal Appeal, March 25, 2003 274
DPP v P&O Ferries (Dover) Limited (1990) 93 Cr. App. R. 72 386
DPP v Power [2007] IESC 31 77
DPP v Pringle, McCann and O'Shea (1981) 2 Frewen 57 377
DPP v Ramachchandran [2000] 2 I.R. 307 182
DPP v Redmond [2006] 3 I.R. 188 .... 39n
DPP v Reilly [2005] 3 I.R. 111 .... 297–298, 310
DPP v Rose, unreported, Court of Criminal Appeal, February 21, 2002 .... 367–368, 374
DPP v Ryan [2006] IECCA 47 285
DPP v Santana-Bermudez [2004] Crim L.R. 471 88
DPP v Stonehouse [1978] A.C. 55 .... 335n
DPP v Valentine [2009] 4 I.R. 33 .... 196, 197n
DPP v Withers [1975] A.C. 842 .... 345n, 346n
DPP v X, unreported, Central Criminal Court, *The Irish Times*, May 20, 1995 149
DPP (Broderick) v Flanagan [1979] 1 I.R. 265 50
DPP for Northern Ireland v Lynch [1975] A.C. 653 .... 274, 275
DPP for Northern Ireland v Maxwell [1978] 3 All E.R. 1140 371
Du Cros v Lambourne [1907] 1 K.B. 40 366
Dullaghan v Hillen and King [1957] Ir. Jur. Rep. 10 187
Dunbar v Plant [1997] 3 W.L.R. 1261 127
Dunlop and Sylvester v R (1979) 47 C.C.C. (2d) 93 366
Dunnes Stores v Director of Consumer Affairs [2005] IEHC 242 .... 51n

Table of Cases xxiii

EC v Clinical Director of the Central Mental Hospital [2012] IEHC 152. . . . . 323n
Elliott v C (A Minor) [1983] 2 All E.R. 1005 66
Ellis v DPP [1990] 2 I.R. 291 316
Engel and Others v The Netherlands (1979) 1 E.H.R.R. 647 . . . . 17, 18, 19, 20
England v DPP, unreported, High Court, Kearns J., February 14, 2003 15
Enright v Ireland [2003] 2 I.R. 321 . . . . 46, 165, 166
Equality Authority v Portmarnock Golf Club [2009] IESC 73 . . . . 51n

Fagan v Metropolitan Police Commissioner [1969] 1 Q.B. 439 83
Fairclough v Whipp (1951) 35 Crim. App. R. 138 154
Faulkner v Talbot [1981] 1 W.L.R. 1528 . . . . 153n, 169n
Flood v Lawlor, unreported, Supreme Court, December 12, 2001 225
Fretwell (1862) Le. & Ca. 161 . . . . 370n

Gammon Ltd v AG of Hong Kong [1985] 1 A.C. 1 . . . . 70, 71
Gillick v West Norfolk and Wisbech Area Health Authority [1986] A.C. 112 . . . . 370n
Gilligan v Murphy [2011] IEHC 465 . . . . 18, 19–20, 46n
Gilligan v Special Criminal Court [2006] 2 I.R. 389 14
Goldman, Re [1968] 3 N.S.W.R. 325 . . . . 226n
Goodman v Hamilton (No.1) [1992] 2 I.R. 542 11–12
R. v Gray [1900] 2 Q.B. 36 228

Hardy v Ireland [1994] 2 I.R. 562 . . . . 40, 42, 45
Haughey, In re [1971] I.R. 217 . . . . 26, 224
Haughton v Smith [1975] A.C. 476 338
Haystead v DPP [2000] 3 All E.R. 890 171
Hegarty v Governor of Limerick Prison [1998] 1 I.R. 412 339
Hibernia National Review Ltd, Re [1976] I.R. 388 227
Hudson v MacRae (1863) 4 B. & S. 585, D.C. 246n
Hui Chi-ming v R [1992] 1 A.C. 3 . . . . 377n
Hyam v DPP [1975] A.C. 55 . . . . 54, 55, 57, 58, 109

Jaggard v Dickinson [1981] 2 W.L.R. 118 215
JB v Mental Health (Criminal Law) Review Board and Ors [2008] IEHC 303 . . . . 325n
Jennison v Baker [1972] 2 Q.B. 52 . . . . 226n
Johnson v DPP [1994] Crim. L.R. 673 215
Jones v Brooks (1968) 52 Cr. App. R. 614 . . . . 335n

Kafkaris v Cyprus [2008] ECHR 143 (App. No. 21906/04) 109n
Kamara v DPP [1974] 1 A.C. 104 342
Kane v Governor of Mountjoy Prison [1988] I.L.R.M. 724 188
KAS (An Infant), Re, unreported, High Court, Budd J., May 22, 1995 232
Kelly v DPP [2003] Crim. L.R. 45 181
Kelly v National University of Ireland [2009] 4 I.R. 163 222
Kelly v O'Neill [2000] 1 I.R. 354 . . . . 230, 231, 235n
Kelly v O'Sullivan (1990) 9 I.L.T.R. 126 242
Kelly and Deighan, In Re [1984] I.L.R.M. 424 231
Kennedy and McCann, Re [1976] I.R. 382 . . . . 226, 227, 232
Kilbride v Lake [1962] N.Z.L.R. 590 82
King v Attorney General [1981] I.R. 233 . . . . 47, 48, 49, 244, 326
KM v DPP [1994] 1 I.R. 514 302

Knuller v DPP [1973] A.C. 435...345n, 346
Kostan v Ireland [1978] I.L.R.M. 12..29
Kyprianou v Cyprus [2004] ECHR 43 (App. No. 73797 of 2001).................234

L v Kennedy [2010] IEHC 195...325n
Laskey and others v United Kingdom [1997] ECHR
    (App. Nos 21627/93, 21826/93)..175n
Lloyd v DPP [1992] 1 All E.R. 982..215
Ludlow v DPP [2008] IESC 54..125n
Lynch v DPP [2010] IEHC 284...208
Lynch and Whelan v The Minister for Justice [2010] IESC 34....................108

M v D [1998] 3 I.R. 178...13
M v Ireland [2007] IEHC 280...152n
M (Michael) v Superior Court of Sonama County 450 U.S. 464..................163n
Magee v Culligan [1992] 1 I.R. 233...46n
Maguire v Shannon Regional Fisheries Board [1994] 2 I.L.R.M. 253...........71, 72
Maidstone Borough Council v Mortimer [1980] 3 All E.R. 552, D.C..............246n
Mallon v Minister for Agriculture, Food and Fisheries [1996] 1 I.R. 517..............28
MB (Medical Treatment), In Re [1997] 2 F.L.R. 426..............................133
McAdam v Dublin United Tramways Co. Ltd [1929] I.R. 327......................71
McBoyle v United States 283 US 25 (1931)...47n
McCann v Judges of the Monaghan District Court [2010] 1 I.L.R.M. 517...........17
McConnell v Chief Constable Manchester [1990] 1 W.L.R. 364..................242
McGee v Attorney General [1974] I.R. 284...326
McLoughlin v Tuite [1989] 1 I.R. 82..8
MD (A Minor) v Ireland, Attorney General and the Director of Public Prosecutions
    [2010] IEHC 101; [2012] IESC 10..163
Mead's and Belt's Case (1828) 1 Lewin 184 assizes................................289
Meagher v O'Leary [1998] 1 I.L.R.M. 211..28
Melling v O'Mathghamhna [1962] I.R. 1...................6–8, 14, 20, 25, 27, 28
Meridian Global Funds Management (Asia) Limited v Securities
    Commission [1995] 2 A.C. 500.................................387, 388, 389
Minster for the Environment v Leneghan [2009] IEHC 226........................77
Minister for Justice, Equality and Law Reform v Bailey [2012] IESC 16............98n
Minister for Justice, Equality and Law Reform v Dolny [2008] IEHC 326;
    [2009] IESC 48...172
Minister for Justice, Equality and Law Reform v Tighe [2010] IESC 61............328
Minister for Posts and Telegraphs v Campbell [1966] I.R. 69....................210n
MM and HM, In Re [1933] I.R. 299...231
M'Naghton Case [1843] 4 St. Tr. (N.S.) 817...................315, 316, 317, 318, 323
Moore v Bresler [1944] 2 All E.R. 515..384n
Morris v The Crown Office [1970] 1 All E.R. 1079................................226
Mulllins v Hartnett [1998] 4 I.R. 426..51n
Murphy v GM [2001] 4 I.R. 113..14, 15, 19
Myles v Sreenan [1999] 4 I.R. 294..345n, 346

National Coal Board v Gamble [1959] 1 Q.B. 11..................................370
Nicklinson v Ministry of Justice [2012] EWHC 304 (QB)....................133n, 283

O'Brien v Parker [1997] 2 I.L.R.M. 170..314
O'Callaghan v DPP [2011] IESC 30..322n

Table of Cases

O'Connor v O'Neill [2011] IEHC 118 77
O'Kelly, Re (1974) 108 I.L.T.R. 97 226
O'Leary v Attorney General [1993] 1 I.R. 102 37
O'Leary v Attorney General [1995] 1 I.R. 254 .... 40, 41, 45
O'Sullivan v Hartnett [1983] I.L.R.M. 79 .... 26, 29

People v Conroy (No.2) [1989] I.R. 160 110
People v Muldoon, unreported, Court of Criminal Appeal, Keane C.J., July 7, 2003 164
People v O'Neill [1964] Ir. Jur. Rep. 1 .... 116, 125
People v Quinlan (1962) 96 I.L.T. 123 .... 125n
PH v Ireland and Ors [2006] IEHC 40 166
Pharmaceutical Society of Great Britain v Storkwain Lttd [1986] 2 All E.R. 635 68
PJ Carey Contractors Ltd v DPP [2011] IECCA 63 .... 45n
Potts v Minister for Defence [2005] 2 I.L.R.M. 517 17

Pretty v UK (2002) 35 E.H.R.R. 1 .... 129n

Quinlivan v Conroy [1999] 1 I.R. 271 307

R. v A [2010] EWCA Crim 1622 .... 377n
R. v ABCD [2010] EWCA Crim 1622 .... 377n
R. v Abdul-Hussain [1999] Crim. L.R. 570 273
R. v Adomako [1995] 1 A.C. 171 .... 117, 118, 119, 121
R. v Allen [1988] Crim. L.R. 698 .... 299n
R. v Anderson [1986] A.C. 27 345
R. v Anderson and Morris [1966] 2 Q.B. 110 .... 373, 376
R. v B [2006] EWCA Crim 2945 148
R. v Badza [2010] EWCA Crim 1363 .... 377n
R. v Bailey [1983] 3 All E.R. 503 313
R. v Bainbridge [1960] 1 Q.B. 129 .... 370, 371
R. v Baker [1924] N.Z.L.R. 865 .... 335n
R. v Ball [1989] Crim. L.R. 730 .... 122n
R. v Banks (1873) 12 Cox CC 393 .... 337, 350n
R. v Barraclough [1906] 1 K.B. 201 .... 243n
R. v Bateman (1925) 19 Cr. App. R. 8 116
R. v Becerra (1975) 62 Cr. App. R. 212 .... 348n, 354n, 379
R. v Bedder [1954] 2 All E.R. 801 .... 262, 263
R. v Blaue (1975) 61 Cr. App. R. 271 92
R. v Boston (1923) 33 C.L.R. 386 .... 346n
R. v Boulton (1871) 1 Cox CC 87 .... 339n
R. v Bourne [1938] 3 All E.R. 615 282
R. v Bow Street Metropolitan Stipendiary Magistrate [1999] 4 All E.R. 1 219
R. v Brain (Eliza) (1834) 172 E.R. 1272 .... 136n
R. v British Steel Plc [1995] 1 W.L.R. 1356 386
R. v Brown [1985] Crim. L.R. 212 207
R. v Brown [1994] 1 A.C. 212 .... 148n, 173–176, 302, 379
R. v Browne [1973] N.I. 96 285
R. v Bryce [2004] EWCA Crim 1231 .... 370n
R. v Bubb [1851] 4 Cox CC 455 85
R. v Burgess [1991] 2 W.L.R. 1206 312
R. v Caldwell [1982] A.C. 341 .... 65, 66, 67

R. v Calhaem [1985] 1 Q.B. 808 363
R. v Camplin [1978] A.C. 705 263
R. v Cheshire [1991] 1 W.L.R. 844 93
R. v Church [1966] 1 Q.B. 59 83
R. v City of Sault Ste Marie [1978] 2 S.C.R. 1229 .... 69, 72, 76
R. v Clarke [1949] All E.R. 481 142
R. v Clarkson [1971] 3 All E.R. 344 .... 366, 367
R. v Clarence (1888) 22 QBD 23 .... 146, 148
R. v Clegg [1995] 1 A.C. 482 268
R. v Codère (1916) 2 All E.R. 1 .... 316n
R. v Cogan and Leak [1976] Q.B. 217 358
R. v Collins [1973] Q.B. 100 .... 204, 205, 206, 209n, 251, 252, 253n
R. v Coney (1882) 8 QBD 534 .... 365, 366
R. v Conway [1988] 3 All E.R. 102 280
R. v Corbett [1996] Crim. L.R. 594 95
R. v Court [1988] 2 All E.R. 221 155
R. v Creighton (1908) 14 Can. Crim. Cas. 349 .... 317n
R. v Cuerrier [1998] 2 S.C.R. 371 147
R. v Cunningham [1957] 2 Q.B. 396 .... 64, 65
R. v Dee (1884) Cox CC 579; (1884) 14 Law Reports (Ireland) 468 145
R. v De Kromme (1892) 17 Cox CC 492 .... 337, 349n
R. v Deller (1952) 36 Cr. App. R. 184 81
R. v Denton [1981] 1 W.L.R. 1446 215
R. v Dhaliwal [2006] 2 Cr. App. R. 24 95
R. v Dica [2004] EWCA Crim 1103 148
R. v Doherty [1887] 16 Cox 306 294
R. v Doot [1973] A.C. 807 340
R. v Doughty (1986) 83 Cr. App. R. 319 .... 137n
R. v Dudley and Stephens (1884) 14 QBD 273 .... 281, 282
R. v Duffy [1949] 1 All E.R. 932 267
R. v Duguid (1906) 75 L.J.K.B. 470 .... 342n
R. v Dytham [1979] Q.B. 722 .... 88, 89
R. v Eagleton (1855) Dears 515 .... 330n, 331, 332, 333, 335n
R. v Emmett, *The Times*, October 15, 1999 176
R. v Evans [2009] EWCA Crim 650 .... 119, 120, 121, 124
R. v Evans [2009] 1 W.L.R. 1999 .... 87, 88
R. v Feely [1973] Q.B. 530 .... 193n
R. v Fennell [1971] 1 Q.B. 428 285
R. v Field [1972] Crim. L.R. 435 .... 285n
R. v Fitzmaurice [1983] Q.B. 1083 (CA) 353n
R. v Fitzpatrick [1977] N.I. 20 275
R. v Flattery [1877] 2 Q.B. 410 145
R. v Folkes [2011] EWCA Crim 325 .... 123n
R. v Foxford [1974] N.I. 181 301
R. v Fury [2006] EWCA Crim 1258 362
R. v G [2008] UKHL 37 .... 296n
R. v G and R [2004] 1 A.C. 1034 66–67
R. v Ghosh [1982] Q.B. 1053 193
R. v Giannetto [1996] Crim. L.R. 722 361
R. v Gibbons and Proctor (1918) 13 Cr. App. R. 134 86
R. v Gnango [2012] 2 W.L.R. 17 79

Table of Cases xxvii

R. v Gore [2007] EWCA Crim 2789 ....139, 140
R. v Gorrie (1919) 83 J.P. 136 302
R. v Gotts [1992] 1 All E.R. 832 ....274n
R. v Grimwood [1962] 3 All E.R. 285...102n
R. v Hancock and Shankland [1986] A.C. 455 ....55, 57
R. v Hardie [1984] 3 All E.R. 848 299
R. v Heard [2008] Q.B. 43..296
R. v Hennessy [1989] 2 All E.R. 9..313
R. v Hennigan (1971) 55 Cr. App. R. 262 ....92n
R. v Hess and Nguyen [1990] 2 S.C.R. 906 75
R. v Hicklin (1868) L.R. 3 Q.B. 360 ....243n
R. v Hills [2001] 1 F.C.R. 569..181
R. v Holzer [1968] V.R. 481 123
R. v Hood (2004) 1 Cr. App. R. (S) 431 86
R. v Howe (1958) 100 C.L.R. 448..269
R. v Howe [1987] A.C. 417..275
R. v Howes (1971) 2 S.A.S.R. 293 ....346n
R. v Howell [1981] 3 All E.R. 383 241
R. v Hudson and Taylor [1971] 2 Q.B. 202.............................272, 273, 278
R. v Hutty [1953] V.L.R. 338..98n
R. v Iby (2005) 63 N.S.W.L.R. 278...99
R. v ICR Haulage Limited [1944] 1 K.B. 551.......................................384n
R. v Inglis [2010] EWCA 2637 132
R. v Instan [1893] 1 Q.B. 450 86
R. v Ireland [1998] 1 A.C. 147...170, 171, 180n
R. v Jarmain [1946] 1 K.B. 74 102
R. v Jones [2005] Q.B. 259 216
R. v Jones [2007] EWCA Crim 1118..350
R. v Jones and Smith [1976] W.L.R. 672....................205, 209n, 252, 253n
R. v Jordan (1956) 40 Cr. App. R. 152 ....92, 93
R. v Kaitamaki [1985] A.C. 147 ....84, 143
R. v Kai-Whitewind [2005] EWCA Crim 1092.......................................138
R. v Kemp [1957] 1 Q.B. 399 316
R. v Kennedy (No.2) [2008] 1 A.C. 269 ....120, 124, 125n
R. v Kennedy (No.2) [2007] UKHL 38................................88n, 94, 355
R. v Khan [1990] 1 W.L.R. 813..................................209n, 331n, 336
R. v Kimber [1983] 1 W.L.R. 1118 ....149, 301
R. v King [2003] NSWCCA 399..98
R. v Kingston [1995] 2 A.C. 355..299, 314
R. v Konzani [2005] EWCA Crim 706 ....148n
R. v Larsonneur (1933) 24 Cr. App. R. 74...82, 238n
R. v Latimer [1886–1887] 17 QBD 359 78
R. v Lawrence [1981] 1 All E.R. 974 66
R. v Le Brun [1992] 1 Q.B. 61 83
R. v Lewis [2010] EWCA Crim 151 95
R. v Lewis [2010] EWCA Crim 496 ....377n
R. v Linekar [1995] 3 All E.R. 69 146
R. v Lipman [1970] 1 Q.B. 152 ....299, 310
R. v Looseley; Attorney General's Reference (No.3 of 2000) [2001] 1 W.L.R. 2060....305
R. v Loughnan [1981] V.R. 443...279, 280
R. v Lowe [1973] Q.B. 702 84

R. v Luffman [2008] EWCA Crim 1752 363
R. v Malcherek and Steel [1981] 1 W.L.R. 690. 93
R. v Malone (1998) 2 Crim. App. R. 447 149
R. v Martin [2010] EWCA Crim 1450. 366
R. v Matthews [2003] Crim. L.R. 553. . . . . 56, 57
R. v Mawgridge (1706) Kel. 119. 262
R. v Mawji [1957] 1 A.C. 125 341
R. v Mendez and Thompson [2010] EWCA Crim 516 362
R. v McCalla (1988) 87 Cr. App. R. 372 211
R. v McDonnell [1966] 1 Q.B. 233 341
R. v McInnes [1971] 3 All E.R. 295 286
R. v Meade and Belt (1823) 1 Lew C.C. 184 170
R. v Mendez [2010] EWCA Crim 516. . . . . 377n
R. v Michael (1840) 9 C. & P. 356. 358
R. v Miller [1954] 2 Q.B. 282 142
R. v Miller [1983] 2 A.C. 161 . . . . 87, 88
R. v Misra [2004] EWCA Crim 2375 . . . . 118, 121
R. v Mitchell [1983] 2 W.L.R. 938 123
R. v Moloney [1985] A.C. 905 . . . . 55, 56, 57
R. v Moore (Hannah) (1852) 175 E.R. 501 . . . . 136n
R. v Morgan [1975] 2 All E.R. 347 . . . . 300, 301
R. v Most (1881) 7 QBD 244. . . . . 350, 352
R. v Murphy (1837) 8 C. & P. 297. 340
R. v Murray (1982) 75 Cr. App. R. 58. . . . . 223n
R. v Nedrick [1986] 3 All E.R. 1. . . . . 55–56, 57
R. v Ness and Awan [2011] Crim. L.R. 645. . . . . 275n
R. v O'Brien [1954] S.C.R. 666. . . . . 344, 345
R. v O'Connor (1980) 146 C.L.R. 64 295
R. v Olugboja [1981] 3 All E.R. 443 149
R. v Pagett (1983) 76 Cr. App. R. 279. . . . . 93, 122
R. v Paine, *Times*, February 25, 1880 84
R. v Parnell (1881) 14 Cox CC 508. . . . . 230, 340n, 342
R. v Pearson (1835) 2 Lewin 144 299
R. v Pembliton [1874] 12 Cox CC 607 78
R. v Pigg [1982] 1 W.L.R. 762 . . . . 209n, 331n, 336n
R. v Pittwood [1902] 19 T.L.R. 37. 88
R. v Pommell (1995) 2 Cr. App. R. 607. 280
R. v Powell and Daniels [1997] 4 All E.R. 545. . . . . 377n
R. v Prince (1875–1877) 13 Cox CC 138 . . . . 68, 160
R. v Quayle [2005] 1 W.L.R. 3642 281
R. v Quick [1973] 3 All E.R. 347 313
R. v R [1991] 4 All E.R. 481 142
R. v R [1992] 1 A.C. 599. . . . . 49n
R. v Rabey [1980] 2 S.C.R. 513 . . . . 309n, 311
R. v Rahman [2008] UKHL 45 . . . . 377n, 378
R. v Roberts (1971) 56 Cr. App. R. 95. . . . . 94, 95
R. v Robertson [1968] 3 All E.R. 557 322
R. v Safety-Kleen Canada Inc (1997) 145 D.L.R. (4th) 276. 385
R. v Saik [2007] 1 A.C. 18. . . . . 340, 341n
R. v Sainsbury (1989) 11 Cr. App. R. (S) 533 137
R. v Salvo [1980] V.R. 401 193

Table of Cases xxix

R. v Sang [1980] A.C. 402. . . . . .304, 305
R. v Sargeant [1997] Crim. L.R. 50. 153
R. v Saunders and Archer (1573) 2 Plowd 473 77
R. v Scott [1967] V.R. 276. 83
R. v Senior [1832] 1 Mood CC 346. . . . . .99, 100
R. v Shepherd (1988) 86 Cr. App. R. 47 276
R. v Sheppard [1980] 3 W.L.R. 960. . . . . .246n
R. v Sirat (1985) Cr. App. R. 41. 349
R. v Smith [1959] 2 All E.R. 193. 93
R. v Steele (1977) 76 Cr. App. R. 22 142
R. v Stone and Dobinson [1977] Q.B. 354 86
R. v Stringer [2011] EWCA Crim 1396. 362
R. v Stringer and Banks (1991) 94 Cr. App. R. 13 . . . . .358, 359
R. v Sweeney (1986) 8 Cr. App. R. (S) 419. 127
R. v Taafe [1983] 1 W.L.R. 627. 338
R. v Taktak [1988] 14 N.S.W.L.R. 226 87
R. v Thabo Meli [1954] 1 All E.R. 373 83
R. v Thompson (1965) 50 Cr. App. R. 1 345
R. v Thomson Newspapers Limited *Ex p.* Attorney General [1968] 1 All E.R. 268. 230
R. v Tolson (1889) 23 QBD 168 301
R. v Tomlinson [1895] 1 Q.B. 707. 191
R. v Tyrell [1894] 1 Q.B. 710 . . . . .357n, 378, 379
R. v Valderrama-Vega [1985] Crim. L.R. 220. 273
R. v Wacker [2002] EWCA Crim 1944. 118
R. v Walkington [1979] 1 W.L.R. 1169 207
R. v Wallis (1983) 5 Crim. App. R. (S) 342. 127
R. v Walters (Ann) (1841) 174 E.R. 455 . . . . .136n
R. v Webster [2006] EWCA Crim 415 366
R. v Webster and Warwick [1995] 2 All E.R. 168. 217
R. v Welsh (1869) 11 Cox CC 674. 262
R. v White [1910] 2 K.B. 124 91
R. v Whitechurch (1890) 24 Q.B. 420. . . . . .342n
R. v Whitehouse [1977] Q.B. 868 . . . . .349, 357n, 378
R. v Whybrow (1951) 35 Cr. App. R. 141. . . . . .337n
R. v Williams [1923] 1 K.B. 340. 145
R. v William (Gladstone) (1984) 78 Cr. App. R. 276 288
R. v Williams and Davis [1992] 1 W.L.R. 380 95
R. v Willoughby [2004] EWCA Crim 3365. 118
R. v Wilson [1955] 1 W.L.R. 493 170
R. v Wilson [1997] Q.B. 47. . . . . .175, 176
R. v Windle [1952] 2 All E.R. 1. 316
R. v Woollin [1999] 1 A.C. 82. . . . . .56, 57
R. v Z (otherwise known as Hasan) [2005] 2 A.C. 467. . . . . .273, 276, 278
R. (on the application of Pretty) v DPP [2001] UKHL 61. . . . . .128, 129, 131n
R. (on the application of Purdy) v DPP [2009] UKHL 45. . . . . .129, 130n
Reference re Section 94(2) of the Motor Vehicle Act [1985] 24 D.L.R. (4th) 536 73
Registrar of Companies v Judge David Anderson and Anor [2004] IESC 103. 9
Reilly v Judge Pattwell [2008] IEHC 446. 77
Reniger v Fogossa (1552) 1 Plowd 1. 293
Royal Dublin Society v Yates [1997] IEHC 144. 180
Ryan v DPP [1989] I.R. 399 . . . . .37n

S v Goliath [1972] (3) SA 1..274n
S v Nkosiyana (1966) 4 S.A. 655 350
Scott v Metropolitan Police Commissioner [1975] A.C. 819 ....345n, 347
Semayne's Case (1604) 5 Co. Rep. 91a..289
Shannon Regional Fisheries Board v Cavan County Council [1996] 3 I.R. 267...72, 73, 76
Shermsan v United States 356 U.S. 369 (1958)..................................305
Shillitani v United States 384 U.S. 364 (1966) 224n
SM v Ireland (No.2) [2007] 4 I.R. 369 327
Southwark London Borough v Williams [1971] Ch. 734 ....131n, 279n
SR (A Minor), In the Matter of; An Irish Hospital v RH and JMcG and SR
   (Notice Party) [2012] IEHC 2 134
State (Commins) v McRann [1977] I.R. 78.......................................224
State (DPP) v Walsh and Connelly [1981] I.R. 412..............226, 227, 233, 234, 276
State (Keegan) v De Burca [1973] I.R. 223.....................................224
State (M) v O'Brien [1972] I.R. 169 208
State (Trimbole) v Governor of Mountjoy Prison [1985] I.R. 550 309
St Regis Paper Co. Limited v R [2011] EWCA 2527 388
Stubing v Germany [2012] ECHR 656 (App. No. 43547/08).........................157
Superwood Holdings Plc v Sun Alliance Assurance Plc [1995] 3 I.R. 330.........392
Supply of Ready Mixed Concrete (No.2), Re [1995] 1 A.C. 456 387
Sweet v Parsley [1970] A.C. 132....................................70, 250n, 251
Syon v Hewitt and McTiernan [2008] 1 I.R. 168 ....308, 309

Tesco Supermarkets v Natrass [1972] A.C. 153 ....384, 385, 388, 389
Texeira de Castro v Portugal (1998) 28 E.H.R.R. 101...........................306
Thorne v Motor Trade Association [1937] A.C. 797..............................190
Thorpe v DPP [2007] 1 I.R. 502 ....242, 243
Tuberville v Savage (1669) 2 Keb. 545; 1 Mod. Rep. 3; 86 Eng. Rep. 684 169
Tuck v Robson [1970] 1 All E.R. 1171 366

United States v Holmes 26 Fed. Cas. 360 (1841) 282n
United States v Lumumba 741 F 2nd 12 (2nd Cir. 1984) 226
United States v Sorrells 287 U.S. 435 (1932) 306

Walsh v United Kingdom [2006] ECHR 1154 (App. No. 43384 of 2005).............49n
Ward of Court (No.2), In Re a [1996] 2 I.R. 79......................90, 134–135, 326
Wilcox v Jeffrey [1951] 1 All E.R. 464.......................................368n
Wilmott v Atack [1977] Q.B. 498 ....246n
Winterwerp v The Netherlands (1979) 2 E.H.R.R. 387............................321
Winzar v Chief Constable of Kent, *The Times*, March 28, 1983..................82
Woolmington v DPP [1935] A.C. 462 ....36, 38, 39

ZS v DPP [2011] IESC 49 ....162n

TABLE OF LEGISLATION

Bunreacht na hÉireann

Art.15.5.1°.	46
Art.15.13.	21n
Art.29.8.	98
Art.34.1.	8
Art.37.1.	5
Art.38	5, 9, 12, 25
Art.38.1.	8, 11, 12, 15, 37, 40, 41, 42, 43, 45, 46, 48, 161, 166, 326
Art.38.2.	25
Art.38.5.	6, 232, 235
Art.39	22
Art.40	161, 248
Art.40.1.	48, 152n, 163, 164, 247, 327
Art.40.3.	48, 247, 287
Art.40.3.1°.	75, 289, 326
Art.40.3.3°.	99
Art.40.4.1°.	30, 48, 247
Art.40.4.6°.	30, 50
Art.40.5.	289
Art.40.6.1°.	243

Pre-1922 Acts

Accessories and Abettors Act 1861	356
s.8	360
Criminal Law Amendment Act 1885	
s.5	378
Customs Consolidation Act 1876	
s.186	6, 7, 25
s.197	7
s.204	7
s.205	7
s.223	7
s.256	7
Sch.C.	7
Explosive Substances Act 1883	
s.3(a)	371
s.3(b)	371
s.4	41
s.4(1)	40
Forgery Act 1913	212
Larceny Act 1861	192, 211

Larceny Act 1916 . . . . 190, 192, 196, 203, 211
    ss.29–31 190
Malicious Damage Act 1861 213
Offences Against the Person Act 1861. . . . . 152n, 167, 171, 173
    s.9 98
    s.20 . . . . 180n
    s.55 160
    s.62 326
    s.63 142
Offences Against the Person Act 1861
    s.23 64
Perjury Act 1586 (28 Eliz. c.1) 220n
Perjury Act 1729 (3 Geo. II c.4) 220n
Perjury Act 1791 (31 Geo. III c.18). 220n
Petty Sessions (Ireland) Act 1851
    s.22 357
Punishment of Incest Act 1908 . . . . 157n
    s.1 . . . . 156n
    s.2 . . . . 156n
Trial of Lunatics Act 1883 . . . . 321, 323
Vagrancy Act 1824. . . . . .47, 326
    s.3 247
    s.4 244

Post-1922 Acts of the Oireachtas

Bail Act 1997. . . . . 30–31, 32
    s.1 31
    s.2(1). 30
    Sch. 31

Central Bank and Financial Services Authority of Ireland Act 2003. 11
Children Act 2001 304
    s.52 . . . . 303, 304
    s.246 86
Child Trafficking and Pornography Act 1998 . . . . 164, 166
    s.3 154
    s.3(2). 154
Civil Partnership and Certain Rights and Obligations of Cohabitants Act 2010. 346
Commission to Inquire into Child Abuse Act 2000
    s.1(1). 32n
Commission to Inquire into Child Abuse (Amendment) Act 2005
    s.3 . . . . 32n
Commissions of Investigation Act 2004 11
Communications (Retention of Data) Act 2011
    s.1 . . . . 32n
Companies Act 1963
    s.125 9
Control of Horses Act 1996
    s.48 368

Table of Legislation

Criminal Damage Act 1991 .... 62, 213–219
    s.1 214
    s.2(1) 216
    s.2(2) 53, 216
    s.2(3) 217
    s.2(4) 218
    s.2(6) 258
    s.3 218
    s.4 218
    s.5 .... 200, 216, 218
    s.6 .... 279n
    s.6(2) 214
    s.6(2)(c) 214
    s.6(3) 214
    s.9 .... 4n
Criminal Justice Act 1951
    s.6 .... 23n
Criminal Justice Act 1964 .... 100, 102
    s.4 .... 60, 61, 100, 112, 153, 269
    s.4(1) 80, 102, 337n
    s.4(2) 60, 114
Criminal Justice Act 1967
    s.4B 23n
    s.4C 23n
Criminal Justice Act 1984
    s.13 89
Criminal Justice Act 1990 .... 22, 103
    s.1 .... 22n
    s.3 103
    s.3(2)(a) 104
    s.4 .... 22n
    s.4(a) 104n
    s.5(1) 104n
Criminal Justice Act 1993 .... 157n
    s.5 .... 4n
Criminal Justice Act 1994 15
    s.4 .... 14, 15
    s.39 15
Criminal Justice Act 1999
    s.9 .... 23n
    s.38 96
    s.41 223
Criminal Justice Act 2003
    s.269 .... 132n
    Sch.21, para.11(f) 132n
Criminal Justice Act 2006 .... 304, 339
    Pt 7 .... 32, 255n
    s.6 .... 34n
    s.8 .... 32n
    s.70 .... 32n, 339
    s.71 339

s.71(4)...339
s.71A..355n
s.72..355n
s.74...98n
s.176..164
s.185...189n
Criminal Justice Act 2011
　s.3..382
　s.3(2)...382
　s.19..35, 89
　s.19(1)...382
　Sch.1...382
Criminal Justice (Amendment) Act 2009 223
　s.19..24n, 357
　s.19(2)(a)..34n
Criminal Justice (Female Genital Mutilation) Act 2012
　s.3...39
Criminal Justice (Miscellaneous Provisions) Act 1997
　s.10..34n
Criminal Justice (Public Order) Act 1994 .... 190, 242, 243, 244, 249, 250, 256
　s.3...236, 237, 239
　s.4...23, 24, 236, 237, 238, 239, 244
　s.4(4)..238
　s.5...236, 238, 239, 244
　s.5(3)..238
　s.6..58, 64, 236, 239, 240, 241, 243, 244
　s.6(1)..239
　s.7..236, 243, 244
　s.7(1)..243
　s.8..236, 244, 245
　s.8(1)..244, 245
　s.8(2)..245
　s.8A..245
　s.8A(1)...245
　s.8A(2)...245
　s.8A(4)...245
　s.9..236, 244, 246, 247
　s.11...251n, 252, 253, 254
　s.11(1)(a)..253
　s.11(1)(b)..253
　s.13..253, 254
　s.13(1)..251n
　s.14..255
　s.14(2)(a)..255
　s.14(2)(c)..255
　s.15..256
　s.15(2)(b)...256n
　s.15(3)...256
　s.15(5)...256
　s.15(6)..256n
　s.16..257

s.16(2)(a)	257
s.16(2)(b)	257
s.16(3)	258
s.17(1)	190
s.17(2)(a)	190
s.17(2)(b)	190
s.18	189
s.19	189
s.19(3)	246, 247
s.19(3)(a)	246
s.19(3)(b)	246, 247
s.19(3)(c)	246
s.19(3)(d)	246, 247
s.19(6)	246
s.19A	254
s.19C	254
s.19C(3)	254
s.19D	254
s.19G(1)	254
s.19G(2)	254
Criminal Justice (Public Order) Act 2011	247, 248
s.1	250
s.1(2)	248
s.1(2)(a)	248
s.2	248, 249
s.3	249
s.3(6)	249
s.5	249, 250
s.6	249, 250
s.11	250
s.13	250
s.14	374
s.15	374
Criminal Justice (Surveillance) Act 2009	34, 330
s.4(1)	34n
Criminal Justice (Theft and Fraud Offences) Act 2001	192, 193, 194, 195, 197, 198, 200, 201, 204, 373
Pt 3	201
Pt 4	212
Pt 5	213
s.2	194, 197, 211
s.2(1)	193, 196, 199
s.2(2)	198, 199
s.2(3)	198
s.2(4)	196
s.(4)(b)–(e)	196
s.4	192, 193, 194, 197, 211
s.4(1)	193
s.4(2)	197
s.4(4)	194
s.4(5)	195, 196

s.4(6)	373
s.5	196
s.6	194, 197, 198, 199, 200, 212
s.6(1)	198
s.7	194, 197, 199, 200, 212
s.7(1)	199
s.7(2)	199
s.7(3)	199
s.8	194, 197, 200
s.8(1)	199
s.8(2)	200
s.9	194, 197, 200
s.10	194, 197, 201
s.10(1)	201
s.10(2)	201
s.11	194, 197, 201
s.11(2)(a)	201
s.12	203, 209
s.12(1)	34
s.12(1)(a)	208
s.12(1)(b)	208
s.12(2)	207
s.12(3)	373
s.12(4)	204, 208
s.13	209, 211
s.13(2)	209
s.14	211, 360
s.15	212
s.15(1)	212
s.15(1A)	212
s.15(2)	212
s.15(2A)	212
s.16	202
s.17	194, 201, 202, 212
s.17(2)	202
s.17(3)	201
s.18	202
s.18(1)	202
s.18(2)	202
s.18(3)	201
s.19	203
s.20	201
s.24	213
s.25	212
s.26	213
s.27	213
s.28	213
s.29	213
s.30	213
s.31	213
s.32	213

Table of Legislation xxxvii

    s.33 213
    s.34 213
    s.35 213
    s.36 213
    s.37 213
Criminal Law Act 1976
    s.11 187
Criminal Law Act 1997 ....21, 32, 33, 356–357, 381
    s.1 32
    s.2 382
    s.3(1) 21
    s.4 ....21, 33
    s.4(1) 33, 34
    s.4(2) 33, 34
    s.4(3) 33
    s.4(4) 33
    s.4(5) 33
    s.5 21
    s.6 21
    s.7 ....21, 127, 357, 374
    s.7(1) 337, 343, 349, 356, 357, 367, 382
    s.7(1A) 24
    s.7(2) 34, 381, 382
    s.7(3) 381
    s.7(4) 381
    s.8 ....21, 35
    s.8(1) 357, 381, 382
    s.15(4) 21
    s.16 356
Criminal Law Amendment Act 1935 ....74, 152n
    s.1 160
    s.1(1) 73, 74, 76, 161, 162n, 326
    s.2 ....160, 161
    s.2(1) 162n
    s.2(2) 162n
    s.4 ....157, 158
    s.12 ....156n
    s.17 326
Criminal Law (Defence and the Dwelling) Act 2011 ....287, 288, 289, 292, 293
    s.1(1) 292
    s.2(1) 292
    s.2(4) 293
    s.2(5) 293
    s.2(7) 293
    s.3 293
    s.4 292
Criminal Law (Human Trafficking) Act 2008 ....154, 166
    s.4 166
    s.5 166
Criminal Law (Incest Proceedings) Act 1995 ....156, 157n
    s.5(1) 156n

Criminal Law (Insanity) Act 2006 . . . . 39, 136, 315, 320, 321, 324n, 325, 326
    s.3 . . . . 323n
    s.4 . . . . 321–322, 323n
    s.4(8) 323n
    s.5 323
    s.5(1)(b)(iii) 323
    s.5(2) 324
    s.6 . . . . 39n, 260, 323
    s.6(2) 323
    s.6(3) 137, 323n
    s.13 325
    s.22 . . . . 136n
Criminal Law (Insanity) Act 2010 325
Criminal Law (Rape) Act 1981 . . . . 141, 152
    s.2 . . . . 143, 359
    s.2(1) 141
    s.2(1)(b) 149
    s.2(2) 151, 152, 301
Criminal Law (Rape) (Amendment) Act 1990 . . . . 142, 143, 144, 152, 153, 156
    s.1(2) 142
    s.2 . . . . 31n, 152
    s.3 . . . . 153, 162
    s.4 . . . . 143–144, 153, 158, 162, 304
    s.4(1) 143
    s.5 142
    s.5(2) 142
    s.6 303
    s.9 144
    s.10 . . . . 24n
Criminal Law (Sexual Offences) Act 1993 . . . . 158, 159
    s.5 . . . . 158, 159
    s.5(4) 158n
    s.9 249
    s.10 250
    s.13 . . . . 378n
Criminal Law (Sexual Offences) Act 2006 . . . . 137, 162, 163, 302
    s.2 162
    s.3(1) 162, 163, 327
    s.3(2) 162
    s.5 . . . . 163, 164, 327
Criminal Law (Sexual Offences) (Amendment) Act 2007
    s.6 . . . . 164n
Criminal Law (Suicide) Act 1993
    s.2(1) 126
    s.2(2) 127
Criminal Procedure Act 1967
    s.13(1)(a) 24n
Criminal Procedures Act 2010
    s.4 . . . . 4n

Table of Legislation

Defamation Act 2009
    s.32(2) 4n

European Arrest Warrant Act 2003 ....98n
European Convention on Human Rights Act 2003 ....17, 19
Extradition (European Convention on the Suppression of Terrorism) Act 1987......30, 31
    s.1 30

Fines Act 2010...24n, 27
Firearms and Offensive Weapons Act 1990
    s.9 ....210, 329n
    s.9(4)..210
    s.9(5)..210
    s.9(6)..210
Fisheries (Consolidation) Act 1959 71

Gaming and Lotteries Act 1956...29, 206
    s.39 206

Immigration Act 2004
    s.12 ....48, 49
Income Tax Act 1967
    s.500 ....8, 9
    s.508 ....8, 9
Infanticide Act 1949..136, 140
    s.1(3)(b)..140
Interception of Postal Packets and Telecommunications Messages (Regulation)
    Act 1993
    s.1 ....32n
International Criminal Court Act 2006
    s.62 ....32n
Intoxicating Liquor Act 2008
    s.19 245

Mental Health Act 2001...324, 325, 326
Misuse of Drugs Act 1977
    s.15A..42, 77
    s.29 ....43, 44
    s.29(2)(a)...42, 43, 44

Non-Fatal Offences Against the Person Act 1997 .... 62, 124, 167, 168, 169, 170,
              172, 173, 177, 179, 180, 184, 187, 188, 214, 216, 268, 270, 287
    s.1 ....171, 172, 177, 184
    s.2 ....167, 168, 169, 170, 171, 172, 173
    s.2(1)(a)..168
    s.2(1)(b)..168
    s.2(2)..169
    s.2(3)..168
    s.3 ....171, 173
    s.4 ....24, 172, 302, 365

s.5	176, 177
s.6	80, 177
s.6(1)	177, 178
s.6(2)	178
s.6(3)	178
s.6(5)	178
s.6(5)(a)	178
s.6(5)(b)	178
s.6(5)(c)	178
s.7	178
s.8	178
s.8(1)	178
s.8(2)	179
s.9	179
s.10	180, 181
s.10(3)	182n
s.10(4)	182n
s.10(5)	182n
s.11	183
s.12	183
s.12(2)	183n
s.13	49n, 63, 184, 186, 187, 217, 329n, 337
s.13(1)	63
s.14	186
s.15	187, 188
s.16	188
s.17	188
s.18	270, 283, 284, 285, 287, 291
s.18(1)	283, 284, 288
s.18(5)	288n
s.18(7)	285
s.19	283, 285, 287
s.19(1)	288n
s.19(3)	288n
s.20	283
s.20(1)	286
s.20(2)	285
s.20(3)	286
s.20(4)	286
s.21	283
s.22	283
s.22(1)	287
s.22(2)	270, 287
s.24	169

Nurses and Midwives Act 2011

s.27(2)	27n

Offences Against the State Act 1939 103

s.21	41
s.24	41, 42
s.30	33n

Table of Legislation xli

Offences Against the State (Amendment) Act 1998 . . . . 31, 32
    s.8 . . . . 32n
    s.9 . . . . 32n, 89

Proceeds of Crime Act 1996 . . . . 13, 14, 19, 20
    s.8(2) 14
Prohibition of Incitement to Hatred Act 1989
    s.2 354
    s.3 354
    s.4 354
Protection of Animals Acts 1911 and 1965
    s.1(1)(a) 368

Residential Institutions Redress Act 2003
    s.28 . . . . 32n
Road Traffic Act 1961
    s.49 28
    s.49(1) 26
    s.52 . . . . 68, 126
    s.53 125
    s.112 212
Road Traffic Act 1994
    s.13 . . . . 73, 77
    s.23 73
Road Traffic Act 2010
    s.12 89

Safety Health and Welfare at Work Act 1989
    s.50 . . . . 45n
Sex Offenders Act 2001 . . . . 46, 164, 165, 166
    s.7(2)(b)(i) 46
Sexual Offences (Jurisdiction) Act 1996 165

Treason Act 1939 22
    s.1(3) 22n
    s.2(2) 22n
Tribunals of Enquiry (Evidence) Act 1921 11

UNITED KINGDOM ACTS

Children and Young Person Act 1963 303
Coroners and Justice Act 2009
    s.54 263
    s.55 263
    s.56 263
    s.57 139
    s.59(1) 127n
Corporate Manslaughter and Homicide Act 2007 391–392
Crime and Disorder Act 1998 303
Criminal Attempts Act 1981

s.1 .... 336n
Criminal Damage Act 1971 214
   s.1(2) 336
Criminal Law Act 1977
   s.1(1) 345n
Dangerous Drugs Act 1965 70
Homicide Act 1957
   s.2 320
   s.4(1) 126
Infanticide Act 1938 139
   s.1(1) 140
Law Reform (Year and a Day Rule) Act 1996 96
Police and Criminal Evidence Act 1984 305
   s.78 305
Proceeds of Crime Act 2002 19
   s.241(1) 19
Protection of Harassment Act 1997 181
Public Order Act 1986
   s.1 255
   s.6(1) 255
Restrictive Trade Practices Act 1976 387
Sexual Offences Act 2003 .... 152, 296n
   s.1 .... 152n
   s.3 .... 296n
   s.74 .... 145n
   s.75 .... 145n
Sexual Offences (Amendment) Act 1976
   s.1(1) 151
Suicide Act 1961 .... 126, 127n
Theft Act 1968 .... 193, 205, 208, 252
Trade Descriptions Act 1968 385

SECONDARY LEGISLATION

Aliens Order 1920 .... 82, 238n
Pollution Prevention and Control (England and Wales) Regulations 2000 389

AUSTRALIAN LEGISLATION

Crime (Sexual Offences) Act 1980 (Victoria) 144n

CANADIAN LEGISLATION

Canadian Charter of Rights and Freedoms 75
   Art.1 75
   s.7 73
Quebec Charter of Human Rights and Freedoms 85
   s.2 .... 85n

Table of Legislation

UNITED STATES LEGISLATION

United States Constitution
    Art.III, section 2 .... 22n

12 Vt. Stat. Ann. s.519 (Emergency Medical Care). 84

INTERNATIONAL CONVENTIONS

European Convention on Human Rights 16, 19, 20, 105, 108, 109, 128, 129, 306
    art.2 128
    art.3 .... 109, 128
    art.5 109
    art.5(1)(e) 321
    art.5(4). 105
    art.6 .... 16, 18, 20, 119, 234
    art.6(1). 19, 307
    art.6(2). 19
    art.7 .... 17, 19, 20, 119
    art.7(1). 46, 49n
    art.8 .... 128, 129, 157, 175
    art.8(2). 128, 129, 157, 175
    art.9 .... 128n
    art.10(1). 243
    art.14 .... 128n
United Nations Universal Declaration of Human Rights 1948
    art.11 37
    art.38 37

Chapter 1

GENERAL PRINCIPLES

Defining the Criminal Law

Background

Crime is by far the most visible face of the law, with intense media coverage of trials, arrests, and all the other aspects of the criminal justice system. As Kenny put it in his classic 1902 text, there is a public fascination with the "vivid and violent nature of the events which criminal courts notice and repress, as well as of those by which they effect the repression".[1] Over a century later this remains true. As such, there is no difficulty in understanding in general terms what is meant by "crime" and the "criminal law". However, when we try to formalise that understanding, to examine precisely what we mean by "crime" and the "criminal law", we run into difficulties.[2]

To begin with, we must point out that the public face of criminal law can be misleading. Although most coverage is of serious crimes, the day-to-day work of the criminal justice system is more mundane and deals with such matters as road traffic offences, littering and public order offences. The high-profile jury trials which dominate the media are a small minority of all criminal cases. Instead, the overwhelming majority take place in the District Court before a judge without a jury—or never see a courtroom at all, being dealt with by the payment of a fixed penalty notice. In 2010, the most recent year for which statistics are available, the District Court disposed of 498,672 offences, while between them the Circuit Court, Central Criminal Court and Special Criminal Court disposed of only 4,229 more serious offences—less than one per cent of the total.[3]

We must also take into account the fact that the content of the criminal law is far from fixed—whether particular conduct is subject to criminal sanctions at any particular time depends strongly on the social and political context. The decriminalisation of male homosexual behaviour in 1993 (following a long campaign for law reform and an adverse judgment of the European Court of Human Rights) reflected an important change in social norms and a political acceptance that the role of the criminal law in sexual matters should be limited.[4] At the same time, however, the use of the criminal law has been greatly expanded in other areas such as competition law, environmental

---

[1] Courtney Stanhope Kenny, *Outlines of Criminal Law* (Oxford: Oxford University Press, 1902), p.2.
[2] See, e.g. Lindsay Farmer, "The Obsession with Definition: The Nature of Crime and Critical Legal Theory" (1996) 5 S. & L.S. 57.
[3] Courts Service, *Annual Report 2010* (Dublin, 2011), Ch.4.
[4] Decriminalisation was finally achieved by the Criminal Law (Sexual Offences) Act 1993. For background, see Richard Dunphy, "Sexual identities, national identities: The politics of gay law reform in the Republic of Ireland" (1997) 3(3) *Contemporary Politics* 247.

law and safety in the workplace where recent legislation now criminalises conduct which was previously considered solely a matter for the civil law.[5] In short, societal views as to what should be criminalised can and do change significantly in a relatively short period of time.

An added complication is a deliberate government strategy, in recent years, to straddle the civil–criminal divide by making use of civil law procedures to address what would otherwise be considered criminal behaviour. In areas such as the proceeds of crime and anti-social behaviour, legislation has sidestepped procedural protections for the individual, e.g. by substituting the lower civil standard of proof, on the balance of probabilities, for the criminal standard of proof, beyond a reasonable doubt. As Kilcommins and Vaughan note:

> "The employment of criminal law as the monopoly mechanism for dealing with deviant behaviour is also beginning to fragment and blur. In particular, the diversification and diffusion of the State into the civil sphere as a means of crime control is becoming more visible in Ireland. This move away from the traditional condemnatory 'prosecution-conviction-sentencing' approach to deviant behaviour may to some extent be seen (through a benevolent lens) as a willingness to move beyond the harsh consequences of criminalisation. It seems more likely however that recent embrace of civil measures is more closely connected with the perceived ineffectiveness of the criminal law mechanism. The principled protections of the criminal process—premised on a criminal sanctioning model of justice—can more easily be circumvented by directing the flow of power into this parallel system of civil justice."[6]

Finally, before any attempt to define the "criminal law" we must ask ourselves—for what purpose? What do we hope to achieve by a definition? Here we can separate the concerns of the lawyer from those of the criminologist or others who might study crime. The lawyer will usually wish to find out whether a particular matter should be treated as criminal because of the practical consequences which flow from this— whether an individual enjoys a right to silence or presumption of innocence, for example. Consequently the perspective of the lawyer is internal to the legal system. The perspective of the criminologist is external to the legal system and generally seeks to locate the concept of crime within a wider social context. For example, the criminologist might ask why it is that certain behaviours are criminalised and not others, or how crime is understood and regarded by the public.[7] Bearing this in mind, this chapter will first give a short introduction to the nature of the criminal law, before going on to consider the narrower question of the rules by which the Irish courts differentiate civil from criminal matters.

---

[5] See, e.g. Patrick Massey, "Criminal Sanctions for Competition Law: A Review of the Irish Experience" (2004) 1(1) Comp. L.R. 23; Shelley Horan, *Corporate Crime* (Dublin: Bloomsbury, 2011).

[6] Shane Kilcommins and Barry Vaughan, "Reconfiguring State-Accused Relations in Ireland" (2006) 41(1) Ir.Jur. 90. See also, Claire Hamilton, "Anti-Social Behaviour Orders and the Presumption of Innocence" (2005) 23 I.L.T. 215.

[7] See, e.g. Grant Lamond, "What is a Crime?" (2007) 27(4) O.J.L.S. 609; Lucia Zedner, *Criminal Justice* (Oxford: Oxford University Press, 2004), Ch.2.

General Principles 3

Nature of the criminal law

While there is no single purpose to the criminal law we can identify a number of functions which it serves and some broad areas where it differs from the civil law. At its core it identifies certain conduct as being particularly reprehensible and censures and condemns those who engage in this conduct. As Lamond puts it:

> "Crimes are not simply artificial creations of the law, like a *cestui que trust*, or a negative covenant. Instead, criminal law has a crucial social dimension. A successful prosecution does not simply result in a defendant being held liable for the breach of a legal prohibition—instead she is convicted of committing a crime—she is found guilty of the charge against her. These are socially expressive terms. The criminal law serves an important condemnatory function in social life—it marks out some behaviour as specially reprehensible, so that the machinery of the state needs to be mobilized against it."[8]

This expressive function marks out civil from criminal outcomes even though they might otherwise appear similar. For example, the convict who is ordered to pay a fine may suffer precisely the same harm to his wallet as the civil defendant who is ordered to pay compensation for damage caused by negligence, but the societal disapproval expressed through the fine gives it an additional symbolic significance.[9]

The criminal law does not, however, merely censure those who offend against social order. By setting rules for conduct it also acts as a guide to the individual, enabling him to know what he is and is not permitted to do and setting out the consequences of prohibited behaviour. This in turn has both a negative and positive dimension: negative in that it helps to deter unwanted behaviour and positive in that the individual can be secure that he will not be "singled out for punishment" unless it has been "established beyond reasonable doubt that he has deviated from a clearly prescribed standard of conduct".[10]

To a limited extent we can say that the criminal law is characterised by the severity of harms it deals with and the moral nature of the acts it prohibits. In identifying certain conduct as worthy of condemnation or as causing harm to the community as a whole the criminal law does often reflect these factors. Certainly, the most well-known crimes—such as murder, rape or burglary—can be said to share the characteristics of having a significant harmful impact on others and being intrinsically morally wrong (*"mala in se"*) rather than simply being wrong because they are prohibited (*"mala prohibita"*). That said, however, these characteristics are at best an unreliable guide. There are many crimes where the harm caused by the offence is relatively minor, while many instances of moral wrongdoing (such as lying or infidelity) are not in themselves criminal.[11]

---

[8] Grant Lamond, "What is a Crime?" (2007) 27(4) *Oxford Journal of Legal Studies* 609 at 610.
[9] See, e.g. Joel Feinberg, "The Expressive Function of Punishment" in *Doing and Deserving: Essays in the Theory of Responsibility* (Princeton N.J.: Princeton University Press, 1970).
[10] Per Henchy J. in *King v Attorney General* [1981] I.R. 233.
[11] See, e.g. Andrew Simester et al., *Criminal Law: Theory and Doctrine*, 4th edn (Oxford: Hart Publishing, 2010), pp.2–3. The extent to which the criminal law should be used to enforce societal morality is also controversial—see, e.g. John Paul McCutcheon, "Morality and the Criminal Law: Reflections on Hart-Devlin" (2002–2003) 47 Crim.L.Q. 15.

Criminal law is also marked out by its focus on punishment as compared with a focus on compensation in the civil law, although again this is not an infallible distinction. There are instances in which the civil law provides for punitive damages to mark special disapproval of a defendant's conduct,[12] while the criminal justice system in a number of situations seeks to provide compensation for victims of crime.[13] Nevertheless, as a general rule we can say that the primary outcome of criminal proceedings is the punishment of the person found to have committed a crime and the severity of punishment is gauged mainly by the quality of the defendant's actions while in the civil law the level of compensation is generally measured by the harm suffered by the injured party.[14]

In looking at the moral quality of actions the criminal law generally takes a subjective approach which focuses on the defendant's mental state at the time of an alleged crime to determine if punishment is merited. This is a key contrast with the civil law where, as a rule, an objective approach is taken which looks to the behaviour of the defendant, not his subjective beliefs or intentions. While this subjective approach is not always adopted in the criminal law—there are offences of strict liability which do not require proof of fault on the part of the defendant—recent case law has suggested that the Irish courts will look sceptically at attempts to criminalise defendants who are "mentally innocent", at least in relation to serious criminal offences.[15]

Finally, it is customary to distinguish crimes as "public wrongs" which harm the interests of the State or public as a whole, not merely the interests of the particular injured party. Blackstone explains this as follows:

> "The distinction of public wrongs from private, of crimes and misdemeanour from civil injuries, seems principally to consist in this: that private wrongs, or civil injuries, are an infringement or privation of the civil rights which belong to individuals, considered merely as individuals; public wrongs, or crimes and misdemeanors, are a breach and violation of the public rights and duties, due to the whole community, considered as a community, in its social aggregate capacity."[16]

This public wrong view of crime is closely linked with the manner by which the criminal law is enforced. In the case of the civil law, enforcement is largely in the

---

[12] See, e.g. s.32(2) of the Defamation Act 2009 which provides for punitive damages where a defendant knowingly or recklessly publishes defamatory material.

[13] See, e.g. s.9 of the Criminal Damage Act 1991 which allows a court to make compensation orders requiring a person convicted of an offence to pay compensation to any injured party.

[14] Though the criminal law does increasingly focus on the harm suffered by the injured party, as exemplified by the development of the victim impact statement in Irish law. See s.5 of the Criminal Justice Act 1993, as substituted by s.4 of the Criminal Procedure Act 2010; Anthony McGrath, "Is anybody listening and why do they hear? The use of victim impact statements in Ireland" (2008) 15(1) *Dublin University Law Journal* 71.

[15] See *CC v Ireland* [2006] 4 I.R. 1, though compare David Prendergast, "The Constitutionality of Strict Liability in Criminal Law" (2011) 18(1) D.U.L.J. 285, suggesting that constitutional limits on strict liability have been overstated.

[16] William Blackstone, *Commentaries on the Laws of England* (Oxford: Clarendon Press, 1753), Vol.4, Ch.5.

hands of the individual. If a person is affected by a tort or breach of contract then only that person may sue and he may settle or discontinue those proceedings freely. In the criminal law, by contrast, violations are felt to injure the community as a whole and so enforcement is not left to the victim but is in the hands of public bodies, and the consent of the victim is not required before a prosecution is brought. For the same reason, if the prosecution succeeds the victim cannot pardon the offender; this power is reserved to the State.

Effect of the civil–criminal distinction

There is an overlap between the civil and criminal law in that a particular set of facts may give rise to legal consequences in both domains. For example, should one punch another person one may be liable to criminal prosecution but also to a tort action seeking compensation for the injuries suffered. Consequently, as Glanville Williams points out, we must differentiate "not between crimes and civil wrongs but between criminal and civil proceedings" so that a crime can be understood as "an act that is capable of being followed by criminal proceedings".[17]

Bearing this point in mind, what is the significance of a finding that a particular matter should be treated as criminal in its nature? In Irish law the distinction between civil and criminal proceedings is of considerable practical importance. The law treats criminal proceedings as being especially serious so that once we identify a matter as criminal then the accused person will benefit from a number of rules designed to minimise the risk of injustice to him. Most fundamentally, the trial of criminal matters is governed by Art.38 of the Constitution, which provides that:

1. No person shall be tried on any criminal charge save in due course of law.
2. Minor offences may be tried by courts of summary jurisdiction ...
5. Save in the case of trial of offences under s.2, no person shall be tried on any criminal charge without a jury.

In addition, Art.38 must be read in conjunction with Art.37.1, which allows for limited powers and functions of a judicial nature to be carried out by persons who are not judges appointed under the Constitution, or bodies which are not courts established under the Constitution (e.g. the Employment Appeals Tribunal or the Labour Court). However, Art.37.1 is limited to "matters other than criminal matters".

The net effect of these two Articles is, therefore, that once we determine that a matter is criminal, it must be tried before courts established under the Constitution, with a jury (unless the matter is minor), and in due course of law. We will see that this last phrase encompasses certain rules of law, such as the presumption of innocence, the requirement of proof of guilt beyond a reasonable doubt and the right to silence, which are not applicable to civil matters.

---

[17] Glanville Williams, "The Definition of Crime" (1955) Vol.8 Curr. Leg. Probl. 107 at 123.

The *indicia* of a criminal offence

Melling v O'Mathghamhna

The key factors or *indicia* which identify a criminal matter in Irish law have been authoritatively set out in the Supreme Court decision in *Melling v O'Mathghamhna*.[18] In this case the plaintiff was a commercial traveller who was charged in the District Court with 15 charges relating to the smuggling of butter into the State, contrary to s.186 of the Customs Consolidation Act 1876. The possible sanction was a fine of £100 on each charge or treble the value of the smuggled goods, with six to 12 months' imprisonment in lieu of payment. The plaintiff brought an action seeking a declaration that the District Court had no jurisdiction on the basis that these were criminal charges, were not of a minor nature, and as such could only be tried by a judge and jury.

The first question faced by the Supreme Court was whether the proceedings were criminal.[19] The members of the Supreme Court unanimously held that the charges were criminal in character but took different approaches as to the test that should be used. Lavery J. (with whom Maguire C.J. and Maguire J. agreed) looked primarily to the procedural nature and possible outcome of the proceedings as the *indicia* of a criminal offence:

> "It seems to me clear that a proceeding, the course of which permits the detention of the person concerned, the bringing of him in custody to a Garda station, the entry of a charge in all respects appropriate to the charge of a criminal offence, the searching of the person detained and the examination of papers and other things found upon him, the bringing of him before a District Justice in custody, the admission to bail to stand his trial and the detention in custody if bail be not granted or is not forthcoming, the imposition of a pecuniary penalty with the liability to imprisonment if the penalty is not paid has all the *indicia* of a criminal charge."[20]

A similar approach was taken by Ó Dálaigh J., who also stressed the fact that the terminology used was that of the criminal law:

> "One of the chief characteristics of civil liability (as contrasted with criminal liability) is the obligation to make reparation and, in our times, not to have to suffer imprisonment if unable to make such reparation … There are, of course, instances, such as that of defamation, when because of the circumstances of the injury the law allows the reparation to be by such a sum as will be not only reparation but also a mark of disapproval or punishment. Moreover, it need hardly be said that certain acts, such as assaults, may be the subject of criminal as well as civil proceedings.
>
> It is not, however, a feature of civil proceedings that the plaintiff can have the defendant detained in jail before the proceedings commence and keep him

---

[18] [1962] I.R. 1.
[19] Whether the proceedings constituted a "minor offence" for the purposes of Art.38.5 will be addressed later in this chapter.
[20] [1962] I.R. 1 at 9.

there unless he can obtain bail. Nor may he obtain a warrant to enter and search the defendant's house or shop and seize goods and if obstructed break open any door and force or remove any impediment to such search, entry or seizure (see s.205 of the Customs Consolidation Act, 1876). Nor yet is it a feature of civil proceedings that a plaintiff can put the defendant in jail because he cannot pay the damages awarded.

The vocabulary of s.186 of the Act of 1876 is the vocabulary of the criminal law; the preliminary detention in jail unless bail be found (s.197) and the right to enter, search and seize goods in a defendant's house or premises (ss.204 and 205) are, as yet, unfamiliar features of civil litigation. In their initiation, conclusion and consequences proceedings under s.186 have all the features of a criminal prosecution. Note that Parliament in inserting directions in the form of conviction (set out in Schedule C to the Act and directed by s.223 of the Act to be used) speaks unequivocally: I quote:—

'Where the party has been convicted of an offence punishable by pecuniary penalty and imprisonment in default of payment.'

Finally, the mode of withdrawal of proceedings is the time-honoured formula employed by the Attorney General in criminal charges — nolle prosequi (s.256). Well might Mr. Justice Murnaghan say, as he did in Gettins' Case:—

'the proceedings before the District Justice have all the marks of criminal procedure and are in no way distinguishable from criminal proceedings for which the punishment is a penalty with imprisonment in default of payment.'

Unless I am to hold that, as in some strange, unreal, 'Kafka-esque' world, what it is not, I must come to the conclusion that the offences comprised in s.186 are 'criminal charges.'"[21]

By contrast, Kingsmill Moore J. took a more abstract approach, holding that a criminal charge was distinguished by three elements: its nature as an offence against the community at large, the punitive rather than compensatory nature of the sanction, and the requirement of mens rea:

"What is a crime? The anomalies which still exist in the criminal law and the diversity of expression in statutes make a comprehensive definition almost impossible to frame ... A recent text-book, Cross and Jones, suggests as a definition: 'A crime is a legal wrong the remedy for which is the punishment of the offender at the instance of the State.' Professor Kenny in the earlier editions of his Outlines of Criminal Law says that 'crimes are wrongs whose sanction is punitive and is remissible by the Crown if remissible at all.' If we regard the Revenue Commissioners as a branch of the executive acting for the State (and in discharging their functions under the Customs Acts I think they must be so regarded) an offence under s.186 would fall within both those definitions. Moreover, the offences enumerated in s.186 possess several features which are regarded as indicia of crimes.

---

[21] [1962] I.R. 1 at 40–41.

(i) They are offences against the community at large and not against an individual. Blackstone defines a crime as 'a violation of the public rights and duties due to the whole community, considered as a community.' ...
(ii) The sanction is punitive, and not merely a matter of fiscal reparation, for the penalty is £100 or three times the duty-paid value of the goods; and failure to pay, even where the offender has not the means, involves imprisonment.
(iii) They require *mens rea* for the act must be done 'knowingly' and 'with intent to evade the prohibition or restriction...' *Mens rea* is not an invariable ingredient of a criminal offence ... but where *mens rea* is made an element of an offence it is generally an indication of criminality."

Since then, as we shall see, *Melling v O'Mathghamhna* has generally been the starting point for cases which consider whether a particular matter should be considered as criminal, with those cases looking primarily to the criteria elaborated by Lavery J. and Ó Dálaigh C.J. It should be noted, however, that there is an element of circularity in those criteria: in effect, the majority approach asks whether a matter *should be* treated in the way associated with a criminal matter by looking to whether it *already is* so treated. Campbell, for example, has criticised the decision on these grounds:

"Thus, the courts have held, using somewhat circular logic, that a procedure is not a criminal process if it does not involve characteristics such as arrest or detention. However, it appears that it is the avoidance of these aspects at the stage of enactment which facilitates the depiction of forfeiture as civil. For example, while the lack of detention under the Proceeds of Crime Acts may be cited as evidence that the proceedings are not criminal, the initial classification of the process as civil in nature by the legislature has resulted in the fact that an individual may not be detained."[22]

Administrative penalties

An important application of the *Melling* reasoning is that the use of administrative penalties—even where these are expressly intended to have a deterrent effect—may not constitute punishment for criminal offences within the meaning of Art.38.1 of the Constitution. Consequently, legislation providing for administrative penalties may be constitutionally permissible so long as the other *indicia* of the criminal law are not present and the other constitutional requirements (such as the Art.34.1 requirement that justice shall be administered in courts) are met.

An example can be seen in the Supreme Court decision in *McLoughlin v Tuite*.[23] This case (like *Melling*) involved a revenue matter, and concerned s.500 of the Income Tax Act 1967 which imposed a fixed penalty on any person failing to comply with a notice to make income tax returns. This penalty could then be recovered by the Revenue by civil proceedings under s.508 of the 1967 Act. The plaintiff in this case—faced with a cumulative total penalty of £5,500 for failure to make returns

---

[22] Liz Campbell, "The Recovery of 'Criminal' Assets in New Zealand, Ireland and England" (2010) 41 Vic. U. Well. L. Rev. 15 at 23.
[23] [1989] 1 I.R. 82.

General Principles

from 1973 to 1983 inclusive—brought an action seeking a declaration that s.500 was invalid as it imposed a criminal penalty other than in accordance with Art.38.

The Supreme Court rejected this argument, holding that although the penalty payment was punitive in effect, the proceedings did not otherwise have the *indicia* of a criminal offence. In particular: mens rea was not required, no question of detention or arrest arose and imprisonment could not be imposed in default of payment. In addition, the sum could be recovered from the estate of a deceased taxpayer, in a way which was characteristic of a civil debt, but inconsistent with a criminal penalty. According to Finlay C.J.:

> "In the instance of a penalty under s.500 of the Act of 1967 no question of *mens rea* arises at all. It is of importance that in other provisions of the income tax code which expressly and explicitly create criminal offences which are punishable either by a fine with imprisonment in default of payment, or by imprisonment without a fine, clearcut and explicit *mens rea* is clearly provided for. Such offences are found to be knowingly, wilfully or fraudulently committed. The provision for the recovery of this penalty against the estate of a deceased taxpayer is, again, quite inconsistent with its existence as a criminal offence.
>
> In short, the only feature which could be said to be common between the provisions of s.500 and s.508 and the ordinary constituents of a criminal offence is that the payment of a sum of money is provided for which is an involuntary payment and which is not related to any form of compensation or reparation necessary to the state but is rather a deterrent or sanction. The Court is not satisfied that the provision for a penalty in that fashion in a code of taxation law, with the general features which have been shortly outlined in this judgment, clearly establishes the provisions of the section as creating a criminal offence."[24]

A similar result was reached in *Registrar of Companies v Judge David Anderson and Another*,[25] where the Supreme Court considered late filing fees imposed on a company for failure to make annual returns to the Registrar of Companies. In this case, the respondent company failed to file its 2000 and 2001 returns on time, therefore incurring an automatic late filing fee of €1,579 when it did file. The company was later selected for prosecution by the Registrar of Companies for the failure to make annual returns on time, which was an offence contrary to s.125 of the Companies Act 1963 as amended.

Before the District Court the company challenged the prosecution on the basis that it exposed it to a risk of double jeopardy—that is, that it would be punished again in relation to offences which it had already been punished by the late filing fee. The District Court agreed and struck out the proceedings, prompting the Registrar of Companies to judicially review the decision. In the Supreme Court it was held that there was no risk of double jeopardy as the late filing fee did not constitute a criminal penalty; instead, the court ruled, it was a permissible administrative sanction which was intended to encourage prompt filing rather than to act as a punishment. Per Murray C.J.:

---

[24] [1989] 1 I.R. 82 at 90.
[25] [2004] IESC 103.

> "In an ideal world all such returns should be made in time and it seems to me a legitimate administrative objective to seek, by administrative means, to encourage timely filing of returns and discourage late ones. It is by no means an unfamiliar administrative phenomenon for incentives to be provided so as to encourage such matters as the timely payment of bills or the making of reservations in relation to a particular event, or, to discourage late payers or late compliers with a deadline specified in relation to a particular matter, by charging higher or additional fees.
>
> In this case the liability to pay higher fees is an automatic consequence to the objective fact of a certain statutory deadline having passed. The amount or amounts are fixed and there is no discretion. It is a foreseeable, objective and automatic consequence for lateness in filing an annual return by any company. It is clearly designed to encourage timely filing and discourage the dilatory. That is something which is clearly in the interest of good and efficient administration.
>
> It is manifest that the statutory requirement to pay late filing fees is not in any sense something which involves a criminal process let alone a criminal prosecution.
>
> Therefore, from a formal point of view I have no hesitation in concluding that the obligation to pay extra fees for a later return of a company's annual report is in form an administrative sanction. That is to say a sanction that does not have as its purpose the punishment of an offence but the achievement of a legitimate administrative objective."

Significantly, however, the court went on to indicate that if an administrative sanction were to be excessive and disproportionate to its objective then it might be found to be in substance a criminal penalty. Per Murray C.J.:

> "It may not necessarily follow that something which is in the form of an administrative sanction for failing to comply with a statutory obligation could never be considered to be in substance a criminal penalty. It might be argued for example that a sanction which was so excessive and disproportionate to the administrative objective to be achieved was in substance if not in form the imposition of a criminal penalty. I do not think it is necessary to decide whether the imposition of the late return fees in this case could, even arguably, (which I doubt), be considered as being in substance the imposition of a criminal penalty. The reason is that if the late return fees could be classed as the imposition of a criminal penalty, then it would be one which was imposed outside the criminal process automatically and without discretion. Then it is the relevant statutory provisions imposing such fees which would be open to challenge by reason of the fact that it did not involve a criminal process, with all the due process constitutional protections that the latter would entail.
>
> In this case the company were not charged with any offence, no decision or judgment was made by any person or body concerning the individual company, there was no trial of any issue and of course there was no conviction or acquittal."

It should be noted also that these cases dealt with administrative penalties only in the context of automatic and fixed sanctions for breaches of procedural rules. A much more difficult situation arises in the context of civil fines, where a regulatory body is given the power to impose financial penalties on a discretionary basis for the breach of substantive rules—for example, the power of the Financial Regulator to impose financial penalties under the Central Bank and Financial Services Authority of Ireland Act 2003. This power has been used to impose very large fines indeed—in one case, €3.35 million against an insurance company for sustained breaches[26]—which raises a significant question as to whether such a sanction may be constitutionally suspect as being in effect either punishment in a criminal matter or the administration of justice by a body other than a court.[27]

Tribunals of inquiry

An important aspect of Irish public life in recent years has been the use of tribunals of inquiry, set up under the Tribunals of Inquiry (Evidence) Act 1921 as adapted and amended, to investigate "matters of urgent public importance". Although generally chaired by judges, these tribunals are not courts and instead are established by Dáil Éireann as inquisitorial bodies to inquire into and report on particular matters—usually, though not always, involving allegations of political corruption.[28] Consequently, tribunals of inquiry present an important issue: does Art.38.1 preclude the Dáil from establishing a body with the express aim of investigating and reporting on whether conduct amounting to a criminal offence has taken place? Will the work of such a body amount to the trial of a "criminal charge" within the meaning of that Article?[29]

This issue came before the Supreme Court in *Goodman v Hamilton (No. 1)*.[30] This case involved what was commonly known as the Beef Tribunal, a tribunal of inquiry chaired by the President of the High Court and set up in 1991 following a *World in Action* television investigation which exposed very serious wrongdoing (including criminal activity) in the Irish meat industry. The applicants—a company accounting for a large part of the industry and the principal behind that company—brought an application for judicial review claiming, amongst other things, that the work of the

---

[26] Simon Carswell, "Regulator sends clear warning to all firms", *Irish Times*, December 20, 2011.
[27] On the question of civil fines see, e.g. Noreen Mackey, "Expanding Civil Penalties Constitutionally: Punishment without Crime?" (Paper delivered at Competition Press Conference, Dublin, September 28, 2006); Michael McDowell, "Non-Criminal Penalties and Criminal Sanctions in Irish Regulatory Law" in Shane Kilcommins and Ursula Kilkelly (eds), *Regulatory Crime in Ireland* (Dublin: First Law, 2010); Gerald FitzGerald and David McFadden, "Filling a gap in Irish competition law enforcement: the need for a civil fines sanction" (Paper delivered at Civil Fines Condition in the EU/IMF MoU: the Competition Authority's Perspective, Dublin, June 9, 2011).
[28] See, e.g. Gary Murphy, "Payments for no political response? Political corruption and tribunals of inquiry in Ireland, 1991–2003" in John Garrard and James Newell (eds), *Scandals in Past and Contemporary Politics* (Manchester: Manchester University Press, 2004), p.91.
[29] Although tribunals of inquiry have now fallen into disfavour, similar questions will apply to other public investigative bodies such as commissions of investigation under the Commissions of Investigation Act 2004. See, e.g. Keith Spencer, "A New Era of Tribunalism–The Commissions of Investigation Act 2004" (2005) 23 I.L.T. 105.
[30] [1992] 2 I.R. 542.

Tribunal amounted in substance to the trial of a "criminal charge" other than in due course of law and without a jury. In particular, the applicants pointed to the fact that the Tribunal was composed of a High Court judge and would only make findings of criminality if satisfied beyond reasonable doubt that the allegation was established—claiming that these were strong indications that the Tribunal was carrying out what was in effect a criminal trial.

This argument was, however, rejected by the Supreme Court, which held that although the Tribunal was investigating allegations of criminal misconduct, it was not conducting a criminal trial. In particular, Finlay C.J. noted that:

> "Article 38 of the Constitution is exclusively confined to the trial of persons on criminal charges or the trial of offences. I am quite satisfied that an inquiry, conducted as this resolution provides, into the question as to whether criminal acts have been committed, even to the extent of inquiring whether criminal acts have been committed by a named person or persons, and the reporting of the truth or falsity of such an allegation to the Legislature by the sole member of the Tribunal cannot under any circumstances be construed or deemed as a trial on a criminal charge or of an offence within the meaning to be attached to those phrases in Article 38 of the Constitution.
>
> The essential ingredient of a trial of a criminal offence in our law, which is indivisible from any other ingredient, is that it is had before a court or judge which has got the power to punish in the event of a verdict of guilty. It is of the essence of a trial on a criminal charge or a trial on a criminal offence that the proceedings are accusatorial, involving a prosecutor and an accused, and that the sole purpose and object of the verdict, be it one of acquittal or of conviction, is to form the basis for either a discharge of the accused from the jeopardy in which he stood, in the case of an acquittal, or for his punishment for the crime which he has committed, in the case of a conviction.
>
> The proceedings of the inquiry to be held by this Tribunal have none of those features. The Tribunal has no jurisdiction or authority of any description to impose a penalty or punishment on any person. Its finding, whether rejecting an allegation of criminal activity or accepting the proof of an allegation of criminal activity, can form no basis for either the conviction nor acquittal of the party concerned on a criminal charge if one were subsequently brought, nor can it form any basis for the punishment by any other authority of that person. It is a simple fact-finding operation, reporting to the Legislature."[31]

This approach takes a relatively narrow view of the guarantee in Art.38.1 and holds that there is no "trial" of a criminal offence unless the outcome of a particular procedure is to determine the guilt or innocence of a person charged with a crime and to decide on the punishment which might be inflicted upon him. As such, it has been criticised as being "unduly formalistic" and failing to protect the individual from the burden of an official finding that he has committed a criminal act. Hogan and Whyte in particular have argued that:

---

[31] [1992] 2 I.R. 542 at 587–588.

> "It is certainly true that one could scarcely raise a constitutional objection just because a tribunal or other administrative body is required to consider allegations of criminal impropriety, but it is surely a different matter where the Tribunal is empowered to bringing [sic] in specific findings of criminal wrong-doing. In such circumstances it is surely cold comfort to the citizen concerned to be told that no specific *penalty* had been or could be imposed if he has nonetheless been stigmatised by a public finding that he has engaged in (possibly very serious) criminal wrongdoing."[32]

Proceeds of crime legislation

One of the most significant recent developments in Irish criminal law has been the establishment of a system which crosses the civil–criminal divide by using the civil law to seize criminal profits. This system is made up of legislation which allows for the forfeiture of "the proceeds of crime" along with a designated state agency (the Criminal Assets Bureau) which deals solely with forfeiture. It was adopted in some haste in the summer of 1996 following the assassination of crime journalist Veronica Guerin, an event which shocked Irish society and led to an outpouring of public concern (some would say a "moral panic") which demanded an immediate legislative response.[33]

The legislation which resulted—in the form of the Proceeds of Crime Act 1996—reflected a widespread view that the criminal law had failed to protect society as a result of difficulties in securing convictions and an inadequate deterrent effect of sentencing.[34] The comments of Moriarty J. in *M v D*[35] exemplify this perspective:

> "It seems to me that I am clearly entitled to take notice of the international phenomenon, far from peculiar to Ireland that significant numbers of persons who engage as principals in lucrative professional crime, particularly that referable to the illicit supply of controlled drugs, are alert and effectively able to insulate themselves against the risk of successful criminal prosecution through deployment of intermediaries and that the Act of 1996 is designed to enable the lower probative requirements of civil law to be utilised in appropriate cases, not to achieve penal sanctions, but to effectively deprive such persons of such illicit financial fruits of their labours as can be shown to be the proceeds of crime."

---

[32] Gerard Hogan and Gerry Whyte (eds), *J.M. Kelly, The Irish Constitution*, 4th edn (Dublin: LexisNexis Butterworths, 2003), p.1041 (emphasis in original). See also, Una Ní Raifeartaigh, "Goodman v The Beef Tribunal" (1992) 2(2) I.C.L.J. 141 who argues that: "While the tribunal is certainly not in a position to deprive an individual of his liberty, it may be in a position to hit his pocket and reputation as much as a court. Arguably, its public finding (if such is the case) that an individual has violated the criminal law would inflict a stigma analogous to the stigma of a criminal conviction. It appears also that it is in a position to deprive the citizen of money, by making an award of costs."

[33] John Meade, "Organised Crime, Moral Panic and Law Reform: the Irish Adoption of Civil Forfeiture" (2000) 10(1) I.C.L.J. 11.

[34] See, e.g. Fachtna Murphy and Barry Galvin, "Targeting the Financial Wealth of Criminals in Ireland: The Law and Practice" (1999) 9(2) I.C.L.J. 133.

[35] [1998] 3 I.R. 178.

As can be seen from these comments, the key tactic which the 1996 Act adopted was to make use of "the lower probative requirements of civil law", permitting the High Court to make orders for forfeiture of property alleged to constitute the proceeds of crime on the basis of proof on the balance of probabilities and allowing for the use of hearsay evidence. Lest there be any doubt on this point, s.8(2) explicitly provided that "[t]he standard of proof required to determine any question arising under this Act shall be that applicable to civil proceedings".

The 1996 Act was, unsurprisingly, challenged on the basis that in substance proceedings under the Act were criminal rather than civil in nature. This issue came before the Supreme Court in *Murphy v GM*[36] in which a number of individuals sought declarations that, amongst other things, the Act was invalid on the basis that it deprived them of significant safeguards associated with the criminal law. Relying on *Melling*, they argued that the forfeiture scheme had many of the *indicia* identified by that case, in particular that:

"(i) it was of general application;
(ii) it made no provision for compensation or reparation being paid to any of the victims of the alleged crimes;
(iii) its clear policy was the deterrence of crime;
(iv) relief under the Act could only be obtained where the assets were shown to be the proceeds of crime;
(v) the necessity for *mens rea*, an ingredient associated exclusively with the criminal law, was implicit in the jurisdiction given to the court to grant relief to the persons affected where there was 'a serious risk of injustice';
(vi) the applicant in each case was a senior garda officer attached to the Criminal Assets Bureau;
(vii) powers exclusively associated with the criminal law, e.g. the use of search warrants, were used to assist in the plaintiff's case."[37]

The Supreme Court, however, held that the forfeiture provisions of the Act could not be considered to be criminal in their nature. Applying *Melling*, it noted that the elements which were decisive in that case (arrest, detention, admission to bail, imposition of a fine and imprisonment in default of payment) were absent. Crucially, forfeiture was held not to be a punishment as it did not relate to any valid constitutional right to property—any property forfeited was not property which the individual had a right to retain in the first place. In addition, it held there was no requirement of *mens rea* for forfeiture to take place, while as a historical matter the forfeiture of the proceeds of crime had always been considered to be civil in nature.

Since then a number of decisions have applied this reasoning to find that other schemes for the forfeiture of property are civil in nature. For example, in *Gilligan v Special Criminal Court*,[38] the plaintiff had been convicted in the Special Criminal Court of the importation of cannabis. Under s.4 of the Criminal Justice Act 1994, the courts, on convicting a person of a drug trafficking offence, could make a

---

[36] [2001] 4 I.R. 113.
[37] [2001] 4 I.R. 113 at 132.
[38] [2006] 2 I.R. 389.

confiscation order covering the proceeds of the drug trafficking. This confiscation order jurisdiction applied a civil standard of proof, created a number of presumptions which would apply against the person convicted, created powers of search, and provided for imprisonment where a person failed to comply with the confiscation order. In this case, the confiscation order assessed that the defendant had benefited to the tune of approximately €17 million, and required him to pay that sum within 12 months.

The plaintiff challenged the jurisdiction of the Special Criminal Court to make the confiscation order as well as the constitutionality of a number of provisions of the Act. In particular, he argued that this s.4 forfeiture system amounted to a criminal procedure contrary to Art.38.1 of the Constitution. Ultimately the Supreme Court found that the Special Criminal Court did not have jurisdiction to make such an order and declined to consider the constitutionality point; in the High Court, however, McCracken J. applied *Murphy v GM* to hold that this forfeiture system did not amount to the trial of a criminal charge. The judgment emphasised in particular that the section 4 procedure did not operate as a punishment:

> "[P]enalties by way of punishment [are] an essential element of a criminal charge. However what the 1994 Act deals with is not penalising the person for having committed drug trafficking offences, but rather it is seeking to recover from that person the value of the benefits which accrued through drug trafficking ... This is unlike financial penalties imposed for criminal offences, which are absolute, irrespective of the defendant's means."[39]

A similar result can be seen in *England v DPP*.[40] In that case, the applicant while travelling through Dublin Airport in 1998 was found to be carrying approximately £80,000 in cash, despite having no visible source of income. The DPP applied to the Circuit Court for forfeiture of that sum under s.39 of the Criminal Justice Act 1994, on the basis that the money was either the proceeds of drug trafficking, or was intended for use in drug trafficking. The trial judge adjourned the application to allow the DPP to put in additional evidence—however, the defendant objected on the basis that this was a criminal matter and as such the evidence was closed at this point and he was entitled to a ruling on the merits of the case as it then stood. On application to the High Court for judicial review, Kearns J. held that this was not a criminal matter, and therefore the trial judge was permitted to adjourn the case to allow further evidence to be put in. While the court acknowledged this could be described as a "hybrid" jurisdiction, Kearns J. held that it was essentially civil in nature, since:

> "Section 39 provides for a forfeiture proceeding which is *in rem*. It is the monies or the proceeds which are proceeded against, whereas in a criminal prosecution it is the wrongdoer in person who is proceeded against, convicted and punished. No part of Section 39 provides for the creation of a criminal offence, nor does this section in substance appear to me to have that effect."

---

[39] [2006] 2 I.R. 389 at 401–402.
[40] Unreported, High Court, Kearns J., February 14, 2003.

It should be noted, however, that this line of cases has been strongly criticised on the basis that they fail to take into account the imbalance of power between the individual and State in this area, the expressed aim of forfeiture laws being to punish by hitting "criminals where it hurts most—in their pockets, bank accounts, fancy houses and fast cars", and the role which forfeiture laws play in censuring and shaming those against whom proceedings are brought. Campbell in particular has suggested that, at the least, it would be desirable to see a middle-ground jurisprudence in this area—one where the seriousness of the matter would be reflected in a greater set of procedural protections for the individual, even though falling short of the standards which would apply to a fully criminal matter.[41] It seems clear from the case law, however, that any such approach would require legislative intervention.

Criminal offences under the European Convention on Human Rights

The preceding sections have looked at the definition of a "criminal matter" as a matter of domestic law. It should be noted, however, that the civil–criminal distinction also arises under the European Convention on Human Rights (ECHR) where certain rights are guaranteed to persons charged with a criminal offence within the meaning of the ECHR. The most important of these provisions are as follows:

> Article 6—Right to a fair trial
> 1. In the determination of his civil rights and obligations or of any criminal charge against him, everyone is entitled to a fair and public hearing within a reasonable time by an independent and impartial tribunal established by law. Judgment shall be pronounced publicly but the press and public may be excluded from all or part of the trial in the interest of morals, public order or national security in a democratic society, where the interests of juveniles or the protection of the private life of the parties so require, or the extent strictly necessary in the opinion of the court in special circumstances where publicity would prejudice the interests of justice.
> 2. Everyone charged with a criminal offence shall be presumed innocent until proved guilty according to law.
> 3. Everyone charged with a criminal offence has the following minimum rights:
>   (a) to be informed promptly, in a language which he understands and in detail, of the nature and cause of the accusation against him;
>   (b) to have adequate time and the facilities for the preparation of his defence;
>   (c) to defend himself in person or through legal assistance of his own choosing or, if he has not sufficient means to pay for legal assistance, to be given it free when the interests of justice so require;

---

[41] Liz Campbell, "The Recovery of 'Criminal' Assets in New Zealand, Ireland and England" (2010) 41 Vic. U. Well. L. Rev. 15. See also, John Meade, "The Disguise of Civility: Civil Forfeiture of the Proceeds of Crime and the Presumption of Innocence in Irish Law" (2000) 1 Hibernian L.J. 1; Claire Hamilton, "Presumed Guilty? The Summer Anti-Crime Package Of 1996 And The Presumption Of Innocence" (2002) 10 I.S.L.R. 202.

(d) to examine or have examined witnesses against him and to obtain the attendance and examination of witnesses on his behalf under the same conditions as witnesses against him;

(e) to have the free assistance of an interpreter if he cannot understand or speak the language used in court.

Article 7—No punishment without law

1. No one shall be held guilty of any criminal offence on account of any act or omission which did not constitute a criminal offence under national or international law at the time when it was committed. Nor shall a heavier penalty be imposed than the one that was applicable at the time the criminal offence was committed.

2. This Article shall not prejudice the trial and punishment of any person for any act or omission which, at the time it was committed, was criminal according to the general principles of law recognised by civilised nations.

Following the European Convention on Human Rights Act 2003 these rights have been incorporated into Irish law so that the courts are obliged to interpret and apply statutory provisions and rules of law (so far as possible) in a manner compatible with the ECHR. Significantly, a "criminal offence" or "criminal charge" under the ECHR is an autonomous concept—one which is independent of the categorisations used by national legal systems.[42] Consequently, the fact that Irish law classifies a matter as being civil in nature is not conclusive as to whether or not these rights will apply—instead, we must also consider whether the matter is criminal under the criteria which have been developed by the European Court of Human Rights.

The starting point for this assessment is the judgment of the European Court of Human Rights in *Engel and Others v the Netherlands*[43] which sets out three primary criteria to be taken into account: (1) the domestic classification of the offence; (2) the nature of the offence; and (3) the severity of the penalty the individual risks incurring. Of these the first is a starting point only—if a matter is classified as criminal by national law then this will be conclusive but if not the assessment then proceeds to the second and third criteria. These are more significant and have been interpreted to require the court to consider factors such as the punitive or deterrent purpose of the legal rule, the nature of the possible punishment and whether a conviction may involve deprivation of liberty, the comparative classification of the offence in other states, whether the legal rule is addressed solely to a particular group or is of general application, whether a penalty requires a finding of guilt before it can be imposed, and whether an adverse finding will give rise to a criminal record.[44]

To date there have been surprisingly few Irish cases which address the question of whether a matter should be treated as a criminal one using the *Engel* criteria.[45] However, two recent cases do provide some guidance as to how the Irish courts will

---

[42] *Engel and Others v the Netherlands* (1979) 1 E.H.R.R. 647.
[43] (1979) 1 E.H.R.R. 647.
[44] See, e.g. Paul Mahoney, "Right to a Fair Trial in Criminal Matters under Article 6 ECHR" (2004) 4(2) J.S.I.J. 107; Audrey Guinchard, "Fixing the Boundaries of the Concept of Crime: The Challenge for Human Rights" (2005) 54 Int'l & Comp. L. Q. 719.
[45] The point was raised but not decided in *Potts v Minister for Defence* [2005] 2 I.L.R.M. 517 and *McCann v Judges of the Monaghan District Court* [2010] 1 I.L.R.M. 517.

approach this issue. Both concerned the same individual, John Gilligan. In the first case, *Gilligan v Murphy*,[46] he faced criminal charges arising out of his possession of a mobile phone while in prison. He had previously been subject to a prison disciplinary inquiry in respect of this, and argued that the later charges put him at risk of double jeopardy. In a case stated by the District Court, the question presented was whether the disciplinary inquiry amounted to a criminal charge for the purposes of art.6 of the ECHR. The High Court, applying *Engel*, held that the internal and limited nature of the inquiry, along with the very limited punishment available (loss of 14 days' remission), meant that the inquiry should not be treated as criminal. Per Ryan J.:

> "The European Court of Human Rights cases are the basis of [the] argument. But they do not say that double jeopardy arises in these circumstances. Those cases focus on the nature of prison disciplinary procedures with a view to whether art 6 rights are engaged. The question is whether a prisoner is entitled, for example, to legal representation in such proceedings. In that sense the issue arose as to whether such disciplinary inquiries were to be regarded as criminal and not purely matters of internal enforcement of rules. This is not to say that the European Court of Human Rights cases … are irrelevant. Far from it. But they must be considered in a context that is quite different from the particular double jeopardy issue that is raised in this case.
>
> Applying the jurisprudence of these European Court cases, bearing in mind the limitation I have mentioned, three tests have been approved as to whether a proceeding should be considered criminal so as to give rise to art 6 entitlements. First is how the matter is treated in national law. Obviously, this is not decisive because that could exclude art 6 by the local categorisation alone. It is nevertheless relevant at the initial stage. This point is of more than nominal importance in Ireland because the Constitution prohibits the trial of offences otherwise than in a court.
>
> The second criterion is the nature of the acts that constitute the breach of discipline. In this case, the facts are essentially the same that amount to breach of prison rules and for the criminal charge. The European Court recognises that some acts will constitute both disciplinary breaches and crimes against the public peace.
>
> The third and most important point is the punishment. It is relevant to consider the range of penalty or sanction that may be imposed, as well as the actual imposition in the particular case. It is clear that the disciplinary sanction of depravation of prison privileges in this case would not invoke art 6. The maximum sentence that is provided for a breach of rules is deprivation of remission up to fourteen days and the European Court has not decided that that indicates criminal proceedings.
>
> My conclusion is that the cumulative effect of the sanction imposed, the maximum sanction as described and the fact that it is in the nature of reduction of remission do not bring the prison disciplinary regime into the criminal category where art 6 would be engaged."

---

[46] [2011] IEHC 465.

In the second case, *Gilligan v Murphy*,[47] the plaintiff and his wife brought an action seeking a declaration that the provisions of the Proceeds of Crime Act 1996 were incompatible with the ECHR. This was, in effect, an attempt by him to reopen the arguments in his earlier unsuccessful constitutional challenge to that Act which had been rejected by the Supreme Court in the case entitled *Murphy v GM*.[48] A number of issues arose as a result, including whether the proceedings constituted an abuse of process and the extent to which the European Convention on Human Rights Act 2003 could apply to matters which had been litigated before it came into force. Leaving those other issues aside, however, the High Court was in any event not persuaded that the forfeiture of property should be viewed as a criminal matter within the meaning of art.7 of the ECHR. Per Feeney J.:

> "Article 7 of the Convention applies only to criminal proceedings which can result in a conviction or the imposition of a criminal penalty. Even though Article 7 does not generally apply to civil proceedings, the jurisprudence of the European Court of Human Rights has established that proceedings which are defined as civil in domestic law may in certain limited circumstances nevertheless qualify as criminal proceedings for the purposes of Article 7 …
>
> When one has regard to each of those matters by reference to the Act of 1996, one finds that the position is that the legislation is directed against property (i.e. *in rem*) rather than against a Defendant or Respondent that the proceedings are heard by a civil court and that a Defendant's or Respondent's guilt is not in issue and that the Defendant or Respondent is not facing a criminal charge nor can he be arrested or remanded or compelled to attend and that the proceedings can lead to no criminal conviction or any finding of guilt or the imposition of any sentence and that the determination of the civil court leads to no order which could form part of a criminal record and that the proceedings are not related to any particular criminal proceedings nor can they lead to any criminal proceedings being re-opened. That analysis using and adopting the identification of relevant matters for consideration and applying those matters to the scheme and procedures of the Act of 1996 leads to the conclusion that the Act of 1996 is civil rather than penal.
>
> The European Court of Human Rights in the case of *Walsh v United Kingdom*[49] dealt with a challenge to UK Proceeds of Crime Act 2002 under which application may be made to the High Court for the civil recovery of property rights claimed to represent the proceeds of unlawful conduct. The definition of unlawful conduct is contained in s 241(1) of that Act as 'conduct occurring in any part of the United Kingdom is unlawful conduct if it is unlawful under the criminal law of that part'. In *Walsh* the applicant contended that the proceedings brought for the recovery of his assets were not 'civil' but 'criminal' and that the guarantees of Article 6(1) and 6(2) applied. He argued that the presumption of innocence was not present contrary to Article 6(2). The court held that applying the *Engel* criteria namely the classification of the

---

[47] [2011] IEHC 465.
[48] [2001] 4 I.R. 113.
[49] [2006] ECHR 1154 (App. No. 43384 of 2005).

matter in domestic law, the nature of the charge and the penalty, if any, that none of those criteria were established by *Walsh* and that the proceedings fell outside the criminal head of art 6. The European Court held that proceeds of crime proceedings, similar to the Act of 1996, do not involve a criminal charge

...

> The court is satisfied that the provisions contained in the Act of 1996 and the scheme of the Act for the preservation and, where appropriate, the disposal of the proceeds of crime are not penal in character and do not engage either art 6 or art 7 of the Convention as they are clearly civil proceedings."

This case illustrates the point that following the incorporation of the ECHR into Irish law the courts, in deciding whether a particular matter should be regarded as criminal in nature, will now often have to engage in a parallel analysis which applies both the *indicia* of an offence set out in *Melling v O'Mathghamhna*[50] along with the criteria established in *Engel and Others v the Netherlands*.[51] It may well be that in most cases—as in *Gilligan v Murphy*—both tests will lead to the same result. However, the differences in emphasis between the two suggest that differing outcomes may become more common in future.

CLASSIFICATION OF CRIMES

Not all crimes are of equal magnitude. To take an extreme example, murder and littering are both crimes yet the legal response which we would expect for the one would be entirely inappropriate for the other. For this reason, the law has classified offences in a number of different ways: as felonies or misdemeanours, indictable or summary, arrestable or non-arrestable, minor or non-minor and serious or non-serious.

These classifications, broadly speaking, reflect two principles. The first is that State powers and restrictions on individual liberty should be proportionate to the gravity of the offence under investigation. Consequently, whether there is a power to arrest and question a suspect, to intercept telephone calls, to issue search warrants, to refuse bail or to plant covert surveillance devices will in each case depend on the seriousness of the crime. The second principle is that the trial of criminal offences should provide safeguards for the accused person commensurate with the possible consequences of a guilty verdict. For that reason, the availability of procedural protections such as pre-trial disclosure of evidence and trial by jury will depend on the nature of the charge and in particular the severity of the sentence which might be imposed and the moral stigma of a finding of guilt.

Felonies, misdemeanours and treason

Until 1997, the most important classification was the common law distinction between felonies and misdemeanours. The term "felony" was applied to those crimes such as rape, murder and burglary which resulted in automatic forfeiture

---

[50] [1962] I.R. 1.
[51] (1979) 1 E.H.R.R. 647.

General Principles 21

of the offender's property and which carried a possible capital punishment, while lesser offences were termed "misdemeanours".[52] As a historical matter, the felony–misdemeanour distinction was of fundamental importance to the trial process: for example, an accused felon could not initially call witnesses in his defence nor could he have counsel to defend him.[53]

While the differences between felonies and misdemeanours were gradually reduced over time, a number of contrasts remained. Most significantly, whether a power of arrest without warrant existed for a particular crime depended on whether the crime was a felony or a misdemeanour; in the same way, the possible liability of third parties for the criminal acts of another was much wider where the underlying crime was a felony rather than a misdemeanour. These differences were, however, often anomalous in their nature and stemmed from historical accident rather than conscious design, so that by 1902 Kenny could say that:

> "There can be little doubt that, of all parts of our criminal law, none is in greater need of a thorough reconstruction than that which concerns the classification into Felonies and Misdemeanors."[54]

This reconstruction eventually took place in Irish law through the Criminal Law Act 1997 which in s.3(1) abolished "all distinctions between felony and misdemeanour".[55] In relation to powers of arrest the 1997 Act substituted instead a new category of arrestable offences (ss.4–6), while in relation to third parties who became involved in the crimes of another the 1997 Act provided for wider liability depending on whether the primary crime was either arrestable or indictable (ss.7 and 8). Both of these categories will be considered further below.

Within the felony–misdemeanour classification, a special place was reserved for the crime of treason. Treason itself was at common law a type of felony but one

---

[52] Not all felonies carried the death penalty, nor did all crimes carrying the death penalty amount to felonies. Blackstone explains that: "Felony may be without inflicting capital punishment, as in the cases instanced of self-murder, excusable homicide, and petit larceny; and it is possible that capital punishments may be inflicted and yet the offence be no felony; as in the case of heresy by the common law, which, though capital, never worked any forfeiture of lands or goods, an inseparable incident to felony. And of the same nature was the punishment of standing mute without pleading to an indictment, which at the common law was capital, but without any forfeiture, and therefore such standing mute was no felony. In short, the true criterion of felony is forfeiture..."; William Blackstone, *Commentaries on the Laws of England* (Oxford: Clarendon Press, 1753), Vol.2, Ch.7.

[53] See Courtney Stanhope Kenny, *Outlines of Criminal Law* (Oxford: Oxford University Press, 1902), pp.91–100.

[54] Courtney Stanhope Kenny, *Outlines of Criminal Law* (Oxford: Oxford University Press, 1902), p.100.

[55] The felony–misdemeanour distinction lives on to a very limited extent as a result of Art.15.13 of the Constitution, which provides that members of each House of the Oireachtas shall be privileged from arrest while going to, within and returning from the Oireachtas, except in cases of treason, felony or breach of the peace. Section 15(4) of the Criminal Law Act 1997 takes account of this by providing that: "For the purpose of Article 15.13 of the Constitution and for that purpose only, offences which were felonies immediately before the commencement of this Act shall continue to be treated as felonies and, accordingly, for all other purposes any rule of law or enactment whereby an offence is, or is regarded as, a felony shall be construed as relating to an indictable offence."

which was regarded as "the most heinous of all crimes" and therefore carried special rules in relation to matters such as the manner of trial and the liability of accomplices. Most famously, the punishment for treason was unique to the crime:

> "Treason, like all felonies, was punished with death. But the execution of a traitor was accompanied with special circumstances of horror, to mark the supreme heinousness of his crime. Instead of being taken in a cart to the scaffold, he was drawn to it on a hurdle, hanged only partially, cut down alive and then disembowelled, beheaded and quartered. The head and quarters were permanently exposed in some conspicuous place, after being boiled in salt to prevent putrefaction, and in cummin seed to prevent birds pecking at them."[56]

While this and other features of treason have for the most part been repealed, the special position of treason still survives in modern Irish law. In particular, treason is the only offence defined by the Constitution. This reflects a historical tendency by governments to abuse laws of treason to target political opponents and Art.39 specifically guards against this by restricting the scope of the offence:

> Treason shall consist only in levying war against the State, or assisting any State or person or inciting or conspiring with any person to levy war against the State, or attempting by force of arms or other violent means to overthrow the organs of government established by this Constitution, or taking part or being concerned in or inciting or conspiring with any person to make or to take part or be concerned in any such attempt.[57]

Similarly, the Treason Act 1939 creates a safeguard against wrongful accusations by providing that a person shall not be convicted of treason (or encouraging, harbouring, or comforting persons guilty of treason) on the uncorroborated evidence of one witness.[58] The Criminal Justice Act 1990 also reflects the particular gravity of treason by establishing a mandatory life sentence and requiring that the court, in passing sentence, shall specify a minimum of 40 years' imprisonment to be served.[59]

Summary and indictable offences

Summary trial and trial on indictment

There are two ways in which a criminal offence can be tried in Irish law: either summarily or on indictment. Summary trials are restricted to minor offences and take place using a relatively informal procedure in the District Court before a judge without a jury.[60] As explained by Gannon J. in *Clune v DPP and Clifford*:

---

[56] Courtney Stanhope Kenny, *Outlines of Criminal Law* (Oxford: Oxford University Press, 1902), pp.275–276.
[57] See, e.g. *Report of the Constitution Review Group* (Dublin: Stationery Office, 1996), pp.185–186. The restriction of the crime of treason is modelled in part on Art.III, s.2 of the United States Constitution.
[58] Sections 1(3) and 2(2).
[59] Sections 1 and 4.
[60] See, e.g. Vicky Conway, Yvonne Daly and Jennifer Schweppe, *Irish Criminal Justice: Theory, Process and Procedure* (Dublin: Clarus Press, 2010), Ch.7.

"A summary trial is a trial which could be undertaken with some degree of expedition and informality without departing from the principles of justice. The purpose of summary procedures for minor offences is to ensure that such offences are tried as soon as reasonably possible after their alleged commission so that the recollection of witnesses may still be reasonably clear, that the attendance of witnesses and presentation of evidence may be procured and presented without great difficulty or complexity, and that there should be minimal delay in the disposal of the work load of minor offences."[61]

Trials on indictment, on the other hand, involve a significantly greater degree of formality, take place before the Circuit Criminal Court, Central Criminal Court or Special Criminal Court and are tried before a judge and jury (except in the case of the Special Criminal Court, where cases are tried before three judges).[62]

The policy behind this distinction balances judicial economy with safeguards for the defendant and seeks to ensure that the procedure to be followed at trial is proportionate to the gravity of the case. For example, when a matter is to be tried on indictment the prosecution must provide the accused in advance with a collection of documents known as the book of evidence which sets out in detail the evidence which the prosecution intend to advance at the trial.[63] This ensures that the accused has full notice of the case against him pre-trial. In contrast, there is no such general duty in summary trials—advance disclosure will only be ordered on a case-by-case basis where special circumstances mean that disclosure is necessary in the interests of justice.[64]

Defining and identifying "summary" offences and "indictable" offences

Whether a particular offence can be tried summarily or on indictment depends, in the first instance, on the offence itself. A summary offence is one which can *only* be heard in the District Court before a judge sitting without a jury while an indictable offence is one which either *may or must* be tried before a judge and jury.[65]

To identify whether a particular offence is summary or indictable we look to the source of the offence. All common law offences are indictable, while in the case of statutory offences the legislation creating the offence will specify whether the offence is summary or indictable. For example, public drunkenness contrary to s.4 of the Criminal Justice (Public Order) Act 1994 is a summary offence:

---

[61] [1981] I.L.R.M. 17 at 19.
[62] See, e.g. Vicky Conway, Yvonne Daly and Jennifer Schweppe, *Irish Criminal Justice: Theory, Process and Procedure* (Dublin: Clarus Press, 2010), Ch.8.
[63] Under ss.4B and 4C of the Criminal Justice Act 1967, as inserted by s.9 of the Criminal Justice Act 1999.
[64] *DPP v Doyle* [1994] 2 I.R. 286.
[65] There is one exception to this general rule. Under s.6 of the Criminal Justice Act 1951, where a person is sent forward for trial on an indictable offence he may also be sent forward for trial on any summary offence which arises out of the same set of facts. By consolidating the charges, this avoids the need for two separate trials arising out of the same facts. It also avoids the problem whereby any pending summary charges would have to be adjourned until the trial on indictment had been finally disposed of. The maximum penalty for the summary offence remains the same as would apply on summary conviction.

4.—(1) It shall be an offence for any person to be present in any public place while intoxicated to such an extent as would give rise to a reasonable apprehension that he might endanger himself or any other person in his vicinity.

(2) A person who is guilty of an offence under this section shall be liable *on summary conviction* to a [class E fine].[66]

By comparison, the offence of causing serious harm under s.4 of the Non-Fatal Offences Against the Person Act 1997 is indictable:

4.—(1) A person who intentionally or recklessly causes serious harm to another shall be guilty of an offence.

(2) A person guilty of an offence under this section shall be liable *on conviction on indictment* to a fine or to imprisonment for life or to both.[67]

The fact that an offence is indictable does not necessarily mean that it can only be prosecuted on indictment. While there are some especially grave offences which may only be tried on indictment (in particular genocide, treason, murder and related offences, piracy, rape and aggravated sexual assault), the majority of indictable offences can be dealt with in the District Court where the facts of a particular case constitute a minor offence.[68] In the case of these "each way" offences, a complex set of rules determine whether the accused person or the prosecutor has the right to opt for summary trial or trial on indictment.[69]

Other effects of the summary–indictable distinction

Apart from the procedural issue of how a particular matter is to be tried, the distinction between summary and indictable offences is also relevant in a number of other contexts. For example, s.7(1A) of the Criminal Law Act 1997[70] provides that a person outside the State may face criminal liability where he aids, abets, counsels or procures the commission of an offence within the State—but only where the offence in question is an indictable one. Similarly, it is common for legislation to provide for disqualification or removal from a profession where a person is convicted of an indictable (but not a summary) offence.[71]

---

[66] Emphasis added, and fine updated in accordance with the Fines Act 2010.
[67] Emphasis added.
[68] The offences which must be tried on indictment are set out in s.13(1)(a) of the Criminal Procedure Act 1967 and s.10 of the Criminal Law (Rape) (Amendment) Act 1990.
[69] See generally, James Hamilton, "The Summary Trial of Indictable Offences" (2004) 4(2) J.S.I.J. 154; Office of the Director of Public Prosecutions, *Guidelines for Prosecutors* (Dublin: revised edition, 2007), Ch.13; Vicky Conway, Yvonne Daly and Jennifer Schweppe, *Irish Criminal Justice: Theory, Process and Procedure* (Dublin: Clarus Press, 2010), paras 7–19 to 7–24.
[70] As inserted by s.19 of the Criminal Justice (Amendment) Act 2009.
[71] Section 27(2) of the Nurses and Midwives Act 2011, for example, provides that a member of the Irish Nursing Board automatically ceases to hold office if convicted of an indictable offence. Conviction of a summary offence will only have this effect if the offence involves fraud or dishonesty or results in a term of imprisonment.

Minor and non-minor offences

Article 38.2 of the Constitution provides that "minor offences may be tried by courts of summary jurisdiction". Article 38 goes on to provide that with the exception of minor offences and offences tried by special courts or military tribunals, no person may be tried on any criminal charge without a jury. There is, therefore, a constitutional imperative to consider whether a charge relates to a "minor" offence—only minor offences may be tried summarily by a judge alone in the District Court, while non-minor offences must generally be tried on indictment before a jury in the Circuit Court or High Court.

The Constitution does not, however, define the term "minor", which has led to a significant body of cases considering the matters which should be taken into account in deciding how a particular offence should be categorised.[72] The most important of these is *Melling v O'Mathghamhna*[73] in which the Supreme Court set out four factors to be taken into account:

1. the severity of the punishment prescribed for the offence;
2. the moral quality of the act constituting the offence;
3. the state of the law when the Constitution was enacted;
4. public opinion at the time of enactment of the Constitution.

These factors are not, however, of equal importance. With the passage of time, the courts have given much less weight to the third and fourth factors (which are historical in nature, looking backwards to conditions in 1937) and have instead focused on crimes in their modern context.[74] Consequently, the cases applying the test in *Melling* have focused on the first and second factors with the greatest weight being given to the severity of punishment. In *Conroy v Attorney General*,[75] for example, the Supreme Court explicitly accepted that "the primary consideration in determining whether an offence be a minor one or not is the punishment it may attract",[76] so that "the moral quality of the act is a relevant though secondary consideration".[77]

Despite the apparent simplicity of this test the courts have had difficulty applying it to individual cases. In *Melling* itself the members of the Supreme Court differed as to whether the penalty for smuggling of butter contrary to s.186 of the Customs Consolidation Act 1876 (a fine of £100 or six months' imprisonment in lieu of payment) took it outside the realm of minor offences. While the majority opinion by Lavery J. took the view that this should be regarded as a minor offence, it also acknowledged an element of subjectivity in the test by admitting that "[i]n the end, it is a matter of first impression whether a particular offence is of a minor character or not and a Judge can only express his own view thereon".[78]

---

[72] For discussion of these cases see the Law Reform Commission Consultation Paper, *Penalties for Minor Offences* (LRC CP18–2002).
[73] [1962] I.R. 1.
[74] See in particular, *State (Rollinson) v Kelly* [1984] I.R. 248.
[75] [1965] I.R. 411.
[76] [1965] I.R. 411 at 430 per Walsh J.
[77] [1965] I.R. 411 at 436 per Walsh J.
[78] [1962] I.R. 1 at 17.

Maximum penalty or penalty actually imposed?

The courts have also differed as to whether the severity of a penalty should be measured according to the maximum penalty authorised by law, or rather by the punishment which a particular offence would attract in the event of conviction. In *Conroy v Attorney General*[79] the Supreme Court assessed the offence of drink driving contrary to s.49(1) of the Road Traffic Act 1961 by reference to the maximum possible penalty (six months' imprisonment and/or a £100 fine) rather than the penalty actually imposed. This approach was explicitly approved by the Supreme Court in *In re Haughey*,[80] in which Ó Dálaigh C.J. stated:

> "Of the relevant criteria, the most important is the severity of the penalty which is authorised to be imposed for commission of the offence ... This Court sees no reason for departing from the test it laid down in Conroy's Case ... To apply the test of the penalty actually imposed would, in effect, be to deny to an accused the substance of the right to trial by jury."[81]

Against this, however, there is a conflicting line of authority which focuses on the penalty actually imposed. This is exemplified by the Supreme Court decision in *O'Sullivan v Hartnett*[82] where Henchy J. expressed the view of the court as follows:

> "It may be necessary in an appropriate case to review the criteria laid down in the decided cases for deciding whether an offence is minor or not. For example, the penalty laid down by the statute can scarcely be held to be a primary consideration in all cases ... Whatever the applicable criteria may be or the priority of those criteria inter se where a statute lays down a fixed penalty or a minimum penalty, *in cases such as the present where the extent of the penalty depends on the circumstances of the case the line of demarcation between minor and non-minor offences must be drawn in the light of those circumstances.*"[83]

Not long after that decision, however, the Supreme Court muddied the waters in *State (Rollinson) v Kelly*,[84] where the court split evenly on this point. Two members of the court (O'Higgins C.J. and Hederman J.) expressed the view that the relevant test was the maximum penalty which the offence might attract, while two other members of the court (Henchy and Griffin JJ.) held that the penalty actually imposed on conviction was the key factor. The fifth judge, McCarthy J., did not address this point. Consequently, the Law Reform Commission summarises the current position as follows:

---

[79] [1965] I.R. 411.
[80] [1971] I.R. 217.
[81] [1971] I.R. 217 at 247–248.
[82] [1983] I.L.R.M. 79.
[83] [1983] I.L.R.M. 79 at 80. Emphasis added.
[84] [1984] I.R. 248.

"[I]t would seem that the law is still somewhat undecided on this particular point. James Woods, however, an authority on practice and procedure in the District Court, and an experienced District Court Clerk, has stated that the deciding criterion [used by District Court judges in deciding whether to accept jurisdiction] is the penalty actually imposed, in other words following the line taken by Henchy and Griffin JJ in *State (Rollinson) v Kelly*."[85]

Fines to be measured according to the current value of money

In *State (Rollinson) v Kelly*,[86] the majority of the Supreme Court held that the severity of a monetary penalty must be gauged according to standards at the time the fine is imposed, rather than the severity the fine would have had at the time it was first enacted. In that case, therefore, a revenue offence carrying a £500 fine was accepted as being minor, having regard to the value of money in the early 1980s, notwithstanding that £500 would have been a very substantial sum at the time the offence was created in 1926.

Although the point was not expressly considered in that case, the logic of *State (Rollinson) v Kelly*[87] would also suggest that the moral quality of an offence should be gauged according to the prevailing mores at the time of trial, rather than the time the offence was enacted. It may well be the case that a particular offence will cease to be a minor one if public opinion changes and societal attitudes harden against it.

Maximum permissible punishments

Because the value of money varies over time it can be difficult to determine from the case law the maximum fine which the courts will accept as consistent with a minor offence. In the 1962 decision in *Melling*, for example, Lavery J. stated that "a penalty of £1,000 or, indeed, much less" would place the offence above the threshold.[88] By the 1984 decision in *State (Rollinson) v Kelly*, however, the majority accepted that a fine of £500 was consistent with a minor offence, while Griffin J. added that even "a sum fairly considerably in excess of that sum" would be within the minor offence threshold.[89]

We can gain some guidance, however, by considering how legislation has capped fines in relation to summary offences. In legislation between 1980 and 1982 the general level of fines for such offences was between £500 (€635) and £800 (€1,016).[90] By the early 1990s a fine of £1,000 (€1,270) appeared to be the maximum considered acceptable,[91] a sum which had jumped to €3,000 by 2002.[92] Most recently, the Fines

---

[85] Law Reform Commission Consultation Paper, *Penalties for Minor Offences* (LRC CP18–2002), p.15.
[86] [1984] I.R. 248.
[87] [1984] I.R. 248.
[88] [1962] I.R. 1 at 18.
[89] [1984] I.R. 248 at 263.
[90] See the judgment of Griffin J. in *State (Rollinson) v Kelly* [1984] I.R. 248 at 263–264.
[91] Hogan and Whyte (eds), *J.M. Kelly, The Irish Constitution*, 4th edn (2003), p.632.
[92] Hogan and Whyte (eds), *J.M. Kelly, The Irish Constitution*, 4th edn (2003), p.1183.

Act 2010 has updated and consolidated the monetary penalties which can be imposed on summary conviction in five bands: from Class A (fine up to €5,000) to Class E (fine up to €500). Consequently, at the time of writing it seems that the Oireachtas considers a fine of €5,000 to be the maximum which is consistent with the definition of a minor offence.

The maximum sentence of imprisonment consistent with a minor offence has also presented some difficulties. In *Melling* the majority opinion of Lavery J. reluctantly accepted that a sentence of nine months would be permissible but indicated that a penalty of 12 months' imprisonment would take a case outside the realm of minor offences. Later cases have, however, shown a judicial willingness to accept a slightly longer period. In particular, the Supreme Court decision in *Mallon v Minister for Agriculture, Food and Fisheries*[93] appears to have implicitly accepted that a possible sentence of up to one year is acceptable in respect of a minor offence, a point reinforced by the comments of Moriarty J. in *Meagher v O'Leary*[94] who states that:

> "[I]t is uncontested in argument, and indeed was set forth in the Supreme Court judgments in the *Mallon* case supra, that a maximum penalty of two years' imprisonment for a single offence takes that offence beyond the category of a minor one, whereas a maximum penalty of one year's imprisonment does not ..."[95]

What constitutes "punishment"?

In some cases a criminal conviction may carry consequences which are additional to any fine or sentence of imprisonment. For example, a conviction for drink driving may carry with it a driving ban, or a conviction for breach of the liquor licensing laws may result in the forfeiture of a licence to sell alcohol. Should this be taken into account as part of the "punishment" in deciding whether the offence is a minor one?

In *Conroy v Attorney General*,[96] the Supreme Court considered this issue in the context of a drink driving conviction under s.49 of the Road Traffic Act 1961, which automatically led to a disqualification from driving for a minimum of 12 months for a first offence. The Supreme Court held that this should not be taken into account as an aspect of the punishment, ruling that it was not part of the "primary punishment" for the offence but rather a secondary consequence of conviction imposed in the interests of public safety:

> "It may well be ... that to some people a driver's licence may be just as valuable as a licence to engage in an occupation or profession. That, however, does not determine the matter. In the opinion of this Court, so far as punishment

---

[93] [1996] 1 I.R. 517.
[94] [1998] 1 I.L.R.M. 211.
[95] [1998] 1 I.L.R.M. 211 at 218. By comparison, the Law Reform Commission has recently recommended that terms of imprisonment of greater than six months should only be imposed following a jury trial, in order to fully respect the constitutional right to personal liberty. See Law Reform Commission Consultation Paper, *Penalties for Minor Offences* (LRC CP18–2002), p.69; Law Reform Commission Report, *Penalties for Minor Offences* (LRC 69–2003), Ch.2.
[96] [1965] I.R. 411.

is concerned, the punishment which must be examined for the purpose of gauging the seriousness of an offence is what may be referred to as 'primary punishment.' That is the type of punishment which is regarded as punishment in the ordinary sense and, where crime is concerned, is either the loss of liberty or the intentional penal deprivation of property whether by means of fine or other direct method of deprivation. Any conviction may result in many other unpleasant and even punitive consequences for the convicted person. By the rules of his professional association or organisation or trade association or any other body of which he is a member he may become liable to expulsion or suspension by reason of his conviction on some particular offence or perhaps on any offence. His very livelihood may depend upon the absence of a conviction in his record. These unfortunate consequences are too remote in character to be taken into account in weighing the seriousness of an offence by the punishment it may attract ...

Undoubtedly disqualification may have a deterrent quality but that does not make it a punishment. It is a regulation of the exercise of a statutory right in the interest of public order and safety."[97]

This distinction between primary and secondary punishments has been applied in a number of cases since, but remains problematic. Particularly in cases involving some form of forfeiture—whether revocation of a licence or the seizure of property—the outcomes are difficult to reconcile. For example, in *Kostan v Ireland*[98] McWilliam J. held that the forfeiture of all fishing gear onboard a foreign fishing boat (worth £102,040) on foot of a fisheries conviction was intended as a penalty and therefore took the matter outside the category of a minor offence given the value of the property at stake. A similar result was reached by the Supreme Court in *O'Sullivan v Hartnett*[99] where the court held that the forfeiture of 900 salmon alleged to have been illegally caught (valued at several thousand pounds) was a particularly severe consequence of conviction which in and of itself would mean that the offence would no longer be a minor one.

By contrast, in *Cartmill v Ireland*,[100] the forfeiture of £120,000 of gaming machines following a conviction under the Gaming and Lotteries Act 1956 was described as a mere secondary punishment. Similarly, in *Charlton v Ireland*[101] and *State (Pheasantry Ltd) v Donnelly*,[102] the High Court held that the revocation of a bookmaker's licence and liquor licence, respectively, did not constitute primary punishment and should therefore be disregarded in assessing the severity of the penalty in each case.

In light of these conflicting decisions, Hogan and Whyte have suggested that the primary/secondary punishment reasoning is "highly questionable" and that statutory outcomes which involve a deprivation of liberty in a particular sphere—such as the revocation of a licence—should properly be considered "a real punishment". They go on to argue that "the superficial distinction between the modalities of punishment

---

[97] [1965] I.R. 411 at 438–442.
[98] [1978] I.L.R.M. 12.
[99] [1983] I.L.R.M. 79.
[100] [1987] I.R. 192.
[101] [1984] I.L.R.M. 39.
[102] [1982] I.L.R.M. 512.

which underlies the words 'primary' and 'secondary' does not seem significant in appraising the gravity of the offence".[103] Whether the Supreme Court will ultimately be persuaded by these criticisms remains to be seen.

Serious and non-serious offences

Background

The concept of a serious offence seems to have first been introduced in Irish law by the Extradition (European Convention on the Suppression of Terrorism) Act 1987. That Act widened extradition powers for politically-motivated offences where a person was alleged to have committed a serious offence, defined in s.1 as:

> [A]n offence which, if the act constituting the offence took place in the State, would be an offence for which a person aged 21 years or over, of full capacity and not previously convicted may be punished by imprisonment for a term of 5 years or by a more severe penalty.

This section—by defining a "serious offence" as one which carries a possible five-year prison sentence—set a basic pattern for later legislation. However, subsequent laws have adopted their own varying definitions. Consequently—and confusingly—there is no single concept of a serious offence in Irish law but rather a number of similar definitions depending on the precise context.

Bail Act 1997

The most well-known example of the serious–non-serious offence distinction relates to the grant or refusal of bail. In *Attorney General v O'Callaghan*,[104] the Supreme Court held that bail could not be refused to an accused person on the basis that if released from custody he might commit further offences while on bail. As explained by Walsh J., to detain a person on the basis that he may commit offences in the future would be a form of "preventative justice which has no place in our legal system and is quite alien to the true purposes of bail".[105]

Following a 1996 referendum, however, the Constitution was modified to allow for the refusal of bail as a precautionary measure, and Art.40.4.6° now provides:

> Provision may be made by law for the refusal of bail by a court to a person charged with a serious offence where it is reasonably considered necessary to prevent the commission of a serious offence by that person.

The Bail Act 1997 gives effect to this constitutional amendment in s.2(1) which provides that:

---

[103] Hogan and Whyte (eds), *J.M. Kelly, The Irish Constitution*, 4th edn (2003), pp.1186–1189.
[104] [1966] I.R. 501.
[105] [1966] I.R. 501 at 507.

General Principles

> Where an application for bail is made by a person charged with a serious offence, a court may refuse the application if the court is satisfied that such refusal is reasonably considered necessary to prevent the commission of a serious offence by that person.

It is necessary to consider both the crime with which the accused is charged and the crime which it is alleged he might commit if granted bail: both must constitute a serious offence before bail can be refused. The term "serious offence" is then defined in s.1 to mean:

> [A]n offence specified in the Schedule for which a person of full capacity and not previously convicted may be punished by a term of imprisonment for a term of 5 years or by a more severe penalty.

The Schedule to the 1997 Act specifies a large number of crimes which shall be treated as serious offences, including murder, manslaughter, kidnapping, false imprisonment, rape, grave offences against the person, sexual offences, explosives and firearms offences, robbery, burglary, offences of dishonesty, offences against the State, serious public order offences, and certain attempts and conspiracies, amongst others. The Bail Act 1997 therefore follows the approach taken by the Extradition (European Convention on the Suppression of Terrorism) Act 1987 in that it sets the threshold for a serious offence at a possible sentence of five years. However, the 1997 Act is narrower than the 1987 Act in an important way: while the 1987 Act defines a "serious offence" as *any* offence which has a possible five-year sentence, the 1997 Act definition includes only those offences which carry a possible five-year sentence and are also included in the Schedule. Consequently, where a person is charged with an offence which is not listed in the Schedule he may not be refused bail on the ground that he might go on to commit a further offence.

It should also be noted that whether an offence is serious under the Bail Act 1997 is determined by the crime charged rather than the circumstances of the individual case, unlike the test for minor offences. For example, as the maximum penalty for sexual assault is five years' imprisonment then any alleged sexual assault will constitute a serious offence under the 1997 Act, even though a particular case might be towards the lower end of the scale and would be unlikely to attract anywhere near that sentence.[106]

Other legislation

The serious–non-serious classification appears in numerous other pieces of legislation, but must be treated with caution as there is very little consistency between these laws: instead, each new piece of legislation tends to include its own slightly different definition of a serious offence.

An early example came with the Offences Against the State (Amendment) Act 1998, which creates an offence of failing to report to Gardaí information which might be of assistance in preventing or prosecuting a serious offence. In this Act, however,

---

[106] The penalty for sexual assault is set by s.2 of the Criminal Law (Rape) (Amendment) Act 1990.

the term is defined as meaning an offence which may attract five years' imprisonment and which also involves "loss of human life, serious personal injury (other than injury that constitutes an offence of a sexual nature), false imprisonment or serious loss of or damage to property or a serious risk of any such loss, injury, imprisonment or damage".[107] Consequently, a crime such as rape would not constitute a serious offence for the purposes of the 1998 Act, though it would under the Bail Act 1997.

Part 7 of the Criminal Justice Act 2006 shows a similar inconsistency. That Part creates a number of new offences relating to criminal organisations, where a "criminal organisation" is defined as a structured group, comprising three or more persons, which is established over a period of time, and which has as its main purpose the commission of serious offences. Contrary to earlier practice, however, a "serious offence" is here defined as one for which a person may be punished by imprisonment for a term of *four* years or more.[108]

These and other inconsistencies create a trap for the unwary: while Irish law might appear at first glance to recognise a single distinction between serious and non-serious offences, when examined more closely it contains numerous such distinctions which can and do differ significantly from each other.[109]

Arrestable and non-arrestable offences

When the Criminal Law Act 1997 abolished the felony–misdemeanour distinction it had a substantial impact on several areas of criminal law. Many procedural matters—such as the power to arrest without a warrant—hinged on whether an offence constituted a felony, as did the substantive law in relation to matters such as participation in crime and inchoate offences. For that reason, the 1997 Act creates a new classification, that of the arrestable–non-arrestable offence, which acts as a substitute for the felony–misdemeanour distinction. An offence is arrestable if it carries a possible five-year term of imprisonment and s.1 of the 1997 Act provides:

> "[A]rrestable offence" means an offence for which a person of full capacity and not previously convicted may, under or by virtue of any enactment or the common law, be punished by imprisonment for a term of five years or by a more severe penalty and includes an attempt to commit any such offence.[110]

This definition overlaps substantially with definitions of serious offences, so that the majority of serious offences will be arrestable offences and vice versa.

---

[107] Sections 8 and 9.
[108] Section 70.
[109] For further examples of inconsistent definitions of a "serious offence" see, e.g. s.1 of the Interception of Postal Packets and Telecommunications Messages (Regulation) Act 1993; s.1(1) of the Commission to Inquire into Child Abuse Act 2000 (as amended by s.3 of the Commission to Inquire into Child Abuse (Amendment) Act 2005); s.28 of the Residential Institutions Redress Act 2003; s.62 of the International Criminal Court Act 2006; and s.1 of the Communications (Retention of Data) Act 2011.
[110] As amended by s.8 of the Criminal Justice Act 2006.

Powers of arrest

As the name suggests, the main function of the arrestable–non-arrestable distinction is to determine whether there is a power of arrest without warrant for a particular offence. Prior to the Criminal Law Act 1997 there were wide common law powers of arrest without warrant for felonies but not misdemeanours.[111] The effect of the 1997 Act is that these common law powers of arrest have now been repealed[112] and s.4 of that Act now creates three general powers of arrest without warrant.[113]

The first of these relates to situations where a crime is in progress. Under s.4(1) of the 1997 Act "any person may arrest without warrant anyone who is or whom he or she, with reasonable cause, suspects to be in the act of committing an arrestable offence". This is available to any person—both to Gardaí and to private individuals—and is, therefore, sometimes referred to as a citizen's arrest. This power is, however, limited to arrests during the offence, and does not allow arrests after the fact.

The second power of arrest is contained in s.4(2) which provides that "where an arrestable offence has been committed, any person may arrest without warrant anyone who is or whom he or she, with reasonable cause, suspects to be guilty of the offence". This is again open to any person—including private individuals—and allows for arrests after a crime has been committed. It is, however, limited in that it only allows for an arrest where an arrestable offence has in fact been committed. McMahon and Binchy point out that this puts the person relying on this power at some risk:

> "[F]or example, if a store detective reasonably believes that a customer committed a shop-lifting offence and it turns out that no such offence occurred ... then the arrest will be unlawful and the store detective is open to civil liability for false imprisonment, battery, assault and perhaps defamation."[114]

Both the section 4(1) and 4(2) powers are secondary to Garda powers of arrest and this is reflected in two further provisions which are intended to minimise the risks of a private individual taking the law into his own hands. Under s.4(4) an arrest by a private individual may only be carried out where that person has reasonable cause to suspect that the person to be arrested would attempt to avoid arrest by a member of the Garda Síochána, while under s.4(5) a person who is arrested by a private individual must be transferred into the custody of the Garda Síochána as soon as practicable.

The third power of arrest is contained in s.4(3), is limited to members of the Garda Síochána and provides that "[w]here a member of the Garda Síochána, with reasonable cause, suspects that an arrestable offence has been committed, he or she may arrest without warrant anyone whom the member, with reasonable cause,

---

[111] See Courtney Stanhope Kenny, *Outlines of Criminal Law* (Oxford: Oxford University Press, 1902), pp.95–96.
[112] With the exception of arrest for breach of the peace, as to which see *Thorpe v DPP* [2006] IEHC 319.
[113] There are, however, numerous specific statutory powers of arrest which will not be considered here, such as the power of arrest and detention under s.30 of the Offences Against the State Act 1939.
[114] Bryan McMahon and William Binchy, *Law of Torts*, 3rd edn (Dublin: Tottel Publishing, 2000), p.648.

suspects to be guilty of the offence". This power goes further than the powers of arrest under s.4(1) and 4(2) and in particular authorises arrests where a Garda reasonably suspects that an arrestable offence has been committed, even though such a suspicion might later turn out to be ill-founded.

Other situations

Apart from powers of arrest, the arrestable–non-arrestable classification is important in numerous other areas. Many powers of investigation hinge on whether an offence is an arrestable one: for example, under the Criminal Justice (Surveillance) Act 2009 members of the Garda Síochána may use certain surveillance devices only in operations which concern arrestable offences or the security of the State.[115] Similarly, whether the District Court has the power to issue search warrants in relation to a particular matter will often depend on whether the offence in question is an arrestable one.[116]

For the purposes of this book, however, the distinction is most important in that it forms a key part of several substantive criminal offences. For example, the concept of an arrestable offence is central to burglary which is defined in s.12(1) of the Criminal Justice (Theft and Fraud Offences) Act 2001 as follows:

> A person is guilty of burglary if he or she—
> (a) enters any building or part of a building as a trespasser and with intent to commit an arrestable offence, or
> (b) having entered any building or part of a building as a trespasser, commits or attempts to commit any such offence therein.

It can be seen from this that in order to secure a conviction for burglary the prosecutor must show that the accused person committed, attempted to commit or intended to commit an arrestable offence.

In the same way, criminal liability for assisting offenders after an offence has been committed (by concealing or failing to report crimes) will generally depend on whether the underlying crime constitutes an arrestable offence. For example, s.7(2) of the Criminal Law Act 1997 provides that:

> Where a person has committed an arrestable offence, any other person who, knowing or believing him or her to be guilty of the offence or of some other arrestable offence, does without reasonable excuse any act whether inside or outside the State with intent to impede his or her apprehension or prosecution shall be guilty of an offence.[117]

This would criminalise, for example, the provision of a "safe house" for a fugitive or the deliberate destruction of evidence where the intention was to enable the offender

---

[115] Section 4(1). See generally, T.J. McIntyre, "Criminal Justice (Surveillance) Act 2009" [2009] I.C.L.S.A. 15.
[116] See s.10 of the Criminal Justice (Miscellaneous Provisions) Act 1997, as amended by s.6 of the Criminal Justice Act 2006.
[117] As amended by s.19(2)(a) of the Criminal Justice (Amendment) Act 2009.

to evade justice—but only where the original act constituted an arrestable offence. In the same way, s.8 of the Criminal Law Act 1997 creates a crime of concealing an offence for reward and s.19 of the Criminal Justice Act 2011 creates a crime of failing to disclose information relating to certain crimes—but in each case liability depends on whether the underlying offence constitutes an arrestable offence.

FUNDAMENTAL PRINCIPLES OF CRIMINAL LAW

The presumption of innocence

One of the most important procedural safeguards in criminal law is the principle that a person shall be presumed innocent unless and until proved guilty beyond a reasonable doubt.[118] This has a number of distinct but related aspects: in particular it first places the *burden* of proof on the prosecution which is then required to demonstrate the guilt of the accused to a very high *standard* of proof.[119] In this, it reflects a longstanding view that the criminal law should err on the side of caution so as to minimise erroneous convictions—most famously expressed by Blackstone who wrote that "the law holds that it is better that ten guilty persons escape than that one innocent suffer".[120]

This principle serves a number of different purposes. It helps to level the playing field in criminal trials, acting as a "counterweight to the immense power and resources of the State compared to the position of the defendant".[121] More fundamentally, it protects the dignity of the individual, guards against the serious moral wrong done to a person who is wrongfully convicted and in that regard also helps to uphold the moral authority of the criminal law itself. As explained by Brennan J. in the United States Supreme Court decision *In re Winship*[122]:

> "The requirement of proof beyond a reasonable doubt has this vital role in our criminal procedure for cogent reasons. The accused during a criminal prosecution has at stake interests of immense importance, both because of the possibility that he may lose his liberty upon conviction and because of the certainty that he would be stigmatized by the conviction. Accordingly, a society that values the good name and freedom of every individual should not condemn a man for commission of a crime when there is reasonable doubt about his guilt ...

---

[118] See generally, Claire Hamilton, *Whittling the Golden Thread: The Presumption of Innocence in Irish Criminal Law* (Dublin: Irish Academic Press, 2007).

[119] For discussion of the relationship between the presumption of innocence and the burden of proof in Irish law see, e.g. Claire Hamilton, "Threats to the presumption of innocence in Irish criminal law: an assessment" (2011) 15(3) I.J.E.P. 181 at 188.

[120] William Blackstone, *Commentaries on the Laws of England* (Oxford: Clarendon Press, 1753), Vol.4, Ch.27. For an alternative perspective, see Alexander Volokh, "Guilty Men" (1997) 146 U. Pa. L. Rev. 173.

[121] Andrew Ashworth, *Principles of Criminal Law*, 5th edn (Oxford: Oxford University Press, 2006), p.83.

[122] 397 U.S. 358 (1970).

Moreover, use of the reasonable-doubt standard is indispensable to command the respect and confidence of the community in applications of the criminal law. It is critical that the moral force of the criminal law not be diluted by a standard of proof that leaves people in doubt whether innocent men are being condemned. It is also important in our free society that every individual going about his ordinary affairs have confidence that his government cannot adjudge him guilty of a criminal offense without convincing a proper factfinder of his guilt with utmost certainty."[123]

Perhaps the most famous statement of the principle is the decision of the House of Lords in *Woolmington v DPP*.[124] In this case the appellant was a farm labourer charged with the murder of his estranged wife. He admitted shooting her with a shotgun he had brought with him, but claimed that the gun went off accidentally and that his intention was merely to frighten her by threatening to kill himself. The trial judge directed the jury that the burden of proof rested on the appellant to show that the killing was accidental:

"Once it is shown to a jury that somebody has died through the act of another, that is presumed to be murder, unless the person who has been guilty of the act which causes the death can satisfy a jury that what happened was something less, something which might be alleviated, something which might be reduced to a charge of manslaughter, or was something which was accidental, or was something which could be justified ... The Crown has got to satisfy you that this woman, Violet Woolmington, died at the prisoner's hands. They must satisfy you of that beyond any reasonable doubt. If they satisfy you of that, then he has to show that there are circumstances to be found in the evidence which has been given from the witness-box in this case, which alleviate the crime so that it is only manslaughter, or which excuse the homicide altogether by showing that it was a pure accident."

Following his conviction, Woolmington appealed to the House of Lords, which held that the trial judge had misdirected the jury and reaffirmed the significance of the presumption of innocence. Per Viscount Sankey L.C.:

"[I]t is not for the prisoner to establish his innocence, but for the prosecution to establish his guilt. Just as there is evidence on behalf of the prosecution so there may be evidence on behalf of the prisoner which may cause a doubt as to his guilt. In either case, he is entitled to the benefit of the doubt. But while the prosecution must prove the guilt of the prisoner, there is no such burden laid on the prisoner to prove his innocence and it is sufficient for him to raise a doubt as to his guilt; he is not bound to satisfy the jury of his innocence ... Throughout the web of the English Criminal Law one golden thread is always to be seen, that it is the duty of the prosecution to prove the prisoner's guilt subject to what I have already said as to the defence of insanity and subject also

---

[123] 397 US 358 (1970) at 363–364.
[124] [1935] A.C. 462.

General Principles 37

to any statutory exception. If, at the end of and on the whole of the case, there is a reasonable doubt, created by the evidence given by either the prosecution or the prisoner, as to whether the prisoner killed the deceased with a malicious intention, the prosecution has not made out the case and the prisoner is entitled to an acquittal. No matter what the charge or where the trial, the principle that the prosecution must prove the guilt of the prisoner is part of the common law of England and no attempt to whittle it down can be entertained."[125]

Constitutional status

Although the presumption of innocence is not expressly stated in the Constitution, it has been held to be implicit in the Art.38.1 guarantee that "no person shall be tried on any criminal charge save in due course of law".[126] The first case to rule on this point appears to have been *O'Leary v Attorney General* in which Costello J. stated that:

"I have little difficulty in … construing the Constitution as conferring on every accused in every criminal trial a constitutionally protected right to the presumption of innocence. This right is now widespread and indeed enjoys universal recognition. Article 11 of the United Nations Universal Declaration of Human Rights, 1948, provides that 'Everyone charged with a penal offence has the right to be presumed innocent until proved guilty according to law.' … The Constitution of course contains no express reference to the presumption but it does provide in Article 38 that 'no person shall be tried on any criminal charge save in due course of law.' It seems to me that it has been for so long a fundamental postulate of every criminal trial in this country that the accused was presumed to be innocent of the offence with which he was charged, that a criminal trial held otherwise than in accordance with this presumption would, prima facie, be one which was not held in due course of law."[127]

Jury directions on the presumption of innocence

Case law has established a number of guidelines for trial judges when explaining the presumption of innocence (including the burden and standard of proof) to jurors. One of the most important cases on point is *Attorney General v Byrne*[128] which sets out the following principles:

"The correct charge to a jury is that they must be satisfied beyond reasonable doubt of the guilt of the accused, and it is helpful if that degree of proof is contrasted with that in a civil case. It is also essential, however, that the jury should be told that the accused is entitled to the benefit of the doubt and that

---

[125] [1935] A.C. 462 at 481–482.
[126] For a recent example, see *DPP v DO'T* [2003] 4 I.R. 286.
[127] [1993] 1 I.R. 102 at 107. This was confirmed by the Supreme Court on appeal ([1995] 1 I.R. 254). Prior cases which appeared to implicitly recognise a constitutional guarantee of the presumption of innocence include *Attorney General v O'Callaghan* [1966] I.R. 501 and *Ryan v Director of Public Prosecutions* [1989] I.R. 399.
[128] [1974] 1 I.R. 1.

when two views on any part of the case are possible on the evidence, they should adopt that which is favourable to the accused unless the State has established the other beyond reasonable doubt.

In this case the trial judge used the words 'satisfied' and 'to your satisfaction' on many occasions when explaining the onus of proof. He then said that 'being satisfied' means the same thing as 'beyond a reasonable doubt.' This is not correct because one may be satisfied of something and still have a reasonable doubt. The judge made no attempt to explain to the jury what degree of satisfaction is required and it is in this respect that the time-honoured words 'beyond reasonable doubt' are of such assistance; nor did the judge tell the jury that the accused were entitled to the benefit of the doubt. The Court thinks that jurymen understand the meaning of the expression 'beyond reasonable doubt', particularly when it is associated with a comparison of the standard of proof in a civil case.

For these reasons the Court is of opinion that the judge's charge to the jury was not correct and, as the error related to a vital matter, it has decided that the conviction should be set aside and a new trial ordered."[129]

More recently, *DPP v DO'T*[130] has reaffirmed the importance of the presumption of innocence and has stated that the jury should be directed as to the presumption as a separate matter in its own right. Per Hardiman J.:

"The presumption of innocence, thus so securely entrenched nationally and internationally, is not only a right in itself: it is the basis of other aspects of a trial in due course of law at common law. The rule that, generally speaking, the prosecution bears the burden of proving all the elements of the offence necessary to establish guilt is a corollary of the presumption. To state the incidence of the burden of proof without indicating its basis in the presumption is to risk understating its importance and perhaps relegating it to the status of a mere technical rule. The presumption is the basis of the rule as to the burden of proof and not merely an alternative way of stating it ... It is therefore important that the presumption itself should be explained as an essential feature of the criminal trial. The prosecution's burden of proof, the corollary of the presumption, should be itself separately explained. There must then be a treatment of the standard of proof, which is proof beyond reasonable doubt, and which itself entails the corollary that the defendant is entitled to the benefit of any reasonable doubt."[131]

Exceptions to the presumption of innocence

Insanity and diminished responsibility

The decision in *Woolmington v DPP* was careful to note that the defence of insanity was an exception to the general rule that it is the duty of the prosecution to prove

---
[129] [1974] 1 I.R. 1 at 9 per Kenny J.
[130] [2003] 4 I.R. 286.
[131] [2003] 4 I.R. 286 at 290–291.

guilt. This reflected a common law presumption of sanity so that in cases where insanity was raised as a defence the onus of proof rested on the defendant to establish that he was insane at the time of the crime. While one Irish case—*Attorney General v Fennell*[132]—has suggested that the defendant had to meet the criminal standard of proof to rely on the defence, later cases have made it clear that "the onus of proof of establishing insanity when it rests on the defence is to the standard of the balance of probabilities".[133]

Although this defence has now been put on a statutory basis, the Criminal Law (Insanity) Act 2006 does not address the question of the burden of proof. It therefore appears that the common law rules still apply, so that the burden of proof still rests on the defendant.[134] The failure to make this explicit is, however, a surprising gap in the legislation. Elsewhere in that Act a new defence of diminished responsibility is created which expressly places the burden of proof on the defendant, providing that where a person is on trial for murder "it shall be for the defence to establish that the person is, by reason of this section, not liable to be convicted of that offence".[135] Consequently, it is difficult to see why the burden of proof was not also addressed in the context of the insanity defence.

Other statutory exceptions

The decision in *Woolmington* also noted that statute may reverse the burden of proof regarding particular matters and an increasing number of pieces of legislation now provide that some aspect of an offence shall be presumed unless the contrary is shown. To take a recent example, s.3 of the Criminal Justice (Female Genital Mutilation) Act 2012 establishes an offence of removing a girl from the State for the purpose of carrying out female genital mutilation on her and creates a presumption that the accused had this purpose:

> (1) A person is guilty of an offence if the person removes or attempts to remove a girl or woman from the State where one of the purposes for the removal is to have an act of female genital mutilation done to her ...
> (3) In proceedings for an offence under subsection (1), it shall be presumed, until the contrary is shown, that one of the purposes for the removal from the State by the accused person of the girl or woman concerned was to have an act of female genital mutilation done to her if—
> > (a) the accused person removed the girl or woman from the State in circumstances giving rise to the reasonable inference that one of the purposes for such removal was to have an act of female genital mutilation done to her, and

---

[132] [1940] 1 I.R. 445.
[133] Per Kearns J. in *DPP v Redmond* [2006] 3 I.R. 188 at 213.
[134] See Darius Whelan, "Criminal Law (Insanity) Act 2006" [2006] I.C.L.S.A. 11. Cases such as *DPP v Mulder* [2009] IECCA 45 and *DPP v Kieran Smyth Senior and Kieran Smyth Junior* [2011] 1 I.L.R.M. 81 have accepted that the onus of proof remains on the defendant. See also, Timothy Jones, "Insanity, Automatism and the Burden of Proof on the Accused" (1995) 111 L.Q.R. 475.
[135] Section 6.

(b) an act of female genital mutilation was done to her after she was removed from the State and, where she subsequently returned to the State, before that return.

Reversed burdens of proof, however, create an obvious tension with the presumption of innocence and given the status of the presumption in Ireland such provisions come with a constitutional question mark attached.[136] This issue has been addressed in three key judgments in *Hardy v Ireland*,[137] *O'Leary v Attorney General*,[138] and *DPP v Kieran Smyth Senior and Kieran Smyth Junior*,[139] though, as we shall see, none of these decisions provides a conclusive answer as to when a reversed burden of proof will be unconstitutional.

In *Hardy v Ireland*, the Supreme Court was asked to consider the constitutionality of s.4(1) of the Explosive Substances Act 1883, which criminalises possession of explosives under circumstances giving rise to "a reasonable suspicion that [the defendant] does not have it in his possession ... for a lawful object", unless the defendant "can show that he ... had it in his possession ... for a lawful object". The plaintiff, who had been convicted of possession of a number of explosives, claimed that the effect of this was to impermissibly undermine the presumption of innocence in that it required him to prove his innocence on the balance of probabilities. This argument was rejected by the Supreme Court, but in a way which appeared to show that it was divided as to what the constitutional guarantee of the presumption of innocence required.

All the members of the court accepted that the presumption of innocence was a necessary component of a trial in due course of law pursuant to Art.38.1. However, they differed as to whether the burden of proof can be shifted in a way which is compatible with the presumption of innocence.

The majority judgment, delivered by Hederman J., solved the problem by reading the section narrowly, so as to shift only an evidential burden of proof to the accused to point to some evidence which raised the issue of a lawful purpose. Consequently, on this interpretation, the legal burden of proof always remained on the prosecution to prove beyond reasonable doubt that the accused did not have the items in his possession for a lawful purpose:

"[T]he prosecution has to prove beyond reasonable doubt ... (1) that the accused knowingly had in his possession a substance which it proves is an explosive substance; (2) that he had it under such circumstances as to give rise to a reasonable suspicion that he did not have it in his possession for a lawful object and that, in turn, means that there is an onus on the prosecution to prove that the accused could not show that he had it in his possession for a lawful object. Once those ingredients are in place, it is still open to the accused to demonstrate in any one of a number of ways, such as by cross-examination,

---

[136] See, e.g. Claire Hamilton, "Threats to the presumption of innocence in Irish criminal law: an assessment" (2011) 15(3) I.J.E.P. 181; Una Ní Raifeartaigh, "The criminal justice system and drug relating offending: some thoughts on procedural reform" (1998) 4(1) B.R. 15.
[137] [1994] 2 I.R. 562.
[138] [1995] 1 I.R. 254.
[139] [2011] 1 I.L.R.M. 81.

submissions or by giving evidence, that a *prima facie* situation pointing to his guilt should not be allowed to prevail ... [T]his analysis ... protects the presumption of innocence; it requires that the prosecution should prove its case beyond all reasonable doubt; but it does not prohibit that, in the course of the case, once certain facts are established, inferences may not be drawn from those facts ...".[140]

This strained reading (Campbell, Kilcommins and O'Sullivan describe it as "an exercise in extreme interpretive construction")[141] essentially side-stepped the issue of whether a statute may require an accused to prove a particular defence on the balance of probabilities, from which it might be inferred that this issue presented some difficulties for the majority.

By contrast, the minority judgments of Murphy and Egan JJ. took the view that the section did impose an onus on the accused to prove on the balance of probabilities that he had the explosives in his possession for a lawful purpose, but held that such a shifting of the legal burden of proof with regard to a defence would not violate Art.38.1. Egan J. noted that the effect of the section was to create an excusatory defence and drew an analogy with insanity to hold that "[t]here is nothing in the Constitution to prohibit absolutely the shifting of an onus in a criminal prosecution or to suggest that such would inevitably offend the requirements of due process".[142] Murphy J. similarly reasoned that:

"[T]he second limb of the section [i.e. possession for a lawful object] deals not with the charge but with a statutory exoneration or exculpation from a charge already made and sustained beyond reasonable doubt. I am convinced that the burden which the accused must discharge if he is to avail of that procedure is a duty to satisfy the jury of the statutory condition, that is to say, the existence of a lawful object on the balance of probabilities ... I do not see that there is any inconsistency between a trial in due course of law as provided for by Article 38(1) of the Constitution and a statutory provision such as is contained in s.4 of the Explosive Substances Act, 1883, which affords to an accused a particular defence of which he can avail if, but only if, he proves the material facts on the balance of probabilities."[143]

The presumption of innocence again came before the Supreme Court in *O'Leary v Attorney General*. In this case, the plaintiff was convicted of membership of an unlawful organisation contrary to s.21 of the Offences Against the State Act 1939. A significant part of the prosecution case had been his possession of 37 posters bearing a picture of a gunman and the words "IRA calls the shots". These were claimed by the prosecution to be "incriminating documents" within the meaning of the 1939 Act so as to constitute evidence of membership under s.24:

---

[140] [1994] 2 I.R. 562 at 564.
[141] Liz Campbell, Shane Kilcommins and Catherine O'Sullivan, *Criminal Law in Ireland: Cases and Commentary* (Dublin: Clarus Press, 2010), p.349.
[142] [1994] 2 I.R. 562 at 566.
[143] [1994] 2 I.R. 562 at 568.

On the trial of a person charged with the offence of being a member of an unlawful organisation, proof to the satisfaction of the court that an incriminating document relating to the said organisation was found on such person or in his possession or on lands or in premises owned or occupied by him or under his control shall, without more, be evidence until the contrary is proved that such person was a member of the said organisation at the time alleged in the said charge.

The plaintiff brought a challenge to s.24, claiming that by providing for evidence of membership "until the contrary is proved" it negated the presumption of innocence and placed on him the burden of disproving his guilt. The Supreme Court, however, rejected this argument. The relatively short judgment of the court, delivered by O'Flaherty J., took a similar approach to that in *Hardy v Ireland* and interpreted the section so as to shift an evidential burden only. Per O'Flaherty J. at 265:

"In the opinion of the Court, the section permits no more than the following: if an incriminating document is proved to be in the possession of a person (and that is all that the Court has to consider in this case because actual possession of the documents was proved and, indeed, admitted by the accused) that shall, without more, be evidence until the contrary is proved that such person was a member of an unlawful organisation. It is clear that such possession is to amount to evidence only; it is not to be taken as proof and so the probative value of the possession of such a document might be shaken in many ways: by cross-examination; by pointing to the mental capacity of the accused or the circumstances by which he came to be in possession of the document, to give some examples. The important thing to note about the section is that there is no mention of the burden of proof changing, much less that the presumption of innocence is to be set to one side at any stage."

As a result, the Supreme Court again took a narrow interpretation of the section and avoided the question as to when a reversed legal (as opposed to evidential) burden of proof would be constitutional—suggesting again, perhaps, that the narrow interpretation was prompted by a desire to avoid a possible conflict with Art.38.1.

Most recently, the presumption of innocence and reversed burdens of proof have been considered by the Court of Criminal Appeal in *DPP v Kieran Smyth Senior and Kieran Smyth Junior*.[144] In this case the applicants were a father and son who had been charged with possession of cannabis with intent to supply contrary to s.15A of the Misuse of Drugs Act 1977. Their case was that the son had been asked by a friend to collect parcels containing computer parts. As the son was unable to drive, the father agreed to help by driving a van. At no stage, they claimed, were they aware that the parcels contained cannabis.

The prosecution case relied on s.29(2)(a) of the 1977 Act which reverses the burden of proof in relation to a person's knowledge of what is in his possession. Under that section:

---

[144] [2010] 3 I.R. 688.

> In any such proceedings in which it is proved that the defendant had in his possession a controlled drug ... it shall be a defence to prove that—
> (a) he did not know and had no reasonable grounds for suspecting—
>   (i) that what he had in his possession was a controlled drug ..., or
>   (ii) that he was in possession of a controlled drug.

In his charge to the jury based on this section, the trial judge gave conflicting instructions, stating that the burden of proof always rested with the prosecution but also directing the jury that if they were satisfied beyond a reasonable doubt that the applicants did not know what was in the parcels then the applicants were entitled to be acquitted. The applicants were convicted and appealed to the Court of Criminal Appeal.

In a detailed judgment the court (Charleton J.) found that the trial judge had erred in telling the jury that they must be satisfied beyond a reasonable doubt that the applicants did not know what was in the parcel and went on to consider in some detail the direction which should be given.

Section 29(2)(a) had previously been considered by the Court of Criminal Appeal in *DPP v Byrne, Healy and Kelleher*[145] which had held that its effect was to shift the legal burden of proof to the accused to prove, on the balance of probabilities, that he did not know and had no reasonable grounds for suspecting that what he had in his possession was a controlled drug. In *DPP v Kieran Smyth Senior and Kieran Smyth Junior*, however, the Court of Criminal Appeal departed from that decision and instead held that the section placed a substantially weaker burden of proof on an accused, which was merely to show the existence of a reasonable doubt. Per Charleton J.:

> "[T]he court considers that an evidential burden of proof is cast on the accused by s.29 of the Misuse of Drugs Act 1977, as amended, which is discharged when the accused proves the existence of a reasonable doubt that he did not know, and had no reasonable ground for suspecting that what he had in his possession was a controlled drug. This is not a burden merely of adducing evidence. It is a legal burden discharged on the lowest standard of proof, namely that of proving a reasonable doubt."

In reaching this conclusion and taking a narrow interpretation of s.29(2)(a), the court was influenced by the need to ensure that any reversed burden of proof would be compatible with the constitutional presumption of innocence. Consequently, the judgment engaged in a detailed assessment of what was required by Art.38.1, stating that:

> "The fundamental principle of our criminal justice system is that an accused should not be convicted unless it is proven beyond reasonable doubt that the accused committed the offence. The legal presumption that the accused is innocent, until his guilt is proven to that standard, operates to ensure objectivity within the system. It is a matter for the Oireachtas to decide whether on a

---

[145] [1998] 2 I.R. 417.

particular element of the offence an evidential burden of proof should be cast on an accused person. Of itself, this does not infringe the constitutional principle that the accused should be presumed to be innocent until found guilty. Reasons of policy may perhaps require that any reversed element of proof cast on the accused should be discharged as a probability. That should either be stated in the legislation or be a matter of necessary inference therefrom. The construction of a criminal statute requires the court to presume that the core elements of an offence must be proven beyond reasonable doubt; otherwise the accused must be acquitted. A special defence, beyond the core elements of the offence, may carry a different burden; insanity and diminished responsibility are examples of such a defence which casts a probability burden on the accused. Where, however, in relation to an element of the offence itself, as opposed to a defence, a burden is cast upon the accused, the necessary inference that the accused must discharge that burden on the balance of probability is not easily made. The court notes that bearing the burden of proving a defence as a probability could have the effect that in respect of an element of the offence an accused person might raise a doubt as to his guilt, but not establish it as a probability. This might lead to a situation where the charge was not proven as to each element of the offence beyond reasonable doubt, but nonetheless the accused could be convicted. That would not be right. Proof of a guilty mind is integral to proof of a true criminal offence, in distinction to a regulatory offence. In s. 29 of the Misuse of Drugs Act 1977, as amended, the normal burden of proving the mental element of possession of a controlled drug is removed from the prosecution and the accused is required to prove that it did not exist.

In consequence, the court considers that an evidential burden of proof is cast on the accused by s. 29 of the Misuse of Drugs Act 1977, as amended, which is discharged when the accused proves the existence of a reasonable doubt that he did not know, and had no reasonable ground for suspecting that what he had in his possession was a controlled drug. This is not a burden merely of adducing evidence. It is legal burden discharged on the lowest standard of proof, namely that of proving a reasonable doubt."[146]

This is a significant decision, though also one which is in some ways difficult to interpret. The judgment appears to blur the former understanding of the distinction between legal and evidential burdens of proof by describing s.29(2)(a) as creating both a legal and an evidential burden. It also refers to what seems to be a new type of reversed legal burden—one which requires the accused to "prove the existence of a reasonable doubt"—though it is not entirely clear how this differs from an evidential burden to introduce some evidence which casts doubt as to whether the accused was aware of what was in his possession. It may be, therefore, that further judgments will be necessary to clarify what is meant by these points.

Leaving aside these issues, however, the core of the judgment is clear and indicates that s.29(2)(a) would be unconstitutional unless given a restrictive interpretation which protects the presumption of innocence. The judgment goes further in

---

[146] [2010] 3 I.R. 688 at 696.

its analysis than either *Hardy* or *O'Leary* and adopts a two-part classification differentiating "core elements" of an offence from "special defences". It suggests that it would be contrary to Art.38.1 to adopt a reversed burden of proof on the balance of probabilities in relation to a core element of an offence (in this case, knowledge of the contents of the parcels). Consequently, it would seem likely that other reversed burdens of proof will also be given a restrictive interpretation.[147] The judgment does, however, indicate that such reversed burdens of proof would be permissible in relation to special defences such as insanity or automatism and also in relation to regulatory crimes rather than "true criminal" offences—though, as with the case of strict liability, this will present the fresh difficulty of identifying where the truly criminal ends and the merely regulatory begins.

The principle of legality

The rule of law is well established in Irish jurisprudence as a constitutional value and requires that restrictions on the liberty of the individual must be prescribed by law. In general terms, it demands that the law should be predictable, accessible and certain. As Gardner explains:

> "According to the ideal of the rule of law, the law must be such that those subject to it can be reliably guided by it, either to avoid violating it or to build the legal consequences of having violated it into their thinking about what future actions may be open to them. People must be able to find out what the law is and to factor it into their practical deliberations. The law must avoid taking people by surprise, ambushing them, putting them into conflict with its requirements in such a way as to defeat their expectations and frustrate their plans."[148]

When applied in the specific context of the criminal law, the rule of law is often termed the principle of legality and can be summarised by the maxim *nullum crimen, nulla poena sine lege*—that is, that there should be no crime or punishment except in accordance with a (prior) law.[149] For analytical purposes, it is helpful to disaggregate the contents of this far-reaching principle and this section will therefore follow the approach of Ashworth who suggests that the principle of legality should be understood as encompassing three distinct principles: the principle of non-retroactivity, the principle of maximum certainty and the principle of strict construction of penal statutes.[150] Each of these will be considered in turn.

---

[147] See, e.g. *PJ Carey Contractors Ltd v DPP* [2011] IECCA 63, which relied upon *DPP v Kieran Smyth Senior and Kieran Smyth Junior* in giving a narrow interpretation to the reversed burden of proof in s.50 of the Safety, Health and Welfare at Work Act 1989.

[148] John Gardner, "Introduction" in HLA Hart, *Punishment and Responsibility*, 2nd edn (Oxford: Oxford University Press, 2008), p.xxxvi.

[149] For an account of the development of the principle and a critique of the liberal individual values it is said to embody, see Finbarr McAuley and John Paul McCutcheon, *Criminal Liability* (Dublin: Round Hall Sweet & Maxwell, 2000), pp.42–56.

[150] Andrew Ashworth, *Principles of Criminal Law*, 5th edn (Oxford: Oxford University Press, 2006), p.68. See also, Thomas O'Malley, "Common Law Crimes and the Principle of Legality" (1989) 7 I.L.T. 243.

The principle of non-retroactivity

One implication of the principle *nullum crimen, nulla poena sine lege* is that legislation should not be retroactive in its effect so as to make conduct criminal which was not a crime at the time of its commission, nor should it increase the penalty for a crime above that which applied at the time the crime took place. As Simester and Sullivan put it, "criminal liability is not the sort of nasty surprise that should be sprung on citizens *ex post facto*".[151] This reflects important moral and practical considerations: there is an obvious injustice in stigmatising an individual for failure to meet standards of conduct which did not apply until after the conduct in question, while the role of the law in guiding conduct becomes meaningless if an individual can later find himself penalised for conduct which was permitted by the law at the time.

This principle has constitutional status in Ireland and Art.15.5.1° of the Constitution provides that "[t]he Oireachtas shall not declare acts to be infringements of the law which were not so at the date of their commission".[152] The text of this provision applies only to retroactive creation of crimes and not the retroactive increase of criminal penalties; however, the High Court in *Enright v Ireland*[153] has accepted that the concept of trial in due course of law under Art.38.1 includes "the right only to be punished for a crime in accordance with the law which existed at the date of commission of the crime"[154] so as to rule out retroactive increases in penalties. As such, the constitutional principle now more closely matches art.7(1) of the ECHR which provides:

> No one shall be held guilty of any criminal offence on account of any act or omission which did not constitute a criminal offence under national or international law at the time when it was committed. Nor shall a heavier penalty be imposed than the one that was applicable at the time the criminal offence was committed.[155]

It should be noted, however, that the decision in *Enright v Ireland* leaves it open to the legislature to introduce retroactive consequences to criminal convictions provided that these do not constitute penalties. In *Enright*, the plaintiff had been convicted of a number of sexual offences in 1993. The Sex Offenders Act 2001 subsequently introduced a number of obligations on convicted sex offenders following their release (notably registration with the Garda Síochána and notification of whereabouts) and s.7(2)(b)(i) applied these obligations to those who had been convicted prior to the 2001 Act but who were still serving their sentences when it came into force. The plaintiff challenged the constitutionality of this provision on the basis that it imposed on him a retroactive criminal penalty. However, his claim was dismissed on the basis that the requirements placed on released sex offenders—although retroactive—did

---

[151] Andrew Simester et al, *Criminal Law: Theory and Doctrine*, 4th edn (Oxford: Hart Publishing, 2010).
[152] It should be noted that this is not limited to criminal matters and Art.15.5.1° has also been held to apply to retrospective civil wrongs—see *Magee v Culligan* [1992] 1 I.R. 233 at 272.
[153] [2003] 2 I.R. 321.
[154] [2003] 2 I.R. 321 at 331 per Finlay Geoghegan J.
[155] See also, *Gilligan v Murphy* [2011] IEHC 465.

not constitute a penalty. In reaching this conclusion the court held that in order for the requirements to constitute a penalty they would have to be punitive either in their intent or their effect: in this case, the legislation was found to be intended to promote rehabilitation of the offender and the protection of the public and the requirements were not so onerous that they should be treated as in effect a penalty.

The principle of maximum certainty

The principle of maximum certainty reflects the need for clarity in the definition of criminal offences if citizens are to have reasonable notice of the type of conduct which may give rise to criminal liability. This is often referred to as the requirement of fair warning, following United States authority that criminal statutes should provide "fair warning ... in language that the common world will understand, of what the law intends to do if a certain line is passed. To make the warning fair, so far as possible the line should be clear".[156] In addition to a warning function this also has an important institutional or structural effect. That is, by ensuring clarity in the law it minimises areas in which there is unaccountable police discretion and thereby tends to reduce arbitrary or selective enforcement of the law.[157]

The principle has constitutional status and has been used on a number of occasions to invalidate criminal legislation which does not meet the requisite standard of clarity. The leading authority in this area is *King v Attorney General*[158] in which the Supreme Court found inconsistent with the Constitution provisions in the Vagrancy Act 1824 which created an offence of "loitering with intent" by "every suspected person or reputed thief" who frequented certain places. Per Kenny J.:

> "It is a fundamental feature of our system of government by law (and not by decree or diktat) that citizens may be convicted only of offences which have been specified with precision by the judges who made the common law, or of offences which, created by statute, are expressed without ambiguity ... In my opinion, both governing phrases 'suspected person' and 'reputed thief' are so uncertain that they cannot form the foundation for a criminal offence ... a person may be convicted of a criminal offence only if the ingredients of, and the acts constituting, the offence are specified with precision and clarity."[159]

In that case Henchy J. considered in more detail the constitutional basis for the principle in a passage which also reflects on the concerns mentioned earlier that vague offences may give rise to selective enforcement and unaccountable police discretion:

> "In my opinion, the ingredients of the offence and the mode by which its commission may be proved are so arbitrary, so vague, so difficult to rebut,

---

[156] *McBoyle v United States* 283 US 25 (1931) at 27 per Holmes J.
[157] See, e.g. Gearóid Carey, "The Rule of Law, Public Order Targeting and the Construction of Crime" (1998) 8(1) I.C.L.J. 26; Thomas O'Malley, "Common Law Crimes and the Principle of Legality" (1989) 7 I.L.T. 243.
[158] [1981] I.R. 233.
[159] [1981] I.R. 233 at 263.

so related to rumour or ill-repute or past conduct, so ambiguous in failing to distinguish between apparent and real behaviour of a criminal nature, so prone to make a man's lawful occasions become unlawful and criminal by the breadth and arbitrariness of the discretion that is vested in both the prosecutor and the judge, so indiscriminately contrived to mark as criminal conduct committed by one person in certain circumstances when the same conduct, when engaged in by another person in similar circumstances, would be free of the taint of criminality, so out of keeping with the basic concept inherent in our legal system that a man may walk abroad in the secure knowledge that he will not be singled out from his fellow-citizens and branded and punished as a criminal unless it has been established beyond reasonable doubt that he has deviated from a clearly prescribed standard of conduct, and generally so singularly at variance with both the explicit and implicit characteristics and limitations of the criminal law as to the onus of proof and mode of proof, that it is not so much a question of ruling unconstitutional the type of offence we are now considering as identifying the particular constitutional provisions with which such an offence is at variance.

I shall confine myself to saying, without going into unnecessary detail, that the offence, both in its essential ingredients and in the mode of proof of its commission, violates the requirement in Article 38, s. 1, that no person shall be tried on any criminal charge save in due course of law; that it violates the guarantee in Article 40, s. 4, sub-s. 1, that no citizen shall be deprived of personal liberty save in accordance with law which means without stooping to methods which ignore the fundamental norms of the legal order postulated by the Constitution; that, in its arbitrariness and its unjustifiable discrimination, it fails to hold (as is required by Article 40, s. 1) all citizens to be equal before the law: and that it ignores the guarantees in Article 40, s. 3, that the personal rights of citizens shall be respected and, as far as practicable, defended and vindicated, and that the State shall by its laws protect as best it may from unjust attack and, in the case of injustice done, vindicate the life, person, good name, and property rights of every citizen."[160]

A similar result was reached in *Dokie v DPP*[161] where the High Court applied the decision in *King v Attorney General* to find s.12 of the Immigration Act 2004 inconsistent with the Constitution. That section required every non-national within the meaning of the Act to produce on demand a valid passport or equivalent document when requested to do so by an immigration officer or member of the Garda Síochána. Failure to do so constituted an offence unless "he or she gives a satisfactory explanation of the circumstances which prevent him or her from so doing"—however, the term "satisfactory explanation" was nowhere defined in the legislation. In finding this provision to be unconstitutional, Kearns P. noted the section had "considerable potential for arbitrariness in its application by any individual member of An Garda Síochána", before going on to hold that:

---

[160] [1981] I.R. 233 at 257.
[161] [2011] 1 I.R. 805.

"There is no requirement in s.12 that the demanding officer should have formed any reasonable suspicion that the non-national has committed a crime, is about to commit a crime or is otherwise behaving unlawfully before he/she can require the non-national to provide a 'satisfactory' explanation for the absent documents ...

In my view s.12 is not sufficiently precise to reasonably enable an individual to foresee the consequences of his or her acts or omissions or to anticipate what form of explanation might suffice to avoid prosecution. Furthermore, there is no requirement in the section to warn of the possible consequences of any failure to provide a 'satisfactory' explanation.

As a result, the offence purportedly created by s.12 is ambiguous and imprecise. In my view it lacks the clarity necessary to legitimately create a criminal offence."[162]

An as yet unresolved issue in this context is the relationship of the principle of maximum certainty with the judicial interpretation and development of common law offences. Two issues arise. First, the elements of a common law offence might themselves be so uncertain as to fail to meet the requirements of this principle. Secondly, the evolutionary nature of the common law may have the effect of widening the elements of a common law offence and thereby also infringing the principle of non-retroactivity.[163]

These issues are illustrated by *Attorney General (Society for the Protection of Unborn Children) v Open Door Counselling*[164] in which Hamilton P. held that the common law offence of conspiracy to corrupt public morals formed part of Irish law, despite the vagueness inherent in that offence, the impossibility of defining what is meant by the term "public morals" and the risk that juries will reach subjective and inconsistent decisions as to the social values which they consider should be protected under this heading. Consequently, O'Malley has pointed out that this decision appears to be incompatible with *King v Attorney General*:

"Let us suppose that the Oireachtas enacted a statute creating an offence of conspiracy to corrupt public morals. Would this statute survive constitutional challenge in light of the *King* judgment among others? There is a strong argument to be made that it should not and an even stronger argument for the proposition that the courts in considering the existence or otherwise of a common law offence should apply the same criteria as they would employ in considering the validity of a penal statute."[165]

---

[162] [2011] 1 I.R. 805 at 818–819. Compare *Cagney v Director of Public Prosecutions* [2008] 2 I.L.R.M. 293 in relation to the principle of certainty and the "notably open ended" offence of endangerment under s.13 of the Non-Fatal Offences Against the Person Act 1997. See also the decision in *Dillon v DPP* [2008] 1 I.R. 383.

[163] For an example of the common law boundaries of an offence being widened see the House of Lords decision in *R. v R* [1992] 1 A.C. 599 which abolished (with retrospective effect) the common law rule that a husband could not be guilty of the rape of his wife. The European Court of Human Rights decision in *SW v UK* (1995) 21 E.H.R.R. 363 ultimately held that this did not give rise to a violation of the rights of defendants under art.7(1).

[164] [1988] I.R. 593.

[165] Thomas O'Malley, "Common Law Crimes and the Principle of Legality" (1989) 7 I.L.T. 243.

By comparison, the Supreme Court in *Corway v Independent Newspapers*[166] has taken an approach which is more restrictive and which suggests that the courts should be careful to ensure that common law offences are closely circumscribed. In that case the applicant sought leave from the court to bring a criminal prosecution for blasphemy against the respondents in relation to a cartoon about the 1995 divorce referendum. However, leave was refused on the basis that the offence was too vague to allow a criminal trial to proceed. In particular, the court held that despite the constitutional status of blasphemy (Art.40.6.1(i) provides that "[t]he publication or utterance of blasphemous ... matter is an offence which shall be punishable in accordance with law"), the reliance on the common law offence and the failure to introduce a legislative definition meant that the law was so vague as to be unenforceable. Per Barrington J.:

> "From the wording of the Preamble to the Constitution it is clear that the Christian religion is one of the religions protected from insult by the constitutional crime of blasphemy. But the Jewish religion would also appear to be protected as it seems quite clear that the purpose of the fifth amendment to the Constitution was certainly not to weaken the position of the Jewish congregations in Ireland but to bring out the universal nature of the constitutional guarantees of freedom of religion. What then is the position of the Muslim religion? Or of Polytheistic religions such as Hinduism? Would the constitutional guarantees of equality before the law and of the free profession and practice of religion be respected if one citizen's religion enjoyed constitutional protection from insult but another's did not? ...
>
> In this state of the law, and in the absence of any legislative definition of the constitutional offence of blasphemy, it is impossible to say of what the offence of blasphemy consists. As the Law Reform Commission has pointed out neither the *actus reus* nor the *mens rea* is clear. The task of defining the crime is one for the Legislature, not for the Courts. In the absence of legislation and in the present uncertain state of the law the Court could not see its way to authorising the institution of a criminal prosecution for blasphemy against the Respondents."[167]

The principle of strict construction of penal statutes

Finally, it is a well-established rule, and part of the principle of legality, that if any ambiguity in a penal statute leaves a reasonable doubt as to the meaning of the law then that doubt must be resolved in favour of the accused. As explained by Henchy J. in *DPP (Broderick) v Flanagan*[168]:

> "It is, in my view, a cardinal principle in the judicial interpretation of statutes that the range of criminal liability should not be held to have been statutorily extended except by clear, direct and unambiguous words. If the lawmakers

---

[166] [1999] IESC 5.
[167] [1999] IESC 5 at paras 501–502.
[168] [1979] 1 I.R. 265.

wish to trench on personal liberty by extending the range of the criminal law, they may do so, within constitutional limitations; but an intention to do so should not be imputed to them when the statute has not used clear words to that effect. No man should be found guilty of a statutory offence when the words of the statute have not plainly indicated that the conduct in question will amount to an offence. The requirement of guilty knowledge for the commission of the offence pre-supposes as much."[169]

It should be noted that the courts have moved away from describing this as a rule of strict construction, though this remains commonly used as a shorthand term for the principle. Instead, recent case law has tended to describe this rule as an aspect of a wider principle against doubtful penalisation.[170]

---

[169] [1979] 1 I.R. 265 at 280–281.
[170] See, e.g. *Mullins v Harnett* [1998] 4 I.R. 426; *Dunnes Stores v Director of Consumer Affairs* [2005] IEHC 242; *DPP v Martin Lynch* [2008] IEHC 183; *Equality Authority v Portmarnock Golf Club* [2009] IESC 73.

Chapter 2

MENTAL ELEMENT OF CRIMES

Introduction

"Mens rea" is the Latin term for the mental element of a criminal offence and loosely translates as "guilty mind". As a general rule, in order for a crime to be committed a person must have a culpable state of mind. This principle is summed up in the maxim *actus non facit reum nisi mens sit rea*—an act does not make a person guilty unless the mind is also guilty.

The concept of mens rea reflects a social judgment that a person should not be convicted of a crime unless he is morally blameworthy or otherwise at fault.[1] He should therefore not be convicted unless he was culpable in bringing about the actus reus of the crime charged. If, for example, A inadvertently takes B's umbrella, believing it to be his own, then it cannot be said that A is at fault. A should not be convicted of theft. It also reflects the deterrent purpose of the criminal law: if a person does not realise that he might be punished, convicting that person can have no deterrent effect.

It must be remembered, however, that mens rea is distinct from motive. The law does not concern itself with motive. A motiveless, random assault is regarded as being as illegal as a crime that is carefully planned. A contract killer and a mercy killer will both be guilty of the same offence. Where motive may be relevant is at the sentencing stage as judges will look to surrounding circumstances for aggravating and mitigating factors.

Every crime has its own mens rea. The law does not always require the same level of moral culpability before a person can be convicted of a crime. Depending on the crime, the mens rea may be intentionally bringing about a result, being reckless as to whether a certain result occurs or negligently bringing about a certain result. Indeed, in some cases a person can be convicted of a crime where he causes a certain result irrespective of whether he was at fault. Consequently, we can identify five separate categories of mens rea. In descending order of moral culpability they are:

1. intention;
2. recklessness;
3. criminal negligence;
4. negligence;
5. strict or absolute liability.

---

[1] For an interesting account of the historical development of mens rea, see McAuley and McCutcheon, *Criminal Liability* (2000), Ch.6.

We will consider each type of mens rea in turn. However, before we turn to the categories of mens rea it is important to note that we must show mens rea for each element of a criminal offence, although the type of mens rea required may vary as between the elements.

Consider the offence of capital murder, as discussed in *DPP v Murray*[2] and examined in detail in Ch.4. The actus reus of that offence consisted of two parts: (i) the murder (ii) of a Garda acting in the course of his duty. Accordingly, the mens rea required for the offence also had two parts: (i) the necessary mens rea for murder, i.e. an intention to kill or cause serious injury and (ii) either knowledge that the victim was a Garda acting in the course of his duty or recklessness as to that fact. This case also demonstrates that the mens rea may differ as between each element of the offence. In this case, while it was necessary that there was an *intention* to kill or cause serious injury, it was sufficient that the defendant was *reckless* as to the identity of the victim.

Similarly, if we consider the offence of damaging property with intent to endanger life (or recklessness as to whether life is endangered), contrary to s.2(2) of the Criminal Damage Act 1991, we again see that there must be mens rea as regards both elements of the offence: the damage must be intentional or reckless and the endangerment must also be either intentional or reckless. If a person deliberately damages property in a way which does in fact endanger life, but he fails to appreciate that risk, then he must be acquitted of this offence as he lacks mens rea as regards the endangerment element.

INTENTION

Defining "intention"

The concept of intention is important for the criminal law as it is the most culpable state of mind: an intentional killing is regarded as more blameworthy than one which is merely reckless or accidental. Consequently, intention is the mens rea for some of the most serious criminal offences, including the crime of murder. However, despite the importance of this concept, it is nowhere defined in statute and the courts have struggled to find an acceptable definition.

The core meaning of "intention" is reasonably clear: a person intends particular results when they are his conscious aim, object or purpose; where he has "sought to bring them about, by making it the purpose of his acts that they should occur".[3] This core meaning can be considered in a different way. We can say that a person intends a result if he would regard himself as having failed if that result is not achieved. Suppose that A sets fire to a building knowing that B is inside. A clearly intends to kill B if he would consider his actions a failure if B survived. Defining "intention" becomes more difficult as we move away from this core meaning and towards more borderline cases. Before discussing these, it may be helpful to contrast intention with other concepts.

---

[2] [1977] I.R. 360.
[3] Law Commission of England and Wales, *Legislating the Criminal Code: Offences Against the Person and General Principles* (Law Com. No. 218, 1993), para.7.5.

"Intention" does not necessarily mean to *desire* a result. If A is strapped for cash and decides to kill B and collect on the life insurance policy, then A intends to kill B, notwithstanding that A is genuinely fond of B and will miss him. We might not say that A desires B's death, except as a means to an end. Nevertheless, in most cases, the intended result will also be the desired result.

Nor does intention require that the result is *likely to be achieved*. If A shoots at B intending to kill B, then if the bullet does in fact kill B the crime of murder is committed. This is so notwithstanding that A knows he is a poor shot, was shooting from a great distance and was exceptionally lucky to hit B.

Nor is intention the same as *motive*. Suppose that A murders B for no apparent reason. The absence of motive might make it more difficult to link the crime to A but it remains a crime nevertheless.

Finally, intention should not be confused with *pre-meditation*. Planning, forethought and preparation are all aspects which prove intention but they are not necessary for intention to exist. A spontaneous act or even an instinctive reaction is equally capable of being intentional.

The problem of indirect/oblique intention

Problems arise in cases of indirect or oblique intention: cases where an accused foresees that he might or will cause an outcome but does not have as his aim or purpose that outcome. For example, suppose that A has cargo on board an airplane and puts a bomb on board, intending to destroy the cargo in order to collect on an insurance policy. A knows that it is very likely that the bomb will kill all those on board. However, A does not wish them dead and would be happy in the unlikely event that they survived. Does A intend to kill the passengers and crew? Or is A merely reckless as to their deaths? Can we equate foresight of consequences with an intention to bring about those consequences?

The English approach to oblique intention

The courts have had great difficulty with this issue and a series of cases before the English courts illustrates the problems caused.

In *Hyam v DPP*,[4] the defendant was a woman whose relationship with a man, Jones, had broken down, with Jones subsequently becoming engaged to another woman, Booth. The defendant went to Ms Booth's house late at night, poured petrol through the letter box, stuffed newspaper through and lit it. She had previously made sure that Jones was not in the house. The resulting fire caused the death of two of Ms Booth's children. Her defence was that she had set the fire only in order to frighten Ms Booth and did not intend to cause death or grievous bodily harm. The jury were directed that the intention for murder was present if the defendant foresaw death or grievous bodily harm as a "highly probable" result of her actions, even if she did not aim at that result. On appeal, the House of Lords approved of this direction, effectively equating foresight of high probability with intention.

---

[4] [1975] A.C. 55.

In *R. v Moloney*,[5] however, a very different result was reached. Here a man was killed by his stepson. After heavy drinking at a wedding anniversary they played a drunken game with loaded shotguns to see who was quicker on the draw. The victim then taunted his stepson to pull the trigger, which he did, killing the victim. The stepson was charged with murder but claimed that the game was "just a lark" and that he had no idea that firing the gun would injure his stepfather. The jury were directed that the stepson had the necessary intention for murder if either (a) he desired to kill the victim whether or not he had foreseen that it would probably happen, or (b) he foresaw that his conduct was likely to kill or cause serious bodily harm, regardless of whether he desired to do so. However, the House of Lords held that such a direction was incorrect. Departing from *Hyam*, it held that foresight that a result was probable was not the same as intending that result. Instead, the question of foresight belonged not to the substantive law, but rather to the law of evidence. Consequently, the jury should be told that if the defendant foresaw that a result was a "natural consequence" of his actions then that was evidence from which the jury could properly *infer* that he intended that result.

Shortly afterwards, in *R. v Hancock and Shankland*,[6] the House of Lords adopted yet another position. The events in this case took place during the bitter miners' strike in England. Two miners on strike attempted to intimidate "scab" workers by pushing concrete blocks from a bridge over the road along which the workers were driving with a police escort. One block hit the windscreen of a car, killing the driver. The defendants were charged with murder and raised the defence that they did not intend to kill or cause serious injury but to block the road and frighten the workers. The jury was directed in accordance with *R. v Moloney* that intent could be inferred if the defendants foresaw that death or serious injury was a "natural consequence" of their actions. However, this direction was found by the House of Lords to be inadequate, which held that the jury should also be referred to the issue of probability and told that they could infer intention where a result is a "natural and probable consequence" of the defendants' actions. In addition, the jury should be told that the more probable the result, the more likely that it was intended by the defendants.

In *R. v Nedrick*,[7] the Court of Appeal attempted to reconcile the effects of the previous decisions. The facts in this case were very similar to *Hyam v DPP*. The defendant had poured paraffin through the letter box of a woman against whom he had a grudge and set it alight. The woman's child died in the fire. The jury were directed that the defendant had the necessary intention if he knew that it was "highly probable" that what he did would cause serious injury to somebody in the house. This direction was clearly incorrect in light of *Moloney* which made it clear that foresight was *evidence* from which intention could be inferred, but was not sufficient evidence in itself. Accordingly, his conviction was quashed by the Court of Appeal, and Lord Lane C.J. proceeded to set out guidelines for dealing with these cases:

> "It may be advisable to explain first to the jury that a man may intend to achieve a certain result whilst at the same time not desiring it to come about. 'A

---

[5] [1985] A.C. 905.
[6] [1986] A.C. 455.
[7] [1986] 3 All E.R. 1.

man who, at London Airport, boards a plane which he knows to be bound for Manchester, clearly intends to travel to Manchester, even though Manchester is the last place he wants to be and his motive for boarding the plane is simply to escape pursuit.'[8]

When determining whether the defendant had the necessary intent, it may therefore be helpful for the jury to ask themselves two questions: (1) How probable was the consequence which resulted from the defendant's voluntary act? (2) Did he foresee that consequence?

If he did not appreciate that death or serious harm was likely to result from his act, he cannot have intended to bring it about. If he did, but thought that the risk to which he was exposing the person killed was only slight, then it may be easy for the jury to conclude that he did not intend to bring about that result. On the other hand, if the jury are satisfied that at the material time the defendant recognised that death or serious harm would be virtually certain (barring some unforeseen intervention) to result from his voluntary act, then that is a fact from which they may find it easy to infer that he intended to kill or do serious bodily harm, even though he may not have had any desire to achieve that result ...

Where a man realises that it is for all practical purposes inevitable that his actions will result in death or serious harm, the inference may be irresistible that he intended that result, however little he may have desired or wished it to happen."[9]

As a result of *Nedrick*, therefore, a formula was adopted whereby the jury were instructed that they could infer intention from foresight only where the defendant realised that the outcome was "virtually certain".

The House of Lords approved of the *Nedrick* formula soon afterwards in *R. v Woollin*.[10] In this case the accused was charged with murdering his three-month-old son by throwing him on the ground and thereby fracturing his skull. It was agreed that he did not desire to cause serious bodily harm to the infant and so the issue was whether he nevertheless had an intention to cause serious bodily harm. The trial judge directed the jury that they could infer the necessary intention if they were satisfied that the defendant appreciated that by throwing his son he was creating a substantial risk of serious injury. The House of Lords, however, held that this direction was incorrect—the reference to "substantial risk" was broader than the *Nedrick* "virtual certainty" formula and tended to blur the distinction between recklessness and murder.

Finally, the facts of *R. v Matthews*[11] illustrate the application of the *Nedrick–Woollin* formula. The defendants attacked and robbed a young student, stealing his bank card. They were unable to take any money from his account and they returned to him, forced him into a car, and drove him to a bridge. There they threw him into the river, despite his saying that he couldn't swim. He fell about 25 feet into the river and drowned. The defendants were charged with murder and the trial judge directed

---

[8] Quoting from the judgment of Lord Bridge in *R. v Moloney* [1985] A.C. 905 at 926.
[9] [1986] 3 All E.R. 1 at 3.
[10] [1999] 1 A.C. 82.
[11] [2003] Crim. L.R. 553.

the jury that they must find the necessary intention if they were satisfied that the defendants appreciated that it was virtually certain that the student would die as a result of their actions. On appeal, this direction was held to be incorrect: according to the Court of Appeal, under *Nedrick* and *Woollin* a jury is entitled to find intention where there is foresight of virtual certainty, but is not bound to do so. Consequently, the trial judge had mistakenly presented a rule of evidence by which the jury could find intent as a rule of law by which the jury must find intent.

If we attempt to summarise these (rather confusing) cases, we see that the English position has evolved substantially since *Hyam*. In that case the House of Lords equated foresight of a highly probable result with intention. In *Moloney*, however, this approach was rejected and foresight became evidence from which the jury could *infer* intention. In addition, *Moloney* refined the standard of probability by referring to a "natural consequence" rather than a "highly probable" result. *Hancock and Shankland* refined the standard of probability further, by requiring that the jury find a "natural and probable consequence" before they could infer intention. *Nedrick* and *Woollin* both seem to raise the standard of probability required still further, to require that a defendant realised that an outcome was "virtually certain" before the jury can find that he intended that outcome. However, as *Matthews* illustrates, this is a rule of evidence, not of law, and the jury are not bound to find intention even if they find that a defendant foresaw a consequence as virtually certain.

It is worth noting that this limitation of cases of oblique intent to cases of "virtual certainty" results in quite a narrow test and will result in many borderline cases being regarded as manslaughter rather than murder. Suppose, for example, that A plants a bomb in a building hoping to destroy it. He telephones a warning, resulting in the building being evacuated. However, a member of the bomb disposal squad is killed while trying to defuse the bomb. In this case, it is not A's purpose to kill and it would be difficult to say that he foresaw the death as a "virtually certain" outcome. Consequently it would seem that A lacks the necessary intention for murder and Lord Steyn in *Woollin* has acknowledged that such a case would be likely one of manslaughter not murder.

The Irish approach to oblique intention

Until recently, the Irish courts did not have to grapple with the question of oblique or indirect intention in any detail. While some earlier Irish cases do mention the issue, they generally do so only tangentially. For example, in *DPP v Murray*,[12] Walsh J. took quite a restrictive view of intention, drawing a sharp distinction between a desired outcome, on the one hand, and foresight of consequences on the other. If followed, this distinction would seem to rule out oblique intention completely as a species of intention:

> "To intend to murder, or to cause serious injury ... is to have in mind a fixed purpose to reach that desired objective. Therefore, the state of mind of the accused person must have been not only that he foresaw but also willed the possible consequences of his conduct."[13]

---

[12] [1977] I.R. 360.
[13] [1977] I.R. 360 at 386.

The most important case until recently in this area was the decision of the Court of Criminal Appeal in *DPP v Douglas and Hayes*.[14] In that case the defendants, in the course of a robbery, opened fire on a Garda car, hitting it with three bullets. They were charged with shooting with intent to commit murder and were convicted by the Special Criminal Court on the basis that:

> "[I]t must have been apparent that the natural consequence of the shooting would be to cause death or serious personal injury to one or more of the guards in the car and secondly, the person who fired the shots did so with reckless disregard of the risk of killing a guard and in the legal sense, he had the intent to commit murder. It is not necessary to constitute the intent to kill that that should be the desired outcome of what was done. It is sufficient if it is a likely outcome and that the act is done with reckless disregard of that outcome."[15]

This approach of the Special Criminal Court echoed the judgment of the House of Lords in *Hyam*, inasmuch as it held that foresight of a "likely" outcome was sufficient intention. On appeal, however, the Court of Criminal Appeal quashed the convictions. The court held that foresight and recklessness could not be equated with intention but went on to say that foresight of consequences could constitute evidence from which an inference of intention could be drawn:

> "[E]vidence of the fact that a reasonable man would have foreseen that the natural and probable consequence of the acts of an accused was to cause death and evidence of the fact that the accused was reckless as to whether his acts would cause death or not is evidence from which an inference of intent to cause death may or should be drawn, but the court must consider whether either or both of these facts do establish beyond a reasonable doubt an actual intention to cause death.
>
> ...
>
> Although it may be accepted that it is not necessary to constitute an intent to kill that that should be the desired outcome of what was done, a reckless disregard of the likely outcome of the acts performed is not of itself proof of intent to kill but is only one of the facts to be considered in deciding whether the correct inference is that the accused had an actual intent to kill."[16]

However, the most comprehensive and recent judgment on the Irish approach to intention, both direct and oblique, is the judgment of Charleton J. in *Clifford v DPP*.[17] Much of the analysis is obiter, however, as the facts of the case did not disclose any oblique intention. The defendant was charged with a breach of the peace contrary to s.6 of the Criminal Justice (Public Order) Act 1994. The offence is committed by using or engaging in any threatening, abusive or insulting words or behaviour with

---

[14] [1985] I.L.R.M. 25.
[15] [1985] I.L.R.M. 25 at 26.
[16] [1985] I.L.R.M. 25 at 29 per McWilliam J.
[17] [2008] IEHC 322.

intent to provoke a breach of the peace or being reckless as to whether a breach may be occasioned.

Charleton J. stated that:

> "[A]n intent to commit the external element of an offence occurs where an accused person goes about the conduct in question with the purpose of bringing about the wrong ... A person may intend to blow up a plane in flight and so kill the passengers. That is direct intention. A person may claim to intend only to blow up a suitcase in a plane in flight but hope, that through some miracle, all the passengers in the plane will survive. It might usefully be noted, on the relevant case law, that the closer the impugned conduct comes to inevitably causing the consequence charged, as for instance in that example intending the death of the plane passengers, the more readily a court may feel able to infer that intention ... The more obscure the consequence, the less readily can the inference of an intention in that regard be made. In no instance, whether of direct or oblique intention, is the inference that the accused intended either an act or its consequences automatically to be inferred from particular behaviour. In each instance it is a matter of judgment for the court."

Charleton J. addressed the place of motive in criminal law as follows:

> "Intention, in this context, has nothing to do with motive. The motive in destroying the luggage in the plane may be, for instance, to hide a serious act of bank fraud. That is irrelevant to any definitional element of the charge ... The fact that it may be very difficult for a particular accused to achieve the wrong which is the subject matter of the charge does not mean that he did not have an intent to bring it about."[18]

Charleton J. added:

> "[T]he fact that the accused did everything logically necessary to cause an explosion on board an aircraft may, but not must, lead to an inference that this was his purpose. The fact that the scale of that explosion was highly likely to destroy the plane may, but not must, lead to an inference that that was his purpose. The fact that people die when a plane explodes in mid air may, but not must, lead to an inference that he intended to kill."[19]

It would appear, therefore, from the limited Irish authorities on the point, that intention may be defined more broadly in Irish law than in England and Wales. It does not appear that "virtual certainty" is the test, but intention can be inferred if the result was "highly likely" to occur. A definitive judicial analysis of the issue is awaited.

---

[18] [2008] IEHC 322 at paras 10 to 12.
[19] [2008] IEHC 322 at para.12.

The presumption of intention

Irish law recognises a presumption of intention: it is presumed that a person intends the natural and probable consequences of his actions. This presumption applies to all offences and, as regards murder, has also been put in statutory form by s.4(2) of the Criminal Justice Act 1964. However, this presumption is rebuttable and it does not affect the burden of proof, which remains with the prosecution at all times. The Court of Criminal Appeal, in *DPP v McBride*,[20] has explained the way the presumption operates as follows:

> "The jury ought to have been told that while there was a presumption that the applicant intended the natural and probable consequences of his act, this was only a presumption and could be rebutted, [and] one of the things that they had to consider was whether the State had satisfied them beyond reasonable doubt that the presumption had not been rebutted."[21]

DPP v Hull[22] gives an example of the use of the presumption. In that case the defendant was a middle-aged married man who was infatuated with a young co-worker. She repelled his advances and subsequently found a boyfriend in Galway. The defendant went to Galway and knocked on the door of the boyfriend. After an argument the boyfriend returned inside, at which point the defendant fired a shotgun through the door, killing him. The defendant was charged with murder but argued that the firing was accidental and that, as such, he lacked an intention to kill or cause serious injury. The trial judge directed the jury that under s.4 their task was "[f]irstly, to decide whether the natural and probable consequence of the applicant firing at the door was to cause death or serious injury, and secondly, if they decided this in the affirmative, to go on to consider whether the firing had been deliberate or accidental".

The defendant was convicted of murder and, on appeal, argued that the trial judge had not correctly directed the jury on the presumption of intention. This argument was, however, rejected by the Court of Criminal Appeal:

> "The Court considers that this was a reasonable way to put the matter to the jury. If they decided that the natural and probable consequence of firing at the door was to cause death or serious injury, then the presumption arose that this was the applicant's intention, but the question remained as to whether that presumption had been rebutted and this had to be decided by considering whether the firing had been deliberate or accidental. So, in instructing the jury to acquit the defendant if the firing was accidental, the learned trial judge was in effect correctly telling them that, if they took this view, it meant that the presumption that the applicant intended to cause death or serious injury had been rebutted and so he was entitled to be acquitted."[23]

---

[20] [1996] 1 I.R. 312.
[21] [1996] 1 I.R. 312 at 317 per Blayney J.
[22] Unreported, Court of Criminal Appeal, July 8, 1996.
[23] Unreported, Court of Criminal Appeal, July 8, 1996 at 16 per Blayney J.

Mental Element of Crimes

The Court of Criminal Appeal addressed s.4 in *DPP v McDonagh*[24] in the context of the trial for murder of a man who had allegedly stabbed his wife in the back having dragged her apart from her sister with whom she was having a violent altercation. Evidence was given that he then said he was very sorry and took her in his arms and attempted to stop the bleeding. It was held that this subsequent remorse was not evidence rebutting the presumption that the accused had intended the natural and probable consequences of his action.

Reform of intention

The Law Reform Commission has commented that the definition of "intention" in Irish law is very unclear and recommended the following definition of "direct" and "oblique intention" in the context of murder:

"(1) Where a person kills another unlawfully it shall be murder if:
    (a) the accused person intended to kill or cause serious injury to some other person, whether that other person is the person actually killed or not; or
    (b) the killing is committed recklessly under circumstances manifesting an extreme indifference to the value of human life.
...
(3) A result is intended if:
    (i) it is the defendant's conscious object or purpose to cause it; or
    (ii) he is aware that it is virtually certain that his conduct will cause it, or would be virtually certain to cause it if he were to succeed in his purpose of causing some other result.
(4) The accused person shall be presumed to have intended the natural and probable consequences of his conduct, but this presumption may be rebutted.[25]"

We have seen that intention as a form of mens rea has presented a number of difficulties, almost always in the context of murder trials. Consequently, it can be argued that the problems associated with intention could be resolved by widening the mens rea of murder to specifically include cases of oblique intention or reckless killings. This issue is discussed in Ch.4.

RECKLESSNESS

Recklessness exists where a person does not intend to bring about a particular result but runs an unjustifiable risk of bringing that result about. By "unjustifiable" we mean a risk without good cause, having regard to the gravity of the risk and the social utility of the activity involved.

---

[24] [2001] 3 I.R. 201.
[25] Law Reform Commission, *Report on Homicide: Murder and Involuntary Manslaughter* (LRC 87–2008), para.3.78.

For example, a surgeon who carries out an essential operation involving a risk of the patient dying as a result is taking a substantial risk but one which is justifiable in the circumstances. By way of contrast, in *Chief Constable of Avon and Somerset Constabulary v Shimmen*[26] the defendant accidentally broke a shop window while showing off his martial arts skills to a friend. In this situation, the desire to show off clearly did not justify even a slight risk that he might misjudge matters and hit the window.

This form of mens rea is common in Irish law and applies to a wide range of crimes, including the offences of assault, assault causing harm, causing serious harm and endangerment under the Non-Fatal Offences Against the Person Act 1997 and the offence of damaging property under the Criminal Damage Act 1991.

One issue that is central to any analysis of recklessness is whether it is defined as objective or subjective in nature. Suppose that a person creates an unjustifiable risk in circumstances where it is not clear that he is aware of that risk. If he is aware then he is clearly reckless. But suppose that, despite the risk being obvious, he fails to recognise it and is blissfully unaware of the risk his conduct poses. Is that person reckless? In other words do we describe somebody as reckless only if he is aware of a risk (a subjective approach) or will failure to recognise an obvious risk suffice (an objective approach)?[27]

Irish approach

Irish law has generally taken the subjective approach: for an accused to be found reckless as to a particular risk, he must have foreseen the risk but proceeded with his conduct regardless. The leading Irish case is *DPP v Murray*.[28] In this case, the two accused were husband and wife and jointly held up a bank at gunpoint. They fled but were pursued by an off-duty Garda who was out of uniform. The wife shot and killed him. Both were charged with capital murder, which was committed where a person murdered a Garda acting in the course of his duty. Their defence was that the necessary mens rea was not present for all of the elements of the offence: although there may have been an intention to kill or cause serious injury, they did not know that their pursuer was a Garda and they therefore lacked mens rea as to an essential part of the crime.

The Supreme Court, in dealing with this argument, accepted the general principle that mens rea must be shown in respect of each component of an offence. In particular, it noted that the offence was meant to have a deterrent effect, which was lacking where a person was not aware that his intended victim was a Garda. Equally, it pointed out that a much more severe penalty was attached to capital murder and it was unfair and arbitrary to impose that higher penalty on the basis of a circumstance which the defendant knew nothing about.

It was argued for the prosecution that the necessary mens rea was present if the wife *was or should have been aware* that the pursuer was a Garda—that is, objective recklessness would suffice. The Supreme Court, however, rejected objective

---

[26] (1987) 84 Cr. App. R. 7.
[27] Mary McAleese, "Just what is recklessness?" (1981) D.U.L.J. 29.
[28] [1977] I.R. 360.

Mental Element of Crimes

recklessness. It held that Irish criminal law had, at its core, the determination of moral blameworthiness, which could only be decided based on the subjective state of mind of the person charged. Walsh J. remarked that "[i]n this context objective recklessness is really constructive knowledge: and constructive knowledge has no place in our criminal system in establishing intent".[29] The Supreme Court required that a defendant be subjectively reckless as to the identity of his victim before he could be convicted of capital murder. As to what was meant by subjective recklessness, Henchy J. adopted the following definition from the American Law Institute's Model Penal Code[30]:

> "A person acts recklessly with respect to a material element of an offence when he consciously disregards a substantial and unjustifiable risk that the material element exists or will result from his conduct. The risk must be of such a nature and degree that, considering the nature and purpose of the actor's conduct and the circumstances known to him, its disregard involves culpability of high degree."

This result was widely accepted in the Irish legal system on the grounds of fairness:

> "All modern common law systems reject a criminal law which imposes blame on the basis of what a reasonable man would have known, intended or suspected in the situation under analysis."[31]

Surprisingly, there were no significant cases on recklessness in Irish law for 30 years. However, there have been two recent Irish cases confirming that recklessness is subjective in this jurisdiction.

In *DPP v Cagney and McGrath*,[32] the Supreme Court was asked to consider recklessness in the context of the offence of endangerment contrary to s.13(1) of the Non-Fatal Offences Against the Person Act 1997. The deceased had been hit just above the ear and fell onto the road, struck his head, and died. Hardiman J. emphasised that recklessness involves not merely the taking of a risk but the advertent taking of the risk:

> "I believe that this approach is consistent with the authoritative statement of the requirements of recklessness in this jurisdiction. The *locus classicus* on this topic is the decision of this Court in *The People v Murray* ... As a result of the judgment in *Murray*, an accused in Ireland must have foreseen the risk that his conduct would bring about the relevant result, but have elected to proceed with his conduct nonetheless."[33]

Geoghegan J. also endorsed the subjective approach, holding that "[i]t seems clear therefore that for the purpose of a count under section 13 based on recklessness as

---

[29] [1977] I.R. 360 at 386.
[30] Section 2.02(2)9c.
[31] Peter Charleton, *Criminal Law – Cases and Materials* (Dublin: Butterworths, 1992), p.52.
[32] [2008] 2 I.R. 111.
[33] [2008] 2 I.R. 111 at 127.

was the case here the accused would have had to consciously disregard a risk not of just causing harm but of causing serious injury or death".[34]

The Supreme Court quashed the convictions because neither the prosecution nor the trial judge had referred to the necessity to establish advertence by the applicants to the serious risk of death or serious harm.

Recklessness was again considered, this time by the High Court, in *Clifford v DPP*.[35] Here Charleton J. considered the issue in the context of whether a breach of the peace might be occasioned, contrary to s.6 of the Criminal Justice (Public Order) Act 1994. He defined recklessness as follows:

> "Recklessness consists of an accused subjectively taking a serious risk, involving high moral culpability, that his conduct will bring about the wrong defined by the charge ... Recklessness involves a subjective element in Irish law, and so it is different from criminal negligence which is the mental element of one aspect of criminal negligence manslaughter. For an accused to be reckless, it must occur to the mind of accused that his conduct will bring about the consequence impugned but, nonetheless, he proceeds to act. Moral culpability is necessary in this context because all life is at risk. To decide to build a major tunnel through a mountain involves a risk of accidental death to the workers. Where all proper precautions are taken, there is no moral culpability should someone die in the accident. Failing to avoid a serious risk of which you are aware can involve a high degree of moral fault. An example incorporating the necessary elements in recklessness of the subjective taking of a serious risk in culpable circumstances is this. A man is driving a car at speed along a country road and sees a stop sign at a crossroads. He knows that a car may cross the road in front of him but, notwithstanding that risk, he powers ahead without stopping, causing death or injury. He may in these circumstances be charged with manslaughter as his mental state is even more serious than the mental element of criminal negligence required for that offence. That man is reckless as to the death or injury caused."[36]

This preference for subjective tests over objective tests is a motif that repeats itself throughout Irish criminal law, particularly in the field of defences.

The approach in England and Wales

English law has had rather more difficulty with the concept of recklessness. For many years it was considered that recklessness could only exist where a defendant perceived a risk. The leading authority was *R. v Cunningham*.[37] In this case the defendant stole money from a gas meter, fracturing the gas pipes and causing gas to leak into a neighbouring house, where it asphyxiated a person asleep in a bed. The defendant was charged with unlawfully and maliciously causing the victim to take a noxious thing, thereby endangering her life, contrary to s.23 of the Offences Against

---

[34] [2008] 2 I.R. 111 at 138.
[35] [2008] IEHC 322.
[36] [2008] IEHC 322 at para.14.
[37] [1957] 2 Q.B. 396.

the Person Act 1861. The trial judge, addressing the jury, stated that it was enough that the defendant acted "wickedly" without requiring that he should be aware of the danger he was creating. The Court of Appeal, quashing the conviction, held that this direction was incorrect. Malice could not be equated with a vague concept of "wickedness" but rather referred to either intention or recklessness, and the court went on to describe the latter as meaning that the defendant foresaw that a particular kind of harm might be done and yet went on to take that risk.

This so-called *Cunningham* recklessness was, however, departed from in two House of Lords decisions in 1981. The first of these was *R. v Caldwell*.[38] In that case, the defendant set fire to a hotel, avenging a supposed grievance against the proprietor. He was charged with arson, for which the mens rea was intention to endanger the life of another or recklessness as to whether the life of another would be endangered. His defence was that he was so drunk at the time he did not appreciate the risk he was creating.

In dealing with this defence, it was necessary for the House of Lords to decide whether a person could be said to be reckless where he fails to recognise a risk. The House of Lords held that a person in these circumstances was reckless. Lord Diplock stated that:

> "Reckless ... is an ordinary English word. It had not by [the date of the legislation] become a term of legal art with some more limited esoteric meaning than that which it bore in ordinary speech – a meaning which surely includes not only deciding to ignore a risk of harmful consequences resulting from one's acts that one has recognised as existing, but also failing to give any thought to whether or not there is any such risk in circumstances where, if any thought was given to the matter, it would be obvious that there was."[39]

In reaching this conclusion, Lord Diplock was influenced by a moral judgment that a person who failed to appreciate an "obvious risk" should not be allowed to escape liability, by concern over practical difficulties of proving the defendant's state of mind, and by some disapproval of the use of drunkenness as a defence in this way. He stated:

> "Neither state of mind [i.e. appreciating or failing to appreciate a risk] seems to me to be less blameworthy than the other; but if the difference between the two constituted the distinction between what does and what does not in legal theory amount to a guilty state of mind ... it would not be a practicable distinction for use in a trial by jury. The only person who knows what the accused's mental processes were is the accused himself ... If the accused gives evidence that because of his rage, excitement or drunkenness the risk of particular harmful consequences of his acts simply did not occur to him, a jury would find it hard to be satisfied beyond reasonable doubt that his true mental process was [that he recognised a risk]."[40]

---

[38] [1982] A.C. 341.
[39] [1982] A.C. 341 at 353.
[40] [1982] A.C. 341 at 352.

Accordingly, *R. v Caldwell* adopted a standard of objective recklessness, at least in respect of obvious risks. Immediately after this decision, on the same day, the House of Lords decision in *R. v Lawrence*[41] confirmed the application of this standard of recklessness to the crime of reckless driving.

These decisions were almost immediately heavily criticised as a substantial departure from the law as it had previously stood in both England and numerous other common law countries, as being difficult to apply in practice, and as possibly leading to substantial unfairness. Academics pointed out what became known as the "*Caldwell* lacuna"—that a person who considered whether a risk existed and mistakenly concluded that there was not would not be deemed reckless under this definition of recklessness.

One obvious risk of injustice arose where a risk might be obvious to a reasonable person, but was not obvious to the particular accused by reason of age, disability, lack of experience or understanding. In *Elliott v C (a minor)*[42] a 14-year-old girl set fire to a shed by pouring white spirit onto the floor and throwing a lighted match onto the spirit. She had given no thought to the possibility of the shed being destroyed as a result and, as she suffered from a slight mental handicap, would not have appreciated the risk even if she had considered the matter. She was, nonetheless, convicted. The Court of Appeal took the view that whether a risk was obvious was to be judged by the standards of a "reasonably prudent person", not whether it was obvious to this particular accused.

These criticisms were eventually heeded by the House of Lords 20 years later in *R. v G and R*[43] which departed from *R. v Caldwell* and returned to a test of subjective recklessness. In this case two young boys, aged 11 and 12 years, entered the back yard of a shop in the early hours of the morning. Finding bundles of newspapers, they set fire to some of the newspapers and threw them under a plastic dustbin. After leaving the yard, the fire spread to the dustbin and thence to the shop itself and adjoining buildings, causing approximately £1 million worth of damage. They were charged with arson in respect of the damage to the shop and convicted on the basis that their conduct created a risk which would have been obvious to an adult, notwithstanding that neither of them appreciated that there was any risk of the fire spreading.

On appeal, the House of Lords considered that *Caldwell* recklessness was wrong in principle. Lord Bingham commented that:

> "First ... conviction of serious crime should depend on proof not simply that the defendant caused (by act or omission) an injurious result to another but that his state of mind when so acting was culpable ... It is clearly blameworthy to take an obvious and significant risk of causing injury to another. But it is not clearly blameworthy to do something involving a risk of injury to another if ... one genuinely does not perceive the risk. Such a person may fairly be accused of stupidity or lack or imagination, but neither of those failings should expose him to conviction of serious crime or the risk of punishment. Secondly,

---

[41] [1981] 1 All E.R. 974.
[42] [1983] 2 All E.R. 1005.
[43] [2004] 1 A.C. 1034.

the present case shows, more clearly than any other reported cases since *R. v Caldwell*, that [*Caldwell* recklessness] is capable of leading to obvious unfairness ... It is neither moral nor just to convict a defendant (least of all a child) on the strength of what someone else would have apprehended if the defendant himself had no such apprehension."[44]

Instead, the House of Lords held that a person acts recklessly when he is aware of a risk and it is in the circumstances (as known to him) unreasonable to take the risk. The House of Lords also rejected the argument, central to *Caldwell*, that a subjective test of recklessness would lead to difficulties in proving a defendant's state of mind and thus to unjustified acquittals. Lord Bingham remarked:

"There is no reason to doubt the common sense which tribunals of fact bring to their task. In a contested case based on intention, the defendant rarely admits intending the injurious result in question, but the tribunal of fact will readily infer such an intention, in a proper case, from all the circumstances and probabilities and evidence of what the defendant did and said at the time. Similarly with recklessness: it is not to be supposed that the tribunal of fact will accept a defendant's assertion that he never thought of a certain risk when all the circumstances and probabilities and evidence of what he did and said at the time show that he did or must have done."[45]

Lord Steyn commented on the *R. v Caldwell* decision as follows:

"The surest test of a new legal rule is not whether it satisfies a team of logicians but how it performs in the real world. With the benefit of hindsight the verdict must be that the rule laid down by the majority in *R. v Caldwell* failed this test. It was severely criticised by academic lawyers of distinction. It did not command respect among practitioners and judges. Jurors found it difficult to understand: it also sometimes offended their sense of justice. Experience shows that in *Caldwell* the law took a wrong turn."[46]

In *Attorney General's Reference (No. 3 of 2003)*,[47] the Court of Appeal applied subjective recklessness to an offence of wilful misconduct in a public place and the consensus among academics is that subjective recklessness now applies to any crime for which the mens rea is recklessness, not just offences of criminal damage.[48]

---

[44] [2004] 1 A.C. 1034 at 1055.
[45] [2004] 1 A.C. 1034 at 1057.
[46] [2004] 1 A.C. 1034 at 1063.
[47] [2004] EWCA Crim 868.
[48] Richard Card, *Card, Cross and Jones Criminal Law* (Oxford: Oxford University Press, 2010), p.94; David Ormerod, *Smith and Hogan's Criminal Law* (Oxford: Oxford University Press, 2011), p.125.

CRIMINAL NEGLIGENCE

This particular class of mens rea is confined to the offence of manslaughter. It is a higher standard than that required for negligence in the law of tort and is discussed in detail in Ch.4.

NEGLIGENCE

This type of mens rea corresponds to the civil standard of negligence in the law of tort and refers to conduct falling below the standard of a reasonable and prudent person. An example of a crime having this mens rea is driving without due care and attention contrary to s.52 of the Road Traffic Act 1961. While negligence overlaps somewhat with recklessness, it is important to remember that the test of negligence is entirely objective: it is not necessary to show that the defendant was aware that his conduct fell below the necessary standard.

STRICT OR ABSOLUTE LIABLITY

Introduction

Strict liability (sometimes described as absolute liability) exists where there is an absolute prohibition on the doing of a particular act and where a person who voluntarily does that act is subject to punishment regardless of any further intention, negligence or other fault on his part.[49] Liability is described as "strict" or "absolute" because the prosecution does not have to prove mens rea as to one or more of the elements of the actus reus.

For example, in *Pharmaceutical Society of Great Britain v Storkwain Ltd*,[50] the defendant firm of pharmacists supplied drugs in good faith under a prescription which transpired to be a forgery. It was convicted of the offence of supplying drugs without a prescription, notwithstanding that it reasonably believed the prescription to be valid.

Strict liability offences raise obvious concerns about the fairness of punishing a person who is not morally blameworthy. In particular, it can be said that it is unjust to punish a person for an outcome where he has taken all reasonable steps to prevent that outcome. Strict liability offences are also criticised on the basis that they improperly impose the stigma of a criminal conviction on a person who may be blameless. A well-known example of strict liability is *R. v Prince*,[51] where the accused was charged with abducting an unmarried girl under the age of 16 years out of the possession of her father. The girl was 14 years but the accused reasonably and honestly believed her to be 18 years. This was held to be irrelevant; the crime was

---

[49] See McAuley and McCutcheon, *Criminal Liability* (2000), Ch.7.
[50] [1986] 2 All E.R. 635.
[51] [1875–1877] 13 Cox CC 138.

created for the protection of young girls and the court held that this statutory purpose would be frustrated if the absence of intention was accepted as a defence.

As against that, however, arguments can be made in favour of strict liability. One of the most common is that strict liability is necessary for the protection of the public. Many strict liability offences apply to areas (such as transport, or the supply of food or drugs) which have innate risks. A related point is sometimes made that a person who chooses to engage in activities which he knows to be risky must be prepared to take the consequences should those risks become reality.

Another commonly-made argument is that offences of strict liability are not "truly criminal". Such offences are sometimes described as "quasi-criminal" or "public welfare offences" and are distinguishable from "true crimes" on the basis that they carry minor punishments and little or no social stigma.

Finally, one pragmatic argument in favour of strict liability is that it is sometimes necessary in order to make a particular law enforceable, by easing what would otherwise be insurmountable difficulties of proof. An example given by one author is that speeding cases would be almost impossible to prove if the prosecution had to prove that the motorist knew he was speeding.[52]

Strict liability versus absolute liability

There is a tendency for the terms "strict liability" and "absolute liability" to be used interchangeably in this jurisdiction, particularly in older cases. However, it is important to note that the terms have distinct meanings. In *R. v City of Sault Ste Marie*,[53] the Canadian Supreme Court held that the law should distinguish between offences of absolute liability, where it is not open to the accused to exculpate himself by showing that he was not at fault, and offences of strict liability, where there is no necessity for the prosecution to prove mens rea, but where it will be open to the accused to establish a defence by proving that he took all reasonable care. This approach effectively mitigates the harsh effects of the doctrine by allowing a defendant to establish a defence of reasonable diligence, while at the same time easing enforceability by relieving the prosecution of the need to establish mens rea and shifting the burden of proof to the person in the best position to prove that due care was taken.

Determining whether an offence is one of strict liability

Almost all offences of strict liability are statutory offences, the only common law offences being the anomalous crimes of public nuisance and criminal libel. Consequently, in deciding whether an offence is one of strict liability, the starting point must be to look at the language of the statute. If the statute itself deals with the matter by specifying what mens rea, if any, is required, then there is no difficulty. Unfortunately, it is common for legislation to be silent on the question which requires the courts to consider whether to interpret the offence as one of strict liability or to read in a mens rea requirement.

---

[52] Alan C. Michaels, "Constitutional Innocence" (1999) 112 *Harvard Law Review* 828.
[53] [1978] 2 S.C.R. 1229.

There is a strong presumption in favour of mens rea. Lord Reid in *Sweet v Parsley*[54] summarised it as follows:

> "[T]here has for centuries been a presumption that Parliament did not intend to make criminals of persons who were in no way blameworthy in what they did. That means that, whenever a section is silent as to *mens rea*, there is a presumption that, in order to give effect to the will of Parliament, we must read in words appropriate to require *mens rea* ... *mens rea* is an essential element of every offence unless some reason can be found for holding that it is not necessary."[55]

The defendant in that case was a landlady who was charged, under the Dangerous Drugs Act 1965, with "being concerned in the management of premises used for the smoking of cannabis." Evidence was given that she only visited the house periodically to collect rent from the student tenants. The House of Lords quashed her conviction and held that the prosecution was required to prove mens rea in view of the serious criminal offence involved.

This presumption can, however, be rebutted. Lord Scarman, in the leading case of *Gammon Ltd v AG of Hong Kong*,[56] set out the five principles to be considered in deciding whether it has been rebutted:

1. There is a presumption of law that mens rea is required before a person can be found guilty of a criminal offence.
2. This presumption is particularly strong where the offence is "truly criminal" in character.
3. The presumption applies to statutory offences and can be displaced only if this is clearly, or by necessary implication, the effect of the statute.
4. The only situation in which the presumption can be displaced is where the statute is concerned with an issue of social concern, and public safety is such an issue.
5. Even where the statute is concerned with such an issue, the presumption of mens rea stands unless it can also be shown that the creation of strict liability will be effective to promote the objects of the statute by encouraging greater vigilance to prevent the commission of the prohibited act.

From these principles it can be seen that the factors to be taken into account include whether the offence is "truly criminal", whether the statute involves a matter of "public concern" such as public safety and whether strict liability is necessary to "promote the objects of the statute". Later cases, discussed below, have also added other factors such as the severity of punishment and whether a social stigma attaches to the crime.

---

[54] [1970] A.C. 132.
[55] [1970] A.C. 132 at 148–149.
[56] [1985] 1 A.C. 1.

The Irish approach pre-*CC v Ireland*

In *McAdam v Dublin United Tramways Co. Ltd*,[57] the defendant company was charged with overloading a tram. The defendant claimed that it had done all that it possibly could to prevent its conductors from allowing overloading to take place. However, the court held that the defendant could not rely on this absence of fault:

> "[T]he prohibitions contained in that regulation are absolute. The object of the regulation is to protect the public against the danger that may result from the overloading of an omnibus, and that object could be achieved only by absolutely prohibiting the carriage in any omnibus of more than a limited number of passengers, and by penalising the owner for any breach of such [a] prohibition, irrespective of his knowledge of such breach.
>
> The acts in this case are not in any real sense criminal, but in the public interest they are prohibited under a penalty. Having regard to that fact, and to the terms of the regulation and the object it had in view, I am of opinion that *mens rea* is not an essential ingredient in the offences charged against the defendants."[58]

The modern Irish approach to strict liability was developed in a series of cases beginning in the mid-1990s. The first was *Maguire v Shannon Regional Fisheries Board*.[59] This concerned the Fisheries (Consolidation) Act 1959 which provides that any person who causes to fall into any waters any deleterious matter shall be guilty of an offence. The defendant operated a piggery near a river; a pipe fractured, resulting in the pollution of the river. The defendant was found to have taken all reasonable steps to prevent any accident of this sort and to prevent the pollution of the river once the accident had taken place. The question presented was whether the offence was one of strict liability.

In deciding that it was, Lynch J. approved *Gammon Ltd v AG of Hong Kong* and held as follows:

1. as a rule, mens rea is required for every offence;
2. however, this presumption can be rebutted where, as here, the offence created was regulatory rather than truly criminal;
3. in such situations, creating strict liability would promote the policy of the underlying legislation, while if mens rea was required the policy of the legislation would be undermined since it would be very difficult to establish that an offence had been committed. Consequently, the offence was one of strict liability;
4. despite the absence of any fault on the part of the accused, he had caused the pollution by virtue of the running of his piggery and was therefore guilty of the offence.

---

[57] [1929] I.R. 327.
[58] [1929] I.R. 327 at 333 per O'Sullivan P.
[59] [1994] 2 I.L.R.M. 253.

The later case of *Shannon Regional Fisheries Board v Cavan County Council*[60] is on the same point. Here the Supreme Court had to deal with a situation where Cavan County Council had caused sewage to enter the water. Despite a statutory duty to provide sewage treatment, the County Council had not been provided with sufficient funds from central government to carry out that duty and was therefore unable to process the sewage, which it discharged in its untreated form. The County Council was charged under the Fisheries Acts. In the High Court, the decision in *Maguire v Shannon Regional Fisheries Board* was followed and the offence found to be one of strict liability. This was accepted by the majority in the Supreme Court, which also found on the facts that the County Council was in fact acting with mens rea in that it was deliberately discharging untreated sewage.

However, the dissenting judgment of Keane J. is particularly interesting. He outlined the historical development of offences of strict liability in "public welfare" or "regulatory" areas of the law and went on to question whether it is appropriate that this particular fisheries offence, which carried a maximum penalty of £25,000 or five years' imprisonment, or both, should be held to be one of strict liability. In particular, he questioned whether to make such a serious crime into one of strict liability would be compatible with the constitutional guarantee of trial in due course of law. He accepted that not all crimes need have some moral culpability attached to them, but rejected the argument that there was no need for moral culpability in the present case as this sort of crime carries no real stigma. Instead, he argued, such an offence would in fact carry a social stigma, making it unjust for a person to be convicted without any blame on his part.

Keane J. also pointed out that to allow a defence of taking all reasonable care would encourage greater vigilance on the part of potential offenders. To deny such a defence would in effect force the accused to act at his peril and would be a disincentive to maintaining standards. Since the expenditure of time and money on improving standards would not be acknowledged by the courts, then some people in the position of the accused might not bother to take adequate precautions.

Keane J. referred to the position taken in Canadian law as set out in *R. v City of Sault Ste Marie* and proposed that the middle ground established in that case should be adopted in Irish law, holding that:

> "[T]he law should recognise that there is an intermediate range of offences, of which this is one, in which, while full proof of *mens rea* is not required and the proof of the prohibited act *prima facie* imports the commission of the offence, the accused may escape liability by proving that he took reasonable care."[61]

He went on to argue that the County Council did in fact take all reasonable care to prevent the discharge of sewage and should not, therefore, be found guilty of the crime.

In *Director of Corporate Enforcement v Gannon*,[62] the High Court held that the offence of acting as an auditor to a company while disqualified is one of strict

---

[60] [1996] 3 I.R. 267.
[61] [1996] 3 I.R. 267 at 291.
[62] [2002] 4 I.R. 439.

liability. In reaching this conclusion, Ó Caoimh J. relied on the fact that the penalties involved were "relatively limited" and as such the offence could not be described as "truly criminal". He also ruled that the issue was one of social concern, in respect of which strict liability would encourage greater vigilance.

In *DPP v Behan*,[63] the High Court had to consider whether the offence of refusing or failing to give a specimen of breath under s.13 of the Road Traffic Act 1994 should be interpreted as one of strict liability. In this case s.13 created a requirement to give two samples of breath but s.23 went on to provide a defence whereby a defendant could avoid liability by satisfying the court that there was a special or substantial reason for the failure to give specimens. In holding that the offence was one of strict liability, the court was particularly influenced by two factors. First, the offence was one of "failing" or "refusing" to give a specimen and while the word "refuse" might involve an element of intention, a "failure" could take place without any intention. Secondly, the court was influenced by the fact that s.23 created a limited right of defence, which it took to indicate a legislative decision to rule out other defences such as the lack of mens rea.

The constitutional status of strict liability offences and *CC v Ireland*

We have already noted that in *Shannon Regional Fisheries Board v Cavan County Council* Keane J., in his dissenting judgment, raised a query as to the constitutionality of strict liability offences, particularly where an offence does not permit a defence of reasonable care to be established. That analysis drew on Canadian jurisprudence, where it has been held that absolute liability crimes may be invalid where there is the possibility of imprisonment.

The leading Canadian case is *Reference re Section 94(2) of the Motor Vehicle Act*.[64] That case concerned an offence of driving without a valid driver's licence, which carried a minimum sentence of imprisonment and which was an offence of absolute liability, irrespective of any knowledge on the part of the driver and with no defence of reasonable diligence. It was held by the Canadian Supreme Court that a law with the potential of convicting a person who was in no way at fault offends the principles of fundamental fairness and violates a person's right to liberty under s.7 of the Canadian Charter of Rights and Freedoms, if imprisonment is available as a penalty.

In this jurisdiction there had, until recently, been no comparable constitutional challenge to the principle of strict liability. However, this changed with the Supreme Court decision in *CC v Ireland*.[65] The case concerned the offence of unlawful carnal knowledge, commonly known as statutory rape, as provided for in s.1(1) of the Criminal Law Amendment Act 1935. This offence was committed where a man engaged in sexual intercourse with a girl under 15 years of age and her consent was deemed to be irrelevant. The Supreme Court held that a reasonable but mistaken belief

---

[63] Unreported, High Court, Ó Caoimh J., March 3, 2003.
[64] [1985] 24 D.L.R. (4th) 536.
[65] [2006] 4 I.R. 1. For a thoughtful and comprehensive discussion of strict liability and *CC v Ireland*, see two articles by David Prendergast: "Strict Liability and the Presumption of Mens Rea after CC v Ireland" (2011) 46(1) *Irish Jurist* 211; "The Constitutionality of Strict Liability in the Criminal Law" (2011) 33(1) D.U.L.J. 285.

that the girl was older than 15 years would not be a defence. While the presumption of mens rea was applied, it was held (by the majority, Denham J. dissenting) that this presumption had been rebutted. The provision was therefore characterised as creating an offence of absolute liability. The Supreme Court traced the legislative history of s.1(1). The provision which had applied prior to the enactment of the 1935 Act had contained a defence of reasonable mistaken belief as to the age for girls between 13 and 16 years (a misdemeanour offence) and this defence had not been available for offences against younger girls (where the offence was a felony). Fennelly J. reasoned:

> "The presence of this defence to the misdemeanour charge coupled with its absence in the case of the felony seems to me *necessarily to imply* that the enacting legislature did not intend such a defence to be available in the latter case ... When the Oireachtas of Saorstát Eireann came to amend that statute in 1935, it took the further step of removing any possibility of raising such a defence of mistake ... How can the legislature, at the same time, be taken to have intended that it should be available in defence of a charge to which it had never previously been a defence? The intention of the Oireachtas is further clarified by the exclusion of the defence also in the case of a charge of abducting an unmarried girl under the age of eighteen contrary to s.7 of the Act of 1885, while effectively retaining it in the case of mentally impaired victims (s.4). It is, to my mind, compellingly clear that the Oireachtas, as a matter of deliberate policy, deprived accused persons of the defence of mistake as to age made on reasonable grounds in all cases, but one, in which it had previously been expressly available. It is, therefore, also compellingly clear that the Oireachtas did not intend that such a defence should be available in the case of a charge of the newly enacted offence of unlawful carnal knowledge of a girl under the age of fifteen. A contrary view would make nonsense of the legislation and would, furthermore, run counter to the commonly accepted interpretation of the section which has prevailed for the seventy years since its enactment."[66]

The Supreme Court proceeded to strike down the provision as being unconstitutional because the penalty provided for was life imprisonment and it was unjustifiable not to require mens rea for an offence of such gravity.

Hardiman J. stated that the provision was one capable of "criminalising, and of jailing, the mentally blameless".[67] He noted the absolute nature of the offence: that it afforded absolutely no defence once the actus reus was established, no matter how extreme the circumstances. He rejected the argument that those not truly blameworthy would only receive a light sentence and noted that the offence was one where even a mere conviction carried a social stigma and required a defendant to be enrolled on the Sex Offender's Register. Such a conviction resulted in "intense shame"[68] for both the offender and his family. Hardiman J. commented that to criminalise somebody

---

[66] [2006] 4 I.R. 1 at 64.
[67] [2006] 4 I.R. 1 at 75.
[68] [2006] 4 I.R. 1 at 76.

Mental Element of Crimes

who is mentally innocent was to treat him as merely a means to an end; albeit that the end (the protection of young girls from engaging in consensual sexual intercourse) was a legitimate one to be pursued by appropriate means:

> "I cannot regard a provision which criminalises and exposes to a maximum sentence of life imprisonment a person without mental guilt as respecting the liberty or the dignity of the individual or as meeting the obligation as imposed on the State by Article 40.3.1° of the Constitution."[69]

Hardiman J. considered the utilitarian justification of absolute liability as advocated by McLachlin J. of the Canadian Supreme Court in her dissenting judgment in *R. v Hess and Nguyen*[70] in relation to equivalent Canadian legislation. McLachlin J.'s approach was based on a balancing exercise and Hardiman J. commented that "[t]his is an exercise not infrequently required of judges in an appropriate case, but it can also be employed by a judge who is unwilling to take a particular right as seriously as it deserves to be taken".[71] McLachlin J. found that the Canadian provision contravened two Articles of the Canadian Charter of Rights and Freedoms relating to liberty and security of the person and equal treatment and the right to equal protection and equal benefit of the law. However, she held that the provision was saved by Art.1 of the Charter which guaranteed rights and freedoms subject only to such reasonable limits prescribed by law as can be demonstrated in a free and democratic society. As Hardiman J. stated:

> "McLachlin J. was straightforward in her analysis of the effect of the section ... 'Without wishing to commit the crime or intending to commit the crime of having intercourse with a girl of less than fourteen years, an accused may stand convicted.' McLachlin J.'s justification of this is wholly utilitarian. She does not deny the injustice: she embraces it on the basis that its operation tends the greater good. This works, according to McLachlin J. in the following way ... 'it effectively puts men who are contemplating intercourse with a girl who might be under fourteen years of age on guard. They know that if they have intercourse without being certain of the girl's age, they run the risk of conviction, and may conclude that they will not take the chance. That wisdom forms part of the substratum of consciousness with which young men grow up, as exemplified by terms such as 'jailbait'."[72]

McLachlin J.'s approach did not find favour with Hardiman J.:

> "... McLachlin J. does not conceal the logical conclusion of her position: she sees nothing wrong in convicting a person, however young, who specifically contemplates the age of the girl and who is freely shown by her documentation appearing to prove that she is of legal age. Even that, in her view, does not exempt him from guilt of a crime which carries a sentence of up to life

---

[69] [2006] 4 I.R. 1 at 80.
[70] [1990] 2 S.C.R. 906.
[71] [2006] 4 I.R. 1 at 82.
[72] [2006] 4 I.R. 1 at 82–83.

imprisonment. McLachlin J. is not insensitive to the fact that the regime for which she contends gives rise to constitutional and indeed to moral difficulties ... Nevertheless she justifies it on a basis which is crudely utilitarian. It may be unjust – indeed it is unjust – but it is constitutionally allowable because it has a deterrent effect ... This, it seems, is a classic utilitarian argument. It permits the imposition of an admitted injustice on a discrete class of person on the sole justification of effectiveness. The measure, or its predecessors, is thought to be effective because its *in terrorem* effect has been so successful that it has entered into 'the substratum of consciousness with which young men grow up.' The psychology of this is debatable. Certainly it is also wholly unsupported by evidence, as far as one can tell in the Canadian case and certainly in this case. One should be under no illusion as to what McLachlin J. is supporting: the complete objectification of a whole group of a community – young men – and a disregard for their human and constitutional rights ..."[73]

The defence of due diligence to offences of absolute liability was also considered by Hardiman J.:

"On the existing jurisprudence and in particular the judgment of the Canadian Supreme Court in *R. v City of Sault Ste Marie* [1978] 2 S.C.R. 1299, and the dissenting judgment of Keane J. in *Shannon Regional Fisheries Board v Cavan County Council* [1996] 3 I.R. 267, it might appear that a defence of due diligence would suffice to justify a regulatory offence of strict liability ... Whether it would suffice for a true criminal offence carrying a sentence of life imprisonment is not a matter which arises for decision in this case. There is simply no such defence available here. No form of due diligence can give rise to a defence to a charge under s.1(1), even where the defendant has been positively and convincingly misled, perhaps by the alleged victim herself."[74]

The Irish approach since *CC v Ireland*

It would appear that, despite *CC v Ireland,* the courts have not altered their approach to strict liability significantly. Prendergast remarks:

"Hardiman's judgment may give the impression that strict liability in serious offences, as distinct from regulatory offences, is to be regarded as prima facie unconstitutional and requiring strong justification in order to survive constitutional scrutiny. Doubt about this is raised not just by the absence of constitutional challenges to offences such as causing death by dangerous driving but also by cases since *CC* where the superior courts have countenanced strict liability in serious offences outside the area of statutory rape."[75]

---

[73] [2006] 4 I.R. 1 at 83–84.
[74] [2006] 4 I.R. 1 at 78.
[75] David Prendergast, "Strict Liability and the presumption of mens rea after CC v Ireland" (2011) 46(1) *Irish Jurist* 211.

In *Reilly v Judge Pattwell*,[76] the presumption of mens rea was rebutted in relation to litter offences. McCarthy J. listed a number of factors to be used in ascertaining whether the presumption has been rebutted. He emphasised that the list was non-exhaustive:

"1. The moral gravity of the offence.
2. The social stigma attached to the offence.
3. The penalty.
4. The ease (or difficulty) with which a duty is discharged or the law obeyed.
5. Whether or not absolute liability would encourage obedience.
6. The ease or difficulty with which the law might be enforced.
7. The social consequences of non-compliance.
8. The *desideratum* to be achieved when considering the statutes."[77]

The presumption of mens rea was also rebutted in relation to sheep grazing within a forbidden zone in *Minister for the Environment v Leneghan*,[78] where Hedigan J. applied McCarthy J.'s list of factors. Prendergast comments that there is an implication in *Leneghan* that if the subject matter of the offence was not regulatory but truly criminal then the presumption of mens rea may not have been rebutted.[79]

In *DPP v Power*,[80] the Supreme Court held that mens rea was not required in respect of the value of drugs for the purposes of s.15A of the Misuse of Drugs Act 1977, in respect of which a mandatory minimum sentence of 10 years attached for a value of €13,000 or more. Finnegan J. held that any other interpretation would make s.15A unworkable.

More recently, Hanna J. in *O'Connor v O'Neill*[81] held that s.13 of the Road Traffic Act 1994, providing for the offence of refusing or failing to provide breath specimens, did not require mens rea.

THE DOCTRINE OF TRANSFERRED MALICE

Suppose A intends to shoot and kill B, but misses and hits and kills C; murder will still have been committed by virtue of the doctrine of transferred malice. This doctrine provides that where A has the mens rea required for a particular crime, and carries out the actus reus of that crime, he will be found to have committed that crime notwithstanding that the final result (with regard to the identity of the victim) is unintended. The doctrine does not only apply to "malice" but to every type of mens rea. An ancient illustration of the doctrine dating from 1573 can be found in *R. v Saunders and Archer*.[82] Saunders wished to poison his wife in order to be free

---

[76] [2008] IEHC 446.
[77] [2008] IEHC 446 at para.52.
[78] [2009] IEHC 226.
[79] David Prendergast, "Strict Liability and the presumption of mens rea after CC v Ireland" (2011) 46(1) *Irish Jurist* 211.
[80] [2007] IESC 31.
[81] [2011] IEHC 118.
[82] (1573) 2 Plowd 473.

to marry another. He gave his wife a poisoned apple and she took one bite before handing it to their daughter to eat. The child died and Saunders was found guilty of her murder by virtue of the doctrine. Another example is *R. v Latimer*.[83] Here A hit B with his belt but the belt glanced off B and hit C instead, cutting her severely. This ricochet was held by the jury to be accidental and unforeseeable; nevertheless, the accused was found guilty of unlawfully wounding C.

However, the doctrine is limited. It applies only where the actus reus and mens rea are of the same crime. If A shoots at a window, misses, and kills a person who unknown to him is standing close by, then he has not committed murder: the actus reus of murder and the mens rea of a crime against property do not together add up to the crime of murder. Similarly, in *R. v Pembliton*[84] the defendant was acquitted of intentional damage to property in a situation where he threw a stone intending to hit a person but missed and broke a pub window instead.

The doctrine was considered by the House of Lords in *Attorney General's Reference No. 3 of 1994*.[85] The defendant stabbed his pregnant partner in the stomach and she gave birth prematurely. Their baby daughter died after four months because of her prematurity and the defendant was charged with her murder. The House of Lords was asked to consider whether the defendant's intention to kill or do grievous bodily harm to the mother was sufficient to ground the charge of murder, given that it was accepted that no ill will was directed towards the unborn child. The Court of Appeal held that the defendant could be charged with murder as the foetus was an integral part of the mother just like an arm or a leg and the relevant mens rea was directed towards her. The House of Lords disagreed and characterised the foetus as a unique organism. Where an assailant intended to harm a woman, the doctrine of transferred malice did not extend to harming the future human being that the foetus would become, so as to satisfy the requirements of the mens rea for murder.[86] Lord Mustill characterised the doctrine as:

> "'[R]ather an arbitrary exception to general principles'. Like many of its kind this is useful enough to yield rough justice, in particular cases, and it can sensibly be retained notwithstanding its lack of any sound intellectual basis. But it is another matter to build a new rule upon it."[87]

Lord Mustill continued:

> "My Lords, the purpose of this inquiry has been to see whether the existing rules are based on principles sound enough to justify their extension to a case where the defendant acts without an intent to injure either the foetus or the child which it will become. In my opinion they are not. To give an affirmative answer requires a double 'transfer' of intent: first from the mother to the foetus and then from the foetus to the child as yet unborn. Then one would have to

---

[83] [1886–1887] 17 QBD 359.
[84] [1874] 12 Cox CC 607.
[85] [1998] 1 A.C. 245.
[86] However, the House of Lords held that the defendant could be guilty of manslaughter. See Ch.4 for further analysis of this case.
[87] [1998] 1 A.C. 245 at 261.

employ the fiction (or at least the doctrine) which converts an intention to commit serious harm into the mens rea of murder. For me, this is too much. If one could find any logic in the rules I would follow it from one fiction to another, but whatever grounds there may once have been have long since disappeared. I am willing to follow old laws until they are overturned, but not to make a new law on a basis for which there is no principle.

Moreover, even on a narrower approach the argument breaks down. The effect of transferred malice, as I understand it, is that the intended victim and the actual victim are treated as if they were one, so that what was intended to happen to the first person (but did not happen) is added to what actually did happen to the second person (but was not intended to happen), with the result that what was intended and what happened are married to make a notionally intended and actually consummated crime. The cases are treated as if the actual victim had been the intended victim from the start. To make any sense of this process there must, as it seems to me, be some compatibility between the original intention and the actual occurrence, and this is, indeed what one finds in the cases. There is no such compatibility here. The defendant intended to commit and did commit an immediate crime of violence to the mother. He committed no relevant violence to the foetus, which was not a person, either at the time or in the future, and intended no harm to the foetus or to the human person which it would become. If fictions are useful, as they can be, they are only damaged by straining them beyond their limits. I would not overstrain the idea of transferred malice by trying to make it fit the present case."[88]

The most recent analysis of the doctrine of transferred malice was in the Supreme Court of England and Wales in *R. v Gnango*.[89] This was an unusual case with a very complicated factual scenario. The defendant was engaged in a shoot-out with a member of a rival gang (known only as "Bandana Man") when a bullet from his rival, who was aiming at him, killed a Polish care worker who happened to be walking across the carpark. The court held that he could be convicted of her murder by a combination of the common law principles relating to aiding and abetting and the common law doctrine of transferred malice.[90]

The court drew an analogy between a consensual gunfight and a duel or prize fight and noted that case law indicated that all who are present at such an event would be guilty of aiding and abetting each of the protagonists in his attempt to kill the other:

"If one is killed, all who gave encouragement will be guilty of murder ... It logically follows that each protagonist will be party to the violence, or attempted violence, inflicted on himself by his opponent ... A guilty verdict in this case involves a combination of common law principles in relation to aiding and abetting and the common law doctrine of transferred malice. In *Attorney General's Reference No. 3 of 1994* ... Lord Mustill commented of the latter doctrine: 'Like many of its kind this is useful enough to yield rough justice, in

---

[88] [1998] 1 A.C. 245 at 262.
[89] [2012] 2 W.L.R. 17.
[90] Another possible basis for conviction was held to be by way of joint enterprise and the court held that it did not matter by which of the two routes the jury had arrived at a guilty verdict.

particular cases, and it can sensibly be retained notwithstanding its lack of any sound intellectual basis. But it is another matter to build a new rule upon it.' We have considered whether to hold the defendant guilty of murder would be so far at odds with what the public would be likely to consider the requirements of justice as to call for a reappraisal of the application of the doctrine in this case. We have concluded to the contrary. On the jury's verdict the defendant and Bandana Man had chosen to indulge in a gunfight in a public place, each intending to kill or cause serious injury to the other, in circumstances where there was a foreseeable risk that this result would be suffered by an innocent bystander. It was a matter of fortuity which of the two fired what proved to be the fatal shot. In other circumstances it might have been impossible to deduce which of the two had done so. In these circumstances it seems to us to accord with the demands of justice rather than to conflict with them that the two gunmen should each be liable for Miss Pniewska's murder."[91]

Despite the comments of the English Supreme Court to the contrary, it is submitted that this case can be criticised for stretching the doctrine of transferred malice to its limits and an Irish court might not find it a persuasive precedent.

It should be noted that the doctrine is not only a common law one but has been put on a statutory footing in respect of murder, by virtue of s.4(1) of the Criminal Justice Act 1964: "Where a person kills another unlawfully the killing shall not be murder unless the accused person intended to kill, or cause serious injury to, some person, *whether the person actually killed or not.*"[92] Similarly, s.6 of the Non-Fatal Offences Against the Person Act 1997 provides for the doctrine in relation to syringe offences.

---

[91] [2012] 2 W.L.R. 17 at 35–36.
[92] Emphasis added.

CHAPTER 3

ACTION ELEMENT OF CRIMES

Introduction

The actus reus is the action element of a crime. It may be contrasted with the mens rea, the mental element. For example, a person cannot be convicted of murder unless both the required mental state (intention to kill or cause serious personal injury) and the action element of the crime are present (he has caused the death of his victim). A person who intends to kill or cause serious personal injury, yet does nothing but daydream about it, will not be guilty of any crime.

It is, however, misleading to speak of the actus reus as if it is always an "act". It may be limited to the acts of the defendant (and indeed to his omissions in certain cases as will be discussed below) but it may also be defined to include consequences. For example, the actus reus of murder includes the requirement that the victim must die as a result of the perpetrator's action. Similarly, the actus reus may include the circumstances surrounding the defendant's actions. For example, the offence of capital murder requires that the injured party come within a particular category before the offence is committed (e.g. the injured party is a Garda).

There must be an actus reus before any crime can be committed. With crimes of strict liability a defendant may be convicted on the basis of actus reus alone but the converse is never true: a person can never be convicted on the basis of mens rea alone.[1] In *R. v Deller*,[2] the accused was charged with obtaining a car by false pretences. He represented that he owned the vehicle he had traded in for the car but, in fact, he believed that a hire purchase company owned it. This turned out to be untrue as, due to an error in registering the hire purchase agreement, the accused was legally the owner of the vehicle. Deller was acquitted, as although he had the necessary mens rea, he was actually telling the truth when he claimed that the car was free from any encumbrances. There was no actus reus even though he had believed he was committing a crime.

Actus Reus as a State of Affairs

The actus reus does not always amount to an action. In certain circumstances it may be defined as a state of affairs not including an act at all. This is illustrated by the

---

[1] Crimes of strict liability are discussed in Ch.2.
[2] (1952) 36 Cr. App. R. 184.

case of *R. v Larsonneur*[3] in which the accused was convicted of "being found" in a particular situation. An alien who had been refused leave to land, she was convicted under the Aliens Order 1920 of being found in the United Kingdom even though the police had brought her from Ireland against her will. Larsonneur had initially been required to leave the United Kingdom by a certain date and had travelled to the Irish Free State. She was deported from Ireland and brought to Holyhead in the custody of the Irish police. It was held that the woman had "in circumstances which are perfectly immaterial as far as this appeal is concerned, come back to Holyhead". A similar result was reached 50 years later in *Winzar v Chief Constable of Kent*.[4] Winzar was taken to hospital but was found to be intoxicated and asked to leave. Eventually the police were called and he was removed from the hospital to the public highway outside. Once there, he was charged by the police with being found drunk in the highway and was subsequently convicted. The court rationalised as follows:

> "Suppose a person was found as being drunk in a restaurant ... and was asked to leave ... [H]e would walk out the door of the restaurant and would be in a public place ... of his own volition ... because he had responded to a request ... [I]f [he] refused to leave ... he would not be there of his own volition ... It would be nonsense if one were to say that the man who responded to the plea to leave could be found drunk in a public place or in a highway, whereas the man who had been compelled to leave could not."[5]

Larsonneur and *Winzar* have been severely criticised as being contrary to the general principle that the action element of a crime must be voluntary. For example, a conviction for assault cannot be sustained if the accused's hand was forcibly grabbed by another and used to strike a third party. Voluntariness is an essential attribute of the actus reus. If the act is done without any control by the mind, such as a spasm or reflex action, then the accused may be able to rely on the defence of automatism.[6] It is unclear how an Irish court would deal with the issue but other jurisdictions have declined to follow the *Larsonneur* approach. *Larsonneur* has been rejected by the Supreme Court of New Zealand in *Kilbride v Lake*.[7] In that case a driver was charged with failing to display a current warrant of fitness on his motor car. It was accepted that the warrant had disappeared from his vehicle while he was absent from it. In finding the accused not guilty of the offence, Woodhouse J. remarked:

> "[I]t is a cardinal principle that ... a person cannot be made criminally responsible for an act or omission unless it was done or omitted in circumstances where there was some other course open to him. If this condition is absent, any act or omission must be involuntary or unconscious, or unrelated to the forbidden event in any causal sense regarded by the law as involving responsibility."[8]

---

[3] (1933) 24 Cr. App. R. 74.
[4] *The Times*, March 28, 1983.
[5] *The Times*, March 28, 1983.
[6] Automatism is discussed in Ch.11.
[7] [1962] N.Z.L.R. 590.
[8] [1962] N.Z.L.R. 590 at 593.

ACTUS REUS AND MENS REA MUST COINCIDE

In examining the actus reus, it is important to note that a crime is committed only when the actus reus and the mens rea exist at the same time. Suppose a husband decides to kill his wife by poisoning her at dinner that evening. However, that afternoon his careless driving causes a crash in which his wife, a passenger in the car, is killed[9]. We have the actus reus of murder: he caused the death of his wife. We have the mens rea of murder: he intended to kill her. However, this is clearly not a case of murder, since the two did not coincide.

R. v Scott[10] was an Australian case in which the defendant escaped from prison after suffering a blow to the head. He claimed that he did not know what he was doing until two days after he escaped, at which point he decided not to give himself up. Charged with escape from lawful custody, his defence was that he was incapable of forming the necessary mens rea at the time of the escape, although he later formed the intent to remain at large. This defence was accepted by the Supreme Court of Victoria, which held (per Gillard J.) that the two elements necessary to constitute the crime were never brought together as an unlawful action and an evil intention never concurred.

However, where the actus reus is an ongoing act, then it is sufficient if the mens rea coincides with part of the actus reus: it need not coincide with the whole. This principle was illustrated by *R. v Thabo Meli*.[11] A group of men decided to commit a murder and make it appear to be an accident. They struck the victim on the head and, presuming he was dead, then threw him off a cliff. The victim was not dead when thrown off the cliff but died of exposure some time later. The accused argued that there had been no coincidence of actus reus and mens rea—they had mens rea when they struck him but there had been no actus reus as he had merely been stunned. However, when the actus reus occurred there had been no mens rea as they had believed him to be already dead. This argument was rejected and the court characterised the events as a single transaction that could not be divided up in the manner argued by the defendants. Lord Reid commented that it was "much too refined a ground of judgment to say that, because the appellants were under a misapprehension at one stage and thought that their guilty purpose had been achieved before, in fact, it was achieved, therefore they are to escape the penalties of the law".[12]

---

[9] This is an example of coincidence in motivation. Here the problem is that the mens rea did not motivate the actus reus and there is therefore no offence as a result.
[10] [1967] V.R. 276.
[11] [1954] 1 All E.R. 373.
[12] [1954] 1 All E.R. 373 at 374. *R. v Thabo Meli* was applied in *R. v Church* [1966] 1 Q.B. 59 and also in *R. v Le Brun* [1992] 1 Q.B. 61. In the latter case, a husband had an argument in the street with his wife and struck her without intending to do her really serious harm. His wife was rendered unconscious and the defendant then moved her in an effort to conceal what had happened. While being moved the wife hit her head on the pavement and was fatally injured. The Court of Appeal held that there was coincidence of actus reus and mens rea, despite the delay between the striking and the moving, as the incident was viewed as a continuing act. Lord Lane C.J. said that it was particularly appropriate to view the events as one transaction where the defendant's subsequent action, which caused death, was designed to conceal his commission of the original assault.

A further example is the case of *Fagan v Metropolitan Police Commissioner*.[13] In that case the defendant accidentally drove his car onto the foot of a policeman, and then deliberately left it there. Charged with assault, his defence was that his conduct was complete before he formed any intention. However, this argument was rejected. His conduct was treated by the court as continuous and the crime was committed when he decided to *leave* the car on the policeman's foot. *R. v Kaitamaki*[14] applied similar reasoning in the case of rape. The defendant became aware that the woman was not consenting after intercourse had begun. It was held that sexual intercourse is a continuing act and, if the defendant became aware of lack of consent at any stage during intercourse and did not withdraw, he would be guilty of the offence of rape.

The Actus Reus may be an Omission

Under most circumstances the criminal law does not punish failure to act. Suppose A is on a beach and sees B struggling in the sea. A stands by and watches B drown, despite the fact that A is a strong swimmer and could easily rescue B without any danger to himself. A is not guilty of a crime, however morally reprehensible his conduct is. As Hawkins J. put it in *R. v Paine*:

> "If I saw a man, who was not under my charge, taking up a tumbler of poison, I should not be guilty of any crime by not stopping him. I am under no legal obligation to protect a stranger."[15]

This reasoning was echoed almost a century later in *R. v Lowe*:

> "We think that there is a clear distinction between an act of omission and an act of commission likely to cause harm. Whatever may be the position with regard to the latter it does not follow that the same is true of the former. In other words, if I strike a child in a manner likely to cause harm it is right that, if the child dies, I may be charged with manslaughter. If, however, I omit to do something with the result that it suffers injury to health which results in its death, we think that a charge of manslaughter should not be an inevitable consequence, even if the omission is deliberate."[16]

However, not every jurisdiction is of the view that there is no general duty to act. The State of Vermont has enacted a law creating a liability for failure to act in certain circumstances:

> A person who knows that another is exposed to grave physical harm shall, to the extent that the same can be rendered without danger or peril to himself or without interference with important duties owed to others, give reasonable assistance to the exposed person unless that assistance or care is being provided by others.[17]

---

[13] [1969] 1 Q.B. 439.
[14] [1985] A.C. 147.
[15] The *Times*, February 25, 1880.
[16] [1973] Q.B. 702 at 709.
[17] 12 Vt. Stat. Ann s.519 (Emergency Medical Care).

The statute specifically excludes civil liability for a person providing such reasonable assistance, unless his acts amount to gross negligence. This removes one perceived objection to the enactment of such "Good Samaritan" provisions.

Similarly, the Quebec Charter of Human Rights and Freedoms provides the following:

> Every human being whose life is in peril has a right to assistance. Every person must come to the aid of anyone whose life is in peril either personally or by calling aid, or by giving him the necessary and immediate physical assistance, unless it involves danger to himself or a third person, or unless he has some further valid reason.[18]

Ashworth has commented as follows on the issue:

> "Individuals need others, or the actions of others, for a wide variety of tasks which assist each one of us to maximise the pursuit of our personal goals. A community or society may be regarded as a network of relationships which support one another by direct or indirect means ... It follows that there is good case for encouraging co-operation at the minimal level of the duty to assist persons in peril, so long as the assistance does not endanger the person rendering it ... The foundation of the argument is that a level of social co-operation and social responsibility is both good and necessary for the realisation of individual autonomy. Each member of society is valued intrinsically, and the value of one citizen's life is generally greater than the value of another citizen's temporary freedom. Thus it is the element of emergency which heightens the social responsibility in 'rescue' cases, and which focuses other people's vital interests into a 'deliberative priority' and it is immediacy to me that generates my obligation. The concepts of immediacy and the opportunity of help (usually because of physical nearness) can thus be used to generate, and to limit the scope of, the duty of assistance to those in peril."[19]

Although the law in this jurisdiction, and in most other jurisdictions, does not recognise a general duty to act, there are many specific situations where the law does recognise a positive duty to act.

Duty of parents towards their children

The most obvious example is the duty of parents towards their children. If a parent deliberately fails to feed a child, intending to cause death or serious injury, then the crime of murder is committed if the child dies. In the case of *R. v Bubb*[20] the

---

[18] Cl.2.
[19] Andrew Ashworth, "The Scope of Liability for Omissions" (1989) 105 L.Q.R. 424 at 430–434. See Glanville Williams's response to Ashworth's arguments: Glanville Williams, "Criminal omissions – the conventional view" (1991) 107 L.Q.R. 86. See also, Joshua Dressler, "Some brief thoughts (mostly negative) about 'Bad Samaritan' laws" (2000) 40 *Santa Clara L. Rev.* 971.
[20] [1851] 4 Cox CC 455.

defendant was an aunt of a child and was in loco parentis. She was charged with causing the child's death by deliberate neglect. It was held that the defendant, on those facts, had a duty to care for the child. It is probable that this category is not limited to parents and children but includes other similar familial/marital ties. In *R. v Hood*[21] a man was convicted of gross negligence manslaughter when he failed to call for medical help for three weeks for his wife who had fallen and broken bones. There is also a statutory duty imposed on persons who have the custody, charge or care of children to protect them from assault, ill-treatment or neglect pursuant to the child cruelty provision in s.246 of the Children Act 2001.

Duty voluntarily assumed

The law has recognised several further categories where such a duty arises. One is where a duty has been voluntarily assumed. In *R. v Stone and Dobinson*,[22] a man of low intelligence and his cohabiting girlfriend kept his elderly sister as a lodger. She refused to eat and lived in her room in appalling conditions of her own making. The girlfriend attempted to wash her when she became bedridden and made inadequate efforts to summon medical help. The defendants had decided to contact the deceased's doctor but she had refused to tell them his name. The defendants walked a considerable distance in their search for the doctor but it transpired that they had walked to the wrong village. Efforts were made to contact a local doctor but the neighbour who volunteered to do the telephoning (as the defendants were incapable of managing the instrument themselves) was unsuccessful. The deceased's clothes had to be cut off in an effort to wash her and her back was covered with sores. Her bedclothes and mattress were soiled and sodden. When she died soon afterwards it was discovered that her body was ulcerated and infested with maggots. Evidence was given that she could have been saved had she received the appropriate medical attention three weeks before her death. The defendants were convicted of manslaughter by criminal negligence because they had accepted responsibility for the deceased and owed a duty to help her even though her death had been largely caused by her own behaviour. The court also emphasised that the deceased was a blood relative of Stone's.

R. v Instan[23] was an earlier case decided along similar lines. The defendant lived with her elderly aunt who developed gangrene in her leg as she was nearing death. She was unable to fend for herself and the only person aware of her predicament was the defendant. The defendant failed to provide her aunt with any food for 12 days and when she died she was charged with manslaughter. The court held that the defendant had a duty to feed her aunt as "it was only through the instrumentality of the prisoner that the deceased could get the food".[24]

R. v Gibbins and Proctor[25] is an example of voluntary assumption of a duty and also of parental responsibility. The wife of Gibbins had left him and he began to live with Proctor, the co-accused. The couple allowed Gibbins's seven-year-old

---

[21] (2004) 1 Cr. App. R. (S) 431.
[22] [1977] Q.B. 354.
[23] [1893] 1 Q.B. 450.
[24] [1893] 1 Q.B. 450 at 454.
[25] (1918) 13 Cr. App. R. 134.

daughter to starve to death while ensuring that his other children and those of Proctor were well provided for. Both defendants were convicted of manslaughter. Gibbins argued that he had given money to Proctor to feed the children and therefore bore no responsibility for his daughter's death. However, the court held that he had lived in the same household as the deceased and could not have failed to notice her plight. Proctor argued that she had no duty towards the child, but this argument failed as she was deemed to have assumed responsibility for her welfare and had in fact excluded the child's mother from her life.

In the Australian case of *R. v Taktak*,[26] the principle of voluntary assumption of risk was applied to find the defendant guilty of manslaughter. He had hired a prostitute for a party but left her for a while. On his return he became aware that the prostitute was unconscious as a result of an overdose. The defendant took her away from the party and attempted to revive her. By the time he decided to summon medical help, however, she was already dead. It was held that he had assumed responsibility for her by removing her from the party, thereby preventing others from potentially coming to her aid.[27]

Creation of a danger

If a person creates a danger, there may be a duty to act to minimise the dangerous situation. In *R. v Miller*,[28] a vagrant accidentally set fire to a mattress by dropping a cigarette. He failed to take steps to put out the fire and was found to have been under a duty to do so and was convicted of arson. The Court of Appeal had dealt with the matter by applying the continuing act theory to find him guilty.[29] However, the House of Lords preferred the "duty" rationale. Lord Diplock explained that he saw:

> "no rational ground for excluding from conduct capable of giving rise to criminal liability conduct which consists of failing to take measures that lie within one's power to counteract a danger that one has oneself created, if at the time of such conduct one's state of mind is such as constitutes a necessary ingredient of the offence".[30]

---

[26] [1988] 14 N.S.W.L.R. 226.
[27] A modern Irish example of the principle of voluntary assumption of risk can be found in the trial in December 2011 in relation to the death of Evelyn Joel. She was a Wexford woman who suffered from multiple sclerosis and who came to live with her daughter and the daughter's partner. There was evidence that she was unwilling to go for medical treatment and attempts by nursing staff to make contact with her were often unsuccessful. Ms Joel died from pneumonia and complicating sepsis syndrome because of infected bedsores. She had been found in a filthy bed in the upstairs bedroom of her daughter's house by ambulance staff a week before her death in hospital. Her daughter and daughter's partner were tried for her unlawful killing by neglect. Evidence was given that they had failed to ensure that the deceased received nourishment, to attend to her sanitary requirements, to attend to her lack of mobility and to obtain timely medical attention. After an 18-day trial the jury failed to reach a verdict. A re-trial has been ordered. *Irish Times*, July 9, 2012.
[28] [1983] 2 A.C. 161.
[29] [1982] 1 Q.B. 532.
[30] [1983] 2 A.C. 161 at 176.

The *Miller* reasoning was recently applied to those who supply drugs. In *R. v Evans*,[31] the defendant sourced heroin for her half-sister and then failed to summon medical help when she overdosed. The Court of Appeal, in finding the defendant guilty of manslaughter, held that the omission to call an ambulance resulted in the finding of culpability since she had a duty to the deceased arising from having created the danger by supplying the heroin.[32] The prosecution did not rely on a duty arising out of familial ties (in any event the court expressly stated that the relationship of half-sister was too remote) nor did it base the case on a voluntary assumption of duty. The latter was surprising as the defendant admitted to the police that her half-sister would have expected her to look after her during the night. Ormerod makes the point that *Evans* has extended the *Miller* doctrine in one important respect: in *Miller* the duty only arose once the defendant had become subjectively aware of the danger, whereas in *Evans* it was held that the duty arose once the defendant realised or ought to have realised that the danger existed.[33]

DPP v Santana-Bermudez[34] is another example of a duty arising because of the creation of a danger. The defendant injured a police officer by allowing her to search him, knowing that he had hypodermic needles in his pockets. The police officer asked him if he had removed all the items from his pocket himself and he replied "Yes". She then asked him if he was sure he did not have any needles or sharps on him and he said he did not. The police officer was injured by a needle. She noticed that the defendant had a smirk on his face when this occurred. It was held that when someone, by act or word or a combination of the two, creates a danger and thereby exposes another to a reasonably foreseeable risk of injury which materialises, there is an evidential basis for the actus reus of an assault. However, the prosecution still has to prove an intention to assault or appropriate recklessness. In this case the defendant had given the police officer a dishonest answer when questioned about his pockets and had thereby exposed her to a reasonably foreseeable risk of injury.

Duty under contract

A positive duty to act can also be created under contract or by virtue of one's status as a public official. In *R. v Pittwood*,[35] a gatekeeper who failed to close the gate at a level crossing, resulting in a death, was found guilty of manslaughter on the basis of his obligations under contract. *R. v Dytham*[36] was a case where a policeman

---

[31] [2009] 1 W.L.R. 1999.
[32] The reasoning in *Evans* does not sit well with that in *R. v Kennedy (No. 2)* [2007] UKHL 38 (discussed below in relation to novus actus interveniens) and has been met with criticism by academics. *Kennedy (No. 2)* established that a defendant could not be guilty of unlawful act manslaughter when the deceased had self-injected as that broke the chain of causation. The only type of manslaughter that could have resulted in a conviction was therefore that based on gross negligence. See critiques of the case by Jonathan Rogers, "Death, drugs and duties" (2009) *Archbold News* 6; Glenys Williams, "Gross negligence manslaughter and duty of care in 'drugs' cases: R. v Evans" [2009] Crim. L.R. 631.
[33] David Ormerod, "Case comment: R. v Evans (Gemma): manslaughter – gross negligence – deceased supplied by defendant with heroin which proved fatal" [2009] Crim. L.R. 661.
[34] [2004] Crim. L.R. 471.
[35] [1902] 19 T.L.R. 37.
[36] [1979] Q.B. 722.

failed to intervene in a brawl to come to the aid of the deceased. The deceased had been ejected from a nightclub and violently kicked to death in the vicinity of the policeman. The defendant observed what was taking place and, when the assault was over, merely adjusted his helmet, said he was going off duty and drove away. He was found guilty of misconduct of an officer of justice in that he wilfully omitted to take any steps to preserve the peace.

Dytham was expressly approved in Ireland by Carney J. in the Central Criminal Court case of *DPP v Bartley*.[37] A woman who was being abused by her step-brother made a complaint to the Gardaí which was not acted on. The result was that she was abused for a further 25 years. Carney J. re-iterated that where a credible serious complaint is made to a Garda, he has no discretion not to investigate it and a failure to carry out this duty can render him liable to prosecution.

Statutory duties to act

Certain statutory offences also create a positive duty to act. Section 12 of the Road Traffic Act 2010 provides that a motorist who has been brought to a Garda station and who fails to provide a specimen of breath when properly requested to do so is guilty of an offence. Section 13 of the Criminal Justice Act 1984 places an obligation on a person who has been released on bail in criminal proceedings to appear before a court in accordance with his recognisance. A further example is s.9 of the Offences Against the State (Amendment) Act 1998, which creates the offence of withholding information which might be of material assistance in preventing the commission by any other person of a serious offence. A similar duty is contained in s.19 of the Criminal Justice Act 2011 where a person may be guilty of an offence if he or she has information which he or she knows or believes might be of material assistance in preventing the commission by any other person of a relevant offence or securing the apprehension, prosecution or conviction of any other person for a relevant offence, and fails without reasonable excuse to disclose that information as soon as practicable to a member of the Garda Síochána. In 2012 the Minister for Justice announced the publication of a new Bill, the Criminal Justice (Withholding of Information on Offences Against Children and Vulnerable Persons) Bill 2012, which would place on obligation on persons who have any knowledge of any serious offence, including sexual offences, against a child or a vulnerable adult, to inform the Gardaí.

Is the act–omission distinction artificial?

It has been argued that the act–omission distinction is an artificial one that can result in criminal liability being imposed as a result of semantics. This is best illustrated by cases dealing with the withdrawal of feeding tubes from patients in a persistent vegetative state. Lord Goff in *Airedale NHS Trust v Bland*[38] characterised a doctor's conduct in discontinuing life support as an omission, although he might take some positive step to bring the life support to an end. A doctor in such a situation was simply allowing his patient to die of a pre-existing condition and such an omission would not be unlawful unless it constituted a breach of duty to the patient. He added:

---

[37] Unreported, Central Criminal Court, Carney J., June 13, 1997.
[38] [1993] 1 All E.R. 821.

> "[T]he law draws a crucial distinction between cases in which a doctor decides not to provide, or to continue to provide, for his patient treatment or care which could or might prolong his life, and those in which he decides, for example by administering a lethal drug, actively to bring his patient's life to an end ... Even though that course is prompted by a humanitarian desire to end his suffering, however great that suffering may be ... [s]o to act is to cross the Rubicon which runs between on the one hand the care of the living patient and on the other hand euthanasia – actively causing his death to avoid or to end his suffering."[39]

Lord Goff made a clear distinction between the stranger who removes a tube or turns off a life support machine and a doctor who does the same thing:

> "I also agree that the doctor's conduct is to be differentiated from that of, for example, an interloper who maliciously switches off a life support machine because, although the interloper may perform exactly the same act as the doctor who discontinues life support, his doing so constitutes interference with the life-prolonging treatment then being administered by the doctor. Accordingly, whereas the doctor, in discontinuing life support, is simply allowing his patient to die of his pre-existing condition, the interloper is actively intervening to stop the doctor from prolonging the patient's life, and such conduct cannot possibly be characterised as an omission."[40]

The judgments in the leading Irish case on withdrawal of medical treatment, *In Re a Ward of Court (No. 2)*,[41] illustrate different approaches to the issue. The mother of a woman who had suffered cardiac arrest during minor surgery, and had been in a near persistent vegetative state for over 20 years, asked the court to permit doctors to cease artificially feeding her daughter. Hamilton C.J. said that the true cause of the patient's death would not be the withdrawal of nourishment but the injuries she had sustained over 20 years previously; whereas Egan J. was of the view that "[t]he removal of the tube would, as already stated, result in death within a short period of time. It matters not how euphemistically it is worded. The inevitable result of removal would be to kill a human being".[42]

Actus Reus and Causation

Before a defendant can be found to be criminally liable, it must be shown that his conduct caused the prohibited outcome (for example, death in the case of homicide).[43]

---

[39] [1993] 1 All E.R. 821 at 867.
[40] [1993] 1 All E.R. 821 at 868.
[41] [1996] 2 I.R. 79.
[42] [1996] 2 I.R. 79 at 136. This case is discussed in length in Ch.4.
[43] Causation is an issue only for so-called "result" crimes where the actus reus is defined as including a particular consequence that results from the physical action. "Conduct" crimes, in contrast, are crimes where the actus reus is confined to the physical action and does not also encompass its consequences. The offence of dangerous driving would be a conduct crime whereas the offence of dangerous driving causing death is a result crime.

In *R. v White*,[44] the defendant was charged with the murder of his mother, by putting cyanide into her drink. However, medical evidence established that she died of heart failure after drinking the drink, but before the poison could have had any effect. Consequently, the defendant could not be said to have caused her death. He was, however, convicted of her attempted murder.

One test of causation is asking whether the outcome would have happened "but for" what the defendant did. This test can be criticised, however, as being far too broad and unlimited. For example, if a little girl is knocked down by the driver of a speeding car a number of acts would fall within the "but for" test: the driver might not have had access to the car "but for" the fact that his wife did not need it that morning. He might not have had to drive at all "but for" the fact that his son had forgotten to bring his lunch box to school. The driver would not exist "but for" the fact that his parents met in the first place, and so on. The test concentrates on factual responsibility rather than criminal responsibility. It is very inappropriate in certain circumstances. For example, suppose A and B independently stab C who dies. Medical evidence proves that either wound would have been fatal. It could not be the position that A and B could each rely on the "but for" test to argue that C would have died in any event from the other person's wound and that the test had not been made out. In such a case both stab wounds should be seen as causes of death provided that they were more than a minimal cause (the de minimis rule).

The "but for" test is not regarded as the definitive test for causation but is a useful tool to exclude those factors that have no role to play in causing the required result. The test now applied in Ireland is that set out in *DPP v Davis*.[45] Here the deceased had been savagely assaulted by the applicant who then carried her home over his shoulder, dropping her along the way. There was also some evidence that she had fallen down the stairs in her house; that she had been chased by two other men earlier in the evening causing her trousers to be torn and that she had been injured by attempts made to resuscitate her when she suffered a heart attack on her way to hospital. However, Hardiman J. held that "[i]t seems overwhelmingly probable that the applicant's attack was the sole cause of all significant injuries. In point of law, however, it is unnecessary to go so far: it is sufficient if the injuries caused by the applicant were related to the death in more than a minimal way".[46]

This "more than a minimal" cause of death test appears on first reading to be much broader than the equivalent test in England and Wales. In that jurisdiction jurisprudence has developed the "operating and substantial cause of death" requirement which would appear to rule out actions which were more than a minimal cause of death but were not substantial causes of death. However, Coonan and Foley have argued that this is a false distinction, and English judges have frequently upheld the "more than de minimis cause of death" test while, confusingly, approving jury directions which imply that the action must have been a substantial or significant cause of death.[47] "[T]he word 'substantial' ... is clearly a convenient word to use to indicate to the jury that there must be something more than de minimis, and also

---

[44] [1910] 2 K.B. 124.
[45] [2001] 1 I.R. 146.
[46] [2001] 1 I.R. 146 at 149.
[47] See Genevieve Coonan and Brian Foley, *The Judge's Charge in Criminal Trials* (Dublin: Round Hall, 2008), pp.246–251.

to avoid possibly having to go into details of legal causation, remoteness and the like."[48]

It should be noted that the "eggshell skull rule" applies in the criminal law as well as the law of torts. This holds that an accused must take his victim as he finds him. If the victim has a particular weakness (such as a very thin skull) which makes him far more susceptible to injury than the average person, this cannot be used to reduce the liability of the accused. For example, if a victim dies from an assault that would not have killed the average person, the victim's vulnerability is legally irrelevant.

Break in the chain of causation?—Novus actus interveniens

This principle relates back to the idea of the defendant's conduct being an "operating" cause. If some other factor intervenes it may be held that the defendant may not have caused the outcome. Suppose that A is stabbed by B with a knife. A is rushed to hospital where she is advised that a blood transfusion is necessary to save her life. She refuses the transfusion on religious grounds and dies. Is A guilty of murder? These were the facts of *R. v Blaue*[49] and in that case it was held that B was guilty of murder. B was not entitled to argue that the religious beliefs of A were unreasonable: those who use violence on other people must take their victims as they find them (an "egg-shell skull" rule similar to that found in the law of torts). Lawton L.J. commented that:

> "It has long been the policy of the law that those who use violence on other people must take their victims as they find them. This in our judgment means the whole man, not just the physical man. It does not lie in the mouth of the assailant to say that his victim's religious beliefs which inhibited him from accepting certain kinds of treatment were unreasonable. The question for decision is what caused her death. The answer is the stab wound. The fact that the victim refused to stop this end coming about did not break the casual connection between the act and death."[50]

If the stab wound was still an operating and substantial cause of death, then death was still a consequence of the wound. Only if another cause was so overwhelming as to make the wound merely part of the history would it be possible to say that death had not been caused by the original action.

R. v Jordan[51] involved a very particular set of circumstances. The deceased had been the victim of a stabbing but was making a good recovery. However, he died from pneumonia as a result of being given an antibiotic to which he was intolerant, in circumstances where it was grossly negligent for him to be given this treatment. The conviction of the accused for murder was quashed: the Court of Appeal accepted that the direct and immediate cause of death was the treatment the victim received. The medical treatment had caused the death at a time when the original wound had almost completely healed.

---

[48] *R. v Hennigan* (1971) 55 Cr. App. R. 262 at 264.
[49] (1975) 61 Cr. App. R. 271.
[50] (1975) 61 Cr. App. R. 271 at 274.
[51] (1956) 40 Cr. App. R. 152.

Jordan was distinguished in *R. v Smith*.[52] A soldier stabbed another soldier during a barrack-room fight. While being carried to a doctor the injured man was dropped twice. He was subsequently given incorrect medical treatment and died. Evidence was given that had the correct medical treatment been given there was a 75 per cent chance that he would have survived. The conviction for murder was upheld despite arguments that there had been no less than three breaks in the chain of causation. The court held that the test was whether the original wound was still an operating and substantial cause at the time of death, notwithstanding that some other cause also operated. "Only if it can be said that the original wounding is merely the setting in which another cause operates can it be said that the death does not result from the wound. Putting it another way, only if the second cause is so overwhelming as to make the original wound merely part of the history can it be said that the death does not flow from the wound."[53] The court emphasised that *Jordan* was a very particular case depending on its facts.

Novus actus interveniens was also at issue in *R. v Malcherek and Steel*.[54] The victim's injuries required treatment on a life support machine but a decision was made by doctors to switch the machine off when it became apparent that recovery was impossible. The accused argued that disconnecting the life support machine had caused death and that this had broken the chain of causation. Again the "operating and substantial cause at the time of death" test was applied by the court and the accused's argument failed.

R. v Cheshire[55] was another case concerning medical negligence as a possible novus actus interveniens. The deceased, the victim of a shooting, developed respiratory problems following surgery. His medical team failed to diagnose the cause of the problem and he died in hospital two months after the shooting. The court accepted that medical negligence was the immediate cause of death but held that the defendant's acts could be regarded as causing the death, even though they were not the sole or main cause, if they contributed significantly to it. The medical negligence would only relieve the defendant of responsibility for death if it was so independent of his acts and so potent in causing death that the defendant's actions could be regarded as insignificant. Beldam L.J. explained what he meant by "significantly":

"We think the word 'significant' conveys the necessary substance of a contribution made to the death which is more than negligible."[56]

An interesting issue arose in *R. v Pagett*[57] where the accused used his victim as a "human shield" during a shoot out with the police. The victim was killed by a bullet fired by the police. The question arose whether this had broken the chain of causation and it was held that it had not. Lord Goff explained the reasoning of the court as follows:

---

[52] [1959] 2 All E.R. 193.
[53] [1959] 2 All E.R. 193 at 198 per Lord Parker C.J.
[54] [1981] 1 W.L.R. 690.
[55] [1991] 1 W.L.R. 844.
[56] [1991] 1 W.L.R. 844 at 852.
[57] (1983) 76 Cr. App. R. 279.

"There can, we consider, be no doubt that a reasonable act performed for the purpose of self-preservation, being of course itself an act caused by the accused's own act, does not operate as a *novus actus interveniens* ... [Take for example] an act by the victim in attempting to escape from the violence of the accused, which in fact resulted in the victim's death ... [I]f the victim acted in a reasonable attempt to escape the violence of the accused, the death of the victim was caused by the act of the accused. Now one form of self-preservation is self-defence; for present purposes, we can see no distinction in principle between an attempt to escape the consequences of the accused's act, and a response which takes the form of self-defence. Furthermore, in our judgment, if a reasonable act of self-defence against the act of the accused causes the death of a third party, we can see no reason in principle why the act of self-defence, being an involuntary act caused by the death of the accused, should relieve the accused from criminal responsibility for the death of the third party. Of course, it does not necessarily follow that the accused will be guilty of the murder, or even the manslaughter, of the third party; though in the majority of cases he is likely to be guilty at least of manslaughter."[58]

The House of Lords has recently applied the principle of novus actus interveniens in *R. v Kennedy (No. 2)*,[59] a case involving a drug supplier whose client took a fatal overdose. The defendant had supplied the heroin and prepared the syringe but the deceased's decision to inject himself, made freely and voluntarily, broke the chain of causation and resulted in the defendant's acquittal on a charge of unlawful act manslaughter.

Can a victim of crime break the chain of causation by his own actions?

Whether a victim of crime can himself break the chain of causation was examined in *R. v Roberts*.[60] A young girl took a lift in the defendant's car and injured herself by jumping out of the moving vehicle. She claimed she had been escaping the defendant's sexual advances. The question was whether he was responsible for the injuries sustained. The court set out the test to be applied: whether the injuries were the natural result of what the alleged assailant said and did, in the sense that they were something that could reasonably have been foreseen as a consequence of what he was doing or saying:

> "If the victim does something so daft ... or so unexpected ... not that this particular assailant did not actually foresee it but that no reasonable man could be expected to foresee it, then it is only in a very remote and unreal sense a consequence of his assault ... [It] breaks the chain of causation between the assault and the harm or injury."[61]

The defendant was convicted of assault occasioning actual bodily harm.

---

[58] (1983) 76 Cr. App. R. 279 at 289.
[59] [2007] UKHL 38.
[60] (1971) 56 Cr. App. Rep. 95.
[61] (1971) 56 Cr. App. Rep. 95 at 102 per Stephenson L.J.

This precedent was followed in *R. v Corbett*.[62] The defendant was convicted of the manslaughter of a mentally handicapped man who was also an alcoholic. Both men had spent the day drinking and during an argument later in the evening the defendant began to head-butt the deceased. The deceased ran away and fell into a gutter where he was struck by a car and killed. The court applied *Roberts* and held that only a daft reaction on the part of a victim, which would be beyond the foreseeable range of consequences of what the defendant had done, would suffice to break the chain of causation.

In *R. v Williams and Davis*,[63] the deceased was a hitch-hiker who jumped out of a moving car during an attempt to rob him and suffered fatal injuries. Stuart-Smith L.J. commented that it was important that "the deceased's conduct was proportionate to the threat; that is to say that it was within the ambit of reasonableness and not so daft as to make it his own voluntary act which amounted to a *novus actus interveniens* and consequently broke the chain of causation. It should of course be borne in mind that a victim may in the agony of the moment do the wrong thing."[64] This quote was cited with approval in the recent case of *R. v Lewis*[65] where the deceased ran across a busy road during an altercation between friends who were alighting from a taxi and a driver whose way had been impeded by the pedestrians.

In *R. v Dhaliwal*,[66] a man struck his partner on the forehead and she subsequently committed suicide. There was a long history of abuse amounting to psychological (but not psychiatric) injury to the deceased. The charge of manslaughter was dismissed since the psychological injury was deemed incapable of amounting to actual bodily harm and thus the prosecution's case that the abusive relationship was an unlawful and dangerous act was not made out. However, the Court of Appeal did comment that, with different facts, a conviction might have followed. "… subject to evidence and argument on the critical issue of causation, unlawful violence on an individual with a fragile and vulnerable personality, which is proved to be a material cause of death (even if the result of suicide) would at least arguably, be capable of amounting to manslaughter."[67]

This case suggests that there could be circumstances where the act of the victim to kill himself may not break the chain of causation. It is dangerous to over-analyse the decision, given that the comments were obiter and the case was ultimately decided on other grounds, but it may well be the case that a court could hold that an act of suicide, brought on by a long history of abuse by a defendant, might not be seen as the type of free and autonomous decision needed to amount to a novus actus interveniens. An alternative, and perhaps more controversial rationale, is that a court could characterise the act of suicide as a response that was reasonably foreseeable in the circumstances and therefore would not break the chain.[68]

---

[62] [1996] Crim. L.R. 594.
[63] [1992] 1 W.L.R. 380.
[64] [1992] 1 W.L.R. 380 at 388–389.
[65] [2010] EWCA Crim 151.
[66] [2006] 2 Cr. App. R. 24.
[67] [2006] 2 Cr. App. R. 24 at para.8.
[68] See discussion in Richard Card, *Cross, Card and Jones Criminal Law*, 19th edn (Oxford: Oxford University Press, 2010), p.70.

Chapter 4

HOMICIDE

General Principles

The term "homicide" is a general description for crimes which result in death. There are a number of such crimes in Irish law; however, for the purposes of this discussion, the primary ones which will be examined are murder, manslaughter, suicide and infanticide.

Year-and-a-day rule

Under common law all homicide crimes were subject to the year-and-a-day rule. This rule existed until recent times. This meant that, for a homicide crime to be committed, the victim had to die within a year and a day of the infliction of the injury.

This rule had a complicated origin but served at least two purposes. First, it was adopted at a time when medical science was rudimentary so that it was difficult or impossible to tell if deaths after longer intervals were in fact caused by the original injury. Secondly, it protected defendants by ensuring that if they injured someone they would not be at risk of prosecution for murder indefinitely into the future.

The rule, however, became increasingly outdated. The advance of medical science meant that causation could be determined more accurately. In addition, the rule failed to recognise that modern medicine might well keep a victim alive in a coma or with severe brain damage for a number of years before death finally occurs, or before life support is finally removed. Similarly, after a syringe or needle attack, a victim may be healthy for years before developing AIDS and eventually dying. Should a defendant responsible for the death of such a victim escape conviction for murder due to an arbitrary time limit?

These considerations led to the repeal of the rule by s.38 of the Criminal Justice Act 1999 and there is no longer any requirement that the victim die within a year and a day. A prosecution can be brought no matter what the interval between the injury and the death, so long as causation can be proved. The first murder trial involving a victim who died more than a year and a day after the original incident took place in January 2012.[1]

However, s.38 has been criticised. Carey points out that in England the equivalent Law Reform (Year and a Day Rule) Act 1996 abolished the rule but substituted some procedural safeguards for a defendant.[2] These include the requirement that the

---

[1] *Irish Times*, January 20, 2012. Jonathan Dunne was convicted of the murder of Ian Kenny.
[2] Gearóid Carey, "The Year and a Day Rule in Homicide" (2001) 11(1) I.C.L.J. 5.

special consent of the Attorney General be sought before a prosecution is brought in cases where the victim dies more than three years after the injury, or where the defendant has already been convicted of an offence arising out of the same facts. The Irish position includes no such safeguards, leading Carey to argue that there is a risk of unfairness to defendants who might be exposed to a trial in cases where causation is unclear.

Absence of a body

Even if a corpse is not found, a conviction for an offence of homicide can follow if circumstantial evidence proves that such an offence has taken place. This was illustrated by the old Irish case of *Attorney General v Ball*.[3] The defendant claimed that his mother, with whom he lived, had committed suicide in her bed with the aid of a razor and that he had dumped her body in the sea. However, a bloodstained hatchet was found in their home together with very large amounts of blood in several rooms. It was held that there was sufficient evidence to go to the jury that the deceased had met her death at the hands of the defendant.

Murder

The crime of murder has never been put on a purely statutory basis. Instead, it is a hybrid crime with some parts deriving from common law and other parts governed by statute. Consequently, we must first examine the common law definition of "murder" before going on to consider the statutory modifications.

The elements of murder at common law were defined in a famous passage from Coke dating from 1640:

> "Murder is when a man of sound memory, and of the age of discretion, unlawfully killeth within any county of the realm, any reasonable creature *in rerum natura*, under the King's Peace, with malice aforethought either expressed by the party or implied by law, so as the party wounded or hurt, etc. die of the wound or hurt, etc. within a year and a day after the same."[4]

We will look at each element of this definition separately.

Of sound memory and of the age of discretion

This simply means that the defendant must be unable to raise either the defence of insanity or the defence of infancy.[5]

---

[3] (1936) 70 I.L.T.R. 202.
[4] Sir Edward Coke, 3 *Institutes of the Law of England* 47.
[5] Both defences are considered further in Ch.11.

Unlawfully killeth

The killing must be unlawful to constitute murder. Examples of lawful killing would include a reasonable and proportionate killing in self defence[6] and, until it was abolished, the infliction of the death penalty.

Within any county of the realm

In order for a court to try any person for murder that court must have jurisdiction. At common law, this meant that the crime must have taken place within the geographic boundaries of the State; a crime which took place abroad was not the concern of the Irish courts. While this generally remains true today, Art.29.8 of the Constitution allows the Oireachtas to legislate with extraterritorial effect and in the case of some particularly serious crimes the Irish courts can try a defendant regardless of where the crime is alleged to have taken place.[7] Murder is one such crime and s.9 of the Offences Against the Person Act 1861 allows an Irish court to try an Irish citizen[8] for murder irrespective of where the crime is alleged to have been committed.

Any reasonable creature *in rerum natura*

For a murder charge to be brought the victim must be a live human being. Suppose, for example, that A shoots B as B lies in bed. Unknown to A, B has already died in his sleep. In that case A could not be guilty of murder as he had not caused B's death.

There are some difficulties in the case of unborn children. At common law the view was taken that life begins at birth so murder could not be committed until the child was born alive and completely outside the mother (although the umbilical cord need not have been cut). Death must have occurred after "the child is fully extruded from the mother's body and is living by virtue of the functioning of its own organs".[9] Until the child had an existence which was separate from, and independent of, the mother it was not regarded as an independent life. Consequently, killings of unborn children did not amount to murder. This remains the position in many common law countries and the Court of Appeal in New South Wales has considered the issue in two modern cases.

In *R. v King*[10] the accused was convicted of maliciously causing grievous bodily harm to a woman who was pregnant with his child. He had tried to persuade her to terminate the pregnancy and had offered money to others to assault her in an effort to cause a miscarriage. When the woman was between 23 and 24 weeks pregnant the accused punched and stamped on her stomach causing an abruption of the placenta and the death of the foetus. The "born-alive" rule meant that a conviction for murder was impossible. An argument was made that the charge of grievous bodily harm was not appropriate as the foetus was not part of the mother. This was rejected by the

---

[6] Considered further in Ch.11.
[7] See s.74 of the Criminal Justice Act 2006.
[8] See the discussion of extraterritoriality pursuant to s.44 of the European Arrest Warrant Act 2003 in the recent Supreme Court decision of *Minister for Justice, Equality and Law Reform v Bailey* [2012] IESC 16.
[9] *R. v Hutty* [1953] V.L.R. 338.
[10] [2003] NSWCCA 399.

Court of Criminal Appeal which relied on the close physical bond between foetus and mother which meant that it should be regarded as part of the mother for the purposes of assault.

In *R. v Iby*,[11] injury in a road traffic accident to a 38-week pregnant woman caused the death of the subsequently born child. The baby had been delivered by caesarean section after the accident and placed on a respirator but died a short time later. The Court of Criminal Appeal held that the child had had an independent existence for a number of hours and the defendant was convicted of manslaughter. The court commented on the "born-alive" rule, remarking that it had developed in times when live birth could not be taken for granted and was akin to an evidentiary proof that the child "was alive at the time of the alleged criminal conduct and that the child would have lived but for that act".[12] Spigelman C.J. remarked that "[t]he viability of a foetus can now be both established and ensured in a manner which was beyond the realms of contemplation when the 'born-alive' rule was adopted".[13] He noted that many states of the United States have abandoned the rule entirely either by statute or by judicial decision. However, certain commentators have suggested that courts should be cautious about abandoning the rule. Savell writes that abandoning the rule would mean courts would have to make decisions about the point at which a foetus becomes protected by the criminal law. She argues that the legal significance of birth remains a crucial factor in safeguarding the autonomy of women in decisions concerning pregnancy termination and obstetric treatment and offers a measure of protection against oppressive state supervision in the interests of the foetus. She concludes that it is arguable, in light of contemporary attitudes to autonomy, that there are substantive reasons for continuing to regard birth as legally significant, even if the historical basis for the "born-alive" rule no longer seems appropriate.[14]

In Irish law it is not clear whether the common law approach has survived the Eighth Amendment to the Constitution which acknowledges, in Art.40.3.3°, the right to life of the unborn. Charleton, McDermott and Bolger argue that the Eighth Amendment guarantees "[e]qual treatment of unborn and born life"[15] so that the crime of murder would now extend to unborn children also.

It may be possible to prosecute in respect of injuries inflicted prior to birth. Suppose that A assaults a pregnant woman B, causing injuries to her unborn child C. C is born alive but dies soon afterwards from the injuries sustained while in the womb. Can A be prosecuted for the death of C? In a number of cases where this situation has arisen it has been held that A can be prosecuted, notwithstanding that C did not have an independent life at the time of the attack.

This point was accepted in the old case of *R. v Senior*[16] where a midwife, who negligently injured a child during delivery, resulting in its death soon after birth, was convicted of manslaughter.

---

[11] (2005) 63 N.S.W.L.R. 278.
[12] (2005) 63 N.S.W.L.R. 278 at 284.
[13] (2005) 63 N.S.W.L.R. 278 at 284.
[14] Kristin Savell, "The Legal Significance of Birth" (2006) 29(2) *University of New South Wales Law Journal* 200.
[15] Peter Charleton, Paul Anthony McDermott, Marguerite Bolger, *Criminal Law* (Dublin: Butterworths, 1999), p.517.
[16] [1832] 1 Mood CC 346.

More recently, the issue came before the House of Lords in *Attorney General's Reference No. 3 of 1994*.[17] The victim was a young woman who was between 22 and 24 weeks pregnant. Her partner, the father of the child, stabbed her several times with a kitchen knife. This injured her severely and also injured her unborn child and caused her to give birth prematurely. The child died 121 days later from complications associated with the premature birth but not connected directly to the stabbing. The father had pleaded guilty to the offence of attacking the mother but when the baby died he was charged with murder. The House of Lords approved *R. v Senior*, a manslaughter charge, but went on to consider the issue of mens rea as the charge in this case was one of murder. It appeared that the intention of the defendant was to injure the mother, not the unborn child, so the defendant lacked the necessary intention for murder as regards the child. Consequently, the defendant could not be found guilty of murder unless either the mother and unborn child could be considered as a single victim for the purpose of mens rea, or the doctrine of transferred malice applied.[18] The House of Lords rejected both arguments holding that the unborn child was a unique organism, distinct from the mother, and could not therefore be considered as the same "victim" as the mother. It also considered that it would be stretching the doctrine of transferred malice too far to apply it in these circumstances because the unborn child was a foetus and not yet fully human when the assault occurred. This decision will make it very difficult to prosecute for murder in these situations since it requires that the defendant intends to harm not only the mother but also the unborn child. It does not, however, prevent such a defendant from being prosecuted for manslaughter since the mens rea for manslaughter does not require an intention directed towards a particular individual.

Under the King's peace

This phrase indicates that the killing of enemy aliens during a time of war, under battle conditions, will not amount to murder.

With malice aforethought

This refers to the mens rea for the crime of murder. At common law the mens rea was originally described as being "malice aforethought". This is now, however, a misleading phrase. It suggests that malice (i.e. spite, hatred or ill will) should be present and also suggests that there should be planning or premeditation. As the common law developed both requirements were dropped so that eventually neither malice nor premeditation was required for murder. A "mercy killing" amounts to murder despite the absence of what we would ordinarily understand as malice. Similarly, an impulsive attack could amount to murder despite the lack of premeditation.

The common law mens rea was changed in Ireland by the Criminal Justice Act 1964. The mens rea for murder is now set out in s.4, which provides:

---

[17] [1998] A.C. 245.
[18] This doctrine is discussed in Ch.2.

(1) Where a person kills another unlawfully the killing shall not be murder unless the accused *intended to kill, or cause serious injury* to, some person, whether the person actually killed or not.
(2) The accused person shall be presumed to have intended the natural and probable consequences of his conduct; but this presumption may be rebutted. (emphasis added).

Consequently, in order for murder to be established, it must be shown that the defendant intended to kill or cause serious injury. Any lesser intention will not suffice. For example, suppose that A slaps B intending merely to bruise him. B, however, suffers from a rare medical condition and dies soon after as a result. In this case the defendant should not be convicted of murder, since he lacked an intention to kill or cause *serious* injury.[19]

On the other hand if, as in *DPP v Doohan*,[20] A inflicted a "punishment beating" on B intending that B would receive broken arms or legs, this would be sufficient to show an intention to cause serious injury and a death resulting from such a beating would be murder, notwithstanding that there might not be an intention to cause death. In *Doohan* the Court of Criminal Appeal found that the defendant had fully intended, expected and contemplated that the deceased would be seriously injured by the attack. It was accepted that the defendant had said that he did not wish the victim to be killed but he did say that he wanted the deceased to be so badly injured that he would have to be hospitalised for a number of weeks. In those circumstances Denham J. found that sufficient mens rea for murder was present.

Either expressed by the party or implied by law

At common law the mens rea for murder was extremely wide. In addition to an express intention to kill or cause serious harm, the necessary intention was also implied if the defendant killed (even accidentally) while committing any felony. This was known as the doctrine of constructive malice or the felony-murder rule. For example, suppose that A, while carrying out a robbery, accidentally drove into and killed B. Under the felony-murder rule this would amount to the crime of murder notwithstanding the lack of any intention to harm B.

The rule was explained by Coke as follows:

"If the act be unlawful it is murder. As if A meaning to steal a deer in the park of B, shooteth at the deer, and by the glance of the arrow killeth a boy that is hidden in a bush: this is murder, for that the act was unlawful, although A had no intent to hurt the boy, nor knew not of him ... [so also if one] had shot at a cock or hen, or any tame fowl of another man's, and the arrow by mischance had killed a man, this had been murder, for the act was unlawful."[21]

---

[19] He may, however, be convicted of manslaughter.
[20] [2002] 4 I.R. 463.
[21] Inst., Pt III, Ch.8, p.56.

An example of the rule is *R. v Jarmain*,[22] where the defendant pointed a gun at a cashier during an armed robbery. He maintained that he had only intended to frighten the woman but the gun discharged inadvertently resulting in the death of the cashier. The reasoning behind this harsh rule was summarised by Wrottesley J.:

> "We think that the object and scope of this branch of the law is at least this, that he who uses violent measures in the commission of a felony involving personal violence, does so at his own risk and is guilty of murder if those violent measures result even inadvertently in the death of the victim."[23]

The rule was criticised on the basis that it could lead to results which were arbitrary and disproportionate. It also conflicted with the modern view that persons ought not to be punished for outcomes which they neither intended nor foresaw. In many jurisdictions the rule has now been repealed and in Ireland it was abolished by s.4(1) of the Criminal Justice Act 1964 as outlined above.

So as the party, wounded or hurt, etc. die of the wound or hurt, etc. within a year and a day after the same

We have already considered the year-and-a-day rule earlier in this chapter.

Attempted murder

The mens rea for attempted murder differs from that for murder in one important respect. Murder is a result crime and can only be committed where the result of the defendant's conduct is death. In order to convict a person of attempted murder it must be shown that he intended to bring about that result, i.e. that he intended to kill. An intention to cause serious injury is not enough to ground a conviction for attempted murder.

Suppose for example that A fires a gun at B intending to wound but not to kill. If A hits and kills B the crime of murder has been committed. If A misses, however, he will only be guilty of an attempt to cause serious harm not of attempted murder.[24]

This point is considered further in Ch.12 in relation to the mens rea required for attempts generally.

Aggravated murder

Until 1964 a verdict of murder carried a mandatory death sentence. By that stage, however, public sentiment was turning against the death penalty and the death sentence was generally commuted to a sentence of life imprisonment. The Criminal

---

[22] [1946] 1 K.B. 74.
[23] [1946] 1 K.B. 74 at 80.
[24] See *DPP v Douglas and Hayes* [1985] I.L.R.M. 25 on this point. See also, *R. v Grimwood* [1962] 3 All E.R. 285 where the accused attempted to strangle his wife by stuffing pyjamas into her mouth. It was held that the direction to the jury was incorrect as it might have led them to believe that if they were satisfied that all the accused intended to do was to cause grievous bodily harm, that was sufficient to ground a charge of attempted murder.

Justice Act 1964 recognised this shift by abolishing the death penalty for most killings but retaining an offence of capital murder punishable by death as a deterrent in respect of certain, particularly reprehensible, killings.

An example of capital murder was the killing of a member of the Garda Síochána acting in the course of his duty. As was pointed out by Henchy J. in *DPP v Murray*,[25] the purpose behind this offence was "to give an added protection to the members of an unarmed police force by making death the penalty for murdering one of its members on duty".[26] The crime also extended to other killings such as the murder of foreign leaders and diplomats.

In *Murray* the defendants were a husband and wife who participated in an armed robbery. Their getaway car collided with a car being driven by an off-duty Garda. A car chase followed and the robbers jumped out and began to run across a park. The Garda gave chase on foot and was about to capture Noel Murray when Marie Murray fatally shot him with a revolver. There was no evidence that the deceased had made the defendants aware that he was a member of the Garda Síochána and they appealed their convictions for capital murder. The Supreme Court held that the offence of capital murder requires proof of mens rea in relation to each of its elements. In other words, it would not be sufficient that after a person was murdered it transpired that he was an off-duty Garda. The defendants must have known at the time of the killing that the deceased was an off-duty Garda or have been reckless as to whether that was the position. Henchy J. remarked:

> "If capital murder were to depend on the purely adventitious circumstance that the victim turned out to be a Garda acting in the course of his duty, and not on any moral culpability of the killer in that respect, the awesome distinction in penal severity between murder and capital murder would have no ethical or rational foundation. It would be repugnant to reason and fairness if the death penalty were to depend on the outcome of what, in effect, would have been a lottery as to the victim's occupation and activity."[27]

Since then the death penalty has been abolished entirely by the Criminal Justice Act 1990 and replaced by a sentence of imprisonment for life. However, that Act still recognises the need to treat particular killings as being especially serious and therefore creates the offence of aggravated murder in s.3. This is essentially the former crime of capital murder and applies to:

(1) The murder of a member of the Garda Síochána acting in the course of his duty;
(2) The murder of a prison officer acting in the course of his duty;
(3) Murder in the course of specified offences under the Offences Against the State Act 1939, or in the course of the activities of an unlawful organisation under that Act; and

---

[25] [1977] I.R. 360.
[26] [1977] I.R. 360 at 402.
[27] [1977] I.R. 360 at 397.

(4) The murder of the head of a foreign state, or a member of the government of a foreign state, or a diplomat of a foreign state, when the murder is committed within the State for a political motive.

Section 3(2)(a) deals with the mens rea required for aggravated murder and puts in legislative form the principle in *Murray* that a person shall not be convicted of the offence unless it is proved that he knew of the existence of each ingredient of the offence or was reckless as to whether or not that ingredient existed.

In summary, therefore, the offence of aggravated murder is the offence of murder with the aggravating factor of the identity of the victim, or the subversive nature of the activities being carried out, together with the fact that the defendant knew or was reckless as to the existence of the aggravating factor.

Aggravated murder carries a mandatory life sentence of not less than 40 years.[28] In addition, the Act requires that the defendant must serve a minimum of 40 years before becoming eligible for remission, commutation of sentence or temporary release.[29]

Murder and the defences

The interaction between the crime of murder and the various defences will be discussed in Chs 10 and 11. It should be noted at this point that two defences are *unavailable* to a charge of murder (duress and necessity) while three defences are available *only* to a charge of murder and operate to reduce the crime to manslaughter (provocation, excessive self defence and diminished responsibility).

Mandatory sentence for murder

Murder carries a mandatory sentence of imprisonment for life. In practice, however, "life" does not mean the rest of the prisoner's lifetime. It is open to the Minister for Justice, advised by the Parole Board, to grant temporary or early release to life-sentence prisoners. A life-sentence prisoner may have his situation reviewed by the Parole Board after seven years. The Board will interview the prisoner and make a recommendation to the Minister. In deciding whether to recommend temporary or early release the Parole Board will take into account factors including:

(1) nature and gravity of the offence;
(2) period of sentence served at the time of the review;
(3) threat to safety of members of the community from release;
(4) risk of further offences being committed while on temporary release;
(5) conduct while in custody;
(6) extent of engagement with the therapeutic services;
(7) likelihood of period of temporary release enhancing reintegration prospects.[30]

---

[28] Section 4(a).
[29] Section 5(1). See the recent High Court decision of Hanna J. in *Callan v Ireland and the Attorney General* [2011] IEHC 190 on remission in cases of capital murder.
[30] The Parole Board Annual Report 2010.

The role of the Board is advisory only and the final decision on release is the Minister's. However, in the majority of cases to date the Minister has implemented the recommendations of the Board in full or in part.[31]

The average time served before release has increased dramatically in the past 20 years. In 1990 it was between 8 and 10 years[32] and by March 1999 this had increased to between 8 and 12 years.[33] In 2004 Minister Michael McDowell and the chairman of the Parole Board both indicated that, even where there are no aggravating factors, murderers should expect to serve a term of at least 12 to 14 years before being considered for release.[34] Minister McDowell also indicated that murders in the course of other violent crime such as robbery, gangland activity or drug crime would see a minimum of 15 to 20 years' imprisonment before release would be considered. The Parole Board noted in 2010 that a life-sentence prisoner will serve a custodial period of about 17 years.[35]

Where early release is granted it is always conditional and on licence. Restrictions may be imposed, such as a requirement to report regularly to a particular Garda station, or to live at a particular address. If these restrictions are breached, or the released prisoner is thought to present a risk, he can be rearrested and taken back into custody.

McCutcheon and Coffey have raised serious questions about the compatibility of the operation of the Parole Board with the ECHR.[36] Under art.5(4) of the ECHR a person has the right to have the lawfulness of his or her detention reviewed by a court and life-sentence prisoners are entitled to a frequent and speedy review of their cases by courts or a "court like" body. A "court like" body must have the power to determine the lawfulness of detention; it is not enough that it acts in an advisory capacity to the executive. Furthermore, McCutcheon and Coffey argue that the remedy of judicial review of an executive decision is too limited a relief to satisfy ECHR requirements. They conclude that the current state of the law does not comply with European human rights law and recommend the enactment of legislation placing the Parole Board on a statutory footing. Minister Shatter indicated in 2011 that he intends to enact legislation to place the Board on a statutory footing in 2012.[37]

Academic commentators have raised doubts about the appropriateness of a mandatory sentence for the crime of murder.[38] Arguments include that it is very difficult to plan a programme of rehabilitation for a prisoner whose release date

---

[31] During 2010 recommendations were sent to the Minister in 79 cases reviewed by the Parole Board and 72 recommendations were accepted in full. Just one recommendation was not accepted.
[32] Law Reform Commission, *Consultation Paper on Sentencing* (March 1993), para.10.30.
[33] Charleton, McDermott and Bolger, *Criminal Law* (1999), p.542.
[34] Ian O'Donnell, "When has a prisoner been punished enough?", *Irish Times*, July 14, 2004.
[35] The Parole Board Annual Report 2010. In England and Wales statistics provided by the National Offender Management Service at the Ministry of Justice show that mandatory life sentence meant an average of 15-and-a-half years in prison before being released on licence; Barry Mitchell and Julian V. Roberts, *Public Opinion and Sentencing for Murder. An Empirical Investigation of Public Knowledge and Attitudes in England and Wales* (Nuffield Foundation, 2010), p.20.
[36] Paul McCutcheon and Gerard Coffey, *Report into Determination of Life Sentences* (Irish Human Rights Commission, 2006).
[37] Annual Lecture of the Irish Penal Reform Trust (September 16, 2011).
[38] e.g. O'Malley, "Sentencing murderers: the case for relocating discretion" (1995) 5(1) I.C.L.J. 31.

is so uncertain; that a mandatory sentence is a blunt instrument when applied to difficult cases such as so-called mercy killings or those who kill under duress; and that vesting discretion in the executive arguably violates the constitutional vision of the separation of powers. On this last point, it could also be said that vesting this discretion in a politician may lead to popular sentiment controlling the early release system, with decisions being made for electoral advantage rather than on the merits. Bacik has commented that more defendants would plead to murder if it did not carry a mandatory sentence and she argues that to impose the same indeterminate sentence on every murderer, irrespective of mitigating factors, amounts to injustice for many.[39]

Mandatory life sentences have been abolished in several Australian states.[40] In England, both the House of Lords Select Committee on Murder and Life Imprisonment and the Prison Reform Trust Committee have recommended that the mandatory life sentence for murder should be replaced by determinate sentencing with a maximum sentence of life.[41] In this jurisdiction, the call for reform has also been joined by a number of judges, including Keane C.J. who has suggested that the mandatory life sentence for murder might be abolished as "the gradations of culpability in the crime of murder are almost as infinite as the variations in the human psyche itself".[42]

The Law Reform Commission has addressed the issue of the mandatory life sentence for murder in various reports over the years and with differing outcomes. In its 1996 Report on Sentencing it recommended that mandatory sentences of imprisonment for indictable offences should be abolished, saying that its members were unanimous that there are degrees of seriousness even in the most serious of crimes such as murder. The Commission examined the general deterrent argument for mandatory life sentences but could find no evidence that they deter potential killers. In the Australian State of Victoria, where the mandatory sentence became discretionary in 1986, there had been no increase in homicide.[43] It concluded that "a mandatory sentence on conviction on indictment was a blunt instrument which would not be tolerated in any sentencing scheme with the slightest sensitivity to a 'just deserts' approach".[44]

The Law Reform Commission's *Report on Homicide: Murder and Involuntary Manslaughter* revisited the issue in 2008.[45] The Report first set out a number of arguments for maintaining the mandatory life sentence:

---

[39] Ivana Bacik, "Review of the Law Reform Commission Consultation Paper on Homicide: The mental element in murder" (2000) 22 D.U.L.J. 264.
[40] New South Wales in 1982 and Victoria in 1986 (see discussion in Law Reform Commission *Consultation Paper on Sentencing* (March 1993), para.10.35.
[41] House of Lords, *Report of the Select Committee on Murder and Life Imprisonment* (HL Paper 78-1) ("Nathan Committee", 1989); *Report of the Committee on the Penalty for Homicide* (Prison Reform Trust, 1993) ("Lane Committee").
[42] The Hon. Mr Justice Ronan Keane, "Homicide: The Mental Element in Murder" (2001) 2(1) J.S.I.J. 66 at 78.
[43] Law Reform Commission, *Consultation Paper on Sentencing* (March 1993), para.10.36.
[44] Law Reform Commission, *Report on Sentencing* (LRC 53–1996), para.5.7.
[45] Law Reform Commission, *Report on Homicide: Murder and Involuntary Manslaughter* (LRC 87–2008). See generally, Ch.1.

(1) murder is the most heinous crime so it is appropriate that punishment is life in every case;
(2) the replacement of the mandatory life sentence with a discretionary sentence would blur the distinction between murder and manslaughter;
(3) the mandatory penalty is necessary to protect the public against the threat of a murderer killing again on release;
(4) a discretionary penalty for murder would undermine confidence in the administration of justice;
(5) sentencing judges would be faced with difficult sentencing decisions if the penalty became a discretionary one;
(6) the mandatory life sentence acts as a deterrent.

The arguments in favour of abolishing the mandatory life sentence were then discussed, including:

(1) all murders are not equally heinous;[46]
(2) "life" does not mean life;
(3) the duration of the term which the murderer will actually spend in prison is not determined by the trial judge, who can weigh up all aspects of the offence and offender, but by the Minister for Justice and Equality following the advice of the non-statutory Parole Board which may or may not be followed;
(4) under the current system many juries acquit of murder and substitute a conviction for manslaughter on grounds of sympathy;
(5) deciding on the appropriate sentence for a murderer would not be any more difficult for a judge than sentencing in other serious crimes;
(6) the deterrent effect of mandatory sentencing is questionable as most murders are the result of sudden emotions rather than premeditation.

The Law Reform Commission ultimately recommended that the mandatory life sentence for murder be abolished and replaced with a discretionary maximum sentence of life imprisonment.

In 2011 the Law Reform Commission again considered the issue of mandatory sentencing in a consultation paper devoted entirely to the issue.[47] It set out the arguments against mandatory sentences, including that:

---

[46] This was explained eloquently by Lord Irvine of Lairg Q.C. (HL Hansard, November 6, 1989, Col. 521): "A mercy killing is of a different moral order from a sadistic sex-based child murder. Where murder has a much more extended definition so that the mental element is satisfied by an intention to cause serious bodily harm, combined if need be with an awareness of the possibility of death, I would suggest that it is beyond argument that murder embraces such a multitude of diverse sins that a single mandatory life sentence must be inappropriate." A similar comment was made by Keane C.J. (writing extra-judicially): "The time is long overdue for abolishing the mandatory life sentence in cases of murder and recognising ... that the gradations of culpability in the crime of murder are almost as infinite as the variations in the human psyche itself": "Homicide: The Mental Element" (2001) 2(1) J.S.I.J. 66 at 78.
[47] See generally, Law Reform Commission, *Consultation Paper on Mandatory Sentences* (LRC CP66–2011), and especially paras 2.89 to 2.112. See also, O'Malley, *Sentencing Law and Practice*, 2nd edn (Dublin: Thomson Round Hall, 2006), pp.451–452.

(1) they preclude judicial discretion and give rise to disproportionate sentencing;
(2) there is no incentive for entering a guilty plea;
(3) they cause a transfer of discretion from courts to prosecutors;
(4) They amount to a "one-strike" rule as they do not make an exception for first-time offenders;
(5) those convicted can be at the lower end of criminal activity as criminal masterminds distance themselves from the activity;
(6) their deterrent effect is questionable.

However, this time the Commission came down in favour of mandatory sentencing for murder, commenting that mandatory sentences are appropriate for offences at the highest end of the criminal calendar which were previously punishable by death. Indeed, it added that there was a good argument that the principle of proportionality requires the mandatory life sentence to be reserved for the most serious criminal offence. However, it highlighted that every person convicted of murder receives a life sentence, regardless of his circumstances or the facts of the murder. It also questioned whether "a decision regarding release that is made by the Executive without any input from the sentencing court, often many years after the decision regarding sentencing has been made"[48] is fully compatible with the ECHR. It therefore provisionally recommended that the mandatory sentencing regime for murder should provide that, on the sentencing date, the court should recommend a minimum sentence of imprisonment that should be served taking into account all the circumstances. This means that while murder would retain a mandatory life sentence, the actual amount of time spent in prison would be at the discretion of the sentencing judge and would vary from defendant to defendant depending on his circumstances.

The constitutionality of the mandatory sentence for murder, and its compatibility with the ECHR, were both challenged in the recent Supreme Court decision of *Lynch v The Minister for Justice*.[49] Murray C.J. gave the unanimous decision of the court upholding mandatory sentences as both constitutional and compatible with the ECHR. Two arguments were put forward challenging the constitutionality of mandatory sentences for murder. The first was based on the doctrine of proportionality. It was submitted that the imposition of a mandatory sentence offended against the doctrine because no account was taken of the various mitigating or aggravating factors attaching to each case. This was rejected by Murray C.J. who emphasised that the crime of murder is of exceptional gravity and one which the legislature is entitled to mark with punishment at the highest level. The doctrine of proportionality is therefore not infringed by the imposition of a mandatory life sentence on a defendant who, by definition, has unlawfully killed with the intention of killing or causing serious injury. Such defendants can be differentiated from other defendants who have committed homicide.

The second constitutional argument was that mandatory sentencing contravened the separation of powers as the executive, and not the judiciary, determines the length of time actually spent in custody. The Supreme Court held that a life sentence is

---

[48] Law Reform Commission, *Consultation Paper on Mandatory Sentences* (LRC CP66–2011), p.5, para.25.
[49] [2010] IESC 34.

wholly punitive and does not incorporate any element of preventative detention. As such, deciding to release such a prisoner on licence does not amount to a termination or determination of the sentence judicially imposed. Any release on licence is the grant of a privilege in the exercise of an autonomous, discretionary power vested in the executive and this is in accordance with the doctrine of the separation of powers.

The Supreme Court also rejected the challenge to mandatory life sentences on ECHR grounds. The appellants claimed that a system whereby the length of time actually served in custody is determined by the executive breached art.5 of the ECHR which guarantees the right to liberty and security of person and the lawful detention of a person after conviction by a competent court. Murray C.J. analysed ECHR jurisprudence in some detail and noted that the imposition of a life sentence is not per se prohibited by the ECHR.[50] He added that the possibility of review of a life sentence with a view to its commutation by the executive was also permissible and indeed may actually be required to prevent incompatibility with art.3.[51]

The issue of mandatory life sentences has also been the subject of recent public debate in England and Wales. The Homicide Review Advisory Group, a body made up of judges and academics issued a statement in December 2011 saying that mandatory life sentences are unjust and outdated.[52] It highlighted that mercy killings and serial killings attract the same mandatory penalty and referred to research carried out in 2010 by the Nuffield Foundation indicating that there is no general public support for mandatory life sentences for murder.[53] The Nuffield Foundation Report concluded that:

> "There is clarity with respect to the issue of the mandatory life sentence for murder ... Advocates of the mandatory sentence of life imprisonment have long argued that this sentence is important because of the high level of public support which it attracts. We have provided in this report a scientific evaluation of the degree of public support for the mandatory life sentence. It is clear that whatever other arguments may be advanced for applying a mandatory life sentence to all offenders convicted of murder, regardless of the circumstances of the offence, strong public support is not one of them."[54]

The murder–manslaughter distinction

There is ongoing debate concerning whether the law should merge both murder and manslaughter into a single offence of unlawful killing. Suggestions of a merger are not new. In *Hyam v DPP*[55] Lord Kilbrandon said:

---

[50] *Kafkaris v Cyprus* [2008] ECHR 143 (App No. 21906/04).
[51] *Kafkaris v Cyprus* [2008] ECHR 143 (App No. 21906/04). Article 3 prohibits torture and inhuman or degrading treatment or punishment.
[52] December 6, 2011. Statement reported in the *Guardian* newspaper and BBC News.
[53] Mitchell and Roberts, *Public Opinion and Sentencing for Murder: An Empirical Investigation of Public Knowledge and Attitudes in England and Wales* (2010).
[54] Mitchell and Roberts, *Public Opinion and Sentencing for Murder: An Empirical Investigation of Public Knowledge and Attitudes in England and Wales* (2010), p.42.
[55] [1975] A.C. 55.

"There does not appear to be any good reason why the crimes of murder and manslaughter should not both be abolished, and the single crime of unlawful homicide substituted; one case will differ from another in gravity, and that can be taken care of by variation of sentences downwards from life imprisonment. It is no longer true, if ever it were true, to say that murder as we now define it is necessarily the most heinous example of unlawful homicide."[56]

Proponents of a merger argue that the distinction between murder and manslaughter is often arbitrary and unclear and that a less serious murder might well deserve to be treated more leniently than a more serious case of manslaughter. "'More serious' and 'less serious' killings do not drop neatly into the murder/manslaughter categories in practice."[57] The latter point was made by Finlay C.J. when he noted that manslaughter may be as serious as, or even more serious than, the crime of murder:

"Having regard to the multiple factors which enter into consideration of sentence in the case of a homicide, there would not appear to me to be any grounds for a general presumption that the crime of manslaughter may not, having regard to its individual facts and particular circumstances be in many instances, from a sentencing point of view, as serious as, or more serious than, the crime of murder."[58]

The same point was made by Keane C.J. writing extra-judicially:

"Some would say that the time has come to recognise that unlawful killings may range all the way across the spectrum from the cold blooded act of terrorism which kills tens or even hundreds ... to the impetuous assault which results in a tragedy never intended by the assailant. Why should not the law provide for one crime of homicide and allow the courts then to impose the appropriate sentence taking into account all the circumstances which led to the death?"[59]

It is also argued that there would be practical benefits to a merger. Carney J. has noted that, in the overwhelming majority of murder trials, the defence accepts that the accused unlawfully killed the deceased and would be willing to plead to manslaughter. However, defendants are unwilling to plead to murder because of its mandatory life sentence. He argues that:

"[T]he fact that the unlawful killing of the deceased by the accused is scarcely ever in issue suggests that if the crimes of murder and manslaughter were merged in a crime to be known as unlawful homicide, or unlawful killing, the contested murder trial might become a rarity and almost a thing of the past. There would be no reason why there should not be a plea of guilty in nearly every case."[60]

---

[56] [1975] A.C. 55 at 98.
[57] Ivana Bacik, "'If It Ain't Broke' – a Critical View of the Law Reform Commission Consultation Paper on Homicide: The Mental Element in Murder" (2002) 12(1) I.C.L.J. 6 at 7.
[58] *People v Conroy (No. 2)* [1989] I.R. 160 at 163.
[59] The Hon. Mr. Justice Ronan Keane, "Homicide: The Mental Element in Murder" (2001) 2(1) J.S.I.J. 66 at 78.
[60] The Hon. Mr Justice Paul Carney, "Decriminalising Murder?" (2003) 8(6) *Bar Review* 254 at 254.

Homicide 111

Carney J. goes on to argue that this would have significant benefits in clearing backlogs before the criminal courts and creating substantial savings. He also suggests that a desirable side effect would be to spare the relatives of victims the disappointment and trauma occasioned to them by a manslaughter verdict, suggesting that relatives often feel that a finding of manslaughter means that they have not "got justice". A related argument has been made by Victim Support in England and Wales: that there is an advantage to ridding the law of the adversarial dimension to trials caused by the attempt of defendants to reduce their crime from murder to manslaughter, which often involves a bid to blame the deceased as part of a defence.[61]

The Law Reform Commission, on the other hand, has recommended that the distinction be retained.[62] It argued that the law should distinguish between more serious and less serious killings, and that a merged offence would "lump together into a single category the most cold-blooded killers with the least blameworthy manslaughters".[63] The Law Reform Commission took the view that murder is popularly understood as the most serious crime and carries a unique stigma which emphasises the gravity of the offence and may also have a deterrent value. It also expressed concern that abolishing the distinction would effectively shift the centre of gravity of homicide trials to the sentencing stage, marginalising the role of the jury. Finally, it noted that many of the difficulties associated with the distinction could be dealt with by means other than abolition, including the removal of the mandatory life sentence for murder.

The "unique stigma" rationale for maintaining the crime of murder was one of the main reasons given by the Law Commission of England and Wales for rejecting abolition of the distinction. "It would very likely be seen as a signal that the law did not regard murder as a specially or uniquely grave crime. It is wrong to give out such a signal."[64]

It was also one of the reasons that New South Wales legislators have preserved murder as a separate crime to manslaughter. The Attorney General of New South Wales remarked:

> "In our culture, to describe someone as a 'murderer' is to employ the most bitterly and effectively stigmatising epithet available in the language. To remove that term from the law would be to risk possible public misapprehension and to invite the criticism (rightly or wrongly) that the moral force of the law was being lessened."[65]

---

[61] The Law Commission (CP No. 177), *A New Homicide Act for England and Wales?* (2005), para.2.33.
[62] Law Reform Commission, *Consultation Paper on Homicide: The Mental Element in Murder* (LRC CP17–2001). The Law Reform Commission, *Report on Homicide: Murder and Involuntary Manslaughter* (LRC 87–2008) reiterated the arguments set out in its consultation paper seven years previously and again firmly recommended that the distinction should be retained, mainly because of what it perceived as the moral distinction between those who commit murder and those who commit manslaughter. See generally, Ch.1.
[63] Law Reform Commission, *Consultation Paper on Homicide: The Mental Element in Murder* (LRC CP17–2001), p.3.
[64] The Law Commission (CP No. 177), *A New Homicide Act for England and Wales?* (2005), para.2.31.
[65] Mr Frank Walker Q.C., Attorney General of New South Wales, in 1982. Carney J. has questioned

Michael McDowell SC, when Minister for Justice, was of the view that abolishing the murder–manslaughter distinction would simply move lengthy hearings from the trial to the sentencing stage:

> "The suggestion that amalgamating the crimes of murder and manslaughter into a crime of homicide would lead to more pleas of 'guilty' thereby saving court time ignores several fundamental problems. To take away from juries the function of deciding whether a crime of homicide was intentional but to allow a judge alone to impose radically different sentences by reference to a judge-only determination of the same factual issue decision might be convenient but would be very doubtful in constitutional terms. The question of intention is a central question of fact which must surely be left to juries. Otherwise trial by jury in homicide cases would be reduced to simply deciding the identity of the culprit and causation. Pleas of guilty under such a system would be followed by hugely lengthy hearings on sentencing in which the accused, once convicted, would still be 'on the back foot' disputing the issue of intention. Instead of solving a problem we would just be moving it around."[66]

Should the mens rea for murder include an intention to cause serious injury?

As we have seen, under s.4 of the Criminal Justice Act 1964 a conviction for murder is not confined to those who have an intention to kill but includes those who merely have an intention to cause serious injury. The Law Reform Commission considered this issue in 2001[67] and again in 2008 when it set out arguments for and against the retention of the "serious injury" rule.[68]

The following were some arguments in favour of abolishing the "serious injury" rule:

(1) where causing serious injury is the most intended the fault element does not correspond with the outcome (death);[69]
(2) the law should differentiate between the moral culpability of those who intend causing death and those who intend causing serious injury;

"… whether this order of expenditure [contested murder trials] continues to be justified because our culture has bestowed a particular mystique, gravity and aura of heinousness on the word 'murder' over and above the word 'killing'". The Hon. Mr Justice Paul Carney, "Decriminalising Murder?" (2003) 8(6) *Bar Review* 254 at 255. Bacik has argued that it would be possible to accommodate the "unique stigma attaching to murder" argument by creating different degrees of a single homicide offence: Bacik, "Law Reform Commission Consultation Paper on Homicide: The Mental Element in Murder" (2000) 22 D.U.L.J. 264 at 265.

[66] Address to the First Edward O'Donnell McDevitt Annual Symposium, "Sentencing in Ireland", February 28, 2004.
[67] Law Reform Commission, *Homicide: The Mental Element in Murder* (LRC CP17–2001).
[68] Law Reform Commission, *Homicide: Murder and Involuntary Manslaughter* (LRC 87–2008), paras 2.60 to 2.67.
[69] This was the point made by Robert Goff, "The mental element in the crime of murder" (1988) 104 L.Q.R. 30 at 48: "The most fundamental objection is the crime of murder is concerned with unlawful killing of a particularly serious kind; and it seems very strange that a man should be called a murderer even though not only did he not intend to kill the victim, but he may even have intended that he should not die."

Homicide 113

(3) the crime of manslaughter is adequate to deal with cases of intentionally causing serious injury which result in death;
(4) "serious injury" has not been defined and is too vague;
(5) juries may be unwilling to convict people of murder who intended to cause serious injury falling short of death.

The arguments in favour of retaining the "serious injury" rule included:

(1) the fragility of the human body means that death can often result from serious injury and those who intend to cause serious injury demonstrate sufficient disregard for human life to make it morally justifiable to convict them of murder should death result;
(2) related to the above is the idea that a person cannot claim not to have believed that his action could have had a fatal result since knowledge of the frailty of the body is basic to the human experience;
(3) if the "serious injury" rule were to be abolished it would make it more difficult for prosecutions for murder to succeed since defendants could claim that they merely intended to cause serious harm to the deceased but did not intend to cross the line into causing death.

In both 2001 and 2008 the Law Reform Commission recommended that intention to cause serious injury be retained as an element of the mens rea for murder[70]:

> "[T]hose who intentionally inflict serious injury on others cannot deny the latent knowledge they possess about the fragility of the human body. These defendants display a culpability very close to the culpability of intentional killers. Therefore, they deserve to be guilty of murder if death results from the serious injuries they inflict with intent."[71]

The Law Commission for England and Wales dealt with the issue by recommending that the law of homicide be restructured by splitting murder into first degree murder (intention to kill or intention to cause serious injury together with an awareness of a serious risk of causing death) and second degree murder (intention to cause serious injury or intention to cause some injury or risk of injury together with an awareness of a serious risk of causing death).[72]

Should the mens rea for murder be expanded to include other fault elements?

This issue was examined by the Law Reform Commission in 2001 and it recommended that the fault element for murder be expanded to include elements of foresight of a

---

[70] Law Reform Commission, *Homicide: Murder and Involuntary Manslaughter* (LRC 87–2008), paras 3.40 to 3.45.
[71] Law Reform Commission, *Homicide: Murder and Involuntary Manslaughter* (LRC 87–2008), para.3.44.
[72] The Law Commission (Law Com. No. 304), *Murder, Manslaughter and Infanticide* (2006).

risk of death resulting which would not amount to intention.[73] This would embrace reckless killings manifesting an extreme indifference to human life and was based on a section of the American Penal Code. The Law Reform Commission reiterated this recommendation in 2008, explaining that there were actions outside the current legal definition of "murder" that it regarded as morally culpable and deserving of being treated as murder.[74] This definition would include, for example, arsonists and terrorists intending to damage property but indifferent as to whether fatalities would result. This recommendation was criticised by Bacik when it was first made in 2001.[75] She said that the proposal would represent a "drastic departure"[76] from the present law and that the application of s.4(2) of the Criminal Justice Act 1964, which contains the rebuttable presumption that a person intends the natural and probable consequences of his conduct, would adequately deal with the terrorist bomb scenario. Bacik goes on to argue that the proposal would make it much more difficult to justify a distinction between murder and manslaughter and would make the category of murder absurdly broad.

The Law Reform Commission considered recommending a completely new homicide structure based on varying degrees of culpability.[77] It considered an offence of first degree murder where a person killed intentionally or where there was an intention to do serious injury, together with an awareness of serious risk of causing death. This would attract a mandatory life sentence. Second degree murder, attracting a discretionary maximum penalty of life imprisonment, would arise where there was an intention to cause serious injury or an intention to cause injury or a risk of injury coupled with an awareness of a serious risk of causing death or where there was a partial defence to first degree murder. However, the Law Reform Commission ultimately decided that this would be too radical a departure.

Manslaughter

Murder is committed when the accused intends to kill or cause serious injury and death results. Manslaughter, which is also an offence at common law, is committed when unlawful death is caused but the mens rea falls short of that for murder. This is the case either where there is no intention to kill or cause serious injury, or where there is such an intention but culpability is lessened by defences of provocation, excessive self defence or diminished responsibility.

The lower level of culpability is reflected in a lower level of punishment. Manslaughter, unlike murder, does not carry a mandatory life sentence. While it

---

[73] Law Reform Commission, *Homicide: The Mental Element in Murder* (LRC CP17–2001), pp.43–63.
[74] Law Reform Commission, *Homicide: Murder and Involuntary Manslaughter* (LRC 87–2008), pp.51–62.
[75] Ivana Bacik, "'If It Ain't Broke' – A Critical View of the Law Reform Commission Consultation Paper on Homicide: the Mental Element in Murder" (2002) 12(1) I.C.L.J. 6.
[76] Bacik, "'If It Ain't Broke' – A Critical View of the Law Reform Commission Consultation Paper on Homicide: the Mental Element in Murder" (2002) 12(1) I.C.L.J. 6 at 6.
[77] The Law Commission of England and Wales recommended re-structuring the law of homicide along similar lines: Law Commission for England and Wales (Law Com. No. 304), *Murder, Manslaughter and Infanticide* (2006).

carries a maximum penalty of life imprisonment, in practice sentences tend to be substantially lower. In fact, it is not unusual for suspended sentences to be imposed for manslaughter convictions where there are mitigating circumstances.

Manslaughter has never been defined by statute and covers a wide variety of killings, from the deliberate to the accidental, making it impossible to offer a single, comprehensive definition of the crime. Instead, it is customary to divide manslaughter into a number of categories:

(1) where A kills B intending to kill or cause serious injury but where the defence of *provocation* applies;
(2) where A kills B intending to kill or cause serious injury believing he was acting in self defence but where the force used was excessive (*excessive self defence*);
(3) where A kills B intending to kill or cause serious injury but where the defence of *diminished responsibility* applies;
(4) where A kills B without intending to kill or cause serious injury but by virtue of *criminal negligence*;
(5) where A kills B without intending to kill or cause serious injury but as a result of a *criminal and dangerous act*.[78]

Categories 1 to 3 are usually described as cases of voluntary manslaughter while categories 4 and 5 are described as cases of involuntary manslaughter. This description is misleading since the distinction has nothing to do with voluntariness or the defence of automatism. Instead, the distinction relates to whether the accused intended to kill or cause serious injury. If he did, but can rely on provocation, excessive self defence or diminished responsibility, this is voluntary manslaughter. If he did not have this intention, this is involuntary manslaughter. Categories 1, 2 and 3 are dealt with in Ch.10. Here we will analyse involuntary manslaughter.

Manslaughter by criminal negligence

This crime is committed when a person causes death by virtue of conduct which is criminally or grossly negligent: that is, so negligent that any reasonable person would have realised that the conduct created a high degree of risk of serious injury to others. This is an objective test and differs from the subjective test applied to intention and recklessness; for manslaughter by criminal negligence, it is not necessary to show that the accused realised that he was creating such a risk. It is, therefore, something of an anomaly in Irish law: an accused can be convicted of this very serious crime without having any element of subjective fault or actual awareness that he was creating a risk. Given this anomalous status, it is important to remember that criminal negligence is a much higher standard than the standard of negligence in tort.

---

[78] Certain academics add a further category: where A kills B without intending to kill or cause serious injury but as the result of an *assault*. See, e.g. Peter Charleton, *Criminal Law – Cases and Materials* (London: Butterworths, 1992), p.356. However, more recently this assault category has been treated by academics and by the Law Reform Commission as a subset of the criminal and dangerous act category and this is how it will be treated in this chapter.

The leading Irish case on criminal negligence is *People (AG) v Dunleavy*.[79] Here the accused was charged with manslaughter, having killed a cyclist while driving without lights on the wrong side of a busy city road. The jury was directed that it was to decide whether the conduct of the accused showed such a disregard for the lives and safety of others as to amount to a crime deserving punishment, but was not explicitly directed as to what degree of negligence was needed. The Court of Criminal Appeal held that this direction was inadequate: the jury should have been directed as to the different degrees of negligence and as to the very high degree of negligence required in the case of manslaughter. The jury should be told that the negligence required goes beyond a mere matter of compensation, showing a disregard for the life and safety of others, and that the negligence required must be:

> "[O]f a very high degree and of such a character that any reasonable driver, endowed with ordinary road sense and in full possession of his faculties, would realise, if he thought at all, that by driving in the manner which occasioned the fatality he was, without lawful excuse, incurring, in a high degree, the risk of causing substantial personal injury to others."[80]

This definition is an extension of the definition which was previously laid down in the case of *R. v Bateman*.[81] In that case a doctor was charged with the manslaughter of a woman who had died while giving birth. Hewart C.J. stated that the jury should be told that the negligence required "went beyond a mere matter of compensation ... and showed such disregard for the life and safety of others as to amount to a crime against the State and conduct deserving punishment", but did not also require that the jury be directed as to the very high degree of negligence required.[82]

Although *Attorney General v Dunleavy* sets a high standard for criminal negligence manslaughter, there have been several cases since where this standard has been met. For example, in *Attorney General v Crosby*[83] a motorist was found guilty of manslaughter where he was very drunk, approached a bridge at high speed on the wrong side of the road, and struck three pedestrians, killing one. Similarly, in *People v O'Neill*[84] a motorist was found guilty of manslaughter where he caused an accident by driving at excessive speed, on the wrong side of the road, approaching a blind bend.

The most recent Irish case in this area, although it dates from 1999, is *DPP v Cullagh*.[85] The appellant was convicted of manslaughter at a fairground in Tipperary which he owned and operated. The victim was killed when the chairoplane she was being carried in became detached from the metal arm holding it to the central equipment, causing her to fall to the ground. At trial it was shown that the ride was over 20 years old, had not been properly inspected or maintained, had lain in a field for several years and was in appalling condition. The Court of Criminal Appeal approved of the trial judge's direction that the standard of negligence required

---

[79] [1948] I.R. 95.
[80] [1948] I.R. 95 at 102 per Davitt J.
[81] (1925) 19 Cr. App. R. 8.
[82] (1925) 19 Cr. App. R. 8 at 13.
[83] (1961) 1 Frewen 231.
[84] [1964] Ir. Jur. Rep. 1.
[85] Unreported, ex tempore, Court of Criminal Appeal, Murphy J., March 18, 1999.

was gross negligence, not the ordinary standard of civil negligence, and that mere inadvertence, which would attract liability in a civil action, was insufficient. The court also noted that the test was objective, acknowledging that the particular factor that caused the death would not have been apparent to the defendant but going on to say that he should have been aware of it nevertheless, particularly since he "was making available for entertainment equipment which was of its nature to some degree hazardous and undoubtedly old".

The *Dunleavy* test in Irish law is a broad one encompassing risk of death or substantial personal injury but English law takes a narrower approach requiring risk of death. Risk of serious injury does not suffice. The Law Commission of England and Wales reiterated this requirement in 2006 and stated that to do otherwise would be to make the offence of manslaughter over-broad. It reasoned that if a conviction for manslaughter is to be justified where a person is subjectively unaware of any risk, then the risk must be one of death.[86]

The leading English case on criminal negligence manslaughter is *R. v Adomako*.[87] The appellant was an anaesthetist who failed to notice for six minutes that a tube supplying oxygen to his patient had become disconnected. The patient suffered a heart attack and died as a result. The appellant was convicted of manslaughter by gross negligence and appealed on the basis that the trial judge had misdirected the jury on the definition of "gross negligence". The House of Lords held that the appellant was properly convicted. According to Lord Mackay L.C., the ingredients of gross negligence manslaughter were fourfold:

(1) the defendant must owe the victim a duty of care;
(2) there must be a breach of that duty;
(3) the breach must cause the death of the victim;
(4) the breach must amount to gross negligence.

In relation to the fourth point, Lord Mackay stated that the jury should be told to consider whether the defendant's conduct was "so bad" as to deserve a criminal conviction, not merely to require the payment of compensation:

> "[G]ross negligence [depends] on the seriousness of the breach of the duty committed by the defendant in all the circumstances in which he was placed when it occurred. The jury will have to consider whether, having regard to the risk of death involved, the conduct of the defendant was so bad in all the circumstances as to amount in the jury's judgment to a criminal act or omission."[88]

This definition was criticised by counsel for the appellant on the basis that it was circular, since the jury was being told in effect to convict of a crime if they thought a crime had been committed. Lord Mackay acknowledged that there was an element of circularity in the definition, but stated that whether negligence rises to the standard

---

[86] Law Commission of England and Wales (Law Com. No. 304), *Murder, Manslaughter and Infanticide* (2006), para.3.58.
[87] [1995] 1 A.C. 171.
[88] [1995] 1 A.C. 171 at 187.

of gross negligence is a question of degree, and ultimately the jury must decide whether the negligence involved is such that it should attract a criminal sanction.

The case of *R. v Wacker*[89] established that a duty of care can exist even where the deceased and the defendant have engaged in unlawful activity together. Here the defendant was a lorry driver engaged in smuggling 60 Chinese illegal immigrants from Rotterdam to Dover. The immigrants were placed in the container and, in order to ensure they would not be discovered by anybody overhearing the noise of their conversation, it was necessary to close an air vent for the ferry crossing. Upon arrival in Dover customs officials opened the container and discovered that 58 of the immigrants had suffocated. The defendant was convicted of 58 counts of manslaughter. The Court of Appeal held that the criminal law would not refuse to hold one person liable for the death of another simply because they were engaged in unlawful activity at the time or because the deceased might have accepted some degree of risk to further the unlawful activity. It stated that the defendant had voluntarily assumed the duty of care for the safety of the immigrants and that he was aware that he was the only person whose actions could prevent suffocation by the stowaways.

An attempt to distinguish *Wacker* was made in *R. v Willoughby*.[90] The appellant was the owner of a disused public house which was destroyed by fire and an explosion. The prosecution claimed that the appellant had hired a local taxi driver to help him to set fire to the building for insurance purposes. The resulting explosion caused the building to collapse and the local man was killed and the appellant was found outside the premises in a state of shock. He was convicted of manslaughter. The appellant said that he and the deceased had gone to the building to check for squatters and that he had gone back outside to look for a torch while the deceased had remained inside. Counsel for the appellant argued that *Wacker* could be distinguished as being a relationship between vulnerable immigrants and a driver who had control over their ventilation. Here, it was submitted, both men were involved in a dangerous operation as part of insurance fraud and they were of equal degree. The Court of Appeal, however, held that the appellant did owe a duty to the deceased as he was the owner of the public house who stood to gain financially from the enterprise. He had enlisted the deceased and the deceased's role was to spread the petrol inside the premises.

R. v Misra[91] was an unsuccessful challenge to *Adomako*. Here the deceased died of toxic shock syndrome four days after an operation on his knee. The appellants were doctors involved in his post-operative care and each was convicted of manslaughter by gross negligence. It was alleged that neither doctor had appreciated that the deceased was seriously ill. Blood tests had not been ordered and help was not sought

---

[89] [2002] EWCA Crim 1944.
[90] [2004] EWCA Crim 3365. This case could also have been presented as unlawful act manslaughter but the prosecution chose to characterise it instead as gross negligence manslaughter. Indeed, the Court of Appeal commented that it was entirely unnecessary to have recourse to the principles of manslaughter by gross negligence as it was a straightforward case of manslaughter, death having resulted from the unlawful and dangerous act of spreading petrol pursuant to a plan to set fire to the building. The court emphasised that the categories of manslaughter are not mutually exclusive.
[91] [2004] EWCA Crim 2375.

from senior colleagues, despite input from nursing staff that this was necessary. Blood tests ordered by another doctor were entirely disregarded by the defendants who never made any attempt to review the results. The day of the deceased's death, as his condition worsened, one of the defendants misread his fluid chart and failed to look at his observation chart. He went off duty saying that he thought his patient had improved and did not participate in the ward round. When the other defendant came on duty he did not ask to see the blood test results as he presumed he would be told by the laboratory if there was anything abnormal in them. Expert evidence was given that the quality of care provided did not even begin to approach the standard expected of doctors at their level.

The defendants argued that the *Adomako* test for gross negligence was a circular one (as one ingredient was that the jury had to decide whether the conduct amounted to a crime) and therefore gross negligence manslaughter was an offence lacking certainty. They invoked art.6 of the ECHR (the right to a fair trial) and art.7 (prohibiting retrospective criminalisation) but to no avail. The Court of Appeal rejected the uncertainty argument, stating that the question for the jury was not whether the negligence was gross and whether, additionally, it was a crime but whether the behaviour was so grossly negligent that it amounted to a crime. The contrast was between negligence which would not be a crime at all and gross negligence which involves the commission of a criminal offence. The Court of Appeal held that:

> "In our judgment the law is clear. The ingredients of the offence have been clearly defined, and the principles decided in the House of Lords in *Adomako*. They involve no uncertainty. The hypothetical citizen, seeking to know his position, would be advised that, assuming he owed a duty of care to the deceased which he had negligently broken, and that death resulted, he would be liable to conviction for manslaughter if, on the available evidence, the jury was satisfied that his negligence was gross. A doctor would be told that grossly negligent treatment of a patient which exposed him or her to death, and caused it, would constitute manslaughter."[92]

The court concluded that art.7 demanded sufficient rather than absolute certainty and that the degree of vagueness was acceptable. This case has been criticised by academics as failing to clarify the law in this area.[93] Quick argues that the current test for gross negligence manslaughter is unclear, unprincipled and often unfair and states that the Court of Appeal's reasoning is unconvincing. He points out that an application for leave to appeal to the House of Lords was rejected and states that this was a regrettable missed opportunity to clarify the gross negligence test once and for all.

R. v Evans[94] concerned the thorny question of making those who supply drugs to a deceased liable for their manslaughter. Manslaughter by criminal and dangerous act on similar facts will be discussed below, but in *Evans* the issue was treated as an example of gross negligence manslaughter and the defendant, and her mother, were

---
[92] [2004] EWCA Crim 2375 at para.64.
[93] See Oliver Quick, "Medicine, mistakes and manslaughter: a criminal combination?" (2010) C.L.J. 186.
[94] [2009] EWCA Crim 650.

both convicted. The defendant was the older half-sister of the deceased, a teenage girl who had been released on licence from prison. The deceased and the defendant and their mother were all chronic heroin addicts. The defendant sourced heroin from her usual supplier and gave some to the deceased who self-injected and later began to exhibit the signs of an overdose. The defendant had herself taken a heroin overdose in the past and knew that her half-sister was very ill. Both the defendant and her mother, who was also present in the house, were too afraid to call emergency services as they thought they would get into trouble and that the deceased would be re-imprisoned. They decided to let the teenager sleep and after a few hours they believed she was recovering. They themselves slept in her bedroom to look after her but the following morning they realised she was dead. The Court of Appeal emphasised that, in order to find the defendant culpable, in circumstances where the facts indicated that the defendant had omitted to do something, a legal duty to act must be established.[95] The court characterised the issue as follows:

> "The question in this appeal is not whether the appellant may be guilty of manslaughter for having been concerned in the supply of the heroin which caused the deceased's death. It is whether, notwithstanding that their relationship lacked the features of familial duty or responsibility which marked her mother's relationship with the deceased, she was under a duty to take reasonable steps for the safety of the deceased once she appreciated that the heroin she procured for her was having a potentially fatal impact on her health."[96]

The Court of Appeal held that:

> "The duty necessary to found gross negligence manslaughter is plainly not confined to cases of familial or professional relationship between one defendant and the deceased ... [F]or the purposes of gross negligence manslaughter, when a person has created or contributed to the creation of a state of affairs which he knows, or ought reasonably to know, has become life threatening, a consequent duty on him to act by taking reasonable steps to save the other's life will normally arise."

The court indicated that, without the defendant's involvement in supplying the heroin to the deceased, there was no duty to act to save her half-sister even after she had become aware of the effect of the heroin on the deceased.

This decision has been the subject of much academic commentary.[97] Rogers argues that *R. v Evans* is fundamentally inconsistent with *R. v Kennedy (No. 2)*[98] where the House of Lords held that a drug supplier would not be guilty of criminal and

---

[95] See discussion of acts and omissions in Ch.3.
[96] [2009] EWCA Crim 650 at para.20.
[97] See Jonathan Rogers, "Death, Drugs and Duties" [2009] *Archbold News* 6; Glenys Williams, "Gross Negligence Manslaughter and duty of care in 'drugs' cases: R. v Evans" [2009] Crim. L.R. 631; David Ormerod, "Case comment R. v Evans (Gemma): manslaughter – gross negligence – deceased supplied by defendant with heroin which proved fatal" [2009] Crim. L.R. 661.
[98] [2008] 1 A.C. 269. Discussed below under criminal and dangerous act manslaughter.

dangerous act manslaughter where the deceased had injected himself with the drug. This was because the deceased's injecting of the drug breaks the chain of causation. Rogers argues that in *Evans* the deceased had similarly broken the chain of causation by taking the drugs. He suggests that *Evans* creates a disincentive for drug suppliers to stay with their clients after drugs have been taken because it is only when the supplier knows or should reasonably know that the client has become seriously ill that the duty arises. This means that friends and families of drug addicts who supply them with drugs are much more likely to be criminalised than more professional drug suppliers because they are much more likely to have contact with them after the drug taking has taken place. "Any policy based reasoning which accepts that the dealer, who knowingly supplies potentially lethal drugs for profit, should not be guilty of any form of manslaughter when a client dies – but which tolerates the punishment of any one else who was involved with the victim – is seriously flawed."[99]

The Law Reform Commission considered the issue of gross negligence manslaughter in 2008.[100] It evaluated the *Dunleavy* test for gross negligence manslaughter and recommended that it should be amended to make the capacity of the accused to advert to risk or attain the expected standard a relevant factor, thereby proposing a departure from the purely objective test hitherto applied. It also considered bringing the Irish test for gross negligence manslaughter (risk of death or serious injury as per *Dunleavy*) into line with the English test (risk of death only suffices as per *Adomako* and *Misra*); however, it ultimately decided not to advise a change to the Irish test.

Manslaughter by criminal and dangerous act

Charleton explains that:

> "The doctrine of criminal and dangerous act manslaughter occurred as a development of constructive malice. In the early period of the common law any unlawful act or omission which caused the death of the victim amounted to manslaughter. The rule was subsequently modified to require the accused to be committing a criminal offence."[101]

What forms of criminal and dangerous act are included in this category of manslaughter? It is not enough for an act to be illegal or tortious: it must be criminal and objectively dangerous. This is illustrated by *Attorney General v Maher*[102] where the defendant, while driving a car without a licence, killed a man without any evidence of negligence. It was held that there was insufficient evidence to convict for manslaughter. The mere fact that the driving of the car was unlawful was not enough—it had to be shown that the act was both criminal and dangerous.

---

[99] Rogers, "Death, Drugs and Duties" [2009] *Archbold News* 6 at 7.
[100] Law Reform Commission, *Homicide: Murder and Involuntary Manslaughter* (LRC 87–2008). See generally, Ch.5.
[101] Charleton, *Criminal Law – Cases and Materials* (1992), p.363.
[102] (1937) 71 I.L.T. 60.

In *Attorney General v Crosbie and Meehan*,[103] the question of what constituted a criminal and dangerous act was again considered. The victim, a docker, died from a knife wound during an altercation in a crowded room. It was not clear how the wound was inflicted or with what intention: the defendant claimed that he had brought the knife in self defence and said that, while waving the knife around to frighten off attackers, he must have accidentally hit the deceased. There were over 500 people in the room when the altercation broke out. The Court of Criminal Appeal held that this could amount to manslaughter by criminal and dangerous act. If the knife was produced to frighten or intimidate, and not in self defence, then the crime of assault was committed. Waving the knife around in a crowded room was an objectively dangerous act and if death resulted that death would be manslaughter as a result of a criminal and dangerous act. Kenny J. held as follows:

> "When a killing resulted from an unlawful act, the old law was that the unlawful quality of the act was sufficient to constitute the offence of manslaughter. The correct view, however, is that the act causing death must be unlawful and dangerous to constitute the offence of manslaughter. The dangerous quality of the act must however be judged by objective standards and it is irrelevant that the accused person did not think that the act was dangerous."[104]

In *R. v Pagett*,[105] the accused was convicted of manslaughter when he forcefully used a girl as a shield to protect himself from shots fired by the police, causing her to be killed by police bullets. The court held that the accused had committed two unlawful and dangerous acts: the act of firing at the police and the act of using the girl as a shield, by force and against her will, when the police might fire in his direction in self defence. Either act was deemed to constitute the actus reus of manslaughter.

The relatively recent case of *DPP v Horgan*[106] again held that for an act to be "unlawful" it must constitute a criminal offence and dangerousness must be considered objectively. The defendant was convicted of the rape and manslaughter of a woman who had been walking her dogs in a park. Her body was found concealed in undergrowth and a post-mortem revealed that she had suffered compression to her neck, probably as the result of an arm lock. Kearns J. summarised the Irish position as follows:

> "In Ireland a conviction for unlawful and dangerous act manslaughter (where the unlawful act is an assault) arises where:—
> (a) the act which causes death constitutes a criminal offence and poses the risk of bodily harm to another;

---

[103] [1966] I.R. 490.
[104] [1966] I.R. 490 at 495. *R. v Ball* [1989] Crim. L.R. 730 reiterated that the dangerousness of the act is to be judged objectively. Here the defendant had shot his neighbour who was trespassing on his land. He gave evidence that he had always kept live and blank cartridges together in the pocket of his overalls and had grabbed a handful when he picked up his gun. He claimed that he had intended only to frighten the deceased and thought he had loaded the gun with blank cartridges. The dangerous act in question was the taking of the handful of cartridges from a pocket containing both live and blank ones.
[105] (1983) 76 Cr. App. R. 279.
[106] [2007] 3 I.R. 568.

(b) the act is one which an ordinary reasonable person would consider to be dangerous, that is, likely to cause bodily harm;
(c) in this regard 'dangerousness' is to be judged objectively."[107]

An act does not become a criminal and dangerous act where the act carried out is normally lawful and becomes unlawful only because it is negligently carried out. Otherwise, every death due to careless or inconsiderate driving (which could amount to minor road traffic offences) would be manslaughter.

In *DPP v O'Donoghue*,[108] the Court of Criminal Appeal considered the type of acts that could constitute dangerous acts for the purpose of manslaughter. The applicant had been acquitted of the murder, but found guilty of the manslaughter, of an 11-year-old neighbour who had died due to neck compression when he had been caught in an arm lock. The sentencing judge had characterised the applicant's actions as horseplay rather than a violent and prolonged assault. Macken J. commented that "[h]is conclusions from the evidence that the actions of the accused could be set at the 'horseplay end of things' is also not inconsistent with the description of the same action in the evidence as being 'dangerous'".[109]

It is not necessary that the unlawful and dangerous act be aimed at or directed at the deceased. In *R. v Mitchell*[110] the accused attempted to skip a queue in a post office and hit a man who objected. The man fell against an 89-year-old woman who suffered a broken femur necessitating an operation. While recovering from surgery she died suddenly as a result of a blood clot of the left leg caused by the fracture. The accused was convicted of manslaughter.

Mitchell illustrates that a manslaughter charge can be appropriate where the accused did not intend to cause serious injury but did intend to injure. In many cases the accused will have been "unlucky", in that a seemingly minor crime will have had the unforeseen effect of the victim's death.[111] An example is *R. v Holzer*[112] where the accused got into a fight with the deceased and punched him in the face. The deceased fell backwards and hit his head on the road and later died from his injuries. The accused testified that he did not intend to cause serious injury but only to cut or bruise his lip. It was held that, unless the physical injury intended was merely trivial or negligible, such as a scuff or a slap to the hand, then assault resulting in death would be manslaughter.

The Law Reform Commission considered that the main scenario where unlawful and dangerous act manslaughter was in need of reform was in the "one punch" situation. In particular it highlighted the "shove in a queue" scenario where a minor act causes an unforeseen fatality, often because of an inherent weakness of the

---

[107] [2007] 3 I.R. 568 at 574.
[108] [2007] 2 I.R. 336.
[109] [2007] 2 I.R. 336 at 351.
[110] [1983] 2 W.L.R. 938.
[111] See *Attorney General's Reference (No. 60 of 2009) (Appleby)* (2010) 2 Cr. App. R. (S) 46 for a review and discussion of "one-punch" manslaughter cases. *R. v Folkes* [2011] EWCA Crim 325 is a recent example. See also, Barry J. Mitchell, "More thoughts about unlawful and dangerous act manslaughter and the one-punch killer" [2009] Crim. L.R. 502.
[112] [1968] V.R. 481.

deceased.[113] It recommended that a new offence called "assault causing death" be enacted which would rank below manslaughter, and recommended the following wording:

> "Assault causing death occurs where an accused commits an assault which causes death and a reasonable person would not have foreseen that death or serious injury was likely to result in the circumstances."

The Non-Fatal Offences Against the Person Act 1997 defines "assault" as intentionally or recklessly, directly or indirectly, applying force to or causing an impact on the body of another, or causing another to believe on reasonable grounds that he or she is likely immediately to be subjected to any such force or impact. Consequently, a defendant may be guilty of manslaughter even though he might not have struck the deceased but merely threatened to do so. For example, suppose that A runs towards B with a knife, shouting threats. B, trying to escape, falls and hits his head and dies soon afterwards. Since A's actions would amount to an assault, A could be convicted of manslaughter. *DPP v Daley and McGhie*[114] supports this view. In that case the defendants chased the victim and threw stones at him. In attempting to escape, he tripped and fell and was subsequently found to be dead. It was unclear whether the fatal injury had been caused by the stones or the fall. The defendants were convicted of manslaughter. On appeal to the Privy Council it was held that the trial judge was correct in directing the jury that "where one person causes in the mind of another by violence or the threat of violence a well-founded sense of danger to life or limb as to cause him to suffer or to try to escape and in the endeavour to escape he is killed, the person creating that state of mind is guilty of at least manslaughter".

The position of a drug supplier whose customer dies from taking drugs has been the subject of some comment in recent years. We have already considered, in *Evans* above, whether a drug supplier could be convicted of criminal negligence manslaughter. The House of Lords was asked to address the issue of criminal and dangerous act manslaughter in *R. v Kennedy (No. 2)*[115] where the certified point of law of general public importance was:

> "When is it appropriate to find someone guilty of manslaughter where that person has been involved in the supply of a class A controlled dug, which is then freely and voluntarily self administered by the person to whom it was supplied, and the administration of the drug then causes his death?"

The appellant lived in a hostel with the deceased and they were drinking together with another hostel resident. The deceased told the appellant that he wanted "a bit to make him sleep" and the appellant told the deceased to take care that he did not go asleep permanently. The appellant prepared a syringe of heroin and gave it to the

---

[113] Law Reform Commission, *Homicide: Murder and Involuntary Manslaughter* (LRC 87–2008). See generally, Ch.5.
[114] [1980] A.C. 237.
[115] [2008] 1 A.C. 269. See also, Jonathan Rogers, "Death, drugs and duties" [2009] *Archbold News* 6; David Ormerod, "Case Comment R. v Evans (Gemma): manslaughter – gross negligence – deceased supplied by defendant with heroin which proved fatal" [2009] Crim. L.R. 661.

deceased who injected himself and returned the empty syringe to the appellant, who then left the room. The deceased appeared to stop breathing and was later pronounced dead. The House of Lords made it clear that the case had been prosecuted on the basis of manslaughter arising out of a criminal and dangerous act and not criminal negligence. They held that the deceased was an informed adult of sound mind and therefore an autonomous being who had chosen to inject himself. The appellant had therefore not "caused" the drug to be administered. The court commented that there could be scenarios in which a drug could be jointly administered but that this was not the case here.

No Irish case has considered the drug supplier manslaughter dilemma but the Law Reform Commission recommended that where death was caused by a drug injection it should not be regarded as unlawful and dangerous act manslaughter because of the absence of causation.[116]

Death on the roads

Cases such as *Attorney General v Dunleavy*,[117] *Attorney General v Crosby*[118] and *People v O'Neill*[119] demonstrate that while killing in the course of driving may amount to manslaughter, the prosecution must show a very high standard of negligence. However, this standard is not appropriate for all cases of negligence on the roads; there is a need for an intermediate offence which will address cases where death is caused due to negligent driving which falls short of criminal negligence.

Consequently, s.53 of the Road Traffic Act 1961 creates an offence of causing death by dangerous driving. The standard of carelessness which is required for dangerous driving is intermediate, between "ordinary" negligence and criminal negligence: the test is objective and dangerous driving occurs where a person drives in a manner which a reasonable man "would clearly recognise as involving a direct and serious risk of harm to the public".[120] This test has been explicitly approved by the Court of Criminal Appeal in *DPP v Connaughton*.[121]

In deciding whether driving is dangerous, s.53 directs that all the circumstances of the case must be taken into account, including speed, the condition of the vehicle, the nature and condition of the place and the amount of traffic. This offence carries a maximum penalty of 10 years' imprisonment and often results in a custodial sentence. Hardiman J. has noted that "[e]xperience shows that it is almost unique, amongst offences not requiring a specific intent, in carrying a real possibility of a significant custodial sentence for a convicted person of good character".[122]

The Law Reform Commission considered motor manslaughter and related driving offences in 2008 and concluded that the law relating to dangerous driving

---

[116] Law Reform Commission, *Consultation Paper on Involuntary Manslaughter* (LRC CP44–2007), para.5.91. Note that the consultation paper was published before the House of Lords appeal in *R. v Kennedy (No. 2)*.
[117] [1948] I.R. 95.
[118] (1961) 1 Frewen 231.
[119] [1964] Ir. Jur. Rep. 1.
[120] *People v Quinlan* (1962) 96 I.L.T. 123 at 123 per O'Briain P.
[121] Unreported, Court of Criminal Appeal, April 5, 2001.
[122] *Bowes v DPP and McGrath v DPP* [2003] 2 I.R. 25 at 41. Hardiman J. reiterated this sentiment in *Ludlow v DPP* [2008] IESC 54.

causing death and careless driving should continue to co-exist with more serious cases of manslaughter.[123] It acknowledged that manslaughter is only ever charged where the driver's culpability is extremely high and gave examples such as death occurring during joyriding or after high levels of alcohol had been consumed. The Commission recommended that the offence of careless driving set out in s.52 of the Road Traffic Act 1961 should be amended so that a driver could be prosecuted for "careless driving causing death" rather than careless driving simpliciter where a death occurs. This offence should have a higher maximum penalty than careless driving because, although objectively culpability may be similar whether or not death is caused, the fact that a person has been killed makes careless driving causing death a more serious offence.

Suicide

Legality of suicide

Suicide itself is no longer a crime, having been decriminalised by s.2(1) of the Criminal Law (Suicide) Act 1993, a piece of legislation that recognises the absurdity of criminalising conduct which, by definition, leaves the offender beyond the jurisdiction of any court. This reform of the law is somewhat belated, coming more than 30 years after the Suicide Act 1961 which decriminalised suicide in England and Wales.

Suicide pacts

However, the decriminalising of suicide does not entirely remove the criminal law from the field of voluntary decisions to die: there are still difficulties when more than one person is involved. It is still murder to kill another intentionally, notwithstanding that the killing was done at the request and therefore with the consent of the deceased. Consent is not a defence to murder. If, therefore, a doctor administers a fatal dose of morphine with the intention of killing, that doctor is guilty of murder notwithstanding that the fatal dose was administered at the request of the patient.

This rule of law can have harsh results in the area of suicide pacts. Suppose A and B both decide to commit suicide, with each agreeing to inject each other with a fatal drug. They carry out their plan but only B dies. A is found in time and an antidote administered to him. In this jurisdiction A is guilty of murder, notwithstanding the surrounding circumstances. By comparison, in England and Wales s.4(1) of the Homicide Act 1957 recognises a lesser offence in this situation by providing that:

> It shall be manslaughter, and shall not be murder, for a person acting in pursuance of a suicide pact between him and another to kill the other or be a party to the other killing himself or being killed by a third party.

---

[123] Law Reform Commission, *Homicide: Murder and Involuntary Manslaughter* (LRC 87–2008). See generally, Ch.5.

R. v Sweeney[124] illustrates the English position. Here a man pleaded guilty to the manslaughter of his wife. His wife suffered from muscular dystrophy and he suffered from depression. They decided to commit suicide by swallowing tablets and then setting fire to their car while they were inside it. They both tried to escape from the burning car. The husband escaped with serious burns and permanent scarring but his wife was killed. The court held that even desperate people must be deterred from taking life and sentenced him to two years' imprisonment.

Assisted suicide

The position is different if the scenario is one of assisted suicide rather than involvement in a suicide pact, where A merely intends to supply B with the means to kill himself. Suppose, for example, that A sources an unusually sharp kitchen knife on the internet for B knowing that B intends to use it to commit suicide by slashing his wrists. In those circumstances it would not be appropriate to charge A with murder or manslaughter since it cannot be said that his act caused the death of B. The act which causes the death of B is the act of B himself, not the act of A. There is an intervening decision on B's part which breaks the chain of causation.

Nor, in these circumstances, would A face any criminal liability as an accessory under s.7 of the Criminal Law Act 1997 as suicide is no longer a crime.[125] Section 2(2) of the Criminal Law (Suicide) Act 1993 anticipates this situation by creating an offence of assisted suicide:

> A person who aids, abets, counsels or procures the suicide of another, or an attempt by another to commit suicide, shall be guilty of an offence and shall be liable on conviction on indictment to imprisonment for a term not exceeding fourteen years.[126]

There is no Irish authority on assisted suicide.[127] There have been a number of English cases on the topic. In *Dunbar v Plant*[128] (a civil case), it was held that a woman aided and abetted the suicide of her fiancé where they simultaneously attempted to hang themselves, she unsuccessfully. Similarly, in *R. v Wallis*[129] a defendant pleaded guilty to aiding and abetting the suicide of a flatmate in circumstances where he

---

[124] (1986) 8 Cr. App. R. (S) 419.
[125] Section 7 is limited to the case of a person who aids, abets, counsels or procures the commission of any *crime*.
[126] Since the terminology used in this section is identical to that used in s.7 of the 1997 Act, case law on what constitutes aiding, abetting, counselling or procuring under s.7 would also be relevant in this context. See also, Ch.13. Section 59(1) of the UK Coroners and Justice Act 2009 amends the Suicide Act 1961 and dispenses with the words "aids, abets, counsels or procures" in favour of the more modern concepts of assisting and encouraging.
[127] However, an Irish woman was reported to have made internet contact with David George Exoo, a prominent euthanasia campaigner and Unitarian minister from West Virginia, and paid for him to travel to Ireland and assist her with taking her own life. Exoo allegedly advised her how to commit suicide and sat beside her as she swallowed pills and put a plastic bag over her head before inhaling helium. No prosecution ever took place due to extradition difficulties: "US Judge refuses to extradite Unitarian minister", *Irish Times*, October 27, 2007.
[128] [1997] 3 W.L.R. 1261.
[129] (1983) 5 Crim. App. R. (S) 342.

bought the necessary tablets and alcohol, sat with the flatmate while she took the mixture and refrained from calling an ambulance until she was dead. The potential scope of the offence is shown by *Attorney General v Able*[130] where an injunction was sought restraining the publication of a pamphlet by the Voluntary Euthanasia Society entitled "A Guide to Self-Deliverance" which provided practical advice on killing oneself. Although the application was ultimately unsuccessful on the facts, it was accepted by Woolf J. that supplying this information could amount to an offence where: the pamphlet was supplied to a person contemplating suicide; the supplier acted with the intention of assisting or encouraging the person to commit suicide; a person did in fact read it and as a result was assisted in or encouraged to commit or attempt suicide; and that person did in fact commit or attempt suicide.

Several very high-profile cases of assisted suicide in England in recent years have necessitated the publication of policy guidelines by the Director of Public Prosecutions on the prosecution of such offences in England and Wales.

The first case was *R. (on the application of Pretty) v DPP*[131] where a woman who was suffering from motor neurone disease judicially reviewed the Director of Public Prosecutions' refusal to give an undertaking that, should her husband assist her in dying, he would not be prosecuted for aiding and abetting her suicide. She claimed that the refusal to give such an undertaking was incompatible with her rights pursuant to the ECHR. The House of Lords held that Mrs Pretty's right to life under art.2 had not been contravened as "[w]hatever the benefits which, in the view of many, attach to voluntary euthanasia, suicide, physician-assisted suicide and suicide assisted without the intervention of a physician, these are not benefits which derive protection from an article framed to protect the sanctity of life".[132] Article 3 prohibiting torture was also deemed not to have been contravened as the suffering being inflicted on Mrs Pretty derived from her disease and was not being inflicted by the Director. The House of Lords found that art.8, which provides the right to respect for private and family life, had not been infringed as the article protected personal autonomy while individuals lived their lives and there was nothing to suggest that the right extended to the choice to stop living. The court held that Mrs Pretty's rights under art.8 were not engaged at all, but that if they were, such infringement was justified under art.8(2) in order to protect vulnerable members of society.[133] Article 8(2) states that:

> There shall be no interference by a public authority with the exercise of this right except such as is in accordance with the law and is necessary in a democratic society in the interests of national security, public safely or the economic well-being of the country for the prevention of disorder or crime, for the protection of health or morals, or for the protection of the rights and freedoms of others.

---

[130] [1984] 1 Q.B. 795.
[131] [2001] UKHL 61.
[132] [2001] UKHL 61 at para.6 per Lord Bingham.
[133] Article 9 (freedom of thought) and art.14 (prohibition of discrimination) were also invoked, unsuccessfully, by lawyers for Ms Pretty.

An appeal was taken to the European Court of Human Rights where the court took a different view on art.8. It was held that art.8 had been engaged but that this interference was necessary and in pursuit of the legitimate aim of safeguarding life.[134] States are entitled to regulate activities detrimental to the life and safety of individuals. The law was designed to safeguard the weak and vulnerable and it was for states to assess the likely incidence of abuse if the general prohibition on assisted suicides was to be lifted in certain circumstances. The court explained that the blanket ban on assisted suicide was neither disproportionate nor arbitrary and pointed out that the consent of the Director of Public Prosecutions was required to prosecute such cases.

R. (on the application of Purdy) v Director of Public Prosecutions[135] was a House of Lords decision eight years later with a similar factual background. A woman with progressive multiple sclerosis sought clarification as to whether her husband would be prosecuted for assisting suicide should he assist her in travelling to Switzerland to die in a clinic there. Significantly, she did not seek immunity from prosecution but the promulgation of guidelines on the factors the Director of Public Prosecutions would take into account in exercising his discretion to prosecute.[136] The successful argument was made that, in the absence of sufficient clarity, the infringement of art.8 rights would not be "in accordance with the law" as required by art.8(2). The House of Lords agreed that the Director of Public Prosecutions must issue a policy on assisted suicide detailing the considerations to be taken into account when deciding whether to prosecute in such cases. The court preferred the European Court of Human Rights' approach in *Pretty* that these scenarios do engage art.8 and based their reasoning on the idea of autonomous choice. Baroness Hale stated that:

> "It is not for society to tell people what to value about their own lives ... If it is the Convention which is leading us to ask the Director for greater clarity, a relevant question must be in what circumstances the law is justified in interfering with a genuinely autonomous choice."[137]

She summarised her position as follows:

> "What to my mind is needed is a custom-built policy statement indicating the various factors for and against prosecution ... factors designed to distinguish between those situations in which, however tempted to assist, the prospective aider and abettor should refrain from doing so, and those situations in which he or she may fairly hope to be, if not commended, at the very least forgiven, rather than condemned, for giving assistance."[138]

---

[134] (2002) 35 E.H.R.R. 1.
[135] [2009] UKHL 45.
[136] Only 8 of the 115 known cases of assisting to die in Switzerland were referred to the DPP and none of them resulted in a prosecution, according to Lord Hope in *Purdy* [2009] UKHL 45 at para.30. See the following academic commentaries on *Purdy*: Rob Heywood, "R (on the application of Purdy) v DPP: Clarification on assisted suicide" [2010] L.Q.R. 5; Kate Greasley, "R (Purdy) v DPP and the case for wilful blindness" [2010] O.J.L.S. 301; Michael Hirst, "Suicide in Switzerland: complicity in England?" [2009] Crim. L.R. 335; Alex Solomon, "Assisted suicide and identifying the public interest in the decision to prosecute" [2010] Crim. L.R. 737.
[137] [2009] UKHL 45 at para.68.
[138] [2009] UKHL 45 at para.86.

The Director of Public Prosecutions for England and Wales issued his interim policy for prosecutors in respect of cases of encouraging or assisting suicide in September 2009 and the final policy in February 2010.[139] The policy document sets out 16 factors tending in favour of prosecution and six factors tending against prosecution, although it is made clear that these factors are not exhaustive. A number of anti-prosecution factors were dropped from the interim policy statement. For example, the fact that the deceased may have tried to take his own life on a previous occasion was removed as some unsuccessful attempts at suicide are cries for help rather than evidence of a wish to die. That the deceased was a close friend or family member of the defendant was also dropped due to concerns that family members may have the most influence (whether for good or bad) over such persons and can more easily manipulate vulnerable persons.

It is interesting to note that there is no legal exemption for physician-assisted suicide under English law. The House of Lords Select Committee on Medical Ethics, which reported in 1994, was of the view that "[w]e identify no circumstances in which assisted suicide should be permitted, nor do we see any reason to distinguish between the act of a doctor or of any other person in this connection".[140]

Euthanasia

Euthanasia, or "mercy killing", is when a person, usually a relative, undertakes an act to bring about the death of another for humanitarian reasons in order to prevent

---

[139] See http://www.cps.gov.uk/publications/prosecution/assisted_suicide_policy.html. The final policy was published after almost 5,000 public responses had been received. The DPP has issued statements on specific decisions not to prosecute for assisted suicide, both before and after the *Purdy* decision. In December 2008 he stated that he was not prosecuting the parents of a man who had gone to Switzerland to die, despite there being sufficient evidence for a realistic prospect of conviction. This would not be in the public interest. Daniel James had suffered serious spinal injury in a rugby accident which had left him paralysed from the chest down. He frequently stated that he wished to die and made several suicide attempts. He contacted the Dignitas clinic in Zurich despite numerous attempts by his parents to dissuade him. His parents finally agreed to help him with travel arrangements and correspondence with the clinic and accompanied him to Switzerland. Nonetheless, the DPP stated that he thought it very unlikely that a court would impose a custodial penalty on the defendants and emphasised that Mr James was a person with full capacity to make decisions about his medical treatment. His decision to end his life was in no way influenced by his parents and in fact it was very much against their wishes although they had come to accept his decision. Neither of his parents stood to gain any advantage by their son's death and, on the contrary, it had caused them profound sadness. This was not a case where an elderly, vulnerable and easily suggestible person had expressed a wish to die (DPP Press Release, December 9, 2008). The DPP issued another statement on assisted suicide in March 2010. This concerned a well-known conductor and his wife who had taken their own lives at the Dignitas Clinic in Switzerland. Lady Downes had discovered she was terminally ill with cancer and her husband, Sir Edward Downes, who was older and very infirm, had expressed a wish not to live after his wife's death. Their son and daughter accompanied them to Zurich and the DPP decided that, while there was sufficient evidence to charge the son with assisted suicide, it would not be in the public interest to do so. The deceased had "reached a voluntary, clear, settled and informed decision" to take their own lives and, in assisting them, Mr Downes was wholly motivated by compassion. Although his parents' wills show that Mr Downes stood to gain substantial benefit upon the death of his parents, there was no evidence to indicate that he was motivated by this prospect (DPP Press Release, March 19, 2010).

[140] House of Lords Select Committee on Medical Ethics (HL 21-1, 1994, p.11, para.26).

suffering.[141] It differs fundamentally from assisted suicide because the act resulting in death is not carried out by the deceased but by another.[142] The wishes of the deceased may have been expressly known to the defendant, or the defendant may have taken it upon himself to kill because of a belief that the deceased would not have wanted to live had he known what his quality of life would be.[143] The latter scenario is obviously more problematic but both may have been motivated solely by compassion. However, consent has never been a defence to murder and the compassionate motive of the perpetrator does not prevent the law treating such acts as murder.[144]

The Law Commission of England and Wales summarised the dilemma for lawmakers as follows:

> "Under the current law, the compassionate motives of the 'mercy' killer are in themselves never capable of providing a basis for a partial excuse. Some would say that this is unfortunate. On this view, the law affords more recognition to other less, or at least no more, understandable emotions such as anger (provocation) and fear (self-defence). Others would say that recognising a partial excuse of acting out of compassion would be dangerous. Just as a defence of necessity 'can very easily become simply a mask for anarchy',[145] so the concept of 'compassion' – vague in itself – could very easily become a cover for selfish or ignoble reasons for killing, not least because people often act out of mixed motives."[146]

---

[141] See the two articles by Rosanne O'Connor, "Physician – assisted suicide: the way forward?" (2004) 22 I.L.T. 182; (2004) 22 I.L.T. 204. O'Connor recommends that Irish law should follow the Death with Dignity Act in Oregon which legalises physician-assisted suicide and prohibits euthanasia.

[142] Lord Steyn in *R. (on the application of Pretty) v DPP* [2001] UKHL 61 commented at para.52: "Secondly, there is a distinction between voluntary euthanasia and assisted suicide. Glanville Williams (*The Textbook of Criminal Law*, 2nd ed. (1983), at p 580) illustrates the difference. If a doctor, to speed the dying of his patient, injects poison with the patient's consent, this is voluntary euthanasia and murder. If the doctor places poison by the patient's side, and the patient takes it this will be assisted suicide …".

[143] O'Connor divides euthanasia into two types: active voluntary euthanasia (the deliberate killing at the request of the competent patient) and active involuntary euthanasia (when others decide on the fate of a patient who is unable to give consent).

[144] Mercy killing was been considered on a number of occasions in the 1970s and 1980s in England and Wales. See the Criminal Law Revision Committee (Report 14), *Offences Against the Person* (1980). In 1989 the Report of the Select Committee of the House of Lords on *Murder and Life Imprisonment* recommended that mercy killing continue to be treated as murder but that the mandatory sentence of life imprisonment in such cases be abolished.

[145] *Southwark London Borough v Williams* [1971] Ch. 734 at 746 per Lord Justice Edmund Davies.

[146] Law Commission of England and Wales (Law Com. No. 304), *Murder, Manslaughter and Infanticide* (2006), Pt 7, para.7.7. The Law Commission recommended that the Government undertake a public consultation on whether the law should either recognise an offence or a partial defence of mercy killing. However, it did not make any recommendations in its Report as a detailed consideration of euthanasia was outside its terms of reference. It did suggest, however, that the defence of diminished responsibility be reformulated in a manner that would encompass many cases of euthanasia (see p.153). However, such reformulation would not assist mercy killers who were acting rationally and were capable of understanding the nature of their conduct, forming a rational judgment and controlling themselves. It would only be of benefit to carers who had become so worn out caring for the deceased that they had developed an abnormality which would explain their decision to kill.

However, the law of England and Wales does recognise euthanasia in one respect: although murder results in a mandatory sentence of life imprisonment, the trial judge must determine the minimum term to be served before the defendant can be considered for release on licence.[147] One of the mitigating factors specified by legislation is a belief by the defendant that the murder was an act of mercy.[148] Because there is no provision for minimum terms of the mandatory life sentence for murder to be set under Irish law, euthanasia is neither a defence nor a factor to be taken into account in sentencing. The defendant is treated wholly without reference to the motivation for his killing.

There have been no Irish reported cases concerning euthanasia, but two recent English cases dealt with the issue with differing outcomes. Kay Gilderdale was a mother who was acquitted by a jury of the attempted murder of her daughter in January 2010 and given a conditional discharge for the offence of assisting a suicide. Her daughter had suffered from chronic fatigue syndrome for 17 years, ultimately resulting in her being unable to move or speak or be fed except through a nasal tube. Her daughter had repeatedly expressed a wish to cease living and finally injected herself with an overdose of morphine. That did not work and she asked her mother to provide her with more morphine which she did and which the deceased again injected via a tube inserted into her vein. That also failed and the defendant then crushed anti-depressants and sleeping pills into a powder and placed them in her daughter's feeding tube. Almost a day later the defendant injected her daughter with more morphine followed by three air bubbles and her daughter finally died. The trial judge queried the decision of the Crown Prosecution Service to proceed with the charge of attempted murder and the Director of Public Prosecutions issued a statement following the acquittal. He stated that there had been sufficient evidence to provide a realistic prospect of conviction for attempted murder.[149] He recognised that the defendant had acted out of love and devotion but the fact remained that where there was evidence to support a charge of attempted murder, the seriousness of that charge would very often mean that it was in the public interest to prosecute so that a jury could return a verdict.

In *R. v Inglis*[150] the deceased had been assaulted in the street and was being taken to hospital by ambulance when the ambulance door opened and he fell out. He suffered catastrophic head injuries which resulted in him being in a vegetative state. However, after several surgeries the prognosis improved and his family was told that he might eventually lead an independent life. Unfortunately, his mother, the defendant, remained convinced that her son would not recover and asked a neighbour to help her find pure heroin to end his life. Some time later, shortly after the defendant had visited her son in hospital, he suffered a cardiac arrest and had to be resuscitated. The defendant admitted that she had injected her son with heroin and she was charged with attempted murder and released on bail subject to a condition that she not visit her son. A psychiatric report concluded that the defendant was mentally disturbed

---

[147] Criminal Justice Act 2003 s.269.
[148] Criminal Justice Act 2003 Sch.21, para.11(f).
[149] Toxicology reports failed to ascertain whether death was caused by the drugs the defendant gave to her daughter, or the morphine that the deceased could self-administer, so the more serious charge of murder was not proceeded with.
[150] [2010] EWCA Crim 2637.

and believed that she was acting in his best interests. The defendant arrived at the hospital one afternoon with heroin, syringes and superglue. She injected him with heroin and, when a nurse came near, she barricaded herself into the room putting the superglue into the door lock. Her son died and the defendant was charged with murder. This case was the first involving euthanasia to come before the Court of Appeal. The court underlined that the law did not distinguish between murder committed for sinister reasons and murder motivated by compassion and love and sentenced the defendant to serve a minimum term of five years of the mandatory sentence for life imprisonment.[151]

The High Court of England and Wales recently gave leave to a man suffering from "locked in" syndrome to seek a declaration that any doctor who ended his life would not be charged with murder.[152] Tony Nicklinson suffered a stroke in 2005 and has been paralysed from the neck down ever since. He retains full mental capacity and communicates via an Eye Blink computer. The full hearing is expected to take place in late 2012.

Discontinuation of medical treatment

It is self-evident that where a patient of sufficient capacity decides to refuse medical treatment or to discontinue it then this wish must be acceded to. This was the factual background to *B v An NHS Hospital Trust*.[153] Ms B, who was tetraplegic, sought a declaration in the High Court that the invasive treatment being given to her by the respondent hospital by way of artificial ventilation was unlawful. She had repeatedly expressed the wish not to be kept alive by artificial means and had made several living wills stating this. Dame Butler-Sloss P. emphasised that the court was not being asked to decide whether Ms B should live or die but whether she was legally competent to make that decision for herself. It was not a case about the best interests of the patient but about her mental capacity. In finding that Ms B had capacity, Dame Butler-Sloss P. reiterated what she had said in *In re MB (Medical Treatment)*[154]:

> "A mentally competent patient has an absolute right to refuse to consent to medical treatment for any reason, rational or irrational, or for no reason at all, even where that decision may lead to his or her own death."[155]

She noted that this approach was identical to that taken by the United States Supreme Court in *Cruzan v Director, Missouri Department of Health*[156]:

> "No right is held more sacred, or is more carefully guarded ... than the right of every individual to the possession and control of his own person, free from all restraint or interference of others, unless by clear and unquestionable authority of law."

---

[151] See commentary by Andrew Ashworth, "Case Comment Sentencing: murder – mercy killing" [2011] Crim. L.R. 243.
[152] *Nicklinson v Ministry of Justice* [2012] EWHC 304 (QB).
[153] [2002] EWHC 429 (Fam).
[154] [1997] 2 F.L.R. 426.
[155] [1997] 2 F.L.R. 426 at 432.
[156] (1990) 110 S. Ct. 2841.

The question of discontinuing medical treatment when the patient cannot make that choice for himself is much more problematic. The Irish Supreme Court in *In re Ward of Court (No. 2)*[157] and the House of Lords in the earlier case of *Airedale NHS Trust v Bland*[158] have both grappled with this issue with similar results.

In *Bland*, doctors treating a teenage victim of the Hillsborough football disaster who had been in a persistent vegetative state for over two years sought a declaration that it was lawful to cease feeding him by tube. It was held that since a PVS patient could not give or withhold consent to medical treatment, it was for medics to decide what was in his best interests. In this case there was no prospect of improvement and it was therefore reasonable for doctors to have concluded that the feeding by tube was not in the patient's best interests and should be stopped. The patient's parents agreed with the medical staff that there was no point in continuing life-sustaining treatment and medical support measures. The House of Lords agreed and distinguished between disconnecting a feeding tube (which was viewed as the withdrawal of life-sustaining treatment) and administering drugs which would kill the patient. It was never lawful to take active steps to accelerate death. Lord Goff summarised this distinction as follows:

> "So to act is to cross the Rubicon which runs between on the one hand the care of the living patient and on the other hand euthanasia – actively causing his death to avoid or to end his suffering. Euthanasia is not lawful at common law. It is of course well known that there are many responsible members of our society who believe that euthanasia should be made lawful; but that result could, I believe, only be achieved by legislation which expresses the democratic will that so fundamental a change should be made in our law, and can, if enacted, ensure that such legalised killing can only be carried out subject to appropriate supervision and control. It is true that the drawing of this distinction may lead to a charge of hypocrisy; because it can be asked why, if the doctor, by discontinuing treatment, is entitled in consequence to let his patient die, it should not be lawful to put him out of his misery straight away, in a more humane manner, by a lethal injection, rather than let him linger on in pain until he dies. But the law does not feel able to authorise euthanasia, even in circumstances such as these; for once euthanasia is recognised as lawful in these circumstances, it is difficult to see any logical basis for excluding it in others."[159]

The facts of *In re Ward of Court (No. 2)* were equally tragic. A young woman had several cardiac arrests during minor surgery in 1972 and was left in a near permanent vegetative state. She had minimal cognitive capacity and required full nursing care. Her heart and lungs functioned normally but she was fed by a gastronomy tube. More than 20 years after the surgery her mother sought an order that all artificial nutrition and hydration cease. The High Court (and on appeal the Supreme Court) followed *Bland* and held that the proper test was whether it was in the patient's best interest

---

[157] [1996] 2 I.R. 79.
[158] [1993] 1 All E.R. 821.
[159] [1993] 1 All E.R. 821 at 865.

to have her life prolonged by the continuation of artificial feeding.[160] The court held that the artificial feeding should be terminated. Hamilton C.J. emphasised that the right to life imposed a strong presumption in favour of taking all steps capable of preserving it but that in exceptional circumstances this presumption would not apply. He stated that:

> "As the process of dying is part, and an ultimate, inevitable consequence of life, the right to life necessarily implies the right to have nature take its course and to die a natural death and, unless the individual concerned so wishes, not to have life artificially maintained by the provision of nourishment by abnormal artificial means, which have no curative effect and which is intended merely to prolong life."[161]

He emphasised that this right did not include the right to have life terminated or death accelerated. The patient's unenumerated constitutional rights to bodily integrity and to individual privacy were in no way lessened by virtue of her incapacity and it was in the patient's best interest to have nature take its course.[162]

In the recent decision of the High Court in *In the matter of SR (a minor); An Irish Hospital v RH and JMcG and SR (Notice Party)*[163] Kearns P. ruled that a six-year-old boy, who had been brain damaged by near drowning as a toddler, should not be resuscitated if his condition deteriorated. The hospital had sought an order that the child, who was a ward of court, not be resuscitated in those circumstances as medics had advised that it would not be in his best interests. The boy's parents wanted him to be resuscitated and believed that experimental stem cell treatment could offer him hope. However the court ruled that his condition was irreversible and that medical evidence was unanimous that reventilation would not be in his best interests. The court held that reventilation would cause the child undue pain and suffering and involve a prolongation of life with no hope of improvement. Kearns P. emphasised that the paramount consideration was the best interests of the child and that this gave rise to a "balancing exercise in which account should be taken of all circumstances, including but not limited to: the pain, suffering that the child could expect if he survives; the longevity and quality of life that the child could expect if he survives; the inherent pain and suffering involved in the proposed treatment and the views of the child's parents and doctors".[164] The court stated that there was a strong presumption in favour of authorising life-saving treatment, given the importance of the sanctity of life, but that this presumption could be rebutted in exceptional circumstances. Kearns P. emphasised that the courts could never sanction the taking of positive steps to terminate life:

> "The court will, in exceptional circumstances, authorise steps not being taken to prolong life, but could never authorise a course of action which would accelerate death or terminate life."[165]

---

[160] Egan J. dissenting.
[161] [1996] 2 I.R. 79 at 124.
[162] See Dermot Feenan, "Death, Dying and the Law" (1996) 14 I.L.T. 90.
[163] [2012] IEHC 2; unreported, High Court, Kearns P., January 11, 2012.
[164] [2012] IEHC 2; unreported, High Court, Kearns P., January 11, 2012 at 35.
[165] [2012] IEHC 2; unreported, High Court, Kearns P., January 11, 2012 at 36.

INFANTICIDE

It is well established that mothers, shortly after giving birth, face special challenges, both physical and psychological. Physical circumstances include the physical exhaustion of pregnancy and birth, and consequent hormonal changes, as the body re-adjusts. Psychological factors, meanwhile, include what is now known as post-natal depression, the stresses inherent in being responsible for a new life, new financial and relationship pressures, and, in some cases, the added strain attached to being a single mother. When a mother facing those circumstances kills her child, the law recognises that a murder conviction may not be appropriate. Throughout history juries have been extremely reluctant to convict such women of murder and this was particularly evident when capital punishment was the penalty.[166]

The crime of infanticide is set out in the Infanticide Act 1949. This offence is unusual, in that it operates both as an offence and a defence. A defendant may be charged with infanticide; alternatively, if a defendant is charged with murder she can raise infanticide as a defence—if successful, she will be convicted of infanticide rather than murder, and will face a lesser punishment. Where a defendant raises this defence, the burden of proof is on the prosecution to establish, beyond a reasonable doubt, that the killing amounts to murder and not infanticide.

The elements of the offence are as follows:

(1) a mother kills her child;
(2) within 12 months of its birth;
(3) in circumstances which would otherwise have amounted to murder; and
(4) at the time of the killing the balance of her mind was disturbed by reason of not having fully recovered from giving birth to the child or by reason of a mental disorder (within the meaning of the Criminal Law (Insanity) Act 2006).

Until 2006 if the balance of the defendant's mind was disturbed by reason of "the effect of the lactation after the birth of the child" this could also result in a verdict of infanticide. However, this factor had been criticised as not reflecting modern medicine and was removed from the offence definition.[167] However the Law Commission of

---

[166] See *R. v Eliza Brain* (1834) 172 E.R. 1272; *R. v Ann Walters* (1841) 174 E.R. 455; and *R. v Hannah Moore* (1852) 175 E.R. 501. See generally, Niamh Mulryan, Pat Gibbons and Art O'Connor, "Infanticide and child murder – admissions to the Central Mental Hospital 1850–2000" (2002) 19(1) *Ir. J. Psych. Med.* at pp.8–12; Katherine O'Donovan, "The Medicalisation of Infanticide" [1984] Crim. L.R. 259; D.R.S.D., "The Infanticide Act, 1938" (1938) 2 M.L.R. 229; Elizabeth Parker and Frances Good, "Infanticide" (1981) 5 *Law and Human Behaviour* 237; Walker, "Case Comment, Infanticide" [2006] Crim. L.R. 348; Robbin Ogle and Daniel Maier-Katkin, "A rationale for infanticide laws" [1993] Crim. L.R. 903.

[167] Section 22 of the Criminal Law (Insanity) Act 2006. See also, *Dáil Debates*, March 23, 2006, speech of Minister McDowell on the removal of the reference to lactation in the 1949 Act: "I have consulted with the Office of the Attorney General on this matter on the basis that there has been some academic and legal criticism of the perceived narrow, medical, psychiatric basis for infanticide as set out in the current law. Accordingly, I have decided to remove the reference to lactation, which is dubious, and to replace it with a reference to mental disorder within the meaning of this new Act … I understand that in 1949 the view was that lactation had an effect on the mind of mothers who were breastfeeding. Medical and psychiatric science

England and Wales has recommended that the reference to lactation be retained in the definition of the offence under English law.[168]

Section 6(3) of the Criminal Law Insanity Act 2006 provides that an offender found guilty of infanticide will be dealt with as if she had been found guilty of manslaughter on the ground of diminished responsibility. Diminished responsibility is discussed in detail in Ch.11.

The most important element in the definition is that the balance of the mother's mind must have been disturbed. An example of the type of disturbance required can be seen in *R. v Sainsbury*.[169] The defendant was a teenage girl who gave birth on her own in a bathroom, took the baby and (with her boyfriend) wrapped it in a blanket and drowned it in a river. She pleaded guilty to infanticide and the trial judge accepted that plea, noting that:

> "Even without the stresses of pregnancy and child-birth, you were emotionally and intellectually a very immature fourteen-year-old. You were a woman in body but a child in mind. You were quite unable to cope with pregnancy and unable to understand its full implications. You were too frightened to confide in your parents or anyone else who could help you. When you had this baby you were not prepared for the consequences and at a loss as to what to do. It is clear on the evidence that the effect of giving birth to this baby left the balance of your mind disturbed so as to prevent rational judgment and decision."

It should be noted that infanticide is only available in the case of mothers who kill; fathers who deliberately kill will still face a charge of murder, notwithstanding that they might be subject to similar stresses.[170] This has not been challenged before the courts. In *D (a minor) v Ireland*,[171] a case challenging the constitutionality of provisions in the Criminal Law (Sexual Offences) Act 2006 as being discriminatory on gender grounds, Dunne J. made the following obiter comment about infanticide:

> "Discrimination on grounds of gender *per se* is not unconstitutional because the discrimination may be legitimated ... by reason of being founded on difference of capacity, physical or moral, or difference of social function of men and women in a manner which is not invidious, arbitrary or capricious. In other words, a statutory provision may amount to discrimination on grounds

---

have moved on from that. Issues such as post-puerperal depression and the like would not necessarily be linked to lactation in the technical sense and it is for that reason that I put forward these amendments."

[168] See Karen Brennan, "Beyond the medical model: a rationale for infanticide legislation" (2007) 58 N.I.L.Q. 505. Her view is that, given the medical evidence referred to by the Law Commission, the removal of lactation from infanticide in Irish law may be misconceived.

[169] (1989) 11 Cr. App. R. (S) 533.

[170] See however the controversial case of *R. v Doughty* (1986) 83 Cr. App. R. 319 where the Court of Appeal held that a father who had killed his newborn baby could avail of the defence of provocation to reduce the offence from murder to manslaughter. The child had been crying uncontrollably and the defendant had attempted to silence him by covering his head with cushions and kneeling on them.

[171] [2010] IEHC 101.

of gender but that does not necessarily mean that the discrimination renders the statute unconstitutional. There may be good reasons for the particular discrimination. In the course of the defendants' written and oral submission reference was made to the offence of infanticide in which women who are involved in the killing of their child in certain circumstances are not subject to a conviction of murder ... That particular provision clearly does not apply to men. However it is a provision which on the face of it could be said to discriminate in favour of women but it is a discrimination which is clearly founded on the physical differences between men and women and the effect of childbirth on women."

There are no Irish modern cases on infanticide. This is in contrast to the position in England where two recent Court of Appeal decisions have resulted in much judicial and academic debate on the issue.

The Court of Appeal in *R. v Kai-Whitewind*[172] highlighted two particular areas of concern in relation to infanticide. The first was whether infanticide should be extended to circumstances subsequent to but not connected with the birth such as stresses due to lack of bonding with the baby, rather than being confined to mental disorder caused by childbirth itself. The second was the problem arising when a woman cannot bring herself to admit that she has in fact killed her baby. The Court of Appeal noted the difficulty in producing psychiatric evidence of the balance of the mother's mind in the second scenario. *Kai-Whitewind* concerned a woman who was convicted of murdering her young baby who had been conceived as a result of rape. She had previously told a health visitor that she was not bonding with her son and felt like killing him but insisted that he had died of natural causes. Infanticide was not raised as a defence and the conviction for murder was upheld. The court did not answer the questions it had posed as outlined above but indicated that these were issues that merited examination by law reformers.

The Law Commission, having consulted widely, noted that there was only limited support for broadening infanticide to include "circumstances consequent upon birth".[173]

However, the Law Commission recommended the adoption of a post-trial procedure in circumstances where a mother is convicted of murder because she refuses to submit to a psychiatric examination because she cannot accept that she killed her baby. This procedure would be used in circumstances where infanticide was not raised as an issue during the trial of a mother for murder of her child aged 12 months or less. After conviction, the Law Commission recommended that the trial judge should have the power to order a psychiatric examination of the defendant to see whether the elements of a charge of infanticide were present at the time of the baby's killing. If such evidence is produced and the defendant wishes to appeal then the judge would refer the case to the Court of Appeal and postpone sentencing pending the determination of the appeal. The Law Commission noted that "in infanticide cases where a mother is suffering from a mental disorder but denies the

---

[172] [2005] EWCA Crim 1092.
[173] The Law Commission (Law Com. No. 304), *Murder, Manslaughter and Infanticide* (2006), p.162, para.8.29.

Homicide

killing, 'the chasm between the disposal which is appropriate and the one which the judge is forced to impose under the present law is vast'".[174]

The case of *R. v Gore*[175] established that the offence, as defined under English law, covers situations much wider than those which would otherwise amount to murder and extends to scenarios that would otherwise amount to manslaughter. There is no requirement that all the ingredients of murder have to be proved before a defendant can be convicted of infanticide. The mens rea of infanticide does not require an intention to kill or cause serious injury. The Court of Appeal emphasised that the test was a subjective one which could encompass recklessness and the recklessness could relate simply to putting a child's health at risk rather than to serious illness or death. This was seen as a good thing as it avoided detailed examination of the circumstances which resulted in a mother killing her child and allowed a woman who may be in total denial as to her mens rea at the time of the killing to bring herself within the definition of "infanticide".[176]

Section 57 of the UK Coroners and Justice Act 2009[177] amended the Infanticide Act 1938 to reflect this aspect of *Gore* but it also narrowed the breadth of *Gore* in one important respect. *Gore* held that the mens rea for infanticide is that the mother acted or failed to act "wilfully". However, there was a concern that a defendant could be charged with infanticide even if she could not be convicted of manslaughter. In other words, the concern was that the term "wilfully" could include negligence that fell below the gross negligence standard for manslaughter and could result in a mother being convicted of a homicide offence (infanticide) notwithstanding that another adult in the same position would not be convicted of any homicide offence at all. A mother cannot now be convicted of infanticide under English law in circumstances that would not amount to either murder or manslaughter.[178]

Andrew Ashworth has commented that the reasoning of the Court of Appeal in *Gore* appears strained:

> "The possibility of reducing manslaughter to infanticide has not been canvassed in the leading textbooks and it might be thought rather late, some 70 years

---

[174] Law Commission of England and Wales (Law Com. No. 304), *Murder, Manslaughter and Infanticide* (2006), p.168.

[175] [2007] EWCA Crim 2789.

[176] [2007] EWCA Crim 2789 per Lady Justice Hallett at para.35 of her judgment: "Although humanity may not be an acknowledged cannon of statutory interpretation, the fortunate consequence of our interpretation is that the offence of infanticide covers a wider range of cases than those covered by the interpretation put forward by Mr Webster. A distressed young mother in a similar position to this appellant is not forced to confront what may be stark truth that, for whatever reason, however disturbed she may have been at the time, she killed her child intending to kill or cause really serious bodily harm. Nor will such a young woman, if she does not accept that she had such an intention, have to face a murder trial. To our mind no useful purpose would be served by restricting the offence of infanticide in such a way. As Mr Reid put it, the present state of the law is that a mother in this position, often a woman in severe distress, is not required to acknowledge that she has murdered her child before she can benefit from a charge of infanticide."

[177] This came into force on October 4, 2010.

[178] See Seminar given by Rudi Fortson Q.C. on October 16, 2010 to the Criminal Bar Association of England and Wales on "Homicide Reforms under the CAJA 2009": *http//www.rudifortson4law.co.uk*.

after the 1938 Act, to give it this expansive meaning ... The Court of Appeal's reinterpretation is, however, a benevolent one. It is desirable that infanticide ... should be capable of being charged both in cases where the offence might otherwise have amounted to murder and in cases where the offence would only have been manslaughter."[179]

Whether this is also the position in Ireland remains to be seen. However, the wording of the Infanticide Act 1949 is not identical to the equivalent English legislation and appears to confine infanticide to any wilful act or omission which would otherwise amount to murder rather than manslaughter. The judgment in *Gore* turned to a large extent on the reading of s.1(1) of the 1938 Act which provided that a woman was guilty of infanticide "notwithstanding that the circumstances were such that but for this Act the offence would have amounted to murder". The Court of Appeal interpreted the word "notwithstanding" to mean that there could be a conviction for infanticide even if the offence otherwise amounted to murder and not only in such circumstances. However, the Irish wording as set out in s.1(3)(b) of the 1949 Act is that "the circumstances are such that, but for this section, the act or omission would have amounted to murder". This appears to confine infanticide to acts or omissions which would otherwise amount to murder rather than manslaughter.

---

[179] Andrew Ashworth, "Commentary on R. v. Gore" [2008] Crim. L.R. 388 at 390.

Chapter 5

SEXUAL OFFENCES

This is an area of the criminal law that has always been heavily influenced by prevailing attitudes and standards. It is not surprising, therefore, that there has been reform of many sexual offences in recent years as new areas of protection were identified and traditional attitudes became increasingly regarded as outmoded. The area of child sexual abuse has undergone recent radical legislative reform and several important cases dealing with the issues are discussed in some detail below.

Rape

Two distinct forms of rape exist in Irish law. The first is usually called "common law rape" since it was originally a common law offence, although it is now contained in s.2(1) of the Criminal Law (Rape) Act 1981 which provides:

> A man commits rape if:
> (a) he has sexual intercourse with a woman who at the time of the intercourse does not consent to it, and
> (b) at the time he knows that she does not consent to the intercourse or he is reckless as to whether she does or does not consent to it.

This section is a useful example of the division between the actus reus and mens rea of an offence, with (a) containing the former and (b) the latter.

Actus reus of common law rape

The actus reus of common law rape is sexual intercourse with a woman who does not consent to it. At common law there was a rule that a wife, by her marriage, gave irrevocable consent to intercourse and therefore a husband could never be guilty of the rape of his wife. Hale summarised the position as follows:

> "The husband cannot be guilty of a rape committed by himself upon his lawful wife, for by their mutual matrimonial consent and contract the wife hath given up herself in this kind unto her husband, which she cannot retract."[1]

The 1981 Act appeared to recognise this rule by referring to "unlawful sexual intercourse", i.e. intercourse outside marriage. However, attitudes began to change

---

[1] M. Hale, *History of the Pleas of the Crown* (1736–1739), p.629.

and in 1987 the Law Reform Commission stated "rape of a particularly violent and degrading nature perpetrated by a spouse is not necessarily less loathsome than such a rape perpetrated by a stranger"[2] and recommended that the exemption be abolished. State papers released under the 30-year rule in December 2011 record that a law on marital rape was not introduced in 1981 partly because it was believed that it might be an obstacle to the reconciliation of the couple. However, the marital rape exemption was widely criticised as being both outmoded and demeaning to women and was abolished in this jurisdiction by s.5 of the Criminal Law (Rape)(Amendment) Act 1990. The 1990 Act removed the word "unlawful" from the definition of rape and provided that "any rule of law by virtue of which a husband cannot be guilty of the rape of his wife is hereby abolished". However, s.5(2) goes on to provide that any criminal proceedings for marital rape must have the consent of the DPP.

The statutory definition of "rape" in England also contained the phrase "unlawful sexual intercourse" and was also assumed to recognise the common law rule. A majority of the Criminal Law Revision Committee supported the retention of the marital rape exemption, commenting that "the criminal law should keep out of marital relationships between cohabiting partners – especially the marriage bed – except where injury arises, when there are other offences which can be charged".[3]

However, the exemption had become qualified over the years in English law and authorities suggested that if a wife had taken steps to separate from her husband then she had revoked the consent which she had given upon marriage and her husband could be charged with rape. In *R. v Miller*,[4] the husband was found not guilty of rape as separation proceedings had not been completed but in *R. v Clarke*[5] a separation order had been obtained and the husband was convicted of rape. *R. v Steele*[6] was a case which resulted in a conviction where a married couple were living apart and a non-molestation agreement was in place. Finally, in *R. v R*,[7] the House of Lords held that the word "unlawful" was simply redundant and that the statutory definition therefore also applied to rape inside marriage. The House of Lords agreed with the Court of Appeal decision that the marital exemption in respect of rape was "a common law fiction which has become anachronistic and offensive".[8] The position in both jurisdictions is that marital rape is now unlawful.[9]

Sexual intercourse for common law rape means vaginal intercourse only. Some degree of penetration by the penis, however slight, is required but ejaculation is not required.[10] This is made clear by s.1(2) which provides that references to sexual intercourse are to be construed as references to carnal knowledge as defined in s.63 of the Offences Against the Person Act 1861 "so far as it relates to natural intercourse (under which such intercourse is deemed complete on proof of penetration only)." Penetration is a continuing act and failure by an accused to withdraw when he

---

[2] Law Reform Commission, *Consultation Paper on Rape* (1987), p.47.
[3] Criminal Law Revision Committee, 15th Report, *Sexual Offences* (Cmnd 9213, 1984), para.2.67.
[4] [1954] 2 Q.B. 282.
[5] [1949] All E.R. 448.
[6] (1977) 76 Cr. App. R. 22.
[7] [1991] 4 All E.R. 481.
[8] [1991] 4 All E.R. 481 at 490.
[9] See Sinéad McMullan, "Marital Rape in Irish Law" (1993) 3 I.S.L.R. 85.
[10] *Attorney General v Dermody* [1956] I.R. 307.

realises that the other is not consenting amounts to rape. This was illustrated by *R. v Kaitamaki*.[11] The argument cannot be made in those circumstances that the actus reus and mens rea did not collide.[12]

Section 4 rape

It was recognised that the common law definition of "rape", now contained in s.2 of the Criminal Law (Rape) Act 1981, was inadequate since it did not deal with anal or oral rape or rape by an object, all of which are as degrading to the victim as common law rape. The Law Reform Commission recommended that the definition of "rape" be extended "so as to include non-consensual penetration of the vagina, anus and mouth of a person by the penis of another person or of the vagina or anus of a person by an inanimate object held or manipulated by another person …".[13] Section 4(1) of the Criminal Law (Rape) (Amendment) Act 1990 was introduced to remedy this and it provides that:

> In this Act "rape under section 4" means a sexual assault that includes—
> (a) the penetration (however slight) of the anus or mouth by the penis, or
> (b) penetration (however slight) of the vagina by any object held or manipulated by another person.

The actus reus of section 4 rape is therefore a sexual assault accompanied by certain acts of penetration. However, penetration of the anus by an object is not included in the definition of "section 4 rape". This goes against the recommendation of the Law Reform Commission in its 1988 Report on Rape. The *Discussion Paper on Sexual Offences* published by the Department of Justice, Equality and Law Reform in 1998 set out the argument in favour of including this in the definition of rape:

> "[I]t is somewhat artificial to attempt to distinguish penetration of any of the body orifices because the attack on the dignity and bodily integrity of the victim, and his or her utter and complete humiliation, is the same in all cases of penetration."[14]

The *Discussion Paper* stated that there were two reasons put forward at the time of the debates on the 1990 Act for not including anal penetration by an object in the legislation. The first was that such activity would come within the definition of an aggravated sexual assault. The second was the rather bizarre comment that "there are times when penetration of the anus might not amount to an aggravated sexual assault, such as horseplay between schoolboys which results in penetration of the anus by an object such as a pencil and it would be wrong to categorise such as rape."[15] This

---

[11] [1985] A.C. 147.
[12] For a discussion on the principle that actus reus and mens rea must coincide, see Ch.3.
[13] Law Reform Commission, *Report on Rape and Allied Offences* (LRC 24–1988), para.14.
[14] Department of Justice, Equality and Law Reform, *The Law on Sexual Offences: A Discussion Paper* (May 1998), para.6.3.4.
[15] Department of Justice, Equality and Law Reform, *The Law on Sexual Offences: A Discussion Paper* (May 1998), para.6.3.4.

issue was addressed subsequently by the Joint Committee on Child Protection[16] who endorsed the recommendation in the *Discussion Paper on Sexual Offences* and added:

> "The possibility of horseplay between boys accidentally resulting in such an act being committed is not, to the Committee's mind, a reason to exclude what in other circumstances would be a very serious penetrative assault from the definition of that type of offence."[17]

In addition there is some uncertainty over whether digital rape is included in the definition. The provision refers to penetration "by any object held or manipulated" and it would not appear that fingers could be described as "objects", although there is no case law on this point to date.[18]

We have yet to look at the definition of "sexual assault"; however, for the moment, it is enough to know that it is an assault with "circumstances of indecency". Consent is a defence just as in common law rape. The mens rea for this offence is also essentially the same as for sexual assault or rape, which will be discussed below.

What are the differences between section 4 rape and common law rape? Common law rape can only be committed by a man while section 4 rape (rape with an object) can be committed by either sex. Common law rape can only be committed against a woman while section 4 rape can be committed against either sex as it includes anal or oral rape of a man.

Consent

Failure to struggle or put up a fight does not amount to consent, despite misconceptions to the contrary. Absence of violence is not presence of consent. The Criminal Law (Rape) (Amendment) Act 1990 sought to put this beyond doubt by providing in s.9 that:

> It is hereby declared that in relation to an offence that consists of or includes the doing of an act to a person without the consent of that person any failure or omission by that person to offer resistance to the act does not of itself constitute consent to the act.

There is no statutory definition of "consent" in Irish sexual offences legislation, despite the Law Reform Commission's recommendation that this be done:

---

[16] Houses of the Oireachtas, Report of the Joint Committee on Child Protection (November 2006).
[17] Report of the Joint Committee on Child Protection Report on Child Protection (November 2006), p.13.
[18] Charleton's view is that "[a] finger is part of the hand, so cannot be held or manipulated"; Charleton, McDermott, Bolger, *Criminal Law* (1999), p.652. However, in 1980 the State of Victoria introduced the Crime (Sexual Offences) Act 1980 which defined "rape" as "an object (not being part of the body) which is manipulated ...", leading to the implication that it was felt that the words "not being part of the body" were necessary as otherwise the term "object" could include parts of the body.

"[W]e recommend that legislation should provide that:–
(1) 'Consent' means a consent freely and voluntarily given and, without in any way affecting or limiting the meaning otherwise attributable to those words, a consent is not freely and voluntarily given if it is obtained by force, threat, intimidation, deception or fraudulent means.
(2) A failure to offer physical resistance to a sexual assault does not of itself constitute consent to a sexual assault."[19]

Consent vitiated by fraud

At first glance consent would seem to be a clear-cut issue: consent is either present or not. Problems arise, however, when consent results from fraud. The deceit can be as to the nature of the act or as to the identity of the defendant.

In the case of *R. v Williams*,[20] a singing teacher persuaded his 16-year-old pupil that intercourse was a necessary operation to improve her breathing control. It was held that there was no consent to intercourse: fraudulently misrepresenting the nature of the act meant that the apparent consent was not real. Similarly, in *R. v Flattery*[21] the accused had intercourse with a girl under the guise of performing an operation to cure her fits. She submitted to what was being done under the belief that he was treating her medically but the accused was convicted of rape as he had fraudulently induced that belief.

In the old Irish case of *R. v Dee*,[22] meanwhile, it was held that there was no real consent where a man induced a woman to have intercourse with him by pretending to be her husband. A wife, whose husband had gone out fishing one night, fell asleep in her bedroom. The accused came into her room and had intercourse with her. She did not at first resist, believing him to be her husband, but shortly afterwards realised her mistake and ran out of the bedroom. He was convicted and the court held that the accused knew that the woman was deceived as she said to him, when he came into her room, "You are soon home tonight" to which he made no reply.

In *DPP v C*[23] a similar issue arose. During a party, the complainant fell asleep in an upstairs bedroom and awoke to find the accused getting into bed with her. She thought he was her boyfriend and they had sexual intercourse. The accused had not done anything to impersonate her boyfriend and it was argued that, in the absence of active impersonation, her consent had not been vitiated by fraud. This submission was rejected by the Court of Criminal Appeal, Murray J. commenting that:

---

[19] Law Reform Commission, *Report on Rape and Allied Offences* (LRC 24–1988), para.17. Interestingly, the Consultation Paper on Rape and Allied Offences had recommended that a statutory definition was not required but this recommendation was changed following submissions made to the Law Reform Commission. English legislation has recently defined "consent" in an elaborate manner. The Sexual Offences Act 2003 defines consent in s.74 as follows: "… a person consents if he agrees by choice, and has the freedom and capacity to make that choice". Section 74 provides for evidential presumptions about consent and s.75 provides for conclusive presumptions about consent.
[20] [1923] 1 K.B. 340.
[21] [1877] 2 Q.B. 410.
[22] (1884) Cox CC 579; (1884) 14 Law Reports (Ireland) 468.
[23] [2001] 3 I.R. 345.

> "Consent means voluntary agreement or acquiescence to sexual intercourse by a person of the age of consent with the requisite mental capacity. Knowledge or understanding of facts material to the act being consented to is necessary for the consent to be voluntary or constitute acquiescence."[24]

The court reiterated that the prosecution must prove that the accused knew that there was an absence of consent or was reckless as to whether or not there was an absence of consent. There could be cases where, notwithstanding the woman's mistake of identity, the accused had reasonable grounds for believing that she consented.

The same factual scenario arose once more in a recent Irish case dating from October 2007 where a burglar pleaded guilty to burglary and procuring sex under false pretences. He had got into bed with the victim who believed he was her boyfriend who had been in bed with her earlier in the night. It is unclear why a charge of rape was not brought instead.[25]

However, in *R. v Linekar*,[26] it was held that consent was present despite fraud. In that case the defendant approached a prostitute and agreed to pay £25 for intercourse. He had no intention of paying and subsequently made off without paying. The Court of Appeal held that, nonetheless, the consent of the victim was real. Fraud as to a collateral matter did not undermine consent, although fraud as to the nature of the act or the identity of the actor would mean that apparent consent was not real.

Fraud as to existence of HIV or other diseases

What about a person who has intercourse knowing that there are surrounding circumstances which, if known to the victim, would have resulted in consent being denied? Can he be said to have engaged in fraud relating to the nature of the act?

The nineteenth-century case of *R. v Clarence*[27] addressed this issue. The accused was a husband who passed gonorrhoea to his wife through sexual intercourse. He knew that he was infected but she did not. He was convicted of grievous bodily harm and actual bodily harm and appealed and his conviction was quashed. The majority judges were of the opinion that to criminalise him would be an over-broad application of the criminal law. Wills J. made the following analogy:

> "Take, for example, the case of a man without a single good quality, a gaol-bird, heartless, mean and cruel, without the smallest intention of doing anything but possessing himself of the person of his victim, but successfully representing himself as a man of good family and connections prevented by some temporary obstacle from contracting an immediate marriage, and with conscious hypocrisy acting the part of a devoted lover, and in this fashion, or perhaps under the guise of affected religious fervour, effecting the ruin of his victim. In all that induces consent there is not less difference between the man to whom the woman supposes she is yielding herself and the man by whom she is really betrayed than there is between the man bodily sound and

---

[24] [2001] 3 I.R. 345 at 360.
[25] See media report at *http://www.rte.ie/news/2009/1218/stanleyd.html*.
[26] [1995] 3 All E.R. 69.
[27] (1888) 22 QBD 23.

the man afflicted with a contagious disease ... Many women would think that of two cruel wrongs the bigamist had committed the worse ... It seems to me, however, that such an extension of the criminal law to a vast class of cases with which it has never yet professed to deal is a matter for the legislature, and the legislature only."[28]

Stephen J. said that if the conviction were to stand then "[a] man who knowing he has scarlet fever or small-pox shakes hands with a friend and so infects him" would be as culpable.[29]

However, the modern view appears to be that intentional or reckless transmission of diseases would not negative the consent required for rape but could result in a conviction for assault causing harm if the victim was infected. The Law Commission of England and Wales acknowledged that there was an argument for treating a deception as to a person's disease-free status as being so fundamental that it should nullify consent; however, it ultimately concluded that the right solution was a matter requiring expertise in public health and social policy rather than the law.[30]

The Canadian case of *R. v Cuerrier*[31] concerned a man who was HIV positive and had been explicitly instructed to inform all sexual partners of this and to use condoms every time he engaged in sexual intercourse. Despite this, the accused had unprotected sexual intercourse with two women without informing them of his medical status. Both women said that if they had known he was HIV positive they would never have consented to unprotected intercourse and he was charged with aggravated assault. The Supreme Court of Canada widened the understanding of fraud to such a scenario, commenting:

> "Why should fraud be defined more broadly in the commercial context, which is designed to protect property interests, than it is for sexual assault, which is one of the worst violations of human dignity?"[32]

McLachlin J. added:

> "It is unrealistic, indeed shocking, to think that consent given to sex on the basis that one's partner is HIV-free stands unaffected by blatant deception on that matter. To put it another way, few would think the law should condone a person who has been asked whether he has HIV, lying about that fact in order to obtain consent. To say that such a person commits fraud vitiating consent, thereby rendering the consent an assault, seems right and logical."[33]

McLachlin J. differentiated between deception as to HIV status or venereal disease and deception as to other inducements, such as promises of marriage, on the basis that consent to unprotected intercourse was consent to the exchange of bodily fluids.

---

[28] (1888) 22 QBD 23 at 30–33.
[29] (1888) 22 QBD 23 at 39.
[30] Law Commission of England and Wales, *Report on Sexual Offences* (2000).
[31] [1998] 2 S.C.R. 371.
[32] [1998] 2 S.C.R. 371 at para.19 per L'Heureux-Dubé J.
[33] [1998] 2 S.C.R. 371 at para.66.

A person does not consent to the transmission of diseased bodily fluids and deception on that matter goes to the very root of consent as it relates to the physical act itself. *R. v Clarence* was described as having been decided due to "fear of unprincipled overextension"[34] and was not followed. McLachlin J. limited the extension to cases where there was a high risk of infection from the disease and where the defendant knew, or ought to have known, that the fraud induced consent.

The English Court of Appeal considered the issue in *R. v Dica*.[35] The defendant was charged with inflicting grievous bodily harm on two complainants as a result of infecting both of them with HIV following unprotected sexual intercourse. The court did not follow *Clarence* and stated that its reasoning had no continuing application in modern times. It held that a victim's consent to sexual intercourse was not to be regarded as consent to the risk of disease unless there was evidence that the victim did in fact consent to such a risk.[36] This would not apply to the case of a person who set out to deliberately inflict grievous bodily harm through transmission of disease, where consent would not be a defence.[37] The court held that:

> "These victims consented to sexual intercourse. Accordingly, the defendant was not guilty of rape … [I]f the defendant concealed the truth about his condition from them, and therefore kept them in ignorance of it, there was no reason for them to think they were running any risk of infection, and they were not consenting to it."[38]

The Court of Appeal in *R. v B*[39] reiterated that a person who does not disclose his HIV status to a person with whom he has consensual intercourse is not guilty of rape:

> "Where one party to a sexual activity has a sexually transmissible disease which is not disclosed to the other party any consent that may have been given to that activity by the other party is not thereby vitiated. The act remains a consensual act. However, the party suffering from the sexual transmissible disease will not have any defence to any charge which may result from harm created by that sexual activity, merely by virtue of that consent, because such consent did not include consent to infection by the disease."[40]

---

[34] [1998] 2 S.C.R. 371 at para.73 per McLachlin J.
[35] [2004] EWCA Crim 1103.
[36] See *Policy for prosecuting cases involving the intentional or reckless sexual transmission of infection* (Crown Prosecution Service, July 15, 2011) where this is discussed. The policy document makes the point that informed consent does not necessarily mean that the risk of disease must have been discussed between the parties. For example, a third party may have made the injured party aware of the defendant's status. The same point is also made in *R. v Konzani* [2005] EWCA Crim 706.
[37] The principle in *R. v Brown* [1994] 1 A.C. 212, that it is not possible to consent to serious harm, would be applicable in such a case. See discussion of this principle in Ch.6.
[38] [2004] EWCA Crim 1103 at 1268.
[39] [2006] EWCA Crim 2945.
[40] [2006] EWCA Crim 2945 at para.17 per Latham L.J.

Consent vitiated by fear

Consent may also be vitiated by fear, as illustrated in *R. v Olugboja*.[41] The defendant told a 16-year-old girl that he had met at a disco in Oxford that he was going to rape her and she complied because of fear. The defendant's friend was also in the vicinity and he had raped the girl's companion a short time earlier. The girl was pushed onto a settee in a darkened room and did not struggle, resist, scream or cry for help. The Court of Appeal emphasised that "there is a difference between consent and submission; every consent involves a submission but it by no means follows that a mere submission follows consent".[42]

Incapacity to give consent

It is clear that there is no consent where the victim is incapable of giving consent. In *DPP v X*,[43] a man was convicted of rape for having intercourse with a woman while she slept. Similarly, the defendant in *R. v Malone*[44] was convicted of raping an intoxicated 16-year-old girl who gave evidence that she been unable to resist because of her condition:

> "Submitting to an act of sexual intercourse, because through drink she was unable physically to resist though she wished to, is not consent ... What occurred ... not wishing to have intercourse but being physically unable to do anything about it ... would plainly, as a matter of common sense, be against her will. It would be without her consent."[45]

It is clear that there are situations where a person cannot legally consent to intercourse but these are dealt with below in the sections on sexual offences against the mentally handicapped and sexual abuse of children.

MENS REA OF SEXUAL OFFENCES

Absence of consent is a prerequisite before most sexual offences can be made out. The mens rea of the offence, therefore, will be that the defendant intended to commit the acts in question either knowing that the victim did not consent or being reckless as to whether or not the victim consented. The first requires that the defendant is conscious of the lack of consent; the second that the defendant was aware that the victim might not be consenting. This mens rea is explicitly set out by statute in the case of common law rape in s.2(1)(b) of the Criminal Law (Rape) Act 1981 and has been held by the courts to apply also in the case of sexual assault in *R. v Kimber*.[46]

---

[41] [1981] 3 All E.R. 443.
[42] [1981] 3 All E.R. 443 at 448.
[43] Unreported, Central Criminal Court, *Irish Times*, May 20, 1995.
[44] (1998) 2 Crim. App. R. 447.
[45] (1998) 2 Crim. App. R. 447 at 452.
[46] [1983] 1 W.L.R. 1118.

Honest but unreasonable belief in consent

Suppose that a defendant honestly believes that a victim is consenting but his belief is unreasonable? Should the defendant be found guilty of a crime? Two approaches to this situation are possible. An objective approach would find a defendant liable if he honestly believed that there was consent but he had no reasonable grounds for his belief. A subjective approach would acquit the defendant, looking solely at his honest belief and not at whether it was reasonable for him to hold that belief.

In *DPP v Morgan*,[47] this precise issue came before the House of Lords. In a bizarre set of facts, a husband invited three drinking partners back to his house to have sexual intercourse with his wife. He told them that she would put up a struggle but that this would simply be an act and that she would in fact welcome having intercourse with them. The men went back to his house and each had sex with her while she was held down, fighting and screaming. The defence of each of the men was that they honestly, though obviously unreasonably, believed that the victim had consented to intercourse. The trial judge directed the jury that this could not amount to a defence unless the defendants had reasonable grounds for their belief. The defendants were convicted.

On appeal to the House of Lords it was held, by a majority, that the defendants could not be convicted of rape if they had genuinely believed that the victim was consenting. Lord Hailsham L.C. held that:

> "Once one has accepted ... that the prohibited act in rape is non-consensual sexual intercourse, and that the guilty state of mind is an intention to commit it, it seems to me to follow ... that there is no room either for a 'defence' of honest belief or mistake ... Either the prosecution proves that the accused had the requisite intent, or it does not. In the former case it succeeds, and in the latter it fails. Since honest belief clearly negatives intent, the reasonableness or otherwise of that belief can only be evidence for or against the view that the belief and therefore the intent was actually held ..."[48]

Outrage followed this decision, which was described by some as "A Rapists' Charter".[49] Pressure was exerted to change the mens rea of rape to an objective test, asking whether the accused had reasonable grounds for his belief that the victim was consenting. However this was not done. The English Advisory Group on the Law of Rape (The Heilbron Committee) accepted that *DPP v Morgan* was correct in principle.[50] Nevertheless, the Advisory Group did advise that legislation should clarify that:

1. an honest belief in consent would negative mens rea; and
2. this belief did not need to be based on reasonable grounds; but
3. the jury may take into account whether reasonable grounds existed in deciding whether the belief was honest.

---

[47] [1976] A.C. 182.
[48] [1976] A.C. 182 at 361.
[49] See Hinchcliffe, "Rape Law Reform in Britain" (2000) 37(4) *Society* 57 for a summary of arguments for and against the *DPP v Morgan* approach.
[50] *Report of the Advisory Group on the Law of Rape* (Cmnd. 6352, December 1975).

English legislation adopted this approach in the Sexual Offences (Amendment) Act 1976 s.1(1) and this approach was also adopted in Ireland in the Criminal Law (Rape) Act 1981 s.2(2) which provides:

> It is hereby declared that if at a trial for a rape offence the jury has to consider whether a man believed that a woman was consenting to sexual intercourse, the presence or absence of reasonable grounds for such a belief is a matter to which the jury is to have regard, in conjunction with any other relevant matters, in considering whether he so believed.

This approach is a common-sense compromise: the accused is entitled to claim a genuine belief in consent but the jury is entitled to consider whether such a belief would have been reasonable in deciding whether the accused did in fact have that belief.[51]

It is not necessary that the jury should be directed on the provisions of s.2(2) of the 1981 Act in every case where rape is charged: such a direction only becomes necessary where the defence required is one of mistaken belief in consent. A retrial was ordered in *DPP v Gaffey*[52] because the trial judge had not directed the jury on s.2(2) in circumstances where they had to consider that, even if the complainant had not consented, the accused may have believed that she did or was reckless to it. The issue of consent was very much part of the factual background to the case. In *DPP v F*[53] Finlay C.J. commented that obviously consent is not an issue in every rape case—sometimes the only issue will be the identity of the accused:

> "In cases, however, where knowledge by the accused of the fact that the woman concerned was not consenting to a proved sexual intercourse or recklessness on his part as to whether she was or not, arises as something which the prosecution must establish, the provisions of subsection (2) of section 2 come into operation. It is clear that either in relation to knowledge or recklessness subsection (2) of section 2 does not make the presence or absence of reasonable grounds for a belief that the woman was consenting the determining or only factor, but it is merely something which the jury is to have regard to in conjunction with any other relevant matters."[54]

Similarly, in *DPP v Creighton*,[55] it was held that there is no general requirement for a trial judge to give a direction on s.2(2). The need to do so depends on the nature of the evidence given. In *DPP v McDonagh*[56] the defendants were charged with rape. Their defence was that the complainant had consented to sexual intercourse in return for payment. They were convicted. On appeal it was argued that the trial judge had erred in failing to explain to the jury the effect of s.2(2). It was held by Costello J.

---

[51] It is worth noting that the jurors and all judges who heard the *Morgan* case all came to the conclusion that the story was a fabrication.
[52] Unreported, Court of Criminal Appeal, May 10, 1991 (Finlay C.J., Lynch and Morris JJ.).
[53] Unreported, Court of Criminal Appeal, May 27, 1993 (Finlay C.J., Budd and Geoghegan JJ.).
[54] Unreported, Court of Criminal Appeal, May 27, 1993 at 5.
[55] [1994] 2 I.R. 570.
[56] [1996] 1 I.R. 565.

that s.2(2) was limited in its effect to cases where the defence mounted was one of mistaken belief in consent: it had no application in cases such as the present one where the defence was the existence of consent.

Finally, it should be noted that the English approach was changed by the Sexual Offences Act 2003 which now requires the belief to be a reasonable one.[57]

Recklessness as to consent

Recklessness in this context has the same meaning as in *DPP v Murray*[58]: the accused must be consciously aware of the possibility that the victim is not consenting. Objective recklessness is not enough.

SEXUAL ASSAULT AND AGGRAVATED SEXUAL ASSAULT

Until 1990 the majority of sexual attacks which did not amount to rape amounted to indecent assault. Although statute provided maximum penalties for each offence, there was no statutory definition of either.

There was dissatisfaction with this situation. There was an anachronistic differentiation between indecent assault upon a male and upon a female: until 1981 there were different maximum penalties depending on the sex of the victim but this was remedied by the Criminal Law (Rape) Act 1981.[59] In addition, each offence covered a wide span of behaviour, from relatively minor offences to violent sexual attacks. Consequently, it was felt that the label of indecent assault and the maximum sentence available were inadequate for the more serious offences which were included in the definition of "indecent assault".

The Criminal Law (Rape) (Amendment) Act 1990 was enacted and it combined the offences of indecent assault upon a male and upon a female into one offence, to be known as sexual assault and having a single maximum penalty of five years regardless of the sex of the victim. Section 2 provides:

(1) The offence of indecent assault upon any male person and the offence of indecent assault upon any female person shall be known as sexual assault.
(2) A person guilty of sexual assault shall be liable on conviction on indictment ... [to 10 years imprisonment or 14 years if the victim is a child].

---

[57] Section 1. See Temkin and Ashworth, "The Absence of Reasonable Belief in Consent" [2004] Crim L.R. 328.
[58] [1977] I.R. 360.
[59] In *M v Ireland* [2007] IEHC 280, Laffoy J. found that the disparate sentencing in the pre-1981 law for indecent assaults on males and on females was unconstitutional. The Offences Against the Person Act 1861 as amended imposed a maximum sentence of 10 years' imprisonment for indecent assault upon a male and the Criminal Law Amendment Act 1935 only imposed a maximum of two years' imprisonment for indecent assault upon a female. (The offences in that case had been committed prior to 1981 so the old law applied.) Laffoy J. could find nothing pointing to a legitimate legislative purpose for imposing disparate penalties and came to the conclusion that the relevant provision was inconsistent with Art.40.1 of the Constitution.

Sexual Offences

In addition, the more serious cases of sexual attack are now dealt with in two ways. Those involving penetration will now amount to section 4 rape while other serious sexual attacks fall into a new category of aggravated sexual assault. This is a gender-neutral offence carrying a maximum penalty of life imprisonment. The penalty, life imprisonment, is the same as that for common law rape and section 4 rape, reflecting the fact that some attacks not involving penetration can be just as grave as those involving penetration. Section 3 provides:

> In this Act "aggravated sexual assault" means a sexual assault that involves serious violence or the threat of serious violence or is such as to cause injury, humiliation or degradation of a grave nature to the person assaulted.

It should be noted that the 1990 Act does not define "indecent" or "sexual" assault but simply prescribes a new name and range of penalties for an existing offence at common law. It was argued after the passage of the 1990 Act that there was in fact no offence of indecent assault known to Irish law. If so, then the 1990 Act would have been ineffective as purporting to rename and give new penalties for an offence which did not exist. This argument was, however, rejected by O'Hanlon J. in *Doolan v DPP*[60] and by the Supreme Court in *DPP v EF*,[61] both of which held that an offence of indecent assault existed at common law and that it was permissible to rename the offence and provide new penalties for it without re-enacting it. The 1990 Act therefore creates a mixed statutory and common law offence in much the same way as s.4 of the Criminal Justice Act 1964 does with regard to murder. This means that to define "sexual assault" we have to consider what constituted indecent assault at common law.

Indecent assault at common law

> "An indecent assault has been defined as an assault (including psychic assault) accompanied with circumstances of indecency."[62]

An indecent assault is therefore a species of assault—an act by which one person intentionally or recklessly causes another to apprehend immediate, unlawful personal violence or to sustain such violence.[63] For an assault to take place it is not necessary that there should be any element of hostility or aggression. "Violence" simply means any unlawful touching of the victim without consent or lawful excuse.[64] Additionally, it is not necessary that physical touching takes place. An assault is complete where there is the threat of unlawful violence without any physical contact having to be made. This is illustrated by *R. v Sargeant*[65] where the defendant forced a young boy at knife-point to masturbate in front of him. He was convicted of indecent assault despite there having been no physical contact whatsoever between the parties.

---

[60] [1992] 2 I.R. 399.
[61] Unreported, Supreme Court, February 24, 1994.
[62] Peter Charleton, *Offences Against the Person* (Dublin: Round Hall Press, 1992), p.286.
[63] See Ch.6 on offences against the person.
[64] *Faulkner v Talbot* [1981] 1 W.L.R. 1528.
[65] [1997] Crim. L.R. 50.

However, an invitation to do something cannot be regarded as an assault. In *Fairclough v Whipp*[66] the defendant was acquitted of indecent assault. The allegation was that he had exposed himself to a young girl and invited her to touch his penis. It was not considered to be an indecent assault because no assault had occurred.

This loophole is a controversial one and in 1990 the Law Reform Commission recommended the creation of an offence of sexual exploitation which would cover intentional masturbation in the presence of a child and intentional exposure of the sexual organs in the presence of a child for the purpose of sexual arousal or gratification of the older person.[67]

However this was not done, and in 1996 O'Malley remarked that:

> "[T]he courts have refused to accept the notion of a passive assault. A man who touches the sexual organs of a child is guilty of assault, but if he persuades a young girl to touch his sexual organs, he is not, because there is no assaultive action involved. This is one area of child abuse law in urgent need of reform. If the invitee is a boy, the man may be charged with gross indecency (if the boy cooperated) or with an attempt to commit such an act."[68]

In 2006 the Joint Committee on Child Protection endorsed the Law Reform Commission's approach and recommended the enactment, as a legislative priority, of an offence of child sexual abuse to include forms of sexual act, contact or behaviour falling short of penetrative sexual activity.[69] Gillespie[70] points out that the Oireachtas has not expressly closed this loophole but this may have been done implicitly by the Criminal Law (Human Trafficking) Act 2008 which amended s.3 of the Child Trafficking and Pornography Act 1998. Section 3(2) provides that a person who sexually exploits a child shall be guilty of an offence. "Sexually exploiting a child" is defined to include "inviting, inducing or coercing the child to engage in or participate in any sexual, indecent or obscene act, or inviting, inducing or coercing the child to observe any sexual, indecent or obscene act, for the purpose of corrupting or depraving the child". However, it is unclear whether this offence is restricted to situations where there is trafficking of children. Gillespie comments that:

> "Nothing in the Act other than the marginal note suggests that this offence is restricted to situations where there is trafficking or other commercial exploitation. Obviously marginal notes do not form part of the statute …"[71]

However, Gillespie notes that Brian Lenihan T.D., former Minister of Justice, Equality and Law Reform, was of the opinion that the offence only applied to trafficked persons:

---

[66] (1951) 35 Crim. App. R. 138.
[67] LRC 32–1990.
[68] Thomas O'Malley, *Sexual Offences Law, Policy and Punishment* (Dublin: Round Hall Sweet & Maxwell, 1996), p.102.
[69] Houses of the Oireachtas, *Report of the Joint Committee on Child Protection* (November 2006), p.15,
[70] Alisdair A. Gillespie, *Sexual Exploitation of Children Law and Punishment* (Dublin: Round Hall, 2008).
[71] Alisdair A. Gillespie, *Sexual Exploitation of Children Law and Punishment* (Dublin: Round Hall, 2008), p.79.

"The gist of the offence is the trafficking, not the exploitation. That is the essential proof in this matter. The definition of 'sexual exploitation', therefore only comes into play where a person has been trafficked for the purpose of sexual exploitation. The Act does not supply a general definition of 'sexual exploitation' that can be used elsewhere in the law."[72]

Another difficulty lies in defining "circumstances of indecency". Some circumstances will be obviously indecent, such as an attempt to remove another's clothes, while others may or may not be indecent depending on the circumstances. In *R. v Court*[73] the accused was a shop assistant and struck a 12-year-old girl in the shop several times on her buttocks, outside her shorts. Later asked why he did so he replied "buttock fetish". The House of Lords was asked to determine whether these were circumstances of indecency, given that the girl was unaware of his motive. The court upheld the conviction of the accused and laid down the following guidelines:

1. the assault component of indecent assault includes not just physical violence but conduct which causes another to fear immediate and unlawful physical violence;
2. some circumstances are objectively incapable of being regarded as indecent, regardless of the motive of the accused, for example to remove another's shoe is not capable of being regarded as indecent, even if the accused is a shoe fetishist.
3. some circumstances are inherently indecent, regardless of the motive of the accused: for example, to remove a victim's clothes against her will amounts to indecent assault, regardless of whether the accused had a sexual intention or simply intended to embarrass or humiliate the victim;
4. in other circumstances, the jury may consider all the surrounding factors in deciding whether an assault is in fact indecent, including the relationship between the parties and the motive of the accused (for example for a parent to spank a child is not indecent);
5. it is not necessary to show that the victim was aware of the circumstances of indecency. It was no defence that the victim was unaware of the accused's buttock fetish. An indecent assault can obviously take place on a sleeping or unconscious victim.

As a sexual assault is a type of assault, the case law relating to assault and consent is pertinent. This is discussed in detail in Ch.6 on offences against the person.

INCEST

Incest is a crime governed by the Punishment of Incest Act 1908. The offence consists of sexual intercourse with a close blood relative. The majority of cases are violent or abusive but this is not an element of the crime: consensual intercourse

---

[72] Conduct of the Select Committee on Justice, Equality, Defence and Women's Rights, November 20, 2007, quoted in Gillespie, *Sexual Exploitation of Children Law and Punishment* (Dublin: Round Hall, 2008), p.79.
[73] [1988] 2 All E.R. 221.

between close relatives will still amount to incest. In other words, consent is not a defence. The bulk of incest cases concern fathers abusing daughters and, for that reason, different considerations apply to incest by a male and incest by a female. The age of the victim is also irrelevant to the crime, what matters is the blood relationship between the individuals.

Incest by a male

A man who has sexual intercourse with a woman who is to his knowledge his mother, sister, daughter or granddaughter commits incest. Vaginal intercourse must be established: other forms of abuse or exploitation do not amount to incest. Brother and sister include half-brother and half-sister but not step-brother and step-sister since the offence is limited to blood relations. Consequently, it follows that sexual abuse by adoptive parents does not amount to the crime of incest.

Until the enactment of the Criminal Law (Rape) (Amendment) Act 1990 there was a conclusive presumption that a boy under 14 years of age could not commit incest. This has now been abolished. On this point see Ch.11 on the defence of infancy.

Incest by a female

A female of or above the age of 17 years who permits her father, grandfather, brother or son to have sexual intercourse with her commits incest provided she is aware of the relationship. The offence is the same as incest by a male except that the female is not criminally liable until she reaches the age of 17 years, on the assumption that she is the victim of any incestuous intercourse before that age.

Punishment of incest

Committed by a male, the maximum penalty is life imprisonment.[74] Committed by a female, the maximum penalty is seven years' imprisonment.[75]

Reform

It is well recognised that the crime of incest should be extended to adoptive relationships and step-children. During the passage through the Dáil of the Bill of the Criminal Law (Incest Proceedings) Act 1995, an amendment was proposed which would have had the effect of extending the offence to the non-blood relationships of step-parent and step-child and adoptive parent and adoptive child. However, this was not passed.[76]

---

[74] Section 1 of the Punishment of Incest Act 1908; s.12 of the Criminal Law Amendment Act 1935; s.5(1) of the Criminal Law (Incest Proceedings) Act 1995.
[75] Section 2 of the Punishment of Incest Act 1908.
[76] See discussion in Department of Justice, Equality and Law Reform, *The Law on Sexual Offences: A Discussion Paper* (May 1998). The law of incest covers adoptive families in Iceland, Moldova and Slovenia.

In addition, there has been criticism of the differing penalties for male and female perpetrators. A man convicted for incest is liable to imprisonment for life,[77] whereas a woman will face a maximum sentence of seven years. A new Bill was introduced in May 2012 to increase the penalty for women convicted of incest to life imprisonment.

Furthermore, females under 17 years cannot be charged with incest but there is no such provision for males. This is based on the traditional view of males as instigators and women as victims of incest which may not always reflect reality.

Another issue of debate is whether the offence should be broadened to include types of sexual activity other than sexual intercourse. The narrow definition of "incest" is based on a traditional rationale for the offence: the prevention of birth defects.[78]

There is a wide spectrum of international legal views on the place incest has in the criminal law. In the recent European Court of Human Rights judgment in *Stubing v Germany*[79] it was noted that out of 31 Council of Europe Member States only 16 states criminalised incest. In that case a brother and sister, who had first met when he was 23 years and she was 16 years, were prosecuted for incest under German law. The brother was convicted and it was held that the sister was only partially liable for her actions due to a severe personality disorder characterised by dependency. The brother appealed to the European Court of Human Rights, arguing that his right to a private and family life pursuant to art.8 had been contravened. It was held that Germany had stayed within its margin of appreciation when convicting the applicant of incest and there had therefore been no violation of art.8:

> "An interference with the exercise of the right ... will not be compatible with Article 8(2) ... unless it is 'in accordance with the law', has an aim or aims that is or are legitimate under that paragraph and is 'necessary in a democratic society' for the aforesaid aims ... Where, however, there is no consensus within the Member States of the Council of Europe, either as to the relative importance of the interest at stake or as to the best means of protecting it, particularly where the case raises sensitive moral or ethical issues, the margin will be wider."[80]

Sexual Offences Against the Mentally Handicapped

Until 1993 the only offence of this type was contained in s.4 of the Criminal Law Amendment Act 1935 which made it an offence punishable by two years' imprisonment to have unlawful sexual intercourse with a woman who was "an idiot

---

[77] The penalty for males was first increased from seven years to 20 years by the Criminal Justice Act 1993 and further increased to life imprisonment by the Criminal Law (Incest Proceedings) Act 1995. These changes were brought about by the outcry following the Kilkenny Incest Case where a father committed incest against his daughter. The penalty for women was left unchanged from the seven years specified in the Punishment of Incest Act 1908.
[78] See discussion on this point in Department of Justice, Equality and Law Reform, *The Law on Sexual Offences: A Discussion Paper* (May 1998), para.7.5.1.
[79] [2012] ECHR 656 (App. No. 43547/08).
[80] [2012] ECHR 656 (App. No. 43547/08) at paras 55 and 60.

or an imbecile or feeble-minded". That was unsatisfactory as it employed what is now regarded as offensive terminology and offered no protection against other forms of sexual exploitation of the mentally handicapped. The Criminal Law (Sexual Offences) Act 1993 replaces s.4 of the 1935 Act. Section 5 of the 1993 Act creates three distinct offences:

(1) sexual intercourse with a mentally impaired person (10 years' imprisonment; three years' for attempt on a first conviction and five years' for attempt on second and subsequent conviction);
(2) buggery of a mentally impaired person (penalties as intercourse);
(3) commission of an act of gross indecency by a male with a male who is mentally impaired (two years' imprisonment).

Proceedings against a person charged with an offence under this section may only be taken with the consent of the Director of Public Prosecutions.[81]

Section 5 of the 1993 Act defines "mentally impaired" as follows:

> "[S]uffering from a disorder of the mind, whether through mental handicap or mental illness, which is of such a nature or degree as to render a person incapable of living an independent life or of guarding against serious exploitation."

This definition includes temporary conditions but it is unclear whether it covers the situation where a person is suffering from mental disability resulting from physical injury, i.e. acquired brain damage.

There is a defence where a defendant is married to a mentally impaired person. A defence is also provided where an accused can show that at the time of the alleged commission of the offence he did not know and had no reason to suspect that the person in respect of whom he is charged was mentally impaired. However, consent is not a defence, even assuming that the victim has sufficient mental capacity to give consent.

It should be noted that the 1993 Act is designed for situations where a mentally impaired person *is* capable of giving consent. If a victim is so mentally disabled as to be incapable of consenting, then the accused will also be guilty of rape or sexual assault if he has the necessary mens rea. The necessary mental capacity to give consent is expressed by Glanville Williams to be as follows:

> "[T]he woman must know the physical facts and know that the connection is sexual; failing either knowledge, she does not consent in law."[82]

Sexual activity amounting to rape under s.4 is not covered by the Criminal Law (Sexual Offences) Act 1993. This was highlighted during a trial reported in November 2010 where the trial judge accused the Oireachtas of failing to protect the vulnerable when he was forced to acquit a man of allegedly orally raping a woman with an intellectual disability.[83]

---

[81] Section 5(4).
[82] Glanville Williams, *Textbook of Criminal Law*, 2nd edn (London: Stevens & Sons, 1983), p.571.
[83] Report in the *Irish Examiner*, November 16, 2010.

Sexual Offences

The Law Reform Commission, in its 1990 *Report on Sexual Offences Against the Mentally Handicapped*,[84] emphasised the balance that must be achieved between guarding against sexual exploitation and facilitating the sexual expression of the mentally handicapped. However, the current legislation has been criticised as erring too much on the side of guarding against exploitation. It has been argued that many people who are unable to live independently because of mental handicap are capable of protecting themselves from exploitation and the legislation creates a serious difficulty for them in their sexual relationships. The Law Reform Commission Report concluded that the test of whether a person was capable of living an independent life did not add anything to the definition of the category of persons who should be protected, but the legislators did not follow that recommendation. The Law Reform Commission also recommended that a mentally impaired person should not be charged with any of the prescribed offences against another mentally impaired person, unless the act in question constituted a criminal offence by virtue of some other provision of the law. This was to prevent inappropriate prosecutions but the recommendation was not implemented.

The Law Reform Commission has recently reconsidered the issue of sexual offences and the mentally impaired in its *Consultation Paper on Sexual Offences and Capacity to Consent*.[85] It highlighted a number of problems with the current law, in particular that the 1993 Act is paternalistic in tone and fails to recognise the rights of those with intellectual disability to have a fully expressed consensual life. It highlighted that the 1993 Act fails to protect the mentally impaired from unwanted sexual contact apart from sexual intercourse and that a sexual relationship between two mentally impaired persons may constitute a defence because there is no provision for consent being a defence in respect of a non-marital relationship between two adults who were both capable of giving real consent.[86]

It recommended that s.5 should be replaced by legislation providing for a capacity test based on the ability to understand the nature and consequences of a decision in the context of available choices at the time the decision is to be made. It recommended that a person should be deemed to lack capacity to consent to sexual relations if he or she is unable: (a) to understand the information relevant to engaging in the sexual act; (b) to retain that information; (c) to use or weigh up that information as part of the process of deciding to engage in the sexual act; or (d) to communicate his or her decision (whether by talking, using sign language or any other means).[87]

The Law Reform Commission recommended that there should be a strict liability offence for sexual acts committed by a person in a position of trust or authority with a person with an intellectual disability.

It also recommended that a defence of reasonable mistake should apply but that the defence should not be available to those in positions of trust or authority.[88]

---

[84] Law Reform Commission, *Report on Sexual Offences Against the Mentally Handicapped* (LRC 83–1990).
[85] Law Reform Commission, *Consultation Paper on Sexual Offences and Capacity to Consent* (LRC CP63–2011).
[86] *Consultation Paper on Sexual Offences and Capacity to Consent* (LRC CP63–2011), p.20.
[87] See *Consultation Paper on Sexual Offences and Capacity to Consent* (LRC CP63–2011), p.11.
[88] See *Consultation Paper on Sexual Offences and Capacity to Consent* (LRC CP63–2011), p.11.

Sexual Abuse of Children

There is no specific offence, as such, of sexual abuse of children. However, sexual activity with children may amount to an offence where the child is not old enough to consent to that activity. A person of either sex under 15 years of age cannot consent to activity amounting to a sexual assault by virtue of s.14 of the Criminal Law Amendment Act 1935.

Statutory rape—unlawful carnal knowledge

A girl under the age of 17 years cannot consent to sexual intercourse. Until 2006, under ss.1 and 2 of the 1935 Act, unlawful carnal knowledge of a girl under 15 was an offence punishable by life imprisonment while unlawful carnal knowledge of a girl aged between 15 and 17 years was an offence punishable by five years' imprisonment. This prohibition applied regardless of the age of the offender. Where two 16-year-olds were involved then the male had committed an offence. Arguably, it would have been more appropriate to criminalise sexual intercourse with underage children on a gender-neutral basis, reflecting the fact that a more serious offence is committed where a middle-aged man has intercourse with a 16-year-old girl than where two teenagers are involved.

In this context, "carnal knowledge" simply meant vaginal intercourse and "unlawful" meant that the parties were not married. Otherwise, neither consent nor mistake on the part of the man as to age provided any defence. As regards consent, Maguire C.J. in *AG (Shaughnessy) v Ryan*[89] stated that the sections "were designed to protect young girls, not alone against lustful men, but against themselves".[90] Regarding mistake as to age see *R. v Prince*[91] where even a reasonable mistake as to age was held not to amount to a defence. The accused was charged with the offence of abducting an unmarried girl under the age of 16 years out of the possession of her lawful guardian contrary to s.55 of the Offences Against the Person Act 1861. The girl was 14 years but looked older than 16 and had told the accused she was 18. He believed her and it was held that this belief was reasonable. However, Blackburn J. held that a reasonable belief did not amount to a defence as the offence was one of strict liability:

> "The man who has connection with a child relying on her consent does so at his peril if she is below the statuable age."[92]

The 1990 Law Reform Commission *Report on Child Sexual Abuse*[93] made a series of proposals on reform of the law relating to sexual abuse of children. In relation to statutory rape, it proposed the lowering of the age limit for the more serious offence in s.1 to 13 years but recommended that the offence should remain punishable by a maximum of life imprisonment. It recommended that the maximum sentence for

---

[89] [1960] I.R. 181.
[90] [1960] I.R. 181 at 183.
[91] (1875–1877) 13 Cox CC 138.
[92] (1875–1877) 13 Cox CC 138 at 144.
[93] Law Reform Commission, *Report on Child Sexual Abuse* (LRC 32–1990).

an offence under s.2 be seven years. A further recommendation was that it should not be an offence for a male to have intercourse with a girl aged over 15 years of age unless he is either five years or more older than her or is a person in authority, i.e. any person having even temporary responsibility for her education, supervision or welfare. The existing strict liability relating to rape was criticised and the Law Reform Commission recommended that if the accused genuinely believed that the girl was over 17 years he should have a complete defence unless he was a person in authority or was five years or more older than the girl. If the defendant could demonstrate a reasonable belief that the girl was over 13 years but under 15 years, he should be liable to a maximum sentence of seven years' imprisonment.

The Law Reform Commission also expressed concern about the offence of indecent (now sexual) assault on a person under 15 years of age in s.14 of the Criminal Law Amendment Act 1935. As noted in the section on sexual assault, above, the offence does not cover situations where an adult, without force or threat or touching, induces a child to undress before the adult or to touch him or her indecently. The Commission recommended a new definition of "child sexual abuse" or "sexual exploitation" to cover such scenarios and the Department of Justice *Discussion Paper on Sexual Offences*[94] sought views on this proposal.

However, before any reforming legislation was introduced, the case of *CC v Ireland*[95] came before the courts. This was a challenge to s.1(1) of the Criminal Law Amendment Act 1935, the offence of unlawful carnal knowledge of a girl younger than 15 years. The applicant had been charged with four counts of an offence pursuant to s.1(1) and claimed that he had been told that the girl was 16 years. It was argued that the absence of a defence of honest but mistaken belief that the girl was older than 15 years meant that the offence, a very serious offence with a maximum penalty of life imprisonment, was one of strict liability as to the age of the victim. The Supreme Court confirmed that the offence was one of strict liability.[96] This being so, the offence was an unconstitutional infringement of the defendant's right to a trial in due course of law pursuant to Art.38.1 and the provision was held to be void ab initio[97]:

> "It appears to us that to criminalise in a serious way a person who is mentally innocent is indeed 'to inflict a grave injury on that person's dignity and sense of worth' and to treat him as 'little more than a means to an end' ... It appears to us that this, in turn, constitutes a failure by the State in its laws to respect, defend and vindicate the rights to liberty and to good name of the person so treated, contrary to the State's obligations under Article 40 of the Constitution."[98]

---

[94] *The Law on Sexual Offences: A Discussion Paper* (May 1998).
[95] [2006] 4 I.R. 1.
[96] See Ch.2 on mens rea for an examination of *CC v Ireland* in the context of strict liability offences.
[97] See also, *A v Governor of Arbour Hill Prison* [2006] 4 I.R. 88 where a prisoner who had been convicted of an offence pursuant to s.1(1) of the 1935 Act unsuccessfully challenged the legality of his detention after the *CC* case.
[98] [2006] 4 I.R. 1 at 174 per Hardiman J.

Public outcry followed the decision[99] and emergency legislation in the form of the Criminal Law (Sexual Offences) Act 2006 was enacted to protect children.[100]

Defilement of a child under the age of 15 years and defilement of a child under the age of 17 years

Section 2 of the Criminal Law (Sexual Offences) Act 2006 provides that it is an offence to engage, or attempt to engage, in a sexual act with a child under the age of 15 years. Sexual act is defined as meaning sexual intercourse or buggery or section 4 rape or aggravated sexual assault pursuant to s.3 of the 1990 Act. There is a maximum term of imprisonment of life imprisonment.

Section 3(1) of the 2006 Act states that it is an offence to engage or attempt to engage in a sexual act with a child less than 17 years of age. There is a maximum term of imprisonment of five years and this increases to 10 years if the perpetrator is in a position of authority. A "person in authority" is a parent, step-parent, grandparent, guardian, uncle or aunt; any person acting in loco parentis; and any person responsible for the education, supervision or welfare of the victim.

Consent is not a defence to either offence of defilement and a defence of honest belief is provided for.[101] The burden of proof for establishing this defence is placed on the defendant and the court may take into account whether the defendant had reasonable grounds for such a belief.

Controversially, there is no provision for a "Romeo and Juliet" clause—a defence based on the age of the defendant. This means that a 16-year-old boy who engages in a sexual act with his teenage girlfriend is regarded in the same way as a man in his fifties who also has intercourse with a young girl. However, there is one concession to age: s.3(10) provides that a person convicted of an offence will not be subject to the sex register provisions in the Sex Offenders Act 2001 if he was not more than 24 months older than the victim. In addition, the Director of Public Prosecutions must consent to the bringing of a prosecution under s.3(1) or (2).

---

[99] This resulted in a Government commitment to amend the Constitution to reverse the result of *CC*. The proposed wording of the amendment is as follows: "Provision may be made by law for the collection and exchange of information relating to the endangerment, sexual exploitation or sexual abuse, or risk thereof, of children, or other persons of such a class or classes as may be prescribed by law. No provision in this Constitution invalidates any law providing for offences of absolute or strict liability committed against or in connection with a child under 18 years of age. The provisions of this section of the Article do not, in any way, limit the powers of the Oireachtas to provide by law for other offences of absolute or strict liability."

[100] For an overview of the law in this area, see Alisdair A. Gillespie, "The Future of Child Protection and the Criminal Law" (2007) 17(3) I.C.L.J. 2. See also, *ZS v DPP* [2011] IESC 49 where the constitutionality of s.2(1) of the 1935 Act was challenged. The only real difference between s.2(1) and s.1(1) was that s.2(2) had been amended post-1937 and enjoyed the presumption of constitutionality as a result. However, the Supreme Court held that s.2(1) was, for the same reason as was held in relation to s.1(1) in *CC*, inconsistent with the Constitution and did not survive the entry into force of the Constitution. It was therefore not in force in 1997 when legislation purported to amend it and could not be amended. The Supreme Court granted a declaration that s.2(1) of the Criminal Law Amendment Act 1935 is unconstitutional for the same reasons as s.1(1) was deemed unconstitutional in *CC*.

[101] See *DPP v Egan (Seán)* [2010] IECCA 28 for a discussion of the burden of proof and the defence of honest mistake.

Sexual Offences

The 2006 Act contains a lacuna which has been much criticised.[102] Section 5 states that a female under the age of 17 years shall not be guilty of an offence under the Act by engaging in sexual intercourse. This means that a girl under the age of 17 years who engages in sexual intercourse with a boy under the age of 17 years has committed no offence, whereas the boy has. This criminalises the male who is involved in teenage sexual activity while not criminalising his consensual partner. This was the issue in *MD (a minor) v Ireland, Attorney General and the Director of Public Prosecutions*.[103] The appellant was charged with an offence contrary to s.3(1) of the 2006 Act. At the time of the alleged offences the appellant was 15 years of age and the complainant was 14 years old. The complainant was not charged with any offence. The appellant sought a declaration that s.5 of the 2006 Act was repugnant to the Constitution as it discriminated against him on the basis of gender, contrary to Art.40.1 of the Constitution. As Denham C.J. summarised:

> "The appellant's case, in essence, is that this provision is gender biased and discriminatory and that it exposes the underage male to the real risk of criminal sanctions based on the traditional sexual stereotype where it is legislatively assumed that the male is the guilty predator and the female is the innocent comely maiden. It is submitted that the fact that the female alone can become pregnant is not a ground which justifies an immunity of this kind."[104]

Dunne J. in the High Court concluded that there was discrimination but that it was legitimated because it was founded on difference in capacity, physical or moral or difference of social function of men and women in a manner that was not invidious nor arbitrary nor capricious. The difference was that the risk of pregnancy was only borne by girls. Dunne J. explained this by saying that:

> "The adverse consequences that flow from under age sexual activity fall to a greater extent on girls than on boys. Far from being an example of good old fashioned discrimination against young boys as contended by counsel for the plaintiff or a form of 'rough equalisation', the Act provides a limited immunity to girls in the one area of sexual activity that can result in pregnancy. Society is entitled to deter such activity and to place the burden of criminal sanction on those who bear the least adverse consequences of such activity. The Act goes no further than is necessary to achieve this object."[105]

The Supreme Court noted that s.5 expressly differentiated between males and females but only in relation to sexual intercourse and only where the female is under the age of 17 years. Denham C.J. referred to authorities in other jurisdictions[106] and

---

[102] Houses of the Oireachtas, *Joint Committee on Child Protection Report on Child Protection* (November 2006); Finbarr McAuley, *Report of the Criminal Law Rapporteur for the Legal Protection of Children* (Dublin: Office of the Minister for Children and Youth Affairs, 2007).
[103] [2010] IEHC 101 (High Court decision of Dunne J.); [2012] IESC 10 (Supreme Court).
[104] [2012] IESC 10 at para.6.
[105] [2010] IEHC 101 at para.66.
[106] Notably the United States Supreme Court decision in *Michael M v Superior Court of Sonoma County* 450 US 464 (1981).

commented that decisions on matters of such social sensitivity are a matter for the legislature:

> "The Oireachtas made a choice, and such a legislative decision reflects a social policy on the issue. While the legislature could have enacted another social policy, it was an approach the legislature was entitled to take, it was an issue in society to which the legislature had to respond. The danger of pregnancy for the teenage girl was an objective which the Oireachtas was entitled to regard as relating to 'differences of capacity, physical and moral and of social function', as provided for in Article 40.1 of the Constitution."

The Supreme Court rejected the claim that s.5 was unconstitutional.

Reckless endangerment of children

Section 176 of the Criminal Justice Act 2006 creates the offence of reckless endangerment of children. This applies to a person having authority or control over a child, or over a person who has abused a child, who intentionally or recklessly endangers the child by causing or permitting the child to be placed or left in a situation which creates a substantial risk of serious harm or sexual abuse to the child. The offence is also committed where the person having authority or control over the child fails to take reasonable steps to protect the child from such a risk while knowing that the child is in such a situation.

Child trafficking and pornography

The Child Trafficking and Pornography Act 1998 was enacted to combat international paedophile rings. It became obvious in Europe during the 1990s that children were being kidnapped or brought from developing countries to richer countries for the purposes of sexual exploitation. It was also realised that there was a significant international market for child pornography and that this market was growing with more widespread access to the internet. The offences set out in the Act include child trafficking, taking a child for sexual exploitation, meeting a child for the purpose of sexual exploitation,[107] allowing a child to be used for pornography, producing and distributing child pornography and possession of child pornography. Defendants convicted of offences under this Act may also be subject to the provisions of the Sex Offenders Act 2001.

In *People v Muldoon*,[108] the applicant appealed against the severity of his sentence. He had been convicted of being in possession of and advertising child pornography and was sentenced to two-and-a-half years' imprisonment. The trial judge exercised his jurisdiction under the Sex Offenders Act 2001 to require post-release supervision of the applicant by a probation officer for a period of 11 years. The trial judge imposed a further condition restraining the applicant from having control over a personal computer or from having internet access from his home for the 11-year period. The

---

[107] Inserted by s.6 of the Criminal Law (Sexual Offences) (Amendment) Act 2007.
[108] Unreported, Court of Criminal Appeal, Keane C.J., July 7, 2003.

applicant was only to have access to a personal computer or to the internet under supervision. This aspect of the sentence was appealed on grounds of severity. Keane C.J. dismissed the appeal. He emphasised that the offences were of a very serious nature. The evidence was that the applicant, a person skilled in computer science, had been engaged in conduct amounting to advertising the provision of images involving child pornography which were described as being of a horrific nature. Whilst the restrictions imposed would seriously impinge on the applicant's right to earn a living from his skills in information technology, this was a restriction that he had brought about himself as a result of his criminal activity.

Child sex tourism

The Sexual Offences (Jurisdiction) Act 1996 was passed to deal with the increasing national trend for people to travel abroad to procure children for sexual activity. This legislation applies to Irish citizens and to those ordinarily resident in the country. It provides that Irish courts have jurisdiction to try people suspected of committing sexual offences against children in a foreign country. The activity must have been a criminal offence in the foreign jurisdiction and also be an offence under Irish law. The Act defines "children" as being under the age of 17 years.

Register of sex offenders

The Sex Offenders Act 2001 has significantly altered the way sexual offenders are treated by the criminal justice system. It establishes a register of sex offenders, with particular reference to those who commit offences against children. Such offenders are required to notify Gardaí of their names and addresses. A risk assessment is made of those on the register and the Gardaí are empowered to disclose the names of offenders where necessary to prevent an immediate risk of crime or to alert members of the public to a particular danger. Sex offenders coming into the jurisdiction from abroad are also required to register. A civil sex offenders order is also available against sex offenders whose behaviour in the community gives rise to reasonable concern that such an order is necessary to protect the public. The order is available to prohibit conduct which is not criminal but is nevertheless undesirable, e.g. loitering around school playgrounds. The Act also creates a new offence where sex offenders seek or accept work involving unsupervised contact with children without first notifying the employer of their conviction.

The constitutionality of the Act was challenged unsuccessfully in *Enright v Ireland*.[109] The plaintiff was convicted of sexual offences in 1993 and the Sex Offenders Act 2001 came into force prior to his release. The Act applies to persons convicted before the legislation came into force providing they were still serving a sentence at that date. The High Court held that the fact that a provision had a punitive or deterrent element did not necessarily mean that it should be considered to be part of the criminal penalty for the offence. The registration requirements under the Act did not constitute a penalty for the sex offences committed; therefore, their imposition could not be regarded as inconsistent with the constitutional right

---

[109] [2003] 2 I.R. 321.

under Art.38.1 not to have a penalty imposed which did not exist at the time of the offence. The court remarked that although the notification requirements provided by the Act imposed a burden on the sex offender, they did not restrain him in his movements or place him under a disability. It noted that the Oireachtas, in enacting the Act, was required to weigh up the constitutional rights of convicted persons with the constitutional rights of other citizens who might be at risk of attack from such persons following their release from prison. It was necessary to consider whether this balance was so contrary to reason and fairness as to constitute an unjust attack on the plaintiff's right to fair procedures. The court held that it was not. *Enright v Ireland* was endorsed in *PH v Ireland and Ors*,[110] another unsuccessful challenge to the 2001 Act based on the argument that the burden imposed by the 2001 Act was part of the punishment for the purposes of sentencing and that retrospective registration was therefore unconstitutional.

HUMAN TRAFFICKING

We have seen that child trafficking was criminalised by the Child Trafficking and Pornography Act 1998. However, trafficking for the purposes of sexual exploitation is not limited to children and adults are also protected under the Criminal Law (Human Trafficking) Act 2008. Trafficking is not always for the purpose of sexual exploitation.[111] However, it became apparent that a significant number of women were being trafficked into Ireland, mainly from Eastern Europe and Africa, in order to be used in the sex industry throughout the country and to be transported through this jurisdiction into the United Kingdom and the rest of Europe. Section 4 of the Act criminalises the trafficking of adults if the trafficker coerced, deceived or used force against the trafficked person or anyone in whose care he or she was, or if the trafficker paid for the person trafficked. Section 5 criminalises soliciting a trafficked person for the purpose of prostitution.

---

[110] [2006] IEHC 40.
[111] Forced labour is also a common motivation.

CHAPTER 6

OFFENCES AGAINST THE PERSON

BACKGROUND

Until 1997, the law of non-fatal offences against the person was made up of a variety of statutory and common law offences, the bulk of which were contained in the Offences Against the Person Act 1861. There was a wide range of very specific offences: assault, assault occasioning actual bodily harm, unlawful wounding, wounding with intent, suffocation or strangulation, and so on. The definition of each offence was highly technical and unduly complex. The variety of offences available also caused problems for prosecutors, with cases being lost because the wrong offence was chosen.

The law on this topic has now been comprehensively overhauled by the Non-Fatal Offences Against the Person Act 1997. This Act largely follows the recommendations of the Law Reform Commission made in its *Report on Non-Fatal Offences Against the Person*[1] and creates a simplified hierarchy of offences including assault, assault causing harm, causing serious harm, syringe offences, false imprisonment, coercion, harassment and endangerment.

ASSAULT

Prior to the 1997 Act there were two separate offences: assault and battery. "Assault" was defined as an action causing the victim to *fear* that force would be immediately inflicted upon him, while "battery" was the *actual infliction* of force. For example, if A threatened B, and then struck B, A would have committed an assault when B was caused to fear the imminent use of force and would have committed a battery when he went on to strike B.

Section 2 of the 1997 Act merges both offences under a single offence of assault. "Assault" is now defined as follows:

> A person shall be guilty of the offence of assault who, without lawful excuse [e.g. in the course of making a lawful arrest], intentionally or recklessly—
> (a) directly or indirectly applies force to or causes an impact on the body of another, or
> (b) causes another to believe on reasonable grounds that he or she is likely immediately to be subjected to any such force or impact, without the consent of the other.

---

[1] LRC 45–1994.

Section 2(1)(a) (applying force) corresponds to the old offence of battery, while s.2(1)(b) (causing another to believe that force will be applied) corresponds to the old offence of assault. It is important to note that this legal definition of "assault" does not correspond with the ordinary meaning of the word. Usually, when a person speaks of an "assault" he will have in mind some form of physical contact. Under s.2, however, an assault is committed even where there is no physical contact, provided that the victim was put in fear of imminent unlawful contact.

Consent

Absence of consent is a necessary element of the offence. Consent will be implied in circumstances such as contact sports, where each participant implicitly consents to the use of a certain level of force as part of the sport.

Collins v Wilcock[2] sets out examples of the "exigencies of everyday life" where there is frequently some form of physical contact:

> "So nobody can complain of the jostling which is inevitable from his presence in, for example, a supermarket, an underground station or a busy street; nor can a person who attends a party complain if his hand is seized in friendship, or even if his back is (within reason) slapped ... Although such cases are regarded as examples of implied consent, it is more common nowadays to treat them as falling within the general exception embracing all physical contact which is generally acceptable in the ordinary course of daily life."[3]

As regards ordinary day-to-day conduct (for example tapping a person on the shoulder to attract his attention) s.2(3) provides that no offence is committed if:

- the force or impact is not intended or likely to cause injury; and
- the contact in question is generally acceptable in the ordinary conduct of daily life; and
- the defendant did not know or believe that it was in fact unacceptable to that particular person.

This last point is important, as even innocuous conduct will amount to an assault if a defendant knows that it is unacceptable to a particular person. Suppose A has a phobia about germs, causing him to shun all physical contact. B, knowing this, proceeds to tap him on the shoulder, causing distress to A. B would be guilty of assault.

Corporal punishment

At common law parents (or persons in loco parentis) have long been allowed to use reasonable force for the chastisement or discipline of their children and the 1997 Act does not affect this immunity. Until recently, teachers were also immune

---

[2] [1984] 3 All E.R. 374.
[3] [1984] 3 All E.R. 374 at 378 per Goff. L.J.

Offences Against the Person

from punishment in respect of reasonable corporal punishment. This rule has now, however, been abolished by s.24 of the 1997 Act, which provides:

> The rule of law under which teachers are immune from criminal liability in respect of physical chastisement of pupils, is hereby abolished.

Force

"Force" is defined in s.2(2) to include application of heat, light, electric current, noise or any other form of energy, or application of matter in any form. This definition is extremely wide—it could, for example, amount to an assault if A were to deliberately shine a torch into the eyes of B.

The term "force" here can be misleading. In its everyday meaning it might suggest a requirement of hostility or aggression and in the past it was sometimes stated that battery was committed only where the contact was "angry, or revengeful, or rude, or insolent".[4] However, in modern law it is clear that there is no such requirement—so that if A were to affectionately stroke B's hair, without B's consent, this could be an assault.[5]

There is no minimum threshold for the amount of force required (implied consent to ordinary day-to-day conduct excluded): the slightest touching without consent can amount to an assault, regardless of whether the victim is in fact injured. So in *Collins v Wilcock*[6] it was held to be a battery where a police officer took hold of a woman's arm without her consent. Goff J. stated that:

> "The fundamental principle, plain and incontestable, is that every person's body is inviolate. It has long been established that any touching of another person, however slight, may amount to a battery ... The effect is that everybody is protected not only against physical injury but against any form of physical molestation."[7]

The force need not be applied directly to the body of the victim. It is sufficient if the defendant touches something which is worn or carried by the victim.

Immediacy

Section 2 retains the effect of the prior case law that, for an assault (as distinct from a battery) to occur, the victim must believe that he will be immediately subjected to force or impact. Threats to use force at some future date do not amount to assault, though they may amount to other offences. For the same reason, conduct which would otherwise amount to an assault may be negatived by circumstances which show that the force is not about to be immediately used. In the renowned case of *Tuberville v Savage*[8] it was alleged that the plaintiff had placed his hand on his sword

---

[4] 1 Hawk. P.C. c.62, s.2.
[5] *Faulkner v Talbot* [1981] 1 W.L.R. 1528.
[6] [1984] 3 All E.R. 374.
[7] [1984] 3 All E.R. 374 at 378.
[8] (1669) 2 Keb. 545; 1 Mod. Rep. 3; 86 Eng. Rep. 684.

while saying "if it were not assize time, I would not take such language from you". This was held not to be an assault: placing of the hand on the sword would indicate immediate use of force but the words indicated that the plaintiff would not act and so the defendant could not have believed that force was immediately to be used.

Equally, if A was to wave a knife at B who was on the other side of a gorge and to shout that he intended to kill him, no asault would be committed if the circumstances were that B was safely out of A's range the person would not be put in fear of the immediate application of force.

Causes another to believe

On the same point, an assault is not committed if the victim does not *in fact* apprehend immediate and likely force. Suppose that A is on one side of a gorge and B is on the other. A points a gun at B and threatens to shoot. B is, however, aware that the gun is merely a replica and knows that he is in no danger. In this situation, A has not committed an assault, since B did not apprehend the immediate use of force.

Can words alone amount to an assault?

Before the 1997 Act there was some confusion as to whether words alone, unaccompanied by "menacing gestures" or any physical act, could amount to an assault. For example, in *R. v Meade and Belt*,[9] it was said that "[n]o words or singing are equivalent to an assault, nor will they authorise an assault in return".[10] On the other hand, in *R. v Wilson*,[11] Lord Goddard C.J. held that shouting "get out the knives!" would be an assault.

This supposed rule was often criticised as illogical and arbitrary and in England it was abolished in *R. v Ireland*.[12] In that case, the defendant was alleged to have committed an assault by making silent telephone calls to three women, putting them in fear of violence. It was argued for the defendant that since words alone could not amount to an assault, neither could mere silence. The House of Lords rejected this argument, holding that:

> "The proposition that a gesture may amount to an assault, but that words can never suffice, is unrealistic and indefensible. A thing said is also a thing done. There is no reason why something said should be incapable of causing an apprehension of immediate personal violence, e.g. a man accosting a woman in a dark alley saying, 'Come with me or I will stab you.' I would, therefore, reject the proposition that an assault can never be committed by words."[13]

In this jurisdiction the rule was criticised by the Law Reform Commission and it is clear that the 1997 Act is drafted in such a way as to abolish it. The terms of s.2 ("causes another to believe on reasonable grounds") make it clear that words alone

---

[9] (1823) 1 Lew. CC. 184.
[10] (1823) 1 Lew. CC. 184 at 185.
[11] [1955] 1 W.L.R. 493.
[12] [1998] 1 A.C. 147.
[13] (1823) 1 Lew. CC. 184 at 162 per Lord Steyn.

can now amount to an assault, provided that the words amount to reasonable grounds for the belief that the application of force or impact is immediately likely.

Indirect use of force

Before 1997 the case law was unclear as to whether assault was committed where a person indirectly applied force to another, for example by digging a pit for a victim to fall into, or by derailing a train. On balance, it seemed that it was, as in the case of *DPP v K*[14] where a schoolboy was held to commit assault where he poured acid into a hot air dryer in a bathroom, injuring the next user who switched on the dryer. Section 2 now puts this point beyond doubt and makes it clear that assault can be committed by either the direct or indirect application of force.

This issue arose in England in *Haystead v DPP*.[15] The defendant punched a woman twice in the face, causing her to drop her child. The child struck his head on the floor. The defendant was charged with battery in respect of the injury to the child. He argued that battery at common law could be committed only where there was a direct application of force to the victim. After a comprehensive review of the cases, the court held that battery could be committed indirectly, provided that the physical injury was the direct consequence of the defendant's actions and the chain of causation was not broken by some novus actus interveniens.

Punishment

Simple assault is a summary offence only and carries a maximum fine of €1,500 and/or imprisonment for up to six months.

Assault Causing Harm

The next offence created by the Act is contained in s.3 which provides that "[a] person who assaults another causing him or her harm shall be guilty of an offence". "Harm" is defined in s.1 as "harm to body or mind and includ[es] pain and unconsciousness". This offence is, therefore, an aggravated form of assault made up of the components of assault together with the infliction of harm.

It is significant that harm is defined to include harm to body or mind: an assault which causes the victim no physical harm may nevertheless cause the victim psychological harm and this would seem to fall within the terms of s.3.

Consider *R. v Ireland*.[16] In that case a defendant's silent telephone calls caused a number of victims to suffer psychiatric illness, including severe depression. The House of Lords accepted that this constituted assault causing actual bodily harm under the 1861 Act, on the basis that "the body" included all the organs, including the brain.

Until recently, assault causing harm was presumed to be an aggravated form of assault under s.2. However, the decision of Peart J. in the High Court in *Minister*

---

[14] [1990] 1 All E.R. 331.
[15] [2000] 3 All E.R. 890.
[16] [1998] 1 A.C. 147.

for Justice, Equality and Law Reform v Dolny[17] (which was subsequently approved in a judgment by Denham J. in the Supreme Court) now means that there is some confusion about the matter. This was an extradition decision in the context of which Peart J. held that assault causing harm was a free-standing offence which did not build upon assault in s.2.

The defendant argued that he should not be extradited back to Poland because there was no correspondence between the Polish offence and Irish law. The description of the Polish offence in the warrant did not include the element of lack of consent necessary for the equivalent Irish offence of assault causing harm to be made out. The better view, it is suggested, is that this decision should be seen in the context of extradition law and the principle of correspondence under the European Arrest Warrant procedure and not viewed as changing the substantive criminal law on assault.

Punishment

Assault causing harm is punishable by an unlimited fine and/or imprisonment for up to five years.

Causing Serious Harm

Section 4 creates the offence of causing serious harm:

> A person who intentionally or recklessly causes serious harm to another shall be guilty of an offence.

"Serious harm" is defined in s.1 as meaning:

> [I]njury which creates a substantial risk of death or which causes serious disfigurement or substantial loss or impairment of the mobility of the body as a whole or of the function of any particular bodily member or organ.

This does not follow the recommendations of the Law Reform Commission which advocated the creation of an offence of *assault* causing serious harm. Instead, the 1997 Act simply adopts the concept of *causing* serious harm: it is not necessary that the conduct which causes the harm should also amount to an assault. For example, suppose A knows he is HIV positive; he has unprotected intercourse with B without informing her of his status. B contracts HIV. In these circumstances there is no assault since B consented to the intercourse; nevertheless, if A has the requisite intention then A's conduct may amount to the offence of causing serious harm to B.[18]

The meaning of the phrase "serious harm" was at issue in *DPP v Kirwan*,[19] where it was argued that a "glassing" to the eye did not amount to serious harm. The victim's

---

[17] [2008] IEHC 326 (High Court); [2009] IESC 48 (Supreme Court).
[18] See Ch.5 for a discussion of the transmission of HIV and other diseases by sexual intercourse.
[19] [2005] IECCA 136.

vision had fully recovered following medical treatment. The Court of Criminal Appeal held that this was serious harm, despite the harm not being permanent. Defence submissions that the consequences of the stitching to the victim's eye should not be seen as part of the harm suffered were rejected. The court held that the stitching was intimately associated with the original injury and necessitated by it.

The offence is one of intentionally or recklessly causing serious harm and the requirement of mens rea applies, therefore, both to the conduct in question and to foresight of serious harm. Again, the principles laid down in *DPP v Murray*[20] apply: the defendant must intend serious harm or be subjectively reckless as to whether it results.

Is consent a defence to causing serious harm?

Absence of consent is a constituent part of assault under s.2. Since assault causing harm is generally considered to be an aggravated form of assault, absence of consent is also considered to be a constituent part of assault causing harm contrary to s.3.

Before the 1997 Act consent could only be a defence to the causing of bodily harm under the Offences Against the Person Act 1861 in limited circumstances: consent was not a general defence. The report of the Law Reform Commission[21] recommended that there should be a statutory scheme for determining when consent would be a defence to the infliction of serious harm; however, this recommendation was not followed in the 1997 Act. Consequently, one must look to the case law to see when consent will be a defence.

The issue of consent as a defence to serious harm has generally arisen in three main contexts. The first is that of sport, where players consent to physical contact within the rules of the sport. This will seldom result in serious harm, except in the case of boxing. The second is that of dangerous exhibitions: stunts and the like. The third is that of sadomasochistic sexual activities.

When will consent be a defence in each context? The leading authority is the case of *R. v Brown*.[22] In this case the defendants had consensually and in private inflicted various sadomasochistic tortures on each other. They were unwise enough to video these activities: the video tape fell into the hands of the police and they were charged with occasioning actual bodily harm on each other. The question presented was whether lack of consent was an essential part of the offence.

It was held by the House of Lords that, in the circumstances, consent was irrelevant. As a general rule, a person could not consent to bodily harm: in the words of an earlier case involving a consensual fist fight, "it is not in the public interest that people should try to cause or should cause each other actual bodily harm for no good reason".[23] The House of Lords accepted the decisions in earlier cases that consent was a defence in cases of "properly conducted games and sports, lawful chastisement or correction, reasonable surgical interference, dangerous exhibitions etc. These apparent exceptions can be justified as involving the exercise of a legal

---

[20] See Ch.14 for a discussion of *DPP v Murray*.
[21] Law Reform Commission, *Report on Non-Fatal Offences Against the Person* (LRC 45–1994).
[22] [1994] 1 A.C. 212.
[23] *Attorney General's Reference (No. 6 of 1980)* [1981] Q.B. 715.

right, in the case of chastisement or correction, or as needed in the public interest, in the other cases".[24]

It therefore appears that consent is a defence only where the conduct in question is "in the public interest": needless to say, the House of Lords did not accept that the "gratification of sadomasochistic desires" was in the public interest. Lord Templeman commented that:

> "The violence of sadists and the degradation of their victims have sexual motivations but sex is no excuse for violence ... Society is entitled and bound to protect itself against a cult of violence. Pleasure derived from the infliction of pain is an evil thing. Cruelty is uncivilised."[25]

The minority judgments were given by Lords Mustill and Slynn. Lord Mustill characterised the behaviour as private sexual relations and argued that the criminal law should not intervene in that sphere:

> "... I do not invite your Lordships' House to endorse it as morally acceptable. Nor do I pronounce in favour of a libertarian doctrine specifically related to sexual matters. Nor in the least do I suggest that ethical pronouncements are meaningless, that there is no difference between right and wrong, that sadism is praiseworthy, or that new opinions on sexual morality are necessarily superior to the old, or anything else of the same kind. What I do say is that these are questions of private morality; that the standards by which they fall to be judged are not those of the criminal law ... [T]he state should interfere with the rights of an individual to live his or her life as he or she may choose no more than is necessary to ensure a proper balance between the special interests of the individual and the general interests of the individuals who together comprise the populace at large."[26]

He reviewed the authorities on violence and found that no general theory of consensual violence emerged. He commented on the fact that the majority judgments accepted the legality of boxing:

> "That the court is in such cases making a value-judgment, not dependant upon any general theory of consent is exposed by the failure of any attempt to deduce why professional boxing appears to be immune from prosecution. For money, not recreation or personal improvement, each boxer tries to hurt the opponent more than he is hurt himself, and aims to end the contest prematurely by inflicting a brain injury serious enough to make the opponent unconscious, or temporarily by impairing his central nervous system through a blow to the midriff, or cutting his skin ... The boxers display skill, strength and courage, but nobody pretends that they do good to themselves or others. The onlookers

---

[24] *Attorney General's Reference (No. 6 of 1980)* [1981] Q.B. 715 at 719.
[25] [1994] 1 A.C. 212 at 237.
[26] [1994] 1 A.C. 212 at 273.

derive entertainment, but none of the physical and moral benefits which have been seen as the fruits of engagement in manly sports."[27]

The effect of *R. v Brown* is that, in general, the court will look to the public utility of the act in determining whether consent can amount to a defence. The decision of *R. v Wilson*,[28] decided a short time after *R. v Brown*, controversially came to a different conclusion on similar facts.

The case concerned a husband and wife who had engaged in branding the husband's initials on the wife's buttocks with a hot knife. The uncontroverted evidence was that she had been in full agreement to the branding. On the face of it, the harm caused was very similar to the sadomasochistic acts in *R. v Brown*, albeit in a heterosexual context. The trial judge declared himself bound by *R. v Brown* but the Court of Appeal held that the wife's consent was a defence to a charge of assault occasioning actual bodily harm. The court was of the view that the branding was no more dangerous or painful than tattooing and that it was not in the public interest that consensual activity between a husband and wife in the privacy of the matrimonial home should be a matter for the criminal law.

Russell L.J. commented that there was no factual comparison between the facts of the case and the facts in *R. v Brown*, where:

> "[T]he appellants engaged in sado-masochism of the grossest kind, involving inter alia, physical torture, and as Lord Templeman pointed out ... 'obvious dangers of serious personal injury and blood infection.' The facts of the case were truly extreme ... Mrs Wilson not only consented to that which the appellant did, she instigated it. There was no aggressive intent on the part of the appellant. On the contrary, far from wishing to cause injury to his wife, the appellant's desire was to assist her in what she regarded as the acquisition of a desirable piece of personal adornment, perhaps in this day and age no less understandable than the piercing of nostrils or even tongues for the purposes of inserting decorative jewellery."[29]

Russell L.J. stated that "[i]n this field, in our judgment, the law should develop upon a case by case basis rather than upon general propositions to which, in the changing times in which we live, exceptions may arise from time to time not expressly covered by authority".[30]

After the House of Lords decided *R. v Brown* an appeal was taken to the European Court of Human Rights contending that the applicants' right to privacy had been violated contrary to art.8, but the appeal was rejected as it was held that national authorities were entitled to take such prosecutions for the protection of health within the meaning of art.8(2).[31] The court distinguished *R. v Wilson* on the basis that the

---

[27] [1994] 1 A.C. 212 at 265.
[28] [1997] Q.B. 47.
[29] [1997] Q.B. 47 at 50.
[30] [1997] Q.B. 47 at 50.
[31] *Laskey and others v United Kingdom* [1997] ECHR (Application nos. 21627/93, 21826/93), February 19, 1997 (1997) 24 E.H.R.R. 39. See para.45: "It is evident from the facts established by the national courts that the applicants' sado-masochistic activities involved a significant degree of injury or wounding which could not be characterised as trifling or transient. This, in

injuries inflicted in that case were not comparable in seriousness to those in *R. v Brown*.

The reasons given in *R. v Wilson* for distinguishing *R. v Brown* have been criticised by commentators. Roberts[32] points out that the victims in *R. v Brown* had neither complained to the police nor suffered permanent injury and that Mrs Wilson's scar was a greater and more permanent disfigurement than any suffered during the sadomasochistic activities. He concludes that:

> "Beyond its ephemeral voyeuristic and entertainment value, *Wilson* is an unremarkable case, but it does valuable service by demonstrating that *Brown* was a regrettable decision that has become an unsatisfactory precedent. In an area of the criminal law which bears upon such controversial subjects as surgical intervention, contact sports (including boxing), dangerous exhibitions, and traditional religious practices such as circumcision, as well as the minority sexual practices and tattooing and scarification which arose respectively in *Brown* and *Wilson*, it is inconceivable that the Court of Appeal, much less prosecutors and first instance judges, will be able to turn a blind eye to the leading case indefinitely. Nor should they have to. The criminal law is seriously defective when the Court of Appeal feels obliged to go as far as it did in *Wilson* in taking liberties with their Lordships' decisions so that common sense and justice can prevail. The House of Lords will surely have to reconsider *Brown* before too long …".[33]

Although Roberts made his comments in 1997, this area of the law has not been clarified through the years and *R. v Brown* still remains the leading case. It was followed in another case of sadomasochism in *R. v Emmett*.[34]

Punishment

Causing serious harm may be punished by an unlimited fine and/or life imprisonment.

THREATS TO KILL OR CAUSE SERIOUS HARM

Section 5 of the 1997 Act deals with threats other than in the context of assaults and provides that:

> A person who, without lawful excuse, makes to another a threat, by any means intending the other to believe it will be carried out, to kill or cause serious harm to that other or a third person shall be guilty of an offence.

---

itself, suffices to distinguish the present case from those applications which have previously been examined by the Court concerning consensual homosexual behaviour in private between adults where no such feature was present."

[32] Paul Roberts, "Consent to injury: How far can you go?" (1997) 113 L.Q.R. 27.
[33] Roberts, "Consent to injury: How far can you go?" (1997) 113 L.Q.R. 27 at 35.
[34] *The Times*, October 15, 1999.

Offences Against the Person 177

This section is entirely distinct from assault, even though the same conduct might at the same time amount to both an assault and an offence under s.5. For example, if A stands in front of B with an upraised knife and shouts "I'm going to kill you!" then this would probably amount to both an assault and an offence under s.5. However, if A phones B and says the same words but B knows that A is in another country, then this will not amount to assault: the necessary element of immediacy is lacking. It will, however, amount to an offence under s.5.

This section is also distinct from assault as regards the state of mind of the victim. The crime of assault is established only where a victim actually believes that he is likely to be subjected to immediate force or impact. It is not established where a victim does not so believe. Suppose A threatens B with a replica firearm. If B knows that the firearm is a replica then B may not believe that this is likely. The crime of assault may not have been established. On the other hand, an offence under s.5 will be established: A has made a threat, intending B to believe that it will be carried out, to kill or cause serious injury to B. Under s.5 the subjective state of mind of the victim is irrelevant.

Punishment

Threats to kill or cause serious injury may be punished by an unlimited fine and/or imprisonment for up to 10 years.

Syringe Attacks And Related Offences

During the passage of the 1997 Act there was a wave of public concern about robberies carried out by drug users involving syringes, needles and blood. These robberies appeared especially threatening because of the risk of infection associated with these items. Consequently, s.6 was inserted to create a number of distinct offences relating to syringes, blood and contaminated blood. Before looking at each, terms must be defined. Section 1 defines these as follows:

> "contaminated blood" means blood which is contaminated with any disease, virus, agent or organism which if passed into the bloodstream of another could infect the other with a life threatening or potentially life threatening disease;
> "contaminated fluid" means fluid or substance which is contaminated with any disease, virus, agent or organism which if passed into the bloodstream of another could infect the other with a life threatening or potentially life threatening disease;
> "contaminated syringe" means a syringe which has in it or on it contaminated blood or contaminated fluid;
> "syringe" includes any part of a syringe or needle or any sharp instrument capable of piercing skin and passing onto or into a person blood or any fluid or substance resembling blood.

The offences are then created as follows. First is the offence created by s.6(1) in two components. The first component is injuring another by piercing the skin of that other with a syringe, or threatening to so injure the other with a syringe. The second is that the defendant intends the victim to believe, or it is likely that the victim will be caused to believe, that he may become infected with a disease as a result.

Secondly is the offence created by s.6(2), which is again in two parts. The first is spraying, pouring or putting onto another, blood or any substance resembling blood, or threatening to do so. The second is the same as in s.6(1): that the defendant intends the victim to believe, or it is likely that the victim will be caused to believe, that he may become infected with a disease as a result.

Thirdly is the offence created by s.6(3):

> A person who in committing or attempting to commit an offence under section 6(1) or section 6(2)—
> (a) injures a third person with a syringe by piercing his or her skin, or
> (b) sprays, pours or puts onto a third person blood or any fluid or substance resembling blood, resulting in the third person believing that he or she may become infected with disease as a result of the injury or action caused, shall be guilty of an offence.

This is a secondary offence, which comes into play only once a person is committing or attempting to commit an offence under s.6(1) or (2) and covers the situations where A threatens or attacks B but manages also to injure C. In these circumstances, A is guilty of an offence.

Finally, there are the offences created by s.6(5). These offences are distinguished from the preceding offences in that they involve actual (not merely threatened) attacks with contaminated blood or syringes and therefore a real risk of actually causing disease. Under s.6(5)(a) it is an offence to intentionally injure another by piercing the skin of that other with a contaminated syringe. Under s.6(5)(b) it is an offence to intentionally spray, etc. another with contaminated blood. Under s.6(5)(c) it is an offence, similar to that created by s.6(3), to injure a third person while committing or attempting to commit an offence under s.6(5)(a) or (b).

Punishment

For each of the offences created by subss.(1), (2) and (3), the maximum penalty is an unlimited fine and/or imprisonment for up to 10 years. The maximum penalty for the subs.(5) offence is an unlimited fine and/or life imprisonment.

Possession of syringes

Section 7 creates an offence of possession of a syringe, etc. with intention to cause or to threaten injury or intimidate another. The maximum penalty for this offence is an unlimited fine and/or imprisonment for up to seven years.

Section 8 creates two distinct offences of placing or abandoning syringes in places where they are likely to injure another. The less serious offence (subs.(1)) is committed where a person "places or abandons a syringe in any place in such a manner that it is likely to injure another and does injure another or is likely to injure, cause a threat to or frighten another". This carries a maximum penalty of an unlimited fine and/or imprisonment for up to seven years. The more serious offence is defined by subs.(2) and applies where a person "intentionally places a contaminated syringe in any place in such a manner that it injures another". This requires three distinct elements: there must be an intention to injure, there must be an injury and the syringe must in fact be contaminated. This carries a maximum penalty of an unlimited fine and/or life imprisonment. This section would cover, for example, leaving a syringe hidden in a seat with the intention that the next occupant should injure himself.

COERCION

The 1997 Act creates a general offence of coercion in s.9. Before 1997 there had been only one specific offence of coercion, which was limited in scope. Section 9 is wider and covers various forms of harassment and intimidation intended to coerce:

> A person who, with a view to compel another to abstain from doing or to do any act which that other has a lawful right to do or to abstain from doing, wrongfully and without lawful authority—
> (a) uses violence to or intimidates that other person or a member of the family of the other, or
> (b) injures or damages the property of that other, or
> (c) persistently follows that other about from place to place, or
> (d) watches or besets the premises or other place where that other resides, works or carries on business, or happens to be, or the approach to such premises or place, or
> (e) follows that other with one or more persons in a disorderly manner in or through any public place,
> shall be guilty of an offence.

The offence has two constituent parts: the intention to compel and the use of unacceptable means to do so. However, it seems that the offence will not be committed by, for example, a creditor who resorts to following a debtor around to secure payment: in that case it cannot be said that the debtor has a lawful right to abstain from payment.

Punishment

The maximum penalty for this offence is an unlimited fine and/or imprisonment for up to five years.

HARASSMENT

The Law Reform Commission in its Report identified a need for a new offence to cover acts of harassment that interfere with a person's right to a peaceful and private life, even though those acts might not give rise to a fear of violence. The essence of this offence is not the individual actions, which might not in themselves be illegal, but the distress caused by their repetition.

Suppose, for example, that A engages in what is commonly described as stalking—persistently following B, making silent phone calls to B, and/or sending B numerous letters, with the result that B becomes upset and distressed. Prior to the 1997 Act this conduct would have been difficult to prosecute. In particular, unless B was put in fear of violence, no assault was committed.[35]

The result of this gap in the law was that victims generally had to resort to civil actions for their protection. An example of this can be seen in *Royal Dublin Society v Yates*[36] where the defendant appeared to become besotted by an employee of the plaintiff society and pursued her by way of flowers, poems, letters and even paintings depicting her. He also frequented the premises of the plaintiff and the streets outside and at one point had to be forcibly ejected from those premises. The court accepted that his behaviour amounted to the tort of nuisance and granted an injunction restraining the defendant from communicating with the victim, or with any other employees of the plaintiff.

The recommendation of the Law Reform Commission was followed in s.10 of the 1997 Act, which provides:

(1) Any person who, without lawful authority or reasonable excuse, by any means including by use of the telephone, harasses another by persistently following, watching, pestering, besetting or communicating with him or her, shall be guilty of an offence.
(2) For the purposes of this section a person harasses another where—
    (a) he or she, by his or her acts intentionally or recklessly, seriously interferes with the other's peace or privacy or causes alarm, distress or harm to the other, and
    (b) his or her acts are such that a reasonable person would realise that the acts would seriously interfere with the other's peace and privacy or cause alarm, distress or harm to the other.

Mens rea

The mens rea for this offence presents an unusual problem. In many cases a stalker is likely to be unaware of the effect of his conduct. Typically, the offender may be somewhat unbalanced and will pursue what he perceives to be a romantic interest, being unaware that his conduct is unwelcome. Will this person have the necessary mens rea to be found guilty of harassment, given that he is genuinely oblivious to the effect of his actions?

Under s.10 the offence is committed by a person who "by his or her acts *intentionally or recklessly*, seriously interferes with the other's peace and privacy

---

[35] Although in *R. v Ireland* [1998] 1 A.C. 147 the House of Lords took a creative approach to this problem and held that acts of harassment which resulted in psychological injury could amount to the infliction of grievous bodily harm contrary to s.20 of the Offences Against the Person Act 1861, since that section penalised the infliction of harm irrespective of whether the harm was caused by way of an assault.
[36] [1997] IEHC 144.

or causes alarm, distress or harm to the other". In addition, the actions must be "such that a *reasonable person would realise* that the acts would seriously interfere with the other's peace and privacy, or cause alarm, distress or harm". This wording refers to the defendant's *acts* as being intentional or reckless, rather than the *effect* of those acts. Instead, the effects are judged according to the standard of the reasonable person. Although this wording is cumbersome, it appears clear that it is intended to cover a person who does not realise the effect of his actions, provided that a reasonable person would so realise.

Suppose, for example, a besotted individual stalks his victim while believing that he is merely pursuing her romantically, or that his behaviour is actually welcome to the victim. Section 10 will cover this situation, notwithstanding the absence of understanding on the part of the offender. Indeed, under any other interpretation the most persistent and dangerous offenders might escape liability on the basis that they did not appreciate the effects of their actions.

Persistently

The section applies only where a defendant "persistently" harasses another. Consequently, a single incident will not be sufficient to establish the crime. Instead, the prosecution must show a number of incidents over a period of time. This may present some problems in borderline cases.

Suppose, for example, that A telephones B several times over the space of an hour. Would this conduct be persistent, given that it takes place over a relatively short period of time and might arguably be described as one incident? Alternatively, suppose that A confronts B on two occasions, several months apart, in relation to two separate issues. Would this amount to persistent conduct, given the small number of incidents, the length of time separating them and the lack of any apparent link between the two incidents?

There is, as yet, no Irish case considering this point. However, a number of English decisions have considered the similar requirement under the Protection of Harassment Act 1997 that a defendant's actions must amount to a "course of conduct".

In *Kelly v DPP*,[37] it was held that a defendant who left three messages on the victim's voice mail in the space of five minutes had engaged in a course of conduct for the purposes of the Act: the court was entitled to treat each message as separate and distinct, notwithstanding the defence argument that in reality the three telephone calls amounted to a single incident. It will be interesting to see whether this approach would be followed by an Irish court: arguably, the word "persistently" would require that the conduct extend over a longer period of time.

In *R. v Hills*,[38] the defendant had attacked his partner on two separate occasions, six months apart. Between the two attacks, however, the defendant and the victim had reconciled and lived together. The charge of harassment was dismissed, on the basis that the two attacks did not amount to a course of conduct. The court was particularly influenced by the fact that there were only two incidents, a substantial

---

[37] [2003] Crim. L.R. 45.
[38] [2001] 1 F.C.R. 569.

period of time had elapsed between the two attacks, and the two attacks could not be described as linked to each other by anything other than the identity of the parties.

Lawful authority or reasonable excuse

There is an exception for conduct which is carried out either under lawful authority or with reasonable excuse. For example, overt surveillance by the Gardaí will not be criminalised. The offence is, therefore, not intended to cover situations where there is a good reason for what might otherwise amount to harassment. Another example given by the Law Reform Commission was that of a creditor who pursues a debtor seeking payment:

> "The question may also arise as to whether a creditor who repeatedly seeks to have a bill paid should be guilty of an offence. The answer would seem to be that, while clearly the point can be reached where persistence becomes harassment, the legitimacy or justifiability of the intrusion is a factor to which weight should be attached in determining whether the conduct was worthy of criminal sanction. For this reason we recommend that it should be necessary to prove that the conduct was without lawful authority or reasonable excuse. We appreciate that this introduces an element of uncertainty, but without a proviso on these lines the offence would seem overbroad."[39]

Non-contact orders

If a person is convicted of harassment, the court has the power to order that he not communicate with the victim or approach closer than a specified distance to the victim's home or workplace, for such period as the court determines.[40] It is an offence to fail to comply with such an order.[41] Remarkably, the court is also given the power to make such an order even if the defendant is not convicted, provided that it considers it to be "in the interests of justice to do so".[42] This would seem to include cases where the prosecutor meets the civil standard of proof but not the criminal standard, or where the defendant is dealt with under the Probation Act. However, there must be a question mark over the constitutionality of a power to restrict a defendant's liberty where that person has been acquitted of an offence.

In the first conviction under this section (and the only reported decision on harassment to date), *DPP v Ramachchandran*,[43] the court considered the extent of this power. In that case, the accused was convicted of the harassment of a woman and her daughter. However, his trial was compromised by a number of factors stemming from his insistence on representing himself. The Court of Criminal Appeal overturned his conviction but held that, notwithstanding his acquittal, the court was satisfied on the balance of probabilities that the two victims were in need

---

[39] Law Reform Commission, *Report on Non-Fatal Offences Against the Person* (LRC 45–1994), p.258.
[40] Section 10(3).
[41] Section 10(4).
[42] Section 10(5).
[43] [2000] 2 I.R. 307.

of the protection of the court and therefore granted a non-contact order against him. The case illustrates, therefore, that such orders may be made even where there is no conviction and establishes that the standard of proof for such orders is the civil standard rather than the criminal standard. It also shows how wide such orders may be: amongst other things, the defendant was ordered to remain outside an area three miles in radius, centred on Eyre Square in Galway, thus effectively barring the defendant from the entire city.

Punishment

The maximum penalty for this offence is an unlimited fine and/or imprisonment for up to seven years.

Demands for Payment of Debts

Section 11 of the 1997 Act deals with the special case of demands for the payment of a debt. These may amount to coercion, if the debt is not in fact due, or harassment, but will also be subject to this section which provides:

> A person who makes any demand for payment of a debt shall be guilty of an offence if—
> (a) the demands by reason of their frequency are calculated to subject the debtor or a member of the family of the debtor to alarm, distress or humiliation, or
> (b) the person falsely represents that criminal proceedings lie for non-payment of the debt, or
> (c) the person falsely represents that he or she is authorised in some official capacity to enforce payment, or
> (d) the person utters a document falsely represented to have an official character.

This is a summary offence only and carries a maximum fine of €1,500.

Poisoning

Section 12 creates an offence of poisoning:

> A person shall be guilty of an offence if, knowing that the other does not consent to what is being done, he or she intentionally or recklessly administers to or causes to be taken by another a substance which he or she knows to be capable of interfering substantially with the other's bodily functions.

The section goes on to specify that "a substance capable of inducing unconsciousness or sleep is capable of interfering substantially with bodily functions".[44] Note that the

---

[44] Section 12(2).

section covers both administration of a substance as well as causing it to be taken—if, for example, A were to spike B's drink with a sedative, this could amount to poisoning, notwithstanding that A did not directly administer it to B.

The maximum penalty for this offence is an unlimited fine and/or imprisonment for up to three years.

Endangerment

Prior to the 1997 Act, Irish law recognised a number of specific offences involving the creation of a risk, without any actual injury being caused. It was, for example, an offence to interfere with the railways in a way which created a risk, or to lay a mantrap. There was, however, no general defence of endangerment.

The Law Reform Commission argued that the deliberate or reckless creation of a risk was itself deserving of punishment, notwithstanding that no injury might actually be caused, and therefore recommended that a wider offence of endangerment should be created:

> "Moreover, the right to bodily integrity would be given more comprehensive and consistent protection by the creation of such an offence. In the first place, it would cover the gap in existing law arising from the fact that a person who recklessly creates a risk of serious injury commits no offence although he may be prosecuted for attempt where he does so intentionally, or for causing serious injury where such injury results. In certain cases, where the evidence of intent is insufficient, it may provide a valuable alternative to a charge of attempted murder or attempting to cause serious injury.
>
> ...
>
> In such cases of advertent risk-taking, where the risk of serious injury or death may be said to be 'substantial', there is clearly a strong case for facilitating early intervention by authority to prevent the occurrence of actual harm. The creation of a general offence of endangerment would also give effect to the principle that the wanton disregard of others' safety is in itself deserving of condemnation and sanction as a serious infringement of basic values, irrespective of the manner in which such a risk is taken."

This recommendation was followed in s.13 which creates a general offence of endangerment:

> A person shall be guilty of an offence who intentionally or recklessly engages in conduct which creates a substantial risk of death or serious harm to another.

"Serious harm" is defined in s.1 as:

> [I]njury which creates a substantial risk of death or which causes serious disfigurement or substantial loss or impairment of the mobility of the body as a whole or of the function of any particular bodily member or organ.

Examples of endangerment would include, according to the Law Reform Commission, a builder who constructs a building in a way which he knows to be unsafe and to create a risk of collapse. Charleton, McDermott and Bolger have also suggested that endangerment might be committed in circumstances similar to the Blood Transfusion Board scandal, where officials were aware that blood products were contaminated but failed to take steps to recall the products or warn the users about the products.[45]

The only cases to date on endangerment are the Supreme Court decisions in *DPP v Cagney and McGrath*.[46] These two related cases arose out of a late-night drunken brawl involving the victim, Langan, and the two defendants. During the brawl McGrath attempted to attack Langan but was held back by a friend. McGrath then shouted at Cagney to hit Langan for him. Cagney did so, striking Langan with two blows to the head. Langan fell to the ground, hitting his head, and ultimately dying from the effects of the fall.

McGrath and Cagney were charged with manslaughter and endangerment. Both were acquitted of manslaughter but convicted of endangerment. An appeal was taken to the Court of Criminal Appeal. In the case of Cagney, this verdict presented little difficulty: the Court of Criminal Appeal held that striking somebody in the head is clearly conduct which creates a substantial risk of serious harm.

In the case of McGrath, a more difficult issue was presented. Could McGrath be said to be guilty of endangerment in circumstances where he merely ran after, shouted at and threatened the victim? The defence argued that this was a mere "expression of anger and aggression" and was insufficient to come within the statute. The prosecution, however, argued that McGrath had endangered the victim, and in particular by roaring the words "hit him" had caused the blows that were struck by Cagney.

The Court of Criminal Appeal accepted that McGrath could be found guilty of endangerment, holding that his conduct in pursuing the victim in an aggressive manner, shouting at and threatening the victim and shouting to Cagney in an aggressive manner to hit the victim, together would entitle the jury to find he had created a substantial risk of serious harm to the victim.

However, the Supreme Court came to a different conclusion, allowed the appeal in each case and did not direct a re-trial.

Hardiman J. considered that it was:

> "[U]ndesirable that so vague and open ended a section should be used in circumstances such as those of the present case where the actions of the applicants as alleged by the prosecution would clearly constitute an established and recognised criminal offence, *viz.* assault in one of its variants. In those circumstances, in my view, it is desirable that the obvious offence should be charged ... I wish ... to express concern about the bringing of a charge of endangerment in all its uncertainty where a more specific offence is available."[47]

---

[45] Charleton, McDermott and Bolger, *Criminal Law* (1999), p.736.
[46] [2008] 2 I.R. 111.
[47] [2008] 2 I.R. 111 at 122.

Hardiman J. referred to the Law Reform Commission Report[48] which made it clear that the offence of endangerment was designed to fill a gap in the law where one arose and not as an alternative charge:

> "If an alternative to a charge of manslaughter is needed, because of difficulty in proving causation or otherwise, it already exists in the form of assault either in its basic form or in some aggravated form. In this respect there is no 'gap' to be filled in a case like the present."[49]

Geoghegan J. made the point that the inclusion of endangerment on the same indictment as manslaughter caused a difficulty in respect of ensuring there was a fair trial:

> "I do not know how that could have been achieved in a case such as this where in the case of the more serious offence *i.e.* manslaughter, the jury had simply to consider whether the act was likely to cause some injury above the level of trivial with an objective test in relation to that evaluation, whereas in relation to the lesser offence of endangerment, complex instructions would have to be given to the jury first of all that they had to consider the matter as of the time the danger was created and not have regard to the actual damage that resulted and secondly, that the *mens rea* required an actual subjective appreciation of the likely creation of a substantial risk of death or serious injury, as defined."[50]

The maximum penalty for endangerment is an unlimited fine and/or seven years' imprisonment.

Endangering Traffic

Related to the s.13 endangerment offence, s.14 creates a more specific offence of endangering traffic:

> A person shall be guilty of this offence who—
> (a) intentionally places or throws any dangerous obstruction upon a railway, road, street, waterway or public place or interferes with any machinery, signal, equipment or other device for the direction, control or regulation of traffic thereon, or interferes with or throws anything at or on any conveyance used or to be used thereon, and
> (b) is aware that injury to the person or damage to property may be caused thereby, or is reckless in that regard.

The maximum penalty is the same as for the general offence of endangerment, even though the mens rea is lesser: under s.14 a person need only be reckless as to the

---

[48] Law Reform Commission, *Report on Non-Fatal Offences Against the Person* (LRC 45–1994).
[49] [2008] 2 I.R. 111 at 125.
[50] [2008] 2 I.R. 111 at 139.

possibility of *any* injury or damage to property, while under s.13 a person must be reckless as to the possibility of *serious* injury.

FALSE IMPRISONMENT

Before 1997 there were two distinct offences related to restraints on personal liberty: kidnapping and false imprisonment. The offence of kidnapping was a common law offence and was committed where a person was taken by force or fraud against his will. The offence of false imprisonment was also a common law offence and was committed when the accused "unlawfully impose[d], for any time, a total restraint on the personal liberty of another". Both were declared to be felonies punishable by life imprisonment by s.11 of the Criminal Law Act 1976.

The 1997 Act amalgamates the two offences, reflecting what was happening in practice, with prosecutors relying on the charge of false imprisonment because of ambiguities in the offence of kidnapping.[51]

Section 15 therefore provides:

(1) A person shall be guilty of the offence of false imprisonment who intentionally or recklessly—
    (a) takes or detains, or
    (b) causes to be taken or detained, or
    (c) otherwise restricts the personal liberty of another without that other's consent.
(2) For the purposes of this section, a person acts without the consent of another if the person obtains the other's consent by force or threat of force, or by deception causing the other to believe that he or she is under a legal compulsion to consent.

The provision regarding consent is important: consent is vitiated by force but is only vitiated by fraud if this causes the victim to believe that there is a legal obligation to consent. It is pointed out by the Law Reform Commission that:

"In other cases of deception, the victim is free to withdraw consent at any time without fear of force being used, so that his or her liberty cannot be said to be totally restrained."[52]

As regards the restraint on personal liberty, it is clear that s.15 retains the common law position that a person can be falsely imprisoned without being aware of the fact: *Dullaghan v Hillen and King*.[53] A person can be falsely imprisoned although asleep or mentally handicapped so as to be unable to appreciate the fact.

How severe must the restraint on personal liberty be to amount to false imprisonment? At common law, the imprisonment must be total: that is, a person

---

[51] P.A. Charleton, *Offences Against the Person* (Dublin: Round Hall Press, 1992), p.244.
[52] Law Reform Commission, *Report on Non-Fatal Offences Against the Person* (LRC 45–1994), p.319.
[53] [1957] Ir. Jur. Rep. 10.

must be confined within fixed bounds, so as to prevent movement in all directions. However, those fixed bounds could be quite large: imprisonment in a room, a house or a vast country estate would all amount to a crime. It did not take place where a person was walled in on three sides but free to walk away through the fourth. However, a person was not required to take an unreasonable risk, for example of personal injury, or to undergo some major humiliation to avoid an obstacle created by the defendant. A person would be falsely imprisoned if his clothes were taken away, so that while he was free to leave he would have to appear in public naked.

Section 15 at first glance appears to be wider in scope, in that it refers to "restricting personal liberty", which might be read to include situations where a person's freedom of movement was constrained in some directions but not in others. However, the Law Reform Commission did not recommend such a radical change in the law and it therefore seems that imprisonment must still be total: a mere obstruction in a person's path will not amount to false imprisonment. For the same reason there is no false imprisonment where a person is under close surveillance which does not actually confine them. In *Kane v Governor of Mountjoy Prison*,[54] the applicant was kept under extremely close Garda surveillance while a warrant for his extradition was pending. He alleged that he had in effect been detained by this surveillance. This argument was rejected by the Supreme Court: the surveillance had not interfered with his ability to go where he chose, which was the essence of detention.

False imprisonment carries a maximum penalty of life imprisonment.

CHILD ABDUCTION

The 1997 Act creates two distinct offences of child abduction. The first, contained in s.16, relates to the abduction of a child by a parent or guardian, who takes the child out of the State either in defiance of a court order or without court approval or the consent of each guardian of the child. It does not apply where the person is a parent but is not a guardian. It is a defence that the person was unable to communicate with the other persons from whom consent is required but believed that they would consent; it is also a defence that the person did not intend to deprive others of their rights in relation to the child. The sensitivity of this offence is reflected in the fact that proceedings cannot be instituted without the consent of the Director of Public Prosecutions.

The second relates to abduction of children by other persons. Section 17 makes it an offence for a person, other than one to whom s.16 applies (parents, guardians and persons having custody), to intentionally take or detain or cause to be taken or detained a child under the age of 16 so as to remove or keep the child from the lawful custody of another person having control of the child. This offence does not require that the child be taken out of the jurisdiction. Belief that the child is 16 years or over is a defence. The consent of the child is irrelevant for both this offence and the offence under s.16: the offences are designed to protect parents as well as children who will not be in a position to give an informed consent, particularly where the child is quite young.

---

[54] [1988] I.L.R.M. 724.

Assault with Intent to Cause Bodily Harm or Commit an Indictable Offence

This offence is created by s.18 of the Criminal Justice (Public Order) Act 1994 and is another form of aggravated assault:

> Any person who assaults any person with intent to cause bodily harm or to commit an indictable offence shall be guilty of an offence.

Assault of Certain Classes of Workers

Section 19 of the Criminal Justice (Public Order) Act 1994[55] provides for an offence of assault of certain classes of workers. This offence was enacted due to the perception that, in particular, health workers involved in accident and emergency services in hospitals were being subjected to assaults by people who were often violent due to alcohol or drug-taking:

> (1) Any person who assaults or threatens to assault—
>   (a) a person providing medical services at or in a hospital, or
>   (b) a person assisting such a person, or
>   (c) a peace officer acting in the execution of a peace officer's duty, knowing that he or she is, or being reckless as to whether he or she is, a peace officer so acting, or
>   (d) any other person acting in aid of a peace officer, or
>   (e) any other person with intent to resist or prevent the lawful apprehension or detention of himself or herself or any other person for any offence,
>   shall be guilty of an offence.

There is also an offence of resisting or wilful obstruction or impeding:

> (3) Any person who resists or wilfully obstructs or impedes—
>   (a) a person providing medical services at or in a hospital, knowing that he or she is, or being reckless as to whether he or she is, a person providing medical services, or
>   (b) a person assisting such a person, or
>   (c) a peace officer acting in the execution of a peace officer's duty, knowing that he or she is or being reckless as to whether he or she is, a peace officer so acting, or
>   (d) a person assisting a peace officer in the execution of his or her duty,
>   shall be guilty of an offence.

The term "peace officer" includes ambulance personnel.

---

[55] As amended by s.185 of the Criminal Justice Act 2006.

Blackmail

Section 17(1) of the Criminal Justice (Public Order) Act 1994 creates an offence which is generally described as blackmail:

> It shall be an offence for any person who, with a view to gain for himself or with intent to cause loss to another, makes any unwarranted demand with menaces.

An "unwarranted demand" is defined by s.17(2)(a):

> [A] demand with menaces shall be unwarranted unless the person making it does so in the belief—
> (i) that he has reasonable grounds for making the demand, and
> (ii) that the use of menaces is a proper means of reinforcing the demand.

This is a two-stage test: for a defendant to escape liability he must believe both that the demand is reasonable and that the menaces are reasonable. Threatening to publish nude photographs of a person could not be believed to be a proper way of reinforcing an otherwise legitimate demand for payment of a debt, for example.

In addition, s.17(2)(b) specifies that the nature of the act demanded is immaterial, as is whether the menaces relate to action to be taken by the person making the demand. In other words, it does not matter what is demanded, nor whether the defendant's threat relates to something to be done by him or by others.

The components of the offences are therefore:

(1) an unwarranted demand;
(2) with menaces; and
(3) made with a view to gain for the defendant, or to cause loss to another.

"Menaces" are not defined in the 1994 Act and therefore we must look to the case law on the previous offences of blackmail under ss.29–31 of the Larceny Act 1916. These cases originally defined "menaces" as threats of injury to the person or to property, but later cases gave "menaces" a wider meaning, with Lord Wright stating that:

> "[T]he word menace is to be liberally construed and not as limited to threats of violence but as including threats of any action detrimental to or unpleasant to the person addressed."[56]

In that case, the defendant was a trade association who demanded that a member pay a fine for breach of the rules of the association by selling at or below an agreed price. Failure to pay the fine would result in the member being boycotted by other members. It was held that this did not constitute the offence of demanding money with menaces without reasonable or probable cause (under the 1916 Act) since it did

---

[56] *Thorne v Motor Trade Association* [1937] A.C. 797.

not go beyond the promotion of lawful business interests. However, the definition of "menaces" will encompass, for example, the threat of publication of details of a person's sexual life. So, in *R. v Tomlinson*,[57] the victim was caught with a woman who was not his wife and the defendant threatened to tell the world. This was held to come within the meaning of "menaces", notwithstanding that neither the conduct of the victim, nor the activity of the defendant in revealing this conduct, would in itself be illegal.

---

[57] [1895] 1 Q.B. 707.

CHAPTER 7

OFFENCES AGAINST PROPERTY

CRIMINAL JUSTICE (THEFT AND FRAUD OFFENCES) ACT 2001

Introduction

This area of the law is concerned with offences against property involving an element of fraud or theft.[1] Prior to 2001, the law governing theft and fraud was to be found at common law and also in numerous statutes, such as the Larceny Acts of 1861 and 1913. The Law Reform Commission Reports on the Law Relating to Dishonesty[2] and Receiving Stolen Property[3] recommended comprehensive reform on the law of theft and fraud. After a long wait, the Criminal Justice (Theft and Fraud Offences) Act 2001 was eventually enacted, creating a new statutory scheme governing theft and fraud offences. The Criminal Justice (Theft and Fraud Offences) Act 2001 is largely based on the Law Reform Commission *Report on the Law Relating to Dishonesty* (1992), as well as the *Report of the Government Advisory Committee on Fraud* (1992).[4] It follows that both of these Reports may be relevant to understanding the background to the enactment of the provisions of the 2001 Act. The principal aims of the 2001 Act are to consolidate the law on theft and fraud into a single statute, make the law more accessible and clear by reducing the number of offences on the statute book and to modernise the law by ensuring that the coverage of the Act is adequate to address novel forms of harm that have emerged as a result of advances in technology.[5]

THEFT

Background

The offence of theft in s.4 of the Criminal Justice (Theft and Fraud Offences) Act 2001 covers a wide range of criminal conduct that was previously dealt with by a number of specific offences, including larceny, embezzlement, obtaining by false pretences and fraudulent conversion. By providing for a single comprehensive

---

[1] See Cathal McGreal, *Criminal Justice (Theft and Fraud Offences) Act 2001 Annotated and Consolidated*, 2nd edn (Dublin: Round Hall, 2011), for a comprehensive and detailed analysis of the law relating to theft and fraud in Ireland.
[2] Law Reform Commission, *Report on the Law Relating to Dishonesty* (LRC 43–1992).
[3] Law Reform Commission, *Report on Receiving Stolen Property* (LRC 23–1987).
[4] 527 *Dáil Debates* Col.247 (Second Stage).
[5] 527 *Dáil Debates* Cols 247–248 (Second Stage).

Offences Against Property

definition of "theft" it was intended to depart from the previous legislative approach of having multiple offences dealing with specific instances of conduct that harms property interests.[6] The proliferation of so-called "crimes du jour" can lead to an unprincipled approach to law making if left unchecked, as well as having an adverse impact on the accessibility and comprehensibility of the law due to the volume of law that may build up over a period of time.[7] In this regard, the enactment of the offence of theft in s.4 of the 2001 Act can be viewed as an example of offence consolidation, with a view to streamlining, and modernising, the law relating to theft.

The offence of theft is defined in s.4(1) of the 2001 Act as dishonestly appropriating property without the consent of the owner and with the intention of depriving the owner of the property. Each of the terms contained in the definition of "theft" are defined in further detail elsewhere in the Act.

Dishonestly: without a claim of right made in good faith

The term "dishonestly" is defined in s.2(1) of the Criminal Justice (Theft and Fraud Offences) Act 2001 as meaning "without a claim of right made in good faith". This is in contrast to the position in England. English case law has allowed the meaning of the term "dishonestly" to be defined by "the current standards of ordinary decent folk".[8] In *R. v Ghosh*,[9] a two-fold test was adopted in relation to defining the term "dishonestly" for the purposes of the Theft Act 1968: (1) what was done was dishonest according to the ordinary standards of reasonable and honest people; (2) the accused realised that what he was doing was dishonest according to those standards. The problems associated with the English position on dishonesty relate to the potential for inconsistency in the application of the law; if the term "dishonestly" is left undefined, the interpretation of the meaning of that term may vary considerably from case to case.[10] In the Supreme Court of Victoria decision in *R. v Salvo*, Fulager J. considered some of the difficulties that may arise with the English approach to dishonesty:

> "The public respect for the Courts, upon which the Courts' authority and existence ultimately depend, is held *because* they decide cases according to known legal principles. It is equally important that the principles applied be legal principles and known principles. Feelings and intuitions as to what constitutes dishonesty and even as to what dishonesty means must vary greatly from jury to jury and from judge to judge and from magistrate to magistrate."[11]

In Ireland, the drafters of the Criminal Justice (Theft and Fraud Offences) Act 2001 would appear to have opted against adopting the English approach to the issue of

---

[6] 527 *Dáil Debates* Cols 249–250 (Second Stage).
[7] See Criminal Law Codification Advisory Committee, *Draft Criminal Code and Commentary* (Dublin, 2011), pp.6–7 for further discussion on offence consolidation.
[8] *R. v Feely* [1973] Q.B. 530.
[9] [1982] Q.B. 1053.
[10] Elliot, "Dishonesty in theft: A Dispensable Concept" [1982] Crim. L.R. 395; McGreal, *Criminal Justice (Theft and Fraud Offences) Act 2001 Annotated and Consolidated* (2011), p.23.
[11] [1980] V.R. 401 at 430.

dishonesty, and instead followed the Law Reform Commission recommendation to provide a statutory definition of the term "dishonestly" as meaning without a claim of right made in good faith.[12] The Law Reform Commission sets out the rationale for including a claim-of-right provision in the offence of theft in the following passage:

> "To by-pass the judge and leave the definition of fundamental legal concepts to the jury would be an unwarranted exercise in misguided populism. There must be as many different potential definitions of dishonesty as there are differences in age, social status, moral outlook and nature ... The law must be clearly defined for the judges who in turn, will define it for juries ... Most commentators agree that it was a mistake to introduce dishonesty undefined, and consign it to the jury for definition. All are agreed that the essential ingredient to be maintained is that contained in the Larceny Act, namely the requirement that the act be without a claim of right made in good faith ..."[13]

The element of dishonesty will not be made out in circumstances where the defendant establishes that he or she had an honest belief that he or she was entitled to appropriate the property. Examples include where the defendant believes that he or she is the owner of the property in question, or that he or she has a right to appropriate the property in discharge of a debt. McGreal notes that "[t]he focus of belief in a claim of right, then, is not whether the claim in question is correct or the belief is reasonable but whether it is sincere".[14] Section 4(4) of the 2001 Act provides that in considering the issue of dishonesty the court or the jury shall have regard to the presence or absence of reasonable grounds, in conjunction with any other relevant matters, for holding a belief in a claim of right. The use of the word "shall" would tend to suggest that the court or jury must bear in mind the surrounding facts when considering the issue of dishonesty. McGreal has made the observation that the requirement to consider the presence or absence of reasonable grounds only applies in the case of theft; this requirement is expressly provided for in the offence definition in s.4(4) of the 2001 Act but is not referred to in the definition of the term "dishonestly" in s.2 of the 2001 Act which applies to other fraud offences contained in ss.6–11 and s.17 of the 2001 Act.[15]

The fact that the term "dishonestly" is to be found within the offence definition of "theft" in s.4 would tend to suggest that it is a constituent element of the offence, and that the prosecution must prove the element of dishonesty in accordance with the ordinary rules governing the burden of proof. However, the Criminal Law Codification Advisory Committee, in the course of recommending that the issue of claim-of-right be treated as a defence as opposed to an element of the offence definition, observed that in practice:

---

[12] Law Reform Commission, *Report on the Law Relating to Dishonesty* (LRC 43–1992), p.354.
[13] Law Reform Commission, *Report on the Law Relating to Dishonesty* (LRC 43–1992), pp.143–144.
[14] McGreal, *Criminal Justice (Theft and Fraud Offences) Act 2001 Annotated and Consolidated* (2011), p.20.
[15] McGreal, *Criminal Justice (Theft and Fraud Offences) Act 2001 Annotated and Consolidated* (2011), pp.21–22, 55.

> "The prevailing reality would appear to be that in any trial for a 'dishonesty' offence under the 2001 Act, a defendant seeking to argue that he acted with a claim of right made in good faith must discharge an evidential burden; to all intents and purposes, the matter is treated as a defence. A trial judge will not allow the jury to entertain arguments such as 'I thought I had the right to take it', unless the defence can make out a *prima facie* case."[16]

McGreal, in considering the issue of raising a claim of right, makes the following observations:

> "In practice, a defendant will seldom have the confidence to simply raise honesty in the abstract without pointing to some specific basis upon which he believed himself entitled to appropriate the property ... A claim of right may be successfully raised without the defendant ever giving evidence. However, in some cases this approach can be described, at best, as optimistic."[17]

Intention to temporarily or permanently deprive

Apart from dishonesty, the other mental element of the offence of theft is defined as an intention to deprive the owner of his property. Section 4(5) of the 2001 Act clarifies that depriving includes both temporarily and permanently depriving. Under the old law of larceny, there was a requirement to establish an intention that the property be taken permanently; borrowers of property could not be regarded as having committed larceny. This was the reason why the offence of joyriding was never prosecuted under the Larceny Acts but was instead an offence under the Road Traffic Acts. The Law Reform Commission recommended the removal of the requirement of an intention to permanently deprive the owner of property.[18] The drafters of the 2001 Act followed the recommendation of the Law Reform Commission, broadening the mens rea of the offence of theft to cover an intention to temporarily deprive an owner of his property.

Actus reus of theft

The actus reus of the offence of theft is made up of a number of discrete circumstance-and-result elements:

(1) the appropriation of property;
(2) what is appropriated falls within the definition of the term "property";
(3) the property is owned; and
(4) absence of consent of the owner to the appropriation of property.

---

[16] Criminal Law Codification Advisory Committee, *Draft Criminal Code and Commentary* (Dublin, 2011), pp.145–146.
[17] McGreal, *Criminal Justice (Theft and Fraud Offences) Act 2001 Annotated and Consolidated* (2011), p.22.
[18] Law Reform Commission, *Report on the Law Relating to Dishonesty* (LRC 43–1992), pp.157–164.

The term "appropriates" is defined in s.4(5) as usurping or adversely interfering with the proprietary rights of the owner of the property. The term "appropriates" was given a wide definition to cover a wide range of conduct that was covered by separate offences under the former law. Under the old law, the Larceny Act 1916 required the physical taking and carrying away of the property. Under existing law, there is no requirement of carrying away the property; the definition of "appropriates" is defined more broadly, in such a way that a person who is physically in possession of property can nonetheless steal that property. For example, A gives a valuable string of pearls to B for safekeeping during a trip around the world. B is therefore in possession of the pearls. B can, however, still steal the pearls if he decides not to return the string of pearls to A. By retaining the pearls B is interfering with A's proprietary rights in the jewellery. The term "property" is defined broadly in s.2(1) of the 2001 Act as meaning "money and all other property, real or personal, including things in action and other intangible property". Further clarification is given on the scope of the definition of "property" in s.5 of the 2001 Act, which deals with exceptions to theft, and states inter alia that, in general, a person cannot steal land.

Evidence as to ownership of the property alleged to have been stolen is an essential ingredient of the offence of theft. A comprehensive definition of the term "ownership" is provided for in s.2(4) of the 2001 Act. In general terms, "a person shall be regarded as owning property if he or she has possession or control of it, or has in it any proprietary right or interest". This is a broad definition that goes beyond ownership in the sense of having proprietary interests in the property, and extends to persons who may temporarily have control or possession of property. There may be multiple "owners" of an item of property at any one time; where the person who has a legal interest in the property and the person who has physical control of the property are separate persons both are deemed to be "owners" of the property for the purposes of the offence definition of theft.[19] Section 2(4)(b)–(e) goes on to define "ownership" in further detail in relation to matters such as trusts and the property of a corporation sole.

The issue of ownership was considered in the High Court decision of *DPP v Valentine*.[20] In the District Court proceedings, the prosecution case rested on the evidence of a security guard who was working at Texas Homebase at the time of the alleged theft. He gave evidence that he saw the appellant stealing a rotor saw and related accessories from the store, apprehended the appellant and recovered the items in question. However, no specific evidence was given as to the existence of "Texas Homebase" as a legal person or that "Texas Homebase" owned the property alleged to have been stolen. At the close of the prosecution case, counsel for the appellant applied for a direction that there was no case to answer on the basis that no evidence was given as to ownership of the property and that no evidence was given that the owner did not consent to the property being appropriated by the appellant. These submissions were not accepted in the District Court and the appellant was convicted. The matter was appealed by way of case stated from the District Court to the High Court.

---

[19] McGreal, *Criminal Justice (Theft and Fraud Offences) Act 2001 Annotated and Consolidated* (2011), pp.37–38.
[20] [2009] 4 I.R. 33.

In the High Court, it was held that because the charge sheet and warrant of execution specifically referred to the property being owned by "Texas Homebase" there was a requirement to adduce evidence that the company carried on business in fact as such a company. Birmingham J. went on to state that the production of a Certificate of Incorporation is not an absolute requirement. In the instant case, the High Court found that the appellant was incorrectly convicted in the District Court as no evidence was proffered as to the nature of the entity referred to in the charge sheet or even to its existence. Birmingham J. noted briefly the problems that may arise in proving ownership in cases where it is not possible to establish the identity of the person who is the owner of the property alleged to have been stolen:

> "So far as the obligation to prove the property was owned and that the appropriation was without the owner's consent it is the case of course that from time to time there may be difficulties in establishing an owner, the pickpocket in the crowded street being the obvious example and there the jury or judge will have to consider whether the evidence is such that the property in question is proved to be owned by the person unknown and that an absence of consent can be inferred."[21]

Proof of absence of consent on the part of the owner is an essential element of the offence of theft. The prosecution must establish that the owner of the property did not consent to the appropriation of the property by the defendant. Section 4(2) of the 2001 Act provides that a person does not appropriate property without the consent of its owner if the person believes that he or she has the owner's consent, or the person believes that the owner cannot be discovered by taking reasonable steps. However, consent obtained by deception or intimidation is not a valid consent for the purposes of section 4 theft.

Fraud Offences

Background

Sections 6–11 of the Criminal Justice (Theft and Fraud Offences) Act 2001 provide for a variety of fraud offences. Many of these offences are based on the same legal concepts: deception, dishonesty or making a gain or causing a loss, as defined in the general interpretation section in s.2 of the 2001 Act. In relation to fraud offences, it would seem that the drafters of the 2001 Act opted for having a range of statutory offences dealing with specific instances of fraudulent activity, such as computer fraud or fraudulent accounting, rather than having a single comprehensive offence of fraud that would criminalise fraud generally. Some thought was put into the sequencing of the fraud offences in ss.6–11 of the 2001 Act; the more widely drafted fraud offences of a generic nature are followed by individual fraud offences focusing on the specific means by which the fraud is perpetrated.

---

[21] *DPP v Valentine* [2009] 4 I.R. 33 at 37.

Making a gain or causing a loss by deception

Section 6(1) of the Criminal Justice (Theft and Fraud Offences) Act 2001 provides for a general fraud offence:

> A person who dishonestly, with the intention of making a gain for himself or herself or another, or of causing loss to another, by any deception induces another to do or refrain from doing an act is guilty of an offence.

The actus reus of this offence is made up of both circumstance-and-result elements. First, it must be established that another person was induced to do or refrain from doing an act. While it is often the case that the person induced is the victim of the fraud, this is not an absolute requirement; the person induced could be used as the instrument by which the fraud is perpetrated. Secondly, the inducement must be effected by a deception. The term "deception" is defined in s.2(2) of the 2001 Act as follows:

> For the purposes of this Act a person deceives if he or she—
> (*a*) creates or reinforces a false impression, including a false impression as to law, value or intention or other state of mind,
> (*b*) prevents another person from acquiring information which would affect that person's judgement of a transaction, or
> (*c*) fails to correct a false impression which the deceiver previously created or reinforced or which the deceiver knows to be influencing another to whom he or she stands in a fiduciary or confidential relationship ...

The mens rea of this offence is defined as an intention of making a gain for himself or herself or another, or of causing a loss to another. This is a form of ulterior intention in so far as there would not appear to be any requirement to prove, in terms of the actus reus of the offence, an actual gain or loss.[22] This aspect of the offence is concerned with the mental element only. McGreal notes that:

> "If the induced does an act as a result of the deception and the accused was acting with the requisite mens rea, the offence would appear to be made out even if there were no gain or loss. There is, however, a conspicuous absence of any definition of prejudice in this instance ... [W]hilst the title of the offence in s.6, 'making gain or causing loss by deception', is not a statement of the offence in any legal sense it is, to say the very least, misleading if the offence in s.6 is in fact an offence of deception simpliciter."[23]

The terms "gain" and "loss" are defined broadly in s.2(3) of the Criminal Justice (Theft and Fraud Offences) Act 2001. A "gain" or "loss" may be temporary or permanent, and can only relate to money or property. The term "gain" is defined

---

[22] Criminal Law Codification Advisory Committee, *Draft Criminal Code and Commentary* (Dublin, 2011), p.161.
[23] McGreal, *Criminal Justice (Theft and Fraud Offences) Act 2001 Annotated and Consolidated* (2011), p.70.

Offences Against Property　　　　　　　　　　　　　　　　　　　　　　　　　　　199

as "keeping what one has, as well as a gain by getting what one has not". The term "loss" is defined as including "a loss by not getting what one might get, as well as a loss by parting with what one has". It should also be noted that the term "dishonestly" forms part of the offence definition; the term "dishonestly" is defined in s.2(1) of the 2001 Act as meaning without a claim of right made in good faith. It follows that the fraud offence in s.6 of the 2001 Act will not be made out where it is established that the defendant had a claim of right made in good faith.

Obtaining services by deception

Section 7(1) of the Criminal Justice (Theft and Fraud Offences) Act 2001 defines the offence of obtaining services by deception as follows:

> A person who dishonestly, with the intention of making a gain for himself or herself or another, or of causing loss to another, by any deception obtains services from another is guilty of an offence.

In many respects, this offence is similar to the offence of making a gain or causing a loss by deception provided for in s.6 of the 2001 Act. In fact, the Criminal Law Codification Advisory Committee recommended that the offences in ss.6 and 7 of the 2001 Act be merged together into a single offence on the basis that there is considerable overlap between these offences.[24] The mens rea is the same in relation to both offences, requiring an intention of making a gain for oneself or another, or of causing a loss to another, as well as an element of dishonesty, which is defined in s.2(1) of the 2001 Act as meaning without a claim of right made in good faith.

The offences in ss.6 and 7 of the 2001 Act differ slightly in relation to the objective elements of the offence. The offence in s.7 of the 2001 Act is specifically targeted at criminalising the obtaining of services by deception; the focus is on services as opposed to property. For example, a person pretending to be a member of a gym could be prosecuted for using the gym facilities by deception. The actus reus is similar to the offence of making a gain or causing a loss by deception in s.6 of the Act in so far as there is a circumstance element requiring that the services be obtained by means of a "deception", as defined in s.2(2) of the 2001 Act. Further clarification on the scope of the offence of obtaining services by deception is contained in s.7(2) and s.7(3), which states inter alia that the coverage of the offence extends to loan agreements.

Making off without payment

Section 8(1) of the Criminal Justice (Theft and Fraud Offences) Act 2001 defines the offence of making off without payment:

> [A] person who, knowing that payment on the spot for any goods obtained or any service done is required or expected, dishonestly makes off without having

---

[24] Criminal Law Codification Advisory Committee, *Draft Criminal Code and Commentary* (Dublin, 2011), p.160.

paid as required or expected and with the intention of avoiding payment on the spot is guilty of an offence.

The classic example of this offence is a person who consumes a meal in a restaurant and then deliberately takes off without paying. The actus reus of this offence imposes a result element, requiring proof that the defendant made off without having paid as required or expected for the goods or services in question. In relation to the mens rea, the court or jury must be satisfied that the defendant knew that payment on the spot was required in respect of the goods or services, and that the defendant intended to avoid payment on the spot as required.

As the term "dishonestly" forms part of the offence definition in s.8 of the 2001 Act proof of a claim of right made in good faith will defeat a charge of making off without payment. Section 8(2) of the 2001 Act provides for a possible defence to a charge of making off without payment in circumstances where the supply of the goods or the doing of the service is contrary to law or where the service done is such that payment is not legally enforceable. The remainder of the provisions in s.8 are concerned with powers of arrest, including provision for arrest by a citizen.

Unlawful use of a computer

Section 9 of the Criminal Justice (Theft and Fraud Offences) Act 2001 provides for a specific offence of fraud by using a computer.[25] While the offence can be viewed as an offence against property it might also be classified as a form of cybercrime.[26] Section 5 of the Criminal Damage Act 1991 provided for the offence of computer hacking, but this was inadequate to fully address other forms of dishonesty involving computers. One of the policy reasons behind the enactment of the 2001 Act was to criminalise such behaviour. This offence is more serious than the offence of unauthorised access (computer hacking) as it is indictable and carries a substantial penalty, whereas the offence contained in s.5 of the Criminal Damage Act 1991 is only triable summarily.

Under s.9 of the Criminal Justice (Theft and Fraud Offences) Act 2001 it is a criminal offence to dishonestly, whether within or outside the State, operate or cause to be operated a computer within the State with the intention of making a gain for oneself or another, or of causing loss to another. The offence elements are similar to the other fraud offences contained in ss.6–7 of the 2001 Act; the mental element is identical and the term "dishonestly" also forms part of the offence definition. The actus reus of the offence is distinct from the other fraud offences in that the conduct element of the offence is satisfied where a person operates, whether within or outside the State, or causes to be operated, a computer within the State. Unlike the other fraud offences, specific provision is made in the offence definition in s.9 for part of the actus reus of the offence—the operation of the computer—occurring outside the State.

---

[25] T.J. McIntyre, "Cybercrime in Ireland" in Pauline Reich (ed.), *Cybercrime and security* (Oxford: Oxford University Press, 2008).
[26] Criminal Law Codification Advisory Committee, *Draft Criminal Code and Commentary* (Dublin, 2011), p.146.

Offences Against Property 201

False accounting

The offence of false accounting in s.10 of the Criminal Justice (Theft and Fraud Offences) Act 2001 is a form of white-collar crime, and is designed to combat fraudulent activity in the specific context of accounts. The mens rea is similar to the other fraud offences contained in the 2001 Act, requiring proof of dishonesty and an intention of making a gain for oneself or another, or of causing loss to another. The actus reus of the offence of false accounting is defined in s.10(1) of the 2001 Act as a person who, with the requisite mens rea:

> (a) destroys, defaces, conceals or falsifies any account or any document made or required for any accounting purpose,
> (b) fails to make or complete any account or any such document, or
> (c) in furnishing information for any purpose produces or makes use of any account, or any such document, which to his or her knowledge is or may be misleading, false or deceptive in a material particular.

Section 10(2) of the 2001 Act clarifies that for the purposes of the offence of false accounting a person shall be treated as falsifying an account or other document if he or she "(a) makes or concurs in making therein an entry which is or may be misleading, false or deceptive in a material particular, or (b) omits or concurs in omitting a material particular therefrom".

Suppression, etc. of documents

Section 11 of the Criminal Justice (Theft and Fraud Offences) Act 2001 is concerned with the dishonest use of valuable securities and other documents in order to realise a benefit or cause a loss. A person commits an offence:

> "if he or she dishonestly, with the intention of making a gain for himself or herself or another, or of causing loss to another, destroys, defaces or conceals any valuable security, any will or other testamentary document or any original document of or belonging to, or filed or deposited in, any court or any government department or office".

An example of this offence would be where a person burns a will belonging to a deceased member of his family in order that he will inherit part of the estate or in order to thwart another person obtaining his inheritance. In addition, s.11(2)(a) of the 2001 Act provides that a person who dishonestly, with the intention of making a gain for himself or herself or another, or of causing loss to another, by any deception procures the execution of a valuable security is guilty of an offence.

Handling stolen property

Part 3 of the Criminal Justice (Theft and Fraud Offences) Act 2001 is dedicated to offences relating to stolen property. Provisions concerned with the scope of offences relating to stolen property are provided for in s.20 of the 2001 Act. The offence of handling stolen property is set out in s.17 of the 2001 Act. Sections 17(3) and 18(3) of the 2001 Act clarify that a person may be convicted of the offences of handling stolen property or possession of stolen property irrespective of whether the principal offender who was directly involved in the unlawful taking of the property is tried and convicted, or is amenable to justice; the conviction of the principal offender who carries out the theft does not form part of the proofs for the offences of handling stolen property and possession of stolen property.

The offence of handling stolen property is committed by a person who, otherwise than in the course of stealing, dishonestly, having knowledge or being reckless as to whether the property is stolen, receives or arranges to receive it, or undertakes or assists in its retention, removal, disposal or realisation. Where a defendant engages in any of these acts in circumstances where it is reasonable to conclude that the person knew or was reckless that the property was stolen, s.17(2) states that the defendant will be deemed to have the requisite mental state of knowledge or recklessness unless the court or jury is satisfied that there is a reasonable doubt as to the culpability of the defendant. This provision introduces an element of objectivity into the mens rea requirements of the offence and is designed to ease the task of the prosecution in proving the elements of the offence. The term "recklessness" is modelled closely on the definition contained in s.2.02(2)(c) of the Model Penal Code, and is defined in s.16 of the 2001 Act as follows:

> [A] person is reckless if he or she disregards a substantial risk that the property handled is stolen, and for those purposes "substantial risk" means a risk of such a nature and degree that, having regard to the circumstances in which the person acquired the property and the extent of the information then available to him or her, its disregard involves culpability of a high degree.

As the term "dishonestly" is included in the offence definition of handling stolen property a claim of right made in good faith will negate an essential ingredient of the offence.

Possession of stolen property

Section 18 of the Criminal Justice (Theft and Fraud Offences) Act 2001 provides for an offence of possession of stolen property. This offence is committed by a person who possesses stolen property, otherwise than in the course of stealing, knowing that the property is stolen or being reckless as to whether the property is stolen. The same definition of the term "recklessness" in s.16 of the 2001 Act applies. Section 18(2) of the 2001 Act states that where a person is in possession of stolen property in such circumstances that it is reasonable to infer that the person had knowledge or was reckless as to the fact that the property was stolen then the person will be deemed to have the requisite level of culpability unless the court or jury is satisfied that there is a reasonable doubt as to the mens rea of the defendant. This is a form of objectivisation of the mens rea of the offence and is aimed at easing the task of the prosecution in establishing the mental elements of the offence.

In contrast to the offence of handling stolen property, the term "dishonestly" does not form part of the definition of the offence of possession of stolen property in s.18

of the 2001 Act. A defence of lawful authority or excuse is expressly provided for in respect of the offence of possession of stolen property in s.18(1). Interestingly, there is no provision made for a defence of lawful authority or excuse in relation to the offence of handling stolen property in s.17.

Withholding information regarding stolen property

Section 19 of the Criminal Justice (Theft and Fraud Offences) Act 2001 provides for an offence of withholding information regarding stolen property. Failure or refusal to give an account to a member of the Garda Síochána, when demanded, of property in a person's possession may constitute a criminal offence in the following circumstances:

(1) Where a member of the Garda Síochána—
   (a) has reasonable grounds for believing that an offence consisting of stealing property or of handling stolen property has been committed,
   (b) finds any person in possession of any property,
   (c) has reasonable grounds for believing that the property referred to in *paragraph (b)* includes, or may include, property referred to in *paragraph (a)* or part of it, or the whole or any part of the proceeds of that property or part, and
   (d) informs the person of his or her belief, the member may require the person to give an account of how he or she came by the property.
(2) If the person fails or refuses, without reasonable excuse, to give such account or gives information that the person knows to be false or misleading, he or she is guilty of an offence and is liable on summary conviction to a fine not exceeding £1,500 or imprisonment for a term not exceeding 12 months or both.
(3) *Subsection (2)* shall not have effect unless the person when required to give the account was told in ordinary language by the member of the Garda Síochána what the effect of the failure or refusal might be.
(4) Any information given by a person in compliance with a requirement under *subsection (1)* shall not be admissible in evidence against that person or his or her spouse in any criminal proceedings, other than proceedings for an offence under *subsection (2)*.

BURGLARY

Section 12 of the Criminal Justice (Theft and Fraud Offences) Act 2001 provides for the offence of burglary which is wider than the older version of the offence contained in the Larceny Act 1916. The offence of burglary can be committed in one of two ways. First, the offence can be committed by entering a building or part of a building as a trespasser and with intent to commit an arrestable offence. Alternatively, the offence can be committed in circumstances where a person having entered any building or part of a building as a trespasser, commits or attempts to commit an arrestable offence therein.

Under the old law, burglary could only be committed by entering as a trespasser with intent to steal, inflict grievous bodily harm, rape or do unlawful damage, or, having entered as a trespasser, stealing or attempting to steal, or inflicting grievous bodily harm or attempting to do so. With respect to the limb of the offence concerned with the ulterior intention to commit an offence, burglary is widened under s.12 of the 2001 Act by the use of the term "arrestable offence" as opposed to specifying individual crimes in the offence definition. In a similar vein, the other limb of the offence of burglary is broadened by imposing liability in circumstances where a person commits, or attempts to commit, any arrestable offence, having entered a building or part of a building as a trespasser, rather than listing specific types of offences that must be committed or attempted for the crime of burglary to be made out. The term "arrestable offence" is defined in s.12(4) of the 2001 Act as meaning an offence for which a person of full age and not previously convicted may be punished by imprisonment for a term of five years or by a more severe penalty. Both limbs of the offence of burglary require proof of entry into a building or part of a building as a trespasser. It follows that the case law relating to the definitions of the terms "trespass" and "entering" remains relevant.

Trespass

"Trespass" is generally understood to mean entering the property of another person without that other person's consent. The element of trespass in an essential ingredient of the offence of burglary. As the term "trespasser" is not defined in the Criminal Justice (Theft and Fraud Offences) Act 2001 it is necessary to have regard to case law to gain a fuller understanding of the constituent elements of the concept of trespass in criminal law. The legal definition of the term "trespasser" has been considered in a number of English decisions concerning the offence of burglary.

Prior to the decision of the Court of Appeal in *R. v Collins*,[27] there was some disagreement among academic commentators as to what constituted a trespass in the specific context of the criminal law. Under the law of tort, it was sufficient for establishing trespass that a person entered the property of another person without consent, there being no requirement to prove any mental element for the purposes of imposing civil liability. Archbold expressed the view that in relation to the criminal law:

> "Any intentional, reckless or negligent entry into a building will, it would appear, constitute a trespass if the building is in the possession of another person who does not consent to the entry. Nor will it make any difference that the entry was the result of a reasonable mistake on the part of the defendant, so far as trespass is concerned."[28]

According to Archbold's formulation of trespass, there was no requirement that the accused consciously adverted to the facts that made his or her entry unlawful. In other words, it was suggested that there was no requirement to establish a subjective mental state on the part of the accused in relation to the act of trespass.

---

[27] [1973] Q.B. 100.
[28] Archbold, *Archbold Criminal Pleading Evidence & Practice*, 37th edn (London: Sweet & Maxwell, 1969), para.1505.

A different view was expressed by Professors Smith and Griew, who opined that the subjective fault elements of knowledge or recklessness must be established in respect of the act of trespass. Professor Smith submitted that a person "cannot be convicted of the criminal offence unless he knew of the facts which caused him to be a trespasser or, at least, was reckless".[29] The following passage taken from Professor Griew's commentary on the English Theft Act 1968 expresses a similar view that the fault requirements for criminal trespass are knowledge or recklessness:

> "What if D wrongly believes that he is not trespassing? His belief may rest on facts which, if true, would mean that he was not trespassing: for instance he may enter a building by mistake, thinking that it is the one he has been invited to enter. Or his belief may be based on a false view of the legal effect of the known facts: for instance he may misunderstand the effect of a contract granting him a right of passage through a building. Neither kind of mistake will protect him from tort liability for trespass ... But for the purposes of criminal liability a man should be judged on the basis of the facts as he believed them to be, and this should include making allowances for a mistake as to his rights under the civil law ... Unhappily it is common for Parliament to omit to make clear whether mens rea is intended to be an element in a statutory offence. It is also, though not equally, common for the courts to supply the mental element by construction of the statute."[30]

In *R. v Collins*, the Court of Appeal preferred the view expressed by Professor Smith and Professor Griew, holding that a person cannot be convicted for entering as a trespasser "unless the person entering does so knowing that he is a trespasser and nevertheless deliberately enters, or, at the very least, is reckless as to whether or not he is entering the premises of another without the other party's consent".[31] A similar position was adopted in *R. v Jones and Smith*, where it was noted that the decision in *R. v Collins* "added to the concept of trespass as a civil wrong only the mental element of mens rea, which is essential to the criminal offence".[32] While there would appear to be no Irish authorities touching directly on the issue of the mens rea of criminal trespass there would seem to be some support for the English position that criminal trespass requires proof of knowledge or recklessness on the part of the accused as to the facts that make him or her a trespasser.[33]

Trespass also takes place where a person exceeds his or her right of entry or enters for a purpose other than for which the permission was given. In *R. v Jones and Smith*,[34] the two accused entered a bungalow belonging to the father of one of the accused, stealing two television sets. The father had given the son a general permission to enter the house at any time, and it was therefore argued that the accused had not been trespassing. This was rejected by the Court of Appeal: a person is a trespasser if he or

---

[29] Smith, *The Law of Theft*, 1st edn (Oxford: Oxford University Press, 1968), para.462.
[30] Griew, *The Theft Act 1968*, 2nd edn (London: Sweet & Maxwell, 1974), para.4–05.
[31] [1973] Q.B. 100 at 105.
[32] [1976] W.L.R. 672 at 675.
[33] Charleton, McDermott and Bolger, *Criminal Law* (1999), p.842.
[34] [1976] W.L.R. 672.

she enters a building in excess of any permission that had been given to him or her to enter. In the instant case, while there may have been consent to the son's presence on the premises there was clearly no consent to the son being present on the premises for the purposes of carrying out a theft.

In *DPP v McMahon*,[35] the defendants each owned licensed premises and were charged with offences contrary to the Gaming and Lotteries Act 1956. Evidence was given that members of the Garda Síochána entered the premises in plain clothes without a search warrant and proceeded to gather evidence. The Supreme Court held that members of the Garda Síochána must have a search warrant under s.39 of the Gaming and Lotteries Act 1956 before entering a licensed premises for the purpose of detecting possible offences under that Act. It followed that in the absence of such lawful authority the Gardaí were trespassers. The members of the Garda Síochána did not have any statutory authority to enter the premises and, by reason of their intention in so doing, were outside the implied invitation of the owner of the licensed premises. They were therefore trespassers, and the evidence which they obtained by inspecting the use of gaming machines within these premises was evidence obtained by unlawful means. However, no constitutional rights were infringed and a court had discretion whether to admit such evidence in the circumstances. McGreal has commented on this aspect of the offence of burglary, expressing the view that:

> "The authority to enter may be for a given purpose and this might be abused or exceeded. This will render the entry unlawful just as if no authority was given … Entry through permission obtained by fraud or duress is trespass."[36]

Entering a building or part of a building

Proof of entry to a building or part of a building is an essential ingredient of the offence of burglary. The meaning of the term "entering", in relation to the offence of burglary, was considered in *R. v Collins*. In that case, the defendant looked into the window of a house and saw a female asleep in a bed close to the window. He undressed and crouched on the window-sill of the bedroom. At some point, the complainant awoke, and in the mistaken belief that the defendant was her boyfriend, allowed the defendant to enter the bedroom and have sexual intercourse with her. Crucially, in evidence, the complainant was unable to recall whether the defendant had been sitting on the part of the window-sill that was inside the room, or the part of the window-sill that was outside the room, when she sat up in the bed and gestured as to give him permission to enter the room. If he had been on the part of the sill inside the room he would have, in law, have satisfied the "entry" element of burglary. On the other hand, if he had been sitting on the part of the window-sill outside the room an argument could be made that he had not yet entered the building. Edmund Davies L.J. stated that:

> "Unless the jury were entirely satisfied that the defendant made an effective and substantial entry into the bedroom without the complainant doing or saying

---

[35] [1986] I.R. 393.
[36] McGreal, *Criminal Justice (Theft and Fraud Offences) Act 2001 Annotated and Consolidated* (2011), p.79.

anything to cause him to believe that she was consenting to his entering it, he ought not to be convicted of the offence charged. The point is a narrow one, as narrow maybe as the window sill which is crucial to this case."[37]

In the subsequent English decision of *R. v Brown*,[38] the accused was charged with burglary. Having broken a shop window, he leaned in and rummaged around the shop display. Could this conduct amount to "entering" for the purposes of the offence of burglary? The Court of Appeal answered this question in the affirmative. There was no requirement that a person wholly enter the building. Instead, whether an entry had taken place was a matter for the jury or court to decide, and they should be directed to consider whether an effective entry had taken place.

Section 12(2) clarifies that the definition of the term "building", in relation to the offence of burglary, extends to:

> [A]n inhabited vehicle or vessel and to any other inhabited temporary or movable structure, and shall apply to any such vehicle, vessel or structure at times when the person having a habitation in it is not there as well as at times when the person is there.

It would appear that the key consideration is habitation, but there is no requirement that the inhabitant be present at the time of the burglary. Inhabited house boats or caravans would come within the definition of the term "building".

Burglary can also take place where a person enters part of a building as a trespasser. Consider the case of a person who is invited to apartment 1 and then breaks into and burgles the adjoining apartment 2. Clearly, he did not enter the apartment block as a trespasser; nevertheless, he enters apartment 2, which is a part of the building, as a trespasser and is liable to be convicted of the offence of burglary. In *R. v Walkington*,[39] the accused was present in a department store and entered the area inside a three-sided counter area, in which there was a till. While the accused might have legally entered the building, the department store, as a potential customer, it was alleged that he exceeded the scope of the permission given to him to be on the premises by entering a part of the building where there was no consent given to him to enter, the area around the till. The Court of Appeal held that the area inside this counter area was capable of being a "part of a building", and since it was part of the store from which the public were excluded it was open to the jury to find that the accused had entered that specific part of the building as a trespasser. Geoffrey-Lane L.J. stated:

> "Here, it seems to us, there was a physical demarcation. Whether it was sufficient to amount to an area from which the public were plainly excluded was a matter for the jury. It seems to us that there was ample evidence on which they could come to the conclusion (a) that the management had impliedly prohibited customers entering that area and (b) that this particular defendant knew of that prohibition."[40]

---

[37] [1973] Q.B. 100 at 106–107.
[38] [1985] Crim. L.R. 212.
[39] [1979] 1 W.L.R. 1169.
[40] [1979] 1 W.L.R. 1169 at 1176.

In *R. v Walkington*, it was further held that the offence of burglary can be committed in circumstances where a person enters with a conditional intent, such as an intention to steal if he or she finds anything worth stealing. In that case, the accused went behind the counter area and opened the till to see if there was any money in the till; if there had been money in the till he would have taken it. The Court of Appeal held that conditional intent was sufficient to satisfy the mens rea requirements of burglary; it was irrelevant that, unknown to the accused, there was no cash to be found in the till. In his judgment, referring to the court's determination of the question of conditional intent, Geoffrey-Lane L.J. remarked that:

> "[T]o hold otherwise would be to make a nonsense of this part of the Act and cannot have been the intention of the legislature at the time when the Theft Act 1968 was passed. Nearly every prospective burglar could no doubt truthfully say that he only intended to steal if he found something in the building worth stealing."[41]

Burglary: the mental element

The mens rea requirements for burglary are complex, and differ depending on which limb of the offence is being relied upon. Under s.12(1)(a) of the 2001 Act, it is necessary to establish an ulterior intention to commit an arrestable offence, as defined in s.12(4) of the 2001 Act. In *Lynch v DPP*,[42] the High Court held that a charge of burglary with intent to commit an arrestable offence to wit, burglary, was invalid. Citing the decision of the Supreme Court in *State (M) v O'Brien*,[43] the importance of properly particularising a charge of burglary was emphasised. In *Lynch*, Kearns P. went on to state that:

> "In the present case, the particular arrestable offence referred to on the charge sheet was burglary. At the hearing, it was suggested by the case presenter that burglary was generally understood to mean entering a building to commit a theft. However, it is certainly the case that the offence of burglary may be particularised as involving offences other than theft such as entering with intent to commit such offences as criminal damage or assault causing harm. In my view to particularise the offence of burglary as involving the offence of burglary is meaningless and amounts to a failure to specify an arrestable offence."[44]

Under s.12(1)(b) the mental element is different. Either the mens rea requirements of the arrestable offence committed during the course of the burglary must be established or the mental element of an attempt to commit an arrestable offence must be made out. It follows that the mens rea requirements will differ depending on the specific offence committed in the course of the burglary. For instance, the mental element of rape will differ significantly from the mental element of theft. In

---

[41] [1979] 1 W.L.R. 1169 at 1179.
[42] [2010] IEHC 284.
[43] [1972] I.R. 169.
[44] [2010] IEHC 284.

relation to attempts to commit an arrestable offence, it is necessary to consider the case law governing the mens rea requirements of the inchoate offence of attempt. In summary, the mens rea of attempt has been described as an intention to commit the offence that is targeted by the attempt.[45] However, the mental element in attempt is more nuanced, and may cover culpability states falling short of intention; where the culpability requirement of the target offence relates to a circumstance element there is legal authority to the effect that the mental element for attempt tracks that of the target offence.[46] This means that, in relation to attempt, recklessness may suffice in respect of the fault requirement running to a circumstance element if recklessness is the prescribed mental element in the definition of the target offence.

In addition, in relation to both limbs of the offence of burglary, it is necessary to satisfy the mens rea requirements in respect of the trespass element of the offence.[47] There are English authorities,[48] and some support from Irish commentators,[49] for the proposition that criminal trespass requires proof of knowledge or recklessness on the part of the accused as to the facts that make him or her a trespasser. McGreal has observed that:

> "An important distinction must be made between the trespass and the accompanying offence. There are *two* intentions involved: the intention to enter premises without lawful authority and the intention to commit an arrestable ofence."[50]

Aggravated burglary

Section 13 of the Criminal Justice (Theft and Fraud Offences) Act 2001 provides for the offence of aggravated burglary. This is clearly a more serious offence than burglary simpliciter; the aggravating factor is being in possession of a weapon at the time the burglary is committed. The element of possession of a weapon has the effect of heightening the risk of harm posed to the householder and the criminal law recognises this aggravating factor by having an aggravated offence of burglary.

The offence definition of "burglary" in s.12 is incorporated into the offence definition of "aggravated burglary" in s.13 of the 2001 Act. To be liable for the offence of aggravated burglary, the elements of the offence of burglary as defined in s.12 of the 2001 Act must be established.[51] In addition to proving the actus reus and mens rea requirements of the offence of burglary, the offence definition in s.13 of the 2001 Act requires proof that the burglar had with him or her, at the time of the burglary, any firearm or imitation firearm, or weapon of offence or explosive. The terms "explosive", "firearm", "imitation firearm" and "weapon of offence" are

---

[45] *Attorney General v Thornton* [1952] I.R. 91; *Attorney General v Sullivan* [1964] I.R. 169.
[46] *R. v Pigg* [1982] 1 W.L.R. 762; *R. v Khan* [1990] 1 W.L.R. 813; *Attorney General's Reference (No. 3 of 1992)* [1994] 1 W.L.R. 409.
[47] For detailed analysis of the mens rea requirements of trespass, see above.
[48] *R. v Collins* [1973] Q.B. 100; *R. v Jones and Smith* [1976] W.L.R. 672.
[49] Charleton, McDermott and Bolger, *Criminal Law* (1999), p.842; Criminal Law Codification Advisory Committee, *Draft Criminal Code and Commentary* (Dublin, 2011), pp.183–188.
[50] McGreal, *Criminal Justice (Theft and Fraud Offences) Act 2001 Annotated and Consolidated* (2011), p.79.
[51] See above, section on the offence of burglary, as defined in s.12 of the Criminal Justice (Theft and Fraud Offences) Act 2001.

defined in s.13(2) of the 2001 Act. There is a temporal limitation on the scope of the offence in so far as the defendant must have the weapon with him or her at the time of the burglary; the offence of aggravated burglary will not be made out in circumstances where the element of possession of a weapon occurs before or after the burglary occurs, but not at the time the burglary is carried out. McGreal cites the example of a burglar who leaves the weapon outside the building in a car, committing the burglary unarmed, as not being liable for the offence of aggravated burglary.[52]

In *DPP v Ebbs*,[53] the Court of Criminal Appeal considered the meaning of the legal concept of "having with him or her any weapon" in relation to the possession of weapon offences provided for in s.9 of the Firearms and Offensive Weapons Act 1990. Having considered the case law in the area,[54] the Court of Criminal Appeal was of the view that Irish criminal law required that the mental element of knowledge be established in relation to possession. It was held that the mental element of knowledge runs to the actus reus requirement of the offence of having with him or her a weapon, a legal concept that is closely related to possession. O'Donnell J. set out the reasoning of the court for interpreting the term "has with him" as having a mens rea requirement of knowledge:

> "Firstly, it seems clear that the purpose of introducing the concept of 'having with' is to narrow the physical element of possession and it would be surprising if it were also intended by the same language to make a very dramatic alteration to the historical understanding of the nature of the possession, especially when to do so would at least potentially simultaneously expand the potential range of the offence. It would also be surprising that such an important and significant change would have gone unnoticed until now.
>
> Secondly, both the side notes to s. 9 and the long title to the Act of 1990 refer to 'possession' of offensive weapons. It seems clear, therefore, that the Act itself does not conceive of some dramatic distinction between the concept of possession and the formulation used in s. 9(4). Perhaps more importantly, it was noteworthy that s. 9(5) of the Act of 1990 also makes it an offence for a person to have with them in a public place an article, in this case described as 'intended by him unlawfully to cause injury'. Section 9(6) addresses the question of proof of intent to unlawfully cause injury and states that the court or jury 'may regard *possession* of the article as sufficient evidence of intent in the absence of any adequate explanation by the accused' (emphasis added). In criminal law 'possession' may have a number of features, but its unvarying characteristic is knowledge of the existence of the article in question. It seems to the court that the legislature could not be considered to have intended such an extraordinary result as to create an offence in s. 9(5) which does not require proof of knowledge of the article and at the same time permit proof of an essential ingredient of the same offence by reference to 'possession' which implies knowledge of the article. There is clearly nothing to indicate that the

---

[52] McGreal, *Criminal Justice (Theft and Fraud Offences) Act 2001 Annotated and Consolidated* (2011), p.82.
[53] [2011] 1 I.R. 778.
[54] *Minister for Posts and Telegraphs v Campbell* [1966] I.R. 69; *DPP v Byrne* [1988] 2 I.R. 417.

words 'has with him in any public place' are to have a fundamentally different meaning in s. 9(4) from that in s. 9(5) …

Finally, the virtually identical words of the United Kingdom Prevention of Crime Act 1953 have never been understood to have effected an alteration in the requirement of knowledge. In *R. v. McCalla* (1988) 87 Cr. App. R. 372 it was observed, at p. 378, that every case of 'having with' is a case of 'possessing' but not every case of 'possessing' is a case of 'having with'. In other words 'having with' is a subset of possession, it is not something different in its nature."[55]

In relation to aggravated burglary in s.13 of the 2001 Act, the offence definition is silent as to the issue of mens rea attaching to the element of having a weapon with him or her. Applying the principles of statutory interpretation relating to the presumption of mens rea, and in light of the decision of the Court of Criminal Appeal in *Ebbs*, a court might interpret the statutory definition of the offence of aggravated burglary as imposing a mens rea requirement of knowledge in relation to the part of the offence requiring the defendant to have with him or her a weapon at the time of the burglary.

Robbery

Section 14 of the Criminal Justice (Theft and Fraud Offences) Act 2001 defines the offence of robbery as stealing, and immediately before or at the time of doing so, and in order to do so, using force or putting or seeking to put any person in fear of being then and there subjected to force. This definition is broadly similar to that set out under the former law in the Larceny Acts. In essence, robbery is an aggravated form of theft, the aggravating factor being that force is used or threatened in the course of stealing another person's property. Because of the hybrid nature of the offence, robbery can be viewed as both an offence against the person and an offence against property. Robbery is considered to be a very serious offence because of the harm caused or threatened to a person's bodily integrity.

The term "stealing" is an essential ingredient of the offence definition of "robbery". Section 2 of the Criminal Justice (Theft and Fraud Offences) Act 2001 provides that the term "stealing" means committing an offence of theft under s.4 of the 2001 Act. It follows that all of the elements of the offence of theft in s.4 of the 2001 Act form part of the offence definition of "robbery" in s.14, and must be proven beyond reasonable doubt. In addition to proof of stealing, it must be established that before or at the time of the theft, and in order to do so, the defendant used force or put the other person in fear or was seeking to put the other person in fear. The temporal and purposive limitations on the scope of the offence are important in so far as there is a requirement of a clear link between the stealing and the force used or threatened.

---

[55] [2011] 1 I.R. 778 at 789–790.

Possession of Certain Articles

Section 15 of the Criminal Justice (Theft and Fraud Offences) Act 2001 creates two separate offences aimed at criminalising the possession of articles in circumstances where it can be inferred that the person intended to use those articles in connection with a specified theft or fraud offence. Examples of this type of offence would include possession of a foil-lined shopping bag in a department store or possession of bolt-cutters outside a factory gate late at night.

The offence contained in s.15(1) of the 2001 Act makes it a criminal offence to be in possession of any article with the intention that it be used in the course of or in connection with any of the following offences: theft, burglary, robbery, a fraud offence under s.6 or s.7 of the Criminal Justice (Theft and Fraud Offences) Act 2001, blackmail under s.17 of the Criminal Justice (Public Order) Act 1994 or an offence of taking a vehicle without lawful authority under s.112 of the Road Traffic Act 1961. An offence under s.15(1) can only be committed when the defendant is in a place which is not his or her place of residence; proof that the defendant was at his or her residence at the time of the alleged offence negates an essential ingredient of the offence. Section 15(2) provides that it is a defence to prove that the possession of the article concerned was for a purpose other than the commission of one of the offences specified under the section.

A separate offence is provided for in s.15(1A) of the 2001 Act; it is a criminal offence to be in possession of any article made or adapted for use in the course of or in connection with, the commission of any of the following offences: theft, burglary, robbery, a fraud offence under s.6 or s.7 of the Criminal Justice (Theft and Fraud Offences) Act 2001, blackmail under s.17 of the Criminal Justice (Public Order) Act 1994 or an offence of taking a vehicle without lawful authority under s.112 of the Road Traffic Act 1961. A person has a valid defence to a charge under s.15(1A) where it is shown that the person had lawful authority or a reasonable excuse for being in possession of the article. In addition, s.15(2A) provides that is a defence to prove that the article concerned was not made or adapted for use in connection with a specified offence.

Forgery and Counterfeiting Offences

The former law, as provided for in the Forgery Act 1913, was extremely complex. The Law Reform Commission recommended the adoption of the definition of the term "instrument" in the equivalent English legislation.[56] It was also recommended that cash and credit cards be specifically included. Part 4 of the Criminal Justice (Theft and Fraud Offences) Act 2001 reformed the law relating to forgery providing for a new set of forgery offences and definitions.

The core offence of forgery is provided for in s.25 of the 2001 Act. A person commits the offence of forgery if he or she makes a false instrument with the intention that it shall be used to induce another person to accept it as genuine, and by reason of so accepting it, to do some act, or to make some omission, to the prejudice of that

---

[56] Law Reform Commission, *Report on the Law Relating to Dishonesty* (LRC 43–1992), p.266.

person or any other person. The terms "false", "making", "instrument", "prejudice" and "induce" are defined in ss.24, 30 and 31 of the 2001 Act. An example of an offence under this section would be making a false passport for the purpose of using the passport to travel to another country. Section 26 creates a separate offence of using a false instrument. This offence is committed where a person uses an instrument which is, and which he or she knows or believes to be, a false instrument, with the intention of inducing another person to accept it as genuine and, by reason of so accepting it, to do some act, or to make some omission, or to provide some service, to the prejudice of that person or any other person. This offence would be committed where a person uses a false driving licence when asked to produce his or her licence by the police. Sections 27 and 28 of the 2001 Act provide for the offences of copying a false instrument or using a copy of a false instrument. Finally, s.29 of the 2001 Act makes it an offence to be in custody or control of a false instrument.

Part 5 of the 2001 Act is dedicated to counterfeiting offences. The offence of counterfeiting is defined in s.33 of the 2001 Act as making a counterfeit of a currency note or coin, with the intention that he or she or another shall pass or tender it as genuine. The terms "currency note" and "coin" are defined in s.32 of the 2001 Act. Section 34 makes it an offence to pass or tender a counterfeit of a currency note or coin. It is also an offence to have custody or control of counterfeit currency notes and coins (s.35) or to have custody or control of materials and implements for counterfeiting (s.36). Section 37 of the 2001 Act provides for an offence of importing into or exporting out of, the European Union, a counterfeit of a currency note or coin.

Arson and Criminal Damage

The offences of arson and criminal damage were formerly dealt with under the Malicious Damage Act 1861, a notoriously badly drafted piece of legislation. It created a number of extremely specific offences with highly technical differences between them. The Law Reform Commission recommended that these should be replaced by generic offences of criminal damage, capable of being carried out by means of arson.[57] These recommendations were implemented by the Criminal Damage Act 1991.

This Act creates three distinct offences: damaging property simpliciter, damaging property with an intention to endanger life or recklessness as to whether life is endangered and damaging property with intent to defraud. Each of these offences may be committed by damaging property by fire, in which case they shall be charged as arson. If committed by arson each offence carries a higher penalty, reflecting the danger to third parties which arson represents:

> "Fire is capable of inflicting enormous injury and damage. It respects no legal boundaries. Anyone who starts a fire with the intention of damaging or destroying property is engaging in an act that may be considered distinctively different (at least in its potential implications) from damaging or destroying a house (or other property) by other means."[58]

---

[57] Law Reform Commission, *Report on Malicious Damage* (LRC 26–1988).
[58] Law Reform Commission, *Report on Malicious Damage* (LRC 26–1988), p.27.

Although the Law Reform Commission recommended that arson should not carry a higher penalty than any other means of damaging property, this recommendation was not followed.

"Property" is defined in s.1 as including both property of a tangible nature and data. "Damage" is defined in s.1 so as to include destroying, defacing, dismantling, rendering inoperable and preventing the operation of tangible property. In relation to data, damage is defined as including adding to, altering, corrupting, erasing or moving that data, or doing any act contributing to such addition, alteration, etc.

Defence of lawful excuse

A defence of lawful excuse is provided in s.6(2). The defence applies:

(a) [I]f at the time of the act or acts alleged to constitute the offence he believed that the person or persons whom he believed to be entitled to consent to or authorise the damage to ... the property in question had consented, or would have consented ... if he ... had known of the damage ... and its circumstances, or

(b) ... [I]f he is himself the person entitled to consent to or authorise accessing of the data concerned, or

(c) [I]f he damaged or threatened to damage the property in question ... in order to protect himself or another or property belonging to himself or another or a right or interest in property which was or which he believed to be vested in himself or another and the act or acts alleged to constitute the offence were reasonable in the circumstances as he believed them to be.

Section 6(2)(c) was amended by the Non-Fatal Offences Against the Person Act 1997. The previous wording was "he believed ... that the means of protection adopted or proposed to be adopted were or would be reasonable having regard to all the circumstances". This was a purely subjective test but the amended version adds an element of objectivity as the act or acts now must be "reasonable in the circumstances as he believed them to be". There is still a subjective test as regards the circumstances existing but the reasonableness of the act or acts is to be determined objectively. Section 6(3) states that it is immaterial whether a belief is justified or not if it is honestly held. The provision as originally enacted also required that the defendant believed "that he or that other ... was in immediate need of protection", but this immediacy requirement was not carried over into the amended provision.

It should be noted that the defence of lawful excuse does not apply to damaging property intending to endanger life or being reckless as to whether life would be endangered and does not apply to damaging property with intent to defraud. It is similar to the defence provided for in the English Criminal Damage Act 1971 and English case law on the defence may be persuasive in this jurisdiction. However, the English provision is purely subjective and reasonableness is determined subjectively. The wording of the English provision is almost identical to the Irish provision prior to the 1997 Act amendment.

Offences Against Property 215

The meaning of "lawful excuse" was considered in *Jaggard v Dickinson*.[59] The appellant, late at night and while drunk, broke two windows and damaged a curtain in another person's house while attempting to break into the house, believing it to be the house of a friend in the same street. The two houses were identical and the appellant's relationship with her friend was such that she had his consent to treat the house as if it were her own. It was held that the legislation specifically required the court, when deciding whether there was an honest belief that there was a lawful excuse to damage property, to consider the defendant's actual state of belief. Mustill J. held that the belief could be honestly held even though it was affected by intoxication. The defence was one of honest belief and the cause or soundness of that belief was immaterial.

Another case considering the meaning of "lawful excuse" is *R. v Denton*.[60] The defendant, who was employed at a cotton mill, set fire to machinery in the mill and the machinery and the building were damaged. He was charged with arson but claimed that his employer had asked him to set fire to the machinery so he could make a fraudulent insurance claim. He argued that he therefore had a lawful excuse pursuant to the relevant legislation which afforded him a good defence as he had believed that "the person entitled to consent to the damage to the property in question had consented". It was held that the defendant had not committed the offence of arson. This case has been criticised by commentators. Charleton remarks that "[i]t is difficult to see how subjective integration into a common design to destroy property for the purposes of fraud could possible constitute a lawful excuse".[61]

Lloyd v DPP[62] concerned the cutting of padlocks on a clamped vehicle. The appellant parked his car in a private car park which he was not entitled to use. His car was later immobilised by a security company by the use of wheel clamps. The appellant cut two padlocks and removed the wheel clamps. He was charged with criminal damage to the padlocks. He argued that he had a defence of lawful excuse as, inter alia, the clamping was an unlawful act. It was held that, at best, the appellant had a remedy in civil law against the clampers. Self-help involving the use of force could only be contemplated where there was no reasonable alternative. There was no lawful excuse for damaging the wheel clamps since the appellant had the choice of paying the fine under protest, removing his car and then taking civil action against the security company.

In *Johnson v DPP*,[63] the appellant was a squatter who had damaged the door frame of a house he was occupying by chiselling off the locks and replacing them with a lock of his own. When charged with criminal damage, he argued that he had a defence of lawful excuse because he had caused the damage in order to protect his property, had believed the property to be in immediate need of protection and that the means he adopted were reasonable having regard to all the circumstances. It was held that the damage to the door was not done to protect property and that the appellant had no belief that his property was in immediate need of protection. The test to be

---

[59] [1981] 2 W.L.R. 118.
[60] [1981] 1 W.L.R. 1446.
[61] Charleton, McDermott and Bolger, *Criminal Law* (1999), p.754.
[62] [1992] 1 All E.R. 982.
[63] [1994] Crim. L.R. 673.

applied was whether he believed he had to do something which would otherwise be a crime in order to prevent the immediate risk of something worse happening.

The defendants in *R. v Jones*[64] were charged with damaging property at a military airbase and claimed they were attempting to disrupt what they characterised as the unlawful war in Iraq. While the Court of Appeal commented that the court was concerned simply with the defendant's honestly held beliefs, it held that a court could not enter into a consideration of the legality of the war in Iraq and declined to make a finding in relation to this argument.

The Irish courts were recently asked to consider a similar factual scenario in relation to the defence of lawful excuse. In *DPP v Mary Kelly*,[65] the defendant was charged with causing criminal damage to a US aircraft in Shannon. She claimed she damaged the aircraft "to prevent it going to Iraq, to prevent the killing of innocent Iraqi people". Her trial proceeded, however, as if the lawful excuse defence had never been amended by the Non-Fatal Offences Against the Person Act 1997 and it was argued that the requirement that there was an immediate need of protection (which was not part of the amended provision) was fatally absent from the defendant's defence. The trial judge held that there had to be a connection both in time and space between the action undertaken and the end sought to be achieved. When, several days into the trial, it was realised that the provision had been amended to remove the immediacy requirement, the court accepted the prosecution argument that the immediacy requirement was still part of the defence of lawful excuse as it was implied in the provision. On appeal Hardiman J. refused to follow that logic as that would assume that the 1997 Act amendment had no effect whatsoever and the conviction was quashed.

Damaging property

Section 2(1) provides that "[a] person who without lawful excuse damages any property belonging to another intending to damage any such property or being reckless as to whether any property would be damaged shall be guilty of an offence". We have seen that "property" is defined to include data so the activities of computer hackers will almost invariably fall within the offence of damaging property. Where they do not, they will fall within s.5 of the Act which creates the offence of unauthorised accessing of data.

Damaging property with intent to endanger life or recklessness as to whether life would be endangered

Section 2(2) provides that:

> A person who without lawful excuse damages any property, whether belonging to himself or another—
> (a) intending to damage any property or being reckless as to whether any property would be damaged, and

---

[64] [2005] Q.B. 259.
[65] [2011] IECCA 25.

(b) intending by the damage to endanger the life of another or being reckless as to whether the life of another would be thereby endangered,

shall be guilty of an offence.

Note the overlap between this offence and endangerment contrary to s.13 of the Non-Fatal Offences Against the Person Act 1997 discussed in Ch.6: s.13 covers a larger spectrum of behaviour than damaging property. It is also broader because it is not necessary that a defendant intended or was reckless as to the outcome (i.e. the required level of harm to the injured party). It is sufficient that the harm occurred.

The English decision of *R. v Webster and Warwick*[66] concerned the offence of damaging property with intent to endanger life. Two separate appeals addressing the same point but arising out of different facts were considered. In the first case, the appellants pushed a heavy stone from the parapet of a railway bridge onto a passenger train passing below. The passengers were showered with material from the damaged train roof but no physical injury was caused. In the second case, the appellant drove a stolen car from which a passenger threw bricks at a pursuing police car. One of the bricks smashed the rear window of the police car, showering the officers with broken glass. The appellant then rammed his car into the police car several times. It was held that the prosecution had to prove that the danger to life resulted from the destruction of or damage to property and that it was not sufficient for the prosecution to prove that the danger to life resulted from the defendant's act which caused the destruction or damage. The "damage" referred to the damage in relation to which the defendant had the required mens rea, not the damage which in fact occurred. What had to be considered was not whether and how life was in fact endangered, but whether and how it was intended by the defendant to be endangered or if there was an obvious risk of it being endangered. Where a defendant dropped a stone from a bridge, if he intended that the stone would crash through the roof of the train thereby directly injuring passengers or was reckless as to whether it did, the charge would not be made out if only the roof material fell on the passengers. However, if he intended that the stone would smash the roof so that material from it would or might descend upon passengers or was reckless as to whether it did, thereby endangering life, he was guilty of the offence. Where a defendant threw a brick at the windscreen of a moving vehicle and caused some damage to the vehicle, the question whether he committed the relevant offence did not depend on whether the brick hit the windscreen, but on whether he intended to hit it and intended or was reckless as to whether any resulting damage would endanger life.

Damaging property with intent to defraud

Section 2(3) provides that "[a] person who damages any property, whether belonging to himself or another, with intent to defraud shall be guilty of an offence". This offence is intended to deal with the problem of insurance fraud and therefore applies even where a person damages his own property.

---

[66] [1995] 2 All E.R. 168.

Arson

Section 2(4) provides that "[a]n offence committed under this section by damaging property by fire shall be charged as arson". It has already been noted that this is not a separate offence but the offence of criminal damage committed in a particular way and therefore charged differently and resulting in a more severe penalty.

Threats to damage property

Section 3 provides that an offence is committed by somebody who threatens to damage property belonging to some other person or who threatens to damage his own property in a way which is likely to endanger the life of another person. The threat must have been one intended to cause fear that it would be carried out. It is not necessary that the person to whom the threat is directed be the owner of the property or the person whose life is endangered—the offence is still made out if a third party either owns the property or is being endangered.

Possessing any thing with intent to damage property

It is an offence under s.4 if a person, having any thing in his custody or under his control intends, without lawful excuse, to use it or to cause or permit another to use it to damage any property belonging to some other person or to damage his own or the intended user's property in a way which he knows is likely to endanger the life of a person other than the possessor, or with intent to defraud.

Unauthorised accessing of data

Computer hacking is criminalised in s.5. This provides that a person who without lawful excuse operates a computer (a) within the State with intent to access any data kept either within or outside the State, or (b) outside the State with intent to access any data kept within the State, shall, whether or not he accesses any data, be guilty of an offence. This is an attempt offence as the offence is complete whether or not the offender does in fact access data. The offence is committed by a person who "without lawful excuse" operates a computer with intent to access data, but it is not clear whether the "without lawful excuse" requirement relates to the operating or the accessing or both. If A uses a computer without permission to access his own files is he committing an offence?

There appears to be a lacuna where a person operates a computer with a lawful excuse but then makes use of the authorisation in a way which is not permitted. An example would be an employee, who has permission to operate a company computer, accessing a database for the purpose of selling the information. This issue has been considered by courts in England on two occasions. In *DPP v Bignell*,[67] two police officers who were having an affair instructed a computer operator to retrieve registration and ownership details on cars in order to stalk a former wife and her new partner. They were charged with the equivalent English offence of unauthorised

---

[67] (1998) 1 Cr. App. R. 1.

access and the court held that, as the activity did not involve hacking but misuse of data, it did not fall within the definition of the offence. However, shortly afterwards, another court came to a different conclusion in respect of similar facts. In *R. v Bow Street Metropolitan Stipendiary Magistrate*,[68] it was alleged that the accused had obtained account information from an employee of a charge card company and had used the information to withdraw large sums of money from automatic teller machines. The House of Lords held that this activity did fall within the definition of "unauthorised access" and rejected the *Bignell* rationale. Lord Hobhouse commented that the relevant provision did not leave any room for a person to argue that he was not authorised to access particular data but was authorised to access data of the same kind. There is no Irish authority on this point.[69]

---

[68] [1999] 4 All E.R. 1.
[69] For an analysis of how the Criminal Damage Act 1991 deals with computer crime, see T.J. McIntyre, "Computer Crime in Ireland: a Critical Assessment of the Substantive Law" (2005) 15(1) I.C.L.J. 13.

Chapter 8

OFFENCES AGAINST THE ADMINISTRATION OF JUSTICE

This chapter examines perjury, attempts to pervert the course of justice and criminal contempt of court. The common denominator is that each offence has evolved to protect the dignity and integrity of the legal system. The offences are all common law and, as such, both ancient and notoriously ill-defined. Contempt of court, in particular, is an offence with parameters that are very difficult to set out with certainty, though each of the offences could benefit greatly from legislative reform.

Perjury

Perjury is an offence at common law and is triable either summarily or on indictment. The maximum penalty is imprisonment for seven years. Subornation of perjury, the procuring of another to commit perjury, is also a crime at common law. There are various ancient statutes concerning matters ancillary to perjury but no legislation dealing with the offence of perjury itself.[1]

O'Connor[2] defines the offence as follows:

> "Perjury is the making on oath or affirmation, before a competent court or authority in the course of a judicial proceeding, of any assertion, material to the matter in question in such proceeding which to the knowledge of such person is false, or which, whether true or false, he does not believe to be true, or as to which he knows himself to be ignorant."

On oath or affirmation

The statement must be made in the course of giving evidence on oath or affirmation (an affirmation being the secular equivalent of the religious oath). Statements not on oath or affirmation, even if they are made during court proceedings and are deliberately false, will not amount to perjury. The historical reason for the link between perjury and religion was that people believed that God would strike down anyone who swore false information in his name. Another rationale was that religious

---

[1] Perjury Act 1586 (28 Eliz. c.1); Perjury Act 1729 (3 Geo. II c.4); Perjury Act 1791 (31 Geo. III c.18).
[2] Sir James O'Connor, *The Irish justice of the peace: a treatise on the powers and duties of justices of the peace in Ireland and certain matters connected therewith* (Dublin: E. Ponsonby, 1911).

people would not risk eternal damnation by lying under oath. Indeed, until medieval times, only those who were Christians could give evidence as it was believed that there was no incentive for non-believers to tell the truth.[3]

Before a competent court or authority in the course of a judicial proceeding

For perjury to be committed, the statement must be made in the course of a judicial proceeding before a court or equivalent body. False statements in other contexts, while they might well amount to some other crime, will not amount to perjury. For example, it would not be perjury to lie to the police in the course of an investigation, although this might amount to the offence of attempting to pervert the course of justice.

The term "judicial proceedings" is very wide. A comprehensive definition is given by the Law Reform Commission:

> "'Judicial proceedings', in this context, includes, in addition to the courts established under the Constitution and special criminal courts, other complementary proceedings (e.g. commissions established by order of the court to take evidence), all statutory tribunals at which evidence must be given on oath, and proceedings before persons who are authorised by law to hear, receive and examine evidence on oath. Preliminary proceedings in connection with judicial proceedings (e.g. affidavits, depositions, answers to interrogatories, and examinations) are included, as are proceedings before every officer, arbitrator, commissioner, or other person having, by law or consent of the parties, authority to hear, receive and examine evidence on oath."[4]

Material to the matter in question

The false evidence given must be material—that is, relevant to the determination of the matter. It is not perjury for a vain witness to lie about her age, unless of course her age is relevant to the proceedings.

Which to the knowledge of such person is false, or which, whether true or false, he does not believe to be true, or as to which he knows himself to be ignorant

A person commits perjury if he knows his evidence to be false but also where he is reckless as to whether it is true or false.

Case law

Although most commentators remark that perjury cases are seldom prosecuted in Ireland, there are quite a number of modern examples of such prosecutions.[5] A famous

---

[3] See the very interesting historical discussion in the Law Reform Commission *Report on Oaths and Affirmations* (LRC 34–1990).
[4] Law Reform Commission, *Report on Oaths and Affirmations* (LRC 34–1990), p.21.
[5] e.g. a 23-year-old woman who committed perjury leading to the collapse of a murder trial in 2003 was given 100 hours' community service in July 2006. Amanda McNamara was due to be

example is the trial for perjury of one of the Gardaí involved in prosecuting Colm Murphy for involvement in the Omagh bombing.[6] This was ultimately unsuccessful as the chain of custody in relation to the statement allegedly altered by the Garda was not established.

The effect of perjury on civil cases was addressed in *Kelly v National University of Ireland*.[7] It was held that a court could set aside a judgment where the judgment had been obtained through perjury. The test is on the balance of probabilities and the perjured testimony must have been material to the determination. McKechnie J. emphasised that there would have to be significant evidence adduced before a finding of perjury could be made.

Reform

The Law Reform Commission Report commented that there did not appear to be any deficiencies in the law on perjury, although prosecutions were comparatively rare. It indicated that it would be desirable to set out the law in modern language but, as the crime of perjury was not within its terms of reference, it declined to make any recommendations as to legislative reform.

The then Minister for Justice, Michael McDowell T.D., stated in 2006 that the law relating to perjury was being examined in his Department with a view to the preparation of legislative proposals which would codify the law on perjury.[8] However, this was never done.

In 2011 the Competition Authority's Submission to the Department of Justice on white-collar crime called for a perjury Act to be enacted.[9] It commented that perjury is very difficult to prosecute successfully without legislation.

ATTEMPTING TO PERVERT THE COURSE OF JUSTICE

Attempting to pervert the course of justice is a common law offence but the most common manifestation of this offence, interfering with witnesses, has been set out in

---

one of the key witnesses in the murder trial of Liam Keane in October 2003. She had given a number of statements to Gardaí identifying Keane as the killer of Eric Leamy but then claimed, under oath, that she was a drug addict and alcoholic and could remember nothing of that night. She subsequently admitted she had been intimidated (RTE News report of July 31, 2006). In March 2011 the Court of Criminal Appeal found that a one-year term of imprisonment, imposed on a man who refused to give evidence leading to the collapse of a murder trial, was too lenient. Thomas Morey from Cork was due to give evidence at the trial of two men charged with the murder of John Butler (*Irish Times*, March 3, 2011).

[6] *Donnelly v DPP* [2006] IEHC 158. This citation relates to proceedings taken by the Garda to prohibit his trial for perjury on the grounds that certain evidence had been lost. This was unsuccessful but the reported case discusses the law on prohibition but does not deal with the crime of perjury in any substantive way.

[7] [2009] 4 I.R. 163.

[8] Written answers to Dáil questions, April 4, 2006, question 456 asked by Jim O'Keeffe T.D. [13556/06].

[9] Competition Authority, *Submission on White Collar Crime – Competition Authority Submission to the Department of Justice and Law Reform: White Paper on Crime Discussion Document No. 3 'Organised and white collar crime'* (S – 11 – 002, February 2011), p.11.

statute. Section 41 of the Criminal Justice Act 1999 makes it an offence to harm or threaten, menace or in any other way intimidate or put in fear a person who is assisting in the investigation of an offence, or is a witness or potential witness, or a juror or potential juror, in proceedings for an offence, or a member of his or her family, with the intention of causing the investigation or the course of justice to be obstructed, perverted or interfered with. The original penalty was 10 years' imprisonment but this was increased to 15 years by the Criminal Justice (Amendment) Act 2009. In 2010 43 proceedings were commenced for offences under s.41 and 17 people were convicted.[10]

Examples of actions, other than interference with witnesses, which have resulted in convictions for attempting to pervert the course of justice include: a woman who told Gardaí that her deceased friend had been driving their car when it was involved in a crash, thereby escaping prosecution for dangerous driving causing death[11]; a Garda sergeant who had turned back a doctor at a road block who was on his way to Dundalk Garda Station to take a sample following a drink-driving arrest[12]; and a Garda who redirected CCTV cameras away from the incident during an assault by two other Gardaí on a member of the public.[13]

Making a false allegation against somebody can also amount to attempting to pervert the course of justice. The course of justice includes the Garda investigation of a crime; it is not necessary for the legal proceedings to have begun. Risking the arrest or conviction of an innocent person suffices. The English courts have held that all that has to be shown is that there is a possibility that what is done "without more" might lead to a wrongful consequence such as the arrest of an innocent person.[14]

Contempt of Court

Contempt of court is a common law crime that can be prosecuted summarily or on indictment. The law in this area, however, is complicated by two factors. First, not all contempts are criminal. Some forms of interference with the administration of justice, such as a party refusing to obey an injunction, are treated as a less serious civil contempt of court and not as a crime. It is therefore important to be able to distinguish between civil and criminal contempts. Secondly, criminal contempt of court has some unusual procedural aspects. It can be prosecuted by the Director of Public Prosecutions in the same way as any other crime but in some cases it is also open to the court to deal with a contempt of its own motion and without a full hearing and without some of the procedural safeguards, such as trial by jury, which would otherwise apply to a criminal trial.

---

[10] Dáil written answers, December 1, 2011 [38239/11]; question asked by Bernard J. Durkan T.D. and answered by Minister for Justice and Equality, Alan Shatter T.D.
[11] Report in *http://www.sligotoday.ie* on October 14, 2009. Rebecca McLoughlin was sentenced to three years' imprisonment.
[12] Report in *http://www.independent.ie*, January 14, 1999. The Garda sergeant was given a nine-month suspended sentence but allowed to remain in the Gardaí, but at a reduced rank.
[13] Report in *http://www.breakingnews.ie* on December 12, 2011. This conviction is under appeal.
[14] *R. v Murray* (1982) 75 Cr. App. R. 58.

Civil versus criminal contempt

The leading Irish case on the distinction between civil and criminal contempt is *State (Keegan) v De Burca*.[15] In that case the defendant had refused to answer a question of the court and had been sentenced to imprisonment until she purged her contempt; that is until she agreed to comply with the order of the court to answer the question. The effect was to impose imprisonment for an indefinite period. This would have been the appropriate result if the contempt had been civil but she argued that the contempt was criminal and so she should have been sentenced to a definite period of imprisonment or a fine.

In differentiating between the two forms of contempt, Ó Dálaigh C.J. stated:

> "Criminal contempt consists of behaviour calculated to prejudice the due course of justice, such as contempt *in facie curiae* [in the face of the court], words written or spoken or acts calculated to prejudice the due course of justice or disobedience to a writ of *habeas corpus* by the person to whom it is directed – to give but some examples of this class of contempt. Civil contempt usually arises where there is a disobedience to an order of the court by a party to the proceedings and in which the court generally has no interest to interfere unless moved by the party for whose benefit the order was made. Criminal contempt is a common law misdemeanour and, as such, is punishable by both imprisonment and fine at discretion, that is to say, without statutory limit, its objective is punitive: see the judgment of this Court in *In re Haughey* (1971). Civil contempt, on the other hand, is not punitive in its effect but coercive in its purpose of compelling the party committed to comply with the order of the court, and the period of committal would be until such time as the order is complied with or until it is waived by the party for whose benefit the order was made."[16]

It was then held by the Supreme Court that the refusal to answer a question constituted criminal contempt in the face of the court for which a determinate sentence should have been imposed.[17]

Similarly, in *State (Commins) v McRann*,[18] Finlay P. stated that:

> "The major distinction which has been established over a long period and by a long series of authority between criminal and civil contempt of court appears to be that the wrong of criminal contempt is the complement of the right of the court to protect its own dignity, independence and procedures and that, accordingly, in such cases, where a court imposes sentences of imprisonment its intention is primarily punitive. Furthermore, in such cases of criminal contempt the court moves of its own volition, or may do so at any time.

---

[15] [1973] I.R. 223.
[16] [1973] I.R. 223 at 227.
[17] In the United States, however, refusal to answer a question is deemed to be civil contempt: *Shillitani v United States* 384 U.S. 364 (1966).
[18] [1977] I.R. 78.

In civil contempt, on the other hand, a court only moves at the instance of the party whose rights are being infringed and who has, in the first instance, obtained from the court the order which he seeks to have enforced. It is clear that in such cases the purpose of the imposition of imprisonment is primarily coercive; for that reason it must of necessity be in the form of an indefinite imprisonment which may be terminated either when the court, upon application by the person imprisoned, is satisfied that he is prepared to abide by its order and that the coercion has been effective or when the party seeking to enforce the order shall for any reason waive his rights and agree, or consent, to the release of the imprisoned party."[19]

Analysing those two decisions, the Law Reform Commission has indicated that:

"The primary purpose of civil contempt proceedings is coercive, whereas for criminal contempt the primary purpose is punitive; moreover in civil contempt proceedings the court moves only at the instance of the party whose rights have been infringed whereas no similar inhibition applies in respect of criminal contempt."[20]

However, the issue appears to be far from settled as in the case of *Flood v Lawlor*,[21] which concerned civil contempt. Keane C.J. appeared to reject a clear delineation between civil and criminal contempt:

"[W]hile there may be some room for a difference of view as to whether a sentence imposed in respect of civil contempt is exclusively – as distinct from primarily – coercive in nature in civil proceedings generally, I am satisfied that where, as here, the proceedings are inquisitorial in their nature and the legislature had expressly empowered the High Court to secure compliance with the orders of the tribunal, it cannot be said that a sentence imposed in respect of a contumelious disregard of the orders of the tribunal and the High Court is coercive only in its nature. The machinery available for dealing with contempt of this nature exists not simply to advance the private, though legitimate, interests of a litigant: it is there to advance the public interest in the proper and expeditious investigation of the matters within the remit of the tribunal and so as to ensure that, not merely the appellant in this case, but all persons who are required by the law to give evidence, whether by way of oral testimony or in documentary form, to the tribunal comply with their obligations fully and without qualification."

O'Donnell agrees that civil contempt is not purely coercive in nature:

"It has been said, and correctly in my view, that the public at large no less than the individual litigant have a very real interest in justice being effectively administered."[22]

---

[19] [1977] I.R. 78 at 89.
[20] Law Reform Commission, *Consultation Paper on Contempt of Court* (LRC CP4–1991).
[21] Unreported, Supreme Court, December 12, 2001 at 47–48.
[22] Dónal O'Donnell, "Some reflections on the law of contempt" (2002) 2(2) *Judicial Studies Institute Journal* 87 at 96.

He points out that English judges have observed that the distinction between criminal and civil contempt is "an unhelpful and almost meaningless classification"[23] and "is the sort of nonsense which does no credit to the law".[24]

Types of criminal contempt

Contempt in the face of the court

This refers to conduct which is so direct and immediate as to be deemed to be "in the personal knowledge of the court", as stated by Henchy J. in *State (DPP) v Walsh*.[25] In most cases these contempts will literally be "in the face of the court", that is, they will occur in front of the judge. It is not essential, however, that the contempt takes place before the judge, provided there is a sufficiently close connection in time or space with the court proceedings. For example, where a party in litigation threatened a lawyer for the other side in the public waiting area out of court, this was held to constitute contempt in the face of the court.[26]

Contempt in the face of the court will include cases where individuals set out to disrupt or interrupt court proceedings. For example, in *Morris v The Crown Office*[27] criminal contempt was committed where students protesting in favour of the Welsh language took over a court in session. It will also include threats or abuse directed to the judge, as in *United States v Lumumba*[28] where a lawyer stated in court that a judge was an "outstanding bigot" and a "racist dog". It will also include cases where a witness refuses to answer questions. An example is *Re O'Kelly*,[29] where a journalist employed by RTE was called as a prosecution witness in a trial of a defendant for membership of an illegal organisation. He refused to answer certain questions arising out of an interview with the defendant, claiming journalistic privilege. He was found guilty of contempt and sentenced to three months' imprisonment. On appeal, it was held that journalists did not enjoy any special privilege as regards information received by them in confidence and his conviction for contempt in the face of the court was upheld.

Scandalising the court

This outdated term refers to conduct, usually media comment, calculated to reduce public confidence in the administration of justice. There is a tension here between the right of freedom of expression, including the right to criticise the courts and the judiciary, and the supposed public interest in preventing attacks on the courts, such as allegations of corruption, which undermine public confidence in the judiciary. In *Re Kennedy and McCann*[30] O'Higgins C.J. stated that:

---

[23] *Jennison v Baker* [1972] 2 Q.B. 52 at 61 per Salmon L.J.
[24] *Attorney General v Newspaper Publishing Plc* [1988] Ch. 333 per Lloyd L.J. This decision was in the related area of the distinction between civil contempt for breaching an injunction and criminal contempt for aiding and abetting that breach.
[25] [1981] I.R. 412 at 432.
[26] *Re Goldman* [1968] 3 N.S.W.R. 325.
[27] [1970] 1 All E.R. 1079.
[28] 741 F2nd 12 (2nd Cir. 1984).
[29] (1974) 108 I.L.T.R. 97.
[30] [1976] I.R. 382.

"The right of free speech and the full expression of opinion are valued rights. Their preservation, however, depends on the observance of the acceptable limit that they must not be used to undermine public order or morality or the authority of the State. Contempt of court of this nature carries the exercise of these rights beyond this acceptable limit because it tends to bring the administration of justice into disrepute and to undermine the confidence which the people should have in judges appointed under the Constitution to administer justice in our Courts."[31]

In that case two journalists were found to be in contempt of court where they published "biased and inaccurate" reports of custody proceedings, in breach of an order prohibiting publication, including allegations that the court had ignored the statutory rules on custody and had acted for an improper purpose.

It is not contempt to subject the courts to legitimate discussion and criticism. Lord Atkin has said, in a well-known passage in *Ambard v Attorney General for Trinidad and Tobago*[32]:

"But whether the authority and position of an individual judge, or the due administration of justice, is concerned, no wrong is committed by any member of the public who exercises the ordinary right of criticising, in good faith, in private or in public, the public act done in the seat of justice. The path of criticism is a public way: the wrongheaded are permitted to err therein: provided that members of the public abstain from imputing improper motives to those taking part in the administration of justice, and are generally exercising a right of criticism, and not acting in malice or attempting to impair the administration of justice, they are immune. Justice is not a cloistered virtue: she must be allowed to suffer the scrutiny and respectful, even though outspoken, comments of ordinary men."[33]

This has been accepted as a correct statement of the law by the Supreme Court in *Re Hibernia National Review Ltd*,[34] although in that case the court found that the allegations made by the defendants went beyond good faith criticism, particularly since they involved serious misrepresentations of the facts of the case. Similarly, in *Re Kennedy and McCann*, O'Higgins C.J. stressed that "reasonable criticism" of the courts could not be regarded as contempt.

Allegations were made about the Special Criminal Court in *State (DPP) v Walsh*.[35] The defendants, members of a group called Association for Legal Justice, issued a statement to the media in relation to the trial of Noel and Marie Murray for capital murder of a garda. In that statement they said that the court was made up of "Government-appointed judges having no judicial independence which sat without a jury and which so abused the rules of evidence as to make the court akin to a sentencing tribunal". The Supreme Court found that this allegation of bias or

---

[31] [1976] I.R. 382 at 386.
[32] [1936] A.C. 322.
[33] [1936] A.C. 322 at 335.
[34] [1976] I.R. 388.
[35] [1981] I.R. 412.

corruption amounted to a "classical example" of the offence of scandalising the court.

Similarly, in *Attorney General v Connolly*,[36] an editor was found guilty of contempt when he published comments on a murder trial before the Special Criminal Court, including statements suggesting that the court had prejudiced the case. The offending comments included statements that the defendant "was fast approaching his martyrdom" and that "now he awaits his death which sentence will inevitably be passed on him after the mockery of a trial". The High Court found that this was a wild charge, going far beyond legitimate criticism, and as such amounted to scandalising the court. O'Donnell makes the point that there may be no real benefit in maintaining this distinction as the basis of the test:

> "The decisions of the courts would suggest that the line is drawn when criticism becomes scurrilous abuse or wild and baseless allegations. If there is indeed a clear distinction at this point, is there any real benefit in maintaining it? Allegations which are clearly wild and baseless may in many cases be less damaging than plausible and restrained criticism."[37]

In those cases, the abuse amounted to allegations of corruption or bias. However, the offence can also be committed by other types of attacks, including mere abuse. One famous example is the English case of *R. v Gray*.[38] In that case there was some tension between local newspapers and Darling J., which resulted in Darling J. issuing a warning to the press from the bench. Shortly afterwards the defendant, editor of a local newspaper, published an article criticising Darling J. including the following words:

> "The terrors of Mr. Justice Darling will not trouble the Birmingham reporters very much. No newspaper can exist except upon its merits, a condition from which the Bench, happily for Mr. Justice Darling, is exempt. There is not a journalist in Birmingham who has anything to learn from an impudent little man in horsehair, a microcosm of conceit and empty headedness, who admonished the Press yesterday."

It was accepted that this article, albeit mere scurrilous abuse, amounted to a criminal contempt of court, in that it was an attack on a judge in his capacity as a judge. If it had been an attack on a judge in his personal capacity, discussing for example his private life, it would not have been contempt. The doctrine of scandalising the court applies only to attacks on judges in their role as judges.

Breach of the sub judice rule

A matter is sub judice if it is currently before a court. In order to prevent outside pressure on, or manipulation of, court proceedings, it is a criminal contempt to

---

[36] [1947] I.R. 213.
[37] Dónal O'Donnell, "Some reflections on the law on contempt" (2002) 2(2) *Judicial Studies Institute Journal* 87 at 110.
[38] [1900] 2 Q.B. 36.

publish material which tends to interfere with particular proceedings which are sub judice. This is particularly important in relation to criminal proceedings, where the liberty of an accused person is at stake, where there may be a risk of "trial by media" and where juries might be swayed by irrelevant or prejudicial material, such as disclosure of previous convictions which would not be admissible in evidence. As with the offence of scandalising the court, this creates a tension between freedom of expression and the public interest in ensuring fair trials. The test here is whether a particular publication creates a real risk, not merely a remote possibility, of interference with the administration of justice in particular proceedings. It is not necessary to show that that publication did in fact impair the proceedings; the risk of interference is enough.

Hardiman J. has commented as follows on the importance of the sub judice rule:

> "Although not frequently exercised, it is absolutely essential that the courts should possess a jurisdiction to protect the integrity of their proceedings against loud and plangent assertions of the guilt (or innocence) of a person against whom proceedings are pending, long before the trial begins ...
>
> Although the law of contempt has become encrusted with technicalities over the years, especially in the absence of statutory reform, it is not in any sense a purely technical area. On the contrary, the law which prohibits prejudicial comment one way or the other in a pending criminal trial protects a very basic human and civil right: the right to have the guilt or innocence of persons accused of crime assessed by the proper tribunal, untroubled by outside pressures or by public assertions, express or implied, to the effect that the defendant is or is not guilty or should or should not be convicted.
>
> Many Irish people will remember how strange and utterly unfair it seemed, 30 years ago, when the media in another jurisdiction appeared, with impunity, to assume the guilt of certain Irish people facing criminal charges. It is no less appropriate in this jurisdiction. In relation to almost every sort of criminal charge there are some persons who will be gratified or advantaged if the alleged criminals are 'led out in handcuffs'. But such persons, especially if they are newspapers editors or others who are powerful and influential in the shaping of public opinion, must take care not to pollute the fountain of justice by expressing, or seeming to express, a view as to the guilt or innocence of accused persons, especially in lurid or vivid terms. Apart from anything else, such views are rarely based on an examination of the evidence which will eventually come before the trial court."[39]

In order for the sub judice rule to apply the proceedings must be pending. This has created difficulties in relation to criminal proceedings which are "imminent". Suppose, for example, that a newspaper publishes a story about a suspect implicating him in a particular crime shortly before that suspect is arrested and charged. Clearly such a story is capable of prejudicing a trial. But can a prosecution be said to be pending before a person has been charged? There is some Northern Irish authority

---

[39] *DPP v Independent Newspapers (Ireland) Limited, Gerard O'Regan and Anne-Marie Walsh* [2009] 3 I.R. 598 at 601.

suggesting that the jurisdiction extends to matters which are "imminent".[40] However, Kelly J. confirmed in *DPP v Independent Newspapers*[41] that the contempt jurisdiction only attaches once a person has been brought before the court to be charged.

One of the most serious forms of contempt consists of publications likely to prejudice a jury against an accused. It is contempt to publish details of previous convictions of an accused, or even (if sufficiently prejudicial) to reveal an accused's previous bad character. For example, in *R. v Thomson Newspapers Limited Ex p. Attorney General*,[42] the defendant newspaper was in contempt where it published a story in which the accused was described as a brothel-keeper, procurer and property racketeer.

More recently, photographs of defendants have created problems. In *DPP v Davis*,[43] the Court of Criminal Appeal held that publishing photographs of the accused in handcuffs, during a murder trial, could amount to a contempt of court, in that it was likely to prejudice the jury against the accused and tended to deprive the accused of the dignity associated with the presumption of innocence.

It will also be contempt to publish material which prejudices a case. An example is *R. v Parnell*[44] where a newspaper, the Dublin Evening Mail, was found in contempt for publishing a story during a trial alleging that the case against the defendants for conspiracy to induce tenants to withhold rent (one of whom was Charles Stuart Parnell) was overwhelming and that any acquittal would be against the evidence and could only be procured by intimidation.

In the majority of cases, this form of contempt will arise in respect of trials before a jury, particularly since juries are seen as especially susceptible to outside pressure. However, the rule also applies to matters decided by a judge sitting alone. For example, the Supreme Court in *Kelly v O'Neill*[45] held that the rule applies to publications about defendants after conviction but before sentence, even though the decision on sentencing is made by a judge alone. The Supreme Court in that case acknowledged that judges are, by their training and experience, less susceptible to outside influences, but held that nonetheless there was a possibility that judges could be prejudiced by unnecessary exposure to irrelevant material and also held that there was a risk, in relation to sentencing, that judges might be perceived as imposing sentences in response to popular demand.

The courts have used the "fade factor" test in determining the seriousness of the prejudicial publication. This refers to the time that will elapse between the publication of the material and the determination of the matter, usually by way of jury trial. The greater the period of time that will elapse, the more significant the fade factor and the less damage will be done by publication. Kearns J. in *DPP v Independent Newspapers (Ireland) Limited and Ors*[46] stated that the applicant's trial would not take place at the earliest until 2003 and "[b]y that time, the fade factor will undoubtedly have operated to diffuse further the effect of adverse publicity in

---

[40] *R. v Beaverbrook and Associated Newspapers* [1962] N.I. 15.
[41] [2003] 2 I.R. 367.
[42] [1968] 1 All E.R. 268.
[43] [2001] 1 I.R. 146.
[44] (1881) 14 Cox CC 508.
[45] [2000] 1 I.R. 354.
[46] [2005] IEHC 128 at 145.

the past". He commented that a publication made three or four years before the trial might not be of significance and added that:

> "Obviously the temporal factor is simply one issue to be considered in determining objectively whether a publication has a tendency to interfere with the due administration of justice in a particular case. Nevertheless, I am not of the view that it is a necessary proof in an application of the kind before me that the applicant must indicate to the court when a trial is likely to be heard or, indeed, a precise date upon which a case is going to be heard."

In a more recent case, Hardiman J. and Geoghegan J. emphasised that the fade factor has no relevance to the question of whether or not a publication is a contempt but does has relevance when an application is being brought to prohibit a trial on grounds of adverse publicity.[47]

Other acts which interfere with the course of justice

This catch-all category covers other actions which tend to prejudice the administration of justice. Examples of this form of contempt include attempts to intimidate witnesses or counsel: *In re Kelly and Deighan*[48] and *Brown v Putnam*.[49] Similarly, it would be contempt of court to interfere with a jury: *In re MM and HM*.[50]

Mens rea and criminal contempt

Do the various forms of criminal contempt require an intention to interfere with the administration of justice? Is it sufficient that the defendant was reckless as to the possibility of interference? The mens rea required for contempt is a difficult issue and it seems that mens rea may differ as between the various forms of criminal contempt.

It is unclear whether mens rea is required for contempt in the face of the court. As regards acts, other than publication, which interfere with the course of justice, the mens rea issue is also unclear. Breach of the sub judice rule was originally thought to be an offence of strict liability. However, in *Kelly v O'Neill*,[51] Keane J. expressed some doubt as to whether Irish law would still take this view, stating that the facts of that case:

> "[R]aise the question as to whether the offence of criminal contempt had been committed at all, given the absence of any guilty mind or *mens rea* on the part of the respondents ... While undoubtedly the generally accepted view of the law has hitherto been that the offence is absolute in its nature and does not require the establishment of *mens rea*, one certainly could not exclude

---

[47] *DPP v Independent Newspapers (Ireland) Limited, Gerard O'Regan and Anne-Marie Walsh* [2009] 3 I.R. 598.
[48] [1984] I.L.R.M. 424.
[49] 6 A.L.R. 307 (Sup. Ct N.S.W. Ct App. 1975).
[50] [1933] I.R. 299.
[51] [2000] 1 I.R. 354 at 380.

the possibility that, in the absence of any modern Irish authority, the courts in this country might have come to the conclusion that *mens rea* was a necessary ingredient of the offence."

There is also debate as to whether mens rea is required for scandalising the court. It is an offence of strict liability in England, Australia, New Zealand and Canada, although South African law requires mens rea. In Ireland there is still some confusion on this point. In *Re Kennedy and McCann*,[52] O'Higgins C.J. remarked that "[t]he offence of contempt by scandalising the court is committed when, as here, a false publication is made which intentionally or recklessly imputes base or improper motives and conduct to the judge or judges in question".[53] Although this appears to require mens rea, the Law Reform Commission[54] has suggested that O'Higgins C.J. was referring to an intention to impute improper motives to the judiciary, not an intent to interfere with the administration of justice, so that a person would be guilty of contempt once he deliberately accused a judge of bias, even though he did not intend to interfere with the administration of justice.

The Law Reform Commission's interpretation has since been followed in *Re KAS (an infant)*.[55] In that case, Budd J. held that mens rea is not required in respect of scandalising the court so that lack of intention or knowledge is no excuse, although it may have a bearing on the punishment which the court will inflict.

Of course, it is possible that after *CC v Ireland*[56] a court would hold that characterising contempt as a strict liability offence would be unacceptable.

Procedure

Criminal contempts of court can be prosecuted in the ordinary way by the Director of Public Prosecutions. Any person likely to be affected by a criminal contempt, such as an accused in a criminal trial, can also commence proceedings. In addition, the relevant court has power, of its own motion, to commence proceedings for criminal contempt. This last point makes contempt of court unusual in Irish law. In most cases, the court is passive and must wait for a case to be brought before it. In respect of criminal contempt, however, the court can take an active role and act as prosecutor if necessary. The reasoning behind this rule is, in part, that the doctrine of contempt of court exists to safeguard judicial independence and judicial independence would be compromised if the court was dependent on some other party to commence contempt proceedings. In addition, it may be necessary for the court to deal with contempt urgently in the interests of justice, ruling out any delay to allow the DPP to consider whether to bring proceedings.

There are also some unusual features in respect of the trial of criminal contempts. Since a criminal contempt is a criminal offence, which may attract a substantial sentence, we might expect that it would carry a right to trial by jury under Art.38.5 of the Constitution. However, historically the courts have enjoyed a power to punish

---

[52] [1976] I.R. 382.
[53] [1976] I.R. 382 at 387.
[54] Law Reform Commission, *Consultation Paper on Contempt* (LRC CP4–1991), p.63.
[55] Unreported, High Court, Budd J., May 22, 1995.
[56] [2006] 4 I.R. 1. See Ch.5 on sexual offences and Ch.2 on strict liability.

criminal contempts summarily, that is, without a jury. In fact Geoghegan J. has commented that there has not been a trial upon indictment for contempt of court in England since 1902 and stated that he could only find one such example in Ireland; an 1878 case involving an assault on a judge in the precincts of the court.[57]

The rationale of punishing contempts summarily is the need to deal urgently with certain forms of contempt, such as the disruption of an ongoing trial. In the case of contempt in the face of the court, there has also been a view that the court, having witnessed the contempt, did not need to engage in a full trial to determine the facts. Judges have also expressed concern that a jury might perversely acquit a person who committed a criminal contempt, leaving the court without an effective means of safeguarding its independence.

The Law Reform Commission[58] commented that the law of *in facie* contempt could be criticised for "imposing on the judge such an accumulation of conflicting responsibilities that the result is to deny the defendant the protection of several principles of constitutional and natural justice".[59] It pointed out that the judge will "police" the courtroom by ordering that the disruptive person be physically removed from court. The judge is also the complainant; the prosecutor; the chief prosecution witness; prosecution counsel; judge; juror; and sentencer:

> "This combination of several responsibilities in one person causes two main difficulties. The first relates to bias: how can the victim and prosecutor also be the judge? To allow this appears to offend against the *nemo iudex in causa sua* principle. Secondly there is a problem with the presumption of innocence."[60]

These issues were addressed in *State (DPP) v Walsh*[61] where the defendants, who were accused of scandalising the court, submitted that Art.38.5 required that they should be tried before a jury. This was, however, rejected by the Supreme Court. The court unanimously agreed that judicial independence, as provided for in the Constitution, required that the courts should be able to deal with criminal contempt of court summarily, at least where there were no disputed issues of fact (as in that case where the defendants admitted publishing the material in question).[62] The members of the court differed, however, as to what would happen if a defendant denied that he was responsible for a publication. The majority took the view, per Henchy J., that in such a case the accused person would retain his constitutional right to trial by jury in respect of those issues of fact. The minority, per O'Higgins C.J., believed that while it might be desirable to try the factual issues before a jury, this was not required. Instead, this would be a matter for the discretion of the judge and there might be circumstances where it would be undesirable to do this, for example

---

[57] *DPP v Independent Newspapers (Ireland) Limited, Gerard O'Regan and Anne-Marie Walsh* [2009] 3 I.R. 598 at 609.
[58] Law Reform Commission, *Consultation Paper on Contempt of Court* (LRC CP4–1991).
[59] Law Reform Commission, *Consultation Paper on Contempt of Court* (LRC CP4–1991), p.232.
[60] Law Reform Commission, *Consultation Paper on Contempt of Court* (LRC CP4–1991), p.233.
[61] [1981] I.R. 412.
[62] However, see McDermott's comment that one can never say the facts are not in dispute in a trial. While they may seem clear to the prosecution, the accused might not agree; Paul Anthony McDermott, "Contempt of court and the need for legislation" (2004) 4(1) *Judicial Studies Institute Journal* 185 at 193.

where the issue was whether a defendant had attempted to bribe or intimidate a jury. This discussion was, however, obiter and did not form part of the reasoning of the case. Consequently, it is still unclear whether a defendant in those circumstances would enjoy a right to jury trial in respect of factual issues.

Subsequent to *State (DPP) v Walsh*, the European Court of Human Rights considered the issue in *Kyprianou v Cyprus*[63] where it held that art.6 guaranteeing a fair and impartial trial had been violated:

> "The Court considers that the decisive feature of the case is that the judges of the court which convicted the applicant were the same judges before whom the contempt was allegedly committed. This in itself is enough to raise legitimate doubts, which are objectively justified, as to the impartiality of the court – nemo iudex in causa sua.
>
> The Government's assertion that the judges who convicted the applicant cannot be considered complainants in the proceedings and had no personal interest in the relevant offence but were simply defending the authority and standing of the court is, in the opinion of the Court, theoretical. The reality is that courts are not impersonal institutions but function through the judges who compose them. It is the judges who interpret a certain act or type of conduct as contempt of court. Whether a contempt has been committed must be assessed on the basis of the particular judges' own personal understanding, feelings, sense of dignity and standards of behaviour. Justice is offended if the judges feel that it has been. Their personal feelings are brought to bear in the process of judging whether there has been a contempt of court. Their own perception and evaluation of the facts and their own judgment are engaged in this process. For that reason, they cannot be considered to be sufficiently detached, in order to satisfy the conditions of impartiality, to determine the issues pertaining to the question of contempt in the face of their own court."[64]

The court went on to say that the correct course of action would have been to refer the matter to the competent prosecuting authorities for investigation and, should prosecution result, to have the matter determined by other judges.

Further Irish cases addressing the issue will have to do so in a way that is compatible with this decision.

Reform of the law of contempt of court

Various commentators have called for contempt to be put on a statutory footing, not least Hardiman J., who has said:

> "Fortunately, contempt of court is not a matter which arises very frequently in the courts' work. No doubt it is for this reason that some very basic questions are now the subject of full argument for the first time ... There is clearly a case for the Oireachtas to consider whether, as has been done in the neighbouring

---

[63] [2004] ECHR 43 (App. No. 73797 of 2001).
[64] [2004] ECHR 43 (App. No. 73797 of 2001) at paras 34 and 35.

jurisdiction, the complex and in some respects archaic common law of contempt should not now be placed on a statutory basis."[65]

McDermott has also argued that there is an urgent need for legislative intervention, as "[i]t is ... discouraging to note that contempt of court is an area where almost no two lawyers or commentators can agree on many of the most fundamental aspects".[66]

O'Donnell was also of the view that reform was needed in the area of contempt of court, as "it can be said that there is virtually no fixed or settled point in the Irish jurisprudence of contempt".[67] He gives a number of examples, including:

(1) the question of whether civil contempt is coercive and not punitive and therefore very distinct from criminal contempt;
(2) the question of whether contempt requires mens rea;
(3) the extent to which trial of an issue of criminal contempt requires trial by a jury under Art.38.5.

---

[65] *DPP v Independent Newspapers (Ireland) Limited, Gerard O'Regan and Anne-Marie Walsh* [2009] 3 I.R. 598 at 601. Denham J. had expressed similar sentiments in *Kelly v O'Neill* [2000] 1 I.R. 354 at 368: "In many other jurisdictions the law of contempt of court has been developed by legislation. There is benefit in the legislature addressing such matters of policy so important in a democratic society. However, in Ireland this has not occurred. The law in the United Kingdom has been supplemented by legislation amending the common law."
[66] Paul Anthony McDermott, "Contempt of Court and the need for legislation" (2004) 4(1) *Judicial Studies Institute Journal* 185 at 188.
[67] Dónal O'Donnell, "Some reflections on the law of contempt" (2002) 2(2) *Judicial Studies Institute Journal* 87 at 94.

Chapter 9

PUBLIC ORDER OFFENCES

Core Offences Relating to Public Order

Definition of "public place"

Proof that the offence occurred in a "public place" is an essential ingredient of the core public order offences in ss.4–9 of the Criminal Justice (Public Order) Act 1994. In contrast, the more serious public order offences of affray, violent disorder or riot are broader in this respect, and may be committed in a public place or private place. Section 3 of the Criminal Justice (Public Order) Act 1994 defines the term "public place" as including:

(a) any highway,
(b) any outdoor area to which at the material time members of the public have or are permitted to have access, whether as of right or as a trespasser or otherwise, and which is used for public recreational purposes,
(c) any cemetery or churchyard,
(d) any premises or other place to which at the material time members of the public have or are permitted to have access, whether as of right or by express or implied permission, or whether on payment or otherwise, and
(e) any train, vessel or vehicle used for the carriage of persons for reward.

Section 3 provides for an exclusionary definition of the term "private place": a "private place means a place that is not a public place". Hogan notes "the difficulty in marginal cases of separating public from private places is not easy", and considers, by way of example, the case of university buildings:

> "Many members of the public (such as tourists) have access whether as of right or by express or implied permission, or whether on payment or otherwise to certain parts of the University grounds at certain times of the day. Thus, at least part of the University grounds would appear to be a public place. But does this mean that just because tourists and visitors have ready daytime access to Library Square on their way to see the Book of Kells in Trinity College, Dublin, that students who engaged in insulting behaviour with intent to commit a breach of the peace as part of a protest later that evening (when no tourists or visitors were present) against a visiting dignitary could be convicted of an offence under section 6? Presumably this was not the intention of the draftsmen, but the words of section 3 seem capable of encompassing such actions."[1]

---

[1] Gerard Hogan, *Criminal Justice (Public Order) Act 1994 Annotated ICLSA* (Dublin: Round Hall Press, 1994), p.5.

Intoxication in a public place

Section 4 of the Criminal Justice (Public Order) Act 1994 creates an offence of intoxication in a public place. The offence may only be committed in a "public place", a term that is defined broadly in the interpretation section in s.3, and includes any place to which at the material time the public have access. It follows that no offence is committed where a person is intoxicated in a private place, such as a dwelling. The term "private place" is defined in s.3 as meaning "a place that is not a public place".

In relation to the level of intoxication required to meet the actus reus requirements of the offence, the definition in s.4 requires that a person be "intoxicated to such an extent as would give rise to a reasonable apprehension that he might endanger himself or any other person in his vicinity". The reference to the concept of reasonableness would tend to suggest that a form of objective test is used to determine the issue of intoxication as opposed to having regard to any subjective mental state on the part of the accused.[2] It follows that the element of intoxication is established if it can be reasonably inferred from the surrounding circumstances that the defendant was intoxicated to such an extent that might endanger either the defendant or any other person who is nearby.

Citing with approval a passage taken from Charleton, McDermott and Bolger's textbook *Criminal Law*,[3] the Criminal Law Codification Advisory Committee expressed the view that liability is strict in respect of the offence of intoxication in a public place:

> "Given the nature of drunkenness and the altered state of reality it induces, the prosecution would encounter difficulties in proving that the intoxicated person consciously disregarded a substantial risk that he or she was intoxicated in a public place. Moreover, it would seem that the Oireachtas intended section 4 to be one of strict liability given the low original penalty – a £100 fine ...
>
> Strict liability in relation to the conduct element may seem strange. Ordinarily, under the Code a person would have to know that he or she is moving his or her arm (an act) or failing to do so (an omission), in order to satisfy the conduct requirement. In the context of intoxication in a public place, the conduct element is simply *being somewhere* (wherever the alleged offence takes place). Owing to the fact that the policy considerations underlying the offence are concerned with public protection and safety, it is arguably appropriate to relieve the prosecution of establishing fault in relation to all the objective elements.
>
> The difficulty with this approach is that it seems to dispense with the conduct requirement as normally understood in the criminal law. For example, in circumstances where an intoxicated youth is dumped in the street by a taxi driver, the youth would technically satisfy the conduct element of the offence of intoxication in a public place, despite his absence of knowledge as to his *being* (wherever the alleged offence takes place). But this difficulty

---

[2] Conor Hanly, *An Introduction to Irish Criminal Law*, 2nd edn (Dublin: Gill & McMillan, 2003), p.379.
[3] Charleton, McDermott and Bolger, *Criminal Law* (1999), p.764.

is more apparent than real because the youth should have an involuntariness defence[4] ..."[5]

While intoxication by alcohol is the most common means by which the offence is committed in practice, s.4(4) clarifies that a person may be guilty of an offence if intoxication is effected by the use of drugs or other substances, including solvents or a combination of substances. It is noteworthy that there is no requirement that any drugs used for the purposes of intoxication be illegal; a person may be convicted of an offence under s.4 where he or she abuses legal drugs to reach intoxication, which would cover the phenomena in recent years related to the abuse of "legal highs".

Offensive conduct in a public place

Section 5 provides for an offence of offensive conduct in a public place. The offence can be committed in one of two ways:

(1) by engaging in offensive conduct between the hours of 12 o'clock midnight and 7 o'clock in the morning next following, or
(2) by engaging in offensive conduct at any other time, after having been requested by a member of An Garda Síochána to desist from engaging in such conduct.

The term "offensive conduct" is defined in s.5(3) as meaning "any unreasonable behaviour which, having regard to all the circumstances, is likely to cause serious offence or serious annoyance to any person who is, or might reasonably be expected to be, aware of such behaviour". The test for what constitutes "offensive conduct" would appear to be objective in nature.[6] This element of the offence is satisfied once it can be reasonably inferred from the surrounding circumstances that the defendant's behaviour is such that there is a likelihood that a reasonable bystander would be caused serious offence or serious annoyance. The inclusion of the term "serious" would tend to suggest that the conduct must reach a certain threshold of annoyance or offence before it can be classified as "offensive conduct" for the purposes of the offence in s.5; perhaps mere boisterousness or harmless horseplay outside a pub would lack the requisite degree of seriousness to trigger criminal liability. Charleton, McDermott and Bolger suggest that offensive conduct would cover "urinating on the street or engaging in sexual relations in someone's garden".[7] Another example would include a group of youths congregating at a bus stop or taxi rank late at night, making a lot of noise and engaging in unruly conduct that is causing serious annoyance and offence to members of the public. In the final analysis, it is a matter of interpretation

---

[4] See the problematic case of *R. v Larsonneur* (1933) 24 Cr. App. R. 74 where a woman was deported back to Ireland from Britain and convicted of contravening the Aliens Order 1920. The Court of Appeal dismissed her appeal, in which she argued that her return to England was beyond her control.
[5] Criminal Law Codification Advisory Committee, *Draft Criminal Code and Commentary* (Dublin, 2011), pp.288–289.
[6] Charleton, McDermott and Bolger, *Criminal Law* (1999), p.765.
[7] Charleton, McDermott and Bolger, *Criminal Law* (1999), p.765.

Public Order Offences 239

for the court to determine whether or not the conduct in question is sufficiently offensive to merit penal sanction.

Offence of threatening, abusive or insulting behaviour in a public place

Section 6 of the Criminal Justice (Public Order) Act 1994 is a more serious form of offence than the other offences contained in ss.4–5 of the Act. Section 6 is an aggravated form of public order offence and this is reflected in the fact that the penalty on conviction of an offence under s.6 includes the possibility of a term of imprisonment not exceeding three months; there is no jurisdiction to impose a custodial sentence in respect of the public order offences under ss.4–5 of the Act of 1994.

The basic ingredients of the offence of threatening, abusive or insulting behaviour in a public place were considered, in some detail, in the High Court decision in *Clifford v DPP*.[8] This case arose out of a case stated from the District Court to the High Court, in relation to, inter alia, the proper construction of the elements of the offence of threatening, abusive or insulting behaviour in a public place under s.6 of the Criminal Justice (Public Order) Act 1994. The facts of the case can be summarised as follows. The accused entered a Garda Station and demanded that his mobile phone be returned to him, which would appear to have been seized by the Gardaí earlier that day. He was intoxicated, verbally abusive to the Gardaí and was kicking and banging the door in the public office of the station. Eventually, a member of the Gardaí gave him the SIM card for his mobile phone. However, he proceeded to be abusive and threatening, saying that he would get "Garda Susan McLoughlin" and that "it would not be him who would finish her off". Apart from two other persons who were accompanying the accused at the station, other members of the public were present during the incident. The accused was then arrested on suspicion of having committed an offence under s.6 of the Criminal Justice (Public Order) Act 1994.

During the course of the District Court hearing, under cross-examination, two Garda witnesses gave evidence that the members of the public present avoided any confrontation and that none of them attempted to become involved in the incident. The two Garda witnesses accepted that neither of them would have breached the peace in response to the defendant's conduct, and that it was not likely that a breach of the peace would have resulted from the defendant's behaviour. At the close of the prosecution case, a direction for an acquittal was sought on the basis that there was insufficient evidence to establish that the defendant had the necessary mental elements of intention or recklessness in relation to provoking a breach of the peace.

Charleton J. remarked that "[a] traditional model of criminal offence is created by s.(6)(1) incorporating, as it does, an external element coupled with a requirement that the prosecution prove intent or recklessness, the mental element".[9] The actus reus of the offence requires proof that the defendant, in a public place, used or engaged in any abusive, insulting or threatening words or behaviour. It will be recalled that the term "public place" is defined in s.3 of the Criminal Justice (Public

---

[8] [2008] IEHC 322.
[9] *Clifford v DPP* [2008] IEHC 322 at para.5.

Order) Act 1994.[10] Charleton J. made the following remarks in relation to the proper construction of the external elements of words or conduct that are abusive, insulting or threatening in nature:

> "I do not regard it as helpful to attempt to give a separate definition in relation to every word used in the section, or to explain it disjunctively. By using plain words in the English language, the Oireachtas required the District Court, in looking at any particular set of facts, to ask itself whether threatening words or behaviour were used, or whether the accused was abusive, or whether he was insulting. If he was, then the external element of the offence is perpetrated."[11]

In the instant case, the learned High Court judge was satisfied that any one of a number of actions carried out by the defendant at the Garda Station could be interpreted as falling within the definition of the actus reus of the offence in s.6 of the Criminal Justice (Public Order) Act 1994, including, in particular, the threats made to a member of An Garda Síochána.

In *Clifford*, the High Court clarified that the element of breach of the peace is not part of the actus reus of the offence contained in s.6 of the Criminal Justice (Public Order) Act 1994; the element of breach of peace is only relevant to the mens rea of the offence. This means that there is no requirement on the prosecution to establish that a defendant succeeded in bringing about a breach of the peace. In relation to the element of breach of the peace, the prosecution is only required to adduce sufficient evidence to satisfy the court that the defendant had the necessary intent or was reckless with respect to occasioning a breach of the peace. Charleton J. observed that "... the ease of proof of the mischief of abusive behaviour in public was reformed by relieving the prosecution, where they charge under the section, of proving that a breach of the peace actually occurred ...".[12] This aspect of the mens rea of the offence is a form of ulterior intention in so far as proof is required that the defendant had at the time of the offence intention or recklessness as to causing a breach of the peace.

Charleton J. went on to define the mental element of intention in terms of purposive conduct:

> "An intent to commit the external element of an offence occurs where a person goes about the conduct in question with the purpose of bringing about the wrong ... [A]n intent to provoke a breach of the peace, the mental element encapsulated within s.6 of the Criminal Justice (Public Order) Act 1994, requires that, before conviction, the court should be satisfied beyond reasonable doubt that in doing what he did by way of abusive words or behaviour, or other conduct within the section, the accused's purpose was to provoke a breach of the peace. In this context, provoke is an ordinary word and may be explained, if explanation is necessary, as to inspire or to bring about."[13]

---

[10] See above, section on meaning of the term "public place".
[11] *Clifford v DPP* [2008] IEHC 322 at para.9.
[12] [2008] IEHC 322 at para.7.
[13] [2008] IEHC 322 at para.10.

It was further clarified that the mental element of intention extends to cover oblique intention and that a person may be taken to intend the natural consequences of what he does.

In *Clifford*, the High Court confirmed that recklessness is subjective in nature, in the specific instance of the offence contained in s.6 of the Criminal Justice (Public Order) Act 1994, and as a general principle in relation to other crimes. Charleton J. approved the definition of "recklessness" contained in s.2.02(2)(c) of the American Law Institute Model Penal Code as being the generally accepted definition of recklessness in Irish criminal law. It was held by the High Court that:

> "Recklessness consists of an accused subjectively taking a serious risk, involving high moral culpability, that his conduct will bring about the wrong defined by the charge. Here, the wrong defined by the charge in terms of recklessness is as to whether a breach of the peace may be occasioned, that is brought about, by his conduct. Recklessness involves a subjective element in Irish law, and so it is different from criminal negligence ... For an accused to be reckless, it must occur to the mind of the accused that his conduct will bring about the consequence impugned but, nonetheless, he proceeds to act."[14]

In *Clifford*, after making reference to a well-known passage from the judgment of Watkins L.J. in *R. v Howell*,[15] Charleton J. considered the meaning of the concept of "breach of the peace":

> "A breach of the peace implies conduct which goes beyond mere boisterousness. Instead, the offence involves a situation which imminently threatens a person, through the conduct of those involved in the breach of the peace, but not necessarily directly, of being harmed through an assault, an affray, a riot, an unlawful assembly or any other serious disturbance ... In England, a threat of destruction of property in the presence of its owner is regarded as being sufficient to prove a breach of the peace, as it was reasoned in *Howell*, wrecking somebody's property in his presence is likely to provoke a serious response. This is correct ... [T]he crime of breach of the peace occurs where a person finds himself, or herself, in a situation where they reasonably fear that if they do not withdraw from it quite promptly, they may either be assaulted or that the disturbance in respect of which the accused stands charged may create the risk of a response which is disorderly and in consequence potentially violent whereby, through direct or indirect means, bystanders may be caught up in violence."[16]

Charleton J. cited "shoving, flying missiles, stampeding by a few people or a section of a crowd, and fighting within a group" as examples of conduct that would be sufficient to constitute a breach of the peace.[17]

---

[14] [2008] IEHC 322 at para.14.
[15] [1981] 3 All E.R. 383 at 389.
[16] [2008] IEHC 322 at paras 7–8.
[17] [2008] IEHC 322 at para.8.

Offence of breach of the peace contrary to common law

Apart from the statutory offences contained in the Criminal Justice (Public Order) Act 1994 that have the concept of breach of the peace as a constituent element of the offence definition, there would appear to exist, at common law, an offence of breach of the peace.[18] In *Thorpe v DPP*,[19] the High Court held that breach of the peace contrary to common law was an offence known to law. In reaching this conclusion, it was noted that the Criminal Justice (Public Order) Act 1994 did not abolish the common law offence of breach of the peace, and that the common law version of the offence could be prosecuted in the District Court. Support for this conclusion was derived from *Attorney General v Cunningham*[20] and *Kelly v O'Sullivan*.[21]

In the decision of the Court of Criminal Appeal in *Cunningham*, O'Byrne J. described the offence of breach of the peace as follows:

> "In order to constitute a breach of the peace an act must be such as to cause reasonable alarm and apprehension to members of the public, and it seems to us that this is the substantial element of the offence."[22]

In *Thorpe v DPP*, the High Court noted in relation to the definition of "breach of the peace" that "… there was a surprising lack of authoritative definition of what one would expect to be a fundamental concept in criminal law".[23] Murphy J. went on to make the following observations:

> "While a breach of the peace is supposed to underlie every crime, the narrower meaning encompasses a riot or an unlawful assembly which has not yet become a riot. There may also be a breach of the peace without any general disorder where a unilateral assault or battery is committed.
>
> Each of the instances involve some danger to the person, and it is submitted that this is the general meaning of a breach of the peace in criminal law.
>
> In English law, if there is no threat to the person it seems that a threat to property should generally be regarded as insufficient though it may well be that a threat to attack a dwelling house is looked upon with special severity and so is always a breach of the peace if the attack is imminent."[24]

Citing the decision of *McConnell v Chief Constable Manchester*,[25] the High Court in *Thorpe* held that common law breach of the peace may arise in a private premises as well as in a public place.[26] This is in contrast to the core public order offences contained in the Criminal Justice (Public Order) Act 1994 which may only be committed in a public place.

---

[18] *Thorpe v DPP* [2007] 1 I.R. 502; *Clifford v DPP* [2008] IEHC 322; *Brady v DPP* [2010] IEHC 231.
[19] [2007] 1 I.R. 502.
[20] [1932] I.R. 28.
[21] (1990) 9 I.L.T.R. 126.
[22] [1932] I.R. 28 at 33.
[23] [2007] 1 I.R. 502 at 512.
[24] [2007] 1 I.R. 502 at 512.
[25] [1990] 1 W.L.R. 364.
[26] [2007] 1 I.R. 502 at 519.

This might be an area of the substantive law that would benefit from statutory reform. If it is considered desirable to retain the offence it would be preferable to put the offence on a statutory footing with a view to consolidation with the other public order offences in the Criminal Justice (Public Order) Act 1994. It would enhance legal certainty if the elements of the offence were clarified and defined clearly in a statutory provision. In this regard, Murphy J. remarked in *Thorpe* that "[i]t is anomalous, however, that breach of the peace is not prescribed by law, nor that there is no definition of the categories, nor of a dividing line between the serious and minor breaches".[27]

Display of material which is threatening, abusive, insulting or obscene

The actus reus of the offence under s.7(1) of the Criminal Justice (Public Order) Act 1994 requires proof that a defendant distributed or displayed, in a public place, material which is threatening, abusive, insulting or obscene in nature. In relation to the meaning of the terms "threatening, abusive, and insulting", the dicta of Charleton J. in *Clifford v DPP*,[28] in respect of the same terms contained in the offence definition of s.6 of the Criminal Justice (Public Order) Act 1994, would appear to apply with equal measure in interpreting the offence in s.7. That is to say that the terms "threatening, abusive, and insulting" should be given their ordinary English language meaning. Citing a line of English authorities,[29] Charleton, McDermott and Bolger have expressed the view that:

> "The test of obscenity is whether the tendency of the matter charged as obscenity is to deprave and corrupt those whose minds are open to such immoral influences and into whose hands a publication of this sort may fall."[30]

Clearly, the offence contained in s.7 of the Criminal Justice (Public Order) Act 1994 has the potential to be in conflict with the right to freedom of expression which is protected by Art.40.6.1° of the Irish Constitution and art.10(1) of the ECHR.[31]

The offence definition in s.7 provides for a mental element of intention or recklessness as to whether a breach of the peace may be occasioned. It will be recalled that the same mental element is provided for in the offence of threatening, abusive or insulting behaviour in a public place in s.6 of the Criminal Justice (Public Order) Act 1994. On this basis, the part of Charleton J.'s judgment, in *Clifford v DPP*, dealing with the mental element running to the external element of breaching the peace would appear to apply with equal measure to the interpretation of the mens rea requirements of the offence of distribution or display of material which is threatening, abusive, insulting or obscene in s.7 of the Criminal Justice (Public Order)

---

[27] [2007] 1 I.R. 502 at 520.
[28] [2008] IEHC 322 at para.9.
[29] *R. v Hicklin* (1868) L.R. 3 Q.B. 360 at 371; *R. v Barraclough* [1906] 1 K.B. 201; *Calder Publications Limited v Powell* [1965] 1 Q.B. 509.
[30] Charleton, McDermott and Bolger, *Criminal Law* (1999), p.766.
[31] Charleton, McDermott and Bolger, *Criminal Law* (1999), pp.766–767; Hogan, *Criminal Justice (Public Order) Act 1994 Annotated ICLSA* (1994), p.9.

Act 1994.[32] Similar to the offence in s.6, the offence definition in s.7 does not require any proof that a breach of the peace actually occurred. Instead, the prosecution must adduce sufficient evidence to satisfy the court that the defendant had the necessary intent or subjective recklessness with respect to occasioning a breach of the peace.

Offence of failure to comply with direction of member of An Garda Síochána

Section 8 of the Criminal Justice (Public Order) Act 1994 makes it an offence for a person to fail to comply with a direction of a member of An Garda Síochána in specified circumstances. The offence under s.8 is designed to address forms of anti-social conduct that were previously dealt with under the offence of loitering with intent contained in s.4 of the Vagrancy Act 1824. In *King v Attorney General*,[33] the offence of loitering with intent was declared to be unconstitutional. Following the decision of the Supreme Court in *King*, the drafters of the Criminal Justice (Public Order) Act 1994 decided against criminalising the act of loitering and instead opted for bestowing upon members of An Garda Síochána the power to direct persons suspected of engaging in prescribed forms of anti-social conduct "to move on", on pain of criminal sanction in the event of non-compliance with such a direction. Section 8 of the Criminal Justice (Public Order) Act 1994 is designed to deal with the public order problems associated with persons "hanging around" menacingly in public places by empowering the police to issue directions to such persons to desist from behaving in a manner that threatens the maintenance of public order and to leave the vicinity of the public place concerned. Hogan makes the following observations in relation to the historical background to the enactment of the offence:

> "Unlike the offence of loitering which was declared unconstitutional in *King*, this new offence created by section 8 is not restricted to conduct by a 'suspected person or reputed thief', nor does it consist of the act of loitering itself. Instead, section 8 criminalises the offence of failure to comply with a direction from a member of the Gardaí to desist from such conduct in circumstances where the Garda concerned had a reasonable apprehension for the safety of persons or property or for the maintenance of the public peace."[34]

A member of An Garda Síochána may issue a direction under s.8(1) only where that member finds a person in a public place and forms a reasonable suspicion that either:

(1) the person is or has been acting in a manner contrary to the provisions of ss.4,5,6,7 or 9 of the Criminal Justice (Public Order) Act 1994; or
(2) the person, without lawful authority or reasonable excuse, is acting in a manner which consists of loitering in a public place in circumstances, which may include the company of other persons, that give rise to a reasonable apprehension for the safety of persons or the safety of property or for the maintenance of the public peace.

---

[32] [2008] IEHC 322 at para.7.
[33] [1981] I.R. 233.
[34] Hogan, *Criminal Justice (Public Order) Act 1994 Annotated ICLSA* (1994), p.10.

The first limb permits a member of An Garda Síochána to issue a direction where that member has reasonable grounds to believe that one of the core public order offences under the Act has been committed. The second limb is formulated in objective terms, and allows a member of An Garda Síochána to issue a direction where a person is found loitering in a public place in circumstances that give rise to a reasonable apprehension as to the maintenance of public peace or the safety of members of the public or property.

Once there is a legal basis for issuing the direction, the member of An Garda Síochána may direct a person to desist from engaging in one of the specified forms of anti-social conduct. A member of An Garda Síochána may also issue a direction to leave the vicinity of the place concerned in a peaceable or orderly manner. It is the failure to comply with a direction of An Garda Síochána that constitutes an offence under s.8 of the Criminal Justice (Public Order) Act 1994. In *DPP v Galligan*,[35] the High Court held that in a prosecution for an offence contrary to s.8(2) of the Criminal Justice (Public Order) Act 1994 evidence should be given that the accused was informed or was aware of the fact that if he or she did not comply with the direction being given by a member of An Garda Síochána he or she would be committing a criminal offence. However, Laffoy J. went on to clarify that no particular formula of words need be used to convey such a warning. This means that an accused is entitled to fair notice of the penal consequences that flow from failure to comply with a direction made under s.8(1) of the Criminal Justice (Public Order) Act 1994, and that an accused is entitled to an acquittal if the member of An Garda Síochána has failed to give an adequate warning in relation to the implications of non-compliance with the direction. In *Bates v Brady*,[36] the High Court confirmed the position in *Galligan*, that unless evidence was adduced that the accused was given the warning as to non-compliance with the direction, or knew that the failure to comply with the requirement would result in him committing a criminal offence, the offence itself would not be committed.

Section 8A was inserted into the Criminal Justice (Public Order) Act 1994 by s.19 of the Intoxicating Liquor Act 2008, bestowing upon members of An Garda Síochána powers to give directions in relation to persons who the Gardaí with reasonable cause believe are in the possession of intoxicating substances in circumstances which give rise to a reasonable apprehension for the maintenance of public peace, the safety of other persons or property, or the likely annoyance to other persons or interference with the enjoyment of other persons' property. A member of An Garda Síochána may seek an explanation in relation to the suspected anti-social conduct. If this proves unsatisfactory, the member may request that any bottle or container be given to a member of An Garda Síochána, direct the person to desist from behaving in an anti-social manner within the meaning of s.8A(1), direct a person to leave immediately a place in a peaceable or orderly manner, and request the relevant person to provide his or her name and address. Section 8A(4) provides that it is an offence to fail or refuse to comply with a request or direction made under s.8A(2). It is also an offence to provide a name or address which is false or misleading following a request being made under s.8(2).

---

[35] Unreported, High Court, Laffoy J., November 2, 1995 at 5.
[36] [2003] 4 I.R. 111 at 120.

Obstruction offences

Section 9 of the Criminal Justice (Public Order) Act 1994 provides for the offence of wilful obstruction. This offence may only be committed in a public place and is aimed at penalising unjustifiable acts of interference with the free passage of persons or vehicles. For example, protesters blocking public pathways or roads might come within the scope of the offence.[37] Another example would be a person interrupting the free passage of persons in the course of begging.

The actus reus of the offence would appear to require proof of a result element amounting to actual interference with the free passage of persons or vehicles. The mens rea of the offence is less certain. Hogan has expressed the view that the inclusion of the term "wilful" in the offence definition imports an element of mens rea into the offence.[38] However, there is some uncertainty as to the meaning of the term "wilful". The *Commentary to the Draft Criminal Code*[39] notes that the use of the term "wilfully" in statutory offences is problematic as it is unclear if the term should be interpreted as meaning knowledge,[40] intention[41] or even strict liability.[42]

A more aggravated form of obstruction offence is provided for in s.19(3) of the Criminal Justice (Public Order) Act 1994. Under s.19(3)(c)–(d), it is an offence to resist, wilfully obstruct or impede a peace officer acting in the course of his or her duty, or a person assisting a peace officer in the course of his or her duty. The term "peace officer" is defined in s.19(6) as meaning a "member of the Garda Síochána, a prison officer or a member of the Defence Forces".

Section 19(3)(a)–(b) states that it is an offence to resist, wilfully obstruct or impede a person providing medical services at or in a hospital, or a person assisting such a person. An important spatial limitation on the scope of this limb of the offence is that it can only be committed at or in a hospital. It would appear that the offence is not committed if the offence occurs in a place other than a hospital. This restrictive definition of the actus reus of the offence has been critiqued in the *Commentary to the Draft Criminal Code*:

> "[I]t might be considered unduly restrictive to limit the ambit of that offence to [obstructions occurring] 'at or in a hospital', since many medical services are provided outside the hospital setting, for example at the scene of an accident. Given the fact that the offence of aggravated obstruction ... aims to protect the societal interest of maintaining public order, there is an even stronger argument for stating that ... the offence can be committed in *any* place (public or private)."[43]

---

[37] Hanly, *An Introduction to Irish Criminal Law* (2003), p.381.
[38] Hogan, *Criminal Justice (Public Order) Act 1994 Annotated ICLSA* (1994), p.12.
[39] Criminal Law Codification Advisory Committee, *Draft Criminal Code and Commentary* (Dublin, 2011), pp.297–298.
[40] *R. v Sheppard* [1980] 3 W.L.R. 960; *Attorney General's Reference (No. 3 of 2003)* [2004] EWCA Crim 868.
[41] *Wilmott v Atack* [1977] Q.B. 498.
[42] *Hudson v MacRae* (1863) 4 B. & S. 585, D.C.; *Cotterill v Penn* [1936] 1 K.B. 53; *Maidstone Borough Council v Mortimer* [1980] 3 All E.R. 552, D.C.
[43] Criminal Law Codification Advisory Committee, *Draft Criminal Code and Commentary* (Dublin, 2011), p.301.

Public Order Offences 247

The mens rea of the obstruction offence in s.19(3) is twofold. First, it must be shown that any instance of obstruction is "wilful". The same observations made above, in the context of the offence of wilful obstruction under s.9 of the 1994 Act, regarding the lack of certainty as to the meaning of the term "wilful", apply with equal force in relation to the obstruction offence in s.19(3) of the 1994 Act. Secondly, it must be established that the defendant is reckless or has knowledge in relation to the circumstance element of the injured party being a peace officer or a person providing medical services at or in a hospital. It is not clear from the offence definition whether knowledge or recklessness must be established in relation to the circumstance element of the injured party being a person who assists a peace officer or a person providing medical services at or in a hospital:

> "Section 19(3) of the 1994 Act (as amended) only explicitly states the fault element of knowledge/recklessness with regard to the circumstance elements of the victim being (a) a person providing medical services at or in a hospital and (b) a peace officer acting in the course of his or her duty. Under a contextual interpretation of section 19(3), there is an arguable case that the Oireachtas intended liability to be strict in relation to persons aiding persons providing medical services in hospitals or peace officers. However, it would seem logical and fair to apply the same fault element with respect to the other categories of persons listed in section 19(3)(b) and (d) ... [I]t is suggested that the fault elements of knowledge and recklessness be applied across the board to all the persons listed in section 19(3)."[44]

BEGGING OFFENCES

Background

Irish criminal law relating to begging has been amended by the enactment of the Criminal Justice (Public Order) Act 2011. Statutory reform was deemed necessary following the declaration of the High Court in *Dillon v DPP*[45] that the old law governing begging was unconstitutional. Under the former law, s.3 of the Vagrancy (Ireland) Act 1847, "... every person wandering abroad and begging, or placing himself in any public place, street, highway, court or passage to beg or gather alms ..." was liable to be convicted of the offence of begging. The High Court held that this formulation was unconstitutional on two separate grounds. First, the offence definition, by being too vague and imprecise, violated Arts 40.1, 40.3 and 40.4.1° of the Constitution, failing to satisfy the requirement that the law be sufficiently certain and clear so that persons may have, in advance, fair notice of what forms of conduct constitute a criminal offence.[46] Secondly, the offence was held to be a disproportionate and unreasonable interference with the right to freedom of expression as protected

---

[44] Criminal Law Codification Advisory Committee, *Draft Criminal Code and Commentary* (Dublin, 2011), p.301.
[45] [2008] 1 I.R. 383.
[46] [2008] 1 I.R. 383 at 389.

under Art.40 of the Constitution.[47] The thrust of the High Court decision in *Dillon* appears to be that "an overall ban on all forms of begging is unconstitutional".[48]

The High Court went on to state obiter that the manner in which begging is carried out could be regulated by law, provided that any restrictions imposed are proportionate and within the limits set by the Constitution:

> "[N]othing in this judgment should be construed as preventing the legislature making laws controlling the location, time, date, duration and manner in which begging or the seeking of alms might take place and the age of any person involved in such activity."[49]

The provisions of the Criminal Justice (Public Order) Act 2011 aim to strike a balance between respecting the constitutional rights of the individual beggar and protecting the rights of other persons who may be adversely affected by the activity of begging. Broadly speaking, the new legislation is intended to criminalise begging only in circumstances where the begging is of a nature that it interferes with the rights and interests of other persons. The act of begging in not in itself an offence so long as it is not accompanied by aggressive behaviour, acts of obstruction, or in cases of organised begging.

Offence of begging

Under the Criminal Justice (Public Order) Act 2011, a distinction is drawn between the act of begging and the offence of begging. Section 1(2) of the Criminal Justice (Public Order) Act 2011 defines the act of begging as requesting or soliciting money or goods from another person. It is expressly provided in s.1(2)(a) that where a person requests money pursuant to some form of legal authority, such as authorised collections for charity, this does not constitute "begging" for the purposes of the criminal law relating to begging. It is further clarified that begging may take place in both private and public places. It is important to note that the activity of begging, as defined in s.1(2) of the Criminal Justice (Public Order) Act 2011, does not constitute a criminal offence.

For an offence to be committed, the offence definition in s.2 of the Criminal Justice (Public Order) Act 2011 requires that the act of begging be accompanied by harassment, intimidation, obstructing the passage of persons or vehicles, an assault or the making of threats to another person. During the Parliamentary Debates the following example was given to illustrate the difference between the act of begging (which is lawful) and the offence of begging:

> "If a person who is short of change for a bus fare late at night asks another person at a bus stop for help paying a fare, that person may be said to be begging but an offence is committed only if he or she threatens, assaults or intimidates the other person."[50]

---

[47] [2008] 1 I.R. 383 at 389–390.
[48] [2008] 1 I.R. 383 at 390.
[49] [2008] 1 I.R. 383 at 390.
[50] 207 *Seanad Debates* Col.365 (Second Stage).

Offence of failure to comply with a Garda direction to desist from begging

Section 3 of the Criminal Justice (Public Order) Act 2011 bestows upon members of An Garda Síochána powers, in specified circumstances defined in s.3, to give directions to persons to desist from begging and to leave a particular vicinity in a peaceable and orderly manner. A member of An Garda Síochána may give such a direction where that member reasonably believes that the person is acting, or has acted, in a manner that constitutes an offence of begging as defined in s.2, or that the person is behaving in a manner that gives rise to a reasonable apprehension for the safety of persons or property or for the maintenance of public peace. Alternatively, a member of An Garda Síochána may give a direction to a person near the entrance of a dwelling, an ATM machine, a vending machine or a night safe to desist from begging and to leave that particular location. A member of An Garda Síochána may also give a direction where that member has reasonable grounds for believing that a person's begging near a business premises may be deterring members of the public from entering those premises.

A person who fails to comply with a direction given pursuant to s.3 of the Criminal Justice (Public Order) Act 2011 commits a criminal offence. An important safeguard is provided for in s.3(6) which states that a member of An Garda Síochána shall, upon giving a direction under s.3, inform the person to whom the direction is given, in clear language, that any failure to comply with a direction shall constitute an offence. This requirement that a person be given fair notice of the penal consequences of failure to comply with a direction is in line with the general approach taken by the Irish courts in relation to similar types of offences contained in other sections of the Criminal Justice (Public Order) Act 1994.[51] The intention behind s.3 of the Criminal Justice (Public Order) Act 2011 is that members of An Garda Síochána shall give priority to the utilisation of the powers to move on beggars threatening the maintenance of public order and that initiating prosecutions should be the last resort:

> "Section 3 reflects our policy position that the nuisance created by begging should not, as a rule, result in prosecutions or, indeed, imprisonment. Section 3 provides an alternative means whereby the Garda can address particular cases quickly, fairly and effectively."[52]

Offences related to organised begging

A different, more sinister, form of organised begging is addressed by ss.5–6 of the Criminal Justice (Public Order) Act 2011. This type of begging is of a more serious nature as a result of the organised crime element of the offence and the harm caused through the exploitation of some of the most vulnerable members of society, including children and persons marginalised by poverty. The new offence of organised begging is modelled on the offence definition of the offence of organised prostitution in s.9 of the Criminal Law (Sexual Offences) Act 1993. The offence in s.5 of the Criminal Justice (Public Order) Act 2011 can be committed in a number

---

[51] *DPP v Galligan*, unreported, High Court, Laffoy J., November 2, 1995; *Bates v Brady* [2003] 4 I.R. 111; *DPP v Mulligan* [2009] 1 I.R. 794.
[52] 207 *Seanad Debates* Col.366 (Second Stage).

of ways; by controlling, directing or organising begging, and by forcing or causing another person to beg. It will be recalled that the term "begging" is defined in s.1 of the Criminal Justice (Public Order) Act 2011 as requesting or soliciting money or goods from another person. While s.5 of the Criminal Justice (Public Order) Act 2011 is silent as to the mens rea of the offence of organised begging, given the seriousness of the crime and the possibility of a penalty of a term of imprisonment of five years on conviction on indictment it is likely that the principles of statutory interpretation related to the presumption of mens rea would be applied.[53] It is regrettable that the drafters did not expressly stipulate the mens rea requirements for this offence. There may be some uncertainty as to what particular mens rea requirements run to the various external elements contained in the offence definition.

Section 6 of the Criminal Justice (Public Order) Act 2011 provides for an offence of living off the proceeds of another person's begging. This offence is loosely based around the offence of living on earnings of prostitution in s.10 of the Criminal Law (Sexual Offences) Act 1993, but is different in a number of respects. First, it would seem that liability for an offence under s.6 of the Criminal Justice (Public Order) Act 2011 is contingent on there being the commission of an offence by the defendant of an offence under s.5 of that Act, either by committing the offence of organised begging as principal or by aiding and abetting the commission of that offence. Secondly, while no mens rea requirements are expressly provided for in the offence definition of "living off the proceeds of begging", the offence definition of the offence of living off the earnings of prostitution provides for a fault element of knowledge in respect of the external element of living off the earnings of prostitution. Due to the seriousness of the offence, the social stigma attached to the offence and the possibility of a term of imprisonment not exceeding 12 months it is likely that the presumption of mens rea would apply to the external element of living off the proceeds of begging. However, there would appear to be some uncertainty as to which particular fault requirements would be read in to the offence definition; it is unclear whether recklessness, knowledge or intention would apply.

TRESPASS OFFENCES

Criminal trespass

Trespass is generally understood to mean entering the property of another person without that other person's consent. The element of trespass is an essential ingredient of the offences contained in ss.11 and 13 of the Criminal Justice (Public Order) Act 1994. As the term "trespasser" is not defined in the Criminal Justice (Public Order) Act 1994 it is necessary to have regard to case law to gain a fuller understanding of the constituent elements of the concept of trespass in criminal law. The legal definition of the term "trespasser" has been considered in a number of English decisions in the context of the offence of burglary. The line of jurisprudence on the meaning of the term criminal trespass would appear to be relevant to the interpretation of the trespass offences contained in the Criminal Justice (Public Order) Act on the basis that these offences are of a similar nature to burglary. In light of the fact that these

---

[53] *Sweet v Parsley* [1970] A.C. 132; *CC v Ireland* [2006] 4 I.R. 1.

offences can attract a custodial sentence[54] and the stigma of a criminal conviction, an argument could be made that it is more appropriate to apply the criminal definition of the term "trespass", which contains detailed mens rea requirements, as opposed to the civil definition of "trespass" which necessitates proof of the act of trespass only. This interpretation is in line with the canon of construction that a presumption of mens rea will generally apply in respect of penal statutes.[55] In *Sweet v Parsley*, Lord Reid described the rule in the following terms:

> "Sometimes the words of the section which creates a particular offence make it clear that mens rea is required in one form or another. Such cases are quite frequent. But in a very large number of cases there is no clear indication either way. In such cases there has for centuries been a presumption that Parliament did not intend to make criminals of persons who were in no way blameworthy in what they did. That means that whenever a section is silent as to mens rea there is a presumption that, in order to give effect to the will of Parliament, we must read in words appropriate to require mens rea."[56]

Prior to the decision of the Court of Appeal in *R. v Collins*,[57] there was some disagreement among academic commentators as to what constituted a trespass in the specific context of the criminal law. Under the law of tort, it was sufficient for establishing trespass that a person entered the property of another person without consent, there being no requirement to prove any mental element for the purposes of imposing civil liability. Archbold expressed the view that in relation to the criminal law:

> "Any intentional, reckless or negligent entry into a building will, it would appear, constitute a trespass if the building is in the possession of another person who does not consent to the entry. Nor will it make any difference that the entry was the result of a reasonable mistake on the part of the defendant, so far as trespass is concerned."[58]

According to Archbold's formulation of trespass, there was no requirement that the accused consciously adverted to the facts that made his or her entry unlawful. In other words, it was suggested that there was no requirement to establish a subjective mental state on the part of the accused in relation to the act of trespass.

A different view was expressed by Professors Smith and Griew, who opined that the subjective fault elements of knowledge or recklessness must be established in respect of the act of trespass. Professor Smith submitted that a person "cannot be convicted of the criminal offence unless he knew of the facts which caused him

---

[54] A person who is convicted of an offence of trespass under s.11 of the Public Order Act 1994 shall be liable to a fine of €2,500 or a term of imprisonment not exceeding six months. A person who is convicted of an offence of trespass under s.13(1) of the Public Order Act 1994 shall be liable to a fine of €2,500 or a term of imprisonment not exceeding 12 months.
[55] *Sweet v Parsley* [1970] A.C. 132; *CC v Ireland* [2006] 4 I.R. 1.
[56] [1970] A.C. 132 at 148.
[57] [1973] Q.B. 100.
[58] Archbold, *Archbold Criminal Pleading Evidence & Practice*, 37th edn (1969), para.1505.

to be a trespasser or, as least, was reckless".[59] The following passage taken from Professor's Griew's commentary on the English Theft Act 1968 expresses a similar view that the fault requirements for criminal trespass are knowledge or recklessness:

> "What if D wrongly believes that he is not trespassing? His belief may rest on facts which, if true, would mean that he was not trespassing: for instance he may enter a building by mistake, thinking that it is the one he has been invited to enter. Or his belief may be based on a false view of the legal effect of the known facts: for instance he may misunderstand the effect of a contract granting him a right of passage through a building. Neither kind of mistake will protect him from tort liability for trespass ... But for the purposes of criminal liability a man should be judged on the basis of the facts as he believed them to be, and this should include making allowances for a mistake as to his rights under the civil law ... Unhappily it is common for Parliament to omit to make clear whether mens rea is intended to be an element in a statutory offence. It is also, though not equally, common for the courts to supply the mental element by construction of the statute."[60]

In *R. v Collins*, the Court of Appeal preferred the view expressed by Professor Smith and Professor Griew, holding that a person cannot be convicted for entering as a trespasser "unless the person entering does so knowing that he is a trespasser and nevertheless deliberately enters, or, at the very least, is reckless as to whether or not he is entering the premises of another without the other party's consent".[61] A similar position was adopted in *R. v Jones and Smith*, where it was noted that the decision in *R. v Collins* "added to the concept of trespass as a civil wrong only the mental element of mens rea, which is essential to the criminal offence".[62] While there would appear to be no Irish authorities touching directly on the issue of the mens rea of criminal trespass there would seem to be some support for the English position that criminal trespass requires proof of knowledge or recklessness on the part of the accused as to the facts that make him or her a trespasser.[63]

Offence of entering a building or curtilage with intent to commit an offence

Section 11 of the Criminal Justice (Public Order) Act creates an offence of trespass which is aimed at criminalising acts of trespass which are accompanied with an intent to commit an offence or an intent to unlawfully interfere with property. Charleton, McDemott and Bolger describe this offence as "akin to burglary" and suggest that it might be charged as a fallback in cases "where nothing is stolen or where the prosecution cannot prove an intent to steal".[64] Indeed, it could be argued that this

---

[59] Smith, *The Law of Theft*, 1st edn (1968), para.462.
[60] Griew, *The Theft Act 1968*, 2nd edn (Sweet & Maxwell, 1974), para.4–05.
[61] [1973] Q.B. 100 at 105.
[62] [1976] W.L.R. 672 at 675.
[63] Charleton, McDermott and Bolger, *Criminal Law* (1999), p.842; Criminal Law Codification Advisory Committee, *Draft Criminal Code and Commentary* (Dublin, 2011), pp.183–188.
[64] Charleton, McDermott and Bolger, *Criminal Law* (1999), p.768.

offence has been misclassified as a public order offence and would be more suitably classified as an offence against property on the basis that the principal interest at stake is the protection of property as opposed to the maintenance of public order.[65]

Section 11 of the 1994 Act provides that the offence of trespass can be committed in two different ways. Under s.11(1)(a), a person is guilty of an offence if the person enters any building or the curtilage of any building as a trespasser, in circumstances that give rise to a reasonable inference that such entry was accompanied by an intent to commit an offence or an intent to unlawfully interfere with property. Under s.11(1)(b), a person is guilty of an offence if the person is present in the vicinity of any building or curtilage of a building for the purpose of trespassing, in circumstances that give rise to a reasonable inference that such presence was accompanied by an intent to commit an offence or an intent to unlawfully interfere with property. The reach of the offence of trespass has the potential to be very wide as it applies to acts of trespass on the curtilage of a building which refers to the land surrounding a building, such as a driveway or garden. Both limbs of the offence can be viewed as inchoate in nature.

Because the element of trespass is an essential ingredient of the offence definition, in relation to the formulation under s.11(1)(a), the prosecution must establish that the defendant entered the property of another person without consent, and that the defendant knew that he or she was a trespasser or was reckless as to whether he or she was a trespasser.[66] Under the limb of the offence contained in s.11(1)(b) the court must be satisfied that there is sufficient evidence that the defendant's purpose was to trespass on the property of another person. Apart from the requirement to establish the mental element in respect of the act of trespass, the offence definition creates an objective test based on the concept of reasonableness as to whether the defendant's entry was with an ulterior intention to commit an offence or unlawfully interfere with property; there is no requirement to prove that the defendant in fact committed an offence or interfered with property.

Offence of trespass on a building or curtilage causing fear in another person

Section 13 of the Criminal Justice (Public Order) Act 1994 provides for an offence of trespass that occurs in circumstances where fear is caused, or is likely to be caused, to another person. Similar to the offence of trespass contained in s.11, the offence definition in s.13 makes the element of trespass a core ingredient of the offence. It follows that the prosecution must establish that the defendant entered the building (or curtilage) of another person without consent, and that the defendant knew that he or she was a trespasser or was reckless as to whether he or she was a trespasser.[67]

In addition, the court must be satisfied that the act of trespass caused fear in another person or occurred in a manner that was likely to cause fear in another person. In the absence of evidence that a person was in fear as a result of the trespass, there must be sufficient evidence for the court to draw the inference from the surrounding

---

[65] Criminal Law Codification Advisory Committee, *Draft Criminal Code and Commentary* (Dublin, 2011), pp.7 and 146.
[66] *R. v Collins* [1973] Q.B. 100; *R. v Jones and Smith* [1976] W.L.R. 672.
[67] *R. v Collins* [1973] Q.B. 100; *R. v Jones and Smith* [1976] W.L.R. 672.

circumstances that a person would be likely to be in fear. For instance, it is likely that an injured party would be in fear if a stranger was observed in his home or back garden, without any good reason. In contrast to the offence of trespass under s.11, the offence definition in s.13 requires no proof of any intent to commit an offence; the gravamen of the offence is that a person is put in fear, or likely to be put in fear by the defendant's act of trespass.

Section 13 provides for a defence of reasonable excuse. This defence may exculpate a defendant in circumstances where he or she can offer some reasonable explanation for being present on the property of another person. For example, a defendant in the immediate aftermath of being assaulted by a third party might take refuge in the garden of a householder, without consent, and in circumstances that would be likely to cause fear. While technically speaking the defendant has committed an offence of trespass under s.13, a court might accept his or her excuse for trespassing as being reasonable given the immediate threat to his or her bodily integrity, and direct an acquittal. These types of cases, where a defence of reasonable excuse is raised, are likely to turn on the credibility of the witness giving evidence.

Offences relating to entering and occupying land without consent

Section 19C provides for a trespass-related offence, which prohibits a person from entering and occupying land, or bringing onto or placing on any land any object, without the consent of the owner, where such conduct is likely to:

(1) substantially damage the land;
(2) substantially and prejudicially affect any amenity in respect of the land;
(3) prevent persons entitled to use the land or any amenity in respect of the land from making reasonable use of the land or amenity;
(4) otherwise render the land or any amenity in respect of the land, or the lawful use of the land or any amenity in respect of the land, unsanitary or unsafe;
(5) substantially interfere with the land, any amenity in respect of the land, the lawful use of the land or any amenity in respect of the land.

A detailed interpretation section is contained in s.19A covering a range of definitions relevant to the offence in s.19C. Section 19G(2) creates a presumption that consent was not given until the contrary is shown. It is also worth noting that s.19D creates an ancillary offence of refusing or failing to give a name or address, or failure to comply with a direction to leave the land concerned or remove any object from the land, when such a request or direction is made by a member of An Garda Síochána pursuant to s.19C(3). Section 19G(1) provides that a person guilty of an offence under ss.19C–D shall be liable on summary conviction to a fine not exceeding €4,000 or a term of imprisonment not exceeding one month or both.

Riot, Violent Disorder and Affray

Riot

Historically, offences committed by groups of persons in numbers have been viewed as posing a serious threat to the interests protected by the criminal law.[68] Generally speaking, there is a greater potential for harm where a number of persons are engaging in criminal conduct as opposed to a situation where a single individual commits an offence. Where a group of persons engage in criminal behaviour the level of seriousness of the criminality may escalate very quickly. For example, in the context of a prison, a heightened risk of damage to property or bodily harm to prison staff is posed where a large group of prisoners are rioting as opposed to a situation where a lone prisoner is engaging in criminal conduct. The State's special concern with offending involving more than one person is evident in the recent legislative practice of enacting offences targeted at combating organised crime.[69] It is perhaps for these reasons that a distinct offence of riot, triable only on indictment, is provided for, in order to the mark the seriousness with which the criminal law views group crime.

The actus reus of the offence of riot is made up of a number of discrete external elements. First, the offence of riot may be committed at any place, whether that place is a public or a private place. Secondly, the defendant must be present with 11 or more other persons who are using or threatening to use unlawful violence for a common purpose. This aspect of the actus reus is subject to a form of objective test in so far as the conduct of the 12 or more persons, taken together, is such as would cause a person of reasonable firmness present at that place to fear for his or her or another person's safety. However, s.14(2)(c) states that no person of reasonable firmness need actually be, or likely to be, present at that place. Section 14(2)(a) clarifies that there is no requirement that the group of 12 or more persons use or threaten to use violence simultaneously at any place. Thirdly, a person may be found guilty of riot only where that person has used unlawful violence for the common purpose; liability for riot is not established in circumstances where the defendant has threatened but not used unlawful violence.

It has been observed in the *Commentary to the Draft Criminal Code* that apart from the reference to using or threatening to use violence for a common purpose the offence definition of "riot" is silent on the issue of mens rea:

> "By contrast, the English offence of riot in section 1 of the Public Order Act 1986, which is broadly similar to its Irish counterpart, is subject to explicit mens rea requirements: by virtue of section 6(1) of the 1986 Act the defendant must be shown to have intended to use violence or to have been aware that his conduct may be violent, in addition to sharing a common purpose with 11 other people at the scene.
>
> It appears from the Departmental files on the Criminal Justice (Public Order) Bill 1993 that the reason that an express fault requirement of this kind was not included in section 14 of the 1994 Act had to do with the fact that the offence of riot requires the actual, as opposed to a merely threatened, use of unlawful

---

[68] Simester and Sullivan, *Criminal Law Theory and Doctrine* (Oxford: Hart, 2003), p.225.
[69] See Pt 7 of the Criminal Justice Act 2006 which is dedicated to organised crime offences.

violence by the defendant for a common purpose. Although the Heads of Bill prepared by the Department of Justice, Equality and Law Reform had followed the English approach described in the previous paragraph, the opinion of the Office of the Parliamentary Counsel appears to have been that the express inclusion of mens rea in the form of intention or awareness (in the sense of recklessness) was otiose as these fault elements are already comprehended in the requirement that the defendant must be shown to have used violence for a common purpose."[70]

The *Commentary to the Draft Criminal Code* goes on to recommend expressly providing for mens rea requirements of intention, knowledge or recklessness in respect of the circumstance elements of being present in any place with 11 or more other persons and the use of unlawful violence for a common purpose.

Violent disorder

Section 15 of the Criminal Justice (Public Order) Act 1994 provides for the offence of violent disorder. Section 15(5) states that any reference to the common law offences of riot and tumult in any enactment passed before the commencement of the 1994 Act shall be construed as a reference to the statutory offence of violent disorder as provided for in s.15 of the 1994 Act. The related common law offences of rout and unlawful assembly have been abolished.[71]

Charleton, McDermott and Bolger have commented that "violent disorder is a lesser species of riot and is specifically provided for and may perhaps be charged as a lesser and alternative offence".[72] It is perhaps best to consider the constituent elements of the offence of violent disorder in relation to the offence of riot. Similar to the offence of riot, the offence of violent disorder can be committed in a public place or a private place and there is no requirement that the unlawful violence be used or threatened simultaneously. However, the actus reus requirements of violent disorder are less onerous than riot in a number of respects. In relation to the offence of violent disorder, there need only be a minimum of three persons present together at any place using or threatening to use unlawful violence; the offence of riot requires at least 12 persons to be present. Similar to the offence of riot, this component of the actus reus is subject to an objective test in so far as there is a requirement that the conduct of the three or more persons present, taken together, is such as would cause a person of reasonable firmness present at that place to fear for his or her or another person's safety. It should be noted that no reasonable person is required to be actually present.[73] Unlike the offence of riot which imposes a requirement that the accused actually uses unlawful violence, the offence of violent disorder is broader, as it can be committed where the accused uses or threatens to use unlawful violence.

Mens rea is expressly provided for in s.15(3) which states that "a person shall not be convicted of violent disorder unless the person intends to use or threaten to use

---

[70] Criminal Law Codification Advisory Committee, *Draft Criminal Code and Commentary* (Dublin, 2011), pp.310–311.
[71] Criminal Justice (Public Order) Act 1994 s.15(6).
[72] Charleton, McDermott and Bolger, *Criminal Law* (1999), p.771.
[73] Criminal Justice (Public Order) Act 1994 s.15(2)(b).

violence or is aware that his conduct may be violent or threaten violence". In contrast to riot, there is no requirement that the persons taking part in the violent disorder are acting with a common purpose. The *Commentary to the Draft Criminal Code* makes the observation in relation to the offence of violent disorder that "[e]ach of the three or more persons may have a different purpose or no purpose".[74] In other words, violent disorder may encompass situations where a group of persons by chance happen to be in a particular place together engaging in random acts of violence regardless of whether there is any purpose behind their actions. An example might be a disturbance outside a nightclub that unexpectedly turns violent. Riot is arguably more serious in nature in that there is a specific purpose to the unlawful violent behaviour, such as a violent protest that is politically motivated. A final point to note is that the offence definition is silent on the issue of mens rea as to the circumstance element of being present at a place with two or more persons; it is unclear what specific fault element, if any, is required to be established. The *Commentary to the Draft Criminal Code* has recommended having recklessness, knowledge or intention run to this particular external element of the offence.[75]

Affray

Section 16 of the Criminal Justice (Public Order) Act 1994 abolishes the common law offence of affray and replaces it with a statutory offence of affray which is drafted in a similar style to the cognate "group" offences of riot and violent disorder. While the offence of affray would appear to be aimed at combating the harm posed by public displays of violence, such as street fighting, it is noteworthy that the offence may be committed in a public place or private place. It follows that a person could be found liable for the offence of affray even where the acts of violence occur in a place to which the public do not have a right of access, such as a dwelling or private business premises.

The actus reus of the offence of affray requires that two or more persons use or threaten to use violence towards each other, and that the violence used or threatened by one of those persons is unlawful. This aspect of the actus reus is subject to an objective test; it must be established that the conduct of the persons taken together is such as would cause a person of reasonable firmness present at that place to fear for his or her or another person's safety. In ease of the prosecution, s.16(2)(b) provides that there is no requirement that a person of reasonable firmness need actually be, or likely to be, present at the place where the use or threat of violence occurred. In such circumstances, each person who uses or threatens to use unlawful violence commits the offence of affray. In relation to the term "threats" as it applies to the offence of affray, s.16(2)(a) states that "a threat cannot be made by words alone"; something more is required, such as gestures or some physical act. For example, the production of a weapon would probably satisfy the higher threshold imposed by s.16(2)(a) in respect of the definition of the term "threats".

---

[74] Criminal Law Codification Advisory Committee, *Draft Criminal Code and Commentary* (Dublin, 2011), p.307.
[75] Criminal Law Codification Advisory Committee, *Draft Criminal Code and Commentary* (Dublin, 2011), pp.306–308.

Section 16(3) is concerned with the mens rea of the offence of affray, expressly providing that a person is not guilty of affray "unless the person intends to use or threaten to use violence or is aware that his conduct may be violent or threaten violence". At first glance, the fault requirements of the offence would appear to be intention or knowledge (which is usually equated with awareness). However, Charleton, McDermott and Bolger have expressed the view that the "mental element is intention or recklessness".[76] The reasoning justifying this interpretation of the mens rea requirements of affray is set out in further detail in the *Commentary to the Draft Criminal Code*:

> "Section 16(3) of the 1994 Act deals with the fault requirements for the offence of affray. It provides that a person shall not be convicted of the offence 'unless the person intends to use or threatens to use violence or is aware that his conduct may be violent or threaten violence.' On one view, this language suggests that section 16(3) requires proof of intention or *knowledge* in respect of the objective elements covered by the subsection. In other words, the concept of awareness as used in section 16(3) seems more akin to knowledge than it does to recklessness. At all events, this conclusion seems sound if the phrase 'the person ... is aware that his conduct may be violent or threaten violence' is an ellipsis for the person ... is aware that his conduct may be violent or threaten violence in the ordinary course of events ...
>
> There is also the consideration that the legislature chose not to use the term reckless in section 16(3), notwithstanding that recklessness had been defined in Irish case law as advertence to a risk that something might or may occur, and going on to run that risk; and that the legislature itself had adopted this definition in section 2(6) of the Criminal Damage Act, 1991.
>
> Alternatively, the legislature's apparent disinclination to use the language of recklessness may have been influenced by the contemporary jurisprudence on that subject in England and Wales, which deviated sharply from the subjective approach to the concept of recklessness in Irish law as summarised at the conclusion of the preceding paragraph. In other words, there may have been a concern that, given that background, the mere use of the term recklessness could have given rise to controversy as to whether it implied a subjective or objective standard of culpability. Be that as it may, there is a clear difference between knowingly using or threatening to use violence, in the sense of being aware that violence is a virtually certain by-product of one's conduct, on the one hand, and being aware that one's conduct may be violent, on the other. On any reasonable view, the latter looks more like recklessness than knowledge, and it has accordingly been treated as such in the present draft."[77]

The definition of the offence of affray is silent in relation to the mental element (if any) running to the circumstance element of being present at a place with one or more persons who are using or threatening to use violence towards each other. It

---

[76] Charleton, McDermott and Bolger, *Criminal Law* (1999), p.772.
[77] Criminal Law Codification Advisory Committee, *Draft Criminal Code and Commentary* (Dublin, 2011), p.304.

Public Order Offences

is not entirely clear whether liability is strict in respect of this particular external element or whether a presumption of mens rea applies. The *Commentary to the Draft Criminal Code* has recommended having recklessness, knowledge or intention attach to this particular external element of the offence.[78]

---

[78] Criminal Law Codification Advisory Committee, *Draft Criminal Code and Commentary* (Dublin, 2011), pp.302–305.

Chapter 10

DEFENCES SPECIFIC TO MURDER

Introduction

Defences can be divided into three categories. The first is made up of those defences which are specific to murder and which result in a conviction for the lesser offence of manslaughter if successfully raised. The second category consists of those defences which are available to every offence except for murder. The third category consists of those defences which are generally available.

Three defences are specific to murder: diminished responsibility, provocation and excessive self defence. This is not to say that these matters cannot be raised in relation to offences other than murder: if they are, then they can be taken into consideration as mitigating factors at the sentencing stage. However, it is only in the case of murder that these three defences go to the issue of criminal liability, in so far as the defences operate to reduce a conviction of murder to manslaughter. It follows that allowing these defences in the case of murder does not allow the accused to escape all liability for his actions; a person who successfully raises the defence of provocation or excessive self defence will still be convicted of the offence of manslaughter. The criminal law makes these concessions perhaps because of the particularly grave status of murder, which leads to a reluctance to label as murderers those persons who act under the pressure of the moment, even though that would not amount to a defence in another, less serious context. In making provision for these defences specific to murder the criminal law gives recognition to the lesser degree of culpability that may arise in these types of cases.[1]

Diminished Responsibility

Section 6 of the Criminal Law (Insanity) Act 2006 places on a statutory basis the partial defence of diminished responsibility. Under that section, where the defence is successfully raised, a person may have his conviction reduced from murder to manslaughter. The defence is made out where it is established that the accused did the act alleged, was at the time suffering from a mental disorder, and the mental disorder was not such as to justify finding him or her not guilty by reason of insanity, but was such as to diminish substantially his or her responsibility for the act. This defence is considered in detail alongside the wider defence of insanity in Ch.11.

---

[1] For discussion of the rationale underpinning the defences specific to murder, see Law Reform Commission, *Report on Defences in Criminal Law* (LRC 95–2009), pp.111–122.

Defences Specific to Murder 261

PROVOCATION

Introduction

The existing law on provocation can be traced back to the seminal decision of *DPP v MacEoin*.[2] In that case, the Court of Criminal Appeal approved of a subjective test for the defence of provocation:

> "The trial judge at the close of evidence should rule on whether there is any evidence of provocation which having regard to the accused's temperament, character and circumstances, might have caused him to lose control of himself at the time of the wrongful act and whether the provocation bears a reasonable relation to the amount of force used by the accused."[3]

In *DPP v Byrne*, Keane C.J. made the observation that the law governing provocation "has got into a state of affairs which, one can only say, is not easy for a lay person to follow; some lawyers have difficulty following it too".[4] Perhaps due to the wording of the test in *MacEoin*, which has been the subject of criticism,[5] a large amount of case law has built up around the defence of provocation.[6] Despite some reservation, occasionally, having been expressed as to the manner in which the law has been defined in *MacEoin*, the Superior Courts have consistently held that the law relating to provocation is to be governed by a subjective standard.

In the recent Court of Criminal Appeal decision in *DPP v Curran*,[7] while confirming that the test for provocation in this jurisdiction is "wholly subjective", O'Donnell J. remarked that there was an urgent need for statutory reform to clarify the law in this area:

> "... *MacEoin* was initially seen as an enlightened development in accordance with the best academic analyses. However, it has become increasingly clear that the formulation of the defence in wholly subjective terms is, unless carefully defined and applied, particularly capable of creating a dangerously loose formulation to extend the law's indulgence to conduct that should deserve censure rather than excuse ... The increased incidence of a provocation defence being raised in murder trials, is suggestive more of an expansion of the scope of the defence, rather than a surprising resurgence of the values and behaviour of 'Restoration gallantry'. There is a clear and pressing need for a

---

[2] [1978] I.R. 27.
[3] *DPP v MacEoin* [1978] I.R. 27 at 34.
[4] Unreported, ex tempore, Court of Criminal Appeal, February 24, 2003.
[5] Law Reform Commission, *Report on Defences in Criminal Law* (LRC 95–2009), Ch.4; McAuley and McCutcheon, *Criminal Liability* (Dublin: Round Hall Sweet & Maxwell, 2000), pp.872–877.
[6] *DPP v Kehoe* [1992] I.L.R.M. 481; *DPP v Mullane*, unreported, Court of Criminal Appeal, March 11, 1997; *DPP v Noonan* [1998] 1 I.L.R.M. 154; *DPP v Bambrick* [1999] 2 I.L.R.M. 71; *DPP v Kelly* [2000] 2 I.R. 1; *DPP v McDonagh* [2001] 3 I.R. 201; *DPP v Davis* [2001] 1 I.R. 146; *DPP v Doyle*, unreported, Court of Criminal Appeal, March 22, 2002; *DPP v Byrne*, unreported, Court of Criminal Appeal, February 24, 2003; *DPP v Delaney* [2010] IECCA 123; *DPP v Curran* [2011] IECCA 95.
[7] [2011] IECCA 95.

comprehensive review of this area, and its interaction with other areas of the law of homicide, and at a minimum, a statutory regulation of the scope of the defence ... In the meantime the existing law must be applied."[8]

Historical background

The defence of provocation has a long history and the plea initially developed as a means of avoiding the death penalty in cases of intentional homicides.[9] In *R. v Mawgridge*,[10] the courts recognised four types of provocation which could, in law, form the basis of a plea of provocation: a grossly insulting assault, seeing a friend attacked, seeing an Englishman unlawfully deprived of liberty and catching someone in the act of adultery with one's wife. It has been observed that the provocation defence emerged at a time when it was acceptable to defend an attack on one's honour and that the law was primarily concerned with the nature of the provocative conduct.[11]

Subsequently, there was a shift away from the approach of establishing specific categories of provocation on an incremental basis to an approach based on general principles of liability based on the legal concept of the "reasonable man". This new approach to liability for provocation was based on an objective test and was more concerned with the effect of the provocation on the reasonable man than the inherent wrongfulness in the act of provocation. The "reasonable man" test was set out by Keating J. in *R. v Welsh* as follows:

> "[T]here must exist such an amount of provocation as would be excited by the circumstances in the mind of a reasonable man, and so as to lead the jury to ascribe the act to the influence of that passion."[12]

The rationale behind limiting the availability of provocation to situations in which a reasonable man would have lost self-control is based around the concern that the plea of provocation might be too readily available to persons who are peculiarly temperamental in nature and who plead hot-headedness as a defence in circumstances where a person of ordinary self control would not have reacted by using lethal force.

For many observers, the application of the objective test in the English decision of *R. v Bedder*[13] was unduly harsh on the defendant. In that case, the defendant was aged 18 years and sexually impotent. The defendant attempted to have intercourse with a prostitute; when he failed, she taunted him. A struggle followed, in which she slapped, punched and kicked him in the groin area. In response, the defendant stabbed the victim twice with a knife. It would appear from the facts that the defendant's impotence was the reason underpinning his extreme reaction; it is unlikely that the taunt of impotence would have had the same effect otherwise. However, the

---

[8] [2011] IECCA 95.
[9] See Law Reform Commission, *Report on Defences in Criminal Law* (LRC 95–2009), pp.197–110; McAuley and McCutcheon, *Criminal Liability* (2000), pp.851–853.
[10] (1706) Kel. 119.
[11] Law Reform Commission, *Report on Defences in Criminal Law* (LRC 95–2009), pp.108–109; Power, "Provocation and Culture" [2006] Crim. L.R. 871.
[12] (1869) 11 Cox CC 674.
[13] [1954] 2 All E.R. 801.

Defences Specific to Murder 263

House of Lords held that the defendant's impotence could not be taken into account in assessing the effect of the provocation on him. It was reasoned that since the "reasonable man" was not impotent, and would not have lost his self control as a result of the taunt, therefore the defendant could not raise the defence of provocation notwithstanding that he may have been particularly sensitive to the taunts of the injured party in light of the fact that he actually suffered from impotence.

Following the decision in *Bedder*, the English courts gradually moved away from a strict objective test incorporating some subjective elements into the provocation defence. The partial subjectivisation of the law on provocation in England is evident in the House of Lords decision in *R. v Camplin*.[14] This case involved a 15-year-old-boy who killed the deceased after it was alleged the deceased had forcibly buggered the boy and then jeered him. The trial judge refused to direct the jury to consider the effect of the provocation on a 15-year-old-boy in the same position as the accused. On appeal, the House of Lords departed from *R. v Bedder*, and held that on a proper application of the test:

> "The jury had to consider whether a young man of about the same age as the accused but placed in the same position as that which befell the accused could, had he been a reasonable young man, have reacted as did the accused and could have done what the accused did."

In effect, this is a form of mixed subjective/objective test. It is subjective in so far as the jury are to consider the effect of the provocation on a person in the defendant's circumstances; but it is objective in that the jury are not to consider the effect of the provocation on the defendant himself, but on a reasonable person in the defendant's circumstances. The jury may not, therefore, take into account the fact that the accused had a quick temper or was particularly excitable or pugnacious; they should consider how a hypothetical reasonable 15-year-old would react in all other respects placed in the shoes of the defendant. It was against this backdrop that the Irish law on provocation took the form of a subjective test. It should be noted that, in England, s.56 of the Coroners and Justice Act 2009 abolished the common law defence of provocation, and replaced it with a new defence of "loss of control" which is set out in ss.54 and 55 of that Act.

The Irish position on provocation: subjective test

At around the same time as the English case of *R. v Camplin*,[15] the Irish decision of *DPP v MacEoin*[16] was delivered, in which the Court of Criminal Appeal took a very different view of the law of provocation to its English counterpart. In that case, the accused and deceased lived together in a flat. Both men were heavy drinkers, and on the day of the killing both had been drinking heavily. In the course of the drinking session, the deceased began to behave aggressively towards the defendant, and eventually attacked the defendant with a hammer. The defendant wrestled the

---

[14] [1978] A.C. 705 at 721.
[15] [1978] A.C. 705.
[16] [1978] I.R. 27 at 34.

hammer from the deceased and (as he put it) "simmered over and ... completely lost control", killing the deceased with several blows to the head.

The primary issue before the court was whether a person could rely on the defence of provocation where the person intended to kill or cause serious injury. However, the court also dealt with the correct test to be applied in cases of provocation, and held that the objective test for provocation should not be adopted. The test applied in *DPP v MacEoin* was described by Kenny J. in the following terms:

> "When the defence of provocation is raised, we think that the trial judge at the close of the evidence should rule on whether there is any evidence of provocation which, having regard to the accused's temperament, character and circumstances, might have caused him to lose control of himself at the time of the wrongful act and whether the provocation bears a reasonable relation to the amount of force used by the accused.
>
> If there is evidence on which the jury could reach a decision favourable to the accused on this issue, the trial judge should allow the defence to be considered by the jury and should tell them that, before they find the accused guilty of murder, the prosecution must establish beyond reasonable doubt that the accused was not provoked to such an extent that, having regard to his temperament, character and circumstances, he lost control of himself at the time of the wrongful act. Then the jury should be told that they must consider whether the acts or words, or both, of provocation found by them to have occurred, when related to the accused, bear a reasonable relation to the amount of force he used. If the prosecution prove beyond reasonable doubt that the force used was unreasonable and excessive having regard to the provocation, the defence of provocation fails."[17]

There is a passage in *DPP v MacEoin* which appears to state that the force used should be reasonable in relation to the acts of provocation.

On one reading, it would seem that the court is imposing a requirement that the defendant should exercise self control in respect of the response to the acts of provocation, notwithstanding that he or she has lost self control to a degree that provokes him or her into a violent response. It is, of course, true that the extent of force used is evidence of whether the accused was truly provoked. For example, it will be hard for a defendant to argue provocation in most cases where he or she responds to a minor insult by stabbing, while it might be easier to plead provocation where the defendant responds to the insult by punching the injured party in the stomach. In such circumstances, a more extreme response would tend to weaken a plea of provocation.

In subsequent cases, a different reading has been given by the superior courts, interpreting *MacEoin* as providing for a purely subjective test of provocation. In *DPP v Mullane*,[18] the accused admitted killing his girlfriend who had taunted him about his lack of sexual prowess; the only question left to the jury was whether the defence of provocation was available. The trial judge put the applicable test of provocation to

---

[17] [1978] I.R. 27 at 34–35.
[18] [1998] WJSC-CCA 5885.

Defences Specific to Murder

the jury, and went on to read out two key paragraphs from the judgment in *MacEoin* to the jury. The accused was found guilty. On appeal, it was argued that the judge had erred in simply quoting the passages from *MacEoin*, since this might have given the jury the impression that an objective test applied in relation to the amount of force used, when the test was a subjective one. The Court of Criminal Appeal allowed the appeal and ordered a retrial, stating "that it is necessary to emphasise the subjective nature of the test".

The matter came again before the Court of Criminal Appeal in *DPP v Noonan*,[19] where the trial judge had, in his directions to the jury, put a form of objective test for provocation before the jury, based on a combination of Irish and English case law. Although no objection was taken to this direction at the time, the court held that this was due to an oversight, and that in the interests of justice this point would be addressed. The court went on to hold that the jury may well have been left in confusion as to whether provocation was to be assessed on an objective or subjective basis, and on that ground the appeal was successful. It appears from the decisions in *Mullane* and *Noonan* that the Court of Criminal Appeal has explained away the passage in *DPP v MacEoin* which seems to require an objective test in respect of the amount of force used, and has reaffirmed the principle of a purely subjective test for all aspects of the defence of provocation

A similar conclusion was reached in the Court of Criminal Appeal decision in *DPP v Bambrick*.[20] In that case, the appellant was a person who had a very deprived and unhappy childhood and adolescence, experiencing both physical and sexual abuse. He had a low intelligence level and suffered from alcohol addiction. On the date of the offence, the appellant and the victim had been drinking together. The appellant was intoxicated. The appellant maintained that the victim had made suggestive remarks of a sexual nature to him. He also claimed that the victim had made a sexual advance towards him. The appellant said that this advance brought back memories of childhood abuse to him, and that as a result he lost all control of himself, leading him to kill the victim with a wooden stake. In dealing with the defence of provocation, the trial judge directed the jury that to determine whether the defence is available it was necessary for them to consider the appellant's state of mind. The trial judge directed the jury that if it was "likely" that the appellant came into the category of persons being sensitive to a trigger which would cause him to lose all control, then he should be acquitted of murder. The trial judge also directed the jury that when a defence of provocation is raised, the jury should determine whether they would regard it as being reasonable that the provocation could "probably" have triggered off the uncontrollable reaction which the appellant alleged.

The Court of Criminal Appeal found that this direction to the jury was incorrect. First, the trial judge had misdirected the jury on the question of intention. In particular, the trial judge had erred in linking provocation with intention. The impression was incorrectly given to the jury that the defence of provocation was not available where the accused intended to kill or cause serious injury; for the defence of provocation to succeed it is not necessary to show that the accused lacked an intention to kill or cause serious injury. Secondly, the trial judge had misdirected the jury with regard to the test to be used in determining if provocation had taken place. The test is not

---

[19] [1998] 1 I.L.R.M. 154.
[20] [1999] 2 I.L.R.M. 71.

whether it was "likely" or "probable" that the provocation triggered off the alleged reaction. Finally, the Court of Criminal Appeal reiterated that the test in relation to provocation was a subjective one.

In *DPP v Kelly*, the Court of Criminal Appeal stated that:

> "The problem with *MacEoin* is not with the decision itself but in the way the decision is worded. The difficulty with the wording has not been totally removed by the judgment in *Mullane*. For that reason we consider that a trial judge dealing with a plea of provocation in a murder trial should follow *MacEoin* but he may not find it necessary or helpful to the jury, to quote from it."[21]

Barrington J. also remarked that:

> "[T]he usefulness of the concept of excessive force is equivocal. On the one hand, the jury, looking at provocation, might say 'surely the accused was not provoked by that to use such excessive force against his victim'. On the other hand, they might say: 'Surely this force was so excessive that the accused must have been totally out of control when he used it.'"[22]

In *DPP v Boyle*,[23] it was acknowledged that *MacEoin* does not make it absolutely clear that the test for provocation is entirely subjective but emphasised that the subsequent case law does clarify that the test is a subjective one. Similarly, in *DPP v Heaney*,[24] the court stated that the test to be applied is subjective and that the intention of *MacEoin* was to introduce a purely subjective test and not a test coupled with an element of objectivity.

In *DPP v Davis*,[25] further confirmation was given that the test for provocation is subjective in nature. Hardiman J. stated that the defence was in the nature of a concession to the acknowledged weaknesses of human nature. That concession was based on policy considerations which might change from time to time, and these considerations might dictate that the defence should be circumscribed or even denied in cases where it would promote moral outrage, for example, in cases of road rage. The test for provocation in Ireland was characterised by Hardiman J. as:

> "[A]n extreme form of subjectivity ... to the exclusion of the standards of the reasonable man ... That standard, however, remains relevant on the question of credibility."[26]

In *DPP v Curran*,[27] the Court of Criminal Appeal confirmed that the test in this jurisdiction is wholly subjective. However, the court expressed concern that the emphasis on subjectivity might lead to the defence of provocation being established

---

[21] [2000] 2 I.R. 1 at 9–10.
[22] [2000] 2 I.R. 1 at 10–11.
[23] [2000] 2 I.R. 13.
[24] [1999] WJSC-CCA 1795.
[25] [2001] 1 I.R. 146.
[26] [2001] 1 I.R. 146 at 159.
[27] [2011] IECCA 95.

too easily. Citing *DPP v Davis*,[28] the court in *Curran*[29] stated that "it is important that the structure of the defence is maintained ... and that all the elements of the defence, and in particular those features which distinguish true provocation from mere uncontrolled rage, are maintained". Evidence must be adduced that the accused was in fact provoked to the extent of total loss of control, that the accused killed the deceased while in that state of complete loss of control, in response to the provocation, and without there having been time for his or her passion to cool. It was observed that there is a minimum degree of self control expected of each member of society.

Immediacy requirement

The test in *MacEoin* focuses on a sudden loss of self control. This means that the defence is not generally available in circumstances where it is shown the accused had time to think, cool off and consider his or her actions. In *R. v Duffy*, Devlin J. remarked on this aspect of the defence:

> "Circumstances which induce a desire for revenge are inconsistent with provocation, since the conscious formulation of a desire for revenge means that a person has had time to think, to reflect, and that would negative a sudden temporary loss of self-control, which is of the essence of provocation."[30]

However, the fact that a delay has taken place between the alleged acts of provocation and the loss of control by the accused does not necessarily mean that a plea of provocation will fail, but it is an important factor to be taken into account when considering the loss-of-control element of the defence.

The application of a defence of provocation to "battered women" who kill their aggressors has proved controversial. The defence of provocation is based on the concept of a sudden loss of self control and the law therefore requires the accused to have acted in the heat of the moment. The longer the delay between the act of provocation and the accused's actions, the more likely a court is to view the accused's conduct as a form of vengeance rather than provocation. It has been observed that battered women tend not to react immediately to provocation as they have learned through experience that this is likely to give rise to increased violence from their partner.[31] Women, the subject of abuse in a relationship, have been known to suffer a "slow burn" of anger as a result of cumulative provocation, which eventually comes to a head and results in the killing of the abusive partner, often while he is asleep or drunk. The event which triggers the killing may appear, at first glance, relatively trivial but, can be seen as the last straw in a cycle of abuse.

It could be argued that, in light of *MacEoin*, Irish law does not require a battered woman to react in the heat of the moment. *MacEoin* sets out a subjective test for provocation taking into consideration all the characteristics of the accused. In the case of battered women, evidence of a long history of abuse might be allowed in order to

---

[28] [2001] 1 I.R. 146 at 158.
[29] [2011] IECCA 95.
[30] [1949] 1 All E.R. 932.
[31] K. O'Donovan, "Defences for battered women who kill" (1991) 18 Law and Soc. 219.

explain why the accused took some time before finally killing her partner. However, in *DPP v Davis*, Hardiman J. stated that there must be evidence of a "sudden and temporary loss of self-control, rendering the accused so subject to passion as to make him or her for that moment not master of their mind" and that the reaction came "suddenly and before there was time for the passion to cool".[32] Similarly, in *DPP v Kelly*, the court stated that "there must be a sudden unforeseen onset of passion".[33]

Excessive Self Defence

Self defence is a defence of general application in the criminal law. Where a person uses force which is necessary to ward off an attack, and uses no more force than is necessary, then no crime is committed. In relation to the non-lethal use of force, this defence has been put on a statutory footing following the enactment of the Non-Fatal Offences Against the Person Act 1997.

In relation to the majority of crimes, excessive self defence is not available as a defence, although in appropriate cases it may be taken into consideration as a mitigating factor at the sentencing stage. The decision in *R. v Clegg*[34] confirms that this is also the position in England and Northern Ireland in relation to murder. In that case, the defendant was a British soldier in Northern Ireland who was on duty at a vehicle checkpoint. A car drove through the checkpoint and then accelerated down the road. The defendant fired at the car as it went by, killing a passenger. He claimed that he fired at the car because he believed that the life of another soldier, on the other side of the road, was in danger. This claim was accepted as a defence to three of the shots which were fired, but not the fourth shot which was fired when the car had already passed and was 50 feet further down the road. It was the fourth shot that caused the death of the victim and the defendant was convicted of murder with regard to the death.

On appeal to the House of Lords, it was submitted that there should be a qualified defence available in those circumstances, which would operate to reduce the offence from murder to manslaughter. This was rejected on the basis that it was well established that excessive self defence was not available to reduce murder to manslaughter, and the House of Lords declined to change the law on this point. The court emphasised that the question of whether there should be a qualified defence of excessive self defence was a matter for Parliament. In England, therefore, self defence is an all-or-nothing affair; an accused is either guilty of murder or entirely innocent. There is no halfway house.

The position in Ireland in relation to excessive self defence and murder is different. The Supreme Court dealt with the issue in *Attorney General v Dwyer*.[35] In that case, the defendant had been involved in a fight outside a chip shop. The defendant claimed that he believed that the victim was armed with some item and that he feared for his life. As a result of this fear, he took a knife and stabbed the victim causing death. This was clearly not a proportionate response, meaning that a plea of self defence was not available as a full defence to liability for the homicide.

[32] [2001] 1 I.R. 146 at 156.
[33] [2002] 2 I.R. 1.
[34] [1995] 1 A.C. 482.
[35] [1972] I.R. 416.

But could the defendant's subjective belief that the force was necessary operate as a partial defence to reduce the offence from murder to manslaughter? The Supreme Court, applying the decision of the High Court of Australia in *R. v Howe*,[36] answered this question in the affirmative.

Walsh J. held that the effect of s.4 of the Criminal Justice Act 1964—which replaces the concept of malice aforethought with the modern mens rea of intention—was to make the mental element for murder entirely subjective. It followed that if the defendant honestly believed that the force used was necessary, then he could not be found guilty of murder:

> "Our statutory provision makes it clear that the intention is personal and that it is not to be measured solely by objective standards. In my opinion, therefore, when the evidence in a case discloses a question of self-defence and where it is sought by the prosecution to show that the accused used excessive force, that is to say more than would be regarded as objectively reasonable, the prosecution must establish that the accused knew that he was using more force than was reasonably necessary. Therefore, it follows that if the accused honestly believed that the force that he did use was necessary, then he is not guilty of murder. The onus, of course, is upon the prosecution to prove beyond reasonable doubt that he knew that the force was excessive or that he did not believe it was necessary. If the prosecution does not do so, it has failed to establish the necessary malice."[37]

Butler J. took a different approach; if the accused honestly and primarily intended to defend himself or herself then he or she should not be held to have the necessary intention to kill or cause serious injury. Consequently, the moral culpability of the accused is reduced and the killing would amount to manslaughter only. Butler J. reasoned that:

> "A person is entitled to protect himself from unlawful attack. If in doing so he uses no more force than is reasonably necessary, he is acting lawfully and commits no crime even though he kills his assailant. If he uses more force than may objectively be considered necessary, his act is unlawful and, if he kills, the killing is unlawful. His intention, however, falls to be tested subjectively and it would appear logical to conclude that, if his intention in doing the unlawful act was primarily to defend himself, he should not be held to have the necessary intention to kill or cause serious injury. The result of this view would be that the killing, though unlawful, would be manslaughter only."[38]

Notwithstanding the difference of approach in these two judgments, the overall result is clear: in Irish law, excessive self defence will operate as a partial self defence, reducing murder to manslaughter. "Excessive self defence" may in turn be defined as force used which is greater than that which is objectively necessary, but which the accused honestly believed to be necessary. Clearly, the accused will not be

---

[36] (1958) 100 C.L.R. 448.
[37] [1972] I.R. 416 at 424.
[38] [1972] I.R. 416 at 429.

able to establish the necessary honest belief in situations where the victim presented no threat whatsoever. See, for example, *Attorney General v Commane*,[39] a case in which the victim was immobilised by a blow to the head with a whiskey bottle and subsequently strangled. On those facts, excessive self defence was held not to be available as a defence, since the killing had taken place by strangulation after the victim had been rendered incapable of further aggression.

The rationale for allowing excessive self defence to operate as a partial defence is considered in the following passage from the Law Reform Commission *Report on Defences in the Criminal Law*:

> "[W]here, as in *Attorney General v Dwyer*, disproportionate or excessive force was used because the accused is mistaken in his or her perception of the threat of the use of force he or she faced, the law cannot justify this, but may take the view that while the killing is unlawful the force used can, in part, be excused, resulting in a conviction for manslaughter rather than murder."[40]

The Law Reform Commission went on to recommend that the "half-way house" approach adopted in relation to the use of excessive force in *Dwyer* should remain part of Irish criminal law, so that a plea of excessive self defence may continue to operate as a limited defence where the accused uses force that is more than is reasonably necessary, but no more force than he or she honestly believed to be proportionate in the circumstances.[41]

It should be noted that there is a debate as to whether this defence has survived the passing of the Non-Fatal Offences Against the Person Act 1997. Section 18 of the 1997 Act puts self defence on a statutory footing, but is silent as to the case of excessive self defence, while s.22(2) abolishes common law defences in relation to the use of force in self defence. From this, it could be argued that s.22(2) of the 1997 Act has simply done away with excessive self defence. On the other hand, the Report of the Law Reform Commission on which the 1997 Act was based did not deal with the question of excessive self defence.[42] In addition, excessive self defence is limited to the crime of murder and is, therefore, entirely inappropriate to be dealt with in an Act limited in its scope to non-fatal offences. Finally, the decision in *Attorney General v O'Dwyer*[43] is based largely on the statutory definition of the mental element of murder, which the 1997 Act does not alter.[44]

---

[39] [1965] WJSC-CCA 388.
[40] Law Reform Commission, *Report on Defences in Criminal Law* (LRC 95–2009), p.27.
[41] Law Reform Commission, *Report on Defences in Criminal Law* (LRC 95–2009), pp.73–75.
[42] Law Reform Commission, *Report on Non-Fatal Offences Against the Person* (LRC 45–1994).
[43] [1972] I.R. 416.
[44] Ivana Bacik, *Non-Fatal Offences Against the Person Act 1997 Annotated ICLSA* (Dublin: Round Hall Press, 1994), pp.35 and 40.

Chapter 11

GENERAL DEFENCES

Duress

The defence of duress is, in some ways, the opposite of the defences of provocation and excessive self defence. Those defences are available only to a charge of murder, while the defence of duress is available in respect of most crimes and is only unavailable to a charge of murder. The defence applies in circumstances where a person is compelled to commit a crime by virtue of threats made against him or another person. Clearly, in these circumstances, the moral culpability of the accused is reduced to the extent that his will is overborne. However, there is no question of the accused not possessing the relevant mens rea. He fully intends to commit the offence but his ordinary resistance is overborne to such an extent that the law will not view him as morally responsible for his actions.

The leading Irish case is *Attorney General v Whelan*.[1] In that case the accused was charged with receiving stolen property and his defence was that he acted under threats of extreme violence. The jury returned a verdict to the effect that he received the stolen goods but did so under threat of immediate death or serious violence. The question presented to the Court of Criminal Appeal was whether, on foot of this verdict, the accused was guilty or innocent of the crime charged. The court treated this question as posing a simple issue: was there "such an absence of will as to absolve from guilt?"[2] The prosecution contended that only actual physical force which left the accused no choice of will would absolve him from guilt, while anything else would merely go to mitigation of punishment. This position was, however, rejected by the court, which held that:

> "It seems to us that threats of immediate death or serious personal violence so great as to overbear the ordinary power of human resistance should be accepted as justification for acts which would otherwise be criminal. The application of this general rule must, however, be subject to certain limitations. The commission of murder is a crime so heinous that murder should not be committed even for the price of life and in such a case the strongest duress would not be any justification. We have not to determine what class of crime other than murder should be placed in the same category."[3]

---

[1] [1934] I.R. 518.
[2] [1934] I.R. 518 at 526.
[3] [1934] I.R. 518 at 526 per Murnaghan J.

In addition, it is necessary to show that the threats in question were still in effect at the time that the crime was committed and that the accused did not have any opportunity to extract himself from the effect of the threats":

> "Where the excuse of duress is applicable it must further be clearly shown that the overpowering of the will was operative at the time the crime was actually committed, and, if there were reasonable opportunity for the will to reassert itself, no justification can be found in antecedent threats."[4]

The court held that the coercion was present when the act was committed and the defendant was acquitted.

Murnaghan J.'s judgment illustrates the three elements which must be present before the defence of duress is made out: the threats must be of serious harm or death; the threats must be imminent; and the threats must overbear the will of the accused.

Imminence of threats

Attorney General v Whelan requires that threats should be imminent. There are, it seems, two reasons for this. First, a threat of future violence will be treated as too remote to overbear the will of the accused in the here and now. Secondly, a threat of future violence leaves the recipient of the threats free to seek police protection. In light of these reasons, just how imminent must a threat be before it will ground a defence of duress?

This question was dealt with in *R. v Hudson and Taylor*.[5] The two accused were charged with perjury, having lied about the identification of a man charged with wounding. Their defence was duress: an associate of the man had threatened before the trial to cut them up and at the trial they could see that associate sitting in the public gallery. Was this threat sufficiently imminent and could they plead duress when it was open to them to seek police protection before the threat would be carried out? It was held by the Court of Appeal on the first issue that it was a matter for the jury to decide if the threats were sufficiently imminent, remembering that:

> "[T]he threats of [the associate] were likely to be no less compelling, because their execution could not be effected in the court room, if they could be carried out in the streets of Salford the same night."[6]

The threats, while imminent, did not have to be immediately capable of being carried out.

As regards the availability of police protection, it was held that this would defeat a defence of duress where it was reasonably open to the accused to neutralise a threat:

> "[I]t is always open to [the prosecution] to prove that the accused failed to avail himself of some opportunity which was reasonably open to him to render the

---

[4] [1934] I.R. 518 at 526.
[5] [1971] 2 Q.B. 202.
[6] [1971] 2 Q.B. 202 at 207 per Lord Widgery C.J.

threat ineffective, and that upon this being established the threat in questions can no longer be relied upon by the defence. In deciding whether such an opportunity was reasonably open to the accused the jury should have regard to his age and circumstances, and to any risks to him which may be involved in the course of action relied upon."[7]

This was, however, a question for the jury and since the defence of duress had not been left to the jury the convictions were quashed.

The issue of imminence arose again in the case of *R. v Abdul-Hussain*[8] where the defendants were Iraqis who had hijacked an aircraft because they feared they would be killed if deported to Iraq. The court approved of *R. v Hudson and Taylor* and noted that "the peril must operate on the mind of the defendant at the time when he commits the otherwise criminal act, so as to overbear his will ... but the execution of the threat need not be immediately in prospect".[9] It gave the following example:

> "If Anne Frank had stolen a car to escape from Amsterdam and been charged with theft, the tenets of the English law would not, in our judgment, have denied her a defence of duress of circumstances, on the ground that she should have waited for the Gestapo's knock on the door."[10]

However, *Hudson and Taylor* was subsequently disapproved by the House of Lords in *R. v Z (otherwise known as Hasan)*.[11] Lord Bingham commented that Professor Glanville Williams was of the view that *Hudson and Taylor* was:

> "'[A]n indulgent decision', and it has in my opinion had the unfortunate effect of weakening the requirement that execution of a threat must be reasonably believed to be imminent and immediate if it is to support a plea of duress ... I can understand that the Court of Appeal in *R. v Hudson* had sympathy with the predicament of the young appellants but I cannot, consistent with principle, accept that a witness testifying in the Crown Court at Manchester has no opportunity to avoid complying with a threat incapable of execution then or there."[12]

The nature of the threats

In *R. v Z (otherwise known as Hasan)*,[13] the threat was to the defendant and his family. The House of Lords re-affirmed that the threat must be directed against the defendant, his immediate family or someone close to him. The threat or danger must be of death or serious injury. In *R. v Valderrama-Vega*,[14] a threat to expose a person

---

[7] [1971] 2 Q.B. 202 at 207.
[8] [1999] Crim L.R. 570.
[9] [1999] Crim L.R. 570 at 570.
[10] [1999] Crim L.R. 570 at 571.
[11] [2005] 2 A.C. 467.
[12] [2005] 2 A.C. 467 at 494.
[13] [2005] 2 A.C. 467.
[14] [1985] Crim. L.R. 220.

as a homosexual was deemed insufficient. It also appears that a threat to property will not suffice: *DPP for Northern Ireland v Lynch*.[15]

Objective or subjective test?

The test laid down in *Attorney General v Whelan* seems to be objective: an accused cannot avail of the defence unless the threats in question would have overborne "the ordinary power of human resistance" and not merely his personal power of resistance. The weak-willed accused will not, it seems, be able to plead duress. On principle it seems right to impose an objective test in this area notwithstanding that Irish law leans towards subjective tests. As Charleton points out:

> "Duress ... involves a rational choice between the two evils. The threat made to the accused must be of a grave order of magnitude to excuse the commission of a crime. The law might fail to fulfil its objective of ordering society if petty excuses for criminal action were allowed."[16]

However, two Court of Criminal Appeal decisions, both decided in March 2003, call the objective test into question. In *DPP v Dickey*,[17] no criticism was made by the court of the trial judge's jury direction that the defendant's own human frailties should be taken into account. In contrast, in *DPP v O'Toole*[18] the defendant's argument that the test should not be objective was rejected. Academics have criticised *Dickey* and concluded that the test in Ireland is still an objective one. It has been pointed out that the trial judge in *Dickey* quoted without comment from *Whelan* and Hanly and Campbell, Kilcommins and O'Sullivan agree that *Dickey* is of questionable authority.[19]

Application to murder

It has always been clear that duress does not apply to murder.[20] Blackstone wrote that a person subjected to duress "ought rather to die himself than escape by murder of an innocent".[21] *Attorney General v Whelan* leaves open the question whether there are other, particularly grave offences, to which it also does not apply.[22] It is unclear,

---

[15] [1975] A.C. 653.
[16] Charleton, *Criminal law – cases and materials* (Dublin: Butterworths, 1992), p.201.
[17] Unreported, Court of Criminal Appeal, March 7, 2003.
[18] Unreported, Court of Criminal Appeal, March 25, 2003.
[19] Conor Hanly, *An Introduction to Irish Criminal Law*, 2nd edn (Dublin: Gill & Macmillan, 2006), p.158; Liz Campbell, Shane Kilcommins and Catherine O'Sullivan, *Criminal Law in Ireland Cases and Commentary* (Dublin: Clarus Press, 2010), p.930.
[20] One rationale, however, for allowing the defence to apply to murder was put forward by Rumpff J.A. in the South African case of *S v Goliath* [1972] (3) SA 1: "Only they who possess the quality of heroism will intentionally offer their lives for another. Should the criminal law then state that compulsion could never be a defence to a charge of murder, it would demand that a person who killed another under duress, whatever the circumstances, would have to comply with a higher standard than that demanded of the average person. I do not think that such an exception to the general rule which applies in criminal law is justified."
[21] 4 Bl. Com. 28.
[22] It appears that duress is not a defence to attempted murder: *R. v Gotts* [1992] 1 All E.R. 832.

General Defences

for example, whether the defence can apply to the various degrees of participation in the crime of murder. There is no authority from this jurisdiction on this point and contradictory authority from the House of Lords. In *DPP for Northern Ireland v Lynch*,[23] in which the House of Lords expressly approved *Whelan*, the appellant was charged with aiding and abetting the murder of a police constable by driving three armed men to and from a shooting. He pleaded duress, alleging that a well-known member of the IRA had threatened to kill him if he disobeyed. The trial judge ruled that duress was not a defence to a charge of murder. On appeal it was held that it was open to a person accused as a principal in the second degree to plead duress and a re-trial was ordered. This decision was overruled by the House of Lords some years later in *R. v Howe*.[24] It was held that the defence of duress is not available to a person charged with murder either as a principal in the first degree (the actual killer) or principal in the second degree (the aider and abettor).[25]

However, ultimately it would appear that the exclusion of murder from the operation of the defence of duress is more a policy decision than a matter of legal logic. McAuley and McCutcheon comment:

> "Hale's principle of the sacrosancticity of innocent life[26] certainly entails the conclusion that one is never justified in trading one innocent life for another, as the judges in *Howe* were at pains to emphasise. But it does not follow from this that a defendant should never be excused for doing so. Just as we excuse insane defendants without in any way condoning their actions, the critical question here is whether heavily constrained choice should ever be accepted as an excuse for serious crime. Given that the law's general answer to that question is: Yes, provided the pressure was such that a person of reasonable firmness could not be expected to withstand it, the case for the *a priori* exclusion of murder from the reach of duress looks weak."[27]

Membership of a violent organisation

Suppose an accused voluntarily joins the IRA, commits a crime and then claims that, had he failed to do so, retribution would have been forthcoming. Can a defendant rely on "self-induced duress" in this way? The answer is "no"—the person who voluntarily puts himself in a position where duress will be applied is outside the scope of the defence. *R. v Fitzpatrick*[28] was a case in which the accused was charged with murder, robbery and membership of a proscribed organisation. He was a member of

---

[23] [1975] A.C. 653.
[24] [1987] A.C. 417.
[25] However, McCombe J. in Newcastle Circuit Court held that the defence of duress is available for the offence of conspiracy to murder: *R. v Ness and Awan* [2011] Crim. L.R. 645. He drew a line between preparation for the murder and an attempt to commit the offence.
[26] "If a man be menaced with death, unless he will commit an act of treason, murder or robbery, the fear of death does not excuse him, if he commit the fact; for the law hath provided a sufficient remedy against such fears by applying himself to the courts and officers of justice … he ought rather to die himself, than kill an innocent …"; 1 Hale P.C. 51.
[27] Finbarr McAuley and J. Paul McCutcheon, *Criminal Liability* (Dublin: Round Hall Sweet and Maxwell, 2000), p.834.
[28] [1977] N.I. 20.

the Official IRA and testified that he had attempted to leave but was prevented from doing so by threats of violence to himself and his parents. The trial judge held that the defence of duress was not available on those facts. On appeal, it was contended that duress should be available to members of such organisations, at least where they had made sufficient efforts to disassociate themselves from the organisation. It was held by the Court of Criminal Appeal that duress was a defence having its roots in the absence of moral blameworthiness on the part of the accused and therefore the defence was not available where the accused knowingly and voluntarily joins such an organisation:

> "If a person behaves immorally by, for example, committing himself to an unlawful conspiracy, he ought not to be able to take advantage of the pressure exercised on him by his fellow criminals in order to put on when it suits him the breastplate of righteousness."[29]

The court alluded to the public policy reason behind this stance:

> "… [I]f some such limit on the defendant's duress does not exist, it would be only too easy for every member of an unlawful conspiracy and for every member of a gang except the leader to obtain an immunity denied to ordinary citizens. Indeed the better organised the conspiracy and the more brutal its internal discipline, the surer would be the defence of duress for its members. It can hardly be supposed that the common law tolerates such an absurdity."[30]

For the same reason, it was held to be irrelevant that the accused had tried to leave the organisation.

However, it seems that the accused must have some knowledge of the violent nature of the organisation before he joins: "innocent" membership does not make the accused morally culpable so as to defeat the defence of duress. In *R. v Shepherd*[31] the accused voluntarily joined an organised gang of shoplifters. His evidence was that when he sought to leave the gang he was threatened by violence. In these circumstances it was held that the defence of duress should have been left to the jury: it was arguable that the defendant had failed to appreciate the risk of violence and, if that was the case, then the defence would be open to him.

The leading English case on this issue is *R. v Z (otherwise known as Hasan)*,[32] where the defendant committed aggravated burglary but claimed that he was under duress from a man he knew to be violent and a drug dealer and who had claimed to have committed three murders. At one point the man had offered to show him a corpse in the boot of his car. However, the House of Lords held that the defendant was not entitled to rely on the defence of duress as he had associated voluntarily with known criminals and he ought reasonably to have foreseen the risk of being forced to carry out crimes by threats of violence. Lord Bingham held that it was not necessary that the compulsion should actually have been foreseen:

---

[29] [1977] N.I. 20 at 31 per Lowry L.C.J.
[30] [1977] N.I. 20 at 32.
[31] (1988) 86 Cr. App. R. 47.
[32] [2005] 2 A.C. 467.

"The practical importance of the distinction in this context may not be very great, since if a jury concluded that a person voluntarily associating with known criminals ought reasonably to have foreseen the risk of future coercion they would not, I think, be very likely to accept that he did not in fact do so. But since there is a choice to be made, policy in my view points towards an objective test of what the defendant, placed as he was and knowing what he did, ought reasonably to have foreseen ... The policy of the law must be to discourage association with known criminals, and it should be slow to excuse the criminal conduct of those who do."[33]

Duress and marital coercion

A curious rebuttable presumption existed at common law that a wife who committed a crime in the presence of her husband did so as a result of his coercion and so was immune from punishment, subject to an exception in the case of particularly serious crimes. The Supreme Court, however, in *State (DPP) v Walsh and Connelly*,[34] held that the presumption reflected a disparity in status between husband and wife which ran counter to the modern concept of equality and that the presumption did not, therefore, survive the coming into force of the Constitution.

Law Reform Commission recommendations

The Law Reform Commission produced a *Consultation Paper on Duress and Necessity* in 2006[35] and a *Report on Defences in Criminal Law* in 2009.[36] It made a number of recommendations including that duress should be recognised as a defence and that the features of the defence should include that the threat was imminent, there was no reasonable way to avoid the threat or make it ineffective and that the conduct was a reasonable response to the threat.[37] In establishing the reasonableness of the response to the threat, it recommended that an objective test should be applied, tempered with some subjective elements. For example, the court or jury should be allowed to take into account the age and sex of the defendant, and any other characteristics which bear upon the capacity of the defendant to withstand duress. (However, the Draft Bill prepared by the Law Reform Commission specifically excludes the defendant's "temperament" as a characteristic.)

It recommended that the threat should be one of death or serious harm[38] as the law must draw the line somewhere and therefore threats to property are outside the defence whereas threats to bodily integrity come within it. The Law Reform Commission was of the view that the defence should be available where the threat was directed towards any person whatsoever without restriction as to his relationship

---

[33] [2005] 2 A.C. 467 at 499.
[34] [1981] I.R. 412.
[35] Law Reform Commission, *Consultation Paper on Duress and Necessity* (LRC CP39–2006).
[36] Law Reform Commission, *Report on Defences in Criminal Law* (LRC 95–2009).
[37] Law Reform Commission, *Report on Defences in Criminal Law* (LRC 95–2009), para.5.32.
[38] Law Reform Commission, *Report on Defences in Criminal Law* (LRC 95–2009), para.5.44.

with the defendant.[39] However, it pointed out that the identity of the target will be of relevance in relation to the credibility of the defendant's claim of compulsion.

The Law Reform Commission discussed the issue of imminence and stated a preference for the *R. v Hudson and Taylor* approach over that of the House of Lords in *R. v Z (otherwise known as Hasan)*:

> "In the opinion of the Commission, the just approach to the issue of imminence in relation to the defence of duress is not to limit the availability of the defence on the basis of immediacy. Though the threat should be imminent no requirement of immediacy should exist in relation to the harm threatened. Although there may not be a threat of immediate harm (and the person making the threat may not be present at the time the offence is committed especially given the place of technology) the carrying out of the threat may be inevitable. Thus the Commission re-asserts the view that although the threat should be imminent there is no requirement for the threat to be immediate."[40]

The Report recommended that a person who seeks to avail of the defence of duress may not do so if he ought reasonably to have foreseen the likelihood of being subjected to threats, for example, by voluntarily joining a criminal organisation which subsequently puts pressure on the person to commit offences.[41]

It recommended that the marital coercion defence should be formally abolished by statute.[42]

The Commission addressed the issue of whether the defence should be available in cases of murder:

> "The question of whether the defence of duress should be extended to treason, murder and attempted murder is a difficult and complex one. Arguments in favour of extending duress as a defence to these crimes include self-preservation, heroism and consistency in the law. On the other hand, arguments against extending duress to murder include 'sanctity of life', prosecutorial discretion, fabrication, deterrence and the fact that the threat may never actually eventuate. The arguments from both sides are compelling but, on balance, the Commission has concluded that it is preferable not to extend the defence to these crimes. While this leaves the question of what charge to bring in homicide to prosecutorial discretion, the Commission considers that, on balance, this involves the best approach to take to these difficult cases ... The Commission recommends that the defence of duress should be generally available as a defence, but not in the case of treason, murder or attempted murder."[43]

---

[39] Law Reform Commission, *Report on Defences in Criminal Law* (LRC 95–2009), para.5.51.
[40] Law Reform Commission, *Report on Defences in Criminal Law* (LRC 95–2009), para.5.89.
[41] Law Reform Commission, *Report on Defences in Criminal Law* (LRC 95–2009), para.5.107.
[42] Law Reform Commission, *Report on Defences in Criminal Law* (LRC 95–2009), para.5.154.
[43] Law Reform Commission, *Report on Defences in Criminal Law* (LRC 95–2009), paras 5.140 and 3.141.

General Defences

NECESSITY

The defence of necessity is often described as "duress of circumstances". The defence has the same underlying rationale as the defence of duress: a defendant ought not to be punished for breaking the law where he has no choice in the matter, whether as a result of threats (duress) or surrounding circumstances (necessity). However, duress is considered to be an excuse whereas necessity is usually considered to be a justification.[44] By invoking the defence of necessity the defendant is asking the court to sanction his behaviour because it was the lesser of two evils. With duress the court makes allowances for human frailty but does not sanction the action.[45] Because of this courts have been reluctant to allow the defence of necessity to develop freely.[46] Lord Denning summed up the judicial dilemma as follows:

> "[I]f hunger were once allowed to be an excuse for stealing, it would open a door through which all kinds of lawlessness and disorder would pass ... [I]f homelessness were once admitted as a defence to trespass, no one's house could be safe. Necessity would open a door which no man could shut."[47]

When can necessity be used as a defence?

The parameters of the defence of necessity have been set out by the Supreme Court of Victoria in *R. v Loughnan*.[48] In that case the defendant was charged with escaping from prison. He admitted escaping but claimed that he did so because he believed that he would be attacked and killed by other prisoners if he stayed. The trial judge refused to allow the defence of necessity to go before the jury and the defendant was convicted. On appeal, it was held that, on the particular facts of the case, the defence did not have to go before the jury. However, the court dealt with the wider issue of necessity and held as follows:

> "[T]here are three elements involved in the defence of necessity. First, the criminal act or acts must have been done only in order to avoid certain consequences which would otherwise have inflicted irreparable evil upon the accused or upon others whom he was bound to protect ... The other two elements involved ... can, for convenience be given the labels immediate

---

[44] See the discussion on this point in Law Reform Commission, *Report on Defences in Criminal Law* (LRC 95–2009), pp.194–198.
[45] It should be noted that there are also statutory provisions providing for the defence of necessity, e.g. s.6 of the Criminal Damage Act 1991 which provides for a defence of necessity where property is damaged in order to avoid injury to a person or so save other property.
[46] Of course, in many situations where a person has committed a crime as the lesser of two evils, a prosecution will not be brought at all. For example, during the inquest into the Zeebrugge Herald of Free Enterprise disaster, where many lives were lost when the door of a passenger ferry was not closed, it transpired that one man had frozen in fear on a ladder and blocked many passengers from escaping. Having tried in vain to persuade him to move for about 10 minutes, another passenger eventually pushed him off the ladder into the sea and he was never seen again. It appears that no prosecution was ever contemplated in those circumstances.
[47] *Southwark L.B.C. v Williams* [1971] Ch.734.
[48] [1981] V.R. 443.

peril and proportion ... [T]he accused must honestly believe on reasonable grounds that he was placed in a situation of immediate peril ... The element of proportion simply means that the acts done to avoid the imminent peril must not be out of proportion to the peril to be avoided. Put in another way, the test is: would a reasonable man in the position of the accused have considered that he had any alternative to doing what he did to avoid the peril?"[49]

"The essential conditions, I consider, so far as presently relevant, are that: 1. The harm to be justified must have been committed under pressure either of physical forces or exerted by some human agency so that 'an urgent situation of imminent peril' has been created. 2. The accused must have acted with the intention of avoiding greater harm or so as to have made possible 'the preservation of at least an equal value'. 3. There was open to the accused no alternative, other than that adopted by him, to avoid the greater harm or 'to conserve the value'."[50]

If, therefore, the accused had genuinely escaped with the intention of avoiding a danger to his life, and there was no other alternative open to him, then the defence of duress would have been open to him.

In *R. v Conway*,[51] the defendant was convicted of reckless driving. His defence was necessity or, as it was termed, duress of circumstances. Two young men in civilian clothes had come running towards the car, in which he had a passenger who had been the target of a shooting shortly before. The passenger shouted at the defendant to drive off and the defendant did so believing that the two men were trying to kill the passenger. The car was then chased by the two men in an unmarked vehicle, at which point the driver drove in a reckless manner. It transpired that the pursuers were police officers seeking to arrest the passenger. It was held that the defence of necessity was open to the driver in these circumstances. The Court of Appeal held that "duress" and "necessity" were different terms for aspects of the one underlying defence and that the defence, whatever it was termed, should have been left to the jury. This illustrates the fact that the threat or danger involved need not be to the defendant himself but may be to another person.

The issue of "imminent peril" highlighted in *R. v Loughnan* was addressed by the English Court of Appeal in *R. v Pommell*.[52] The defendant was charged with firearms offences following a search of his residence by police. They discovered him in bed concealing a submachine gun under the duvet. Ammunition was found in a holdall in the bedroom. When asked if the gun was his, the defendant replied "I took it off a geezer who was going to do some people some damage with it". He went on to explain that he had persuaded an acquaintance, who had called to see him the previous evening, to hand over the gun. The acquaintance had told him he intended to kill several people in retaliation for the death of his friend. The defendant claimed that he was going to pass the gun on to his brother who would hand it in to police on his behalf, because his brother was on good terms with the police and had handed in guns to them previously. The defendant pleaded necessity and said that his

---

[49] [1981] V.R. 443 per Young C.J.
[50] [1981] V.R. 443 per Crockett J.
[51] [1988] 3 All E.R. 102.
[52] (1995) 2 Cr. App. R. 607.

General Defences 281

possession of the firearm had come about because he had chosen to prevent a greater evil befalling others. The court held that a person who had taken a gun off another in these circumstances must desist from committing the crime as soon as he reasonably can. There had been a delay of some hours between the departure of the acquaintance and the arrival of the police but the defendant had given an explanation for the delay so the court held that the defence of necessity should have been left to the jury.

R. v Quayle[53] concerned a number of defendants who had been charged with drugs offences as a result of growing or possessing or importing cannabis for the purposes of pain relief. They claimed that they were involved with the drug out of necessity to alleviate suffering. The English Court of Appeal held that for the defence of necessity to be available there had to be extraneous circumstances capable of objective scrutiny by judge and jury. The test could not be satisfied by pain not directly associated with imminent danger. The court held that the requirement of extraneous circumstances was based "on the pragmatic consideration that the defence of necessity ... must be confined within narrowly defined limits or it will become an opportunity for almost untriable and certainly peculiarly difficult issues, not to mention abusive defences".[54] Mance L.J. emphasised that the law "has to draw a line at some point in the criteria which it accepts as sufficient to satisfy any defence of duress or necessity ... [T]here is, on any view, a large element of subjectivity in the assessment of pain not directly associated with some current physical injury".[55]

Necessity and murder

The classic case involving necessity and murder is *R. v Dudley and Stephens*.[56] The defendants and the deceased found themselves adrift at sea, in an open boat, without food or water. After several days the defendants killed the deceased, a 17-year-old boy, and survived on his body and blood for four days, at which point they were rescued by a passing ship. Could they rely on the defence of necessity? The jury found the following: if the defendants had not eaten the boy they would probably have died before being rescued; the boy was likely to have died first; at the time of the killing there was no reasonable prospect of relief; there was no greater necessity for killing the boy than either of the two defendants. Even on those extreme findings, the Queen's Bench Division held that necessity was not available as a defence to murder:

> "To preserve one's life is generally speaking, a duty, but it may be the plainest and the highest duty to sacrifice it ... It is not correct, therefore, to say that there is any absolute and unqualified necessity to preserve one's life ... It is enough in a Christian country to remind ourselves of the Great Example which we profess to follow ... It is not needful to point out the awful danger of admitting the principle which has been contended for. Who is to be the judge of this sort of necessity? By what measure is the comparative value of lives to be measured? ... We are often compelled to set up standards we cannot

---

[53] [2005] 1 W.L.R. 3642.
[54] [2005] 1 W.L.R. 3642 at 3682.
[55] [2005] 1 W.L.R. 3642 at 3683.
[56] (1884) 14 QBD 273.

reach ourselves, and to lay down rules which we could not ourselves satisfy. But a man has no right to declare temptation to be an excuse, though he might himself have yielded to it, nor allow compassion for the criminal to change or weaken in any manner the legal definition of the crime."[57]

The accused were convicted and sentenced to death and ultimately their sentences were commuted to six months' imprisonment.

There appears to be one modern exception to the rule that necessity is not available on a charge of murder. This is where it is medically necessary to prefer one life over another. Two of the authorities relate to abortion and the most recent to the case of conjoined twins.

In *R. v Bourne*,[58] a surgeon who performed an abortion on a 15-year-old girl who had been raped was charged with using an instrument with intent to procure miscarriage. His defence was that his action had been necessary to save the life of the girl and this was accepted by the court. "Saving life" was construed broadly to include preventing the girl from becoming a physical and mental wreck. The Irish Supreme Court in *AG v X*[59] also accepted a defence of necessity in the context of abortion, but only where the life of the mother was at risk.

In *Re A (Children) (Conjoined twins: Surgical separation)*[60] the English Court of Appeal held that it was an act of necessity to separate conjoined twins where one was sure to die within minutes of the separation. It was accepted that, without the operation, both girls would die in a matter of months. The hospital treating the babies had sought a declaration that it could lawfully carry out the surgery, in the absence of consent from the twins' parents. The Court of Appeal considered *Dudley and Stevens* carefully, acknowledging that it was authority for the proposition that necessity can never provide a legal justification for murder, but distinguished it on a number of grounds. Brooke L.J. summed this up as follows:

> "[T]here were two insuperable objections to the proposition that necessity might be available as a defence for the *Mignonette*[61] sailors. The first objection was evident in the court's questions: who is to be the judge of this sort of necessity? By what measure is the comparative value of lives to be measured? The second objection was that to permit such a defence would mark an absolute divorce of law from morality. In my judgment, neither of these objections are dispositive of the present case. Mary is, sadly, self-designated for a very early death. Nobody can extend her life beyond a very short span. Because her heart,

---

[57] Contrast *United States v Holmes* 26 Fed. Cas. 360 (1841) where a shipwrecked crew and passengers took to a boat which began to leak dangerously. In order to keep afloat a decision had to be made to jettison some of the passengers. It appears from the judgment that the custom at the time was that lots should be drawn to determine each person's fate but this was not followed. In fact 16 passengers were thrown overboard but the crew remained. Baldwin C.J. commented on the drawing of lots saying that it was the fairest method and was "in some sort ... an appeal to God, for selection of the victim." However, the suggestion that the drawing of lots could have justified the killing was rejected, obiter, in *R. v Dudley and Stevens*.
[58] [1938] 3 All E.R. 615.
[59] [1992] 1 I.R. 1.
[60] [2001] 2 W.L.R. 480.
[61] The name of the boat in *R. v Dudley and Stevens*.

brain and lungs are for all practical purposes useless, nobody would have even tried to extend her life artificially if she had not, fortuitously, been deriving oxygenated blood from her sister's bloodstream."[62]

Brooke L.J. further commented that an operation on conjoined twins would always be an exceptionally rare event and there would therefore be no room for concern that people might too readily avail themselves of exceptions to the law for their own benefit at the risk of other lives.

The defence of necessity has been recently raised in the English High Court in *Nicklinson v Minister for Justice and Others*[63] by a man who was left with "locked-in syndrome" after a stroke. He sought a declaration that it would not be unlawful, on the grounds of necessity, for his doctors to terminate or assist in the termination of his life. Charles J. ruled that Mr Nicklinson had established an arguable case relating to the availability of a defence of necessity and allowed the case to proceed to a full hearing which is expected to take place towards the end of 2012.

Lawful Use of Force

We have already dealt with the defence of excessive self defence in the context of murder.[64] More generally, the use of force will be lawful in circumstances including self defence, the defence of property, the carrying out of an arrest or the prevention of a crime. The parameters of this defence are now set out in ss.18–22 of the Non-Fatal Offences Against the Person Act 1997, which implement the recommendations of the Law Reform Commission in its *Report on Non-Fatal Offences Against the Person*.[65] Section 18(1) provides:

> The use of force by a person for any of the following purposes, if only such as is reasonable in the circumstances as he or she believes them to be, does not constitute an offence—
> (a) to protect himself or herself or a member of the family of that person or another from injury, assault or detention caused by a criminal act.

Defence of the person

This restates the Irish position that no special relationship to the person threatened is required, which departs from the position in other jurisdictions that there must be "some special nexus or relationship between the person relying on the doctrine to justify what he did in defence of another and that other". The position under English law was illustrated by *Devlin v Armstrong*[66] where the defendant was the activist Bernadette Devlin. She was charged with incitement to riot and other public order offences in the barricades in the Bogside. She had encouraged others to build the

---

[62] [2001] 2 W.L.R. 480 at 572.
[63] [2012] EWHC 304 (QBD).
[64] See Ch.10.
[65] Law Reform Commision, *Report on Non-Fatal Offences Against the Person* (LRC 45–1994).
[66] [1971] N.I. 13.

barricade, throw petrol bombs at the police and so on. Her defence was that she was acting in legitimate self defence and defence of others in the belief that the police, if they entered the Bogside, would commit crimes of assault and unlawful attacks on property. This defence was rejected on a number of grounds, including the ground that she could not act in self defence of persons with whom she had no special nexus. Even though this ground would not be applicable in this jurisdiction, the other grounds would be, in particular, the ground that the alleged danger was not sufficiently specific or imminent to justify the force used, which was, in any event, excessive to the alleged danger.

The position in this jurisdiction was set out in *Attorney General v Keatley*.[67] In that case the defendant was charged with manslaughter, having struck and killed another in defence of his brother. The court held that it was not necessary to prove any special relationship between the defendant and the person being defended: the underlying principle of the defence is the right to prevent the commission of an unlawful act. The question of any special relationship is irrelevant to that principle.

Protection from trespass to the person; defence of property; prevention of crime

Section 18(1) also provides that the use of force by a person will be lawful:

(a) to protect himself or herself or (with the authority of that other) another from trespass to the person; or
(b) to protect his or her property from appropriation, destruction or damage caused by a criminal act or from trespass or infringement; or
(c) to protect property belonging to another from appropriation, destruction or damage caused by a criminal act or (with the authority of that other) from trespass or infringement; or
(d) to prevent crime or breach of the peace.

This does not authorise the use of excessive force to prevent petty crime. The force must still be reasonable in the circumstances and it is debatable whether the use of any force would be reasonable where the offence is trivial. Even where an offence is not trivial, the force used must still be proportionate to the gravity of the offence. Speeding motorists cannot be shot dead.

Section 18 goes on to provide that "crimes" and "criminal acts" include acts which would be criminal but for the fact that an accused would be able to raise a defence of infancy, duress, necessity, involuntariness, intoxication or insanity. In addition, whether an act falls within (a) to (e) of s.18(1) is to be judged by the circumstances as the accused believes them to be, i.e. a subjective approach is taken. This has the consequence that a person cannot rely on a defence which was unknown to him at the time of the use of force. It follows that the use of force without apparent justification at the time, which in retrospect turns out to have been justified, is unlawful.

In addition, this section does not provide a defence for the use of force against a person known to be a Garda acting in the course of duty, unless immediately necessary to prevent physical harm to a person. This preserves the position at

---

[67] [1954] I.R. 12.

common law, illustrated by *R. v Fennell*.[68] In that case the accused was convicted of assaulting a police officer who was attempting to arrest his son. His defence was that he believed, on reasonable grounds, that the arrest was unlawful. This was held not to be a defence in these circumstances.

Preparation in anticipation of an attack

Section 20(2) of the 1997 Act provides that ss.18 and 19 shall apply in relation to acts immediately preparatory to the use of force as they apply in relation to acts in which force is used. The facts of *DPP v Ryan*[69] revolved around preparation in anticipation of an attack. The applicants were eating in a restaurant when they spotted two men coming towards them with a walking stick and snooker cue. The applicants immediately grabbed a baby chair and a plastic sign and a battle ensued in the carpark. The applicants said that they knew that other aggressors were about to arrive to help the other side and the following charge to the jury was upheld by the Court of Criminal Appeal:

> "So in an instance where an attack is anticipated the defence of self-defence is not confined to what an accused does spontaneously and simultaneously with the attack; he can go to the question of preparatory anticipation; the law will allow that and you may take that into account. So self-defence can extend to acts done in advance and in anticipation."[70]

Self-induced self defence

A limitation on this defence is contained in s.18(7) which provides that:

> The defence provided by this section does not apply to a person who causes conduct or a state of affairs with a view to using force to resist or terminate it: But the defence may apply although the occasion for the use of force arises only because the person does something he or she may lawfully do, knowing that such an occasion will arise.

A person may not engineer a situation in which he can use force, but may use force notwithstanding that he foresaw that his conduct might give rise to the need for force. This codifies the rule in *R. v Browne*[71] that a person may not rely on self defence where he has deliberately provoked an attack with a view to using force to resist. It also echoes the inability of a defendant to rely on self-induced provocation or intoxication. However, a person remains free to engage in lawful activities notwithstanding that unlawful violence from others may result.[72] The Law Reform Commission stated that "[f]rom the point of view of public order, the practical conclusion to be drawn from this is that where a danger arises that the lawful exercise

---

[68] [1971] 1 Q.B. 428.
[69] [2006] IECCA 47.
[70] [2006] IECCA 47 at 15.
[71] [1973] N.I. 96.
[72] *R. v Field* [1972] Crim. L.R. 435.

of rights may result in a breach of the peace, the proper remedy is the presence of police in sufficient numbers to preserve the peace and not the legal condemnation of those exercising their rights".[73]

The issue of self-induced self defence is obviously extremely relevant to burglars who are accosted by home-owners. For a discussion of self defence and dwellings see Ch.10.

Force

Section 20(1) defines force as follows:

(a) a person uses force in relation to another person or property not only when he or she applies force to, but also where he or she causes an impact on, the body of that person or that property;
(b) a person shall be treated as using force in relation to another person if—
  (i) he or she threatens that person with its use, or
  (ii) he or she detains that person without actually using it; and
(c) a person shall be treated as using force in relation to property if he or she threatens a person with its use in relation to property.

This definition ensures that both direct and indirect assaults are treated as the use of force, as is the threatened use of force.

Section 20(3) and (4) also set out certain criteria to be followed in deciding whether force used was in fact reasonable. These provide that:

(3) A threat of force may be reasonable although the actual use of force may not be.
(4) The fact that a person had an opportunity to retreat before using force shall be taken into account, in conjunction with other relevant evidence, in determining whether the use of force was reasonable.

This restates the common law position, as set out in *R. v McInnes*,[74] that there is no absolute duty to retreat, but whether the defendant had an opportunity to retreat is relevant in determining whether he acted reasonably. In that case the accused was charged with murder arising out of a fight between two rival groups of youths, which ended in the stabbing of one of the youths. The trial judge directed the jury that there was a duty to retreat as far as possible before self defence could be relied upon, but this direction was held to be incorrect by the Court of Appeal.

It should be noted that the "duty to retreat" is no longer applicable to self defence arising out of defence of the dwelling.

The Law Reform Commission examined the area of legitimate defence in 2006 and reported in 2009. One of its recommendations was that a minimum threshold requirement be imposed on the use of private defensive force. It recommended that

---

[73] Law Reform Commission, *Report on Non-Fatal Offences Against the Person* (LRC 45–1994), p.29.
[74] [1971] 3 All E.R. 295.

lethal defensive force should only be permitted to repel threats of death or serious injury, rape or aggravated sexual assault and false imprisonment by force.[75] It was of the view that the general test of reasonableness failed to provide clarity and that the substantive requirements of the defence should be set out by legislation and a minimum threshold test should be imposed before the defence is raised. The Law Reform Commission commented that:

> "By implementing a threshold test, potential defenders are put on notice as to the minimum requirements for successful pleas; juries are provided with a useful starting point for assessing claims of legitimate defence; and this supports the democratic function of drawing a clear line dividing acceptable and unacceptable defensive conduct.
>
> Furthermore, the Commission believes that it is important to send out a clear message regarding the sanctity of life. Imposing a minimum threshold requirement protects the right to life of the attacker as set out in the Article 40.3 of the Constitution by demanding that lethal defensive force may not be resorted to in response to minor threats and attacks."[76]

Criminal Law (Defence and the Dwelling) Act 2011

See Ch.10 for a full discussion of defence of the dwelling and the Criminal Law (Defence and the Dwelling) Act 2011.

Other defences preserved

The 1997 Act, although it provides new statutory definitions for the use of force, does not rule out the use of other defences which might be available also. This is also clear from s.22(1) which provides that:

> The provisions of this Act have effect subject to any enactment or rule of law providing a defence, or providing lawful authority, justification or excuse for an act of omission.

The Act does, however, do away with the common law defence of lawful use of force, as made clear by s.22(2), which states:

> Notwithstanding subsection (1) any defence available under the common law in respect of the use of force within the meaning of sections 18–19 or an act immediately preparatory to the use of force, for the purposes mentioned in sections 18–19 is hereby abolished.

This subsection abolishes the common law defence of necessary force and makes it clear that any such defence is now entirely contained in ss.18–19. It does not,

---

[75] Law Reform Commission, *Consultation Paper on Legitimate Defence* (LRC CP41–2006); Law Reform Commission, *Report on Defences in Criminal Law* (LRC 95–2009).
[76] Law Reform Commission, *Report on Defences in Criminal Law* (LRC 95–2009), p.39.

however, affect the availability of any other defence. It should be noted that there is an argument that this subsection abolishes the defence of excessive self defence in relation to murder. This point is discussed in Ch.10.

Proportionality of response

The effect of this defence is that only reasonable force can be used: "as is reasonable in the circumstances" (s.18(1)). At the same time, however, the courts will not demand exact precision in the amount of force which is used. As Holmes J. put it in *Brown v United States*,[77] "[d]etached reflection cannot be demanded in the presence of an upturned knife".

The issue was addressed, in the context of a householder who comes upon a burglar in his home, by the Court of Criminal Appeal in *DPP v Barnes*[78]:

> "It is, of course, impossible to lay down any formula with which the degree of force can be instantly calculated. Nor, in our view, would it be just to lay down a wholly objective standard, to be judged by the standards of the hypothetical reasonable person.
>
> The victim of a burglary is not in the position of an ordinary reasonable man or woman contemplating what course of action is best in particular circumstances. He may be ... aging, alone, confronted with numerous and/or much younger assailants ... In almost every case the victim of burglary will be taken by surprise. The victim will, therefore, be in almost every case shocked and surprised and may easily be terrified out of his wits. To hold a person in that situation to an objective standard would be profoundly unjust.
>
> Equally, however, it cannot be left to every person himself to lay down for himself how much force he or she is entitled to use. There must be both a subjective and an objective component in the assessment of the degree of force proper to be used by the victim of a burglar."[79]

Mistake and self defence

If a person mistakenly believes that he is faced with a threat, then he will be judged according to his genuine judgment of the situation. This was the position at common law. In *R. v Williams (Gladstone)*,[80] the Court of Appeal held that the appellant was entitled to be judged according to his view of the circumstances as he had made a genuine error in believing that a youth was being assaulted when in fact he was being arrested for stealing. The 1997 Act preserves this position.[81]

Defence and the dwelling

The law relating to the use of force in defence of the dwelling has been put on a statutory footing following the enactment of the Criminal Law (Defence and the

---

[77] 256 U.S. 335 (1921) at 343.
[78] [2006] IECCA 165.
[79] [2006] IECCA 165 at 39.
[80] (1984) 78 Cr. App. R. 276.
[81] See ss.18(1), 18(5), 19(1) and 19(3).

General Defences 289

Dwelling) Act 2011. Following a series of high-profile cases involving fatalities in the course of burglaries, a consensus emerged that there was a need for a clear statement of the law on the use of force in defence of the dwelling. In *DPP v Barnes*, Hardiman J. made the observation that there was surprisingly no modern Irish authority on this topic which has "troubled the courts of law since time immemorial".[82] The new legislation aims to bring clarity as to the rights of occupiers to defend themselves and others against intruders to the dwelling. It was felt that legislation needed to be introduced to ensure certainty as to the legal position on the use of force in defence of the dwelling as well as reassuring the public that the law had struck the balance in favour of householders over burglars. It was against the backdrop of the Court of Criminal Appeal decisions in *DPP v Barnes*[83] and *DPP v Nally*[84] that the Criminal Law (Defence and the Dwelling) Act 2011 was enacted.

The decision of the Court of Criminal Appeal in *DPP v Barnes* sets out a number of principles that would influence the drafting of the Criminal Law (Defence and the Dwelling) Act 2011.[85] In deciding that a heightened level of protection should be given to persons using force in defence of the dwelling, case law was cited in support of the "castle doctrine". A well known passage from *Semayne's case* was referred to:

> "That the house of everyone is to him as his castle and fortress, as well for his defence against injury and violence as for his repose."[86]

Hardiman J. went on to remark that the special status of a dwelling is linked to the dignity of its occupants, quoting from *Mead's and Belt's* case:

> "[T]he making of an attack upon the dwelling, and especially at night, the law requires as equivalent to an assault on a man's person for a man's house is his castle, and therefore, in the eye of the law, it is equivalent to an assault."[87]

Hardiman J. went on to consider the principle of inviolability of the dwelling in Art.40.5 of the Constitution, remarking that "a person's dwellinghouse is far more than bricks and mortar; it is the home of a person and his or her family, dependents or guests (if any) and is entitled to a very high degree of protection at law for this reason ... the home is, of course, also entitled to protection from criminals".[88]

In *Barnes*, the Court of Criminal Appeal, citing every citizen's right to life under Art.40.3.1° of the Constitution, wished to make it clear that it is not permissible for the occupant of a house to kill a burglar simply for being a burglar:

> "[A] person cannot lawfully lose his life simply because he trespasses in the dwellinghouse of another with intent to steal."[89]

---

[82] [2007] 3 I.R. 130 at 143.
[83] [2007] 3 I.R. 130.
[84] [2007] 4 I.R. 145.
[85] 719 *Dáil Debates* Cols 400–405.
[86] (1604) 5 Co. Rep. 91a.
[87] (1828) 1 Lewin 184.
[88] *DPP v Barnes* [2007] 3 I.R. 130 at 144.
[89] [2007] 3 I.R. 130 at 146.

In other words, there is no general "licence to kill" a burglar. Having considered the relevant legal authorities, the Court of Criminal Appeal adopted the following legal principles, as set out in the judgment of Hardiman J.:

> "Every burglary in a dwellinghouse is an act of aggression. The circumstances may make this element of aggression more or less patent but the violation of a citizen's dwellinghouse is just that, a violation and an act of aggression no matter what the other circumstances.
>
> A person who commits such a violation exposes himself to various legal penalties, if he is detected and convicted. But that is not the limit of his exposure. Although he is not liable to be killed by the householder simply for being a burglar, he is an aggressor and may expect to be lawfully met with retaliatory force to drive him off or to immobilise or detain him and end the threat which he offers to the personal rights of the householder and his or her family or guests ...
>
> The propositions just set out derive from the nature of the dwellinghouse itself, and its constitutional standing as a place required by the dignity of the human person to be inviolable except in accordance with law ... [A] dwellinghouse is at a higher level, legally and constitutionally, than other forms of property."[90]

The Court of Criminal Appeal went on to hold that there is no legal obligation on the occupant of a dwelling to retreat; a householder may stand his ground when faced with a burglar and no adverse legal consequences should flow from the fact that the householder did not retreat, even if he or she had an opportunity to retreat. Hardiman J. stated that:

> "It is, in our view, quite inconsistent with the constitutional doctrine of the inviolability of the dwellinghouse that a householder or other lawful occupant could be ever under a legal obligation to flee the dwellinghouse or, as it might be put in more contemporary language, to retreat from it. It follows from this, in turn, that such a person can never be in a worse position in point of law because he has decided to stand his ground in his house."[91]

As to the degree of force that may be permissibly used by a householder in response to the threat posed by a burglar, the Court of Criminal Appeal was of the opinion that it would be unfair to adopt a wholly objective standard, to be judged by the standards of the hypothetically reasonable person. Victims of burglaries are in a particularly vulnerable position given the uncertain nature of the threat posed by the intruder who may be armed or of a violent disposition. Understandably, a person confronted by a burglar may be so terrified and shocked by the sudden threat posed to his personal safety and family that he is not in a position to consider in a measured way the level of force required as a means of defence. For these reasons, the Court of Criminal Appeal held that there must be both a subjective and an objective component to the test used to assess the appropriate degree of force to be used. In this regard, the court

---

[90] [2007] 3 I.R. 130 at 148.
[91] [2007] 3 I.R. 130 at 150.

General Defences

stated that a useful analogy could be drawn with the statutory criteria for the use of non-fatal force as set out in s.18 of the Non-Fatal Offences Against the Person Act 1997, which permits a person to use force "such as is reasonable in the circumstances as he or she believes them to be".

In *Barnes*, it was the burglar who was seeking to rely on a plea of self defence in response to an alleged attack by the householder. In light of the principle of "self-generated necessity" it was held that there is very limited scope for a burglar relying on self defence:

> "Considering the heinous and inherently aggressive nature of the crime of burglary in a dwellinghouse, there is an air of improbability about the burglar, the initial aggressor, relying on the defence of self-defence when he has violently killed the householder."[92]

The Court of Criminal Appeal went on to state that the killing of a householder by a burglar, during the course of the burglary, can never be less than manslaughter, by reason of the burglar's initial, grave, aggression.

In *DPP v Nally*,[93] the applicant was a householder who had been charged with murdering a man he found trespassing in his home. The applicant gave evidence that he accidentally shot the victim in the loin area and right hand after seeing the victim pushing open the back kitchen door of the house. A ferocious physical struggle then ensued. The applicant was concerned that the victim's son, who had been outside the house earlier, might return with a weapon or reinforcements. The applicant went to the shed and retrieved more cartridges and reloaded the shotgun. As the victim was limping away from the property, the applicant followed him onto a public road and fired a further shot at him from a few yards distance; it was this final shot which proved fatal.

The applicant pleaded not guilty to a charge of murder, raising a plea of self defence. Counsel for the prosecution invited the trial judge to direct that the defence of self defence be allowed to go to the jury in a truncated form, shorn of any possibility that the jury might acquit altogether on the basis that the amount of force used by the applicant was so excessive as to destroy any notion that it was objectively reasonable. In such circumstances it was suggested that it should only be open to the jury to convict of either murder or manslaughter. The trial judge directed the jury to consider a limited form of self defence. The applicant was convicted of manslaughter in the Central Criminal Court.

On appeal, the Court of Criminal Appeal, citing the Supreme Court decision in *DPP v Davis*,[94] held that the constitutional right to trial by a jury had, as a fundamental and absolutely essential characteristic, the right of the jury to deliver a verdict. While there was a right and duty vested in a trial judge at any stage of a criminal case to withdraw the case from the jury and direct them to enter a verdict of not guilty, there was no corresponding right or duty on the part of a trial judge to direct a jury to enter a verdict of guilty. The Court of Criminal Appeal allowed the appeal, quashed the conviction and directed a retrial.

---

[92] [2007] 3 I.R. 130 at 153.
[93] [2007] 4 I.R. 145.
[94] [1993] 2 I.R. 1.

The Criminal Law (Defence and the Dwelling) Act 2011 restates the law on the use of force in the specific context of defence of the dwelling. In relation to the use of excessive lethal force the case of *Attorney General v Dwyer*[95] continues to be the leading authority where the killing occurs in a place other than a dwelling, such as a bar or on a street; *Dwyer* sets out the general principles on excessive self defence, whereas the Criminal Law (Defence and the Dwelling) Act 2011 is limited in its application to offences that occur in the dwelling or the curtilage of a dwelling. Sections 2(1) and 4 of the 2011 Act acknowledge the continuing general application of other general defences alongside the new legislative scheme governing defence and the dwelling. The spatial limitation on the application of the 2011 Act is important as it marks the boundary between the general common law rules and the special statutory rules that apply to defence of the dwelling.[96] Careful consideration was given to the definition of the terms "dwelling" and "curtilage" which are defined respectively in s.1(1) of the 2011 Act:

> "curtilage", in relation to a dwelling, means an area immediately surrounding or adjacent to the dwelling which is used in conjunction with the dwelling, other than any part of that area that is a public place.
>
> "dwelling" includes –
>
> (a) a building or structure (whether temporary or not) which is constructed or adapted for use as a dwelling and is being so used,
> (b) a vehicle or vessel (whether mobile or not) which is constructed or adapted for use as a dwelling and is being so used, or
> (c) a part of a dwelling.

The statutory test for the justifiable use of force in defence of the dwelling is set out in s.2(1) of the 2011 Act:

> [I]t shall not be an offence for a person who is in his or her dwelling, or for a person who is a lawful occupant in a dwelling, to use force against another person or the property of another person where—
>
> (*a*) he or she believes the other person has entered or is entering the dwelling as a trespasser for the purpose of committing a criminal act, and
> (*b*) the force used is only such as is reasonable in the circumstances as he or she believes them to be—
>   (i) to protect himself or herself or another person present in the dwelling from injury, assault, detention or death caused by a criminal act,
>   (ii) to protect his or her property or the property of another person from appropriation, destruction or damage caused by a criminal act, or
>   (iii) to prevent the commission of a crime or to effect, or assist in effecting, a lawful arrest.

---

[95] [1972] I.R. 416.
[96] 719 *Dáil Debates* Cols 402–403.

General Defences 293

The test has both subjective and objective components in that the force used may only be such as is reasonable in the circumstances as the person believes it to be to protect himself or herself or another person from injury, to protect property, to prevent the commission of a crime or to effect a lawful arrest. Section 2(4) states that it is immaterial whether a belief is justified or not if it is honestly held, but in considering whether the person using the force honestly held the belief regard shall be had to the presence or absence of reasonable grounds for holding such a belief. In addition, it must be shown that the person using force believed that the other person entered the dwelling as a trespasser for the purpose of committing a criminal act. The availability of the defence is not limited to owners of property; the defence may also be invoked by lawful occupants of the property. Sections 2(5) and 3 provide that there is no requirement on a person to retreat notwithstanding that the person may have a safe and practicable opportunity to retreat; a person is entitled to stand his ground in his home without any prejudice to his legal position in the event that he uses force against an intruder. Section 2(7) makes it clear that the 2011 Act is applicable in cases where force is used in defence of the dwelling causing death to the intruder. This is an acknowledgment of the fact that deaths may occur in the course of defending the dwelling from an unjustifiable attack:

> "The occupier will obviously have a judgment call to make when using force against an intruder as to the level of force required. Such an event, in most cases, is likely to occur in a situation of great tension and anxiety. The force that may be used is such as is reasonable in the circumstances as the occupier believes them to be at the time of the attack. This will be the case whether the force results in the death of the intruder or not."[97]

INTOXICATION

The availability of intoxication as a defence has always been problematic. Moral disapproval of intoxication contributed to a reluctance to admit that it might mitigate guilt: Aristotle recommended that a person who committed a crime while drunk should be punished twice, once for committing the crime and once for being drunk. The 1552 case of *Reniger v Fogossa*[98] held that "[i]f a person that is drunk kills another this shall be felony, and he shall be hanged for it, and yet he did it through ignorance, for when he was drunk he had no understanding nor memory; but in as much as that ignorance was occasioned by his own act and folly, it shall not be privileged thereby". Sir Edward Coke was of the view that "[a]s for a drunkard who is a 'voluntarius daemon' he shall have no privilege thereby …".[99]

Moral disapproval aside, the large proportion of crimes which are committed as the result of intoxication leads to a justifiable reluctance to admit intoxication as a defence lest the result should be unduly lenient. The fact that a person's inhibitions

---
[97] 719 *Dáil Debates* Col.403.
[98] (1552) 1 Plowd 1. This case, along with several others, was discussed by Hardiman J. in *DPP v Murphy*, unreported, Court of Criminal Appeal, July 8, 2003 in summarising the ancient law on intoxication.
[99] *Coke's Institutes* 247a.

and assessment are lowered while drunk is not, therefore, in itself a defence; it may even be an aggravating factor, as in the case of road traffic offences. There is, it follows, no general defence of intoxication.

However, a so-called defence of intoxication does arise in situations where an offence requires mens rea and the defendant claims that he lacked the mental element through the effects of intoxication. For example, murder requires an intention to kill or cause serious injury: if the accused is too drunk to form that intention, then a conviction for murder cannot be forthcoming. In *R. v Doherty*[100] Stephen J. remarked:

> "It is almost trivial for me to observe that a man is not excused from crime by reason of his drunkenness ... But, although you cannot take drunkenness as an excuse for crime, yet where the crime is such that the intention of the party committing it is one of its constituent elements, you may look at the fact that a man was in drink in considering whether he formed the intention necessary to constitute the crime."

Dutch courage

The defence of intoxication is strictly limited in scope. In the first place, it does not apply in circumstances where a person took drink or drugs in order to give himself Dutch courage to carry out a crime. So, in *Attorney General for Northern Ireland v Gallagher*,[101] the accused was charged with the murder of his wife. The evidence showed that he, while sober, had made up his mind to kill her. He then downed a bottle of whiskey, either for Dutch courage or to drown his conscience after the killing. While drunk he killed his wife. His argument was simple: at the time of the killing he was so drunk as to lack the intention to kill or cause serious injury. Although he had, earlier, intended to kill his wife, the actus reus and mens rea did not coincide. This was, unsurprisingly, rejected by the House of Lords:

> "If a man, whilst sane and sober, forms an intention to kill and makes preparation for it, knowing it is a wrong thing to do, and then gets himself drunk so as to give himself Dutch courage to do the killing, and whilst drunk carries out his intention, he cannot rely on this self-induced drunkenness as a defence to a charge of murder, nor even as reducing it to manslaughter. He cannot say he got himself into such a stupid state that he was incapable of an intent to kill ... The wickedness of his mind before he got drunk is enough to condemn him, coupled with the act which he intended to do and did do."[102]

Basic/specific intent

The second major limitation on the availability of the defence is imposed by the distinction between basic and specific intent. This is an artificial distinction, best explained in terms of *intention to carry out an action* and *intention to achieve a*

---

[100] [1887] 16 Cox 306.
[101] [1963] A.C. 349.
[102] [1963] A.C. 349 at 382 per Lord Denning.

General Defences

result. If a crime merely requires intention to perform a particular act, then it is a crime of basic intent. An example is the crime of assault, which simply requires an intention to inflict force on another without their consent. If, however, a crime requires an intention to achieve a particular result by that act, then the crime is one of specific intent. An example is the crime of murder which requires both a particular act and an intention as a result of that act to cause serious injury or death. Another explanation of the distinction that has been proffered is that specific intent exists in respect of those crimes where intent or foresight is a component of the offence (e.g. murder) whereas crimes in respect of which the mens rea is recklessness are classified as crimes of basic intent (e.g. manslaughter, rape, assault).[103]

This distinction was elaborated upon in the context of intoxication by the House of Lords in *DPP v Majewski*.[104] In that case, the accused was charged with assault occasioning actual bodily harm and assault on a police officer in the course of his duty. He was a drug addict and had taken a large quantity of drugs and alcohol before the offences. He claimed to have blanked out and not to have known what he was doing and there was some medical evidence to the effect that this was possible. The trial judge directed the jury not to treat intoxication as being in any way a defence to the charges. On appeal, this direction was upheld. The basic position was expressed as being that voluntary drunkenness is never an excuse, to which an exception existed only in the limited class of offences which require proof of a specific intent. Where a person becomes voluntarily drunk, then the mens rea required is in effect supplied by his conduct in becoming drunk:

> "A man who by voluntarily taking drink and drugs gets himself into an aggressive state in which he does not know what he is doing and then makes a vicious assault can hardly say with any plausibility that what he did was a pure accident which should render him immune from any criminal liability."[105]

This approach has not met with universal approval. The distinction between basic intent and specific intent is admitted to be arbitrary and for that reason the High Court of Australia has adopted a different approach in *R. v O'Connor*,[106] holding that evidence of intoxication, however caused, is admissible to show absence of intent. The accused was observed stealing from a police car and he subsequently stabbed a police man in his pursuit. He had taken a mixture of drink and drugs and claimed to have had no recollection of the incident. Evidence was given that the drug taken was hallucinatory and in association with alcohol could have rendered the accused incapable of reasoning or forming intent to steal or wound. The High Court rejected the basic intent–specific intent distinction. Barwick C.J. stated that:

> "With great respect to those who have favoured this ... it is to my mind not only inappropriate but it obscures more than it reveals ... It seems to me completely inconsistent with the principles of the common law that a man

---

[103] This was how the specific–basic intent distinction was explained in *Metropolitan Police Commissioner v Caldwell* [1981] 1 All E.R. 981.
[104] [1976] 2 All E.R. 142.
[105] [1976] 2 All E.R. 142 at 157 per Lord Salmon.
[106] (1980) 146 C.L.R. 64.

should be conclusively presumed to have an intention which, in fact, he does not have ..."[107]

It was held that evidence of intoxication should have been allowed to go to the jury in order for the jury to decide whether it had deprived the defendant of the requisite mens rea.

The basic intent–specific intent dichotomy has also been rejected in New Zealand and South Africa.[108] The Law Commission of England and Wales[109] recommended that the distinction be abandoned due to the:

> "[P]resent confusion caused by the terminology which has developed in this context, that is, the references to 'offences of basic intent' (voluntary intoxication irrelevant) and 'offences of specific intent' (intoxication relevant). We believe that this distinction is ambiguous, misleading and confusing, and that it should be abandoned."[110]

The Law Commission pointed out that even the Law Lords in *Majewski*, while unanimous that there was a distinction, failed to agree on the definition of each form of intent. It referred to the confusing case of *R. v Heard*[111] where the Court of Appeal "recently went so far as to suggest (we believe, wrongly) that the notion of 'specific intent' also extends to a requirement of recklessness as to something beyond the requirements of the offence's external element and which, for that reason, could be classified as an 'ulterior intent'".[112] However, the Law Commission ultimately opted to take the "unattractive" option of preserving the *Majewski* rule, while simplifying its application and removing the categorisations of offences as ones of basic or specific intent.[113]

---

[107] (1980) 146 C.L.R. 64 at 81.
[108] See the discussion on the reaction to *Majewski* in McAuley and McCutcheon, *Criminal Liability* (2000), pp.592–598.
[109] Law Commission (Law Com. No. 314), *Intoxication and Criminal Liability* (January 2009).
[110] Law Commission (Law Com. No. 314), *Intoxication and Criminal Liability* (January 2009), para.1.28.
[111] [2008] Q.B. 43.
[112] Law Commission (Law Com. No. 314), *Intoxication and Criminal Liability* (January 2009), para.2.8. *R. v Heard* held that "intentionally" in s.3 of the Sexual Offences Act 2003 (sexual assault) requires nothing more than proof that the defendant's conduct was non-accidental. It held that the word "intentionally" was not to be interpreted as requiring a specific intent. It remarked that there is no universally logical test for distinguishing between crimes where intoxication can be a defence and those where it cannot. There is a large element of public policy involved and categorisation can only be achieved on a case-by-case basis. However, the Law Commission points out that the equivalent requirement of "intentional" penetration of a child under 13 years set out in the 2003 Act was interpreted as a fault element, not a requirement of volition, by the House of Lords in *R. v G* [2008] UKHL 37.
[113] The recommendation is that a statutory framework should replace the basic–specific offence distinction, listing "integral fault elements" (intention, knowledge, belief, fraud and dishonesty). If a defendant is charged with an offence requiring an "integral fault element" voluntary intoxication may be a defence.

Intoxication under Irish law

Until very recently the law in Ireland was unclear.[114] The Law Reform Commission, in its *Consultation Paper on Intoxication as a Defence to a Criminal Offence*[115] appeared to suggest that intoxication was never a defence under Irish law. However, a line of Irish case law has supported the view that evidence of intoxication is relevant to the question of whether the accused had the relevant mens rea.

In *Attorney General v Manning*,[116] the question of intoxication was treated as being directly relevant to mens rea. The defendant was found guilty of murdering a nurse. Evidence was given that he had consumed alcohol on the evening in question. He replied to Garda questioning by saying "I will tell you all, drink was the cause of it". He argued that he had been unable to form the necessary intention for murder as a result. On appeal it was held that the following jury direction was correct:

> "[D]rink is no defence if the only effect of the drink is the more readily to allow a man to give way to his passions ... The effect of drink has to go much further. It has to go so far as either to render him incapable of knowing what he is doing at all, or, if he appreciated that, of knowing the consequences or probable consequences of his actions ..."

Another example of this approach was *People (DPP) v McBride*.[117] The defendant was tried for assault on his niece with a pickaxe handle. He made a statement to the Gardaí that he had been drinking prior to the incident: "[m]y mind just went blank and I started hitting her with the handle". The trial judge directed the jury that intoxication is not a defence to a criminal charge. Counsel for the defence argued before the Court of Criminal Appeal that this direction was incorrect: intoxication as such is not a defence but it can be relevant on the question of whether the accused was capable of forming intent. The Court of Criminal Appeal directed a re-trial on other grounds and observed that there was no evidence that the accused was intoxicated at the time of the assault on his niece. The court did not comment adversely on the submission of defence counsel on the effect of intoxication.

It appeared from the above cases that the basic–specific distinction had no place in Irish law and that the sole question to be considered was whether the intoxication had negatived the requisite mens rea.

However, this interpretation is no longer accurate. The Irish courts have now clearly embraced the *Majewski* reasoning and, by default, divided all Irish offences into two separate categories of basic and specific intent.[118]

The case to do so was the decision of the Court of Criminal Appeal in *DPP v Reilly*.[119] The accused had stayed the night at his cousin's house where the group

---

[114] See Thomas O'Malley, "Intoxication and Criminal Responsibility" (1991) 1 I.C.L.J. 86; Finbarr McAuley, "The Intoxication Defence in Criminal Law" (1997) 32 Ir. Jur (N.S) 243.
[115] February 1995.
[116] (1953) 89 I.L.T.R. 155.
[117] [1996] 1 I.R. 312.
[118] Michael Dillon, "Intoxicated Automatism is no Defence: Majewski is law in Ireland" (2004) 14(3) I.C.L.J. 7.
[119] [2005] 3 I.R. 111. The issue was mentioned briefly in *DPP v Murphy*, unreported, Court of Criminal Appeal, July 8, 2003 where Hardiman J. referred to the basic–specific intent distinction without commenting on whether it formed part of Irish law.

became intoxicated. In addition, he drank at least one glass of poitín before calling it a night. He slept downstairs in the same room as his cousin's 18-month-old child. During the night the accused leapt to his feet, unsheathed a knife he always kept on his possession, stabbed the child and killed him. The little boy was found the next morning by his mother. The accused had no recollection of the killing and was extremely upset when he realised what had happened. McCracken J. expressly endorsed *Majewski* by citing the quote that:

> "If a man by his own volition takes a substance which causes him to cast off the restraints of reason and conscience, no wrong is done by holding him answerable criminally for any injury he may do in that condition. His course of conduct in reducing himself by drugs and drink to that condition in my view supplies the evidence of *mens rea*, of guilty mind certainly sufficient for crimes of basic intent."

The applicant's conviction for manslaughter was allowed to stand. McCracken J. characterised *Majewski* as "undoubtedly illogical" but concluded that:

> "[W]hatever may be the logic, the court is here concerned with the commission of actions of violence by one person against another. It is not sufficient to make decisions on such issues in a purely theoretical manner. The court must have regard to the rights of an accused person, but it also must have regard to the interest of the public at large who are entitled to be protected from acts of violence."[120]

The basic intent–specific intent dichotomy has been criticised extensively. It was also characterised by the Law Reform Commission as illogical. It moves away from the subjective recklessness test which has been a feature of Irish criminal law for so long. It is based on the notion that recklessness in taking an intoxicant is sufficient to amount to the recklessness which is the mens rea required for offences of basic intent. This is, of course, not logical and does not sit well with the principles underpinning the criminal law.

Despite this, it appears that *DPP v Reilly* accurately reflects current judicial attitudes to intoxication. The rationale behind the decision appears to be judicial enthusiasm for applying common sense rules. The current climate of intolerance for binge-drinking and the recognition that Irish society does not deal well with alcohol may make it less likely that the decision will be overruled, despite criticisms from legal purists. In addition, the terrible facts of the case may have influenced the court in coming to a decision. Spencer, who characterises this recent endorsement of *Majewski* in Irish law as "a rule of ... doubtful provenance and ... dubious merit" is of the view that "[t]he *Majewski* rule is now embedded in our law and it will take an exorcism of supreme proportions to purge it from our legal system".[121]

---

[120] [2005] 3 I.R. 111 at 121.
[121] Keith Spencer, "The Intoxication Defence in Ireland" (2005) 15(1) I.C.L.J. 3.

Intoxication by other drugs

The operation of the basic intent–specific intent distinction can be seen in *R. v Lipman*[122] which also demonstrates the application of the defence in the case of intoxication by drugs other than alcohol. In this case the accused took LSD and, in the course of hallucinating that he was being attacked by snakes, killed his girlfriend. Charged with murder, he claimed that he had no knowledge of what he was doing and no intention to harm her. He was found guilty of manslaughter and appealed. It was held by the Court of Appeal that, where a killing results from an unlawful and dangerous act, no specific intent is required for the crime of manslaughter: consequently, self-induced intoxication is no defence to a charge of manslaughter.

An interesting case on intoxication by drugs is *R. v Hardie*[123] where the accused was upset after the breakdown of his relationship with his girlfriend and took several valium pills to calm his nerves. In fact, he ended up starting a fire in her flat. Could he rely on the defence of intoxication? It was held that he could. Although he was involuntarily intoxicated he did not know, nor should he have known, that valium in that quantity could produce aggressive effects. He reasonably believed that it would merely have a sedative effect. Had he known that it might produce aggression, then he would not have been able to rely on his self-induced intoxication. Since he did not, he was not morally blameworthy in simply taking the drug and the issue of intoxication should have been left to the jury, who should have been directed to consider whether he was being reckless in taking the drug.

Involuntary intoxication

The parameters of the intoxication defence are set, consciously or otherwise, by judicial disapproval of those who voluntarily drink to excess or engage in drug-taking. This disapproval has no place in situations where a person is involuntarily intoxicated and intoxication is available as a defence in those situations, even to crimes of basic intent. This has been accepted since the case of *R. v Pearson*[124] in which Parke B. stated that "if a party be made drunk by the stratagem or fraud of another, he is not responsible".[125] However, involuntary intoxication is given a rather narrow ambit. Where a person knows he is drinking alcohol, but is not aware of how strong it is, his intoxication is not involuntary.[126]

In addition, the defence applies only where the involuntary intoxication is such as to negative intent. It does not apply where the accused, though intoxicated through no fault of his own, still has the capacity to form an intention, although his inhibitions might be lowered. This can be seen in *R. v Kingston*[127] in which the

---

[122] [1970] 1 Q.B. 152. This case pre-dates *Majewski* but illustrates that the distinction between offences of basic and specific intent did not begin with *Majewski* but can be traced back at least as far as *DPP v Beard* [1920] A.C. 479. However, it has been surmised that Lord Birkenhead in *Beard* may not have intended to create the category of "specific intent" offences at all—the word "specific" may have been superfluous to his judgment.
[123] [1984] 3 All E.R. 848.
[124] (1835) 2 Lewin 144.
[125] (1835) 2 Lewin 144 at 145.
[126] *R. v Allen* [1988] Crim. L.R. 698.
[127] [1995] 2 A.C. 355.

accused was a man with paedophiliac tendencies. Another man, in order to blackmail the accused, lured a boy to his flat and drugged him. He then laced the accused's coffee with a drug. The accused, involuntarily intoxicated, but aware of what he was doing, sexually abused the boy. The defence of intoxication was rejected, even on the assumption that without the spiked drink the accused would not have given in to his tendencies. The House of Lords held that the jury had been properly directed that even a drugged intention was still an intention. The fact that the accused's self-control had been lowered by deception was a factor going to mitigation of penalty only.

Law Reform Commission

The Law Reform Commission[128] was of the view that self-induced intoxication should never ground a defence to any criminal charge. It recommended that a distinct offence of committing a criminal act while intoxicated should be created. This would have the advantage of marking society's disapproval of intoxication while not artificially distorting the elements of criminal offences in order to ensure intoxication could not excuse behaviour that would otherwise be criminal.

The Commission characterised the basic–specific intent dichotomy as illogical and noted that it had been criticised by academics. It emphasised that involuntary intoxication should always be a defence and that a person's intoxication should be regarded as involuntary if the person took the intoxicant solely for a medicinal purpose and either was not aware that taking it would or might give rise to aggressive or uncontrollable behaviour, or took it on medical advice and in accordance with any directions given by the person providing the advice.

MISTAKE

Mistake, like intoxication, is not a general defence.[129] Like intoxication, however, mistake may neutralise an element of the mens rea of the offence in question. This is subject to one obvious limitation: if the offence in question is one of strict liability, then any mistake will be of no effect, since there is no mens rea requirement to be defeated. An example of mistake as a defence can be seen in *R. v Morgan*[130] where an honest though unreasonable belief in consent was held to be a defence to a charge of rape. Similarly, the shooting of a person mistaken for a deer will not amount to murder, nor will the taking of an article believed to be the accused's own amount to theft.

A mistake must go to an element relevant to the offence: if A thinks that he is killing B when in fact he is killing C, then the offence of murder is still committed. Mistake of law is not generally a defence. If one believes it is legal to kill a person who burgles one's home one may nevertheless be guilty of murder. However, mistake

---

[128] Law Reform Commission, *Report on Intoxication* (LRC 51–1995).
[129] For a comprehensive examination of mistake in criminal law, see McAuley and McCutcheon, *Criminal Liability* (2000), Ch.12.
[130] [1975] 2 All E.R. 347. See Ch.5 on sexual offences for a detailed discussion of this case.

of law will be relevant in some cases. In theft, for example, an essential part of the offence is that the defendant should act without a claim of right made in good faith. If a person holds a mistaken view of the law, leading him to the belief that he has a legitimate claim to a particular piece of property, then he will have a claim of right sufficient to defeat the charge of theft.

At common law a mistake, in order to constitute a defence, had to be reasonable. In *R. v Tolson*,[131] the defendant believed on reasonable grounds that her husband was dead, having been lost at sea. She remarried, only to be charged with bigamy when her husband reappeared several years later. She was acquitted, but only on the ground that her belief was reasonable. However, *R. v Morgan* expresses a more modern view and makes it clear that in some circumstances an unreasonable mistake will amount to a defence. The Court of Appeal in *R. v Kimber*[132] emphasised that *Morgan* was not limited to the case of rape and a genuine though mistaken belief will generally excuse liability. The House of Lords endorsed the *Morgan* principle as a general principle in *B v DPP*.[133] Similarly, *DPP v Murray*[134] makes it clear that an assessment of criminal responsibility in this jurisdiction is normally to be conducted on subjective standards. It follows that the defence of mistake is to be judged on subjective grounds.

There are, however, exceptions to this. If the mens rea of a crime is negligence, then clearly a negligent mistake will afford no defence. So, in the case of *R. v Foxford*[135] the accused was a soldier on patrol in Northern Ireland who shot and killed a 12-year-old boy when firing at a gunman. His defence was that he had mistaken the boy for the gunman but it was held that since this mistake was in itself grossly negligent it could not afford a defence to a charge of manslaughter.

Whether a mistake was reasonable may be taken into account by a jury in deciding whether it was in fact made. This is set out by statute in the case of rape in s.2(2) of the Criminal Law (Rape) Act 1981:

> It is hereby declared that if at a trial for a rape offence the jury has to consider whether a man believed that a woman was consenting to sexual intercourse, the presence or absence of reasonable grounds for such a belief is a matter to which the jury is to have regard, in conjunction with any other relevant matters, in considering whether he so believed.

However this section merely restates the existing law, by which the reasonableness of a belief may be taken into account in deciding whether it was honestly held.

For the controversial issue of mistake as regards the age of the person with whom one engages in sexual activity, see Ch.5.

---

[131] (1889) 23 QBD 168.
[132] [1983] 1 W.L.R. 1118.
[133] [2000] 2 A.C. 428.
[134] [1977] I.R. 360.
[135] [1974] N.I. 181.

Consent

Whether consent will be a defence varies from offence to offence and from victim to victim. For example, consent is no defence to a charge of murder. The Criminal Law (Sexual Offences) Act 2006 provides that children under 17 years of age cannot consent to engaging in a sexual act. Equally, it appears from *R. v Brown*[136] that consent will not be a defence to a charge of causing serious harm contrary to s.4 of the Non-Fatal Offences Against the Person Act 1997. Consent is discussed further in the chapters dealing with sexual offences and offences against the person, Chs 5 and 6.[137]

Infancy

> "Criminal law is essentially an adult business. Prisons are designed to punish and rehabilitate mature offenders. Children have no place within a system which may corrupt them further or which may break an undeveloped spirit."[138]

The criminal liability of children was governed at common law by the doctrine of doli incapax. This had two parts: a conclusive presumption and a rebuttable presumption. First, a child under the age of seven years was conclusively presumed to be incapable of committing a crime. While this was phrased in the form of a presumption, it is important to note that it had the effect of a substantive rule of law: a crime could not be committed by a child under seven years of age. Secondly, a child aged between seven and 14 years was presumed to be incapable of committing a crime, but this presumption could be rebutted if it could be shown that the child realised that what he was doing was wrong, or, as some older cases put it, that the child had a "mischievous discretion".

This was quite a high standard and it was not enough to show that the child knew that his conduct was merely naughty or mischievous. The test was set out in the English decision of *R. v Gorrie*[139] and approved by the Irish courts in *KM v DPP*,[140] where Morris J. accepted that it must be shown that the child knew that what he was doing was gravely or seriously wrong. In that case, a child was charged with sexual assaults on other children when he was aged 13 years. It was accepted that his threats to kill the children if they told anyone what he had done could establish that he knew the conduct was seriously wrong and not just mischievous. The doctrine of doli incapax was criticised by the English High Court in *C (a minor) v DPP*[141] and the House of Lords decision in the same case emphasised that urgent statutory reform was necessary. Laws J. in the High Court set out a number of difficulties with the

---

[136] [1994] 1 A.C. 212.
[137] For a theoretical discussion of the role of consent see McAuley and McCutcheon, *Criminal Liability* (2000), Ch.11.
[138] Charleton, *Criminal law—Cases and Materials* (1992), p.271.
[139] (1919) 83 J.P. 136.
[140] [1994] 1 I.R. 514.
[141] [1994] 3 W.L.R. 888. The House of Lords decision, which highlighted the urgent need for legislation in the area, can be found at [1995] 2 W.L.R. 383.

General Defences 303

doctrine's application to modern times. He pointed out that there may be no evidence available to rebut the presumption as the child may have answered no questions at the police station and may decline to give evidence in court. In addition, the requirement of an understanding that the act was seriously wrong was conceptually obscure as it could not mean that the act was against the law (as ignorance of the law is no defence) but case law had indicated that it did not mean morally wrong either. Furthermore, Laws J. argued that the rule was perverse as it tended to absolve the children most likely to engage in criminality from criminal responsibility:

> "[D]elinquents under the age of 14, who may know no better than to commit antisocial and sometimes dangerous crimes, should not be held immune from the criminal justice system, but sensibly managed within it. Otherwise they are left outside the law, free to commit further crime, perhaps of increasing gravity, unchecked by the courts whose very duty it is to bring them to book. It is precisely the youngster whose understanding of the difference between right and wrong is fragile or non-existent who is most likely to get involved in criminal activity. Yet this outdated and unprincipled presumption is, no less precisely, tailored to secure his acquittal if he is brought before the court. The prosecution are in effect required to prove, as a condition of his guilt, that he is morally responsible: But it is because he is morally irresponsible that he has committed the crime in the first place."[142]

It should be noted that the offence of rape was treated differently to other offences. At common law, a conclusive presumption existed that a boy under the age of 14 years could not commit rape. This presumption was limited to cases of rape (or other offences involving intercourse) and did not extend to any other forms of sexual offence. The presumption was therefore an anomaly and a boy under 14 years could be charged with indecent assault on facts which would otherwise amount to rape. This presumption was removed by s.6 of the Criminal Law (Rape) (Amendment) Act 1990.

The age at which a child faced criminal responsibility under Irish law was strikingly low: Canada, another common law jurisdiction, had chosen the age of 12 years and in England 10 years was the age of responsibility. It is interesting to note that the common law originally set the age of criminal responsibility at 12 years, during a time when childhood was not as protracted as it is today. The English position had been modified in stages by legislation. First, the age at which criminal responsibility begins was raised to 10 years by the Children and Young Persons Act 1963. Subsequently, the Crime and Disorder Act 1998 abolished the presumption of doli incapax. As a result, English law now takes the straightforward approach that children under the age of 10 years are not criminally responsible, while those over that age are criminally responsible in the ordinary way.

The legislature intended to reform the Irish position by s.52 of the Children Act 2001 which raised the age of criminal responsibility to 12 years and left the rebuttable presumption in place for children between the ages of 12 and 14 years. However, that

---

[142] [1994] 3 W.L.R. 888 at 896. This was also noted in Glanville Williams, *Criminal Law: The General Part* (London: Stevens & Sons, 1961), p.818.

particular section was never brought into force and the Criminal Justice Act 2006 replaced it with a new s.52:

(1) subject to subsection (2), a child under 12 years of age shall not be charged with an offence;
(2) subsection (1) does not apply to a child aged 10 or 11 years who is charged with murder, manslaughter, rape, rape under section 4 of the Criminal Law (Rape) (Amendment) Act 1990 or aggravated sexual assault;
(3) the rebuttable presumption under any rule of law, namely, that a child who is not less than 7 but under 14 years of age is incapable of committing an offence because the child did not have the capacity to know that the act or omission concerned was wrong, is abolished.

This section differs from the 2001 Act provision in a number of significant ways. First, there is a lower age of responsibility for very serious offences: 10 years. Secondly, the rebuttable presumption has been abolished in all cases.

Entrapment

Suppose that A approaches B with the suggestion that they commit a crime together. After some time, A persuades B of the merits of the plan. They carry out the crime only to find the police waiting as they make their exit. It emerges that A is an undercover policeman who was acting with the intention of luring B into committing a crime. Has B committed a crime and, if so, does B have any defence?

Clearly B has voluntarily carried out a particular act with the necessary intention. The fact that this intention was procured by another does not make any difference, so long as the intention was formed freely. The situation would, of course, be different if there was any question of duress.

The question therefore remains whether B has a defence in respect of the crime which he has committed.

Traditional approach to entrapment

The traditional answer was that entrapment was no defence and this was the approach taken by the House of Lords in *R. v Sang*.[143] The defendant was charged with conspiracy to utter counterfeit US bank notes. He claimed that he had been induced to commit the offence by an informer acting on the instructions of the police and that he would not have committed any crime but for the inducement. The House of Lords accepted earlier Court of Appeal authority and held that:

> "It is now well settled that the defence called entrapment does not exist in English law ... A man who intends to commit a crime and actually commits it is guilty of the offence whether or not he has been persuaded or induced to commit it, no matter by whom."[144]

---
[143] [1980] A.C. 402.
[144] [1980] A.C. 402 at 443 per Lord Salmon.

General Defences 305

Of course, even under this view, an entrapment-type situation may be relevant as a mitigating factor when sentence is being passed, a point which was explicitly made in *R. v Sang*.

Modern English approach

The House of Lords substantially altered its attitude towards entrapment in *R. v Looseley; Attorney General's Reference (No. 3 of 2000)*.[145] It held that it was not acceptable that the State, through its agents, should lure its citizens into committing acts forbidden by law and then seek to prosecute them for doing so. Such conduct would be an abuse of process by the courts, while the conduct of the law enforcement agency may be so improper as to bring the administration of justice into disrepute. While entrapment is not a substantive defence, the House of Lords noted that the position had changed somewhat since the *Sang* decision by reason of the enactment of the Police and Criminal Evidence Act 1984. Section 78 of that Act gives a power to exclude prosecution evidence if, considering all the evidence, it is judged that the admission of the evidence would have such an adverse effect on the fairness of the proceedings that the court ought not to admit it. Lord Nicholls set out a useful test in an effort to delineate the boundaries of pro-active policing:

> "[A] useful guide is to consider whether the police did no more than present the defendant with an unexceptional opportunity to commit a crime. I emphasise the word unexceptional. The yardstick for the purpose of this test is, in general, whether the police conduct preceding the commission of the offence was no more than might have been expected from others in the circumstances. Police conduct of this nature is not to be regarded as inciting or instigating crime, or luring a person into committing a crime. The police did no more than others could be expected to do. The police did not create crime artificially."[146]

The House of Lords set out a list of considerations that should be taken into account:

- the nature of the offence,
- the reason for the particular police operation,
- the nature and extent of police participation in the crime, and
- the defendant's criminal record.

United States approach

Other jurisdictions have not taken the same view as is taken in England: for example, in the United States the courts have held that entrapment is a substantive defence which is available to an accused person who can show that he was not predisposed to commit a crime but did so only as a result of the persuasion of agents of the State. This position was adopted in *Shermsan v United States*.[147] In that case the defendant

---

[145] [2001] 1 W.L.R. 2060.
[146] [2001] 1 W.L.R. 2060 at 2069.
[147] 356 U.S. 369 (1958).

was a drug addict who had attended a drug treatment clinic. Another patient of that clinic was an undercover police agent. The agent repeatedly told the defendant that he needed a fix and contrived opportunities to bump into the defendant and ask him to supply him with drugs. The defendant refused on several occasions but eventually agreed to buy heroin for the agent. When he did so he was arrested.

On those facts, the Supreme Court held that a substantive defence of entrapment was open to the defendant. The court indicated that "stealth and strategy" were acceptable parts of police procedure, but only when they were directed towards the prevention and detection of crime: they ceased to be acceptable when they were directed towards the manufacture of crime. Accordingly, the Supreme Court held that the defence was available to a person who had no predisposition to commit the crime alleged but only did so as a result of police persuasion:

> "The function of law enforcement is the prevention of crime and the apprehension of criminals. Manifestly, that function does not include the manufacturing of crime. Criminal activity is such that stealth and strategy are necessary weapons in the arsenal of the police officer. However, a 'different question is presented when the criminal design originates with the officials of the Government, and they implant in the mind of an innocent person the disposition to commit the alleged offence and induce its commission in order that they may prosecute' [*United States v Sorrells* 287 U.S. 435 at 442 (1932)]. Then stealth and strategy become as objectionable police methods as the coerced confession and the unlawful search. Congress could not have intended that its statutes were to be enforced by tempting innocent persons into violations."[148]

The minority were not in favour of a test based on the defendant's character and predisposition and reasoned that a test that looked instead at the conduct of the police was more in keeping with the underlying rationale of the defence of entrapment.

Influence of the European Convention on Human Rights

The decision of the European Court of Human Rights in *Texeira de Castro v Portugal*[149] has determined that the ECHR requires Member States to control the use of *agents provocateurs* and, in particular, requires Member States to limit the use of evidence obtained in such circumstances.

In that case the applicant had been convicted before the national courts of drug trafficking. His name had been supplied to undercover officers by another individual and the officers, accompanied by that individual, went to his house and indicated that they wished to buy a considerable amount of heroin. The applicant agreed to sell it to them and shortly afterwards procured it and brought it to the officers. At this point he was arrested. Before the national court his argument relating to the issue of entrapment was rejected: in particular, the national courts found that the use of *agents provocateurs* was not forbidden under domestic law so long as the use was justified by the seriousness of the offence being investigated.

---

[148] 356 U.S. 369 (1958) at 372 per Warren C.J.
[149] (1998) 28 E.H.R.R. 101.

The applicant submitted that his rights under art.6(1) of the ECHR had been infringed. That article provides that "[i]n the determination of ... any criminal charge against him, everyone is entitled to a fair ... hearing". He submitted that this provision had been infringed in circumstances where, he alleged, he had no previous convictions and would not have committed the offence but for the use of the *agents provocateurs*. In addition, he complained that the activities of the police had been unsupervised by the courts. The respondent made the case that the special circumstances of drug sales, and in particular the secrecy and victimless nature of the crime, made it necessary to use investigative techniques of this kind, which were customary in a number of jurisdictions.

The court took the view that on the facts of this particular case the rights of the applicant under art.6(1) had been infringed as the activities of the undercover agents had prejudiced the fairness of his trial. The activities of the agents had been unsupervised by the courts. No preliminary investigation had been opened and the authorities had no reason to suspect the applicant, who had no criminal record and was at the outset unknown to the police. The drugs which the applicant ultimately supplied were not in his possession but obtained from a third party. The inference which the court drew from these facts was that the applicant was not predisposed to commit such an offence; rather the police officers, instead of investigating in a passive manner, themselves incited the commission of the crime alleged. Accordingly, the court held that:

> "In the light of all these considerations, the Court concludes that the two police officers' actions went beyond those of undercover agents because they instigated the offence and there is nothing to suggest that without their intervention it would have been committed. That intervention and its use in the impugned criminal proceedings meant that, right from the outset, the applicant was definitively deprived of a fair trial. Consequently, there has been a violation of Article 6.1."[150]

Irish approach

For many years the case of *Dental Board v O'Callaghan*[151] was the leading Irish case on entrapment. The Dental Board, a regulatory body, suspected the defendant of practising as a dentist despite being unqualified to do so. To obtain evidence, it sent an inspector to have the defendant carry out work which was reserved for dentists, which he did. An issue arose as to whether, in the circumstances, the evidence obtained by an *agent provocateur* was admissible. Butler J. in the High Court held that it was and approved of English authority to the effect that the methods used by the police in obtaining evidence should not be grounds on which a conviction should be quashed, although the element of entrapment could be taken into account in determining sentence.

However, the case of *Quinlivan v Conroy*[152] suggested that the opposite approach might be taken by the Irish courts. The extradition of the applicant was sought on

---

[150] (1998) 28 E.H.R.R. 101 at para.39.
[151] [1969] I.R. 181.
[152] [1999] 1 I.R. 271.

foot of a number of charges, including charges arising out of an escape from prison. The applicant alleged that this escape was facilitated by a prison officer who was acting as an *agent provocateur* in order to gather evidence on the applicant and his associates. The applicant made the case that, in those circumstances, extradition should not be granted since, under Irish law, no offence would have been committed as a defence of entrapment would be available. Although the Supreme Court did not explicitly rule on this point, it did seem to have some sympathy for the argument that a state which had facilitated the commission of a crime should be debarred from seeking the extradition of a person in relation to that crime. Such an argument would, of course, tend to favour the concept of entrapment as a substantive defence.

The leading case on entrapment in Ireland is now *Syon v Hewitt and McTiernan*[153] which concerned the use of minors by Health Boards to prosecute shop owners for selling cigarettes to underage customers. The Health Boards had arranged for a minor to conduct a test purchase of tobacco products from the defendants' shop. The defendants contended that this amounted to entrapment and that the use of minors in this way was against public policy. Murphy J. held that there was no substantive defence of entrapment in Irish law. Indeed, he commented that there was not even a judicial discretion to exclude evidence obtained by means of test purchases. He went on to say that public policy and the interests of the common good required that children be protected from the danger of smoking and that, in the light of this, the use of minors to conduct test purchases was necessary for the protection of children and not contrary to public policy.

The defendants argued that the operation of the test purchasing scheme had to be authorised by a statute or statutory instrument in order to be permissible. However, the non-statutory protocol under which the test purchases were carried out was examined by the High Court and deemed sufficient. It was held that the protocol ensured that the test purchasing was authorised and included certain safeguards for the protection of children, such as the requirement of parental consent.

Furthermore, Murphy J. found that it was not relevant that the defendants had not been the subject of any prior complaints: random test purchases were permissible and necessary. The court commented that it is unlikely that those involved in consensual crime, such as minors purchasing cigarettes, will report this to the authorities so it did not favour the argument that the Health Boards should target premises with a history of prior offending:

> "In this context not alone is it permissible to carry out random test purchases and to commission independent surveys so as to generate a list of target premises, it is the function of the Office of Tobacco Control to do so."[154]

There are therefore several possible ways of dealing with the entrapment issue. One, exemplified by the US approach, is to allow entrapment as a substantive defence to a criminal charge. Another is to refuse to allow entrapment as a substantive defence but to take it into account as a factor mitigating any punishment which may be imposed. A further possibility is that the courts could take the view that evidence obtained by

---

[153] [2008] 1 I.R. 168.
[154] [2008] 1 I.R. 168 at para.6.12.

General Defences 309

way of entrapment was unfairly obtained and refuse to admit that evidence; or the court could rule that prosecutions founded on entrapment-type situations amount to an abuse of the process of the courts. This latter approach would be similar to that adopted by the Supreme Court in *State (Trimbole) v Governor of Mountjoy Prison*[155] where the court held that the wrongful arrest of a person amounted to a deliberate and conscious breach of his constitutional rights so as to make any subsequent proceedings consequent upon that arrest an abuse of the process of the court. The Canadian position is that proceedings in entrapment-type situations can be stayed as being an abuse of process. It is clear from *Syon v Hewitt* that the Irish courts currently favour an approach that does not allow entrapment as a substantive defence. *Syon* is silent as to whether entrapment could be taken into account for the purposes of mitigation.

AUTOMATISM

Definition

The defence of automatism is available in circumstances where the accused was, at the material time, physically unable to control his actions. Ritchie J. in the Supreme Court of Canada gave the following definition:

> "Automatism is a term used to describe unconscious, involuntary behaviour, the state of a person who, though capable of action, is not conscious of what he is doing. It means an unconscious, involuntary act, where the mind does not go with what is being done."[156]

The Law Reform Commission summarised the defence in its 2009 *Report on Defences*, emphasising that the defence is a negation of actus reus:

> "Automatism occurs where a defendant suffers a complete loss of self-control caused by an external factor such as being hit on the head and then losing all awareness of their actions. Essentially automatism involves more than a claim that the individual lacked *mens rea* (which he or she did); it involves a claim that he or she is not acting – it is a complete denial of the *actus reus*."[157]

Denning L.J. outlined the circumstances in which it can be said an action is involuntary:

> "The requirement that it should be a voluntary act is essential, not only in a murder case, but also in every criminal case. No act is punishable if it is done involuntarily; and an involuntary act in this context – some people nowadays prefer to speak of it as 'automatism' – means an act which is done by the muscles without any control by the mind, such as a spasm, a reflex action or a convulsion;

---

[155] [1985] I.R. 550.
[156] *R. v Rabey* [1980] 2 S.C.R. 513.
[157] Law Reform Commission, *Report on Defences in Criminal Law* (LRC 95–2009).

or an act done by a person who is not conscious of what he is doing, such as an act done whilst suffering from concussion or whilst sleep-walking."[158]

Denning L.J. contrasted automatism with acts which are not to be classed as involuntary just because a person has no memory of doing them. Loss of memory afterwards is never a defence in itself, so long as the person was conscious at the time the act was done. In addition, an act is not involuntary just because a person could not control an impulse to do it, although he pointed out that this scenario could lead to a defence of diminished responsibility being made out. Nor is an act involuntary because it is not foreseen or is unintentional.

Automatism is closely intertwined with the defence of insanity but once the foundations for the defence have been laid it is for the prosecution to disprove the defence, and not for the accused to prove it. Secondly, an acquittal on the ground of automatism is a complete acquittal, unlike an acquittal on the ground of insanity, after which the accused will be held in the Central Mental Hospital until he can demonstrate that he has recovered.

The defence is available only where the accused had no control over his body, as in the case of the sleepwalker, or the driver attacked by a swarm of bees who veers off the road and kills a pedestrian. It is not available in circumstances where the accused had control over his body, but chose to act in a particular way. If a driver sees a swarm of bees ahead, chooses to swerve to avoid them and kills a pedestrian, his defence (if any) would be necessity. Similarly, the defence is not available where the accused had control over his body but that control was lessened due to anger, intoxication, disease of the mind and so forth.

Defence unavailable in cases of voluntary intoxication

Where conduct is involuntary, but results from the self-induced intoxication of the accused, then the accused must rely on the defence of intoxication rather than the defence of automatism.[159] In *R. v Lipman*[160] the defendant was convicted of manslaughter when he killed a woman during hallucinations brought on by LSD. The rule was re-stated in an Irish context in *DPP v Reilly*.[161] The accused was convicted of the manslaughter of his cousin's toddler. He had consumed a large quantity of alcohol, including some poitín, and slept on the living room sofa near the child who was asleep in two armchairs pushed together to make a makeshift cot. He woke up during the night and stabbed the child to death. Evidence was given that he had been in a deep sleep during the stabbing and that even after the child's body was discovered the next morning, the other people in the house had to pour water on him to wake him up. The defence of automatism was raised but the trial judge held that the defence was not open to the accused as the automatism was self induced and caused by voluntary intoxication. The Court of Criminal Appeal held that voluntary intoxication was not a defence to the offence of manslaughter,

---

[158] *Bratty v AG (Northern Ireland)* [1963] A.C. 386 at 409.
[159] See Dillon, "Intoxicated Automatism is no Defence: Majewski is Law in Ireland (2004) 14(3) I.C.L.J. 7.
[160] [1970] 1 Q.B. 152.
[161] [2005] 3 I.R. 111.

General Defences

even where the intoxication had resulted in a state of automatism. An accused who voluntarily consumes alcohol will be held responsible for his actions by the law. Intoxication was a defence to offences requiring specific intent but not to offences, such as manslaughter, requiring only basic intent.[162]

External factors versus internal factors

In addition it seems that the defence is available only when the automatism is a transient state caused by some external factor and is not available where the automatism is caused by a factor internal to the accused. It appears that in cases of an internal factor the courts take the view that the possibility of recurrence of violence justifies the accused being detained rather than completely acquitted. In *Bratty v Attorney General for Northern Ireland*,[163] Lord Denning remarked that any mental disorder which has manifested itself in violence and is prone to recur, is a disease of the mind:

> "Suppose a crime is committed by a man in a state of automatism or clouded consciousness due to a recurrent disease of the mind. Such an act is no doubt involuntary, but it does not give rise to an unqualified acquittal, for that would mean that he would be let at large to do it again. The only proper verdict is one which ensures that the person who suffers from the disease is kept secure in a hospital so as not to be a danger to himself or others. That is, a verdict of guilty but insane."[164]

This appears to be a distinction based purely on policy and a concern for the common good rather than any inherent logic.

In *Bratty*, the accused strangled an 18-year-old girl. He stated that at the time he had "a terrible feeling" and that "a sort of blackness" came over him but he was able to give some account of what had happened. The defences of automatism due to psychomotor epilepsy and insanity were run at trial and the trial judge left the defence of insanity to the jury but refused to so leave the defence of automatism. On appeal, the House of Lords held that the trial judge had been correct. The court drew a distinction between insane and non-insane automatism and held that where the cause alleged for the unconscious act was a disease of the mind (such as psychomotor epilepsy) then the only verdict which could be returned by the jury was one of insane automatism: in other words, the automatism would be characterised as a species of insanity and dealt with by way of the defence of insanity and not the defence of automatism. It was also held that the onus of proving voluntariness in cases of automatism is on the prosecution, once the foundations are laid by the defendant, and that the prosecution must prove voluntariness beyond a reasonable doubt.

This can also be seen in *R. v Rabey*.[165] In that case the defendant was a student who was smitten with another student. The day before the attack, he found a letter

---

[162] See the defence of intoxication for a discussion of the distinction between offences of basic and of specific intent.
[163] [1963] A.C. 386.
[164] [1963] A.C. 386 at 410.
[165] [1980] 2 S.C.R. 513.

she had written complaining about him and expressing an interest in someone else. On the day of the attack he took a rock from the geology laboratory, met the victim (by chance, it seemed), struck her with the rock and attempted to choke her. The defence of automatism was successfully pleaded at trial, on the basis that the accused was in a completely dissociative state. However, on appeal it was held that this defence could not be sustained; any malfunctioning of the mind or mental disorder which had its source primarily in some matter internal to the defendant is a disease of the mind within the meaning of the defence of insanity and cannot form the basis of the defence of automatism:

> "In general, the distinction to be drawn is between a malfunctioning of the mind arising from some cause that is primarily internal to the accused, having its source in his psychological or emotional make-up, or in some organic pathology, as opposed to a malfunctioning of the mind which is the transient effect produced by some specific external factor such as, for example, concussion."[166]

This principle has also been applied in the case of sleepwalking. In *R. v Burgess*,[167] the defendant was watching videos with a neighbour. When she fell asleep he hit her over the head with a bottle and the video recorder and then grabbed her by the throat. When she screamed he "came round", appeared to be concerned and called an ambulance for her. He was charged with wounding with intent, to which his defence was that he was sleepwalking at the time. At trial this was found to amount to a defence of insanity and the defendant was ordered to be detained in a secure hospital. On appeal, the defendant contended that the defence was in fact one of automatism. The Court of Appeal held that the automatism could not be said to be due to an external factor such as a blow to the head; it was caused by an internal factor:

> "The possible disappointment or frustration caused by unrequited love is not to be equated with something such as concussion."[168]

The automatism was also likely to recur, though recurrence in the form of serious violence was unlikely. It followed as a matter of law that, although the automatism was far removed from insanity in a colloquial or psychiatric sense, it amounted to a defence of insanity in legal terms:

> "[T]his was an abnormality or disorder, albeit transitory, due to an internal factor, whether functional or organic, which had manifested itself in violence. It was a disorder or abnormality which might recur, though the possibility of it recurring in the form of serious violence was unlikely. Therefore, since this was a legal problem to be decided on legal principles, it seems to us on those principles the answer was as the judge found it to be."[169]

---

[166] (1980) 2 S.C.R. 513 at 519.
[167] [1991] 2 W.L.R. 1206.
[168] [1991] 2 W.L.R. 1206 at 1210 per Lord Lane C.J.
[169] [1991] 2 W.L.R. 1206 at 1214.

General Defences

This apparently logical distinction, between internal and external factors, breaks down in the case of defendants who suffer from diabetes and who commit crimes while suffering either from high or low blood sugar levels (hyperglycaemia and hypoglycaemia respectively). Are states of automatism resulting from such conditions to be treated as resulting from internal factors (the diabetes) or external factors (failure to take insulin)? In *R. v Quick*[170] the defendant's automatism resulting from hypoglycaemia was held to result from an external factor (self-administered insulin injections without eating regular meals or eating a lump of sugar). In *R. v Hennessy*,[171] however, the defendant's automatism resulting from hyperglycaemia due to his failure to take insulin was held to result from an internal factor (the underlying disease of diabetes). *R. v Quick* was distinguished on the ground that the hypoglycaemia resulted from injections of insulin, not from the underlying diabetes. This is, however, a distinction without a difference.

R. v Hennessy raised the issue of whether automatism resulting from stress and similar situations was to be treated as resulting from internal or external factors. The defendant was arrested in the process of driving a stolen car. One aspect of his defence has already been dealt with: that he was suffering from hyperglycaemia. Another aspect of the defence was that automatism could also have been triggered by his depression and by his marital and employment problems. This aspect of the defence was also rejected by the Court of Appeal. If automatism had been triggered by these factors, then it would still have been caused by internal factors so as to make the defence of insanity applicable:

> "In our judgment, stress, anxiety and depression can no doubt be the result of the operation of external factors, but they are not, it seems to us, in themselves separately or together external factors of the kind capable in law of causing or contributing to a state of automatism. They constitute a state of mind which is prone to recur. They lack the feature of novelty or accident ..."[172]

Self-induced automatism

It is not necessarily fatal to the defence that the automatism was self induced. If, for example, a diabetic fails to eat following an insulin injection and, as a result, commits a crime while in a hypoglycaemic state, then the defence of automatism can be pleaded unless it can be proved that in failing to eat he acted sufficiently recklessly. In *R. v Bailey*,[173] the accused suffered from diabetes. His girlfriend left him and he subsequently attacked the man for whom she had left him, having shortly before drank a sugar and water solution. His defence was that the resulting hypoglycaemia, owing to his failure to take food after drinking the solution, had produced a state of automatism. The trial judge directed the jury not to consider this defence since the state was self induced. On appeal, this direction was held to be incorrect: self-induced automatism (other than by intoxication) could provide a defence, unless the

---

[170] [1973] 3 All E.R. 347.
[171] [1989] 2 All E.R. 9.
[172] [1989] 2 All E.R. 9 at 14 per Lord Lane C.J.
[173] [1983] 3 All E.R. 503.

conduct of the defendant in inducing automatism had been sufficiently reckless to establish the mens rea for the offence.

Loss of control must be total

The loss of control must be total for the defence of automatism to succeed. In *Bratty*, Lord Denning confined the defence to acts done while unconscious and to spasms, reflex actions and convulsions. In *Broome v Perkins*,[174] the defence was unavailable to a defendant who was suffering from hypoglycaemia as he was able to exercise control from time to time.

The matter was also considered in the context of civil proceedings in *O'Brien v Parker*.[175] Here the plaintiff sued in respect of personal injuries suffered in a road traffic accident. The defendant claimed that at the time of the accident he was suffering an epileptic fit by reason of temporal lobe epilepsy, so that he could not have been said to be negligent. The defendant had no history of epilepsy, but claimed that he had, immediately before the accident, experienced heightened sensitivity to light and smells and an "altered state of consciousness" and that the next thing he remembered was the accident itself. Lavan J. in the High Court held that automatism could amount to a defence in a civil context to a claim based on negligence. However, for that to be the case, it would have to be shown that there was:

> "[A] total destruction of voluntary control on the defendant's part. Impaired, reduced or partial control is not sufficient to maintain the defence."[176]

In this case, therefore, the defendant had not made out the defence since he had testified that he was capable of making the decision to continue driving, notwithstanding that his ability to make such a decision was impaired.

If the accused's inhibitions are lowered by the external factor, but he does not have a complete loss of control, then he cannot benefit from the defence of automatism. The classic example of this is *R. v Kingston*,[177] where the accused's drink was spiked by people who wished to blackmail him. He was known to have paedophiliac tendencies and the blackmailers photographed him abusing a 15-year-old-boy who was also drugged. The accused claimed that he would not have abused the boy but for the fact that his defences had been lowered by the drug but the House of Lords refused to allow him to claim automatism. Lord Mustill commented that:

> "In ordinary circumstances the repondent's paedophiliac tendencies would have been kept under control, even in the presence of a sleeping or unconscious boy on the bed. The ingestion of the drug (whatever it was) brought about a temporary change in the mentality or personality of the respondent which lowered his ability to resist temptation so far as his desires overrode his ability

---

[174] [1987] Crim. L.R. 271.
[175] [1997] 2 I.L.R.M. 170.
[176] [1997] 2 I.L.R.M. 170 at 176.
[177] [1995] 2 A.C. 355.

to control them. Thus we are concerned here with a case of disinhibition. The drug is not alleged to have created the desire to which the respondent gave way, but rather to have enabled it to be released."[178]

INSANITY

The Criminal Law (Insanity) Act 2006 sets out the defence of insanity in Irish law. Up until this legislation came into force the area was common law-based. Although the 2006 Act reformulated and expanded insanity, the pre-2006 case law is still highly relevant and must be examined in some detail.

Insanity under Irish law pre-2006

The defence of insanity is distinct from the defence of automatism. It does not apply where the defendant's body is acting without conscious control but instead applies where the defendant is conscious of his actions but his mental state is in some way impaired.

Burden and standard of proof

The burden of proving insanity lies on the accused, contrary to the normal rule that the prosecution bear the responsibility of disproving any defence raised.[179] The accused must prove his insanity, but only on the balance of probabilities, not beyond a reasonable doubt.

The M'Naghten *Rules*

Griffin J. in *Doyle v Wicklow County Council* eloquently summarised the ancient law relating to insanity:

> "Whilst insanity has always exempted from criminal responsibility a person doing an act which would otherwise be a crime, the approach of the courts and writers to the question of insanity has become less rigid with the passage of time, as might be expected. In the time of Coke, insanity did not provide a defence to a criminal charge unless the insanity alleged was of such a nature that the accused resembled a beast rather than a man ... This somewhat extreme approach to the insane persisted into the 18th century at which time the view regularly accepted by the courts was that no mentally disturbed person should be excepted from criminal responsibility unless he 'is totally deprived of his understanding and memory, and doth not know what he is doing, no more than an infant, than a brute, or a wild beast.'"[180]

---

[178] [1995] 2 A.C. 355 at 364.
[179] *DPP v O'Mahony* [1985] I.R. 517.
[180] [1974] 1 I.R. 55 at 66.

The modern law on insanity dates from the mid-nineteenth century and is set out in the *M'Naghten* Rules. The Rules[181] were formulated in 1843 in response to the *M'Naghten* case, in which the defendant shot Edward Drummond, the private secretary to the Prime Minister, Sir Robert Peel, mistaking him for the Prime Minister. His defence was that he believed himself to be persecuted by the Tory party and that consequently his life was in danger. The verdict reached in his case, not guilty by reason of insanity, produced public disquiet, leading the House of Lords to summon the judges before it to answer a series of questions on the law of insanity.

To fall within the *M'Naghten* Rules the following elements are necessary:

The accused must establish that he suffered from a *defect of reason from disease of the mind*. Disease of the mind does not mean mental illness or brain damage but includes, as we saw in the section dealing with the offence of automatism, conditions resulting from diabetes, epilepsy and so on. In *R. v Kemp*,[182] a defendant was found to be suffering from a disease of the mind where he made a senseless attack on his wife with a hammer, which was triggered by arteriosclerosis causing blood congestion in the brain. He argued that this should be treated as automatism rather than falling within the *M'Naghten* Rules, as the condition had not lead to any degeneration of the brain but merely cut off the blood supply in the same way as concussion might. However, this argument was rejected, notwithstanding that this was a transitory and curable physical interference with the workings of the brain. Similarly, in *Ellis v DPP*[183] the defendant was charged with the murder of a man who, he alleged, was blackmailing him. He relied on the defence of automatism, on the basis that he was in an epileptic state at the time of the killing. The trial judge refused to leave the issue of automatism to the jury but did leave the issue of insanity and the accused was found not guilty by reason of insanity.

To fall within the *M'Naghten* Rules there must have been a *causal link* between the defect of reason and the act. If a person believes that the Vatican is bugging his/her phone and goes shoplifting, then there is clearly no such causal link. It is not enough that the defect of reason and the crime should coincide in point of time; there must also be a causal relationship between the two.

Where the defect of reason takes the form of an *insane delusion* then the delusion, if it relates to existing facts, must be one which would mean that the act committed was not a crime. If I shoot a person, believing him to be a tree, then the act would not be a crime if the delusion were true. However, if I shoot a person, believing him to be Barack Obama, then this act would be a crime even if the delusion were true and the defence will not apply.

The accused must establish that he *did not know the nature and quality of his act, or that he did so know but did not know that the act was wrongful*. The nature and quality of the act refers to its physical nature only, not its moral nature.[184] Not understanding the nature and quality of an act would encompass situations of shooting a person thinking he was a tree. A defendant knows that an act is wrongful if he knows it is illegal or, notwithstanding that he does not know it is illegal, he knows it is an act which he ought not to do. It is irrelevant that the defendant thinks

---

[181] [1843] 4 St. Tr. (N.S) 817.
[182] [1957] 1 Q.B. 399.
[183] [1990] 2 I.R. 291.
[184] *R. v Codère* (1916) 12 Cr. App. R. 21.

General Defences 317

a particular act is morally right if he knows it is legally wrong. In *R. v Windle*,[185] the defendant, who was mentally ill, believed he was acting in a moral way by killing his wife by poisoning her, supposing that he was putting her out of her unhappiness. He knew that what he was doing was legally wrong—on arrest he remarked "I suppose they will hang me for this"—but believed, due to his mental illness, that it was morally right. However, it was held that the defence of insanity could not, on those facts, be put before the jury: once the defendant knew that what he was doing was illegal, then he could not avail of the *M'Naghten* Rules and there was no wider defence of insanity open to him.

So to come within the *M'Naghten* Rules, a defendant must show that at the time the offence was committed:

1. he or she was suffering from a defect of reason,
2. arising from a disease of the mind,
3. such that he or she did not know the nature and quality of his or her actions,
4. or, if he or she did know, that he or she did not know that they were wrong, i.e. contrary to law.

Extending insanity beyond M'Naghten

In England, it has been said that the defence of insanity is exclusively encapsulated in the *M'Naghten* Rules. Where a defendant does not bring himself within those rules then a defence of insanity cannot succeed. However, the Irish position pre-2006 was entirely different to the English understanding of insanity, in that it was considered that the *M'Naghten* Rules were not the beginning and the end of the insanity defence. They were considered to be one component of the insanity defence, although they did form the primary test. This was set out by the Supreme Court in *Doyle v Wicklow County Council*[186] where Griffin J. stated that:

> "In my opinion, the M'Naghten Rules do not provide the sole and exclusive test for determining the sanity or insanity of the accused. The questions put to the judges were limited to the effect of insane delusions and I would agree with the opinion expressed by the Court of Criminal Appeal in *Attorney General v O'Brien*[187] that the opinions given by the judges must be read with the same specific limitation."

The *M'Naghten* Rules were quite restrictive and, in particular, did not allow any scope for the defence of volitional insanity. This is a particular form of mental defect covering situations where an accused knows that conduct is wrong (and therefore falls outside the parameters of the *M'Naghten* Rules) but nevertheless has a diminished capacity to act or refrain from acting based on that knowledge. An example of such a situation would be the case where a person claimed to have had an irresistible impulse to commit a specific crime. The defence of irresistible impulse was never accepted under the *M'Naghten* Rules; indeed as one judge stated:

---

[185] [1952] 2 All E.R. 1.
[186] [1974] 1 I.R. 55.
[187] [1936] I.R. 263.

"If you cannot resist an impulse in any other way, we will hang a rope in front of your eyes and perhaps that will help."[188]

However, the Irish defence of insanity did encompass a defence of irresistible impulse which was available to certain defendants who could not bring themselves within the narrow *M'Naghten* Rules. Irresistible impulse was not regarded as a separate defence to insanity but described behaviour that was characterised as insanity under Irish law.

In the 1936 case of *AG v O'Brien* the defendant sought to raise the defence of irresistible impulse but the trial judge refused to leave the defence to the jury on the ground that it was unknown to the law. On appeal, the Court of Criminal Appeal held that the facts of the case were not sufficient to justify leaving the defence to the jury. The defendant had never suggested that he was labouring under or driven by an impulse of any kind and such a contention would have been quite inconsistent with his denial of all knowledge of the events in which he acted, as he had alleged, an unconscious part. The court went on to hold, however, that the *M'Naghten* Rules were not intended to be exclusive and left open for later the decision whether Irish law recognised the defence of irresistible impulse.

Later cases saw trial judges adopt a wider test of insanity which included irresistible impulse. Particularly significant was the case of *Attorney General v Hayes*[189] in which the defendant was charged with murdering his wife. He had, over a long period, built up an irrational sense of grievance against his wife and sought redress for imaginary complaints by killing her, as he claimed, to clear the name of their children. Although this defence would probably not have fallen within the scope of the *M'Naghten* Rules, Henchy J. directed the jury in terms that were wider than the *M'Naghten* Rules, saying that "if the jury was satisfied that at the time of the attack the accused's mind was so affected by illness that he was unable to restrain himself, a verdict of guilty but insane should be returned". Further, Henchy J. gave a detailed judgment regarding the scope of the defence, stating that:

> "The [*M'Naghten*] rules do not take into account the capacity of a man on the basis of his knowledge to act or to refrain from acting and I believe it to be correct psychiatric science to accept that certain serious mental diseases, such as paranoia or schizophrenia, in certain cases enable a man to understand the morality or immorality of his act or the legality or illegality of it, or the nature and quality of it, but nevertheless prevent him from exercising a free volition as to whether he should or should not do that act."[190]

This approach was then affirmed by the Supreme Court in *Doyle v Wicklow County Council*[191] which was a claim for compensation brought by the owner of an abattoir burnt down by an 18-year-old. The claim would succeed only if what had been done was a crime, which made it necessary to consider the defence of insanity. The facts

---

[188] *R. v Creighton* (1908) 14 Can. Crim. Cas. 349 at 350 per Riddell J.
[189] Unreported, Central Criminal Court, November 30, 1967.
[190] Unreported, Central Criminal Court, November 30, 1967. See *Doyle v Wicklow County Council* [1973] IESC 1 at para.14.
[191] [1973] IESC 1; [1974] I.R. 55.

General Defences

showed that the youth was suffering from some sort of mental disorder which led him to believe that setting fire to the abattoir was a justifiable and moral act based on his love of animals. He knew, however, that the act was a criminal one. Griffin J. adopted what had been said by Henchy J. in *Attorney General v Hayes* as being a correct statement of the law and held that the defence of volitional insanity would have been open to the youth.[192] Griffin J. acknowledged that it was unusual that a criminal law concept was being decided in the context of a civil case:

> "[A]nswering of a question in a Case Stated which arises in the course of a claim for compensation for criminal injury is not the most appropriate circumstance in which to consider the application of rules which have been widely applied in criminal trials for upwards of 130 years."[193]

The decision in *DPP v Courtney*[194] provides an example of the defence of irresistible impulse, albeit an unsuccessful example. In that case the accused was charged with murder. He had been a passenger in a car driven by the deceased, who had picked him up while looking for directions. He said that she had taunted him, at which he "blew a fuse and went mad", punching her several times and driving the car into the mountains. When she regained consciousness he hit her with a rock and killed her. He took her clothes off her body, then drove back into the city and abandoned the car.

The defence was that the accused had acted in panic, without any control of himself, and the accused tendered psychiatric evidence to the effect that he was suffering from post-traumatic stress disorder stemming from his tours of duty as a soldier in Lebanon. Based on this evidence, the trial judge left two questions to the jury: was the accused acting under the influence of an irresistible impulse caused by a defect of reason due to mental illness, which debarred him from refraining from killing the victim; and had it been proved beyond a reasonable doubt that the accused intended to kill or cause serious harm to the victim. The trial judge went on to direct the jury that, depending on their answers to these questions, they could find the accused to be: guilty of murder; not guilty by reason of insanity; or guilty of manslaughter (if it had not been proved beyond a reasonable doubt that the accused intended to kill or cause serious injury). The jury found the accused to be guilty of murder. On appeal, the Court of Criminal Appeal upheld the conviction of the applicant. It approved the reference by Henchy J. in *Hayes* to irresistible impulse as being a correct statement of the law:

> "This is a limited form of insanity recognised by our law, commonly called irresistible impulse. This means in this case an irresistible impulse caused by a defect of reason due to mental illness. Merely because an impulse is not in fact resisted does not mean that it is an irresistible impulse. If so, no one could ever be convicted of a crime – they would only have to say, I found the impulse

---

[192] On the facts, however, Griffin J. stated that he did not think that a case for absolving the youth due to legal insanity had been made out, but he conceded that this was something that would have to be determined by the Circuit Court (Griffin J.'s judgment being the answer to a case stated rather than a determination of the ultimate issue).
[193] [1973] IESC 1 at para.7.
[194] Unreported, Court of Criminal Appeal, July 21, 1994.

irresistible. It must be an irresistible impulse, not an unresisted impulse, to constitute that form of insanity. Diminished self-control or weakened resistence to impulse is not necessarily the same as irresistible impulse."[195]

Pre-2006, did Irish law recognise a defence of diminished responsibility?

A defence of diminished responsibility was introduced into English law by s.2 of the Homicide Act 1957. The defence is confined to cases of murder and reduces the charge to one of manslaughter. For the defence of diminished responsibility to be made out, the defendant must have been labouring under mental impairment such that his ability to control his actions and make decisions is defective. This does not necessarily mean that he acted with an irresistible impulse.[196] The impulse might well have been easily resisted but the defendant lacked the insight into his actions to do so.

As we shall see, the defence has now been introduced into Irish law by the 2006 Act but there was some suggestion before that that diminished responsibility might form part of Irish law. The defence of diminished responsibility was not discussed in any great detail in Irish cases but the obiter comments of Finlay C.J. in *DPP v O'Mahony*[197] are interesting. In that case the defendant appealed his conviction for murder on the grounds that the defence of diminished responsibility existed at common law and should have been left to the jury. The Supreme Court rejected the argument that diminished responsibility was part of Irish law, but Finlay C.J. noted that:

> "Having regard to the definition of insanity laid down by this Court in *Doyle v Wicklow County Council* ... it is quite clear that the appellant in *R. v Byrne* ... a sexual psychopath who suffered from violent perverted sexual desires which he found difficult or impossible to control [but did not suffer any other mental illness] if tried in accordance with the law of this country on the same facts, would have been properly found to be not guilty by reason of insanity."[198]

It appears from this quote that a person might have been able to rely on insanity even in circumstances where he might have had *some* control over his actions ("which he found difficult ... to control"), provided his capacity to exercise control was significantly reduced by mental illness. This might also have encompassed situations where, for example, the accused's ability to make decisions was significantly impaired, as in the case of a father who believes that he and his family would be better off dead and therefore kills the other members of his family. In these circumstances it is not the defendant's control over his actions which is in issue, but rather his ability to make decisions concerning his actions.

---

[195] Unreported, Court of Criminal Appeal, July 21, 1994 at 48 per O'Flaherty J.
[196] Irresistible impulse is considered a form of diminished responsibility in English law.
[197] [1985] I.R. 517.
[198] [1985] I.R. 517 at 522.

Reform of defence of insanity

In 1978 the Henchy Report[199] recommended reform of the defence of insanity, to include the power of the court to order immediate release where the insane person was not dangerous. The establishment of an independent review body was recommended to annually review all detentions on foot of an insanity verdict and to monitor conditions of detention generally.

The Criminal Justice (Mental Disorder) Bill 1996, introduced as a private member's Bill by John O'Donoghue T.D., recommended a new defence of diminished responsibility. This failed to be enacted but was followed a number of years later by the Criminal Law (Insanity) Bill 2002 which was finally enacted as the Criminal Law (Insanity) Act 2006.[200]

The Act defines "mental disorder" as including mental illness, mental disability, dementia or any disease of the mind but does not include intoxication.[201] It sets out three ways in which suffering from a mental disorder can impact upon a defendant: is the defendant fit to be tried?; can he benefit from the defence of insanity?; and can he benefit from the defence of diminished responsibility?

It was considered particularly important to put insanity on a statutory basis because of the necessity of complying with the ECHR, art.5(1)(e) of which allows for the detention of persons of unsound mind. In *Winterwerp v The Netherlands*,[202] the European Court of Human Rights emphasised that the determination that a person is of unsound mind should be: (1) made on objective medical evidence; (2) that the detention should be deemed necessary; and (3) that the detention should be under continuous review. The law on insanity prior to 2006 arguably breached each of the three principles: (1) the legal concept of insanity was not the same as the medical concept and conditions such as epilepsy and diabetes could amount to legal insanity; (2) once a person was found guilty but insane there was no discretion not to detain him pursuant to the Trial of Lunatics Act 1883; and (3) there was no system of automatic or independent review of detention—the onus was on the patient to apply for release to the government and the decision to release was one for the executive to make.

Section 4 of the Criminal Law (Insanity) Act 2006: fitness to be tried

The Act provides for a new procedure to determine fitness to be tried.[203] This was previously referred to as "fitness to plead". This concept is distinct from insanity per se and relates not to whether a defendant understood what he was doing at the time of the crime but to whether the defendant is capable of understanding the proceedings

---

[199] Third Interim Report of the Interdepartmental Committee on Mentally Ill and Maladjusted Persons, *Treatment and Care of Persons Suffering from Mental Disorder who Appeal Before the Courts on Criminal Charges* (1978).
[200] There has been criticism of the title of the Act because the term "insanity" was chosen over more modern and less stigmatising terms such as mental disorder or mental health.
[201] Section 1.
[202] (1979) 2 E.H.R.R. 387.
[203] For a detailed discussion of fitness to the tried in the District Court, see Darius Whelan, "Fitness for Trial in the District Court: The Legal Perspective" (2007) 2 *Judicial Studies Institute Journal* 124.

at his trial. The law takes the view that it is unjust to try a person who is incapable of understanding the trial and therefore incapable of adequately defending himself and for that reason a person who is unfit to be tried will be detained in the same way as a person found not guilty by reason of insanity.

It is important to note that unfitness to be tried is entirely distinct from insanity at the time of the alleged offence. The criminal who is insane at the time of the offence may have recovered to the point where he is capable of understanding his trial and the criminal who is entirely sane at the time of the offence may, pending trial, suffer some injury or illness which leaves him incapable of standing trial.

The pre-2006 test of fitness to plead was set out in *R. v Robertson*[204] and looked to whether the accused was able to: understand the charges against him; understand the nature and effect of a plea of guilty or not guilty; challenge a member of the jury to whom he might object; instruct counsel; and understand the evidence which is given. It the accused was unable to do one or more of these things, then he would be found unfit to plead. The decision as to whether a person was unfit to plead was made by a jury.

Section 4 is broadly similar to the common law tests for fitness to plead and provides that an accused person shall be deemed unfit to be tried if he or she is unable by reason of mental disorder to understand the nature or course of the proceedings so as to:

(a) plead to the charge,
(b) instruct a legal representative,
(c) in the case of an indictable offence which may be tried summarily, elect for a trial by jury,
(d) in the case of a trial by jury, challenge a juror to whom he or she might wish to object, or
(e) understand the evidence.

However, the issue of whether an accused is fit to be tried shall be determined by the court rather than by a jury. The court can, having considered the evidence, decide that the accused requires in-patient or out-patient care and commit him or her to a specified designated centre.[205] It can also, having found a person unfit to be tried, allow evidence to be adduced as to whether or not the accused did the act alleged and, if there is reasonable doubt as to this, it can order that the accused be discharged.[206]

---

[204] [1968] 3 All E.R. 557.

[205] Section 3 states that the Central Mental Hospital is a designated centre but states that the Minister may also designate other psychiatric centres as designated centres by ministerial order. To date the only designated centre is the Central Mental Hospital and this has been criticised as creating difficulties for patients who are from outside Dublin and would receive better in-patient or out-patient care nearer to their communities.

[206] Section 4(8). The procedure for determining fitness for trial in relation to a person who had several years previously been found unfit to be tried on the same charges was at issue in *O'Callaghan v DPP* [2011] IESC 30. Here the Supreme Court granted an order prohibiting the trial of an accused where the prosecution had merely entered a nolle prosequi to the original proceedings and re-charged him with the same offences again in order to find him fit to be tried. Hardiman J. pointed out that the correct procedure would have been for the prosecution to re-enter the case for the purpose of hearing evidence on the fitness issue and the judge, had he thought fit, could have decided that the accused was then fit to be tried and continued with

General Defences 323

Section 5: verdict of not guilty by reason of insanity

This section provides for a verdict of not guilty by reason of insanity, if:

> (a) the accused person was suffering at the time from a mental disorder, and
> (b) the mental disorder was such that the accused person ought not to be held responsible for the act alleged by reason of the fact that he or she—
>   (i) did not know the nature and quality of the act, or
>   (ii) did not know that what he or she was doing was wrong, or
>   (iii) was unable to refrain from committing the act.

The scope of the insanity defence is substantially the same as that covered by the *M'Naghten* Rules (although it does not preserve the archaic term "defect of reason") plus behaviour regarded as amounting to an irresistible impulse. Section 5(1)(b)(iii), in effect, puts *Doyle v Wicklow County Council* on a statutory footing. The burden and standard of proof is not enunciated but in the absence of any change it would appear that the common law position remains.

The special verdict is now one of acquittal (not guilty by reason of insanity). Prior to 2006 it was a verdict of guilty but insane pursuant to the Trial of Lunatics Act 1883.

Section 6: diminished responsibility

Section 6 introduces the defence of diminished responsibility to Irish law. It is a partial defence applicable only to murder and operating to reduce murder to manslaughter.[207] It provides that:

> (1) Where a person is tried for murder and the jury or, as the case may be, the Special Criminal Court finds that the person—
>   (a) did the act alleged,
>   (b) was at the time suffering from a mental disorder, and
>   (c) the mental disorder was not such as to justify finding him or her not guilty by reason of insanity, but was such as to diminish substantially his or her responsibility for the act,

---

the proceedings. The prosecution was of the view that the previous judicial finding of unfitness to be tried did not apply to the new charges. However, the Supreme Court held that this attitude ignored the fact that the previous finding of unfitness was a judicial one and constituted an administration of justice by that judge. Hardiman J. held, at p.24 of the unreported decision, that "[i]n my view, the proposition that that determination can be set aside or rendered nugatory by the entry of a *nolle prosequi* and the subsequent preferring of identical charges, pays insufficient respect to the judicial determination thereby deprived of effect." See the recent High Court case of *EC v Clinical Director of the Central Mental Hospital* [2012] IEHC 152 where Hogan J. held that the applicant's detention was not in accordance with law because the District Court judge had not followed the correct procedure as set out in s.4 of the 2006 Act for determining the question of unfitness for trial. The judge had determined, upon reading psychiatric reports, that the accused was unfit for trial but had then neglected to remand him to the Central Mental Hospital in order to receive fresh evidence as to whether the accused needed in-patient care.

[207] See Ch.10 for a discussion of defences only applicable to murder.

the jury or the court, as the case shall be, shall find the person not guilty of that offence but guilty of manslaughter on the ground of diminished responsibility.[208]

Section 6(2) places the burden of proving that an accused should benefit from diminished responsibility on the defence. The Act is silent on the standard of proof, so it would appear that the common law position of proof on the balance of probabilities for the defence of insanity is required.

The Court of Criminal Appeal addressed sentencing for diminished responsibility in *DPP v Leigh Crowe*,[209] where the applicant pleaded guilty to manslaughter by reason of diminished responsibility. The applicant's accomplice shot the deceased at point blank range. The trial judge noted the seriousness of the crime and imposed a life sentence and the applicant appealed against the severity of the sentence. The Court of Criminal Appeal quashed the life sentence and substituted a sentence of 20 years' imprisonment. It held that it was implicit in the acceptance of a plea to manslaughter by reason of diminished responsibility that an accused should not be sentenced as if he were fully responsible for his actions and the applicant was entitled to a sentence falling short of the sentence of life imprisonment which, had there not been diminished responsibility, would have been appropriate due to the very serious facts.

Procedural aspects

As we have noted, prior to 2006 all those benefitting from the insanity defence were detained. This was so even where the disorder which constituted insanity in law was not such a disorder as would make it appropriate for a person to be detained. For example, if a person suffering from diabetic hyperglycaemia was found to be suffering from a disease of the mind within the meaning of the defence of insanity, then it was possible that such a person would be detained in the Central Mental Hospital notwithstanding the fact that he had been found to be innocent of the crime charged and notwithstanding the fact that he posed no danger to himself or anyone else. However, the position post-2006 is more flexible. Section 5(2) provides that the person is only committed to a specified designated centre provided that the court is satisfied, having considered any report submitted to it and such other evidence as may be adduced, that the accused person is suffering from a mental disorder within the meaning of the Mental Health Act 2001[210] and is in need of in-patient care or treatment. Presumably, the vast bulk of people with diabetes or epilepsy will not be in need of in-patient care or treatment. The Act provides that a person found unfit to be tried can be deemed in need of in-patient or out-patient care, but the latter option seems not to be open to a person found to be insane.[211]

---

[208] Section 6(3) provides that a woman found guilty of infanticide may benefit from the defence of diminished responsibility. See Ch.4 for a full discussion of infanticide.
[209] [2010] 1 I.R. 129.
[210] The 2001 Act governs civil law aspects of voluntary and involuntary detention in psychiatric institutions. The definition of "mental disorder" in the 2001 Act is narrower than that in the 2006 Act and is confined to psychiatric disorders necessitating treatment.
[211] See the article by McGillicuddy commenting on this and giving an overview of the 2006 Act: Tony McGillicuddy, "The Criminal Law (Insanity) Act 2006" (2006) 11 *Bar Review* 95.

General Defences 325

The decision as to whether a person found to be insane had recovered was one for the executive prior to 2006. This was held by *DPP v Gallagher*[212] which departed from previous case law which had held that the decision to release such a person was a judicial act forming part of the administration of justice. Instead, the role of the court was said to be to order the detention of a person "until the executive, armed with both the knowledge and the resources to deal with the problem, decides on the future disposition of the person".[213] However, the case made it clear that the executive, in deciding whether a person should be kept in custody, was obliged to consider only whether he was suffering from any mental disorder warranting his continued detention in the public and private interests and was obliged to do so in accordance with fair and constitutional procedures. The decision of the executive was subject to judicial review if necessary. However, the 2006 Act set up the independent Mental Health (Criminal Law) Review Board to govern detention of those found not guilty by reason of insanity. Section 13 requires that the Review Board review the detention of a patient at least every six months. The Review Board can order continued detention, order an unconditional discharge, order a temporary release or order a conditional discharge. The latter power was not used for a number of years as there was no method of enforcing the compliance with conditions.[214] However, the Criminal Law (Insanity) Act 2010 addressed that lacuna and enforcement is now carried out by the Gardaí who can arrest and return a person who breaches a condition to the designated centre.[215]

Although it is widely acknowledged that the 2006 Act has greatly improved the position for those found to be criminally insane, criticisms of the regime remain. Recently, Sheehan J. compared the 2006 Act regime to the protections given to those deemed in need of civil voluntary or involuntary detention pursuant to the Mental Health Act 2001. He remarked in *DPP v B*[216] that:

> "This Court notes that there is a huge discrepancy in the protection afforded to patients detained pursuant to the Criminal Law (Insanity) Act 2006 and those admitted to the Central Mental Hospital pursuant to the Mental Health Act 2001. The purpose of both Acts must be such as to strive for the treatment or care of mentally ill persons in our society whether they are being detained in, or admitted to, the Central Mental Hospital. Yet, persons detained pursuant to the Criminal Law (Insanity) Act 2006 are not granted the same protections as those patients admitted to the Central Mental Hospital pursuant to the Mental

---

[212] [1991] I.L.R.M. 339.
[213] [1991] I.L.R.M. 339 at 344 per McCarthy J.
[214] See *JB v Mental Health (Criminal Law) Review Board and Ors* [2008] IEHC 303 where the failure of the Review Board to conditionally discharge persons was unsuccessfully challenged. An application for habeas corpus on similar grounds was also unsuccessful: *L v Kennedy* [2010] IEHC 195.
[215] See the Irish Human Rights Commission, *Observations on the Criminal Law (Insanity) Bill 2010* (April 2010) where concern is expressed that a situation may arise where a person who is otherwise eligible for a conditional discharge is not able to be so discharged because of lack of services in the community to treat him or her on an out-patient basis. The lack of funding for community-based mental health services means that this scenario may well frequently arise and this may result in the State's obligations pursuant to the ECHR not being met.
[216] [2011] IECCA 1 at para.5.17.

Health Act; namely there is no requirement for the *'best interests of the patient'* to be at the forefront of a court's considerations in making such an order. This, therefore, appears to undermine any requirement for this Court to exercise its role as *pariens patriae*, pursuant to its inherent jurisdiction, at the sentencing stage. It is another cause for concern that the results of this web of legislative provisions is that once a person is found to be not guilty by reason of insanity for an offence in the criminal sense, that person can only be detained if he or she has a mental disorder within the civil law sense. So while a person is detained using civil law criteria, he or she does not have the same rights as patients detained under the Mental Health Act 2001. For example, a person admitted as a patient pursuant to the Act of 2001 can only be detained for an initial period of 21 days within which there must be a review by a Mental Health Tribunal. In contradistinction to this, the requirement to review a person detained pursuant to the Act of 2006, on the basis that they have been found not guilty by reason of insanity, arises only every six months."[217]

Unconstitutionality

Article 38.1 of the Constitution states that no person shall be tried on any criminal charge save in due course of law. While standards of procedural fairness must be adhered to by the police and prosecution, an accused can also rely on constitutional provisions in a substantive manner to render a criminal provision unconstitutional. This happens only rarely, however, as there is a presumption that legislation is constitutional, and the accused must have exhausted all other arguments before relying on unconstitutionality.

The constitutional right to privacy has been invoked on several occasions to render criminally proscribed conduct illegal. For example, in *McGee v AG*,[218] it was held that s.17 of the Criminal Law Amendment Act 1935, prohibiting distribution of contraceptives, violated the guarantee of marital privacy protected by Art.40.3.1°. More recently, the constitutional rights to life and privacy were relied on in *In Re a Ward of Court*[219] to permit medical treatment to be withdrawn from a woman who had been in a persistent vegetative state for over 20 years, conduct which might otherwise have been criminal.

It is clear that legislation creating an offence may be struck down where it creates an offence which is insufficiently clear and precise. The definition of the offence must be certain to enable an accused to prepare a defence; vagueness may prove to be a fatal constitutional defect. So, for example, in *King v AG*[220] various offences of loitering under the Vagrancy Act 1824 were struck down as being unconstitutionally vague.

The courts have addressed the defence of unconstitutionality a number of times recently in relation to sexual offences. In *CC v Ireland*,[221] the Supreme Court agreed

---

[217] [2011] IECCA 1 at para.5.17.
[218] [1974] I.R. 284.
[219] [1996] 2 I.R. 79.
[220] [1981] I.R. 233.
[221] [2006] 4 I.R. 1.

General Defences 327

that the absence of a defence of honest mistake of age in relation to the offence of unlawful carnal knowledge of a child by s.1(1) of the Criminal Law Amendment Act 1935 was unconstitutional.[222] Section 62 of the Offences Against the Person Act 1861 provided different penalties for sexual assaults depending on the victim's gender and this was held to be in breach of Art.40.1 in *SM v Ireland (No. 2)*.[223] The constitutionality of ss.3(1) and 5 of the Criminal Law (Sexual Offences) Act 2006 was challenged in *D(M) (a minor) v Ireland*.[224] It was argued that it was unconstitutional to punish males but not females for engaging in underage sexual intercourse but this was found to be constitutional by the Supreme Court. These cases are discussed in some detail in Ch.5.

---

[222] Although that does not necessarily mean that those who have been previously convicted of the offence will have their convictions quashed. See *A v Governor of Arbour Hill Prison* [2006] 4 I.R. 88.
[223] [2007] 4 I.R. 369.
[224] [2012] IESC 10.

CHAPTER 12

INCHOATE OFFENCES

Introduction

The criminal law has developed a body of rules governing inchoate liability which is aimed at criminalising incipient harm that falls short of completed substantive offences.[1] This chapter examines the law relating to inchoate liability: attempt, conspiracy and incitement. These offences are generally described as being inchoate in nature as they target the criminalisation of criminal actions that are not fully completed. Inchoate liability performs a function of criminalising harm-threatening conduct even though the principal harm targeted by the substantive offence has not yet materialised. For example, attempts, conspiracies and incitements relating to robbery are deemed to be in breach of the criminal law even though the robbery is not in fact committed.

It is important to note that inchoate offences always attach to a substantive offence.[2] For example, there is no such thing as an offence of attempt simpliciter; rather a substantive offence must be attempted, such as attempted rape or attempted murder. This point was addressed in the Supreme Court decision of *Minister for Justice, Equality and Law Reform v Tighe* which related to a European arrest warrant case:

> "[C]onspiracy is *not* in itself an offence: it is criminal only in the context of an agreement to commit a specific unlawful act or (perhaps) a lawful act by an unlawful means."[3]

In a passage cited in the *Tighe* decision, Charleton, McDermott and Bolger note that "[t]here was no general offence of conspiracy at Common Law".[4]

The inchoate offences of attempt, conspiracy and incitement are general principals of criminal liability insofar as they apply generally to the substantive offences in the special part of the criminal law. For instance, the same principles of inchoate liability apply in respect of both attempted theft and attempted rape, even though the target of the attempt may vary significantly. General inchoate liability must be distinguished from specific substantive offences that are inchoate in nature, such as the possession

---

[1] See McAuley and McCutcheon, *Criminal Liability* (2000), pp.401–418, for a comprehensive account of the historical development of the law relating to inchoate offences.
[2] With the exception of conspiracy, which is broader in scope, and can potentially attach to non-criminal acts.
[3] [2010] IESC 61.
[4] Charleton, McDermott and Bolger, *Criminal Law* (1999), p.296.

of a knife offence[5] or the offence of endangerment.[6] In the case of knife crime, the legislature has imposed liability at the point of possession in a public place which is antecedent to the actual infliction of bodily harm with the use of a knife. Similarly, the offence of endangerment criminalises conduct which creates a substantial risk of death or serious harm to another person, imposing liability where the interest of bodily integrity has been threatened, but not yet harmed. There are many examples of offences on the statute book where the offence is complete notwithstanding that the principal harm targeted by the offence has not in fact materialised.

Inchoate liability must be distinguished from secondary liability. Since the liability of secondary participants is derivative in nature, proof that the principal offence occurred is required. In contrast to secondary liability, inchoate liability does not require that the commission of any offence be established. Liability may be imposed in respect of an inchoate offence despite the fact that the wrongdoer has been unsuccessful in his efforts to bring about the commission of the target offence. It follows that if A enters into a conspiracy, incites or attempts to commit an offence, but the target offence is not in fact brought to completion, A may still be liable for the commission of an inchoate offence. However, if A's acts of assistance or encouragement take place in circumstances where the principal offence is actually committed by the principal then the liability of A is more appropriately considered under the principles of secondary liability; A's liability is derivative on the commission of the principal offence.

In Ireland, the rules governing inchoate liability are to be found at common law. While much of the principles on inchoate liability may be distilled from the case law, certain aspects of the law are uncertain and would benefit from being codified in statutory form.[7] The Law Reform Commission *Report on Inchoate Offences* made a series of recommendations on how the law relating to inchoate offences might be reformed.[8]

ATTEMPT

Introduction

It is not an absolute necessity for an offence to be successfully completed for criminal liability to be imposed; an attempt to commit a crime is a criminal offence in itself notwithstanding that the intended harm has not actually materialised. Where a man attempts to rape a woman, and comes close to completing the crime, the criminal law deems such conduct as being worthy of criminal sanction. While the intended harm is not actually inflicted, the woman's bodily integrity is seriously threatened. Equally, the offender who attempts rape has the same level of moral fault as the offender who successfully perpetrates the rape. In terms of culpability, there is little to distinguish between a person who successfully completes the offence and a person who tries but fails to commit a crime—both have guilty minds; the key distinction

---

[5] Firearms and Offensive Weapons Act 1990 s.9.
[6] Non-Fatal Offences Against the Person Act 1997 s.13.
[7] David Prendergast, "Codifying Inchoate Offences" (2008) 26 I.L.T. 134.
[8] Law Reform Commission, *Report on Inchoate Offences* (LRC 99–2010).

in the nature of their wrongdoing lies in the fact that one offender accomplishes his or her criminal objective while the other offender fails to bring about the criminal result targeted by his or her endeavours. Offenders should not escape liability simply because they have not been successful in their endeavours to commit a crime.

The principle of just deserts demands that persons who attempt to commit crimes are punished. Persons who embark on a criminal enterprise but fail to successfully execute the crime pose a serious threat to the interests protected by the criminal law. The protection of the community is enhanced by allowing for criminal liability to be imposed prior to the point when harm is actually caused. The law on attempt recognises that harm-threatening conduct merits criminalisation. Wrongdoers are on notice that liability will be imposed in respect of unsuccessful attempts as well as for the full commission of an offence. This arrangement arguably deters would-be offenders from attempting crime on the basis that people are aware that it is unlawful to attempt to commit an offence. Criminal attempt law also serves a preventative function as it allows for intervention by the police without stifling the possibility of a prosecution. In this regard, Professor Ormerod has suggested that the role of inchoate offences is likely to become more prominent in light of the "recent shift from coercive to 'intelligence-led' policing where new powers and technological advances allow the police to gather evidence and intervene before substantive crimes are committed".[9] In Ireland, the suite of criminal justice legislation enacted in recent years, such as the Criminal Justice (Surveillance) Act 2009, would tend to suggest that a similar trend may emerge in this jurisdiction in coming years, with increased recourse to inchoate offences.

Attempts may cause harm in themselves independently of the harm targeted by the substantive offence the subject of the attempt. For example, in the case of attempted burglary, although the victim's home may not have been broken into and property may not have been stolen, the victim may feel shock and a sense that he has been violated, knowing that a criminal made efforts to enter his home with criminal intent. Such a victim may contemplate what might have happened if the burglar had been successful and fear the possibility that he may be burgled again in the future.

The inchoate offence of attempt consists of three principal elements, each of which will be considered in detail below:

1. the actus reus of attempt is an act done by the accused that is more than merely preparatory, and is proximate to the substantive offence the subject of the attempt;[10]
2. the mens rea of attempt has been described as an intention to commit the offence that is targeted by the attempt.[11] However, the mental element in attempt is more nuanced, and may cover culpability states falling short of intention; where the culpability requirement of the target offence relates to a circumstance element there is legal authority to the effect that the mental element for attempt tracks that

---

[9] Ormerod, *Smith & Hogan Criminal Law*, 13th edn (2011), p.403.
[10] *R. v Eagleton* (1855) Dears 515; *Attorney General v Thornton* [1952] I.R. 91; *Attorney General v Sullivan* [1964] I.R. 169.
[11] *Attorney General v Thornton* [1952] I.R. 91; *Attorney General v Sullivan* [1964] I.R. 169.

Inchoate Offences

of the target offence.[12] This means that in relation to attempt, recklessness may suffice in respect of the fault requirement running to a circumstance element if recklessness is the prescribed mental element in the definition of the target offence;
3. an attempt must attach to a substantive offence ("the target offence"). Consideration must be given to the types of offences that, in law, may be attempted.

Other areas covered in this chapter include the availability of the defences of abandonment and impossibility in Irish law.

Actus reus of attempt

The law relating to criminal attempt imposes a physical act requirement. A person cannot be prosecuted for an attempt on the basis of his thoughts alone; certain physical acts must be established that manifest the person's intent to commit a particular crime.[13] The courts have developed certain legal rules to determine at what point a person's conduct is sufficient to amount to a criminal attempt.

The Irish position on the actus reus of attempt can be traced back to the seminal decision of the English Court of Criminal Appeal in *R. v Eagleton*.[14] In that case, the accused supplied bread to the poor in return for vouchers distributed by the Poor Law Authority. On presenting the vouchers to the Authority, the accused would be paid a specified sum of money for each loaf of bread. After he had presented the vouchers, and after his account had been credited, but before the money was paid over to him, it was discovered that the loaves he supplied had been below the agreed weight. If the money had passed to the accused, he would have been guilty of the offence of obtaining by false pretences. The question to be determined by the Court of Criminal Appeal was whether the acts of the accused were sufficient to constitute the actus reus of an attempt to obtain by false pretences. In finding the accused guilty of attempt to obtain by false pretences, Parke B. made the following observations:

> "The mere intention to commit a [crime] is not criminal. Some act is required; and we do not think that all acts towards committing a [crime] are [themselves criminal]. Acts remotely leading towards the commission of the offence are not to be considered attempts to commit it, but acts immediately connected with it are; and if in this case, after the credit with the relieving officer for the fraudulent overcharge, any further step on the part of the defendant had been necessary to obtain payment, as the making out of a further account, or producing the vouchers to the Board, we should have thought that the obtaining of credit in account with the relieving officer would not have been sufficiently proximate to obtaining the money. But on the statement in this case, no other act on the part of the defendant would have been required. It was the last act depending on himself towards the payment of the money and therefore it is to be considered as an attempt."[15]

---

[12] *R. v Pigg* [1982] 1 W.L.R. 762; *R. v Khan* [1990] 1 W.L.R. 813; *Attorney General's Reference (No. 3 of 1992)* [1994] 1 W.L.R. 409.
[13] *R. v Eagleton* (1855) Dears 515; *Attorney General v Thornton* [1952] I.R. 91.
[14] (1855) Dears 515.
[15] (1855) Dears 515 at 537–538.

This important passage establishes a number of important general principles governing the law of attempt. Attempt liability cannot be established on the basis of intention alone. In addition to the necessary mental element, an act is required on the part of the accused which must be deemed sufficiently proximate to the target substantive offence for criminal liability to be imposed. Subsequent Irish cases have followed the general approach to the actus reus requirement set out in *R. v Eagleton*.[16]

In *Attorney General v Thornton*, the appellant was convicted in the Circuit Court of unlawfully attempting to procure a poison or other noxious thing, called ergot, knowing that it was intended to be unlawfully used or employed to procure the miscarriage of a girl. Evidence was given of a conversation alleged to have taken place between the appellant and a doctor, in the course of which the appellant asked "[w]asn't there some drug named ergot?", and the doctor replied "that no self-respecting doctor would give such a drug under the circumstances". These remarks were expressed on the third occasion on which the appellant had visited the doctor. On the first occasion, the appellant asked whether anything could be done about the girl's case and the doctor said that he could not interfere in any way. At the second meeting, the appellant asked for a prescription for medication to interfere with the pregnancy and the doctor refused and replied that no self-respecting Catholic doctor would have anything to do with that business. On appeal, it was held that the conviction must be quashed. The Court of Criminal Appeal held that "a mere desire to commit the crime, or a desire followed by an intention to do so, is not sufficient to constitute an attempt".[17] Haugh J. went on to state that:

> "[A]n attempt consists of an act done by the accused with a specific intent to commit a particular crime; that it must go beyond mere preparation, and must be a direct movement toward the commission after the preparations have been made; that some such act is required and if it only remotely leads to the commission of the offence and is not immediately connected therewith, it cannot be considered as an attempt to commit an offence."[18]

In Irish law, merely preparatory acts are not sufficient to trigger attempt liability.[19] In *Attorney General v England*,[20] the defendant was charged with attempting to procure the commission of an act of gross indecency with another man. The defendant was friendly with the young man and one day talked to him about sex, and invited him to go to a nearby secluded spot; when the young man agreed the defendant offered him 10 shillings. It was held that this could not amount to a criminal attempt since the acts did not directly approximate to the commission of the offence. The acts could be viewed as mere preparation for the commission of an offence, which falls short of the level of conduct required to impose liability for criminal attempt.

In determining the issue of the threshold of the act requirement for attempt, the Supreme Court in *Attorney General v Sullivan* applied the test of proximity. Since

---

[16] (1855) Dears 515.
[17] [1952] I.R. 91 at 93.
[18] [1952] I.R. 91 at 93.
[19] *Attorney General v England* (1947) 1 Frewen 81; *Attorney General v Thornton* [1952] I.R. 91; *Attorney General v Sullivan* [1964] I.R. 169.
[20] (1947) 1 Frewen 81.

Inchoate Offences

this is the seminal case on attempt in Irish law it is worth setting out the facts in some detail. The defendant was a midwife who was paid a basic salary of £208 per year. She was paid an additional allowance for every case attended by her once the number of 25 cases had been reached in any one year. It follows that until the point in time that 25 cases had been attended by the defendant she was not entitled to the additional allowance. The defendant was charged with the offence of attempting to obtain by false pretences with intent to defraud. The case against her was that she had prepared and handed in claim forms in respect of fictitious patients. This would have facilitated her in reaching the figure of 25 attendances more quickly, which would enable her to make a fraudulent claim for the additional allowance on the basis of work that she had not in fact carried out. Since there was no evidence that the accused had already attended 25 cases at the material time, the Supreme Court proceeded on the assumption most favourable to the defendant: that she had not attended 25 cases and that the cases referred to in the summonses were to be viewed as being the first and second cases respectively in the contract year. It follows that 25 more cases would need to have been attended for her to reach the figure of 25 cases which would have allowed her to claim the additional allowance. The completed crime would have been obtaining the additional allowance by false pretences. Since the fraud was detected before the additional payment had been made to the defendant the issue became whether the defendant's acts were sufficient to constitute an attempt to obtain by false pretences. It was argued on behalf of the defendant that her conduct could not amount to an attempt, since, even had the fraudulent forms been processed in the ordinary way and been accepted as genuine, she would not have received any payment until patient number 26 was reached; 24 more cases were outstanding until the crime could be completed. Instead, it was submitted that the defendant's conduct was mere preparation for the crime, and not, in law, a criminal attempt.

The key issue to be decided in the case was whether the acts of the defendant should be regarded "merely as a preparation for the commission of offences or whether they constituted acts sufficiently proximate to amount to attempts to commit substantive offences". After considering the jurisprudence in the area, the majority of the Supreme Court confirmed that the applicable law on the actus reus of attempt is whether the acts in question are sufficiently proximate to the target offence, and that merely preparatory acts are not criminal attempts. It was noted that the proximity test had been formulated in different forms in various cases. For example, in *R. v Eagleton*, the following formulation was used:

> "[A]cts remotely leading towards the commission of the offence are not to be considered as attempts to commit it, but acts immediately connected with it are."[21]

The majority of the Supreme Court in *Sullivan* viewed the description of the actus reus of attempt in *Eagleton* as a statement in the negative form of what is referred to as the "proximity rule".[22] Following the decision in *Sullivan*, the proximate act approach is the test governing the threshold of the actus reus for attempt in Irish criminal law.

---

[21] (1855) Dears 515 at 537.
[22] *Attorney General v Sullivan* [1964] I.R. 169 at 196 per Walsh J.

In the instant case, the majority of the Supreme Court held that:

> "[E]ach false claim put in, whether it be the first or the twenty-sixth, would, in law, be an act sufficiently proximate to constitute an attempt to commit the substantive offence of obtaining by false pretences …"[23]

Walsh J. went on to state that the issue of proximity is "a question of law only".

The definition of the act requirement in attempt is generally regarded as being both a delicate and complex legal issue. The search for a satisfactory approach to defining the actus reus of attempt has troubled jurists and law makers alike down through the centuries, both in Ireland and other jurisdictions. The Law Reform Commission has commented that there is "both merit and demerit in the distinguishing feature of the proximity test, that distinguishing feature being its flexibility".[24] The concept of proximity is inherently vague; in many cases it is difficult to say with any degree of certainty whether a particular act is sufficiently proximate to constitute an attempt. Much depends on how the facts of a particular case are interpreted. The principal disadvantage of the proximity approach is uncertainty which may lead to inconsistency in the application of the law.

The relationship between criminal attempt and the legality principle was considered in the Law Reform Commission *Report on Inchoate Offences*. Legitimate concerns arise as to whether a vague definition of the act requirement may lead to an undesirable level of uncertainty in the law on attempt. The Law Reform Commission is of the view that the malleable nature of the concept of proximity does not undermine the legality principle:

> "Flexibility suggests uncertainty and indeterminacy, which in turn cause concern for legality. The worry is that with a flexible test for criminal attempt, the point at which attempt liability is imposed will depend as much on judicial discretion as on legal definition. These are real concerns, but some observations tend to blunt them insofar as they are used to attack the proximity approach. First, as argued in the Consultation Paper, for respecting the legality principle it is crucial that the definitions of target substantive offences are certain; it is much less important to have certainty regarding the exact point at which criminal liability is imposed when working towards a substantive offence. Once a citizen can ascertain what the substantive offences are and can know that, roughly speaking, attempting offences is prohibited, they are well on the way to having fair notice of what not to do in order to avoid criminal sanction. Recall that from the point of view of an actor there is no difference between attempting to do a crime and actually doing it. Indeed, all completed acts were initially attempted. There does not seem to be any additional gain in legality to be achieved by allowing citizens to know to what extent they can work towards a crime without criminal liability attaching to their actions. Second, even with a more certain approach to defining criminal attempt, there will still be very substantial indeterminacy in criminal attempt cases. This is because of

---

[23] *Attorney General v Sullivan* [1964] I.R. 169 at 198 per Walsh J.
[24] Law Reform Commission, *Report on Inchoate Offences* (LRC 99–2010), p.39.

the inherent flexibility in characterising the facts in an attempt case. The facts depend on how you look at them; this being an area of law that manifestly bears out legal realist claims that facts decide cases, not law."[25]

The proximity test has the advantage of flexibility. This allows for a certain amount of discretion in determining whether a person's conduct has reached the threshold to impose criminal liability. Such flexibility arguably allows for the justice of the case to be met in individual cases rather than having a rigid test that may lead to undesirable results. For the sake of completeness, it is worth noting that alternative approaches to defining the actus reus of attempt have been adopted, at different times, and in different jurisdictions. Under the last act approach, attempt liability is triggered only when the last act prior to completion of the substantive offence has occurred.[26] While this approach promotes legal certainty it has been criticised for being under-inclusive, and failing to capture a range of inchoate conduct that is worthy of criminalisation. Other approaches include the unequivocality test[27] and the substantial step test.[28]

The Irish position on the actus reus in attempt may be summarised as follows:

(1) acts that are more than merely preparatory, and
(2) acts that are sufficiently proximate to the commission of the substantive offence the target of the attempt.[29]

Mens rea of attempt

In Irish criminal law, the mens rea of attempt is generally understood to be intention. In *Attorney General v Thornton*, the Court of Criminal Appeal described the mental element of attempt as an act done with "specific intent to commit a particular crime".[30] This means that, in criminal attempt cases, the prosecution must prove intention on the part of the defendant even if recklessness is sufficient for the substantive offence the subject of the attempt. It follows that in attempt crimes, generally speaking, the culpability requirements are elevated to intention, imposing a more onerous burden on the prosecution in relation to proof of mens rea. Charleton, McDermott and Bolger have suggested that the intention-based approach to attempt culpability may be justified "on the basis that the requirement for a more blameworthy state of mind than the completed offence is balanced by the fact that the accused need not have done so much, or indeed any, harm in order to be convicted".[31] Because the actus reus of attempt can potentially be any physical act, even seemingly innocuous

---

[25] Law Reform Commission, *Report on Inchoate Offences* (LRC 99–2010), p.37.
[26] *R. v Eagleton* (1855) Dears 515; *DPP v Stonehouse* [1978] A.C. 55.
[27] *R. v Baker* [1924] N.Z.L.R. 865; *Davey v Lee* [1967] 2 All E.R. 423; *Jones v Brooks* (1968) 52 Cr. App. R. 614.
[28] American Law Institute Model Penal Code, s.5.01(2).
[29] *R. v Eagleton* (1855) Dears 515; *Attorney General v Thornton* [1952] I.R. 91; *Attorney General v Sullivan* [1964] I.R. 169.
[30] [1952] I.R. 91 at 93.
[31] Charleton, McDermott and Bolger, *Criminal Law* (1999), p.263.

or harmless acts, "the mental element assumes paramount importance in attempts".[32] The justification typically put forward is that the broad actus reus of attempt is counterbalanced by having more onerous mens rea requirements than the mental elements specified in the target substantive offence.

Concern has been expressed that if intention must be established in respect of every element of the target offence there is a risk that the law may fail to criminalise conduct that merits criminalisation.[33] A good illustration of the potential for under-criminalisation is the inchoate offence of attempted rape. While the substantive offence of rape requires proof of intention in respect of the physical act of sexual intercourse, recklessness suffices in relation to the circumstance element of the absence of consent on the part of the victim. In the case of attempted rape, if the prosecution were required to establish intention in respect of the issue of consent, a defendant who was reckless only as to the absence of consent might be acquitted on the basis that he did not intend or have as his purpose that the victim not consent. Clearly, this would be an undesirable outcome, as the person who attempts rape in circumstances where he is reckless as to whether the woman consents bears a high degree of culpability.

In *R. v Khan*,[34] the English Court of Appeal recognised that there are circumstances in which a fault requirement lesser than intention may suffice for attempt culpability. In that case, it was held that the same culpability requirements apply in respect of both the substantive offence of rape and the inchoate offence of attempted rape: intention as to the act of sexual intercourse and recklessness as to the absence of consent.[35] Under English law, it would appear that recklessness is sufficient in respect of the circumstance element of an attempted offence where recklessness is the specified fault element of the substantive offence the subject of the attempt.[36]

In *Attorney General's Reference (No. 3 of 1992)*,[37] the English Court of Appeal held that on a charge of aggravated arson (as defined in s.1(2) of the Criminal Damage Act 1971), in addition to establishing a specific intent to cause damage by fire, it is sufficient to prove that the defendant was reckless as to whether life would thereby be endangered. Professor Ormerod has expressed the view that "the decision goes beyond *Khan* by allowing a conviction for attempt where D's *mens rea* comprises only recklessness as to the existing *consequences* if there is an intention as to the missing *circumstances*".[38] Since it is unclear to what extent the Irish courts would rely on the English authorities the law relating to the mental element of attempt is uncertain.

The Law Reform Commission has recommended reforming the law on the mens rea of attempt so that the culpability requirements for attempting a substantive offence ought to track the culpability requirements for the target substantive offence the subject of the attempt.[39] Under the proposed scheme, the problem of under-

---

[32] Ormerod, *Smith & Hogan Criminal Law* (2011), p.404.
[33] Law Reform Commission, *Report on Inchoate Offences* (LRC 99–2010), p.53.
[34] [1990] 1 W.L.R. 813.
[35] Under s.1 of the UK Criminal Attempts Act 1981, the mental element of attempt is defined as "intent to commit an offence".
[36] *R. v Pigg* [1982] 1 W.L.R. 762; *R. v Khan* [1990] 1 W.L.R. 813.
[37] [1994] 1 W.L.R. 409.
[38] Ormerod, *Smith & Hogan Criminal Law* (2011), p.407.
[39] Law Reform Commission, *Report on Inchoate Offences* (LRC 99–2010), p.65.

Inchoate Offences

criminalisation would be addressed by clarifying that the fault element of intention is no longer to be the sole fault requirement for attempt liability. Instead, the culpability requirements for the attempted offence would be identical to the fault requirements of the substantive offence attempted. For example, both rape and attempted rape would have the same mens rea requirements.

Finally, special mention needs to be made in relation to the culpability requirements of attempted murder. It would appear that the mens rea for attempted murder is restricted to an attempt to kill,[40] this notwithstanding that the mens rea for the substantive offence of murder is an intention to kill or cause serious injury.[41] This is a departure from the general scheme of attempt culpability. In the context of attempted murder, it seems that an intention to cause serious injury is insufficient to satisfy the culpability requirements of attempted murder; an intention to kill must be established.

Identifying the types of offences that may be attempted

An attempt must attach to a substantive offence; there is no stand-alone offence of attempt. Generally speaking, an attempt will relate to a substantive offence, such as rape or theft. An attempt may also attach to a target offence that is inchoate in nature. In *R. v Banks*,[42] an attempt to incite was recognised as being a possible form of double inchoate liability. In *R. v De Kromme*,[43] an attempt to conspire to commit an offence was considered an acceptable formulation. Other instances include statutory offences that are inchoate in nature, such as the offence of endangerment under s.13 of the Non-Fatal Offences Against the Person Act 1997 which is inchoate in nature insofar as it criminalises the creation of a risk of harm, as opposed to actually causing harm. It follows that a charge of attempted endangerment would be a form of "double inchoate liability". The Law Reform Commission has expressed concern about the possibility of criminalising conduct that is far removed from the central criminal harm targeted by the substantive offence:

> "[C]are must be taken not to let inchoate liability build on top of inchoate liability to an excessive degree. There are many statutory offences that are inchoate in nature in that they can be committed despite no substantive harm having occurred. Prosecutors should refrain from constructing charges such as attempt to incite the commission of endangerment ... A sensible rule of thumb could be that charges involving more than two inchoate offences should be avoided. Double inchoate liability may be acceptable at times, but triple inchoate liability and beyond is not."[44]

The Law Reform Commission went on to express the view that attempt liability cannot attach to secondary liability because an attempt can only attach to an offence; s.7(1) of the Criminal Law Act 1997 does not create an offence of aiding, abetting,

---

[40] *R. v Whybrow* (1951) 35 Cr. App. R. 141; *DPP v Douglas and Hayes* [1985] I.L.R.M. 25.
[41] Criminal Justice Act 1964 s.4(1).
[42] (1873) 12 Cox CC 393.
[43] (1892) 17 Cox CC 492.
[44] Law Reform Commission, *Report on Inchoate Offences* (LRC 99–2010), pp.46–48.

counselling or procuring the commission of an offence, instead that section states that a secondary participant "shall be liable to be indicted, tried and punished as a principal offender".[45]

Legal impossibility and factual impossibility

Legal impossibility arises where a defendant attempts to do something which he or she believes to be illegal, when in fact the objective targeted by the attempt is not a criminal offence. In these types of cases the defendant mistakenly thinks that he is in the process of committing an offence. Since an attempt must attach to an offence, there can be no liability because the defendant is attempting to bring about a result that has not been criminalised by any rule of law. In *R. v Taafe*,[46] the defendant imported cannabis into the United Kingdom believing it to be currency. Since importation of currency was not a criminal offence he could not be guilty of an attempt to import currency. Notwithstanding his erroneous belief as to the illegality of the importation of currency, the defendant could not be found guilty of attempting some form of imaginary offence that did not exist in law.

Factual possibility is concerned with attempts that are impossible on the facts. A classic example is a pickpocket who attempts to steal by putting his hand into the pocket of another person but the pocket turns out to be empty. In *Attorney General v Sullivan*, the Supreme Court considered the possibility that it may have been factually impossible for the defendant midwife to reach the required number of 25 cases to complete the offence of obtaining by false pretences. The Supreme Court went on to state that such factual impossibility, if it arose, would not be a bar to imposing liability for attempt:

> "Even, however, if that should have proved impossible in the event, it is, I think not a matter material to the discussion of this point because it has been well established in various cases that the ultimate impossibility of achieving or carrying out the crime attempted is not a defence to a charge of attempt."[47]

The Law Reform Commission criticised the position taken by the UK House of Lords in *Haughton v Smith*[48] that a factually impossible attempt was not a criminal attempt, and recommended clarifying in statutory form that factual impossibility not preclude liability for a criminal attempt.[49]

Abandonment

In Irish law, there would appear to be no defence available to a person who having satisfied the actus reus requirement of attempt then subsequently withdraws his involvement prior to completion of the offence. In the leading Irish decision on attempt, in *Attorney General v Sullivan*, Walsh J. remarked obiter that the law relating to attempt in Ireland does not recognise a defence of abandonment:

---

[45] Law Reform Commission, *Report on Inchoate Offences* (LRC 99–2010), pp.48–51.
[46] [1983] 1 W.L.R. 627.
[47] *Attorney General v Sullivan* [1964] I.R. 169 at 196 per Walsh J.
[48] [1975] A.C. 476.
[49] Law Reform Commission, *Report on Inchoate Offences* (LRC 99–2010), pp.65–69.

"It might also be suggested that even assuming that she had the criminal intent she might have changed her mind and not gone ahead with the plan some time before the twenty-sixth case was reached. That again, in my opinion, is not a consideration to be taken into account in examining this charge, and indeed there is authority for holding that even if there were evidence that she had in fact changed her mind it would not amount to a defence because the offence charged is that of having the intent at the time the act constituting the attempt is carried out. That cannot be answered by evidence of a subsequent abandonment of the intent."

It would seem that liability is imposed at the point in time when the actus reus of attempt is complete, and is accompanied by the necessary mens rea. Abandonment of the criminal enterprise after this point does not operate as a bar to criminal liability, but goes to mitigation of sentence only.

CONSPIRACY

Introduction

In Ireland, the law relating to conspiracy is governed by both common law rules and statute law. Section 71 of the Criminal Justice Act 2006 enacted a statutory offence of conspiracy that applies in relation to "serious offences", a category which is defined in s.70 of the Act of 2006 as an offence for which a person may be imprisoned for a term of four years or more. Section 71(4) provides that a person charged with an offence of conspiracy under s.71 is liable to be indicted, tried and punished as a principal offender. Since the term "conspiracy" is not defined in the Act of 2006 the case law relating to common law conspiracy would appear to be relevant to the interpretation of the elements of the offence of conspiracy in s.71 of the Act of 2006.

Common law conspiracy is much broader than the statutory form of conspiracy. At common law, there exists a general inchoate offence that covers agreements to commit a criminal offence and certain types of civil wrongs. In contrast to attempt and incitement, a prosecution may lie for both the inchoate offence of conspiracy and the substantive offence to which the conspiratorial agreement relates.[50] There are also several "stand-alone" common law offences based on the concept of conspiracy: conspiracy to corrupt public morals, conspiracy to effect a public mischief, conspiracy to outrage public decency and conspiracy to defraud. First, consideration will be given to the elements of the general inchoate offence of conspiracy. This will be followed by an examination of the various specific common law offences of conspiracy.

Actus reus of conspiracy: an agreement

The inchoate offence of conspiracy is built around the concept of "agreement". In *Hegarty v Governor of Limerick Prison*, Geoghegan J. observed that "... whether a conspiracy is criminal or tortious an absolutely essential element is that there be

---

[50] *R. v Boulton* (1871) 12 Cox CC 87 at 93.

an agreement between the alleged conspirators".[51] In general terms, "conspiracy" is defined as an agreement by two or more persons to do an unlawful act, or to do a lawful act by unlawful means.[52] The common law has developed a number of principles concerning the meaning of the term "agreement". It is important to note that liability for conspiracy is triggered at the point of entering into an agreement; no further acts are required to implement the agreement. In the House of Lords decision in *R. v Doot*, it was held that conspiracy is a continuing offence:

> "[A]lthough a conspiracy was complete as a crime when the agreement was made it continued in existence so long as there were two or more parties to it intending to carry out its design."[53]

In *Attorney General v Oldridge*,[54] the defendant allegedly participated in an elaborate scheme to defraud three banks. It was alleged that his role was during the "lulling phase", following the commencement of the scheme, and consisted of providing assurances to the banks to induce them to forebear from suing. The Supreme Court held that the defendant's role in lulling the banks into a false sense of security was an essential feature of the alleged fraudulent scheme and that he played a vital part in continuing the conspiracy to defraud the banks. The Supreme Court, following *R. v Doot*,[55] approved the statement of the law set out in the direction of Coleridge J. to the jury in *R. v Murphy* that "[i]t is not necessary that it should be proved that these defendants met to concoct this scheme, nor is it necessary that they should have originated it. If a conspiracy be already formed, and a person joins it afterwards, he is equally guilty".[56] It follows that there is no requirement in law that all the parties to an agreement knew each other or were in contact prior to the formation of the conspiracy. Suppose that A recruits B, C, D and E to bomb a building, and that B, C, D and E had never met and were unaware of each other's identities. Notwithstanding this, each is party to the same conspiracy to bomb the building. This is sometimes described as a cartwheel conspiracy, with A at the hub directing the enterprise, and the other parties at each spoke carrying out a specified task. Equally, one can have a chain conspiracy, where A recruits B, B recruits C and so on.

An agreement may be express or implied from the circumstances. In relation to proving the elements of the inchoate offence of conspiracy, there is a requirement that two or more persons are party to an agreement. However, it is possible that only one party to the conspiracy may be ultimately convicted.[57] For liability to be imposed an agreement must in fact be reached; negotiations falling short of actual agreement do not amount to criminal conspiracy. *R. v Saik* is authority for the proposition that a conditional agreement may come within the scope of criminal conspiracy where the agreement:

---

[51] [1998] 1 I.R. 412 at 425.
[52] *R. v Parnell* (1881) 14 Cox 508 at 512.
[53] [1973] A.C. 807 at 823.
[54] [2000] 4 I.R. 593 at 601.
[55] [1973] A.C. 807 at 823.
[56] (1837) 8 C. & P. 297 at 311.
[57] *Attorney General v Keane* (1975) 1 Frewen 392.

Inchoate Offences

> "[I]s expressed to be conditional on the happening, or non-happening, of some particular event. The question always is whether the agreed course of conduct, if carried out in accordance with the parties' intentions, would necessarily involve an offence. A conspiracy to rob a bank tomorrow if the coast is clear when the conspirators reach the bank is not, by reason of this qualification, any less a conspiracy to rob. In the nature of things, every agreement to do something in the future is hedged about with conditions, implicit if not explicit. In theory if not in practice, the condition could be so far-fetched that it would cast doubt on the genuineness of a conspirator's expressed intention to do an unlawful act. If I agree to commit an offence should I succeed in climbing Mount Everest without the use of oxygen, plainly I have no intention to commit the offence at all."[58]

The common law has placed some limitations on the categories of persons who can enter into conspiratorial agreements. *R. v Mawji* is authority for the rule that spouses cannot enter into a conspiracy with one another.[59] This common law rule is an example of the legal fiction that husband and wife are regarded for certain purposes as one person in law. The survival of the spousal immunity rule in conspiracy has been questioned,[60] and the Law Reform Commission has recently recommended abolition of the rule.[61]

In *R. v McDonnell*,[62] the defendant was a director and the sole person in each of two companies responsible for the acts of the company. It was alleged that the defendant had entered into a conspiracy with these companies. Nield J. observed that the basis of conspiracy was the acting in concert of two or more persons and that, although a company was a separate legal entity, where the sole responsible person in a company was the defendant himself, there could not be two or more persons and, therefore, there could be no conspiracy between the defendant and the company. Nield J. went on to say that:

> "[T]hese charges of conspiracy cannot be sustained, upon the footing that in the particular circumstances here, where the sole responsible person in the company is the defendant himself, it would not be right to say that there were two persons or two minds. If it were otherwise, I feel that it would offend against the basic concept of a conspiracy, namely, an agreement of two or more to do an unlawful act, and I think it would be artificial to take the view that the company, although it is clearly a separate legal entity, can be regarded here as a separate person or a separate mind, in view of the admitted fact that this defendant acts alone so far as these companies are concerned."[63]

---

[58] *R. v Saik* [2007] 1 A.C. 18 at 31–32.
[59] [1957] 1 A.C. 125.
[60] Campbell, Kilcommins and O'Sullivan, *Criminal Law in Ireland: Cases and Commentary* (2010), p.305; Charleton, McDermott and Bolger, *Criminal Law* (1999), p.319.
[61] Law Reform Commission, *Report on Inchoate Offences* (LRC 99–2010), p.84.
[62] [1966] 1 Q.B. 233.
[63] [1966] 1 Q.B. 233 at 245.

Certain aspects relating to the actus reus suffer from legal uncertainty. Clarification is needed as to whether a person may be convicted of the inchoate offence of conspiracy in circumstances where his or her co-conspirator lacks capacity or culpability in respect of the offence targeted by the conspiracy.[64] Examples include where the co-conspirator lacks capacity due to young age or mental illness. The Law Reform Commission has recommended that a prosecution for conspiracy should be allowed to proceed in circumstances where only one party has criminal capacity, or where only one party has the requisite culpability.[65]

The object of conspiracy

In contrast to the other inchoate offences of attempt and incitement, at common law, a conspiracy may be entered into in respect of both criminal offences and certain civil wrongs. Under the common law, "[a] conspiracy consists of an agreement of two or more to do an unlawful act, or to do a lawful act by unlawful means".[66] The term "unlawful" is understood as not being restricted to criminal offences, but extends to non-criminal acts. This means that a breach of the civil law that would not be a criminal offence if done by a single actor may be transformed into a criminal offence where two or more persons enter into an agreement to commit that civil wrong. The wider application of criminal conspiracy reflects the traditional concern of the criminal law with group crime. The formation of criminal groups or organisations has always been viewed as presenting a serious threat to society and the interests protected by the criminal law. The rationale for this approach was expressed as follows in *R. v Parnell*:

> "It is obvious that a wrongful violation of another man's right committed by many assumes a far more formidable and offensive character than when committed by a single individual ... The law has therefore, and it seems to us wisely and justly, established that a combination of persons to commit a wrongful act with a view to injure another shall be an offence though the act if done by one would not amount to more than a civil wrong."[67]

In this case, the accused, Charles Stewart Parnell, was charged with conspiracy to prevent tenants paying their rents. Other persons were also charged with conspiracy in similar terms. While Parnell's actions would not have been criminal in nature had he acted alone, it was held that conspiring with others to encourage non-payment of rent could constitute a criminal offence, notwithstanding that the object of the conspiracy was non-criminal.

The leading case in relation to criminal conspiracy to commit torts is *Kamara v DPP*.[68] In this case, a number of students were charged with conspiracy to commit the tort of trespass by agreeing to occupy the premises of the High Commissioner of Sierra Leone, in London. The House of Lords held that that trespass or any other tort

---

[64] *R. v Whitechurch* (1890) 24 Q.B. 420; *R. v Duguid* (1906) 75 L.J.K.B. 470.
[65] Law Reform Commission, *Report on Inchoate Offences* (LRC 99–2010), pp.80–81, 84.
[66] *R. v Parnell* (1881) 14 Cox 508 at 512.
[67] (1881) 14 Cox 508 at 520.
[68] [1974] 1 A.C. 104.

could form the element of illegality necessary in conspiracy, but in addition either (a) the execution of the combination had to involve invasion of the public domain, e.g. the embassy of a friendly power or a building publicly owned, or an infringement of the criminal law, or (b) the execution of the combination had necessarily to involve, and be known and intended to involve, the infliction on its victim of more than purely nominal damage, as in the occupation of premises to the exclusion of the owner's right.[69] A different formulation was put forward in the concurring opinion of Lord Cross, who stated that whether an agreement to commit a tort amounted to conspiracy depended on whether the public had a sufficient interest; that is, whether the execution of the conspiracy would have sufficiently harmful consequences to justify penal sanctions.[70] Lord Cross went on to state that "[i]n the case of an agreement to trespass that might be the case – because, for example, of the nature of the property on which the trespass was to be committed or of the means to be employed in carrying out the trespass or of the object to be achieved by it".

The uncertainty surrounding the potentially wide scope of conspiracy to commit non-criminal wrongs has generated a large amount of criticism. For example, it is unclear to what extent, if it all, criminal conspiracy applies to breach of contract. The Law Reform Commission have made a well-reasoned argument in favour of restricting the scope of the general inchoate offence of conspiracy to agreements the carrying out of which will involve the commission of a criminal offence:

> "Conspiracy, as defined at common law, is an extraordinary tool for expanding criminal liability. It provides that the existence of agreement can render otherwise non-criminal activity criminal. That conspiracy has a very wide ambit is problematic in itself, but the problem is made much worse by the fact that conspiracy's ambit is so uncertain. An agreement to breach a contract, for example, may or may not be considered a conspiracy. Precedents can be found where what was criminalised as a conspiracy was essentially an agreement to breach various contracts. Yet, on the other hand, it is fair to suppose that every day there are agreements to breach contractual obligations (by not honouring them and so on) and the criminal law (specifically conspiracy) is not sought to be applied or even thought appropriate. This state of affairs represents what the legality principle and the rule of law says ought not be, that is, inconsistent application of uncertain laws with the resulting potential for implementation to be arbitrary."[71]

In theory, conspiracy might apply to other inchoate offences, such as attempt or incitement. However, as was previously noted in relation to attempt, caution needs to be exercised so that there are not too many layers of inchoate liability.[72] Equally, conspiracy would not appear to attach to secondary liability on the basis that s.7(1) of the Criminal Law Act 1997 does not create an offence of aiding, abetting, counselling or procuring the commission of an offence; that section states that a secondary participant "shall be liable to be indicted, tried and punished as a principal offender".

---

[69] [1974] 1 A.C. 104 at 130 per Lord Hailsham.
[70] [1974] 1 A.C. 104 at 132 per Lord Cross.
[71] Law Reform Commission, *Report on Inchoate Offences* (LRC 99–2010), p.98.
[72] Law Reform Commission, *Report on Inchoate Offences* (LRC 99–2010), pp.95–97.

Mens rea of conspiracy

There is a good deal of uncertainty as to the precise contents of the mens rea of conspiracy. There are no Irish cases touching directly on the issue of mens rea and regard must be had to common law authorities in other jurisdictions. As there is a conflict between different lines of authority it is unclear what position the Irish courts would take on the matter. Given the lack of legal certainty it is an area of the law that would benefit greatly from statutory reform.

In relation to the agreement itself, it seems clear that intention is required.[73] This would preclude imposing liability in circumstances where a person's external conduct was misinterpreted as evidencing an intention to enter into a conspiracy. A person cannot fall into a conspiratorial agreement accidentally on the basis of an objective assessment of his or her conduct; there must be evidence of an intention to form a conspiracy, a subjective mental state must be established on the part of the alleged conspirator.

It also seems that knowledge may be required in respect of the circumstances that render the objective of the agreement unlawful. In the House of Lords decision in *Churchill v Watson*, observations were made in respect of the relevance of knowledge to the mens rea of conspiracy:

> "[M]ens rea is only an essential ingredient in conspiracy in so far as there must be an intention to be a party to an agreement to do an unlawful act; that knowledge of the law on the part of the accused is immaterial and that knowledge of the facts is only material in so far as such knowledge throws a light on what was agreed ... The question is, 'What did they agree to do?' If what they agreed to do was, on the facts known to them, an unlawful act, they are guilty of conspiracy and they cannot excuse themselves by saying that, owing to their ignorance of the law, they did not realise that such an act was a crime. If, on the facts known to them, what they agreed to do was lawful, they are not rendered artificially guilty by the existence of other facts, not known to them, giving a different and criminal quality to the act agreed upon."[74]

It is clear from this passage that ignorance of the law is no defence to a charge of conspiracy. Interestingly, the House of Lords, in the same passage, appeared to express the view that, conceptually speaking, it is preferable to focus on the concept of "agreement" rather than "mens rea" when considering the elements of conspiracy:

> "[I]n cases of this kind [it] is desirable to avoid the use of the phrase 'mens rea' which is capable of different meanings, and to concentrate on the terms or effect of the agreement made by the alleged conspirators."

In the decision of the Canadian Supreme Court in *R. v O'Brien*,[75] it was held that there must exist, on the part of a conspirator, an intention to put the agreement into effect.

---

[73] *R. v O'Brien* [1954] S.C.R. 666; *Churchill v Watson* [1967] 2 A.C. 224.
[74] [1967] 2 A.C. 224 at 237.
[75] [1954] S.C.R. 666.

A similar position was adopted in England and Wales, in *R. v Thompson*,[76] in relation to common law conspiracy, where it was held that a defendant must intend that the agreement will be implemented and the unlawful objective realised. Subsequently, in *R. v Anderson*,[77] the House of Lords, applying statutory conspiracy,[78] decided that there was no requirement to establish an intention on the part of each conspirator that the offence or offences in question should in fact be committed. As there are two competing lines of authority, there is some uncertainty as to what approach the Irish courts would take to this particular element of the mens rea of conspiracy. Initially, the Law Reform Commission provisionally recommended placing on a statutory basis the common law position in *R. v O'Brien* that requires a specific intention on the part of a conspirator that the unlawful goal of the conspiratorial agreement be carried out.[79] However, at Report stage, the Law Reform Commission revised its position, recommending a novel scheme of mens rea for conspiracy whereby a "conspiratorial agreement must have been entered into and, in doing so, a conspirator must at least have the kind of culpability required for the substantive offence to which the conspiracy relates".[80]

Specific offences of conspiracy

At common law, the courts have developed a number of specific offences of conspiracy. These individual offences belong to the body of offences in the special part of the criminal law and are to be distinguished from the general part doctrine of conspiracy, discussed above. The most noteworthy stand-alone conspiracy-based offences include the following: conspiracy to corrupt public morals,[81] conspiracy to effect a public mischief,[82] conspiracy to outrage public decency[83] and conspiracy to defraud.[84] These specific instance offences exist in their own right at common law and their operation is not dependent upon the operation of the general principles of common law conspiracy set out above.

In relation to conspiracy to effect a public mischief, the Law Reform Commission has made the following observations in the *Consultation Paper on Inchoate Offences*:

> "In *DPP v Carew*[85] Hamilton J recognised the substantive offence of effecting a public mischief. Hence, it can be said there is implicit Irish judicial recognition of conspiracy to effect a public mischief. This is implicit because the existence

---

[76] (1965) 50 Cr. App. R. 1 at 2.
[77] [1986] A.C. 27.
[78] Criminal Law Act 1977 s.1(1).
[79] Law Reform Commission, *Consultation Paper on Inchoate Offences* (LRC CP48–2008), pp.87–89.
[80] Law Reform Commission, *Report on Inchoate Offences* (LRC 99–2010), pp.85–92.
[81] *Knuller v DPP* [1973] A.C. 435; *Attorney General (SPUC) v Open Door Counselling Ltd* [1988] I.R. 593.
[82] In *DPP v Withers* [1975] A.C. 842, the House of Lords held that the law knew no such generalised offence as conspiracy to effect a public mischief.
[83] *Knuller v DPP* [1973] A.C. 435.
[84] *Scott v Metropolitan Police Commissioner* [1975] A.C. 819; *Myles v Sreenan* [1999] 4 I.R. 294; *Attorney General v Oldridge* [2000] 1 I.R. 593.
[85] [1981] 1 I.L.R.M. 91.

of the substantive offence entails the existence of the ancillary conspiracy offence. There is a House of Lords decision[86] stating there is no such offence known to the law. This House of Lords decision predates, but is not mentioned in, Hamilton J's judgment in *Carew*.[87] There are some cases from Australia recognising the offence.[88] Where it is recognised, public mischief is the substantive offence and agreeing to pursue it constitutes conspiracy."[89]

There is no requirement that the conspiracy relates to unlawful conduct; even an agreement to do something lawful may trigger criminal liability if the conduct in question is interpreted as corrupting public morals, effecting a public mischief or outraging public decency. Since the contents of concepts such as "public morals" are uncertain and open to inconsistent interpretation, concern has been expressed that these set of offences may offend the legality principle. There is a strong argument that because these offences are so vaguely defined they fail to give fair notice of what constitutes a criminal offence. The Law Reform Commission put forward the following reasons for abolishing the offences of conspiracy to corrupt public morals, conspiracy to effect a public mischief and conspiracy to outrage public decency:

> "These offences pose serious difficulties in terms of legality. Not only do they have the extraordinary function of rendering criminal quite lawful activity merely because two or more agree to pursue it, there is also great uncertainty as to what constitutes, for example, the corruption of public morals. The Commission notes the two-fold vagueness here: uncertainty as to what 'to corrupt' means and uncertainty regarding the ambit of 'public morals' and the method for ascertaining public morals. Similar comments can be said about effecting a public mischief and outraging public decency. The problem is that precedent is of little guidance because of the shifting nature of public morals and public decency. In 1973, in *Knuller v DPP* the UK House of Lords held that activity designed to promote contact between homosexual men was against public morality. Even if this decision might, at one time, have been followed in Ireland, this could hardly be the case now, particularly in light of the enactment by the Oireachtas of the Civil Partnership and Certain Rights and Obligations of Cohabitants Act 2010, which provides for the recognition in law of the status of civil partnership between same-sex couples. Indeed, if the *Knuller* case was to be applied, it is at least arguable that quite a number of publications in Ireland and the UK, not to mention social website operators, conspire every day to corrupt public morals."[90]

In *Myles v Sreenan*,[91] the High Court held that the common law offence of conspiracy to defraud was carried over by the Constitution as its ingredients had been clearly

---

[86] *DPP v Withers* [1975] A.C. 842.
[87] See Mary McAleese, "Note on Criminal Law – Public Mischief" (1982) 4 D.U.L.J. 110.
[88] *R. v Boston* (1923) 33 C.L.R. 386; *R. v Howes* (1971) 2 S.A.S.R. 293. See Charleton, McDermott and Bolger, *Criminal Law* (1999), p.307.
[89] Law Reform Commission, *Consultation Paper on Inchoate Offences* (LRC CP48–2008), p.95.
[90] Law Reform Commission, *Report on Inchoate Offences* (LRC 99–2010), pp.99–101.
[91] [1999] 4 I.R. 294 at 299–300.

established and no question of uncertainty arose.[92] Geoghegan J. went on to remark obiter that conspiracy to defraud was a common law offence similar in Irish law and English law. In *Attorney General v Oldridge*,[93] the Supreme Court approved the definition of "conspiracy to defraud" in the House of Lords decision in *Scott v Metropolitan Police Commissioner* as "an agreement by two or more by dishonesty to deprive a person of something which is his or to which he is or would be or might be entitled, and an agreement by two or more by dishonesty to injure some proprietary right of his".[94] The Supreme Court, in *Oldridge*, confirmed that conspiracy to defraud is a valid offence in Irish law and that the elements of the offence are specified with sufficient certainty at common law, Keane C.J. citing with approval the following passage from McAuley and McCutcheon:

> "[I]ts incriminating features have been clearly and consistently delineated by the courts for at least two centuries."[95]

Impossibility

The position in relation to legal impossibility is similar in respect of conspiracy and the other inchoate offences of attempt and incitement. A person is not guilty of criminal conspiracy where he agrees with another person to do an act that is not in fact unlawful, notwithstanding that the parties believe that the object of their agreement is criminal or unlawful. The parties' mistaken belief as to the lawfulness of the act does not have the effect of criminalising their agreement to perform what is in reality a lawful act.

The Irish position on factual impossibility is less certain. The Law Reform Commission has expressed the view that it is unclear, as a matter of Irish law, whether it is a criminal conspiracy to enter into an agreement to carry out a specific course of action that would amount to a crime if circumstances were as the alleged conspirators believed them to be, but on the facts as they really are the success of the conspiracy is impossible.[96] On the one hand, there is an argument that the obiter remarks in *Attorney General v Sullivan*[97] that impossibility is no defence to a criminal attempt could apply equally in the context of conspiracy; the reasoning behind precluding a defence of factual impossibility in attempt seems to be transferrable to conspiracy, and perhaps even more compelling given that the point of criminalisation in conspiracy is earlier in time than in attempt.[98] On the other hand, there is legal authority in England and Wales, in the House of Lords decision in *DPP v Nock*,[99] that when two or more persons agreed on a course of conduct with the object of committing a criminal offence but, unknown to them, it was not possible to achieve

---

[92] See Cathal McGreal, *Criminal Justice (Theft and Fraud Offences) Act 2001 Annotated and Conolidated*, 2nd edn (Dublin: Round Hall, 2011), pp.45–46.
[93] [2000] 1 I.R. 593 at 600.
[94] [1975] A.C. 819 at 840 per Viscount Dilholme.
[95] McAuley and McCutcheon, *Criminal Liability* (2000), p.429.
[96] Law Reform Commission, *Report on Inchoate Offences* (LRC 99–2010), pp.107–108.
[97] *Attorney General v Sullivan* [1964] I.R. 169 at 196 per Walsh J.
[98] Campbell, Kilcommins and O'Sullivan, *Criminal Law in Ireland: Cases and Commentary* (2010), pp.256–258.
[99] [1975] A.C. 476.

that object by that course of conduct, they did not commit the crime of conspiracy, and accordingly the limited agreement entered into by the defendants, which could not in any circumstances have involved the commission of the offence created by the statute, did not amount to the crime of conspiracy. In that case, the accused were charged with conspiracy to manufacture cocaine using ingredients which they believed were the raw materials for cocaine. However, it was factually impossible to produce cocaine using these particular ingredients, and on this basis the appellant's conviction was quashed. The Law Reform Commission has recommended that factual impossibility should not preclude liability for criminal conspiracy.[100]

Abandonment

A question arises as to how the criminal law treats a person who after entering a conspiracy subsequently abandons that conspiracy, withdrawing his involvement in the criminal enterprise. The position in Ireland would appear to be that withdrawal from a conspiracy does not absolve a person from criminal liability, but that abandonment may be a relevant mitigating factor at the sentencing stage. While there is no Irish case law touching directly on the issue of the availability of a defence of abandonment in criminal conspiracy, the obiter remarks of Walsh J. in *Attorney General v Sullivan*,[101] that abandonment does not preclude liability in the context of attempt, is of persuasive authority. It is also worth noting that the law relating to secondary participation provides for a defence of withdrawal in limited circumstances.[102]

A restricted form of the defence of abandonment is available in certain US states that have followed the approach taken in s.5.03(6) of the American Law Institute Model Penal Code; a requirement is imposed that the person withdrawing actually thwarts the success of the conspiracy. Justifications put forward in favour of the defence of withdrawal relate both to its potential for preventing crime and recognition of the lesser degree of culpability where a person shows some remorse by withdrawing his involvement. However, the defence is clearly open to abuse by persons who withdraw for less worthy reasons, such as the fear of detection by the police.

INCITEMENT

Introduction

At common law, the inchoate offence of incitement criminalises the incitor's acts of encouragement to another person to commit a crime. An incitement must attach to a criminal offence to trigger inchoate liability. The rules governing incitement liability are of general application to all substantive offences. For example, an order to rob a bank is incitement to robbery, and a request to rape a woman is incitement to rape, and so on. There is some legal authority suggesting that it is possible to have a

---

[100] Law Reform Commission, *Report on Inchoate Offences* (LRC 99–2010), p.108.
[101] *People (Attorney General) v Sullivan* [1964] I.R. 169 at 196 per Walsh J.
[102] *R. v Becerra* (1975) 62 Cr. App. R. 212.

Inchoate Offences 349

combination combining different inchoate offences, such as inciting an incitement[103] and inciting a conspiracy.[104] The Law Reform Commission expressed concern about having too many layers of inchoate liability, and recommended against constructing combinations that go beyond two layers of inchoate liability, such as "attempt to incite endangerment".[105] It was also recommended to avoid creating illogical combinations, such as incitement to attempt. Incitement would not appear to attach to secondary liability on the basis that s.7(1) of the Criminal Law Act 1997 does not actually create an offence of aiding, abetting, counselling or procuring the commission of an offence; that section states that a secondary participant "shall be liable to be indicted, tried and punished as a principal offender".

In *R. v Whitehouse*,[106] it was held that since the defendant's daughter, by virtue of her young age, was incapable of committing the crime of incest, the defendant could not be guilty of the common law offence of inciting her to commit that crime. Because the defendant's daughter belonged to a special category of vulnerable persons protected by statute she was incapable, in law, of committing the crime of incest. Applying the general principles of incitement liability the defendant could not be prosecuted since there was no incitement to commit an offence known to law. While there was an incitement to commit incestuous conduct, there was no incitement to commit an offence. Scarman L.J. observed that:

> "Plainly a gap or lacuna in the protection of girls under the age of 16 is exposed by this decision. It is regrettable indeed that a man who importunes his daughter under the age of 16 to have sexual intercourse with him but does not go beyond incitement cannot be found guilty of a crime."[107]

The Law Reform Commission has identified other instances in which a defendant may, on a strict application of the general principles of incitement, evade criminal liability in circumstances where the conduct involved is highly blameworthy and arguably merits criminalisation.[108] First, an example is given of a deceived incitee who is asked by the incitor to have sexual intercourse with a woman and is falsely told that the woman consents to intercourse. Because the incitee lacks the mens rea for rape an argument could be made that no offence has been incited. Such an outcome would clearly be undesirable as the incitor's conduct is harm-threatening and highly culpable. A second instance relates to where the incitee lacks criminal capacity to commit an offence. Because a child below the legal age of criminal responsibility or an insane person cannot, in law, commit an offence, a defence could be put forward by a person who incites a young child or mentally-ill person to commit a crime, that no criminal incitement has taken place because the incitee is incapable in law of committing an offence. Finally, an incitor who incited another person to commit a crime by the use of threats might argue that no offence has been incited in circumstances where the incitee avoided criminal liability on the

---

[103] *R. v Sirat* (1985) Cr. App. R. 41.
[104] *R. v De Kromme* (1892) 17 Cox CC 492.
[105] Law Reform Commission, *Report on Inchoate Offences* (LRC 99–2010), pp.123–124.
[106] [1977] Q.B. 868.
[107] *R. v Whitehouse* [1977] 1 Q.B. 868 at 875.
[108] Law Reform Commission, *Report on Inchoate Offences* (LRC 99–2010), pp.125–129.

basis of the defence of duress. It is unclear, on the basis of existing common law principles, to what extent a defendant might successfully rely on the above defences to a charge of incitement. In relation to each of the above categories, the Law Reform Commission has recommended that it should be clarified by statutory reform that a person may not evade liability for incitement.[109]

Actus reus of incitement

The actus reus of incitement relates to the act of encouraging another person to commit a criminal offence. The definition of the actus reus of incitement is extremely broad. The forms which the act of incitement may take are abundant, ranging from polite requests to commands accompanied by threats. The act of incitement may be express or implied. The following passage taken from the judgment of Holmes J.A., in *S v Nkosiyana*, captures the breadth of the definition of the act of incitement:

> "An inciter is one who reaches and seeks to influence the mind of another to the commission of a crime. The machinations of criminal ingenuity being legion, the approach to the other's mind may take various forms, such as suggestion, proposal, request, exhortation, gesture, argument, persuasion, inducement, goading or the arousal of cupidity."[110]

For the act of incitement to be complete there must be communication of the incitement to the incitee. If the communication of incitement fails to reach the recipient it is more appropriate to initiate a prosecution based on the double inchoate offence of attempting to incite an offence.[111] In *R. v Most*,[112] it was held that incitements do not need to be directed at a particular person; an incitement can be aimed at the world at large with no specific person in mind. In that case, publishing an article in a newspaper encouraging readers to assassinate political leaders was held to be sufficient to satisfy the act requirement of incitement. *R. v Most* was followed in the more recent decision of the English Court of Criminal Appeal in *R. v Jones*,[113] where it was held that, for the purposes of establishing the actus reus of incitement, it did not matter that an incitement of a child under 13 years to engage in sexual activity was targeted at a specific child or children generally, and that there was no requirement that the intended recipient of the incitement was identifiable prior to the making of the communication.

It is important to note that liability is triggered once the act of incitement is complete; it does not matter that the incitement is unsuccessful, having no effect on the mind of the incitee. In *DPP v Murtagh*, Costello J. observed that "... an offence is completed when the words of incitement are uttered, and so the offence is committed even though the incitement fails".[114] For example, if A requests B to assault another person, the act of incitement is established notwithstanding that B refuses, and in

---

[109] Law Reform Commission, *Report on Inchoate Offences* (LRC 99–2010), p.130.
[110] (1966) 4 S.A. 655 at 658.
[111] *R. v Banks* (1873) 12 Cox CC 393.
[112] (1881) 7 Q.B.D. 244.
[113] *R. v Jones* [2007] EWCA Crim 1118.
[114] [1990] 1 I.R. 339 at 342.

Inchoate Offences 351

reality, would never have carried out A's request. In *DPP v Armstrong*, Tuckey L.J. commented that "... the intention of the persons incited is entirely irrelevant".[115]

It is worth bearing in mind that, of the three inchoate offences, incitement is the furthest removed from the commission of the substantive offence. McAuley and McCutcheon have commented that incitement is:

> "[T]he most remote point on the continuum between intention and execution at which relational liability is normally attached in modern criminal law. Theoretically speaking, incitement marks the threshold of relational liability in the sense that it represents the first stage on a continuum that runs through conspiracy to attempt."[116]

The leading Irish authority on what constitutes incitement is *Attorney General v Capaldi*.[117] In that case, the defendant was a man charged with inciting a doctor to commit the crime of bringing about an abortion. Referring to a girl whom he had brought to the doctor, he asked whether the doctor would "do something for her" in relation to her pregnancy. The doctor replied "do you realise what you are asking me to do, you are asking me to perform an illegal operation", to which the defendant replied "Yes. Would you perform; there is ample money to meet your fees". The doctor refused, and the defendant was ultimately charged with the inchoate offence of incitement.

It was argued for the defendant that this did not amount to incitement, and was no more than the mere expression of a desire. It was further argued on behalf of the defendant that an incitement must include some element of "overcoming the reluctant mind". The Court of Criminal Appeal accepted that incitement must be more than the mere expression of a desire; however, on the evidence, it was clear that the defendant had made a positive request to bring about an abortion, which could not be fairly characterised as the mere expression of a desire. The court rejected the argument that incitement must involve an effort to overcome the reluctant mind: rather, a person may commit incitement by doing something if "but for it, it would not have occurred to the party incited to commit the crime, whether he had any particular reluctance to commit it or not".[118]

Mens rea of incitement

The mens rea of incitement is made up of a number of distinct fault elements. First, intention or knowledge must be established in respect of the act of incitement. Liability is not imposed where a person unknowingly and accidentally incites another person to commit a crime. Equally, criminal incitement will not be established where the incitor's conduct or words unwittingly happen to influence another to commit a crime; there must be some degree of purpose or knowledge in relation to the conduct or words that are alleged to constitute incitement. The following example taken from the Law Reform Commission's *Report on Inchoate Offences* neatly illustrates the

---

[115] [2000] Crim. L.R. 379.
[116] McAuley and McCutcheon, *Criminal Liability* (2000), p.430.
[117] (1949) 1 Frewen 95.
[118] *People (Attorney General) v Capaldi* (1949) 1 Frewen 95 at 97.

mens rea requirement that the incitor's act of communication to the incitee must be intentional:

> "A person could keep a private diary setting out desires for particular offences to be committed and how their commission would be heroic and so on. If by accident this diary was published or read by others, it seems incitement is not committed despite the diarist truly desiring the substantive offences to be committed. This is because the diarist did not take the conscious decision to incite; they did [not intend to] make an incitement to crime, merely desired it, and to punish them in the circumstances would be to punish wicked thoughts alone, albeit ones reduced to private writing.
>
> It might be said that writing down such thoughts is something worth discouraging, that if the diary being 'published' results from negligence or recklessness on the part of the diarist then they can be said to have incited crime ... Though it cannot be stated with certainty, it seems that common law incitement draws the line before recklessness. That is, to commit incitement one must have culpability greater than recklessness in respect of the act of communicating."[119]

A second aspect of the mens rea requirements of criminal incitement relates to proof of intention in respect of the elements of the offence the subject of the incitement. Citing the decision of the English Court for Crown Cases Reserved in *R. v Most*,[120] the Law Reform Commission has expressed the view that the conventional view at common law requires that an incitor have the mental state of intention in relation to the constituent elements of the offence incited, "and this is so even if culpability states other than intention suffice for the particular substantive offence to which the instance of incitement relates".[121] In *R. v Most*, Coleridge C.J. describes the mental element of incitement as an intention to incite another to commit a crime.[122]

The Law Reform Commission has critiqued this aspect of the mens rea of incitement, noting that an elevation of the fault requirements in respect of all elements of the target offence may lead to under-criminalisation.[123] Incitement to rape is cited as an example of an inchoate offence that could potentially result in unmeritorious acquittals if intention is required in respect of both the act of sexual intercourse and the circumstance element of absence of consent on the part of the woman. It is difficult to identify any clear justification for elevating the fault element of recklessness to intention in the context of the circumstance element of absence of consent in rape cases. The person who incites another to rape a woman should not escape liability on the basis that he is merely reckless as to the woman's lack of consent, as opposed to intending that the woman lacks consent; in respect of both reckless and intentional incitement to rape, the incitor's conduct is highly culpable and surely merits criminal sanction. The Law Reform Commission has recommended departing from the intention-only based approach, and adopting a

---

[119] Law Reform Commission, *Report on Inchoate Offences* (LRC 99–2010), pp.118–119.
[120] (1881) 7 QBD 244 at 251.
[121] Law Reform Commission, *Report on Inchoate Offences* (LRC 99–2010), p.120.
[122] *R. v Most* (1881) 7 QBD 244 at 251.
[123] Law Reform Commission, *Report on Inchoate Offences* (LRC 99–2010), pp.120–122.

new approach where incitement culpability tracks the culpability requirements of the offence that has been incited. Under the "tracking approach", the incitor, when making the incitement, must act with the same culpability requirements that are required for the substantive offence incited. This would mean that, in relation to the offence of rape, the incitor, at the time that he incites another to commit rape, must be reckless as to whether, or intend that, the incitee has sexual intercourse with a woman without her consent.

A third aspect of the mens rea of incitement relates to a requirement that the person making the incitement intends that the crime he is inciting will be committed by the incitee. If the incitor is only acting in jest and, in reality, has no intention that the crime incited be carried out that person lacks culpability for criminal incitement. An example might be a group of friends behaving boisterously in a bar, and one member of the group jokingly asks a friend to kill another friend in the group. While in many cases it will be clear from the context and surrounding circumstances that it was never intended for the incited crime to be carried out, in other cases it may be more difficult to ascertain whether the incitor was involved in harmless banter or serious about his wishes for a crime to be committed.

Impossibility

The position in relation to legal impossibility is the same in relation to incitement as it is with the other inchoate offences of attempt and conspiracy. An incitor is not guilty of incitement where he or she incites another person to do an act that is in fact lawful, notwithstanding that he or she believes the act to be criminal in nature. The person's mistaken belief that the conduct he is encouraging is a crime does not transform otherwise lawful conduct into a criminal offence.

There is some authority at common law suggesting that a defence of factual impossibility is available, in limited circumstances, in the context of criminal incitement.[124] However, because there is no Irish authority touching directly on factual impossibility, it is unclear whether such a defence is available under Irish law. Examples of conduct which might raise the issue of the availability of such a defence include the following: (1) where A incites B to steal from C but the crime is impossible because C's pockets are empty; and (2) where A requests that B kills C in circumstances where the crime of murder is impossible because unknown to A and B, C is actually already dead. There is a possibility that the Irish courts would follow the line of reasoning underlying the obiter remarks in *Attorney General v Sullivan*[125] to the effect that impossibility is no defence to a criminal attempt. The rationale for precluding a defence of factual impossibility in attempt could be said to apply equally in the context of incitement: it is preferable to impose liability on a subjectivist basis by reference to the culpability of the incitor at the point in time when the act of incitement is complete. In relation to the inchoate offence of incitement, the Law Reform Commission has recommended against making provision for a defence of factual impossibility in Irish criminal law.

---

[124] *R. v Fitzmaurice* [1983] Q.B. 1083 (CA).
[125] *Attorney General v Sullivan* [1964] I.R. 169 at 196 per Walsh J.

Abandonment

The position under Irish law would appear to be that the withdrawal of an incitement does not absolve a person from criminal liability, but that abandonment may be a relevant mitigating factor at the sentencing stage. While there is no Irish case law touching directly on the issue of the availability of a defence of abandonment in criminal incitement, the obiter remarks of Walsh J. in *Attorney General v Sullivan*,[126] that abandonment does not preclude liability in the context of attempt, are of persuasive authority. It is worth noting that the law relating to secondary participation provides for a defence of withdrawal in limited circumstances.[127]

Specific offences of incitement

In addition to the general principles of incitement liability, there exist a number of specific statutory offences of incitement. These individual offences belong to the body of offences in the special part of the criminal law and are to be distinguished from the general part doctrine of incitement, discussed above. A notable example of stand-alone incitement-based offences include the offences under ss.2–4 of the Prohibition of Incitement to Hatred Act 1989. These specific instance offences exist in their own right in statute law and their operation is not dependent upon the operation of the general principles of common law incitement set out above.

---

[126] *Attorney General v Sullivan* [1964] I.R. 169 at 196 per Walsh J.
[127] *R. v Becerra* (1975) 62 Cr. App. R. 212.

CHAPTER 13

DEGREES OF COMPLICITY IN CRIME

Introduction

Criminal law recognises that there may be more than one participant in a crime. The principal offender has the most direct involvement in the commission of a criminal offence, being the person responsible for the actus reus of the offence. However, the general principles of criminal law provide that other persons who participate in the criminal act of the principal offender may be criminally liable for acts of assistance or encouragement. Glanville Williams succinctly describes the legal distinction between principal offenders and secondary parties in a passage referred to by Lord Bingham in *Kennedy (No. 2)*[1]:

> "Principals cause, accomplices encourage (or otherwise influence) or help. If the instigator were regarded as causing the result he would be a principal, and the conceptual division between principals (or, as I prefer to call them, perpetrators) and accessories would vanish. Indeed, it was because the instigator was not regarded as causing the crime that the notion of accessories had to be developed. This is the irrefragable argument for recognising the *novus actus* principle as one of the bases of our criminal law. The final act is done by the perpetrator, and his guilt pushes the accessories, conceptually speaking, into the background. Accessorial liability is, in the traditional theory, 'derivative' from that of the perpetrator."[2]

Since the conduct of the secondary participant is accompanied by a guilty mind and harms the interests protected by the criminal law such conduct is clearly deserving of criminal sanction.[3] In some cases, the degree of culpability will be higher in respect of the secondary participant. As Glanville Williams put it, "Lady Macbeth was worse than Macbeth".[4] Consider the criminal gang boss who orders a desperate addict to conceal large quantities of drugs inside his body and to board a plane, with a view to facilitating the cross-border transportation of illegal drugs.[5] While the

---

[1] [2007] UKHL 38 at para.17.
[2] Glanville Williams, "Finis for Novus Actus?" [1989] 48(3) C.L.J. 391 at 392.
[3] See McAuley and McCutcheon, *Criminal Liability* (2000), pp.453–456, considering the rationale underpinning the law relating to secondary participation.
[4] Glanville Williams, *Textbook of Criminal Law* (London: Stevens & Sons, 1978), p.287.
[5] While the criminal activities of gang bosses are clearly covered by the general principles of criminal liability relating to complicity in crime, it is worth noting that ss.71A and 72 of the Criminal Justice Act 2006 provide for specific offences relating to directing a criminal organisation and participation in a criminal organisation. See Seán Ó Toghda, *Criminal Justice (Amendment) Act 2009 Annotated* (Dublin: Round Hall, 2011), pp.10–18.

drug mule is the person directly responsible for bringing about the actus reus of the drug trafficking offence, many observers would conclude that both the conduct and culpability of the gang boss is more heinous. In a given case, the motivations of the drug mule might be confined to clearing a drug debt or obtaining a modest payment to finance the person's drug addiction. In contrast, the intentions of the leader of a criminal gang will generally relate to earning huge profits through the illegal drugs trade, with no regard to the massive harm caused to society by his actions.

The liability of secondary participants is derivative in nature. To establish secondary liability, proof that the principal offence occurred is required. In this regard, secondary liability must be distinguished from attempt, conspiracy and incitement. In contrast to secondary liability, inchoate liability does not require that the commission of any offence be established. Relational liability may be imposed in respect of an inchoate offence despite the fact that the wrongdoer has been unsuccessful in his efforts to bring about the commission of the target offence. It follows that if A enters into a conspiracy, incites or attempts to commit an offence, but the target offence is not in fact brought to completion, A may still be liable for the commission of an inchoate offence. However, if A's acts of assistance or encouragement take place in circumstances where the principal offence is actually committed by the principal then the liability of A is more appropriately considered under the principles of secondary liability; A's liability is derivative on the commission of the principal offence.

Prior to 1997, the rules governing the area of participation in crime were to be found in part, at common law, and in part, under the provisions of the Accessories and Abettors Act 1861. Four categories of participants in crime were recognised under the former law:

1. principal in the first degree—the person who actually committed the offence;
2. principal in the second degree—a person who was present at the time of the commission of a felony or misdemeanour and aided or abetted the commission of the felony or misdemeanour;
3. accessory before the fact—a person who gave assistance before a felony or misdemeanour was committed;
4. accessory after the fact—a person who, knowing that a felony had been committed, assisted the criminal in evading apprehension, trial or punishment.

Criminal Law Act 1997

The Criminal Law Act 1997 abolished the above archaic distinction between felonies and misdemeanours, as well as enacting a new set of provisions on secondary participation in indictable crime. Section 16 of the Criminal Law Act 1997 repeals the Accessories and Abettors Act 1861 in its entirety, as well as a range of provisions contained in other statutes relating to secondary liability. Section 7(1) of the Criminal Law Act 1997 sets out the existing law relating to secondary liability for indictable offences as follows:

> Any person who aids, abets, counsels or procures the commission of an indictable offence shall be liable to be indicted, tried and punished as a principal offender.

Degrees of Complicity in Crime 357

While s.7(1) of the Criminal Law Act 1997 is concerned only with indictable offences, it should be noted that the effect of s.22 of the Petty Sessions (Ireland) Act 1851 is that, broadly speaking, the same principles apply to summary offences. It follows that the discussion contained in this chapter relating to complicity in crime is relevant to both summary and indictable offences. It should also be noted that s.19 of the Criminal Justice (Amendment) Act 2009 gives extraterritorial effect to offences committed by persons who, outside the State, aid, abet, counsel or procure the commission of an offence in the State, as provided for under s.7 of the Criminal Law Act 1997. Section 19 of the Act of 2009 also gives extraterritorial effect to offences committed by persons who conceal an offence under s.8(1) of the Criminal Law Act 1997.

Since the rules governing complicity are general principles of criminal liability they are applicable to all offences, unless their application is excluded by some other rule of law. For example, there is legal authority to the effect that victims of crimes will generally not be considered criminally liable for secondary participation in the crime of the principal notwithstanding that the victim has in fact assisted or encouraged the principal to commit an offence.[6]

The above statutory provisions only provide a skeletal outline on the law relating to complicity, stating in rather bald terms that a secondary party may be tried and punished as a principal offender. The detail of the substantive law is to be found at common law. To gain a fuller understanding of the legal rules governing secondary liability reference must be made to the relevant case law. As will be seen in the discussion that follows, there is a great deal of conceptual confusion and uncertainty as to the precise contents of the law relating to secondary liability. Professor Ormerod's comments relating to the state of the law on secondary liability in England and Wales are equally applicable in the Irish context:

> "The current law of secondary liability is unsatisfactorily complex, and displays many of the characteristic weaknesses of common law that has been allowed to develop in a pragmatic and unprincipled way. Reform would be welcome ..."[7]

There is a strong argument for restating the law relating to secondary liability in a more coherent and simplified form, with a view to bringing greater clarity to the contents and limits of the law in this area. The Criminal Law Codification Advisory Committee earmarked the law relating to complicity as an area suitable for codification.[8] Streamlining the rules governing secondary liability in a codified form would enhance accessibility and legal certainty, as well as increasing the likelihood of consistency in the application of the law. At present, common law principles are being stretched to ensure that a just outcome is achieved in individual cases, with the result that the jurisprudence has developed in an unprincipled manner, bringing with it a good deal of confusion and uncertainty. The law relating to complicity in crime would benefit from a rigorous analysis by the Law Reform Commission, with a view to identifying areas in need of reform, and recommending a set of statutory provisions that would bring greater clarity and principle to this area of law.

---

[6] *R. v Tyrell* [1894] 1 Q.B. 710; *R. v Whitehouse* [1977] Q.B. 868.
[7] Ormerod, *Smith & Hogan Criminal Law*, 13th edn (Oxford: Oxford University Press, 2011), p.184.
[8] Criminal Law Codification Advisory Committee, *Annual Report 2007*, p.16.

Innocent Agency

Under the doctrine of innocent agency, a person who causes the actus reus of an offence by using an innocent agent to perpetrate a criminal act is viewed as a principal offender rather than a secondary party. The innocent agent is the means used by the principal offender to commit the crime. For example, instead of directly stabbing an intended victim by his own physical act, a person might use alternative means to stab the proposed victim, such as using an innocent third party to carry out the crime. A person might hand a knife to a child below the age of criminal responsibility or an insane person with instructions to stab another person. Notwithstanding the fact that it is the infant or insane person who commits the actus reus of the offence, the criminal law deems the person who provided the weapon to the innocent agent to be the principal offender. The innocent agent is not criminally liable because the criminal law excuses his or her wrongful conduct due to a lack of criminal responsibility owing to his or her young age or insanity.

In *R. v Michael*,[9] the defendant wished to kill her child. She procured poison and gave it to her nurse, telling the nurse that it was medicine for the child. The nurse decided not to use the "medicine", leaving it on a shelf. Another child, however, came across the "medicine" and administered it to the baby, killing him. The defendant was found guilty as the principal offender, with the court accepting that both the nurse and the child could be described as innocent agents. The nurse is an innocent agent because she lacks mens rea, and the child lacks criminal responsibility by virtue of young age.

Another example of the doctrine of innocent agency is *R. v Stringer and Banks*.[10] In this case, the defendant was a manager who directed employees to pay invoices which (unknown to them) were fraudulent. Charged with theft, he argued that he himself had not appropriated property, but that this was done by the acts of the employees in arranging payment. The court held that since the employees were unaware of the fraud they acted as innocent agents, with the result that the manager was guilty as a principal offender.

In *R. v Cogan and Leak*,[11] it was suggested that the crime of rape could be committed by a principal offender through the use of an innocent agent. In that case, Leak brought Cogan to his home with the intention that Cogan rape his wife, knowing that his wife did not consent to having sexual intercourse with Cogan. Cogan was found not guilty of rape as he lacked the requisite men rea; Cogan believed that Leak's wife was consenting to intercourse. On the other hand, Leak was fully aware of his wife's lack of consent and intended that the crime of rape be perpetrated against his wife by Cogan. Leak's conviction for aiding and abetting the crime of rape against his wife was upheld by the Court of Appeal. Professor Ormerod has argued that there are some crimes to which the doctrine of innocent agency is inapplicable such as bigamy and rape.[12] He goes on to say that "[t]here are *dicta* in *Cogan and Leak* that rape may be committed through an innocent agent but these are contrary to principle". If a female defendant used an innocent agent to

---

[9] (1840) 9 C. & P. 356.
[10] (1991) 94 Cr. App. R. 13.
[11] [1976] Q.B. 217.
[12] Ormerod, *Smith & Hogan Criminal Law* (2011), p.189.

perpetrate the crime of rape against another woman, could that female defendant be properly viewed as the principal offender? It will be recalled that the definition of the offence of rape contained in s.2 of the Criminal Law (Rape) Act 1981 specifies that only a man may commit the offence of rape.

Elements of secondary liability

In *R. v Stringer*, Toulson L.J. observed that "secondary liability requires proof of the necessary conduct element accompanied by the necessary mental element".[13] Similarly to substantive offences, such as murder or rape, it is possible to identify the actus reus and mens rea that must be proven to establish secondary liability. Robinson and Grail say that:

> "Element analysis, by providing a precise statement of all the separate elements of an offence definition, has the increased advantage of conceptual simplicity."[14]

The separation of the doctrine of secondary liability into constituent parts assists in understanding this complex area of law, enables a clearer statement of the law to be provided and helps in identifying weaknesses in existing law.

Secondary liability is made up of a variety of circumstance, conduct and mental elements. Since liability is derivative in nature there is a requirement to identify a principal offence. This aspect of the actus reus might be classified as the core circumstance element in secondary participation. Without proof of a principle offence there is no basis for secondary liability to be imposed; the defendant must assist or encourage the commission of some offence known to law. The other aspects of the actus reus of complicity relate to the physical elements of aiding, abetting, counselling or procuring which will be considered in further detail in the following section.

The mens rea requirements of the secondary participant consist of a number of discrete mental elements:

(1) intention to perform the physical act of assistance or encouragement, and in the case of an omission, an intentional failure to act,
(2) intention that the acts or omissions assist in or encourage the commission of the principal offence, and
(3) the secondary participant must have intended to assist or encourage the principal in the crime proved to have been committed by the principal, or the commission of a crime of a similar nature known to the accused to be the intention of the principal when assisting or encouraging him.

---

[13] [2011] EWCA Crim 1396 at para.40.
[14] Paul H. Robinson and Jane A. Grail, "Element Analysis in Defining Criminal Liability: The Model Penal Code and Beyond" (1983) 35 *Stanford Law Review* 681 at 704.

Secondary liability—the conduct element

The conduct element of the secondary participant consists of "aiding, abetting, counselling or procuring" the commission of the principal offence. There is some uncertainty at common law as to the precise meaning of each of these terms. Differing approaches have been taken as to how these terms should be interpreted. In *Attorney General v Able*, Woolf J. appeared to be suggesting that rather than analyse each term separately, "it is preferable to consider the phrase 'aids, abets, counsels or procures' as a whole".[15] By contrast, in *Attorney General's Reference (No. 1 of 1975)* Lord Widgery interpreted the terms as follows:

> "We approach s.8 of the 1861 Act on the basis that the words should be given their ordinary meaning, if possible. We approach the section on the basis also that if four words are employed here 'aid, abet, counsel or procure', the probability is that there is a difference between each of those four words and the other three, because, if there were no such difference, then Parliament would be wasting time in using four words where three or two would do."[16]

Since a body of case law has developed around each of the terms used to describe the conduct element of the secondary party it is preferable to consider each of the terms separately to obtain a clearer understanding of the legal meaning of each of these terms. McAuley and McCutcheon have stated in clear terms the reason why it is important to identify the contents of the actus reus of secondary participants:

> "Thus, it would appear that there are limits, as yet undefined, to the extent of the cumulative expression 'aids, abets, counsels or procures' and that certain forms of criminal involvement do not come within it."[17]

Many lay observers would probably consider the language used to describe the conduct requirement in secondary liability as being both outmoded and obtuse. The meaning of the terms "aids, abets, counsels and procures" was neatly summarised, in modern English, by the Law Commission of England and Wales as follows:

> "Disregarding 'procuring', it is generally accepted that these specified modes of involvement cover two types of conduct on the part of D, namely the provision of assistance and the provision of encouragement."[18]

In the case of procuring, a person might cause the principal to commit an offence without carrying out acts of assisting or encouraging.

It is worth noting the distinction between the actus reus of full substantive offences and the conduct requirement in secondary liability. The actus reus of the principal offence is prescribed by the statutory provision creating the offence or at common law. For example, the offence of robbery is defined in s.14 of the Criminal

---

[15] [1984] 1 Q.B. 795 at 809.
[16] [1975] Q.B. 773.
[17] McAuley and McCutcheon, *Criminal Liability* (2000), p.462.
[18] Law Commission (Law Com. No. 305), *Participating in Crime* (2007), para.2.21.

Justice (Theft and Fraud Offences) Act 2001 as stealing, and immediately before or at the time of doing so, using force on any person or seeking to put any person in fear of being then and there subjected to force. As noted above, the conduct element in complicity is "aiding, abetting, counselling or procuring" the commission of the principal offence. The type of conduct required on the part of the secondary party covers virtually any form of conduct. Indeed, the degree of conduct required to impose secondary liability may be very minimal. In many cases, there will be a stark difference in the degree of participation in a crime, in terms of actual physical conduct, between the secondary participant and the principal. In the case of robbery, the conduct requirement of the secondary party could be satisfied by a wide range of physical acts along a spectrum ranging from minimal to maximum involvement: encouraging the principal to rob, supplying information, providing a getaway car, carrying out surveillance, or keeping lookout.

R. v Giannetto[19] is a good case to illustrate the point that the threshold is very low in respect of establishing the conduct element of secondary parties. In that case, the defendant was charged with the murder of his wife. The prosecution alleged that either he killed her himself, or he encouraged a third party to kill her. In relation to encouragement, the jury sought guidance from the judge, asking:

> "How much of an involvement in the murder does the defendant need to have in order to convict for murder, i.e. planning, paying for, knew of and didn't prevent."

In response, the trial judge gave the following direction (which was upheld on appeal):

> "Supposing somebody came up to [him] and said, 'I am going to kill your wife', if he played any part, either in encouragement, as little as patting him on the back, nodding, saying, 'Oh goody', that would be sufficient to involve him in the murder, to make him guilty, because he is encouraging the murder."

The Court of Appeal went on to say that "[a]ny involvement from mere encouragement upwards would suffice".

Aiding

The term "aids" is generally understood to mean assisting or helping another person to commit an offence. The jurisprudence has attributed a broad meaning to the term "aids", and it would appear to cover a wide range of conduct. Examples of the type of conduct that would come within the definition of "aids" include the supply of information or weapons, surveillance activities, keeping lookout, and facilitating escape following the commission of the offence. In *DPP v Egan*,[20] the Court of Criminal Appeal held that a person could aid and abet the commission of an offence without being present when the crime was committed. In that case, simply making a workshop available to a group of criminals following the commission of an offence satisfied the conduct element of assisting in the commission of an offence; it was

---

[19] [1996] Crim. L.R. 722 at 723.
[20] [1989] I.R. 681 at 686.

irrelevant that the defendant was not himself present during the commission of the robbery.

There would appear to be no causation requirement between the secondary party's act of aiding and the commission of the principal offence; it is sufficient to show that the secondary party performed some act of assistance that contributes in some way to the commission of the crime. The relationship between causation and secondary liability was considered in the recent judgment of the Court of Appeal in *R. v Stringer*:

> "It is well established that D's conduct need not cause P to commit the offence in the sense that 'but for' D's conduct P would not have committed the offence (see *R. v Mendez and Thompson*[21] at para. 23). But it is also established by the authorities referred to in *R. v Mendez and Thompson* that D's conduct must have some relevance to the commission of the principal offence; there must, as it has been said, be some connecting link. The moral justification for holding D responsible for the crime is that he has involved himself in the commission of the crime by assistance or encouragement, and that presupposes some form of connection between his conduct and the crime."[22]

Toulson L.J. went on to refer to a passage from the Law Commission's *Report on Participating in Crime*:

> "However, the precise nature of this sufficient connection is elusive. It is best understood, at least where D's conduct consists of assistance, as meaning that D's conduct has made a contribution to the commission of the offence."[23]

Accordingly, it would appear that it is sufficient to show that the secondary party participated in the crime of the principal offender by conduct that actually assists in some way in the commission of the crime.

There are dicta in *R. v Fury* that "[t]here is no requirement in law for a secondary party to have planned or agreed the offence committed by the principal".[24] The Court of Appeal went on to quote a passage from Professor Ormerod's *Smith & Hogan Criminal Law* with approval:

> "Aiding does not imply any consensus between D and P. If D sees P committing a crime and comes to his assistance by, for example, restraining the policeman who would have prevented P from committing the crime, D is surely guilty even though his assistance is unforeseen and unwanted by P and unknown to him. The same might apply to aid given beforehand. D, knowing that P is going to meet a blackmailer, V, slips a gun into P's pocket in the hope that he will kill V – which he does."[25]

---

[21] [2010] EWCA Crim 516 at para.23.
[22] [2011] EWCA Crim 1396 at para.48.
[23] Law Commission (Law Com. No. 305), *Participating in Crime* (2007), para.2.33.
[24] [2006] EWCA Crim 1258 at para.16.
[25] Ormerod, *Smith & Hogan Criminal Law* (2011), p.193.

Abetting and counselling

There is considerable overlap between the terms "abetting" and "counselling" in so far as both terms essentially relate to acts of encouragement.[26] It follows that both terms may be discussed together, for the sake of avoiding unnecessary repetition. The terms "abetting" and "counselling" are generally considered to mean encouraging or inciting the commission of the principal offence.[27] Abetting and counselling can be distinguished from the inchoate offence of incitement. In relation to abetting and counselling, the abettor or counsellor will have encouraged the commission of the principal offence; proof is required in respect of both the conduct element of encouragement and the circumstance element of a principal offence having been committed. In contrast, inchoate liability requires that acts of incitement or encouragement of the target offence be established but there is no requirement that the target offence be completed by the person the subject of the incitement; the essence of relational liability is that the target offence is not brought to completion.

It would appear that there is no requirement that acts of abetting, counselling or encouragement cause the commission of the principal offence. In *R. v Calhaem* it was held that:

> "Taking the natural meaning of the word, and there being nothing in the authorities to bind us to adopt one or other construction, we take the view that the approach in *Smith and Hogan* and *Glanville Williams* is correct. The natural meaning of the word does not imply the commission of the offence. So long as there is counselling (and there was ample evidence in this case of that fact), so long as the principal offence is committed by the one counselled and so long as the one counselled is acting within the scope of his authority, and not in an accidental way."[28]

However, in *R. v Luffman*,[29] the Court of Appeal held that there must be some "connection or causal link" between the act of abetting or counselling and the commission of the principal offence. In other words, the secondary party must have actually done some external act that amounts to encouragement of the commission of the principal offence. It follows that while there is no requirement that the act of encouragement caused the commission of the offence, evidence must be adduced establishing conduct on the part of the secondary participant that equates to some form of encouragement to commit the principal offence.

Finally, there must be actual communication of the encouragement from the secondary party to the principal offender. The principal offender must be aware that he is being encouraged by the secondary party. Professor Ormerod has described this aspect of the actus reus of abetting and counselling as the "consensus requirement":

---

[26] Ormerod, *Smith & Hogan Criminal Law* (2011), p.193.
[27] See Charleton, McDermott and Bolger, *Criminal Law* (1999), p.198; McAuley and McCutcheon, *Criminal Liability* (2000), p.464; Ormerod, *Smith & Hogan Criminal Law* (2011), p.193.
[28] [1985] 1 Q.B. 808 at 818.
[29] [2008] EWCA Crim 1752 at para.39.

"It is probably not necessary to prove that P was influenced in any way by D, but P must at least be aware that he has the authority, or the encouragement or the approval, of D to do the relevant acts."[30]

Procuring

The leading case is *Attorney General's Reference (No. 1 of 1975)*,[31] where the term "procuring" was defined as meaning "to produce by endeavour" so that the defendant in some way caused the principal to commit the offence. In that case, the defendant spiked the principal's drink with alcohol, unbeknownst to the principal, knowing that the principal was about to drive home. The principal drove home, and in doing so committed the strict liability offence of drink driving; it was no defence that he was not aware that he had consumed alcohol in excess of the legal limit as the offence definition did not prescribe a mens rea requirement in respect of that aspect of the offence. The defendant was found guilty of procuring the commission of the principal offence on the basis that through his conduct he brought about the actus reus of the offence of drink driving. Lord Widgery set out the constituent elements of the term "procuring" in the following passage:

> "To procure means to produce by endeavour. You procure a thing by setting out to see that it happens and taking the appropriate steps to produce that happening. We think that there are plenty of instances in which a person may be said to procure the commission of a crime by another even though there is no sort of conspiracy between the two, even though there is no attempt at agreement or discussion as to the form which the offence should take ...
>
> Causation here is important. You cannot procure an offence unless there is a causal link between what you do and the commission of the offence, and here we are told that in consequence of the addition of this alcohol the driver, when he drove home, drove with an excess quantity of alcohol in his body.
>
> Giving the words their ordinary meaning in English, and asking oneself whether in those circumstances the offence has been procured, we are in no doubt that the answer is that it has. It has been procured because, unknown to the driver and without his collaboration, he has been put in a position in which in fact he has committed an offence which he never would have committed otherwise."[32]

It is noted in the above passage that the conduct element of procuring contains a causation requirement; it must be established that the conduct of the procurer caused the commission of the actus reus of the principal offence. This is in contrast to the conduct elements of aiding, abetting and counselling which do not require proof of causation. A second point worth noting is that *Attorney General's Reference (No. 1 of 1975)* makes it clear that, in relation to procuring, there is no requirement of a meeting of minds between the secondary party and the principal. In that case,

---

[30] Ormerod, *Smith & Hogan Criminal Law* (2011), p.194.
[31] [1975] Q.B. 773 at 779.
[32] [1975] Q.B. 773 at 779–780.

there was no communication between the principal and secondary participant as to the commission of the principal offence. In fact, the principal's drink was laced surreptitiously by the secondary party. The principal was unaware that the secondary party had taken steps to bring about the actus reus of drink driving. In the words of Professor Ormerod, the case "decides that consensus is immaterial where 'procuring' is relied on".[33]

Failure to act or mere presence as an actus reus

It is necessary to consider whether a failure to act or mere presence at the scene of a crime can satisfy the actus reus requirement of the secondary participant. The general rule is that an omission to act on the part of the secondary party will be insufficient to impose criminal liability. There is no general duty in Irish criminal law to intervene and take steps to prevent the commission of an offence. In *R. v Coney*, Cave J. stated the general principle as follows:

> "Now it [is] a general rule in the case of principals in the second degree that there must be participation in the act, and that, although a man is present whilst a felony is being committed, if he takes no part in it, and does not act in concert with those who commit it, he will not be a principal in the second degree merely because he does not endeavour to prevent the felony, or apprehend the felon."[34]

In the same case, Hawkins J. stated that "it is no criminal offence to stand by, a mere passive spectator of a crime, even of a murder. Non-interference to prevent a crime is not itself a crime".[35]

There are some exceptions to this general rule. First, in exceptional circumstances the criminal law imposes a positive duty on individuals to act. For example, the law imposes a duty on parents towards their children. If a mother intentionally assaults her child causing serious harm to the child she is guilty as principal of the offence of assault causing serious harm under s.4 of the Non-Fatal Offences Against the Person Act 1997. If the father stands by, doing nothing, watching the mother carry out a serious assault on the child, and his failure to intervene to protect his child is accepted as amounting to encouragement to the mother, he may be found guilty as a secondary participant in the offence of assault causing serious harm perpetrated by the mother, provided he also has the requisite mens rea. Since the father has a special duty towards his child, his failure to act is sufficient to satisfy the actus reus requirement of secondary parties. If the person standing by was a stranger, as opposed to the father of the child, secondary liability would not be imposed on the stranger as the law does not oblige him or her to intervene to rescue the child.

A second exception to the general rule applies in circumstances where the secondary party has a power of control over the conduct of the principal offender, and the secondary party fails to exercise that control in such a manner that the

---

[33] Ormerod, *Smith & Hogan Criminal Law* (2011), p.196.
[34] (1882) 8 QBD 534 at 539.
[35] (1882) 8 QBD 534 at 557–558.

omission amounts to assistance or encouragement in the commission of the principal offence. In *Tuck v Robson*,[36] the licensee of a pub was found guilty of aiding and abetting his customers in the offence of the consumption of intoxicating liquor after hours. By failing to exercise his power to remove the customers from the premises, the licensee's tolerance towards after-hours drinking could be viewed as some form of encouragement to commit the offence. Lord Parker C.J. held that secondary liability could be imposed in circumstances of "passive assistance in the sense of presence with no steps being taken to enforce his right either to eject the customers or at any rate to revoke their licence to be on the premises".[37] In *R. v Webster*, the Court of Appeal approved the position in *Du Cros v Lambourne*[38] on the law relating to secondary liability for failure to intervene, "which establishes that a defendant might be convicted of aiding and abetting dangerous driving if the driver drives dangerously in the owner's presence and with the owner's consent and approval".[39] In the related case of *R. v Martin*, the principal offender was a learner driver, and the secondary participant was convicted of the offence of causing death by dangerous driving in circumstances where secondary liability was "based on his failure to act when under a duty by reason of his position as the qualified driver to do so (rather than active encouragement)".[40]

R. v Coney[41] is authority for the general principle that mere presence at the scene of a crime is an insufficient basis, of itself, to establish secondary liability. In general, some participation in the principal offence in the form of a positive act is required, such as shouting encouragement. Notwithstanding the general rule, a line of jurisprudence has developed imposing secondary liability in circumstances where mere presence in fact assists or encourages the principal offender and the secondary party intends that his or her presence be of assistance or encouragement in relation to the commission of the principal offence.

In *R. v Clarkson*,[42] a young woman was brutally raped by a number of soldiers in a British army base in Germany. Two other soldiers heard her screams and came in to watch. They remained there and watched the victim being raped, although they did not actively assist in the rape. Each of the two soldiers was charged with aiding and abetting the rape. However, since there was no evidence that they had taken any active part in the rape, the prosecution case was that their mere presence encouraged the principal offenders who committed the rape. It was accepted by the court that the rapists may have in fact been encouraged by the defendants' presence. In allowing the appeal, the Courts Martial Appeal Court held that "it was not sufficient to establish that the mere presence of the appellants had in fact given encouragement to the crime; it must be proved that the appellants intended to give encouragement".[43] A similar conclusion was reached in *Dunlop and Sylvester v R.*[44] where the charges against two

---

[36] [1970] 1 All E.R. 1171.
[37] [1970] 1 All E.R. 1171 at 1175.
[38] [1907] 1 K.B. 40.
[39] [2006] EWCA Crim 415 at para.28.
[40] [2010] EWCA Crim 1450 at paras 30–32.
[41] (1882) 8 Q.B.D. 534.
[42] [1971] 3 All E.R. 344.
[43] [1971] 3 All E.R. 344 at 347.
[44] (1979) 47 C.C.C. (2d) 93.

defendants included a charge that they stood by and watched a rape being committed, and in doing so aided and abetted the commission of the principal offence. The Supreme Court of Canada applied *Clarkson*, holding that mere presence and passive acquiescence were not enough; there must be actual assistance or encouragement coupled with an intention to assist or encourage.

The approach of the Irish courts to the issue of secondary liability for mere presence at the scene of a crime would appear to be similar to the position in England and Wales. In *Attorney General v Ryan*,[45] the Court of Criminal Appeal held that secondary liability could be imposed where presence at the crime scene assisted or encouraged the principal in committing an offence, and the defendant knew that his presence would have the effect of assisting or encouraging the principal. In that case, the defendant was one of a group of five who attacked another group after a dance. There had been a verbal exchange between the groups earlier, after which the attackers proceeded to arm themselves with car tools. They then confronted the other group and the ringleader (Coffey) struck and killed one victim and seriously injured another. Coffey was convicted of murder. Ryan, although he did not directly take part in the attack, was charged as a secondary party and was convicted of manslaughter.

Ryan appealed, alleging that the trial judge had misdirected the jury in relation to the level of involvement required to trigger secondary liability. In particular, the defence claimed that the trial judge gave the impression to the jury that merely "standing around" in Coffey's presence during the course of the attack was sufficient to incriminate Ryan in the killing. The Court of Criminal Appeal rejected the appeal. While the court accepted that mere presence alone was insufficient to implicate Ryan, it was pointed out that the trial judge had made it clear that Ryan could be convicted if by his presence he was "knowingly giving [Coffey] aid or encouragement ... either by carrying weapons or standing around ...". The Court of Criminal Appeal approved of this direction, and reasoned that:

> "If Coffey was enabled to accost these people by reason of the presence of a superior number in his gang, of whom [Ryan] was one, then mere presence, if it was knowingly to lend him support to his enterprise, could implicate the applicant and others in the crime."[46]

In *DPP v Rose*,[47] the Court of Criminal Appeal considered whether the applicant's participation in the crimes was sufficient to render her liable as a secondary participant under s.7 of the Criminal Law Act 1997. While the decision appears to be based on principles of secondary liability, there are a number of references made to "joint enterprise" and "common design". The loose use of language is unfortunate, as it has the potential to create confusion as to the specific area of criminal liability being considered by the court: secondary liability or joint enterprise. Since the judgment appears to be focused on the issue of secondary liability for mere presence at the scene of a crime, analysis of the case is perhaps most appropriately located within the section dealing with the actus reus of secondary participants.

---

[45] (1966) 1 Frewen 304.
[46] (1966) 1 Frewen 304.
[47] Unreported, Court of Criminal Appeal, February 21, 2002.

In this case, there was an argument at a house between the victim and two men (Roche and Sage) about money. A fight broke out when the two men attempted to take the money from the victim, resulting in the victim being left unconscious. The applicant, Rose, was present during the fight. It was suggested that the victim would be driven to the hospital, accompanied by Roche, Sage and the applicant. In the car, Roche started to punch and kick the victim and demanded his bank card and pin code. At this point, the applicant told Roche to search the victim's pockets. Instead of being driven to a hospital, the car went to a small dirt road, where the victim was taken out and beaten by Roche with a crowbar. During the course of this attack, the applicant said "mind the blood lads". Roche continued to beat the victim, ultimately killing him.

The applicant was convicted of the offences of murder and assault with intent to rob, based on her statements during the course of the attack. It was accepted that she took no physical part in the attack. In determining the appeal, the Court of Criminal Appeal held that the "applicant could not be convicted of anything for mere callousness", and that if she was not a participant in the crime, "but was merely a spectator she had no criminal liability even if she did not express any words or take any steps to prevent what was happening". Consequently, what she said while the attack was being carried out was of vital importance, as these words were the only basis for imposing liability. In respect of the charge of assault with intent to rob, the court held that she was properly convicted, having said the words "search his pockets". However, in relation to the murder charge, the Court of Criminal Appeal quashed that conviction, as there was no evidence of any assistance or encouragement in that crime. The only basis on which it could be argued that she participated in the killing were the use of the words "mind the blood lads", uttered during the course of the attack on the victim. The court found that the import of these words was ambiguous, and could have been intended as "a plea to go easy" so as to prevent the infliction of more serious injuries, rather than forming a warning about the risk of blood stains and avoiding detection by the authorities.

In *DPP v Jordan and Deegan*,[48] the Court of Criminal Appeal held that to establish aiding and abetting of an offence on the basis of encouragement, such encouragement might be implied from the surrounding circumstances. It was also held that mere presence at the scene of a crime did not, of itself, evidence wilful encouragement so as to infer the aiding and abetting of an offence.[49] In this case, the accused were convicted of aiding and abetting the offence of cruelty to animals contrary to s.1(1)(a) of the Protection of Animals Acts 1911 and 1965, as amended by s.48 of the Control of Horses Act 1996. The accused were found guilty on the basis that they

---

[48] [2006] 3 I.R. 425.
[49] See *Wilcox v Jeffrey* [1951] 1 All E.R. 464, a decision which held a spectator liable as a secondary party for attending an illegal jazz concert, notwithstanding that there was no evidence of any positive acts of assistance or encouragement during the course of the performance. It has been observed that "the Court was influenced by the commercial dimension of the appellant's presence at the concert. But there was no evidence of collusion on the part of the appellant or of positive acts of encouragement, such as applauding or cheering. All that was established was that the appellant attended an event with the intention of reporting it in his magazine ... The decision in *Wilcox v Jeffery* is difficult to reconcile with the general principle and is now better considered to be confined to its own facts"; McAuley and McCutcheon, *Criminal Liability* (2000), pp.467–468.

were secondary participants in the principal offence by virtue of their attendance at an event involving two American pit bull terriers fighting each other. In allowing each appeal and quashing the respective convictions, the Court of Criminal Appeal noted that "[a]ll that was proved was presence. There was no evidence of gambling or fleeing from arrest".[50] Geogheghan J. stated that:

> "It is trite law that a person cannot be convicted of an offence by merely being present when it is being committed. There must be some evidence either of common design or of aiding and abetting in the offence. The court would agree with the view taken by the trial judge that the proven encouragement which would be necessary need not be express. It could be implied from the circumstances."[51]

Secondary liability—the mental element

The mens rea requirements of the secondary participant consist of a number of discrete mental elements:

(1) intention to perform the physical act of assistance or encouragement, and in the case of an omission, an intentional failure to act,
(2) intention that the acts or omissions assist in, or encourage, the commission of an offence,
(3) the secondary participant must have intended to assist or encourage the principal in the crime proved to have been committed by the principal, or the commission of a crime of a similar nature known to the accused to be the intention of the principal when assisting or encouraging him.

There would appear to be three separate strands to the culpability requirements of the secondary participant, each of which merits deeper scrutiny.

The aspect of mens rea requiring that the actual physical act or omission of the secondary participant be intentional will be a relatively straightforward matter in the majority of cases. In relation to this particular mental element, intention is to be considered from a very narrow perspective. Specifically, what is envisaged here is intention as to control of the secondary participant over his or her bodily movements. An issue might arise with respect to this particular element if there was some evidence that the defendant's bodily movements were involuntary, and by implication, non-intentional acts. For example, a sudden loss of physical control due to a diabetes attack, or sleepwalking, might raise an issue as to whether the physical actions of the secondary participant were truly intentional acts.

The second aspect of mens rea relates to establishing that the defendant intended that his conduct assisted, encouraged or procured the commission of the principal offence. Despite some judicial remarks to the contrary,[52] there is some support for the proposition that recklessness does not satisfy this particular element of the mens

---

[50] [2006] 3 I.R. 425 at 430.
[51] [2006] 3 I.R. 425 at 428.
[52] *Blakely and Sutton v DPP* [1991] R.T.R. 405.

rea requirements for secondary liability; the minimum culpability requirement is intention.[53] There are two competing lines of authority as to the meaning of the term "intention" in relation to this specific mental element of secondary liability. One view is that oblique intention, in terms of a presumption that a person intends the natural and probable causes of his actions, is sufficient to satisfy this particular fault requirement.[54] In other words, it must be shown that the defendant knows or is aware that his conduct will assist or encourage the principal offender. The other view suggests that direct intent or purpose must be established; the defendant must have as his desire, objective or purpose that his conduct will assist or encourage the principal offender.[55]

In the following example, referred to in *Gamble*,[56] the question of liability hinges on whether or not the term "intention" is viewed as equating to oblique or direct intent. If one man deliberately sells to another a gun to be used for murdering a third party, he may be indifferent about whether the third party lives or dies and interested only in the cash profit to be made out of the sale. In such a case, although he is aware of the intended use, if the seller's motive for the sale is confined to making a profit but he is indifferent as to what use the buyer puts the weapon, the seller lacks mens rea if the term "intention" is defined in terms of desire or purpose. The seller does not care as to what use the weapon is ultimately put; he cannot be said to have as his purpose or desire the killing of another person. On the same facts, the seller will be liable if the term "intention" is defined in terms of knowledge or awareness, as he knows that it is the intention of the principal offender to kill a third party, albeit the seller is indifferent as to whether or not the proposed victim is actually killed. All the seller is concerned with is making a profit from the sale of the gun. It would appear from consideration of the above set of facts that to frame the term "intention" in such a way as to require proof of desire or purpose would have the effect of limiting the reach of criminal liability; persons, such as the unscrupulous gun seller, would escape criminal liability on the basis that it was not their desire to bring about a homicide. Such a narrowing of the scope of secondary liability is perhaps questionable on both moral and policy grounds; is the conduct of the gun seller in the above example not sufficiently blameworthy so as to merit the imposition of criminal liability, and worthy of deterrence?

The third mental element that makes up the mens rea of secondary liability relates to the degree of knowledge required of the secondary party as to the nature of the crime committed by the principal offender. In the English decision of *R. v Bainbridge*,[57] the Court of Criminal Appeal held that "it is not enough that it should be shown that a man knows that some illegal venture is intended". The court went on to hold that it is sufficient to show knowledge of the intention to commit a crime of the type which was committed and that it is not necessary to prove knowledge as to the precise details of the principal offence, such as dates or the location of

---

[53] Ormerod, *Smith & Hogan Criminal Law* (2011), p.204.
[54] *Cook v Stockwell* (1915) 84 L.J.K.B. 2187; *Cafferata v Wilson* [1936] 3 All E.R. 149; *National Coal Board v Gamble* [1959] 1 Q.B. 11; *R. v Bryce* [2004] EWCA Crim 1231.
[55] *Fretwell* (1862) Le. & Ca. 161; *Gillick v West Norfolk and Wisbech Area Health Authority* [1986] A.C. 112; *Attorney General v Able* [1984] Q.B. 795.
[56] [1959] 1 Q.B. 11 at 23.
[57] [1960] 1 Q.B. 129 at 133.

Degrees of Complicity in Crime 371

the offence. In that case, the defendant supplied another person with oxygen-cutting equipment, which was ultimately used to break into a bank. The defendant, charged as an accessory, admitted knowing that the equipment would be used for some illegal purpose, but claimed to have no idea that it would be used to break into a bank, much less that particular bank. It was held that the defendant could be convicted if he knew that the principal offender intended to break and enter premises, and to steal property.

The English approach to this aspect of mens rea is set out in the decision of the House of Lords in *DPP for Northern Ireland v Maxwell*.[58] The appellant was a member of the Ulster Volunteer Force, an illegal organisation responsible for sectarian attacks against Catholics in Northern Ireland. He was told by a member of the organisation to guide a car to a bar located in a remote country area. The evidence suggested that the appellant knew that he was involved in a terrorist enterprise but that he was unaware what precise form it would take. In a separate vehicle, the appellant led another car to the bar. When the defendant arrived at the bar he drove slowly past the bar and continued his journey home. The other car following the appellant stopped opposite the bar, and one of the occupants alighted from the car and threw a pipe bomb into the bar. The bomb attack was unsuccessful due to the intervention of a third party inside the bar. The appellant was convicted of doing an act with intent to cause an explosion by a bomb, contrary to s.3(a) of the Explosive Substances Act 1883 and with possession of a bomb contrary to s.3(b) of that Act, on the basis that he was a secondary participant in those offences. While the appellant admitted knowing that some kind of paramilitary attack was planned against the bar, he argued that since he did not know the form of the proposed crime, and was unaware about the intended use of a pipe bomb, he was not liable for aiding and abetting the crime that was actually committed. The House of Lords approved the general principle laid down in *R. v Bainbridge*,[59] and dismissed the appeal, holding that:

> "A person may properly be convicted of aiding and abetting the commission of a criminal offence without proof of prior knowledge of the actual crime intended if he contemplated the commission of one of a limited number of crimes by the principal and intentionally lent his assistance in the commission of such a crime. It was irrelevant that at the time of lending his assistance the accused did not know which of those crimes the principal intended to commit. On the facts, the appellant must have known when he was ordered to act as a guide for the other car that he was taking part in a terrorist attack and although he may not have known the precise target or weapons to be used, he must have contemplated, having regard to his knowledge of the organisation's methods, that the bombing of the public house was an obvious possibility among the offences likely to be committed and consequently must have contemplated that the men in the second car had explosives."[60]

In the words of Lord Scarman:

---

[58] [1978] 3 All E.R. 1140.
[59] [1960] 1 Q.B. 129.
[60] [1978] 3 All E.R. 1140.

"His guilt springs from the fact that he contemplates the commission of one (or more) of a number of crimes by the principal and he intentionally lends his assistance in order that such a crime will be committed."[61]

The Irish position on the issue of the extent of knowledge required in relation to the principal offence is considered in the Court of Criminal Appeal decisions in *DPP v Madden*[62] and *DPP v Egan*.[63] In *Madden*, O'Higgins C.J. set out the applicable law:

"The kernel of the matter is the establishing of an activity on the part of the accused from which his intentions may be inferred and the effect of which is to assist the principal in the commission of the crime proved to have been committed by the principal, or the commission of a crime of a similar nature known to the accused to be the intention of the principal when assisting him."[64]

In the subsequent decision in *Egan*, the Court of Criminal Appeal applied *Madden*. In *Egan*, the applicant was convicted of robbery. In a statement, the applicant said that he gave permission over the telephone for a van to be left at his workshop, he undertook to be at his workshop door at an arranged time, and that he was aware that a "small stroke" was to be carried out. He went on to say that on the day in question the van arrived at the specified time. Inside the van were a group of armed and masked men with several sacks of jewellery. These men stayed in his workshop for a while and left later in the day. The applicant found a bag containing gold rings in his workshop which he later disposed of. In his defence, the applicant argued that he got frightened when he realised that the "small stroke" was actually a robbery, and that if he had known the nature of the crime he would not have become involved with the criminal enterprise. It was submitted that the applicant lacked the requisite degree of knowledge as to the principal offence on the basis that the crime of robbery was "a fundamentally different crime to the crime he believed he was assisting", namely theft or handling stolen property.

Dismissing the appeal, the Court of Criminal Appeal held that:

"[I]n order to be convicted of the principal offence, it was not necessary for the prosecution to establish that a person who aided and abetted the principal offender before the crime was committed had knowledge of the actual crime intended. It is sufficient that a person who gave assistance knew the nature of the intended crime."[65]

The Court of Criminal Appeal went on to state that it is not necessary to establish that the accused knew the specific details of the principal offence, such as the means employed to commit the offence, the location of the offence or the time of the offence. In the case of theft, there was no requirement to establish knowledge as to the nature of the goods to be stolen or the means used to effect the theft. In *Egan*, the

---

[61] [1978] 3 All E.R. 1140 at 1162.
[62] [1977] I.R. 336.
[63] [1989] I.R. 681.
[64] [1977] I.R. 336 at 341.
[65] [1989] I.R. 681 at 682.

offence of theft was held to be of a similar type to the offence of robbery. It has been suggested that the decision in *Egan* is open to a potentially "expansive reading" and that any offence of which theft is a constituent element might be construed as being an offence of a similar type to the offence of theft simpliciter.[66] Thus, the offences of burglary, aggravated burglary and robbery would be classified as being offences of a similar type to theft, notwithstanding that offences involving a threat of violence to the person are arguably of a more serious, and different, nature to crimes that might be classified as being purely offences against property. It is noteworthy that the offences against property that contain an element of harm to the person carry a more severe penalty than the basic offence of theft: in the Criminal Justice (Theft and Fraud Offences) Act 2001, s.4(6) provides that a person is liable on indictment to a maximum term of imprisonment of 10 years for the offence of theft, s.12(3) provides that a person is liable on indictment to a maximum term of imprisonment of 14 years for the offence of burglary, and in respect of aggravated burglary and robbery the maximum term of imprisonment is life. On the basis of a hierarchy of protected interests in the criminal law one would expect greater concern to be afforded to protecting the interest of bodily integrity than property. Clearly, any scheme that proposes to classify crimes into different types is inherently going to be vulnerable to uncertainty. Professor Ormerod notes that "[w]hether a crime is of the 'same type' as another may not always be easy to discover".[67]

The doctrine of common design/joint enterprise

Closely related to secondary liability is the doctrine of common design, also known as the doctrine of joint enterprise. The core elements of the doctrine are set out in *R. v Anderson and Morris*, and have been approved as representing the law in Ireland in the Court of Criminal Appeal decisions in *DPP v Cumberton*[68] and *DPP v Doohan*[69]:

> "Where two persons embark on a joint enterprise, each is criminally liable for acts done in pursuance of the joint enterprise, including unusual consequences arising from the execution of the joint enterprise; but if one of them goes beyond what has been tacitly agreed as part of the joint enterprise, the other is not liable for the consequences of the unauthorised act."[70]

In essence, where two or more parties enter into an agreement to take part in a criminal enterprise each of the parties will be liable in respect of offences that are committed in furtherance of that enterprise. Liability extends to "unusual circumstances" if they result from the implementation or performance of the criminal enterprise.

Since the constituent elements of secondary liability and the doctrine of joint enterprise are different it is better to view each as forming separate bases of criminal liability. The actus reus and mens rea requirements for secondary liability and joint enterprise are distinct. In relation to the doctrine of common design liability is based

---

[66] McAuley and McCutcheon, *Criminal Liability* (2000), p.479.
[67] Ormerod, *Smith & Hogan Criminal Law* (2011), p.210.
[68] [1995] WJSC-CCA 495 at 497–498.
[69] [2002] WJSC-CCA 2022 at 2036–2037.
[70] [1966] 2 Q.B. 110 at 118.

on the agreement to take part in a criminal enterprise. Secondary liability does not require any agreement or consensus between the parties in respect of the crime to be committed; it is sufficient that the secondary party intentionally assisted or encouraged the principal offender to commit the offence that was in fact committed or an offence of a similar nature.

Several justifications have been offered as to why it is preferable to treat secondary liability and the doctrine of common design as distinct legal concepts. First, since both concepts are structurally distinct it enhances legal clarity to consider each concept separately. A certain degree of confusion has been created where the courts have used the language relating to each concept in an indiscriminate and loose manner. Apart from causing a good deal of conceptual confusion, the lack of clarity and precision in the use of terminology and analysis has the potential to dilute the precedential value of the relevant authorities; sometimes it is difficult to discern if a particular case is legal authority for the principles of secondary liability or joint enterprise. For example, in *DPP v Rose*,[71] the Court of Criminal Appeal appears to conflate both legal concepts in the following passage:

> "The case against the applicant was that she was part of a joint enterprise or venture with two men and that her participation in the crimes was sufficient to render her equally guilty as a principal in accordance with section 7 of the Criminal Law Act 1997."

A second justification for distinguishing between the two concepts relates to the group element specifically targeted by the doctrine of common design. Simester and Sullivan note:

> "The law has a particular hostility to criminal groups ... Criminal associations are dangerous. They present a threat to public safety that ordinary criminal prohibitions, addressed to individual actors, do not entirely address. Moreover, the danger is not just of an immediately physical nature. A group is a form of society that has set itself against the law and order of society at large. Individuals offending alone do not do this. Thus concerted wrongdoing imports additional and special reasons why the law must intervene."[72]

In a similar vein to the "group" offences of riot and violent disorder contained in ss.14 and 15 of the Criminal Justice (Public Order) Act 1994, crimes which carry a maximum penalty of 10 years' imprisonment, one would also expect the criminal law to treat group crime, in the context of complicity, more seriously. In view of the risk that the level of harm threatened may escalate rapidly where crimes are committed by offenders in numbers it seems a logical corollary that the level at which liability is imposed be adjusted accordingly. While this might have been the response in England and Wales where the mental element of foresight of the crime committed is sufficient to trigger joint enterprise liability, in Ireland the degree of

---

[71] Unreported, Court of Criminal Appeal, February 21, 2002.
[72] Simester and Sullivan, *Criminal Law Theory and Doctrine* (2003), p.225.

mens rea does not appear to have been similarly reduced. Campbell, Kilcommins and O'Sullivan have observed:

> "It is difficult to see in Ireland, for example, how a wider door of liability arises through the process of joint enterprise given that it is limited to what is expressly or tacitly agreed between the parties."[73]

While the above observations on the criminal law's heightened concern with offences involving a group element hold true, it is worth noting that secondary liability may also have such a group element. For example, a number of men might agree to take part in a criminal assault on a victim and be found guilty under the doctrine of joint enterprise; it being their common design to attack the victim each party will be liable for the acts of the other in executing the criminal enterprise. Equally, on very similar facts, the principal offender might assault the victim with the assistance and encouragement of a group of men, each secondary party playing a distinct role in participating in the principal offence. Assistance might be offered by supplying a weapon, luring the victim to the crime scene, acting as lookout, facilitating escape or simply being present in numbers so as to overbear the victim's will to such a degree that he is resigned to suffering the attack and offers no resistance. It follows that a group of men may form a criminal group and be dealt with under either the principles relating to secondary liability or the doctrine of joint enterprise. It would appear that the threat posed by group crime might be adequately catered for under both legal doctrines.

DPP v Doohan[74] is a good case demonstrating the application of the general principles on joint enterprise. As a reprisal for previous mistreatment of his father, the applicant paid another man, Heron, to give a "punishment style beating" to the victim. In a statement to the police, the applicant made some remarks as to his intentions in relation to the nature of the proposed assault. The applicant said that as far as he was concerned there was only to be a "beating" to the arms or legs that would require hospitalisation for a couple of weeks. He said that he had expected the attack to have been carried out with a baseball bat or a stick on the legs. He left the means of the attack at the discretion of Heron. The only limitation appeared to be a direction to Heron to stay away from the victim's head. In the end, a gun was used by Heron and the victim died from a shot to his right thigh which resulted in massive blood loss when a major artery and vein were severed.

Lawyers for the applicant argued that the scope of the joint enterprise did not extend either to conduct which would result in the death of the victim or to an enterprise involving the use of the gun. It was submitted that the applicant should not be liable for the unusual consequences flowing from the unauthorised actions carried out by Heron. In an interview, the applicant said that he had never wished for the victim to be killed and that had he known that a shotgun was being used that he would not have authorised its use. The Court of Appeal dismissed the appeal on the basis that there was sufficient evidence that there was an agreement between

---

[73] Campbell, Kilcommins and O'Sullivan, *Criminal Law in Ireland: Cases and Commentary* (2010), p.305.
[74] [2002] 4 I.R. 463.

the applicant and Heron to cause serious injury to the victim. Since an intention to cause serious injury meets the minimum culpability requirements for the offence of murder it was held that the applicant was properly convicted for joint enterprise in the murder of the victim. In terms of liability it was irrelevant that the applicant had never intended or desired to kill the victim; it was enough that the parties had entered into a joint enterprise to cause serious bodily harm to the victim. It follows that the applicant was liable for the unusual consequences—the use of the shot gun and resulting death—arising from the agreement to cause serious injury.

McAuley and McCutcheon have made the observation that the Irish law on joint enterprise has focused on "the extent of the agreement between the parties".[75] To establish liability there must be evidence that the agreement between the parties to the joint enterprise covered the offence that was in fact committed. Such an agreement may be express, but it may also be implied from the surrounding facts. In *R. v Anderson*,[76] it was held that there is no requirement of an express agreement between the parties; it is sufficient that there is evidence of a "tacit agreement", and this is something which can be inferred from the nature of the crime. In *DPP v Cumberton*, Blayney J. stated that "[t]he test is what was tacitly agreed between the parties and whether what happened was within the common design".[77]

In *Anderson*,[78] the two accused, A and M, went together in search of another man, W, who was believed to have made an attempt to strangle A's wife. On finding W, A produced a knife and stabbed W to death. M looked on but had no direct involvement in the fight. On being questioned, M admitted that he had set out with A to give W a beating, but that he had no intention to kill or stab the victim and that he was unaware that A had a knife in his possession. At trial, the jury were directed that they could find M guilty of manslaughter if there was a common intention to attack W, and if M took some part in the fight, even if the use of the knife was entirely outside the contemplation of M and there was no intention on M's part to kill or cause serious bodily harm. This direction was held to be improper by the English Court of Criminal Appeal. The court held that M was not liable for A's conduct since A's stabbing to death of W with a knife fell outside the scope of the common design. No tacit agreement to stab W could be inferred from the facts; there was no evidence suggesting that M had any knowledge that A would produce a knife in the course of the fight. On the other hand, if the facts of the case were slightly different, insofar as M knew that A was armed with a knife, but proceeded to take some part in the attack on W, it would be open to a trier of fact to infer that there was a tacit agreement between the parties to use a knife in the course of the attack.

Since an agreement between the parties is the basic element underpinning joint enterprise liability an issue frequently arises as to whether a particular act falls within the scope of the agreement. In the Supreme Court decision of *DPP v Murray*,[79] the defendants, who were husband and wife, carried out an armed bank robbery together. On leaving the bank, they were pursued by an off-duty police officer, and, to prevent the capture of the husband, the wife shot and killed the officer. In the Special

---

[75] McAuley and McCutcheon, *Criminal Liability* (2000), p.488.
[76] [1966] 2 Q.B. 110.
[77] [1995] WJSC-CCA 495 at 502.
[78] [1966] 2 Q.B. 110.
[79] [1977] I.R. 360.

Criminal Court, both were convicted of capital murder, and sentenced to death. On appeal, the Supreme Court held that while there was clearly a common design, in the execution of the armed robbery, to kill or cause serious injury if necessary, there was no evidence that the parties had agreed to use violence specifically against the police. Because there was no prior agreement to use force against the police there could be no liability in respect of the offence of capital murder which has as one of its constituent elements a requirement that the victim is a member of the police force:

> "As to the appellant Noel Murray, if the recklessness required for the capital murder charged is held to have been proved in the case of Marie Murray, that recklessness could not be imputed to Noel Murray. In the absence of evidence that a decision to shoot a would-be captor, even if there was a risk that he was a Garda, was an express or implied part of the common design, recklessness in this respect on the part of Marie Murray must be deemed to be personal to her and outside the scope of the common design. The activities of the parties to the bank robbery, particularly the carrying and use of loaded guns, amply support the inference that there was a common agreement to shoot to kill or to cause serious injury if necessary. It may, however, have been the case that it was part of the pre-arrangement that a shot would not be discharged at a Garda. At all events, it cannot be fairly inferred from the evidence that the discharge of a shot at a Garda was part of the pre-arranged scheme of things, and more particularly the discharge of a shot at a Garda in the circumstances in which Marie Murray shot Garda Reynolds."[80]

In contrast to *Murray*, two subsequent cases found that there was a common design in respect of capital murder. In *DPP v Pringle*[81] and *DPP v Eccles*,[82] the defendants in both cases took part in armed robberies which involved the lethal shooting of a police officer. In each of those cases, the Court of Criminal Appeal found that there was a common design in respect of capital murder, on the basis that there was evidence of a common intention to overcome any resistance by the police, using firearms if necessary. Apart from the extent of evidence as to an agreement, a distinguishing feature that may have had an impact on the Supreme Court in *Murray* reaching the conclusion that there was no common design in relation to capital murder was the fact that the offence then carried the death penalty.[83]

The English position on common design seems to be distinct in that an offence will be considered to be part of the common design if the offence was within the contemplation, or foresight, of the defendant.[84] Under English law, liability for joint enterprise is based on a test of contemplation or foresight. A party to a joint enterprise is liable for an offence committed by another party if he has foreseen the possibility that the offence might be committed in the course of the joint enterprise.

---

[80] [1977] I.R. 360 at 405.
[81] (1981) 2 Frewen 57.
[82] (1986) 3 Frewen 36.
[83] McAuley and McCutcheon, *Criminal Liability* (2000), p.483.
[84] *Chan Wing-Siu v R.* [1985] A.C. 168; *Hui Chi-ming v R.* [1992] 1 A.C. 34; *R. v Powell and Daniels* [1997] 4 All E.R. 545; *R. v Rahman* [2008] UKHL 45; *R. v ABCD* [2010] EWCA Crim 1622; *R. v Mendez* [2010] EWCA Crim 516; *R. v Lewis* [2010] EWCA Crim 496; *R. v Badza* [2010] EWCA Crim 1363; *R. v A* [2010] EWCA Crim 1622.

Foresight or contemplation in this context is considered to be subjective in nature. Under this arrangement, there is no requirement of any agreement, tacit or otherwise, to commit an offence; it is sufficient that the defendant contemplated or foresaw the possibility of the offence. In *R. v Rahman*,[85] the victim was attacked by a group of men armed with various blunt instruments, including the four defendants. After a severe beating he died. The cause of death was later discovered to be a number of knife wounds. Since it was not possible to establish which person inflicted the fatal injury each defendant was charged as being part of a joint enterprise to kill the victim. The House of Lords held that where a party to a joint enterprise committed an unlawful killing with the requisite intent for murder, other parties could be held liable for murder on the basis of their foresight of what the principal might do. It remains to be seen whether the Irish courts will approach the issue of joint enterprise liability by retaining their focus on the agreement or following the English approach based on foresight.

Victims as participants in crime

In some cases, the conduct of a victim might lend some assistance or encouragement to the commission of an offence against him or her. It would be questionable from a policy perspective if victims were held criminally liable for aiding or abetting an offence against themselves. To ensure that the net of secondary liability does not unduly extend to the victims of crimes, a rule has developed at common law whereby victims will not be held liable if they belong to a class of persons that are protected under the statute that enacted the offence. In *R. v Tyrell*,[86] the underage girl who aided and abetted the principal offender to have unlawful sexual intercourse was held not to be liable for the statutory offence under s.5 of the Criminal Law Amendment Act 1885 which was passed specifically to protect young women like the victim in this case. Clearly, it would be an absurd result, contrary to public policy, if the victim in such a case was to be treated as a criminal and liable to conviction as a secondary participant in the perpetration of a crime against herself. A similar outcome was reached in *R. v Whitehouse*,[87] a case in which the court held that an underage girl was not liable for assisting and encouraging her father in committing the crime of incest, notwithstanding that her conduct may have in fact amounted to aiding and abetting the unlawful sexual acts.

Like many common law rules, the potential scope of the exception in *R. v Tyrell* is far from clear. Further classes of persons may well be added, on an incremental basis, where the courts deem it appropriate to extend the exception to other classes of vulnerable persons. The principle in *Tyrell* could conceivably be applied to a prostitute who assists and encourages a person to commit the offence of brothel-keeping[88] on the basis that the prostitute is a victim of exploitation by the person managing the brothel. Apart from the public order and morality objectives, the statutory offence has as a further policy objective the protection of sex workers, who are clearly a vulnerable class of persons.

---

[85] [2008] UKHL 45.
[86] [1894] 1 Q.B. 710.
[87] [1977] Q.B. 868.
[88] Criminal Law (Sexual Offences) Act 1993 s.13.

McAuley and McCutcheon have considered the application of the rule in *R. v Tyrell* to the facts of *R. v Brown*,[89] which involved the consensual infliction of bodily harm during a sado-masochistic encounter:

> "The decision in *R. v Brown* confirmed the principle that consent is not a defence to offences of violence where actual bodily harm is likely to result. Would the 'victims' in that case escape liability as accessories despite their willing but passive participation, while those who inflicted the violence are convicted as principals?"[90]

Withdrawal

The rules governing complicity in crime provide that a person may have a valid defence where the person terminates his involvement in the commission of the principal offence. The underlying rationale for the defence of withdrawal relates both to the harm and culpability principles. On the one hand, the defence recognises that a defendant who withdraws from a crime reduces his level of culpability to a considerable extent; the blameworthy mental state that led him to participate in the crime would appear to be replaced by some form of remorse that is manifested by his withdrawal from the crime. On the other hand, the defence encourages wrongdoers to withdraw from criminal enterprises, which may have an impact on bringing down the number of crimes committed, thereby reducing the level of harm posed to society.

To ensure that the defence of withdrawal is available only in meritorious cases the jurisprudence has built up around the concept of withdrawal a number of factors limiting the availability of the defence:

(1) there must be timely communication of the intention to withdraw from the accessory to the principal offender(s);
(2) the time of withdrawal is an important factor; it is more difficult to raise the defence where the withdrawal occurs just before or at the time of commission of the offence; the defence is more likely to succeed if notice of the purported withdrawal is given well in advance of the commission of the offence.

The general principles on withdrawal are set out in a passage from Sloan J.A.'s judgment in *R. v Whitehouse*, which was subsequently adopted in its entirety by the English Court of Criminal Appeal in *R. v Becerra*[91] as representing a correct statement of the law:

> "[S]omething more than a mere mental change of intention and physical change of place by those associates who wish to dissociate themselves from the consequence attendant upon their willing assistance up to the moment of the actual commission of the crime [is required]. I would not attempt to define too closely what must be done in criminal matters involving participation in a common unlawful purpose to break the chain of causation and responsibility.

---

[89] [1994] 1 A.C. 212.
[90] McAuley and McCutcheon, *Criminal Liability* (2000), p.472.
[91] (1975) 62 Cr. App. R. 212.

That must depend upon the circumstances of each case but it seems to me that one essential element ought to be established in a case of this kind: where practicable and reasonable there must be timely communication of the intention to abandon the common purpose from those who wish to dissociate themselves from the contemplated crime to those who desire to continue in it. What is a 'timely communication' must be determined by the facts of each case but where practicable and reasonable it ought to be such communication, verbal or otherwise, that will serve unequivocal notice upon the other party to the common unlawful cause that if he proceeds upon it he does so without further aid and assistance of those who withdraw. The unlawful purpose of he who continues alone is then his own and not one in common with those who are no longer parties to it nor liable to its full and final consequences."[92]

Clearly, private repentance without any external manifestation of an intention to withdraw from the crime is insufficient; there must be some objective basis for raising the defence in the form of a positive act communicating withdrawal as opposed to a mere subjective mental state of remorse on the part of the defendant. There are valid policy reasons for restricting the availability of the defence to cases where there is a clear and unequivocal communication of the fact of withdrawal. First, if there were no requirement to give prior notice of withdrawal and the defendant simply fled the crime scene such conduct could be interpreted in a number of different ways: (1) the defendant may have genuinely decided that he wished to take no further part in the criminal enterprise; or (2) the defendant may have fled the crime scene to avoid being apprehended by the police; or (3) the defendant may have decided that he no longer wished to be involved in the crime for some other reason, such as a realisation that there was no gain to be made from committing the crime. There would be too much uncertainty in the law if the test for withdrawal was based solely on the subjective motives of the defendant; legal certainty is enhanced by requiring objective evidence of withdrawal.

A second reason for limiting the defence is that the principal might continue to derive a benefit from the assistance or encouragement in the absence of some external act of withdrawal that is aimed at negativing the prior acts of assistance or encouragement.[93] If the defendant does nothing, in the form of a positive act of withdrawal, his previous acts of assistance or encouragement may remain operative. On the other hand, if the defendant makes efforts to externalise his remorse, by communicating his withdrawal to the principal offender, or attempting to prevent the commission of the offence by his own intervention or by informing the police, such external acts contribute to undoing the harm caused by the original acts of assistance or encouragement.

Assistance after a crime has been committed

Prior to 1997 there were several different offences which could be committed by a person who assisted after the crime had been committed. In the case of felonies, a person could be found liable as an accessory after the fact or for misprision of a

---

[92] [1940] 55 B.C.R. 420.
[93] McAuley and McCutcheon, *Criminal Liability* (2000), p.498.

felony (i.e. concealing a felony which he knew to have been committed). There were also separate offences of compounding a felony and compounding a misdemeanour (i.e. agreeing to conceal an offence in return for a reward). The Criminal Law Act 1997 recasts the law on offences relating to assistance after the offence, providing a range of statutory offences of general application.

Section 7(2) of the Act of 1997 creates an offence of impeding the arrest or prosecution of a person who has committed an arrestable offence:

> Where a person has committed an arrestable offence, any other person who, knowing or believing him to be guilty of the offence or some other arrestable offence, does without reasonable excuse any act with intent to impede his or her apprehension or prosecution shall be guilty of an offence.

This would cover, for example, knowingly harbouring an offender or the destruction of evidence, with the intention of frustrating the offender's arrest or prosecution. Liability is derivative in nature in so far as there must be proof that an arrestable offence was in fact committed, although s.7(3) makes it clear that there is no requirement that the principal offender be convicted of the principal offence. The mental element requiring knowledge of belief as to the principal having committed an arrestable offence is not confined to the offence that was in fact committed; the mens rea extends to other arrestable offences that the accessory believes he has participated in. For instance, if a person believes he is assisting the principal in evading arrest in respect of the offence of burglary, but in fact the principal committed the more serious offence of aggravated burglary involving the use of a knife, the person assisting remains liable notwithstanding that he believes he has assisted the principal to avoid apprehension in relation to an offence of a different nature. Punishment for an offence under s.7(2) is governed by s.7(4) and the maximum term of imprisonment will vary from three years' imprisonment to 10 years' imprisonment depending on the gravity of the principal offence. For example, if the principal offence carries a maximum penalty of life imprisonment, then a person guilty of an offence under s.7(2) will face a maximum penalty of 10 years' imprisonment.

Section 8(1) of the Act of 1997 creates a separate offence of concealing an arrestable offence for a reward:

> Where a person has committed an arrestable offence, any other person who, knowing or believing that the offence or some other arrestable offence has been committed and that he or she has information which might be of material assistance in securing the prosecution or conviction of an offender for it, accepts or agrees to accept for not disclosing that information any consideration other than the making good of loss or injury caused by the offence, or the making of reasonable compensation for that loss or injury, shall be guilty of an offence and shall be liable on conviction on indictment to imprisonment for a term not exceeding three years.

This offence is intended to deal with situations where witnesses are "bought off" and corresponds to the older offences of compounding a felony or misdemeanour. The offence is committed where a person knows or believes that an arrestable offence has been committed, knows or believes that he has information which would assist in the detection or prosecution of the principal offence and that person agrees not to disclose that information in return for some form of consideration. Apart from the defence of reasonable excuse, a separate defence is available where it is shown that the consideration is limited to restitution for a loss or injury suffered as a result of the commission of the principal offence. Consider the following example where A burgles B's house. B discovers that A was responsible and B agrees not to notify the police provided that he is paid compensation for the stolen property. In these circumstances, B will not have committed an offence under s.8(1) so long as the amount agreed is limited to reasonable compensation.

It is important to note that the scope of application of the offences relating to assistance after the commission of an offence in ss.7(2) and 8(1) is limited to arrestable offences. This is in contrast to s.7(1) which refers to aiding, abetting, counselling or procuring the commission of an indictable offence. The term "arrestable offence" is defined in s.2 of the Act of 1997 as meaning "an offence for which a person of full capacity and not previously convicted may, under or by virtue of any enactment, be punished by imprisonment for a term of five years or by a more severe penalty".

Withholding information

Section 19(1) of the Criminal Justice Act 2011 creates a new offence of withholding information. This offence places a duty on persons to disclose information to the police in circumstances specified under that Act. The offence is defined as follows:

(1) A person shall be guilty of an offence if he or she has information which he or she knows or believes might be of material assistance in—
   (a) preventing the commission by any other person of a relevant offence, or
   (b) securing the apprehension, prosecution or conviction of any other person for a relevant offence, and fails without reasonable excuse to disclose that information as soon as it is practicable to do so to a member of the Garda Síochána.

It is important to note that the scope of application of this offence is limited to "relevant offences" as defined in s.3 of the Criminal Justice Act 2011. A "relevant offence" is defined as an arrestable offence that is specified in Sch.1 to the Criminal Justice Act 2011, and includes conspiring to commit, as well as aiding, abetting, counselling, procuring or inciting the commission of a specified offence in Sch.1. Schedule 1 lists a variety of offences covering the following areas of law: offences relating to banking, investment of funds and other financial activities, company law offences, money laundering and terrorist offences, theft and fraud offences, bribery and corruption offences, consumer protection offences and criminal damage to property offences. Subject to limitations prescribed by statute, s.3(2) of the Criminal Justice Act 2011 provides that the Minister for Justice and Equality may by order add further offences to the list of offences contained in Sch.1.

CHAPTER 14

CRIMINAL LIABILITY OF CORPORATIONS

INTRODUCTION

Corporations are legal persons and may be found guilty of crimes. However, there are obvious difficulties in applying the ordinary principles of criminal law to corporations. The most significant of these difficulties comes from the fact that the principle of mens rea breaks down when it is applied to a body which has no mental capacity of its own. In addition, the actus reus, or external element, of an offence involving a corporation must obviously be derived from the actions of persons connected in some way with the company. Other difficulties include the fact that the legal capacity of corporations does not mirror that of natural persons: for example, a corporation cannot marry and therefore cannot be accused of bigamy. From a practical point of view, corporations cannot be imprisoned and this creates problems where the only penalty for an offence is imprisonment, for example the offence of murder.

The common law did not recognise criminal liability of corporations. This appears to have stemmed from the fact that corporations could not appear in person and there was no right to representation under the common law. In addition, felonies were punishable by death—a sanction which had no meaning in the case of a corporation. These practical difficulties were overcome when the right to representation was granted and when fines were introduced as a penalty, thus leaving the way clear for the development of corporate criminal responsibility.

In modern times there has been a movement towards ensuring that corporations are made criminally liable where appropriate. This reflects the important role played by corporations in modern society. Various tragedies over the past decades have highlighted the terrible loss of life that can occur when corporations behave in a manner that is grossly negligent. The Zeebrugge ferry disaster, various rail disasters in England and the blood transfusion scandal in this country have all focused public attention on the necessity to mark society's outrage by having recourse to the criminal law. There has been increased public awareness of how ill-equipped the traditional concepts of the criminal law can be to deal with such harm. It is widely perceived that health and safety legislation can be a poor tool to use against corporations, especially when lives are lost, and it is recognised that a conviction of manslaughter carries a far greater stigma than penalties under health and safety legislation.

This chapter will firstly examine the common law treatment of corporate criminal liability and then discuss recent statutory developments in this jurisdiction and in England and Wales.[1]

---

[1] For a definitive treatment of corporate criminal liability, see Shelley Horan, *Corporate Crime* (Dublin: Bloomsbury Professional, 2011). See also, Amanda Pinto Q.C. and Martin Evans,

The Identification Doctrine—Controlling Mind—Directing Mind Theory

The early cases espousing this doctrine originated in England and Wales in the 1940s and confirmed that a corporation could be identified with its principals. The first of the cases was *DPP v Kent and Sussex Contractors Ltd*[2] where a company was convicted of issuing false records and furnishing false information in order to obtain petrol coupons.[3] Viscount Caldecote L.C.J. held that:

> "[A]lthough the directors or general manager of a company are its agents, they are something more. A company is incapable of acting or speaking, or even thinking except in so far as its officers have acted, spoken or thought."[4]

It was held that the acts and state of mind of the main individuals within the company could be treated as the acts and state of mind of the company itself. This differs from the concept of vicarious liability: with vicarious liability the actions of a company's agents are deemed to be the responsibility of the company but with identification theory the acts and state of mind of the individuals are deemed to be those of the company.

Lord Reid, several decades after *Kent and Sussex Contractors Ltd*,[5] summed up the distinction as follows:

> "[T]he person who acts is not speaking or acting for the company. He is acting as the company and his mind which directs his acts is the mind of the company. There is no question of the company being vicariously liable. He is not acting as a servant, representative, agent or delegate. He is the embodiment of the company, within his appropriate sphere, and his mind is the mind of the company. If it is a guilty mind then that guilt is the guilt of the company."[6]

The *Kent and Sussex Contractors Ltd* line of authority was said to adopt the controlling mind theory, otherwise known as the directing mind theory or identification doctrine. To determine whether the company was criminally liable one had to ask whether the act was committed by a person who could be said to be substantially in control of the company's operations. Thus, the act of a mere employee with little discretion would not suffice: one would have to show that the act was carried out by a person such as a senior manager with the ability to direct the operations of the company.

This test was elaborated upon in the leading English case of *Tesco Supermarkets Ltd v Natrass*.[7] The House of Lords considered whether a supermarket chain could

---

Corporate Criminal Liability, 2nd edn (London: Sweet and Maxwell, 2008). Articles from an Irish perspective include Deirdre Ahern, "Corporate Killing: The Way Forward?" (2003) 13 (2) I.C.L.J. 10; Paul Anthony McDermott, "Defences to Corporate Criminal Liability" (2000) 5 *Bar Review* 170; Gerard Conway, "The Criminal Character of a Company" (1998) 7 I.S.L.R. 23.

[2] [1944] 1 K.B. 146.
[3] The other cases illustrating this doctrine, also reported in 1944, were *R. v ICR Haulage Ltd* [1944] 1 K.B. 551 and *Moore v Bresler* [1944] 2 All E.R. 515.
[4] [1944] 1 K.B. 146 at 155.
[5] *Tesco Supermarkets Ltd v Nattrass* [1972] A.C. 153, discussed below.
[6] [1972] A.C. 153 at 170.
[7] [1972] A.C. 153.

incur criminal liability based on the acts of a regional supermarket manager. The company was prosecuted for an offence pursuant to the Trade Descriptions Act 1968. Evidence was given that the regional supermarket manager had advertised washing powder at a lower price than was available in his store as he had forgotten to check the shelves to ensure that the special offer boxes were still available. The House of Lords concluded that the branch manager was not sufficiently senior to equate to the directing mind and will of the company and the prosecution failed. The board of directors had not delegated part of their management function to the regional managers of their supermarkets. Lord Diplock explained that:

> "What natural persons are to be treated in law as being the company for the purpose of acts done in the course of its business, including the taking of precautions and the exercise of due diligence to avoid the commission of a criminal offence, is to be found by identifying those natural persons who by the memorandum and articles of association or as a result of action taken by the directors or by the company in general meeting pursuant to the articles, are entrusted with the exercise of the powers of the company."

The test is a restrictive one. It requires that any wrongdoing exists at a senior level within the company, effectively excluding liability for criminal offences committed at a lower level. Having said that, it must be remembered that if senior officers are aware of and connive in activities at a lower lever, this will suffice. It means that the identification theory is most suited to smaller companies rather than large corporations with a longer chain of command. Pinto has criticised the rationale of *Tesco* as follows:

> "The division of a corporation into 'brains' and 'hands' is inappropriate in the common situation where the company is diffuse; the board would ordinarily be responsible for the culture of the corporation setting the priorities which affect the behaviour of those on the shop floor. The model of a 'ladder of responsibility' referred to in *Tesco* is a somewhat simplistic tool with which to analyse decision-making in a large modern corporation let alone a multi-national enterprise."[8]

The restrictive nature of the test can be seen from the Canadian case of *R. v Safety-Kleen Canada Inc.*[9] Here the defendant company ran a fleet of waste-oil collection trucks. One of its drivers was found, contrary to Canadian environmental legislation, to have knowingly given false information in a return made to a provincial officer. The driver was the only representative of the company in a wide area and carried out a variety of roles. He was, in effect, the only point of contact for customers in the area and was responsible for administration in the area. However, the employee did not have any managerial or supervisory function and had no power to make policy. The court found no evidence that the truck driver had authority to made corporate decisions which went beyond those arising out of the transfer and transportation of

---

[8] Amanda Pinto Q.C. and Martin Evans, *Corporate Criminal Liability* (2008), p.55.
[9] (1997) 145 D.L.R. (4th) 276.

waste. On this basis, the Ontario Court of Appeal felt that the criminal acts of the employee could not be imputed to the company, notwithstanding the wide discretion which he enjoyed in carrying out his duties.

The inadequacy of the identification approach in certain situations was highlighted in *DPP v P&O Ferries (Dover) Ltd*.[10] This prosecution arose from the sinking of the ferry, Herald of Free Enterprise, just outside the port of Zeebrugge. The tragedy was caused by the assistant bosun's failure to ensure that the bow doors had been closed and the company was charged with manslaughter. The Central Criminal Court held that there was no conceptual difficulty in charging a corporation with manslaughter. Turner J. noted that "where a corporation, through the controlling mind of one of its agents, does an act which fulfils the prerequisites of the crime of manslaughter, it is properly indictable for the crime of manslaughter".[11] However, the judge ultimately directed an acquittal at the close of the prosecution case as there was insufficient evidence identifying the assistant bosun with the company and he was the only person possessing the required mens rea of recklessness.

THE ORGANISATIONAL—AGGREGATION THEORY

The controlling mind theory, convenient as it may be for particular cases, has obvious limitations. One of these is evident when we consider sins of omission rather than commission. Where a company fails to do something then it may not be possible to point the finger of blame at one individual. The fault may lie with the systems in place within the company so that the company, rather than any one individual, is at fault. Another criticism of the controlling mind theory is that it allows companies to escape liability for wrongs committed by more junior employees. The controlling mind theory works best in the context of a small company and is far less suited to larger corporations with more complex management structures. Yet another disadvantage of the theory is that it encourages proceedings to focus, not on the commission of the crime itself, but on the defendant's internal management hierarchy. These faults have resulted in the development of the organisational or aggregate theory of criminal liability, under which courts will look to the structure and decision-making processes within the defendant corporation.

Celia Wells has explained the theory of aggregation as follows:

> "The aggregation of employees' knowledge means that corporate culpability does not have to be contingent on one individual employee's satisfying the relevant culpability criterion ... Aggregation needs to be seen as a recognition that individuals within a company contribute to the whole machine; it is the whole which is judged, not the parts."[12]

An example of this can be seen in *R. v British Steel Plc*,[13] where the defendant corporation was charged with health and safety offences that were offences of strict

---

[10] (1990) 93 Cr. App. R. 72.
[11] (1990) 93 Cr. App. R. 72 at 84.
[12] Celia Wells, *Corporations and Criminal Responsibilty*, 2nd edn (Oxford: Oxford University Press, 2001), pp.154–160.
[13] [1995] 1 W.L.R. 1356.

liability (subject to a defence of reasonable care having been taken). A worker was killed because of the collapse of a steel platform during an operation that should have been recognised as being inherently dangerous. The argument put forward by the defence was that the senior management had taken all reasonable care in the circumstances and that any fault lay with the independent contractors. This defence was not accepted by the Court of Appeal. It took the view that where strict liability had been imposed it would be seriously undermined if the company were to escape liability on the basis that the "directing mind" was not at fault. In reaching this decision, the court was greatly influenced by the fact that practical difficulties had arisen at the trial of corporate offences, with the bulk of trial time being spent arguing whether or not particular employees were part of senior management.

Similarly, in *Director General of Fair Trading v Pioneer Concrete (UK) (Ltd)*,[14] the House of Lords held that a company could be liable where employees acted in breach of court injunctions restraining them from enforcing unlawful agreements in contravention of the Restrictive Trade Practices Act 1976. This was notwithstanding that they did so contrary to express instructions and without the knowledge of senior management, on the basis that any other position would give companies immunity from action.

STATUTORY CONSTRUCTION APPROACH

Another approach that can be taken by courts is referred to as the "attribution" approach. This was applied in *Meridian Global Funds Management (Asia) Ltd v Securities Commission*[15] where it was held that whether an act is to be attributed to a company is a question of statutory construction. In *Meridian*, the chief investment officer of a corporation, acting without the knowledge of the board of directors but within his authority, bought a holding which required to be registered with the Securities Commission. He failed to do so and the Securities Commission instituted proceedings against the company. The officer was not senior enough to be regarded as the directing mind of the company for the purposes of the identification doctrine but the court refused to limit the identification doctrine to those representing the directing mind and will of the company and held that courts should look at each case individually and fashion a rule of attribution for each statutory context. Lord Hoffman stated that if the officer's actions could not be attributed to the company:

> "This would put a premium on the board paying as little attention as possible to what its investment managers were doing."[16]

Lord Hoffman said that the question "was one of construction rather than metaphysics",[17] and rejected an approach that would focus solely on identification.

---

[14] Also known as *Re Supply of Ready Mixed Concrete (No. 2)* [1995] 1 A.C. 456.
[15] [1995] 2 A.C. 500.
[16] [1995] 2 A.C. 500 at 507.
[17] [1995] 2 A.C. 500 at 512.

The attribution approach was distinguished in *Attorney General's Reference (No. 2 of 1999)*[18] which held that it was not appropriate for common law offences and should be limited to regulatory offences. The facts of the case concerned a prosecution of a company for manslaughter. Here the defendant was a train operator and the allegation was that gross negligence had caused a train crash as a result of which seven passengers were killed. The crash was caused by a combination of factors: the train driver had not seen warning signals along the track; two automatic warning systems were not operative; the company did not insist on two drivers manning each train. The trial judge ruled that where a defendant was a corporation it could only be convicted where a human being, with whom the corporation could be identified, had the requisite mens rea. The Court of Appeal agreed that a corporation's liability for manslaughter was based on the identification theory. Unless the actions of a grossly negligent individual could be attributed to the company, it could not be convicted of manslaughter. Rose L.J. characterised *Meridian* as a restatement, not an abandonment, of existing principles. He stated:

> "None of the authorities since *Tesco Supermarkets Ltd v Nattrass* ... supports the demise of the doctrine of identification: all are concerned with statutory construction of different substantive offences and the appropriate rule of attribution was decided having regard to the legislative intent, namely whether Parliament intended companies to be liable. There is a sound reason for a special rule of attribution in relation to statutory offences rather than common law offences, namely there is, subject to a defence of reasonable practicability, an absolute duty imposed by the statutes. The authorities on statutory offences do not bear on the common law principle in relation to manslaughter."[19]

Lord Rose L.J. noted that:

> "Indeed, Lord Hoffmann's speech in the *Meridian* case, in fashioning an additional special rule of attribution geared to the purpose of the statute, proceeded on the basis that the primary 'directing mind and will' rule still applies although it is not determinative in all cases. In other words, he was not departing from the identification theory but re-affirming its existence."[20]

The Law Reform Commission has criticised the *Meridian* approach for introducing vagueness into the criminal law by leaving the choice of principle of corporate criminal liability to the discretion of the court.[21]

The recent Court of Appeal decision in *St Regis Paper Co. Ltd v R.*[22] illustrates that the statutory construction–*Meridian* approach is still applied, particularly in relation to regulatory offences. The court was asked to decide whether a corporation could be held criminally liable for intentionally making a false entry in an environmental pollution control record. The corporation manufactured paper and owned five mills.

---

[18] [2006] 3 All E.R. 182.
[19] [2006] 3 All E.R. 182 at 190.
[20] [2006] 3 All E.R. 182 at 192.
[21] Law Reform Commission, *Consultation Paper on Corporate Killing* (LRC CP26–2003), p.37.
[22] [2011] EWCA Crim. 2527.

The smallest mill, employing 129 employees, employed a Mr Steer as its technical manager who was required to produce daily environmental report sheets monitoring the outflow from the mill into a nearby river. He made false entries and was convicted of offences contrary to the Pollution Prevention and Control (England and Wales) Regulations 2000.

The trial judge held that Mr Steer's actions could be attributed to the corporation as his mind could be identified as the controlling mind of the company. The Court of Appeal applied the *Meridian* statutory construction approach to the Regulations but held that Mr Steer's actions could not be attributed to St Regis. The Regulations did not allow liability to be imposed by virtue of the actions of a person who was not the directing mind and will of the company. Moses L.J. noted that Mr Steer was the technical manager of the smallest of the five mills operated by the company and reported to the mill's operations manager who reported to the mill's managing director. He in turn reported to divisional technical managers and a Divisional Environmental Director who formed part of a team of eight to 10 divisional directors. The court held that Mr Steer did not fall within the category of someone who was in actual control of the operations of a company or part of them and not responsible to another person in the company for the manner in which they were discharged.

Moses L.J. noted that Mr Steer had been found guilty in his personal capacity and held that:

> "There is, in those circumstances, no basis for suggesting that the Regulations, designed as they are to protect the environment and prevent pollution, cannot function without imposing liability on the company in respect of one who is not the directing mind and will of the company. We do not, accordingly, agree with the judge that it is necessary to relax the rule in *Tesco v Nattrass* to avoid emasculating the legislation, as he put it."[23]

The court noted that:

> "It seems to us that the lesson to be learned from *Meridian* is the importance of construing the statute which creates the statutory offence in order to determine the rules of attribution applicable to the statutory offence in question ... If the Regulations, properly construed, imposed criminal liability upon St. Regis for dishonestly making false entries in records, then the fact that it had no knowledge of the dishonesty and that it was contrary to written instructions, would be nothing to the point. But it is not, for the reasons we have given, possible to construe the relevant Regulation in that way."[24]

Restrictions on Corporate Liabilty

Where the corporation is incapable of committing the particular crime

It remains the case that a corporation cannot commit certain crimes by reason of its nature: bigamy and perjury being the obvious ones. Equally, a company cannot

---

[23] [2011] EWCA Crim. 2527 at para.14.
[24] [2011] EWCA Crim. 2527 at paras 20–23.

be convicted of a crime for which the only punishment is imprisonment, such as murder. It is, however, unclear whether a company could be charged with, for example, counselling or procuring the commission of perjury.

Where the corporation is the victim

A corporation will not be criminally liable for the acts of an employee where those acts are directed towards defrauding the corporation. This point was made in *Canadian Dredge & Dock Co. v R.*[25] where the Supreme Court of Canada accepted that where a manager sets out to intentionally defraud a corporation, then it becomes unrealistic in the extreme to identify the manager with the corporation. However, that case also illustrates the difficulties that can arise in establishing the defence. The defendant companies had colluded to bid at rigged prices in respect of public procurement contracts. The employees in question had benefitted from this arrangement, receiving kickbacks for so doing. The defendant companies claimed that they had been defrauded by the collusion and so could not be held responsible for it. This argument was rejected by the court, which noted that the companies had received benefits from the collusion: the employees were acting partly for their own benefit but also partly for the benefit of the companies as the impugned activities formed a "share the wealth project" for the benefit of all concerned except for the public authorities awarding the contracts. The court held that the directing minds aimed to ensure the corporation an enhanced level of profits and in the process also rewarded themselves. The companies were not, therefore, true victims of the conduct in question.

Where employees act contrary to instructions

As we have seen, *Director General of Fair Trading v Pioneer Concrete (UK) Ltd* held that the existence of instructions against a particular course of conduct may not always amount to a defence. A similar view has been taken in Canada in *Canadian Dredge & Dock Co. v R.* where the court expressly held that instructions preventing the conduct in question were irrelevant to the question of guilt. It should be noted, however, that such instructions, or indeed a detailed policy in relation to the conduct, may be an important factor mitigating the penalty to be imposed.

PUNISHMENT OF COMPANIES

Generally, the only sanction that can be imposed on a company that is guilty of a crime is a fine. These fines will often be derisory compared to the profits of the company, particularly where the offence is one prosecuted in the District Court. In such cases the real punishment of the company may come from other sources: unwelcome publicity, increased insurance premia or exclusion from further opportunities such as the tender procedure for government building contracts which asks bidders whether they have been convicted of any health and safety offences.

---

[25] [1985] 1 S.C.R. 662.

Consequently, one can ask whether companies should be fined at a higher level than individuals (as is the case in Australia) or whether alternative sanctions should be imposed. One possibility that has been adopted in the United States is a form of corporate probation, allowing the court to monitor the ongoing conduct of a company. Indeed, one might go further and argue for a corporate death penalty, in other words the winding-up of companies found guilty of serious criminal offences. Alternatively, it has been suggested that regulation of companies should take place in a civil context and that civil law remedies will ease the burden of proof associated with corporate prosecutions. It should be remembered in this context that civil liability is much easier to establish than criminal liability, since in the civil law a company is generally vicariously liable for the acts of its employee acting in the course of his employment, regardless of the seniority or otherwise of the employee.

Corporate Manslaughter and Homicide Act 2007 (UK)

The UK Home Office published a paper in May 2000 proposing that the law on involuntary manslaughter be reformed.[26] One of the proposals was that a new offence of corporate killing be enacted. The paper pointed out that problems with identification theory meant that there had only been three successful prosecutions for corporate manslaughter in the history of English law and all of those were prosecutions of small companies.

The Corporate Manslaughter and Homicide Act 2007 came into force in 2008. The new offence is named corporate manslaughter in England and Wales and Northern Ireland and corporate homicide in Scotland. The Act considers the actions of senior management collectively and does not seek to identify a directing mind. The offence applies to "organisations" and is not confined to corporations: partnerships, trade unions, the police force and bodies listed in the Schedule to the Act are included in the definition of an "organisation". The offence is committed when the way in which the organisation's activities are managed causes a person's death and amounts to a gross breach of the relevant duty of care owed to the deceased.

The organisation is only guilty if its senior management has managed or organised its activities in such a way as to amount to a substantial element of that breach. The term "senior management" is defined to mean those persons who play a significant role in the management of the whole, or a substantial part of, the organisation's activities. This test is a wider one than is found with identification theory, which essentially looks at company directors to ascertain the directing mind. However, it has been criticised as not being wide enough. The UK Law Commission report and draft bill required "management failure", not "senior management failure", and it has been argued that the focus on senior management behaviour will require juries to assess the behaviour of individuals rather than systemic failure. The Guidance Notes to the new legislation issued by the Ministry of Justice state that:

---

[26] Home Office, *Reforming the Law on Involuntary Manslaughter: The Government's Proposals* (May 2000). The paper was based on a Law Commission Report published in 1996: Law Commission (Law Com. No. 237), *Legislating the Criminal Code: Involuntary Manslaughter* (1996).

"[T]he Act does not require the prosecution to prove specific failings on the part of individual senior managers. It will be sufficient for a jury to consider that the senior management of the organisation collectively were not taking adequate care, and this was a substantial part of the organisation's failure."[27]

Another criticism of the legislation is that individuals cannot be prosecuted for corporate manslaughter (although of course they can still be prosecuted for gross negligence manslaughter). As Pinto points out, simultaneous prosecution of corporations and of individuals for manslaughter would be unsatisfactorily complicated given the differing tests of liability for both.[28] Given the expense involved, it is unlikely that two separate trials would take place arising out of the one fatal incident and this could lead, in the future, to individuals hiding behind the culpability of corporations rather than being punished themselves.

The relevant duty of care is that owed under the law of negligence and the organisation's conduct must have fallen far below that which could have been reasonably expected. Any health and safety breaches will be taken into account. The jury may take into account the extent to which the "corporate culture" tolerated or encouraged health and safety breaches.

An organisation found guilty of corporate manslaughter can be penalised by an unlimited fine. The courts can also order publicity orders, requiring that the conviction and fine be published, and remedial orders, requiring the organisation to take steps to remedy the failure or failures that caused the death.

The first conviction under the new legislation was in February 2011 when Cotswold Geotechnical was fined £385,000 over the death of a geologist employee who had been buried in a trench that had collapsed during soil investigation work. The Court of Appeal refused leave to appeal the amount of the fine, commenting that should the fine ultimately result in the company going out of business, that was not an unacceptable consequence. The company had a sole director who was on-site on the day of the fatality so this made it a relatively easy prosecution. Indeed, there is no reason why the company would not have been convicted by using the old controlling mind test. There have been no further convictions to date but the real test for the legislation will come when a bigger and more complex corporation is prosecuted.[29]

THE IRISH POSITION

Common law

In *Superwood Holdings Plc v Sun Alliance Assurance Plc*,[30] the Supreme Court accepted the identification theory in the context of civil liability of corporations.

---

[27] Ministry of Justice, *Guide to the Corporate Manslaughter and Corporate Homicide Act 2007* (October 2007), p.14.
[28] Amanda Pinto Q.C. and Martin Evans, *Corporate Criminal Liability* (2008), p.237.
[29] The second prosecution under the 2007 Act is ongoing with a trial expected in 2012. Lion Steel Equipment has been charged with corporate manslaughter in relation to the death of an employee who fell through a roof on one of the company's sites. The company is a large one with over 100 employees and three of Lion Steel's directors have been charged with gross negligence manslaughter.
[30] [1995] 3 I.R. 303.

Criminal Liability of Corporations

It held that a company could be vicariously liable for fraud, despite having no will of its own, once the directing mind and will of the company could be identified.[31] However, there has been no express judicial consideration of corporate criminal liability in Irish law.

Law Reform Commission proposals

A Corporate Manslaughter Bill was introduced in 2001 but it lapsed. However, public opinion was in favour of punishing corporations responsible for fatal injuries and the Law Reform Commission considered the issue in 2003 in its *Consultation Paper on Corporate Killing*.[32] It concluded that corporations should be subject to criminal liability for corporate killings and provisionally recommended that a statutory offence of corporate killing, equivalent to gross negligence manslaughter, be established. The rationale was explained as follows:

> "The establishment of a specific corporate killing offence would resolve the difficulties created by the residual uncertainty regarding whether corporations can be prosecuted for the common law offence of manslaughter (and indeed other homicide offences). A conviction of a corporation on indictment for an offence of corporate killing would be qualitatively different to a conviction under health and safety legislation, whatever the penalty imposed. It would mark the disapproval of the community and should have a greater deterrent effect than the offences under health and safety legislation. Moreover, its scope need not be limited to the workplace. It is envisaged that a prosecution for such an offence would take place where none of the other available sanctions were adequate to address the gravity of the matter."[33]

The recommendations expanded the definition of the scope of the identification doctrine in a number of important ways: the offence would apply to all "undertakings" and not just incorporated entities; the offence would apply to "high managerial agents" and not just top management; the recommendation embodied the concept of "reckless tolerance". For reckless tolerance to be proved, a high managerial agent of the undertaking must have been aware, or ought reasonably to have been aware, of a high degree of risk of serious personal injury to any person arising from the acts or omissions of another person and he or she must nonetheless have unreasonably disregarded that risk. The Commission recommended that an undertaking should not be found guilty of corporate killing where evidence showed that its highest level of management had done all that was reasonably practicable to prevent the commission of the offence.

The Law Reform Commission *Report on Corporate Killing* was published in 2005 and it recommended a statutory corporate manslaughter offence and a further offence, applicable to individuals, entitled grossly negligent management causing

---

[31] The Supreme Court applied *Lennards Carrying Co. Ltd v Asiatic Petroleum Co. Ltd* [1915] A.C. 705.
[32] Law Reform Commission, *Consultation Paper on Corporate Killing* (LRC CP26–2003).
[33] Law Reform Commission, *Consultation Paper on Corporate Killing* (LRC CP26–2003), p.166.

death.³⁴ Another Corporate Manslaughter Bill was introduced in 2007 but again it lapsed on the dissolution of the Government. However, the Department of Justice and Law Reform's *White Paper on Organised and White Collar Crime* in 2010 stated that the Government was considering the recommendations of the Law Reform Commission in relation to corporate manslaughter and in 2011 another Corporate Manslaughter Bill was published.

Corporate Manslaughter Bill 2011

The Bill defines the offence of corporate manslaughter as "where an undertaking causes the death of a human person by gross negligence".³⁵ An "undertaking" is defined as a body corporate or an unincorporated body of persons engaged in the production, supply or distribution of goods or the provision of a service including those which are Government Departments and statutory bodies whether carried on for profit or not, as well as faith-based organisations and groups.³⁶

The undertaking causes death by gross negligence where (a) it owed a duty of care to the deceased human person; (b) it breached that duty of care in that it failed to meet the standard of care required (defined as to take all reasonable measures to anticipate and prevent risks to human life, having due regard to the size and circumstances of the undertaking)³⁷; (c) the breach of duty was of a very high degree and involved a significant risk of death or serious personal harm; and (d) that breach of duty caused the death of the human person.³⁸

In assessing whether the undertaking owed the deceased human person a duty of care the court shall have regard to any common law or statutory duties imposed on the undertaking, and in particular shall have regard to whether the undertaking owed a duty as (a) an employer; (b) an occupier of land; (c) a producer of goods; or (d) a provider of services.³⁹

In assessing whether the undertaking breached the standard of care the court shall have regard to any or all of the following: (a) the way in which the activities of the undertaking are managed or organised by its high managerial agents; (b) the allocation of responsibility within the undertaking; (c) the procedural decision-making rules of the undertaking; (d) the policies of the undertaking; (e) the training and supervision of employees of the undertaking; (f) the response of the undertaking to previous incidents involving a risk of death or serious personal harm; (g) the stated and actual goals of the undertaking; (h) the adequacy of the communications systems within the undertaking including systems for communicating information to others affected by the activities of the undertaking; (i) the regulatory environment in which the undertaking operates, including any statutory duties to which the undertaking is subject; (j) any assurance systems to which the undertaking has subscribed; or (k) whether the undertaking was operating within the terms of a contract or licence

---

[34] Law Reform Commission, *Report on Corporate Killing* (LRC 77–2005).
[35] Section 3(1).
[36] Section 2.
[37] Section 3(3).
[38] Section 3(2).
[39] Section 3(4).

made or granted under legislation.[40] The court is not prevented from having regard to any other matters it considers relevant.[41]

"High managerial agent" is defined as a person being a director, manager, or other similar officer of the undertaking, or a person who purports to act in any such capacity, whether or not that person has a contract of employment with the undertaking.[42]

The offence of grossly negligent management causing death is set out as follows:

> Where an undertaking has been convicted of corporate manslaughter and a high managerial agent of the convicted undertaking (a) knew or ought to reasonably have known of a substantial risk of death or serious personal harm (b) failed to make reasonable efforts to eliminate that risk (c) that failure fell far below what could reasonably be expected in the circumstances, and (d) that failure contributed to the commission of the corporate offence; that agent shall be guilty of an offence called "grossly negligent management causing death".[43]

For the purposes of assessing whether a high managerial agent ought to have known of a risk, the court shall have due regard to the actual and stated responsibilities of the high managerial agent.[44] For the purposes of assessing whether a high managerial agent failed to make reasonable efforts to eliminate a risk, the court shall have due regard to the actual responsibilities within the undertaking of the high managerial agent and whether it was within the power of the high managerial agent to eliminate the risk.[45] If it was not within the power of the high managerial agent to eliminate a risk then he or she will have failed to take reasonable measures to eliminate the risk if he or she failed to pass on information of the risk to others within the undertaking who were in a position to eliminate the risk.[46]

The penalty for an undertaking convicted of corporate manslaughter is a fine and the penalty for grossly negligent management causing death is a fine or imprisonment for a term not exceeding 12 years.

The Bill provides for remedial orders in certain circumstances.[47] An undertaking convicted of corporate manslaughter may, in addition to, or instead of, any fine imposed, be ordered to remedy the matters which gave rise to the offence. This may include a requirement that prior to imposition of the remedial order the undertaking submits to the court a detailed programme outlining the steps to be taken to remedy the problems that led to the manslaughter. There may also be a requirement to make regular reports on the implementation of the programme and regular, unannounced inspections to assess the implementation may be made. Where the terms of the remedial order are not being complied with, the court may order "supervised management" on the undertaking. Where there is no relevant regulatory or enforcement authority to manage the undertaking, the court may appoint a competent officer to carry out the inspections and make regular progress reports to court.

---

[40] Section 3(5).
[41] Section 3(6).
[42] Section 2.
[43] Section 4(1).
[44] Section 4(2).
[45] Section 4(3).
[46] Section 4(4).
[47] Section 8.

Provision is made for community service orders to be imposed on an undertaking instead or, or in addition to, a fine.[48] Disqualification orders may also be imposed.[49] These apply to high managerial agents convicted of grossly negligent management causing death and disqualify them from acting in a management capacity for a period not exceeding 15 years. It is an offence, triable on indictment, to breach a disqualification order. Adverse publicity orders may also be made in addition to or instead of any fine.[50] These require undertakings to publicise the fact of conviction, details of the offence and the penalty imposed, including remedial, disqualification or community service orders made. Publicising may be done through the print or broadcast media, by signage or leaflets at the principal office or place of business of the undertaking and by letters, emails or telephone to customers. The court can order publicising to be done through any other appropriate means.

It should be noted that both the offence of corporate manslaughter and the offence of grossly negligent management causing death are concerned with the risk of death or serious personal harm. For corporate manslaughter, the test is "significant risk of death or serious personal harm" and for grossly negligent management causing death it is "substantial risk of death or serious personal harm". It is unclear what difference, if any, there is between "significant" and "substantial" risk. Furthermore, the test is a narrower one than the current Irish test for gross negligence manslaughter as set out in *Attorney General v Dunleavy*[51]—a risk of "substantial personal injury".[52] The Law Reform Commission, referring to its test for corporate killing as set out in the 2005 Report,[53] commented on this discrepancy in its 2008 *Report on Homicide*:

> "It would make sense if the degree of risk for the gross negligence manslaughter test and the Commission's corporate killing test were the same. There does not appear to be any good reason for applying a lower test in the former, simply because it targets culpable negligence in individuals rather than corporate entities. Framing the risk in terms of 'death or serious personal harm' is also clearer than 'substantial personal injury', a vague term which no doubt does little to help juries decide whether negligence is of a sufficiently high level to justify a conviction for gross negligence."[54]

---

[48] Section 9.
[49] Section 11.
[50] Section 10.
[51] [1948] I.R. 95.
[52] It is, however, the same as the test for gross negligence manslaughter in England and Wales. For a full discussion of gross negligence manslaughter, see Ch.4.
[53] Law Reform Commission, *Report on Corporate Killing* (LRC 77–2005).
[54] Law Reform Commission, *Report on Homicide – Murder and Involuntary Manslaughter* (LRC 87–2008), p.90.

INDEX

Abandonment
    attempt, 338–339
    conspiracy, 348
    incitement, 354
    secondary liability, 379–380
Abduction of child, 188
Abetting, 363–364
Abortion
    attempt, 332
    defence of necessity, 282
    incitement, 351
Absence of body, 97
Absolute liability, 69
Accessory before/after the fact, 356
Actus non facit reum nisi mens sit rea, 52
Actus reus
    action element, 81
    attempt, 331–335
    causation, and, 90–95
    common law rape, 141–143
    conspiracy, 339–342
    continuing act, 83–84
    incitement, 350–351
    must coincide with mens rea, 83–84
    omission, 84–90
    secondary liability, 359, 360–361
    state of affairs, 81–82
    voluntariness, 82
Administration of justice, offences against
    attempting to pervert course of justice, 222–223
    contempt of court, 223–235
    perjury, 220–223
Administrative penalties, 8–11
Affray, 257–259
After hours drinking
    secondary liability, 366
Aggravated burglary, 209–211
Aggravated murder, 102–104
Aggravated sexual assault, 153
Aggregation theory, 386–387
Agreement
    common design or joint enterprise, 373–378
    conspiracy requirement, 339–342

Aiding, 361–362
Appropriation of property, 196
Arrest
    crime in progress, 33
    Garda power, 33–34
    impeding, 34–35, 381
    private individual's power, 33
    suspicion arrestable offence committed, 33–34
    suspicion person guilty of arrestable offence, 33
    without warrant, 33–34
Arrestable offence
    definition, 32, 382
    arrest without warrant, 33–34
    assisting offender, 34–35, 380–382
    burglary requirement, 34, 204
    concealing for reward, 35, 381–382
    effect of classification, 34–35
    surveillance, 34
Arson
    criminal damage by, 213–214, 218
Assault
    definition, 124, 167–168
    and battery, 167–168
    causes another to believe, 170
    consent, 168
    corporal punishment, 168–169
    force, 169
    immediacy requirement, 169–170
    indirect use of force, 171
    ordinary day-to-day conduct, 168
    punishment, 171
    words alone, 170–171
Assault causing death, 124
Assault causing harm, 171–172
Assault of health worker, peace officer etc, 189
Assault with intent to cause bodily harm or commit indictable offence, 189
Assistance of offender, 34–35
Assisted suicide
    David George Exoo, 127n
    DPP policy document, 130
    English cases, 127–130

Assisted suicide *(continued)*
  euthanasia distinguished, 131
  offence, 127
  Pretty case, 128–129
  Purdy case, 129
Attempt
  abandonment, 338–339
  actus reus, 331–335
  elements, 330–331
  inchoate offences, 337
  Law Reform Commission, 334–335, 336–337, 338
  legal and factual impossibility, 338
  legality principle, 334–335
  mens rea, 335–337
  murder, 102, 337
  obtaining by false pretences, 333–334
  proximity test, 332–335
  purpose of inchoate offence, 329–330
  rape, 336
  recklessness, 336
  secondary liability, 337–338
  substantial step test, 335
  unequivocality test, 335
Attempting to pervert course of justice, 222–223
Attribution approach to corporate liability, 387–389
Automatism
  definition, 309
  availability of defence, 309–310
  diabetes, 312–313
  drink spiked, 314
  epilepsy 314
  external and internal factors, 311–313
  insane and non-insane, 311–313
  insanity defence distinguished, 310
  loss of memory distinguished, 310
  self-induced, 313
  sleepwalking, 312
  stress, 313
  total loss of control, 313–314
  voluntary intoxication, and, 310

Bail
  refusal for serious offence, 30–31
Basic and specific intent, 294–296, 297–298
Battered woman
  defence of provocation, 267–268
Battery, 167–168

Beef Tribunal, 11–13
Begging
  act and offence distinguished, 248
  failure to comply with Garda direction to desist, 249
  offence, 248
  organised begging, 249–250
  unconstitutionality of former offence, 247–248
Blackmail, 190–191
Blasphemy, 50
Blood transfusion
  refusal on religious grounds, 92
Born-alive rule, 98–99
Breach of the peace
  definition, 241
  common law, 242–243
  display of threatening, abusive, insulting or obscene material, 243–244
  recklessness, 64, 241
  statutory offence, 58–59, 239–241
Burden of proof
  constitutionality of reversed burden, 40–45
  diminished responsibility, 39
  female genital mutilation, 39–40
  insanity, 38–39
  presumption of innocence, 35, 36–37
Burglary
  aggravated, 209–211
  arrestable offence, 34, 204
  attempt to commit arrestable offence, 208–209
  building: definition, 207
  conditional intent, 207–208
  entering building or part of building, 206–208
  lawful use of force in defence of dwelling, 288–293
  mens rea, 208–209
  self-defence plea by burglar, 291
  trespass, 204–206
  widening of old offence, 203–204
"But for" test, 91

Capital murder
  actus reus, 81
  common design, 376–377
  death penalty, 102–103
  former offence, 103
  mens rea, 53, 62–63, 103
  now aggravated murder, 103–104

Causation
   "but for" test, 91
   eggshell skull rule, 92
   "more than de minimis cause of death" test, 91–92
   novus actus interveniens, 92–94
   requirement, 90–92
   whether victim breaking chain, 94–95

Causing serious harm
   consent, whether defence, 173–176
   indictable offence, 24
   mens rea, 173
   offence, 172
   punishment, 176
   sadomasochism, 173–176
   serious harm, 172–173

Certainty principle, 47–50
Changing content of criminal law, 1–2
Child
   abduction, 188
   corporal punishment, 168–169
   criminal liability, 302–303
   neglect, 85–86, 87
   rape by, 303
   sexual assault by, 302–303
   sexual offences against
      defilement of child under 15 or 17 years, 162–164
      reckless endangerment, 164
      register of sex offenders, 46–47, 165–166
      sex tourism, 165
      sexual exploitation, 154–155, 164
      statutory rape/unlawful carnal knowledge, 73–76, 160–162
      trafficking and pornography, 164–165

Civil law
   criminal law distinguished, 3–5
   use of procedures in criminal law, 2, 13–16

Claim of right, 193–195
Classification of offences
   arrestable and non-arrestable, 32–35
   felonies and misdemeanours, 20–21
   general principles, 20
   minor and non-minor, 25–30
   serious and non-serious, 30–32
   summary and indictable, 22–24
   treason, 21–22

Coercion, 179
Common design, 373–378

Common law rape, 141–143
Company
   criminal liability *see* Corporate criminal liability
   late filing fee, 9–10

Complicity *see* **Secondary liability**
Compounding felony or misdemeanour, 381–382
Computer
   hacking, 200, 218–219
   unlawful use, 200

Concealing arrestable offence for reward, 35, 381–382
Conduct crime, 90n
Confiscation order
   drug trafficking, 14–15

Conjoined twins, 282–283
Consent
   assault, 168
   causing serious harm, 173–176
   defence, 302
   sexual offences *see* Sexual offences

Consolidation of charges, 23n
Conspiracy
   abandonment, 348
   actus reus, 339–342
   agreement, 339–342
   cartwheel conspiracy, 340
   Charles Stewart Parnell, 342
   civil wrong, 342–343
   common law, 339
   continuing offence, 340
   inchoate offences, 343
   lack of criminal capacity of one party, 342
   Law Reform Commission, 341, 343, 345, 346
   legal and factual impossibility, 347–348
   mens rea, 344–345
   object, 342–343
   secondary liability, 343
   sole director and company, 341
   spouses, 341
   statutory offence, 339
   to corrupt public morals, 345–346
   to defraud, 345, 346–347
   to effect public mischief, 345–346
   to outrage public decency, 345–346

Constitution
   blasphemy, 50
   defence of unconstitutionality, 326–327

Constitution *(continued)*
    judicial powers of bodies hearing matters other than criminal matters, 5
    jury trial, 25
    minor offences, 25
    non-retroactivity, 46
    presumption of innocence, 37
    refusal of bail for serious offence, 30
    trial of criminal matters, 5
Constitutionality of legislation
    Criminal Justice Act 1994, 14–15
    Proceeds of Crime Act 1996, 13–14
Contaminated blood products, 185
Contempt of court
    breach of sub judice rule, 228–231
    civil and criminal contempt distinguished, 224–226
    commencement of proceedings, 232
    contempt in the face of the court, 226
    law reform, 234–235
    mens rea, 231–232
    overview, 223
    scandalising the court, 226–228
    summary punishment or jury trial, 232–234
Continuing act, 83–84
Contraceptives
    distribution, 326
Contractual duty to act, 88–89
Controlling mind theory, 384–386
Corporal punishment, 168–169
Corporate criminal liability
    attribution approach, 387–389
    background, 383
    controlling or directing mind theory, 384–386
    Irish position, 392–393
    manslaughter *see* Corporate manslaughter
    organisational or aggregation theory, 386–387
    punishment, 390–391
    restrictions
        corporation incapable of committing particular crime, 389–390
        corporation victim of crime, 390
        employee acts contrary to instructions, 390
    statutory construction approach, 387–389
Corporate manslaughter
    attribution approach, 388
    identification approach, 386
    Irish Bill 2011, 394–396
    Law Reform Commission, 393–394
    UK legislation, 391–392
Corruption of public morals, 49–50, 345–346
Counselling, 363–364
Counterfeiting offences, 213
Creation of danger, 87–88
Criminal and dangerous act
    drug supplier, 124–125
    form of manslaughter, 121–123
    Law Reform Commission, 123–124
    neck compression, 122–123
    objective test, 121–123
    one-punch cases, 123–124
    threat of violence, 124
Criminal damage
    by arson, higher penalty, 213–214, 218
    damage: definition, 214
    damaging property, 216
    damaging property with intent to defraud, 217
    damaging property with intent to endanger life, or recklessness, 216–217
    lawful excuse defence, 214–216
    offences, 213
    possession of any thing with intent, 218
    threat to damage property, 218
    unauthorised accessing of data, 218–219
Criminal negligence
    deceased engaged in unlawful activity, 118
    drug supplier, 119
    England, 117–121
    form of manslaughter, 115
    jury direction, 116
    Law Reform Commission, 121
    medical negligence, 117, 118–119
    objective test, 115
    standard of negligence required, 115–117
Criminal organisation
    serious offence as purpose, 32
Criminologist's perspective, 2
Cruelty to animals
    secondary liability, 368–369
Cybercrime, 200

Damaging property, 216
Damaging property with intent to defraud, 217

Index 401

Damaging property with intent to endanger life, or recklessness
  mens rea, 53
  statutory offence, 216–217
Data
  unauthorised access, 218–219
Death by dangerous driving
  secondary liability, 366
  statutory offence, 125–126
Death penalty
  abolition, 102–103
  capital murder, 102–103
  crimes carrying, 21n
  treason, 22
Deception
  definition, 198
  making gain or causing loss by, 198–199
  obtaining services by, 199
Defences
  automatism, 309–314
  consent, 302
  diminished responsibility, 260, 323–324
  duress, 271–278
  entrapment, 304–309
  excessive self-defence, 268–270
  infancy, 302–304
  insanity, 315–326
  intoxication, 293–300
  lawful use of force, 283–293
  mistake, 300–301
  murder, 104, 260
  necessity, 279–283
  provocation, 261–268
  unconstitutionality, 326–327
Defilement of child under 15 or 17 years
  background, 160–162
  disparate treatment of boys and girls, 163–164
  honest belief defence, 162
  no "Romeo and Juliet" clause, 162
  offences and penalties, 162
Definition of criminal law
  blurring of civil and criminal law, 2
  changing content, 1–2
  civil and criminal law distinguished, 3–5
  European Convention on Human Rights, 16–20
  indicia of criminal offence, 6–8
  public face misleading, 1
  purpose, 2

Degrees of complicity *see* **Secondary liability**
Demand for payment of debt, 183
Diabetes, 312–313
Diminished responsibility
  burden of proof, 39
  defence to murder, 260, 323–324
  English law, 320
  infanticide, 137, 323n
  pre-2006 Act, 320
Directing criminal organisation, 355n
Directing mind theory, 384–386
Disciplinary inquiry
  whether criminal charge, 18
Discontinuance of medical treatment, 89–90, 133–135
Dishonesty
  theft requirement, 193–195
Display of threatening, abusive, insulting or obscene material, 243–244
Disqualification from profession
  indictable offence, 24
Doctrine of transferred malice, 77–80, 100, 101
Doli incapax, 302–304
Drink driving
  disqualification from driving, 28–29
  refusal to give breath specimen
    statutory duty to act, 89
    whether strict liability, 73
    whether minor or non-minor offence, 26, 28–29
Driving without due care and attention
  mens rea, 68
Drug intoxication as defence, 299
Drug overdose
  criminal and dangerous act of supplier, 124–125
  criminal negligence of supplier, 119–121
  failure to summons medical help, 87–88
  novus actus interveniens, 94
Drug trafficking
  confiscation order, 14–16
  entrapment, 306–307
  liability of gang boss and drug mule, 355–356
Duress
  availability of police protection, 272–273
  defence, 271–272
  imminence of threat, 272–273
  Law Reform Commission, 277–278

Duress *(continued)*
    marital coercion, 277
    membership of violent organisation, 275–277
    nature of threat, 273–274
    non-application to murder, 274–275
    objective or subjective test, 274
Dwelling
    definition, 292
    lawful use of force in defence, 288–293

Eggshell skull rule, 92
Endangering traffic, 186–187
Endangerment
    background, 184
    certainty principle, and, 49n, 185
    examples, 185
    judicial criticism, 185–186
    recklessness, 63–64
    serious harm, 184–185
    statutory offence, 184
Enforcement of criminal law, 4–5
Entering building
    burglary requirement, 206–208
    trespass offences *see* Trespass
Entrapment
    drugs offences, 305–307
    European Convention on Human Rights, 306–307
    example, 304
    Irish approach, 307–309
    minors test purchasing tobacco products, 308
    modern English approach, 305
    traditional English approach, 304–305
    United States approach, 305–306
Entry powers
    exceeding authority, 205–206
Epilepsy
    automatism, 314
European Convention on Human Rights
    assisted suicide, 128–129
    classification of matter as criminal, 17–20
    entrapment, 306–307
    fair trial, 16–17, 234
    incest, 157
    insanity, 321
    mandatory life sentence, 108–109
    no punishment without law, 17
    non-retroactivity, 46
Euthanasia, 130–133

Excessive self-defence, 268–270
Explosives
    reversed burden of proof, 40–41
Extradition
    David George Exoo, 127n
Extraterritorial jurisdiction
    murder, 98
    secondary liability, 24, 357

Factual impossibility
    attempt, 338
    conspiracy, 347–348
    incitement, 353
Fade factor test, 230–231
Failure to act *see* **Omission**
Failure to comply with Garda direction, 244–245
Fair trial
    European Convention on Human Rights, 16–17, 234
Fair warning, 47
False accounting, 201
False imprisonment, 187–188
False instrument
    using, custody or control, 213
Felonies, 20–21
Felony murder rule, 101–102
Female genital mutilation, 39–40
Financial Regulator
    criminal or administrative sanctions, 11
Fine for minor offence, 25–30
Fitness to be tried, 321–322
Foetus *see* **Unborn child**
Force
    assault requirement, 169
    excessive self-defence, 268–270
    lawful use defence *see* Lawful use of force
    robbery requirement, 211
Forfeiture
    effect on classification as minor offence, 28–30
    proceeds of crime, civil nature, 13–16
Forgery, 212–213
Fraud
    conspiracy to defraud, 345, 346–347
    damaging property with intent to defraud, 217
    HIV or other disease, 146–148
    property offences, 197–203
    vitiating consent to sexual intercourse, 145–146
Function of criminal law, 3

Index 403

Gardaí
   direction to person begging, 249
   direction to person in possession of intoxicating substance, 245
   direction to person loitering etc in public place, 244–245
   failure to act, 88–89
Gross negligence manslaughter
   English law, 117–121
Guerin, Veronica, 13
Gunfight
   doctrine of transferred malice, 79–80, 100
   human shield, 93–94, 122

Handling stolen property, 201–202
Harassment
   background, 179–180
   course of conduct, 181–182
   lawful authority or reasonable excuse, 182
   mens rea, 180–181
   non-contact order, 182–183
   persistently, 181–182
   punishment, 183
   statutory offence, 180
Henchy Report, 320–321
Herald of Free Enterprise, 279n, 386
HIV
   non-disclosure of status to sexual partner, 147–148, 172
Homicide
   absence of body, 97
   infanticide, 136–140
   manslaughter *see* Manslaughter
   murder *see* Murder
   suicide *see* Suicide
   year and a day rule, 96–97
Homosexuality
   decriminalisation, 1
   sadomasochism, 173–176
Honest belief defence
   sexual offences, 162
   theft, 194
Hospital staff
   assault, 189
   resisting, wilfully obstructing or impeding, 189, 246–247
Human shield, 93–94, 122
Human trafficking, 166

Identification doctrine, 384–386
Immediacy requirement
   assault, 169–170
   provocation, 267–268
Impeding arrest or prosecution, 34–35, 381
Imprisonment
   minor offence, 28
Incest
   by female, 156
   by male, 156
   consent no defence, 155–156
   European law, 157
   law reform, 156–157
   non-blood relationships, 156
   punishment, 156, 157
Inchoate offences
   attempt, 329–339
   conspiracy, 339–348
   incitement, 348–354
   Law Reform Commission, 329, 334
   overview, 328–329
   secondary liability distinguished, 329, 356
Incitement
   abandonment, 354
   abetting and counselling distinguished, 363
   abortion, 351
   actus reus, 350–351
   communication, 350
   defences of lack of capacity, duress etc, 349–350
   hatred, 354
   incest with girl under 16, 349
   inchoate liability, 348–350
   Law Reform Commission, 349, 351–353
   legal and factual impossibility, 353
   mens rea, 351–353
   secondary liability, 349
   specific offences, 354
   unsuccessful, 350–351
Indecent assault
   common law offence, 153–155
   disparate penalties for male and female victims, 152n
   now sexual assault, 152, 153
***Indicia* of criminal offence**, 6–8
Indictable offence
   definition, 23
   common law offences, 23
   identifying, 23–24

Indictable offence triable summarily, 24
Indirect intention, 54–59
Infanticide
 balance of mind disturbed, 137
 denial of killing, 138–139
 diminished responsibility, 137, 323n
 elements of offence, 136
 failure to bond with child of rape, 138
 father's position, 137–138
 removal of reference to lactation, 136–137
 wider scope of English offence, 139–140
Information on offences
 withholding, 35, 89, 382
Innocence, presumption see **Presumption of innocence**
Innocent agency, 358–359
Insanity
 burden and standard of proof, 38–39, 315
 Central Mental Hospital as designated centre, 322n
 detention and release of criminally insane, 324–326
 diminished responsibility see Diminished responsibility
 European Convention on Human Rights, 321
 fitness to be tried, 321–322
 Henchy Report, 320–321
 law reform, 320–321
 mental disorder: definition, 321
 Mental Health (Criminal Law) Review Board, 325
 not guilty by reason of, 323
 pre-2006 Act
  burden and standard of proof, 315
  diminished responsibility, 320
  extension of defence beyond M'Naghten, 317–319
  irresistible impulse, 317–319
  M'Naghten Rules, 315–317
 procedural aspects, 324–326
Intention
 definition, 53–54
 basic and specific intent, 294–296, 297–298
 desire distinguished, 54
 foresight of consequences as evidence, 55, 58
 foresight of high probability, 54–55
 highly likely test, 59
 indirect or oblique
  English approach, 54–57
  example of problem, 54
  Irish approach, 57–59
 motive distinguished, 54, 59
 natural and probable consequence, 55, 60–61
 pre-meditation distinguished, 54
 presumption, 60–61
 proposed law reform, 61
 virtual certainty, 56–57
 whether result likely to be achieved, 54
Intoxication as defence
 automatism, and, 310, 314
 availability of defence, 293–294
 basic and specific intent, 294–296, 297–298
 drugs, 299
 Dutch courage, 294
 involuntary intoxication, 299–300
 Irish law, 297–298
 Law Reform Commission, 297, 300
 moral issues, 293
Intoxication in public place, 237–238
Irresistible impulse, 317–319

Joint enterprise, 373–378
Journalistic privilege, 226
Joyriding, 126, 195
Judicial proceedings
 definition, 221
Jurisdiction
 extraterritorial, for murder, 98
Jury directions
 criminal negligence, 116
 presumption of innocence, 37–38
Jury trial
 constitutional right, 25

Kidnapping, 187

Late filing fee, 9–10
Law Reform Commission
 attempt, 334–335, 336–337, 338
 causing serious harm, 172, 173
 consent to sexual offences, 144–145
 conspiracy, 341, 343, 345, 346
 corporate killing, 393–394
 criminal and dangerous act manslaughter, 123–124
 criminal negligence manslaughter, 121

Index 405

death by dangerous driving, 125–126
direct and oblique intention, 61
dishonesty and fraud, 192
duress, 277–278
endangerment, 184
excessive self defence, 270
expansion of fault element of murder, 113–114
first and second degree murder, 114
inchoate offences, 329, 334, 349
incitement, 349, 351–353
intoxication as defence, 297, 300
legitimate defence, 286–287
mandatory life sentence, 106–108
maximum penalty or penalty actually imposed, 26–27
merger of murder and manslaughter, 111
serious injury rule, 112–113
sexual exploitation of child, 154
sexual offences against mentally handicapped, 159
statutory rape, 160–161
terms of imprisonment, 28n
theft, 194

Lawful excuse
defence to criminal damage, 214–216

Lawful use of force
defence of dwelling, 288–293
defence of person, 283–284
defence of property, 284
force: definition, 286
Law Reform Commission, 286–287
mistaken belief in threat, 288
opportunity to retreat, 286
other defences preserved, 287–288
person known to be Garda, 284–285
preparation in anticipation of attack, 285
prevention of crime, 284
proportionality of response, 288
reasonableness, 286
self-induced self defence, 285–286
statutory defence, 283
trespass to person, 284

Legal impossibility
attempt, 338
conspiracy, 347
incitement, 353

Legality principle
attempt, and, 334–335
conspiracy to corrupt public morals etc, 346

maximum certainty, 47–50
non-retroactivity, 46–47
nullum crimen, nulla poena sine lege, 45
statement, 45
strict construction of penal statutes, 50–51

Life sentence
aggravated sexual assault, 153
defilement of child under 15 years, 162
false imprisonment, 188
incest, 156
mandatory sentence for murder *see* Mandatory life sentence
rape, 153

Life support, withdrawal
act-omission distinction, 89–90
non-resuscitation order, 135
patient's mental capacity, 133
persistent vegetative state, 89–90, 134–135, 326
whether novus actus interveniens, 93

Locked-in syndrome, 133, 283
Loitering with intent, 47–48, 244

M'Naghten **Rules**, 315–317
Making gain or causing loss by deception, 198–199
Making off without payment, 199–200
Mala in se, 3
Mala prohibita, 3
Malice aforethought, 100–101
Mandatory life sentence
aggravated murder, 104
arguments for and against, 105–106, 107–108
Australia, 106
average time served before release, 105
constitutionality and compatibility with human rights, 108–109
England, 106, 109
Law Reform Commission reports, 106–108
murder, 104–109
review by Parole Board, 104–105

Manslaughter
categories, 115
corporate liability *see* Corporate manslaughter
criminal and dangerous act, 121–125
criminal negligence, 115–121
murder distinguished, 114

Manslaughter *(continued)*
  proposed merger with murder, 109–112
    punishment, 114–115
    road deaths, 116, 121, 125–126
    voluntary and involuntary, 115
Marital coercion, 277
Marital rape, 49n, 141–142
Medical negligence
  criminal negligence, 117, 118–119
  novus actus interveniens, 92–94
Medical treatment
  assault of person providing, 189
  discontinuance, 89–90, 133–135
  failure to summons, 86, 87–88
  non-resuscitation order, 135
  resisting, wilfully obstructing or impeding person providing, 246–247
Member of Oireachtas
  privilege from arrest, 21n
Membership of unlawful organisation
  duress as defence, 275–277
  reversed burden of proof, 41–42
Mens rea
  actus reus must coincide with, 83–84
  alone insufficient for crime, 81
  attempt, 335–337
  categories, 52
  conspiracy, 344–345
  criminal negligence *see* Criminal negligence
  doctrine of transferred malice, 77–80
  for each element of offence, 53, 62–63
  incitement, 351–353
  intention, 53–61
  mental element of crime, 52–53
  motive distinguished, 52
  negligence, 68
  recklessness, 61–67
  secondary liability, 359, 369–373
  strict or absolute liability, 68–77
Mental disorder
  definition, 321
  defence of insanity *see* Insanity
Mental Health (Criminal Law) Review Board, 325
Mentally handicapped
  sexual offences against, 157–159
Mercy killing, 100, 106, 109, 130–133
Minor offence
  factors to be considered, 25
  severity of punishment
    fine measured by current value of money, 27
    maximum penalty or penalty actually imposed, 26–27
    maximum permissible punishments, 27–28
    revocation of licence or seizure of property, 28–30
    what constitutes punishment, 28–30
  summary trial, 22–23, 25
Misdemeanours, 20–21
Mistake
  age of sexual partner, 73–74, 160–161
  consent of sexual partner, 150–152
  defence, 300–301
  identity of sexual partner, 145–146
  self-defence, 288
  trespass, 204–205, 251–252
"More than de minimis cause of death" test, 91–92
Motive, 52, 54, 59
Murder
  definition, 97
  actus reus, 81
  aggravated, 102–104
  any reasonable creature *in rerum natura*, 98–100
  attempt, 102, 337
  capital murder *see* Capital murder
  defences
    diminished responsibility, 260, 323–324
    excessive self-defence, 268–270
    generally, 104, 260
    provocation, 261–268
  doctrine of transferred malice, 79–80
  either expressed by party or implied by law, 101–102
  elements of offence, 97–102
  expansion of fault element, 113–114
  extraterritorial jurisdiction, 98
  first and second degree, 114
  intention to cause serious injury, 112–113
  mandatory life sentence, 104–109
  mens rea, 100–101, 112–114
  of sound memory and age of discretion, 97
  proposed merger with manslaughter, 109–112
  secondary liability, 367–368
  unborn child, 98–100

Index 407

under the King's peace, 100
unlawfully killeth, 98
with malice aforethought, 100–101
within any county of the realm, 98

Nature of criminal law, 3–5
Necessity
abortion, 282
availability of defence, 279–281
conjoined twins, 282–283
duress of circumstances, 279
Herald of Free Enterprise, 279n
locked-in syndrome, 283
shipwreck, 281–282
whether applicable to murder, 281–283
Negligence
criminal negligence, 115–121
form of mens rea, 68
No punishment without law
European Convention on Human Rights, 17
legality principle, 45
Non-contact order, 182–183
Non-fatal offences against the person
assault, 167–171
assault causing harm, 171–172
assault of health worker, peace officer, etc., 189
assault with intent to cause bodily harm or commit indictable offence, 189
background, 167
blackmail, 190–191
causing serious harm, 172–176
child abduction, 188
coercion, 179
demand for payment of debt, 183
endangering traffic, 186–187
endangerment, 184–186
false imprisonment, 187–188
harassment, 179–183
poisoning, 183–184
syringe attacks, etc., 177–179
threat to kill or cause serious harm, 176–177
Non-retroactive effect of legislation, 46–47
Novus actus interveniens, 92–94
Nullum crimen, nulla poena sine lege, 45

Oblique intention, 54–59
Obstruction offences, 246–247
Obtaining services by deception, 199

Offensive conduct in public place, 238–239
Omission
child left to starve, 85–86, 87
contractual duty to act, 88–89
creation of danger, 87–88
elderly relative left without food or medical care, 86
failure to summons medical help, 86, 87–88
no general duty to act, 84–85
parental duty to act, 85–86, 365
Quebec, 85
secondary liability, 365–369
statutory duty to act, 89
Vermont, 84–85
voluntary assumption of duty to act, 86–87
whether act-omission distinction artificial, 89–90
withdrawal of life support, 89–90
Organisational theory, 386–387
Organised begging, 249–250
Ownership
definition, 196

Parent
duty to act, 85–86, 365
Parole Board, 104–105
Participation in criminal organisation, 355n
Passport
failure to produce without satisfactory explanation, 48–49
Peace officer
assault, 189
resisting, wilfully obstructing or impeding, 189, 246–247
Perjury
definition, 220
civil case, 222
Colm Murphy case, 222
judicial proceedings, 221
knowledge or recklessness as to truth or falsity, 221
law reform, 222
material to matter in question, 221
on oath or affirmation, 220–221
punishment, 220, 222n
Persistent vegetative state
withdrawal of feeding tube, 89–90, 134–135, 326

Person
    non-fatal offences against *see* Non-fatal offences against the person
    use of force in defence of, 283–284
Poisoning, 183–184
Police *see also* **Gardaí**
    failure to act, 88–89
Pornography
    child pornography, 164–165
Possession of cannabis
    reversed burden of proof, 42–45
Possession of certain articles
    intent to damage property, 218
    theft and fraud offences, 212
Possession of stolen property, 202
Pre-meditation, 54
Presence at scene of crime, 365–369
Presumption in favour of mens rea, 70
Presumption of innocence
    burden and standard of proof, 35, 36–37
    constitutional status, 37
    exceptions
        constitutionality of reversed burdens, 40–45
        female genital mutilation, 39–40
        insanity and diminished responsibility, 38–39
    jury directions, 37–38
    purpose, 35–36
Presumption of intention, 60–61
Primary and secondary punishments, 28–30
Principle of legality *see* **Legality principle**
Privacy, right to, 326
Private place
    definition, 236
Proceeds of Crime Act 1996
    compatibility with European Convention on Human Rights, 19–20
    constitutional challenge, 13–14
Procuring, 364–365
Property
    lawful use of force in defence, 284
    offences against *see* Property offences
Property offences
    arson and criminal damage, 213–219
    burglary, 203–211
    Criminal Justice (Theft and Fraud Offences) Act 2001, 192
    false accounting, 201
    forgery and counterfeiting, 212–213
    fraud offences, 197–203
    handling stolen property, 201–202
    making gain or causing loss by deception, 198–199
    making off without payment, 199–200
    obtaining services by deception, 199
    possession of certain articles, 212
    possession of stolen property, 202
    property: definition, 196
    robbery, 211
    suppression etc of documents, 201
    theft, 192–197
    unlawful use of computer, 200
    withholding information regarding stolen property, 203
Provocation
    battered women, 267–268
    English law, 262–263
    historical background, 262–263
    immediacy requirement, 267–268
    need for statutory reform, 261–262
    subjective test, 261, 263–267
Proximity test, 332–335
Public decency
    conspiracy to outrage, 345
Public drunkenness
    summary offence, 23–24
Public face of criminal law, 1
Public mischief
    conspiracy to commit, 345–346
Public order offences
    affray, 257–259
    begging, 247–250
    breach of the peace, 242–243
    display of threatening, abusive, insulting or obscene material, 243–244
    failure to comply with Garda direction, 244–245
    intoxication in public place, 237–238
    offensive conduct in public place, 238–239
    public place: definition, 236
    riot, 255–256
    threatening, abusing or insulting behaviour in public place, 239–241
    trespass, 250–254
    violent disorder, 256–257
    wilful obstruction, 246–247
Public wrongs, 4
Publication
    breach of sub judice rule, 228–231
    scandalising the court, 226–228

Index 409

Punishment
    aggravated murder, 104
    aggravated sexual assault, 153
    assault, 171
    assault causing harm, 172
    attempting to pervert course of justice, 223
    causing serious harm, 176
    child pornography, 164–165
    coercion, 179
    corporate offender, 390–391
    defilement of child under 15 or 17 years, 162
    demand for payment of debt, 183
    endangering traffic, 186–187
    endangerment, 186
    false imprisonment, 188
    harassment, 183
    impeding arrest or prosecution, 381
    incest, 156, 157
    manslaughter, 114–115
    murder, 104–119
    organised begging, 250
    perjury, 220, 222n
    poisoning, 184
    primary and secondary, 28–30
    purpose of criminal law, 4
    rape, 153
    severity in classifying as minor offence, 25–30
    sexual assault, 152
    sexual offences against mentally handicapped, 157–158
    syringe attacks, 178–179
    threat to kill or cause serious harm, 177
    threatening, abusing or insulting behaviour in public place, 239
Punishment beating, 101, 375–376

Rape
    attempt, 336
    common law rape, 141–143
    consent
        English law, 145n, 150–152
        failure to put up fight, 144
        fear vitiating, 149
        fraud as to HIV or other disease, 146–148
        fraud vitiating, 145–146
        honest but unreasonable belief in, 150–152
        incapacity, 149
        intoxicated victim, 149
        Law Reform Commission, 144–145
        recklessness as to, 152
    innocent agency, 358–359
    marital rape, 49n, 141–142
    mens rea, 149–152
    punishment, 153
    section 4 rape, 143–144
    standing by and watching, secondary liability, 366–367
    statutory rape, 73–76, 160–162
Reasonable excuse
    defence to trespass, 254
Recklessness
    American definition, 63, 241
    attempt, fault element, 336
    breach of the peace, 240–241
    damaging property with intent to endanger life, or recklessness, 216–217
    English approach, 64–67
    form of mens rea, 61–62
    handling stolen property, 202
    Irish approach, 62–64
    subjective or objective test, 62–67
    trespass, 204–205, 251–252
    unjustifiable risk of result, 61–62
Registration of sex offenders, 46–47, 165–166
Resisting, wilfully obstructing or impeding peace officer or person providing medical services, 189, 246–247
Result crime, 90n
Revenue penalty
    failure to make income tax returns, 8–9
Riot, 255–256
Road deaths, 116, 121, 125–126
Robbery, 211

Sadomasochism, 173–176, 379
Scandalising the court, 226–228
Search warrant
    issue by District Court, 34
Secondary liability
    abetting, 363–364
    aiding, 361–362
    assistance after crime committed, 34–35, 380–382
    attempt, 337–338

Secondary liability *(continued)*
   causation, 362, 363, 364
   conduct element, 359, 360–361
   conspiracy, 343
   counselling, 363–364
   Criminal Law Act 1997, 356–357
   degree of knowledge required, 370–373
   doctrine of common design/joint enterprise, and, 373–378
   elements, 359
   extraterritorial effect, 24, 357
   failure to act, or mere presence, 365–369
   former categories, 356
   inchoate liability distinguished, 329, 356
   incitement, 349
   innocent agency, 358–359
   mens rea, 359, 369–373
   need for law reform, 357
   oblique or direct intent, 370
   principal offender distinguished, 355
   procuring, 364–365
   purpose, 355–356
   recklessness, 369–370
   summary offence, 357
   victim as participant, 378–379
   withdrawal, 379–380
   withholding information, 382
Section 4 rape, 143–144
Self-defence
   lawful use of force *see* Lawful use of force
   mistaken belief in threat, 288
   murder defence, 268–270
   self-induced, 285–286
Sentence *see also* **Punishment**
   life *see* Life sentence; Mandatory life sentence
   sub judice rule, 230
Serious injury rule, 112–113
Serious offence
   definition, 30, 31–32
   criminal organisation, 32
   failure to report information to Gardaí, 31–32
   introduction of concept, 30
   refusal of bail, 30–31
Severity of punishment
   minor offence, 25–30
Sex offenders
   registration, 46–47, 165–166
Sex tourism, 165

Sexual assault
   aggravated, 153
   background, 152, 153
   circumstances of indecency, 155
   indecent assault at common law, 153–155
   punishment, 152
   sexual exploitation of child, 154–155
   statutory offence, 152
Sexual offences
   child, against
      child trafficking and pornography, 164–165
      defilement of child under 15 or 17 years, 162–164
      reckless endangerment, 164
      register of sex offenders, 46–47, 165–166
      sex tourism, 165
      sexual exploitation, 154–155, 164
      statutory rape/unlawful carnal knowledge, 73–76, 160–162
   consent
      English law, 145n, 150–152
      failure to put up fight, 144
      fear vitiating, 149
      fraud as to HIV or other disease, 146–148
      fraud vitiating, 145–146
      honest but unreasonable belief in, 150–152
      incapacity, 149
      intoxicated victim, 149
      Law Reform Commission, 144–145
      mentally handicapped, 158–159
      recklessness as to, 152
   human trafficking, 166
   incest, 155–157
   mens rea, 149–152
   mentally handicapped, 157–159
   rape, 141–144
   sexual assault, 152–155
   unconstitutionality, 326–327
Shipwreck, 281–282
Silent telephone calls, 170, 171
Sleepwalking, 312
Spiked drink, 300, 314, 364–365
Spouses
   conspiracy between, 341
Stalking *see* **Harassment**
Standard of proof
   insanity, 38–39

Index 411

presumption of innocence, 35, 36–37
use of civil standard in criminal law, 2, 14
Starvation
child, 85–86, 87
elderly relative, 86
State of affairs
actus reus as, 81–82
Statistics, 1
Statutory duty to act, 89
Statutory offence
strict liability *see* Strict liability
whether summary or indictable, 23–24
Statutory rape, 73–76, 160–162
Stealing
element of robbery, 211
Stolen property
handling, 201–202
possession, 202
withholding information, 203
Strict construction of penal statutes, 50–51
Strict liability
definition, 68
absolute liability distinguished, 69
arguments for and against, 68–69
Canadian approach, 73, 75
common law offences, 69
constitutionality, and *CC v Ireland*, 73–76
criminal contempt, 231–232
determining whether offence within category, 69–70
health and safety offences, 386–387
intoxication in public place, 237–238
post-*CC v Ireland*, 76–77
pre-*CC v Ireland*, 71–73
presumption in favour of mens rea, 70
statutory rape/unlawful carnal knowledge, 73–76, 160–162
Sub judice rule, 228–231
Subjective approach of criminal law, 4
Suicide
abuse leading to, 95
assisted, 127–130
decriminalisation, 126
pact, 126–127
Summary offence
definition, 23
hearing with indictable offence on same set of facts, 23n
identifying, 23–24
secondary liability, 357

Summary trial
generally, 22–23
minor offence, 25–30
Suppression etc of documents, 201
Surveillance by Gardaí, 34
Syringe attacks, etc.
definitions, 177
offences, 177–178
placing or abandoning syringe, 178–179
possession of syringe, 178
punishment, 178

Theft
definition, 193
absence of owner's consent, 197
actus reus, 195–197
appropriation of property, 196
consolidation of offences, 192–193
dishonestly, without claim of right made in good faith, 193–195
evidence of ownership of property, 196–197
honest belief defence, 194
intention to temporarily or permanently deprive, 195
Threat to damage property, 218
Threat to kill or cause serious harm, 176–177
Threatening, abusing or insulting behaviour in public place, 239–241
Trafficking
adult, 166
child, 164
Transferred malice, 77–80
Treason, 21–22
Trespass
burglary requirement, 204–206
causing fear in another, 253–254
conduct likely to damage land or amenity, 254
conspiracy to commit tort, 342–343
criminal trespass, 250–252
entering building or curtilage with intent to commit offence, 252–253
mens rea, 204–205, 251–252
reasonable excuse defence, 254
Trial on indictment
generally, 22
Tribunals of inquiry, 11–13

Unauthorised accessing of data, 218–219
Unborn child
    born-alive rule, 98–99
    doctrine of transferred malice, 78–79, 100
    right of life, 99
Unconstitutionality
    defence, 326–327
Unlawful carnal knowledge, 73–76, 160–162
Unlawful use of computer, 200

Vague or ambiguous offence
    principle of maximum certainty, 47–50
Verdict
    not guilty by reason of insanity, 323
Victim as participant in crime, 378–379
Victim impact statement, 4n
Violent disorder, 256–257
Voluntariness of actus reus, 82
Voluntary assumption of risk, 86–87
Voluntary manslaughter, 115

Weapon
    aggravated burglary, 209–211
Wilful obstruction, 246–247
Withdrawal from complicity, 379–380
Withholding information
    regarding offences, 35, 89, 382
    regarding stolen property, 203
Witness
    buying off, 381–382
    intimidation or interference with, 222–223, 231
    perjury *see* Perjury
    refusal to answer questions, 226
Words alone
    assault by, 170–171

Year-and-a-day rule, 96–97